AMERICAN GOVERNMENT

Readings and Cases

Second Edition

AMERICAN ✠ ✠ ✠

GOVERNMENT

✠ ✠ ✠ Readings and Cases

PETER WOLL
Brandeis University

Boston
LITTLE, BROWN AND COMPANY

This book is dedicated to
JOHN W. WOLL *and* RUTH C. WOLL

LIBRARY OF CONGRESS CATALOG CARD NO. 65–13915

SIXTH PRINTING

Published simultaneously in Canada
by Little, Brown & Company (Canada) Limited

PRINTED IN THE UNITED STATES OF AMERICA

Preface

THIS BOOK is designed to supplement standard textbooks in the introductory college course in American government. It provides readings, with explanatory notes, to stimulate student interest in the major areas generally covered.

In making the selections for this and the earlier edition strong emphasis has been given to strengthening those materials used for the core parts of the American government course: the nature and origins of constitutional theory and practice; the relationship between the national government and the states; civil liberties and civil rights; the organization and functions of political parties, the role of elections, and the nature of electoral behavior; interest groups; the responsibilities, powers, and limitations of the President; the structure and functions of Congress, and the environment of congressional decision making; the judicial process; and finally, selected problems of government and policy making.

The book offers readings from current research, and cases in politics and in constitutional law. Since the appearance of the first edition, research has provided fresh insights into many areas, including the framing of the Constitution, electoral behavior, the nature of parties, and the role of interest groups. Additional selections from these and other areas of research are included.

The book is arranged by topics to facilitate discussion. Pro and con points of view are given where appropriate, but no attempt is made to fit topics superficially into this mold. Hopefully, then, the plan of the book and the readings themselves will give the student a sense of the historical antecedents and the theoretical background of the American political process, and an understanding of the contemporary political scene.

The author has been helped immeasurably in the preparation of this and the earlier edition by the thoughtful comments of many. I would particularly like to thank George Brasington, Bernard C. Cohen, I. Ridgway Davis, Earl F. Kohler, Robert L. Peabody, Robert L. Peterson, John H. Schaar, Karl M. Schmidt, and Robert G. Thompson for their kind assistance.

Finally, I am especially indebted to my wife, Mary J. Woll, who has made it possible for me to have the time necessary to complete this project, and who did a truly exceptional job in keeping Bob and Cindy Woll happy and creative while I was occupied with the book.

P. W.

Contents

CHAPTER SIX

The Presidency

CHAPTER SEVEN

Congress

CHAPTER ONE

Constitutional Government

The development of constitutional government is of major significance in the study of political science. The term implies a government that is regulated by laws which control *and limit* the exercise of political power. A constitutional democracy is a process in which the people participate in government on a limited basis. A distinction should be made between an unlimited democratic government and a constitutional democracy. In the former "the people" govern through the operation of a principle such as majority rule without legal restraint; in the latter majority rule is curtailed and checked through various legal devices.

1. Introduction

American government is, above all, a constitutional democracy. It was designed to be a government of law and not of men. Many students of American government feel that this is a unique contribution made by the United States to the world; however, the fact is that the idea of constitutional government is as ancient as Western civilization. Aristotle's *Politics* provides us both with an introduction to the study of government in general and of constitutional government in particular. It is chosen as an introductory selection to emphasize that the roots of political science lie deep in our Western heritage.

THE POLITICS OF ARISTOTLE

*Translated by Benjamin Jowett**

The Study of Government

Hence it is obvious that government too is the subject of a single science, which has to consider what kind of government would be best and most in accordance with our aspirations, if there were no external impediment, and also what kind of government is adapted to particular states. For the best is often unattainable, and therefore the true legislator and statesman ought to be acquainted, not only with (1) that which is best in the abstract, but also with (2) that which is best relatively to circumstances. We should be able further to say how a state may be constituted under any given conditions (3) both how it is originally formed and, when formed, how it may be longest preserved. . . .

He ought, moreover, to know (4) the form of government which is best suited to states in general; for political writers, although they have excellent ideas, are often unpractical. We should consider, not only what form of government is best, but also what is possible and what is easily attainable by all. . . . Any change of government which has to be introduced should be one which men will be both willing and able to adopt, since there is quite as much trouble in the reformation of an old constitution as in the establishment of a new one, just as to unlearn is as hard as to learn. And therefore, in addition to the qualifications of the statesman already mentioned, he should be able to find remedies for the defects of existing constitutions. This he cannot do unless he knows how many forms of a government there are. It is often supposed that there is only one kind of democracy and one of oligarchy. But this is a mistake; and, in order to avoid such mistakes, we must ascertain what differences there are in the constitutions of states, and in how many ways they are combined. The same political insight will enable a man to know which laws are the best, and which are suited to different constitutions; for the laws are, and ought to be, relative to the constitution, and not the constitution to the laws. A constitution is the organization of offices in a state, and determines what is to be the governing body, and what is the end of each community. But laws are not to be confounded with the principles of the constitution: they are the rules according to which the magistrates should administer the state, and proceed against offenders.

Forms of Government

In our original discussion about governments we divided them into three true forms: kingly rule, aristocracy, and constitutional government, and three corresponding perversions—tyranny, oligarchy, and democracy. . . . In what follows we have to describe the so-called constitutional government, which bears the common name of all constitutions, and the other forms, tyranny, oligarchy, and democracy.

It is obvious which of the three perversions is the worst, and which is the next in badness. That which is the perversion of the first and most divine is necessarily the worst. And just as a royal rule, if not a mere name, must exist by virtue of some great personal superiority in the king, so tyranny, which is the worst of governments, is necessarily the farthest removed from a well-constituted form; oligarchy is a little better, but a long way from aristocracy, and democracy is the most tolerable of the three.

Forms of Democracy

Of forms of democracy first comes that which is said to be based strictly on equality. In such a democracy the law says that it is just for nobody to be poor, and for nobody to be rich; and that neither should be masters, but both equal. For if liberty and equality, as is thought by some, are chiefly to be found in democracy, they will be best attained when all persons alike share in the government to the utmost. And since the people are the majority, and the opinion of the majority is decisive, such a government must necessarily be a democracy. Here then is one sort of democracy. There is another, in which the magistrates are elected according to a certain property qualification, but a low one; he who has the required amount of property has a share in the government, but he who loses his property loses his rights. Another kind is that in which all the citizens who are under no disqualification share in the government, but still the law is supreme. In another, everybody, if he be only a citizen, is admitted to the government, but the law is supreme as before. A fifth form of democracy, in other respects the same, is that in which, not the law, but the multitude, have the supreme power, and supersede the law by their decrees. This is a state of affairs brought about by the demagogues. For in democracies which are subject to the law the best citizens hold the first place, and there are no demagogues; but where the laws are not supreme, there demagogues spring up. For the people becomes a monarch, and is many in one; and the many have the power in their hands, not as individuals, but collectively. . . . Such a democracy is fairly open to the objection that it is not a constitution at all; for where the laws have no authority, there is no constitution. The law ought to be supreme over all, and the magistracies and the government should judge of particulars. So that if democracy be a real form of government, the sort of constitution in which all things are regulated by decrees is clearly not a democracy in the true sense of the word, for decrees relate only to particulars.

The Best State

We have now to inquire what is the best constitution for most states, and the best life for most men, neither assuming a standard of virtue which is above ordinary persons, nor an education which is exceptionally favored by nature and circumstances, nor yet an ideal state which is an aspiration only, but having regard to the life in which the majority are able to share, and to the form of government which states in general can attain. As to . . . aristocracies . . . , they either lie beyond the possibilities of the greater number of states, or they approximate to the so-called constitutional government, and therefore need no separate discussion. And in fact the conclusion at which we arrive respecting all these forms rests upon the same grounds. For if it has been truly said in the Ethics that the happy life is the life according to unimpeded virtue, and that virtue is a mean, then the life which is in a mean, and in a mean attainable by everyone, must be the best.

Now in all states there are three elements; one class is very rich, another very poor, and a third in a mean. . . . Those who have too much of the goods of fortune, strength, wealth, friends, and the like, are neither willing nor able to submit to authority. . . . On the other hand, the very poor, who are in the opposite extreme, are too degraded. So that one class cannot obey, and can only rule despotically; the other knows not how to command and must be ruled like slaves. . . . But a city ought to be composed, as far as possible, of equals and similars; and these are generally the middle classes. Wherefore the city which is composed of middle-class citizens is necessarily best governed; they are, as we say, the natural elements of a state. And this is the class of citizens which is most secure in a state, for they do not, like the poor, covet their neighbors' goods; nor do others covet theirs, as the poor covet the goods of the rich.

Thus it is manifest that the best political community is formed by
citizens of the middle class, and that those states are likely to be well-
administered, in which the middle class is large, and larger if possible
than both the other classes, or at any rate than either singly; for the addition of the middle class turns the scale, and prevents either of the
extremes from being dominant.

Rule of the Multitude

The principle that the multitude ought to be supreme rather than
the few best is capable of a satisfactory explanation, and, though not free
from difficulty, yet seems to contain an element of truth. For the many,
of whom each individual is but an ordinary person, when they meet
together may very likely be better than the few good, if regarded not
individually but collectively, just as a feast to which many contribute
is better than a dinner provided out of a single purse. For each individual
among the many has a share of virtue and prudence, and when they
meet together they become in a manner one man, who has many feet, and
hands, and senses; that is a figure of their mind and disposition. Hence
the many are better judges than a single man of music and poetry; for
some understand one part, and some another, and among them, they
understand the whole. . . . In some cases [this principle] is impossible
of application; for the argument would equally hold about brutes. . . .
But there may be bodies of men about whom our statement is nevertheless true. And if so, the difficulty which has been already raised, and
also another which is akin to it—viz. what power should be assigned
to the mass of freemen and citizens, who are not rich and have no personal merit—are both solved. There is still a danger in allowing them
to share the great offices of state, for their folly will lead them into error,
and their dishonesty into crime. But there is a danger also in not letting
them share, for a state in which many poor men are excluded from office
will necessarily be full of enemies. The only way of escape is to assign
to them some deliberative and judicial functions. . . . On the other
hand, the popular form of government involves certain difficulties. In
the first place, it might be objected that he who can judge of the healing
of a sick man should be one who could himself heal his disease, and
make him whole—that is, in other words, the physician; and so in all
professions and arts. As, then, the physician ought to be called to account by physicians, so ought men in general to be called to account by
their peers. . . . Yet possibly these objections are to a great extent met
by our old answer, that if the people are not utterly degraded, although
individually they may be worse judges than those who have special

knowledge—as a body they are as good or better. Moreover, there are some artists whose works are judged of solely, or in the best manner, not by themselves, but by those who do not possess the art; for example, the knowledge of the house is not limited to the builder only; the user, or, in other words, the master, of the house will even be a better judge than the builder, just as the pilot will judge better of a rudder than the carpenter, and the guest will judge better of a feast than the cook.

The Rule of Law

It is thought to be just that among equals every one be ruled as well as rule, and that all should have their turn. We thus arrive at law; for an order of succession implies law. And the rule of law is preferable to that of any individual. On the same principle, even if it be better for certain individuals to govern, they should be made only guardians and ministers of the law. For magistrates there must be,—this is admitted; but then men say that to give authority to any one man when all are equal is unjust. There may indeed be cases which the law seems unable to determine, but in such cases can a man? Nay, it will be replied, the law trains officers for this express purpose, and appointed them to determine matters which are left undecided by it to the best of their judgment. Further it permits them to make any amendment of the existing laws which experience suggests. He who bids the law rule, may be deemed to bid God and Reason alone rule, but he who bids man rule adds an element of the beast; for desire is a wild beast, and passion perverts the minds of rulers, even when they are the best of men. The law is reason unaffected by desire. 🖌

Although Aristotle was not of direct significance in the American political tradition, nevertheless there is little doubt that his emphasis upon the importance of democracy and the rule of law reflected parts of the Western heritage that formed a background against which American political philosophy developed. Many political thinkers were of more immediate importance in shaping the American constitutional tradition, and among these we would have to list John Locke as being one of the most dominating figures. It is not suggested that Locke was read by most of the colonists, but only that his ideas invariably found their way into many of the writings of 18th century America, not the least of which was the Declaration of Independence. In a letter to Henry Lee in 1825, Thomas Jefferson wrote that: "When forced . . . to resort to arms for redress, an appeal to the tribunal of the world was deemed proper for our justification. This was the object of the Declaration of Independence. Not to find out new principles, or new arguments, never before thought of, not merely to say things which had never been said before; but to place before mankind the common sense of the subject, in terms so plain and firm as to command their assent, and to justify ourselves in the independent stand we are compelled to take. Neither aiming at originality of principle or sentiment, nor yet copied from any particular and previous writing, it was intended to be an expression of the American mind, and to give to that expression the proper tone and spirit called for by the occasion. All its authority rests then on the harmonizing sentiments of the day, whether expressed in conversation, in letters, printed essays, or in the elementary books of public right [such] as Aristotle, Cicero, Locke, Sidney, etc. . . ." In May of 1790, Jefferson wrote that: "Locke's little book on government is perfect as far as it goes." Although Jefferson's admiration of Locke was perhaps greater than that of many other colonists, his views did reflect a mood of 18th century America. Locke's *Second Treatise, Of Civil Government* attempted to trace the reasons why men enter into political societies in the first place. The 18th century, no less than the 20th century, was an era characterized by attempts to be "scientific" in political formulations. Locke's *Second Treatise* was published first in 1690, and reflected the scientific emphasis that later was to prevail so widely beginning in the 18th century. To Locke, natural law was objectively valid, and therefore once ascertained, governments based upon it would have a superior claim to legitimacy. Locke is notable for his discussions of natural law, from which he derived the "best" form of government. In reading Locke it should be observed how much importance he placed upon property rights, and the right of the people to dissolve government once it no longer meets their legitimate expectations.

SECOND TREATISE, OF CIVIL GOVERNMENT

John Locke

Of the State of Nature

To understand political power aright, and derive it from its original, we must consider what estate all men are naturally in, and that is, a state of perfect freedom to order their actions, and dispose of their possessions and persons as they think fit, within the bounds of the law of

Nature, without asking leave or depending upon the will of any other man.

A state also of equality, wherein all the power and jurisdiction is reciprocal, no one having more than another, there being nothing more evident than that creatures of the same species and rank, promiscuously born to all the same advantages of Nature, and the use of the same faculties, should also be equal one amongst another, without subordination or subjection, unless the lord and master of them all should, by any manifest declaration of his will, set one above another, and confer on him, by an evident and clear appointment, an undoubted right to dominion and sovereignty. . . .

But though this be a state of liberty, yet it is not a state of license; though man in that state have an uncontrollable liberty to dispose of his person or possessions, yet he has not liberty to destroy himself, or so much as any creature in his possession, but where some nobler use than its bare preservation calls for it. The state of Nature has a law of Nature to govern it, which obliges every one, and reason, which is that law, teaches all mankind who will but consult it, that being all equal and independent, no one ought to harm another in his life, health, liberty or possessions . . . And, being furnished with like faculties, sharing all in one community of Nature, there cannot be supposed any such subordination among us that may authorize us to destroy one another, as if we were made for one another's uses, as the inferior ranks of creatures are for ours. Every one as he is bound to preserve himself, and not to quit his station wilfully, so by the like reason, when his own preservation comes not in competition, ought he as much as he can to preserve the rest of mankind, and not unless it be to do justice on an offender, take away or impair the life, or what tends to the preservation of the life, the liberty, health, limb, or goods of another.

And that all men may be restrained from invading others' rights, and from doing hurt to one another, and the law of Nature be observed, which willeth the peace and preservation of all mankind, the execution of the law of Nature is in that state put into every man's hands, whereby every one has a right to punish the transgressors of that law to such a degree as may hinder its violation. For the law of Nature would, as all other laws that concern men in this world, be in vain if there were nobody that in the state of Nature had a power to execute that law, and thereby preserve the innocent and restrain offenders; and if any one in the state of Nature may punish another for any evil he has done, every one may do so. For in that state of perfect equality, where naturally there is no superiority or jurisdiction of one over another, what any may do in prosecution of that law, every one must needs have a right to do.

And thus, in the state of Nature, one man comes by a power over another, but yet no absolute or arbitrary power to use a criminal, when he has got him in his hands, according to the passionate heats or boundless extravagancy of his own will, but only to retribute to him so far as calm reason and conscience dictate, what is proportionate to his transgression, which is so much as may serve for reparation and restraint. . . .

Every offence that can be committed in the state of Nature may, in the state of Nature, be also punished equally, and as far forth, as it may, in a commonwealth. For though it would be beside my present purpose to enter here into the particulars of the law of nature, or its measures of punishment, yet it is certain there is such a law, and that too as intelligible and plain to a rational creature and a studier of that law as the positive laws of commonwealths, nay, possibly plainer; as much as reason is easier to be understood than the fancies and intricate contrivances of men, following contrary and hidden interests put into words. . . .

Of the Ends of Political Society and Government

If man in the state of Nature be so free as has been said, if he be absolute lord of his own person and possessions, equal to the greatest and subject to nobody, why will he part with his freedom, this empire, and subject himself to the dominion and control of any other power? To which it is obvious to answer, that though in the state of Nature he hath such a right, yet the enjoyment of it is very uncertain and constantly exposed to the invasion of others; for all being kings as much as he, every man his equal, and the greater part no strict observers of equity and justice, the enjoyment of the property he has in this state is very unsafe, very insecure. This makes him willing to quit this condition which, however free, is full of fears and continual dangers; and it is not without reason that he seeks out and is willing to join in society with others who are already united, or have a mind to unite for the mutual preservation of their lives, liberties and estates, which I call by the general name—property.

The great and chief end, therefore, of men uniting into commonwealths, and putting themselves under government, is the preservation of their property; to which in the state of Nature there are many things wanting.

Firstly, there wants an established, settled, known law, received and allowed by common consent to be the standard of right and wrong, and the common measure to decide all controversies between them. For though the law of Nature be plain and intelligible to all rational creatures, yet men, being biased by their interest, as well as ignorant for want of study of it, are not apt to allow of it as a law binding to them in the application of it to their particular cases.

Secondly, in the state of Nature there wants a known and indifferent judge, with authority to determine all differences according to the established law. For every one in that state being both judge and executioner of the law of Nature, men being partial to themselves, passion and revenge is very apt to carry them too far, and with too much heat in their own cases, as well as negligence and unconcernedness, make them too remiss in other men's.

Thirdly, in the state of Nature there often wants power to back and support the sentence when right, and to give it due execution. They who by any injustice offended will seldom fail where they are able by force to make good their injustice. Such resistance many times makes the punishment dangerous, and frequently destructive to those who attempt it.

Thus mankind, notwithstanding all the privileges of the state of Nature, being but in an ill condition while they remain in it are quickly driven into society. Hence it comes to pass, that we seldom find any number of men live any time together in this state. The inconveniencies that they are therein exposed to by the irregular and uncertain exercise of the power every man has of punishing the transgressions of others, make them take sanctuary under the established laws of government, and therein seek the preservation of their property. It is this makes them so willingly give up every one his single power of punishing to be exercised by such alone as shall be appointed to it amongst them, and by such rules as the community, or those authorised by them to that purpose, shall agree on. And in this we have the original right and rise of both the legislative and executive power as well as of the governments and societies themselves.

For in the state of Nature to omit the liberty he has of innocent delights, a man has two powers. The first is to do whatsoever he thinks fit for the preservation of himself and others within the permission of the law of Nature; by which law, common to them all, he and all the rest of mankind are one community, make up one society distinct from all other creatures, and were it not for the corruption and viciousness of degenerate men, there would be no need of any other, no necessity that men should separate from this great and natural community, and associate into lesser combinations. The other power a man has in the state of Nature is the power to punish the crimes committed against that law. Both these he gives up when he joins in a private, if I may so call it, or particular political society, and incorporates into any commonwealth separate from the rest of mankind.

The first power—viz., of doing whatsoever he thought fit for the preservation of himself and the rest of mankind, he gives up to be regulated by laws made by the society, so far forth as the preservation of himself and the rest of that society shall require; which laws of the society in many things confine the liberty he had by the law of Nature.

Secondly, the power of punishing he wholly gives up, and engages his natural force, which he might before employ in the execution of the law of Nature, by his own single authority, as he thought fit, to assist the executive power of the society as the law thereof shall require. For being now in a new state, wherein he is to enjoy many conveniences from the labor, assistance, and society of others in the same community, as well as protection from its whole strength, he is to part also with as much of his natural liberty, in providing for himself, as the good, prosperity, and safety of the society shall require, which is not only necessary but just, since the other members of the society do the like.

But though men when they enter into society give up the equality, liberty, and executive power they had in the state of Nature into the hands of the society, to be so far disposed of by the legislative as the good of the society shall require, yet it being only with an intention in every one the better to preserve himself, his liberty and property (for no rational creature can be supposed to change his condition with an intention to be worse), the power of the society or legislative constituted by them can never be supposed to extend farther than the common good, but is obliged to secure every one's property by providing against those three defects above mentioned that made the state of Nature so unsafe and uneasy. And so, whoever has the legislative or supreme power of any commonwealth, is bound to govern by established standing laws, promulgated and known to the people, and not by extemporary decrees, by indifferent and upright judges, who are to decide controversies by those laws; and to employ the force of the community at home only in the execution of such laws, or abroad to prevent or redress foreign injuries and secure the community from inroads and invasion. And all this to be directed to no other end but the peace, safety, and public good of the people. . . .

Of the Extent of the Legislative Power

The great end of men's entering into society being the enjoyment of their properties in peace and safety, and the great instrument and means of that being the laws established in that society, the first and fundamental positive law of all commonwealths is the establishing of the legislative power, as the first and fundamental natural law, which is to govern even the legislative itself, is the preservation of the society and (as far as will consist with the public good) of every person in it. This legislative is not only the supreme power of the commonwealth, but sacred and unalterable in the hands where the community have once placed it. Nor can any edict of anybody else, in what form soever conceived, or by what power soever backed, have the force and obligation of a law which has not its sanction from that legislative which the public has chosen and appointed; for without this the law could not have that which is absolutely necessary to its being a law, the consent of the society, over whom nobody can have a power to make laws but by their own consent and by authority received from them. . . .

These are the bounds which the trust that is put in them by the society and the law of God and Nature have set to the legislative power of every commonwealth, in all forms of government. First: They are to govern by promulgated established laws, not to be varied in particular cases, but to have one rule for rich and poor, for the favorite at Court, and the countryman at plough. Secondly: These laws also ought to be designed for no other end ultimately but the good of the people. Thirdly: They must not raise taxes on the property of the people without the consent of the people given by themselves or their deputies. And this properly concerns only such governments where the legislative is always in being, or at least where the people have not reserved any part of the legislative to deputies, to be from time to time chosen by themselves. Fourthly: Legislative neither must nor can transfer the power of making laws to anybody else, or place it anywhere but where the people have. . . .

Of the Dissolution of Government

. . . The constitution of the legislative [authority] is the first and fundamental act of society, whereby provision is made for the continuation of their union under the direction of persons and bonds of laws, made by persons authorised thereunto, by the consent and appointment of the people, without which no one man, or number of men, amongst them can have authority of making laws that shall be binding to the rest. When any one, or more, shall take upon them to make laws whom the people have not appointed so to do, they make laws without authority, which the people are not therefore bound to obey; by which means they come again to be out of subjection, and may constitute to themselves a new legislative, as they think best, being in full liberty to resist the force of those who, without authority, would impose anything upon them. . . .

Whosoever uses force without right—as every one does in society who does it without law—puts himself into a state of war with those against whom he so uses it, and in that state all former ties are cancelled, all other rights cease, and every one has a right to defend himself, and to resist the aggressor. . . .

Here it is like the common question will be made: Who shall be judge whether the prince or legislative act contrary to their trust? This, perhaps, ill-affected and factious men may spread amongst the people, when the prince only makes use of his due prerogative. To this I reply, The people shall be judge; for who shall be judge whether his trustee or deputy acts well and according to the trust reposed in him, but he who deputes him and must, by having deputed him, have still a power to discard him when he fails in his trust? If this be reasonable in particular cases of private men, why should it be otherwise in that of the greatest moment, where the welfare of millions is concerned and also where the evil, if not prevented, is greater, and the redress very difficult, dear, and dangerous? . . .

To conclude. The power that every individual gave the society when he entered into it can never revert to the individuals again, as long as the society lasts, but will always remain in the community; because without this there can be no community—no commonwealth, which is contrary to the original agreement; so also when the society hath placed the legislative in any assembly of men, to continue in them and their successors, with direction and authority for providing such successors, the legislative can never revert to the people whilst that government lasts; because, having provided a legislative with power to continue for ever, they have given up their political power to the legislative, and cannot resume it. But if they have set limits to the duration of their legislative, and made this supreme power in any person or assembly only temporary; or else when, by the miscarriages of those in authority, it is forfeited; upon the forfeiture of their rulers, or at the determination of the time set, it reverts to the society, and the people have a right to act as supreme, and continue the legislative in themselves or place it in a new form, or new hands, as they think good. 🏴

2. The Separation of Powers: Theory and Mechanism

Hamilton noted in *Federalist 1* that "it seems to have been reserved to the people of this country, to decide by their conduct and example, the important question, whether societies of men are really capable or not, of establishing good government from reflection and choice, or whether they are for ever destined to depend, for their political constitutions, on accident and force." There is little doubt that the framers of our Constitution attempted, as Aristotle suggested was necessary, to devise a constitution particularly suited to function in the American environment, taking into account the needs and aspirations of the people. *The Federalist*, written between October 1787 and August 1788, is one of the few unique contributions that America has made to political theory. It should not only be noted for its general theoretical considerations, but also for providing us with a rare opportunity to lay bare the minds of those who framed the Constitution.

FEDERALIST 1

Alexander Hamilton

I PROPOSE, in a series of papers to discuss the following interesting particulars . . . The utility of the UNION to your political prosperity . . . The insufficiency of the present confederation to preserve that Union . . . The necessity of a government, at least equally energetic with the one proposed, to the attainment of this object . . . The conformity of the proposed constitution to the true principles of republican government . . . Its analogy to your own state constitution . . . and lastly, The additional security, which its adoption will afford to the preservation of that species of government, to liberty, and to property. 🏴

FEDERALIST 47

James Madison

I PROCEED to examine the particular structure of this government, and the distribution of this mass of power among its constituent parts.

One of the principal objections inculcated by the more respectable adversaries to the constitution, is its supposed violation of the political maxim, that the legislative, executive, and judiciary departments, ought to be separate and distinct. In the structure of the federal government, no regard, it is said, seems to have been paid to this essential precaution in favor of liberty. The several departments of power are distributed and blended in such a manner, as at once to destroy all symmetry and beauty of form; and to expose some of the essential parts of the edifice to the danger of being crushed by the disproportionate weight of other parts.

No political truth is certainly of greater intrinsic value, or is stamped with the authority of more enlightened patrons of liberty, than that on which the objection is founded. The accumulation of all powers, legislative, executive, and judiciary, in the same hands, whether of one, a few, or many, and whether hereditary, self-appointed, or elective, may justly be pronounced the very definition of tyranny. Were the federal constitution, therefore, really chargeable with this accumulation of power, or with a mixture of powers, having a dangerous tendency to such an accumulation, no further arguments would be necessary to inspire a universal reprobation of the system. I persuade myself, however, that it will be made apparent to every one, that the charge cannot be supported, and that the maxim on which it relies has been totally misconceived and misapplied.

The oracle who is always consulted and cited on this subject, is the celebrated Montesquieu. If he be not the author of this invaluable precept in the science of politics, he has the merit of at least displaying and recommending it most effectually to the attention of mankind. . . .

From . . . facts, by which Montesquieu was guided, it may clearly be inferred, that in saying, 'there can be no liberty, where the legislative and executive powers are united in the same person, or body of magistrates'; or 'if the power of judging, be not separated from the legislative and executive powers,' he did not mean that these departments ought to have no *partial agency* in, or no *control* over, the acts of each other. His meaning ... can amount to no more than this, that where the *whole* power of one department is exercised by the same hands which possess the *whole* power of another department, the fundamental principles of a free constitution are subverted....

If we look into the constitutions of the several states, we find, that notwithstanding the emphatical, and, in some instances, the unqualified terms in which this axiom has been laid down, there is not a single instance in which the several departments of power have been kept absolutely separate and distinct....

The constitution of Massachusetts has observed a sufficient, though less pointed caution, in expressing this fundamental article of liberty. It declares, 'that the legislative department shall never exercise the executive and judicial powers, or either of them: the executive shall never exercise the legislative and judicial powers, or either of them: the judicial shall never exercise the legislative and executive powers, or either of them.' This declaration corresponds precisely with the doctrine of Montesquieu. ... It goes no farther than to prohibit any one of the entire departments from exercising the powers of another department. In the very constitution to which it is prefixed, a partial mixture of powers has been admitted....

FEDERALIST 48

James Madison

... I SHALL undertake in the next place to show, that unless these departments be so far connected and blended, as to give to each a constitutional control over the others, the degree of separation which the maxim requires, as essential to a free government, can never in practice be duly maintained.

It is agreed on all sides, that the powers properly belonging to one of the departments ought not to be directly and completely administered by either of the other departments. It is equally evident, that neither of them ought to possess, directly or indirectly, an overruling influence over the others in the administration of their respective powers. It will not be denied, that power is of an encroaching nature, and that it ought to be effectually restrained from passing the limits assigned to it. After discriminating, therefore, in theory, the several classes of power, as they may in their nature be legislative, executive, or judiciary; the next, and most difficult task, is to provide some practical security for each, against the invasion of the others. What this security ought to be, is the great problem to be solved.

Will it be sufficient to mark, with precision, the boundaries of these departments, in the constitution of the government, and to trust to these parchment barriers against the encroaching spirit of power? This is the security which appears to have been principally relied on by the compilers of most American constitutions. But experience assures us, that the efficacy of the provision has been greatly overrated; and that some more adequate defense is indispensably necessary for the more feeble, against the more powerful members of the government. The legislative department is everywhere extending the sphere of its activity, and drawing all power into its impetuous vortex. . . .

In a government where numerous and extensive prerogatives are placed in the hands of an hereditary monarch, the executive department is very justly regarded as the source of danger, and watched with all the jealousy which a zeal for liberty ought to inspire. In a democracy, where a multitude of people exercise in person the legislative functions, and are continually exposed, by their incapacity for regular deliberation and concerted measures, to the ambitious intrigues of their executive magistrates, tyranny may well be apprehended on some favorable emergency, to start up in the same quarter. But in a representative republic, where the executive magistracy is carefully limited, both in the extent and the duration of its power; and where the legislative is exercised by an assembly, which is inspired by a supposed influence over the people, with an intrepid confidence in its own strength; which is sufficiently numerous to feel all the passions which actuate a multitude; yet not so numerous as to be incapable of pursuing the objects of its passions, by means which reason prescribes; it is against the enterprising ambition of this department, that the people ought to indulge all their jealousy and exhaust all their precautions.

The legislative department derives a superiority in our governments from other circumstances. Its constitutional powers being at once more extensive, and less susceptible of precise limits, it can, with the greater facility, mask, under complicated and indirect measures, the encroachment which it makes on the co-ordinate departments. It is not infrequently a question of real nicety in legislative bodies, whether the operation of a particular measure will, or will not extend beyond the legislative sphere. On the other side, the executive power being restrained within a narrower compass, and being more simple in its nature; and the judiciary being described by landmarks, still less uncertain, projects of usurpation by either of these departments would immediately betray and defeat themselves. Nor is this all: as the legislative department alone has access to the pockets of the people, and has in some constitutions full discretion, and in all a prevailing influence over the pecuniary rewards of those who fill the other departments; a dependence is thus created in the latter, which gives still greater facility to encroachments of the former. . . . 🖅

FEDERALIST 51

James Madison

To what expedient then shall we finally resort, for maintaining in practice the necessary partition of power among the several departments, as laid down in the constitution? The only answer that can be given is, that as all these exterior provisions are found to be inadequate, the defect must be supplied, by so contriving the interior structure of the government, as that its several constituent parts may, by their mutual relations, be the means of keeping each other in their proper places. . . .

In order to lay a due foundation for that separate and distinct exercise of the different powers of government, which, to a certain extent, is admitted on all hands to be essential to the preservation of liberty, it is evident that each department should have a will of its own; and consequently should be so constituted, that the members of each should have as little agency as possible in the appointment of the members of the others. . . .

It is equally evident, that the members of each department should be as little dependent as possible on those of the others, for the emoluments annexed to their offices. Were the executive magistrate, or the judges, not independent of the legislature in this particular, their independence in every other, would be merely nominal.

But the great security against a gradual concentration of the several powers in the same department, consists in giving to those who administer each department, the necessary constitutional means, and personal motives, to resist encroachments of the others. The provision for defense must in this, as in all other cases, be made commensurate to the danger of attack. Ambition must be made to counteract ambition. The interest of the man must be connected with the constitutional rights of the place. It may be a reflection on human nature, that such devices should be necessary to control the abuses of government. But what is government itself, but the greatest of all reflections on human nature? If men were angels, no government would be necessary. If angels were to govern men, neither external nor internal controls on government would be necessary. In framing a government, which is to be administered by men over men, the great difficulty lies in this: You must first enable the government to control the governed; and in the next place, oblige it to control itself. A dependence on the people is, no doubt, the primary control on the government; but experience has taught mankind the necessity of auxiliary precautions.

This policy of supplying by opposite and rival interests, the defect of better motives, might be traced through the whole system of human affairs, private as well as public. We see it particularly displayed in all the subordinate distributions of power; where the constant aim is, to divide and arrange the several offices in such a manner, as that each may be a check on the other; that the private interest of every individual, may be a sentinel over the public rights. These inventions of prudence cannot be less requisite to the distribution of the supreme powers of the state.

But it is not possible to give to each department an equal power of self-defense. In republican government, the legislative authority necessarily predominates. The remedy for this inconvenience is, to divide the legislature into different branches; and to render them by different modes of election, and different principles of action, as little connected with each other, as the nature of their common functions, and their common dependence on the society will admit. It may even be necessary to guard against dangerous encroachments, by still further precautions. As the weight of the legislative authority requires that it should be thus divided, the weakness of the executive may require, on the other hand, that it should be fortified. An absolute negative on the legislature, appears, at first view, to be the natural defense with which the executive magistrate should be armed. But perhaps it would be neither altogether safe, nor alone sufficient. On ordinary occasions, it might not be exerted with the requisite firmness; and on extraordinary occasions, it might be perfidiously abused. May not this defect of an absolute negative be supplied by some qualified connection between this weaker department, and the weaker branch of the stronger department, by which the latter may be led to support the constitutional rights of the former, without being too much detached from the rights of its own department?

3. The Constitutional Convention of 1787

The preceding selections have emphasized the importance the framers of the Constitution attached to the limitation of the authority of the national government. The separation of powers was an intricate mechanism designed to accomplish this goal. There is little doubt that the effect of the Constitution was to limit the ability of the majority of the people to operate in an unbridled fashion through the machinery of the national government. But it does not necessarily follow that most of the members of the Constitutional Convention were antidemocratic in their views. In attempting to assess motives, historical analysis is confronted with an almost impossible task. Indeed it can be argued that it is not the motives that count, but only the results of the actions that were taken. In this regard the Constitution was a conservative document that carefully provided for indirect rather than direct democracy. But with respect to the times in which it was drafted, the Constitution can be viewed in a different fashion. This is the argument of John P. Roche in the following selection.

THE FOUNDING FATHERS: A REFORM CAUCUS IN ACTION

John P. Roche*

Over the last century and a half, the work of the Constitutional Convention and the motives of the Founding Fathers have been analyzed under a number of different ideological auspices. To one generation of historians, the hand of God was moving in the assembly; under a later dispensation, the dialectic (at various levels of philosophical sophistication) replaced the Deity: "relationships of production" moved into the niche previously reserved for Love of Country. Thus in counterpart to the Zeitgeist, the Framers have undergone miraculous metamorphoses: at one time acclaimed as liberals and bold social engineers, today they appear in the guise of sound Burkean conservatives, men who in our time would subscribe to *Fortune,* look to Walter Lippmann for political theory, and chuckle patronizingly at the antics of Barry Goldwater. The implicit assumption is that if James Madison were among us, he would be Presi-

* Reprinted from *The American Political Science Review* (December 1961) by permission of The American Political Science Association and the author.

dent of the Ford Foundation, while Alexander Hamilton would chair the Committee for Economic Development.

The "Fathers" have thus been admitted to our best circles; the revolutionary ferocity which confiscated all Tory property in reach and populated New Brunswick with outlaws has been converted by the "Miltown School" of American historians into a benign dedication to "consensus" and "prescriptive rights." The Daughters of the American Revolution have, through the ministrations of Professors Boorstin, Hartz, and Rossiter, at last found ancestors worthy of their descendants. It is not my purpose here to argue that the "Fathers" were, in fact, radical revolutionaries; that proposition has been brilliantly demonstrated by Robert R. Palmer in his *Age of the Democratic Revolution.* My concern is with the further position that not only were they revolutionaries, but also they were democrats. Indeed, in my view, there is one fundamental truth about the Founding Fathers that *every* generation of Zeitgeisters has done its best to obscure: they were first and foremost superb democratic politicians. I suspect that in a contemporary setting, James Madison would be Speaker of the House of Representatives and Hamilton would be the *eminence grise* dominating (*pace* Theodore Sorenson or Sherman Adams) the Executive Office of the President. They were, with their colleagues, *political men*—not metaphysicians, disembodied conservatives or Agents of History—and as recent research into the nature of American politics in the 1780s confirms, they were committed (perhaps willy-nilly) to working within the democratic framework, within a universe of public approval. Charles Beard *and* the filiopietists to the contrary notwithstanding, the Philadelphia Convention was not a College of Cardinals or a council of Platonic guardians working within a manipulative, predemocratic framework; it was a *nationalist* reform caucus which had to operate with great delicacy and skill in a political cosmos full of enemies to achieve the one definitive goal—popular approbation.

Perhaps the time has come, to borrow Walton Hamilton's fine phrase, to raise the Framers from immortality to mortality, to give them credit for their magnificent demonstration of the art of democratic politics. The point must be reemphasized; they *made* history and did it within the limits of consensus. There was nothing inevitable about the future in 1787; the *Zeitgeist,* that fine Hegelian technique of begging causal questions, could only be discerned in retrospect. What they did was to hammer out a pragmatic compromise which would both bolster the "National interest" and be acceptable to the people. What inspiration they got came from their collective experience as professional politicians in a democratic society. As John Dickinson put it to his fellow delegates on August 13, "Experience must be our guide. Reason may mislead us."

In this context, let us examine the problems they confronted and the solutions they evolved. The Convention has been described picturesquely as a counter-revolutionary junta and the Constitution as a *coup d'état,* but this has been accomplished by withdrawing the whole history of the movement for constitutional reform from its true context. No doubt the goals of the constitutional elite were "subversive" to the existing political order, but it is overlooked that their subversion could only have succeeded if the people of the United States endorsed it by regularized procedures. Indubitably they were "plotting" to establish a much stronger central government than existed under the Articles, but only in the sense in which one could argue equally well that John F. Kennedy was, from 1956 to 1960, "plotting" to become President. In short, on the fundamental *procedural* level, the Constitutionalists had to work according to the prevailing rules of the game. Whether they liked it or not is a topic for spiritualists—and is irrelevant: one may be quite certain that had Washington agreed to play the de Gaulle (as the Cincinnati once urged), Hamilton would willingly have held his horse, but such fertile speculation in no way alters the actual context in which events took place.

I

When the Constitutionalists went forth to subvert the Confederation, they utilized the mechanisms of political legitimacy. And the roadblocks which confronted them were formidable. At the same time, they were endowed with certain potent political assets. The history of the United States from 1786 to 1790 was largely one of a masterful employment of political expertise by the Constitutionalists as against bumbling, erratic behavior by the opponents of reform. Effectively, the Constitutionalists had to induce the states, by democratic techniques of coercion, to emasculate themselves. To be specific, if New York had refused to join the new Union, the project was doomed; yet before New York was safely in, the reluctant state legislature had *sua sponte* to take the following steps: (1) agree to send delegates to the Philadelphia Convention; (2) provide maintenance for these delegates (these were distinct stages: New Hampshire was early in naming delegates, but did not provide for their maintenance until July); (3) set up the special *ad hoc* convention to decide on ratification; and (4) concede to the decision of the *ad hoc* convention that New York should participate. New York admittedly was a tricky state, with a strong interest in a *status quo* which permitted her to exploit New Jersey and Connecticut, but the same legal hurdles existed in every state. And at the risk of becoming boring, it must be reiterated that the *only* weapon in the Constitutionalist arsenal was an effective mobilization of public opinion.

The group which undertook this struggle was an interesting amalgam of a few dedicated nationalists with the self-interested spokesmen of various parochial bailiwicks. The Georgians, for example, wanted a strong central authority to provide military protection for their huge, underpopulated state against the Creek Confederacy; Jerseymen and Connecticuters wanted to escape from economic bondage to New York; the Virginians hoped to establish a system which would give that great state its rightful place in the councils of the republic. The dominant figures in the politics of these states therefore cooperated in the call for the Convention. In other states, the thrust towards national reform was taken up by opposition groups who added the "national interest" to their weapons system; in Pennsylvania, for instance, the group fighting to revise the Constitution of 1776 came out four-square behind the Constitutionalists, and in New York, Hamilton and the Schuyler *ambiance* took the same tack against George Clinton. There was, of course, a large element of personality in the affair: there is reason to suspect that Patrick Henry's opposition to the Convention and the Constitution was founded on his conviction that Jefferson was behind both, and a close study of local politics elsewhere would surely reveal that others supported the Constitution for the simple (and politically quite sufficient) reason that the "wrong" people were against it.

To say this is not to suggest that the Constitution rested on a foundation of impure or base motives. It is rather to argue that in politics there are no immaculate conceptions, and that in the drive for a stronger general government, motives of all sorts played a part. Few men in the history of mankind have espoused a view of the "common good" or "public interest" that militated against their private status; even Plato with all his reverence for disembodied reason managed to put philosophers on top of the pile. Thus it is not surprising that a number of diversified private interests joined to push the nationalist public interest; what would have been surprising was the absence of such a pragmatic united front. And the fact remains that, however motivated, these men did demonstrate a willingness to compromise their parochial interests in behalf of an ideal which took shape before their eyes and under their ministrations.

As Stanley Elkins and Eric McKitrick have suggested in a perceptive essay [76 *Pol. Science Quarterly* 181 (1961)], what distinguished the leaders of the Constitutionalist caucus from their enemies was a "Continental" approach to political, economic and military issues. To the extent that they shared an institutional base of operations, it was the Continental Congress (thirty-nine of the delegates to the Federal Convention had served in Congress), and this was hardly a locale which inspired respect for the state governments. Robert de Jouvenal observed French politics half a century ago and noted that a revolutionary Deputy had more in common with a non-revolutionary Deputy than he had with a revolutionary non-Deputy; similarly one can surmise that membership in the Congress under the Articles of Confederation worked to establish a continental frame of reference, that a Congressman from Pennsylvania and one from South Carolina would share a universe of discourse which provided them with a conceptual common denominator *vis à vis* their respective state legislatures. This was particularly true with respect to external affairs: the average state legislator was probably about as concerned with foreign policy then as he is today, but Congressmen were constantly forced to take the broad view of American prestige, were compelled to listen to the reports of Secretary John Jay and to the dispatches and pleas from their frustrated envoys in Britain, France and Spain. From considerations such as these, a "Continental" ideology developed which seems to have demanded a revision of our domestic institutions primarily on the ground that only by invigorating our general government could we assume our rightful place in the international arena. Indeed, an argument with great force—particularly since Washington was its incarnation—urged that our very survival in the Hobbesian jungle of world politics depended upon a reordering and strengthening of our national sovereignty.

The great achievement of the Constitutionalists was their ultimate success in convincing the elected representatives of a majority of the white male population that change was imperative. A small group of political leaders with a Continental vision and essentially a consciousness of the United States' *international* impotence, provided the matrix of the movement. To their standard other leaders rallied with their own parallel ambitions. Their great assets were (1) the presence in their caucus of the one authentic American "father figure," George Washington, whose prestige was enormous; (2) the energy and talent of their leadership (in which one must include the towering intellectuals of the time, John Adams and Thomas Jefferson, despite their absence abroad), and their communications "network," which was far superior to anything on the opposition side; (3) the preemptive skill which made "their" issue The Issue and kept the locally oriented opposition permanently on the defensive; and (4) the subjective consideration that these men were spokesmen of a new and compelling credo: *American* nationalism, that ill-defined but none-theless potent sense of collective purpose that emerged from the American Revolution.

Despite great institutional handicaps, the Constitutionalists managed in the mid-1780s to mount an offensive which gained momentum as years went by. Their greatest problem was lethargy, and paradoxically, the number of barriers in their path may have proved an advantage in the long run. Beginning with the initial battle to get the Constitutional Convention called and delegates appointed, they could never relax, never let up the pressure. In practical terms, this meant that the local "organizations" created by the Constitutionalists were perpetually in movement building up their cadres for the next fight. (The word organization has to be used with great caution: a political organization in the United States —as in contemporary England—generally consisted of a magnate and his following, or a coalition of magnates. This did not necessarily mean that it was "undemocratic" or "aristocratic," in the Aristotelian sense of the word: while a few magnates such as the Livingstons could draft their followings, most exercised their leadership without coercion on the basis of popular endorsement. The absence of organized opposition did not imply the impossibility of competition any more than low public participation in elections necessarily indicated an undemocratic suffrage.)

The Constitutionalists got the jump on the "opposition" (a collective noun: oppositions would be more correct) at the outset with the demand for a Convention. Their opponents were caught in an old political trap: they were not being asked to approve any specific program of reform, but only to endorse a meeting to discuss and recommend needed reforms. If they took a hard line at the first stage, they were put in the position of glorifying the *status quo* and of denying the need for *any* changes. More-over, the Constitutionalists could go to the people with a persuasive argument for "fair play"—"How can you condemn reform before you know precisely what is involved?" Since the state legislatures obviously would have the final say on any proposals that might emerge from the Convention, the Constitutionalists were merely reasonable men asking for a chance. Besides, since they did not make any concrete proposals at that stage, they were in a position to capitalize on every sort of generalized discontent with the Confederation.

Perhaps because of their poor intelligence system, perhaps because of over-confidence generated by the failure of all previous efforts to alter the Articles, the opposition awoke too late to the dangers that confronted them in 1787. Not only did the Constitutionalists manage to get every state but Rhode Island (where politics was enlivened by a party system reminiscent of the "Blues" and the "Greens" in the Byzantine Empire) to appoint delegates to Philadelphia, but when the results were in, it appeared that they dominated the delegations. Given the apathy of the opposition, this was a natural phenomenon: in an ideologically nonpolarized political atmosphere those who get appointed to a special committee are likely to be the men who supported the movement for its creation. Even George Clinton, who seems to have been the first opposition leader to awake to the possibility of trouble, could not prevent the New York legislature from appointing Alexander Hamilton—though he did have the foresight to send two of his henchmen to dominate the delegation. Incidentally, much has been made of the fact that the delegates to Philadelphia were not elected by the people; some have adduced this fact as evidence of the "undemocratic" character of the gathering. But put in the context of the time, this argument is wholly specious: the central government under the Articles was considered a creature of the component states and in all the states but Rhode Island, Connecticut and New Hampshire, members of the national Congress were chosen by the state legislatures. This was not a consequence of elitism or fear of the mob; it was a logical extension of states'-rights doctrine to guarantee that the national institution did not end-run the state legislatures and make direct contact with the people.

II

With delegations safely named, the focus shifted to Philadelphia. While waiting for a quorum to assemble, James Madison got busy and drafted the so-called Randolph or Virginia Plan with the aid of the Virginia delegation. This was a political master-stroke. Its consequence was that once business got underway, the framework of discussion was established on Madison's terms. There was no interminable argument over agenda; instead the delegates took the Virginia Resolutions—"just for purposes of discussion"—as their point of departure. And along with Madison's proposals, many of which were buried in the course of the summer, went his major premise: a new start on a Constitution rather than piecemeal amendment. This was not necessarily revolutionary—a little exegesis could demonstrate that a new Constitution might be formulated as "amendments" to the Articles of Confederation—but Madison's proposal that this "lump sum" amendment go into effect after approval by nine states (the Articles required unanimous state approval for any amendment) was thoroughly subversive.

Standard treatments of the Convention divide the delegates into "nationalists" and "states'-righters" with various improvised shadings ("moderate nationalists," etc.), but these are *a posteriori* categories which obfuscate more than they clarify. What is striking to one who analyzes the Convention as a case-study in democratic politics is the lack of clear-cut ideological divisions in the Convention. Indeed, I submit that the evidence—Madison's *Notes,* the correspondence of the delegates, and debates on ratification—indicates that this was a remarkably homogeneous body on the ideological level. Yates and Lansing, Clinton's two chaperones for Hamilton, left in disgust on July 10. (Is there anything more tedious than sitting through endless disputes on matters one deems fundamentally misconceived? It takes an iron will to spend a hot summer as an ideological *agent provocateur.*) Luther Martin, Maryland's bibulous narcissist, left on September 4 in a huff when he discovered that others did not share his self-esteem; others went home for personal reasons. But the hard core of delegates accepted a grinding regimen throughout the attrition of a Philadelphia summer precisely because they shared the Constitutionalist goal.

Basic differences of opinion emerged, of course, but these were not ideological; they were *structural.* If the so-called "states'-rights" group had not accepted the fundamental purposes of the Convention, they could simply have pulled out and by doing so have aborted the whole enterprise. Instead of bolting, they returned day after day to argue and to compromise. An interesting symbol of this basic homogeneity was the initial agreement on secrecy: these professional politicians did not want to become prisoners of publicity; they wanted to retain that freedom of maneuver which is only possible when men are not forced to take public stands in the preliminary stages of negotiation. There was no legal means of binding the tongues of the delegates: at any stage in the game a delegate with basic principled objections to the emerging project could have taken the stump (as Luther Martin did after his exit) and denounced the convention to the skies. Yet Madison did not even inform Thomas Jefferson in Paris of the course of the deliberations and available correspondence indicates that the delegates generally observed the injunction. Secrecy is certainly uncharacteristic of any assembly marked by strong ideological polarization. This was noted at the time: the *New York Daily Advertiser,* August 14, 1787, commented that the " . . . profound secrecy hitherto observed by the Convention [we consider] a happy omen, as it demonstrates that the spirit of party on any great and essential point cannot have arisen to any height."

Commentators on the Constitution who have read *The Federalist* in lieu of reading the actual debates have credited the Fathers with the invention of a sublime concept called "Federalism." Unfortunately *The Federalist* is probative evidence for only one proposition: that Hamilton and Madison were inspired propagandists with a genius for retrospective symmetry. Federalism, as the theory is generally defined, was an improvisation which was later promoted into a political theory. Experts on "federalism" should take to heart the advice of David Hume, who warned in his *Of the Rise and Progress of the Arts and Sciences* that " . . . there is no subject in which we must proceed with more caution than in [history], lest we assign causes which never existed and reduce what is merely contingent to stable and universal principles." In any event, the final balance in the Constitution between the states and the nation must have come as a great disappointment to Madison, while Hamilton's unitary views are too well known to need elucidation.

It is indeed astonishing how those who have glibly designated James Madison the "father" of Federalism have overlooked the solid body of fact which indicates that he shared Hamilton's quest for a unitary central government. To be specific, they have avoided examining the clear import of the Madison-Virginia Plan, and have disregarded Madison's dogged inch-by-inch retreat from the bastions of centralization. The Virginia Plan envisioned a unitary national government effectively freed from and dominant over the states. The lower house of the national legislature was to be elected directly by the people of the states with membership proportional to population. The upper house was to be selected by the lower and the two chambers would elect the executive and choose the judges. The national government would be thus cut completely loose from the states.

The structure of the general government was freed from state control in a truly radical fashion, but the scope of the authority of the national sovereign as Madison initially formulated it was breathtaking—it was a formulation worthy of the Sage of Malmesbury himself. The national legislature was to be empowered to disallow the acts of state legislatures, and the central government was vested, in addition to the powers of the nation under the Articles of Confederation, with plenary authority wherever " . . . the separate States are incompetent or in which the harmony of the United States may be interrupted by the exercise of individual legislation." Finally, just to lock the door against state intrusion, the national Congress was to be given the power to use military force on recalcitrant states. This was Madison's "model" of an ideal national government, though it later received little publicity in *The Federalist*.

The interesting thing was the reaction of the Convention to this militant program for a strong autonomous central government. Some delegates were startled, some obviously leery of so comprehensive a project of reform, but nobody set off any fireworks and nobody walked out. Moreover, in the two weeks that followed, the Virginia Plan received substantial endorsement *en principe;* the initial temper of the gathering can be deduced from the approval "without debate or dissent," on May 31, of the Sixth Resolution which granted Congress the authority to disallow state legislation ". . . contravening *in its opinion* the Articles of Union." Indeed, an amendment was included to bar states from contravening national treaties.

The Virginia Plan may therefore be considered, in ideological terms, as the delegates' Utopia, but as the discussions continued and became more specific, many of those present began to have second thoughts. After all, they were not residents of Utopia or guardians in Plato's Republic who could simply impose a philosophical ideal on subordinate strata of the population. They were practical politicians in a democratic society, and no matter what their private dreams might be, they had to take home an acceptable package and defend it—and their own political futures—against predictable attack. On June 14 the breaking point between dream and reality took place. Apparently realizing that under the Virginia Plan, Massachusetts, Virginia and Pennsylvania could virtually dominate the national government—and probably appreciating that to sell this program to "the folks back home" would be impossible—the delegates from the small states dug in their heels and demanded time for a consideration of alternatives. One gets a graphic sense of the inner politics from John Dickinson's reproach to Madison: "You see the consequences of pushing things too far. Some of the members from the small States wish for two branches in the General Legislature and are friends to a good National Government; but we would sooner submit to a foreign power than . . . be deprived of an equality of suffrage in both branches of the Legislature, and thereby be thrown under the domination of the large States."

The bare outline of the *Journal* entry for Tuesday, June 14, is suggestive to anyone with extensive experience in deliberative bodies. "It was moved by Mr. Patterson [*sic,* Paterson's name was one of those consistently misspelled by Madison and everybody else] seconded by Mr. Randolph that the further consideration of the report from the Committee of the whole House [endorsing the Virginia Plan] be postponed til tomorrow and before the question for postponement was taken. It was moved by Mr. Randolph seconded by Mr. Patterson that the House adjourn." The House adjourned by obvious prearrangement of the two principals: since the preceding Saturday when Brearley and Paterson of New Jersey had announced their fundamental discontent with the representational features of the Virginia Plan, the informal pressure had certainly been building up to slow down the streamroller. Doubtless there were extended arguments at the Indian Queen between Madison and Paterson, the latter insisting that events were moving rapidly towards a probably disastrous conclusion, towards a political suicide pact. Now the process of accommodation was put into action smoothly—and wisely, given the character and strength of the doubters. Madison had the votes, but this was one of those situations where the enforcement of mechanical majoritarianism could easily have destroyed the objectives of the majority: the Constitutionalists were in quest of a qualitative as well as a quantitative consensus. This was hardly from deference to local Quaker custom; it was a political imperative if they were to attain ratification.

III

According to the standard script, at this point the "states'-rights" group intervened in force behind the New Jersey Plan, which has been characteristically portrayed as a reversion to the *status quo* under the Articles of Confederation with but minor modifications. A careful examination of the evidence indicates that only in a marginal sense is this an accurate description. It is true that the New Jersey Plan put the states back into the institutional picture, but one could argue that to do so was a recognition of political reality rather than an affirmation of states'-rights. A serious case can be made that the advocates of the New Jersey Plan, far from being ideological addicts of states'-rights, intended to substitute for the Virginia Plan a system which would both retain strong national power and have a chance of adoption in the states. The leading spokesman for the project asserted quite clearly that his views were based more on counsels of expediency than on principle; said Paterson on June 16: "I came here not to speak my own sentiments, but the sentiments of those who sent me. Our object is not such a Governmt. as may be best in itself, but such a one as our Constituents have authorized us to prepare, and as they will approve." This is Madison's version; in Yates' transcription, there is a crucial sentence following the remarks above: "I believe that a little practical virtue is to be preferred to the finest theoretical principles, which cannot be carried into effect." In his preliminary speech on June 9, Paterson had stated " . . . to the public mind we must accommodate ourselves," and in his notes for this and his later effort as well, the emphasis is the same. The *structure* of government under the Articles should be retained:

> 2. Because it accords with the Sentiments of the People
> [Proof:] 1. Coms. [Commissions from state legislatures defining the jurisdiction of the delegates]
> 2. News-papers—Political Barometer. Jersey never would have sent Delegates under the first [Virginia] Plan—
> Not here to sport Opinions of my own. Wt. [What] can be done.
> A little practicable Virtue preferrable to Theory.

This was a defense of political acumen, not of states'-rights. In fact, Paterson's notes of his speech can easily be construed as an argument for attaining the substantive objectives of the Virginia Plan by a sound political route, *i.e.,* pouring the new wine in the old bottles. With a shrewd eye, Paterson queried:

> Will the Operation and Force of the [central] Govt. depend upon the mode of Representn.—No—it will depend upon the Quantum of Power lodged in the leg. ex. and judy. Departments—Give [the existing] Congress the same Powers that you intend to give the two Branches, [under the Virginia Plan] and I apprehend they will act with as much Propriety and more Energy . . .

In other words, the advocates of the New Jersey Plan concentrated their fire on what they held to be the *political liabilities* of the Virginia Plan —which were matters of institutional structure—rather than on the proposed scope of national authority. Indeed, the Supremacy Clause of the Constitution first saw the light of day in Paterson's Sixth Resolution; the New Jersey Plan contemplated the use of military force to secure compliance with national law; and finally Paterson made clear his view that under either the Virginia or the New Jersey systems, the general government would ". . . act on individuals and not on states." From the states'-rights viewpoint, this was heresy: the fundament of that doctrine was the proposition that any central government had as its constituents the states, not the people, and could only reach the people through the agency of the state government.

Paterson then reopened the agenda of the Convention, but he did so within a distinctly nationalist framework. Paterson's position was one of favoring a strong central government in principle, but opposing one which in fact *put the big states in the saddle.* (The Virginia Plan, for all

its abstract merits, did very well by Virginia.) As evidence for this speculation, there is a curious and intriguing proposal among Paterson's preliminary drafts of the New Jersey Plan:

> Whereas it is necessary in Order to form the People of the U.S. of Amer-
> ica in to a Nation, that the States should be consolidated, by which means
> all the Citizens thereof will become equally intitled to and will equally
> participate in the same Privileges and Rights . . . it is therefore resolved,
> that all the Lands contained within the Limits of each state individually,
> and of the U.S. generally be considered as constituting one Body or Mass,
> and be divided into thirteen or more integral parts.
>
> Resolved, That such Divisions or integral Parts shall be styled Districts.

This makes it sound as though Paterson was prepared to accept a strong
unified central government along the lines of the Virginia Plan if the existing states were eliminated. He may have gotten the idea from his New
Jersey colleague Judge David Brearley, who on June 9 had commented
that the only remedy to the dilemma over representation was ". . . that a
map of the U. S. be spread out, that all the existing boundaries be erased,
and that a new partition of the whole be made into 13 equal parts." According to Yates, Brearley added at this point, ". . . then a government
on the present [Virginia Plan] system will be just."

This proposition was never pushed—it was patently unrealistic—but
one can appreciate its purpose: it would have separated the men from
the boys in the large-state delegations. How attached would the Virginians
have been to their reform principles if Virginia were to disappear as a
component geographical unit (the largest) for representational purposes?
Up to this point, the Virginians had been in the happy position of supporting high ideals with that inner confidence born of knowledge that
the "public interest" they endorsed would nourish their private interest.
Worse, they had shown little willingness to compromise. Now the delegates from the small states announced that they were unprepared to be
offered up as sacrificial victims to a "national interest" which reflected
Virginia's parochial ambition. Caustic Charles Pinckney was not far off
when he remarked sardonically that ". . . the whole [conflict] comes to
this": "Give N. Jersey an equal vote, and she will dismiss her scruples,
and concur in the Natil. system." What he rather unfairly did not add
was that the Jersey delegates were not free agents who could adhere to
their private convictions; they had to take back, sponsor and risk their
reputations on the reforms approved by the Convention—and in New
Jersey, not in Virginia.

Paterson spoke on Saturday, and one can surmise that over the week-end there was a good deal of consultation, argument, and caucusing among the delegates. One member at least prepared a full length address: on Monday Alexander Hamilton, previously mute, rose and delivered a six-hour oration. It was a remarkably apolitical speech; the gist of his position was that *both* the Virginia and New Jersey Plans were inadequately centralist, and he detailed a reform program which was reminiscent of the Protectorate under the Cromwellian *Instrument of Government* of 1653. It has been suggested that Hamilton did this in the best political tradition to emphasize the moderate character of the Virginia Plan, to give the cautious delegates something *really* to worry about; but this interpretation seems somehow too clever. Particularly since the sentiments Hamilton expressed happened to be completely consistent with those he privately—and sometimes publicly—expressed throughout his life. He wanted, to take a striking phrase from a letter to George Washington, a "strong well mounted government"; in essence, the Hamilton Plan contemplated an elected life monarch, virtually free of public control, on the Hobbesian ground that only in this fashion could strength and stability be achieved. The other alternatives, he argued, would put policy-making at the mercy of the passions of the mob; only if the sovereign was beyond the reach of selfish influence would it be possible to have government in the interests of the whole community.

From all accounts, this was a masterful and compelling speech, but (aside from furnishing John Lansing and Luther Martin with ammunition for later use against the Constitution) it made little impact. Hamilton was simply transmitting on a different wave-length from the rest of the delegates; the latter adjourned after his great effort, admired his rhetoric, and then returned to business. It was rather as if they had taken a day off to attend the opera. Hamilton, never a particularly patient man or much of a negotiator, stayed for another ten days and then left, in considerable disgust, for New York. Although he came back to Philadelphia sporadically and attended the last two weeks of the Convention, Hamilton played no part in the laborious task of hammering out the Constitution. His day came later when he led the New York Constitutionalists into the savage imbroglio over ratification—an arena in which his unmatched talent for dirty political infighting may well have won the day. For instance, in the New York Ratifying Convention, Lansing threw back into Hamilton's teeth the sentiments the latter had expressed in his June 18 oration in the Convention. However, having since retreated to the fine defensive positions immortalized in *The Federalist,* the Colonel flatly denied that he had ever been an enemy of the states, or had believed that conflict between states and nation was inexorable! As Madison's authoritative *Notes* did not appear until 1840, and there had been no press coverage, there was no way to verify his assertions, so in the words of the reporter, ". . . a warm personal altercation between [Lansing and Hamilton] engrossed the remainder of the day [June 28, 1788]."

IV

On Tuesday morning, June 19, the vacation was over. James Madison led off with a long, carefully reasoned speech analyzing the New Jersey Plan which, while intellectually vigorous in its criticisms, was quite conciliatory in mood. "The great difficulty," he observed, "lies in the affair of Representation; and if this could be adjusted, all others would be surmountable." (As events were to demonstrate, this diagnosis was correct.) When he finished, a vote was taken on whether to continue with the Virginia Plan as the nucleus for a new constitution: seven states voted "Yes"; New York, New Jersey, and Delaware voted "No"; and Maryland, whose position often depended on which delegates happened to be on the floor, divided. Paterson, it seems, lost decisively; yet in a fundamental sense he and his allies had achieved their purpose: from that day onward, it could never be forgotten that the state governments loomed ominously in the background and that no verbal incantations could exorcise their power. Moreover, nobody bolted the convention: Paterson and his colleagues took their defeat in stride and set to work to modify the Virginia Plan, particularly with respect to its provisions on representation in the national legislature. Indeed, they won an immediate rhetorical bonus; when Oliver Ellsworth of Connecticut rose to move that the word "national" be expunged from the Third Virginia Resolution ("Resolved that a *national* Government ought to be established consisting of a *supreme* Legislative, Executive and Judiciary"), Randolph agreed and the motion passed unanimously. The process of compromise had begun.

For the next two weeks, the delegates circled around the problem of legislative representation. The Connecticut delegation appears to have evolved a possible compromise quite early in the debates, but the Virginians and particularly Madison (unaware that he would later be acclaimed as the prophet of "federalism") fought obdurately against providing for equal representation of states in the second chamber. There was a good deal of acrimony and at one point Benjamin Franklin—of all people—proposed the institution of a daily prayer; practical politicians in the gathering, however, were meditating more on the merits of a good committee than on the utility of Divine intervention. On July 2, the ice began to break when through a number of fortuitous events—and one that seems deliberate—the majority against equality of representation was converted into a dead tie. The Convention had reached the stage where it was "ripe" for a solution (presumably all the therapeutic speeches had been made), and the South Carolinians proposed a committee. Madison and James Wilson wanted none of it, but with only Pennsylvania dissenting, the body voted to establish a working party on the problem of representation.

The members of this committee, one from each state, were elected by the delegates—and a very interesting committee it was. Despite the fact that the Virginia Plan had held majority support up to that date, neither Madison nor Randolph was selected (Mason was the Virginian) and Baldwin of Georgia, whose shift in position had resulted in the tie, was chosen. From the composition, it was clear that this was not to be a "fighting" committee: the emphasis in membership was on what might be described as "second-level political entrepreneurs." On the basis of the discussions up to that time, only Luther Martin of Maryland could be described as a "bitter-ender." Admittedly, some divination enters into this sort of analysis, but one does get a sense of the mood of the delegates from these choices—including the interesting selection of Benjamin Franklin, despite his age and intellectual wobbliness, over the brilliant and incisive Wilson or the sharp, polemical Gouverneur Morris, to represent Pennsylvania. His passion for conciliation was more valuable at this juncture than Wilson's logical genius, or Morris' acerbic wit.

There is a common rumor that the Framers divided their time between philosophical discussions of government and reading the classics in political theory. Perhaps this is as good a time as any to note that their concerns were highly practical, that they spent little time canvassing abstractions. A number of them had some acquaintance with the history of political theory (probably gained from reading John Adams' monumental compilation *A Defense of the Constitutions of Government,* the first volume of which appeared in 1786), and it was a poor rhetorician indeed who could not cite Locke, Montesquieu, or Harrington *in support* of a desired goal. Yet up to this point in the deliberations, no one had expounded a defense of states'-rights or the "separation of powers" on anything resembling a theoretical basis. It should be reiterated that the Madison model had no room either for the states or for the "separation of powers": effectively *all* governmental power was vested in the national legislature. The merits of Montesquieu did not turn up until *The Federalist;* and although a perverse argument could be made that Madison's ideal was truly in the tradition of John Locke's *Second Treatise of Government,* the Locke whom the American rebels treated as an honorary president was a pluralistic defender of vested rights, not of parliamentary supremacy.

It would be tedious to continue a blow-by-blow analysis of the work of the delegates; the critical fight was over representation of the states and once the Connecticut Compromise was adopted on July 17, the Convention was over the hump. Madison, James Wilson, and Gouverneur Morris of New York (who was there representing Pennsylvania!) fought the compromise all the way in a last-ditch effort to get a unitary state with parliamentary supremacy. But their allies deserted them and they demonstrated after their defeat the essentially opportunist character of their objections—using "opportunist" here in a non-pejorative sense, to indicate a willingness to swallow their objections and get on with the business. Moreover, once the compromise had carried (by five states to four, with one state divided), its advocates threw themselves vigorously into the job of strengthening the general government's substantive powers —as might have been predicted, indeed, from Paterson's early statements. It nourishes an increased respect for Madison's devotion to the art of politics, to realize that this dogged fighter could sit down six months later and prepare essays for *The Federalist* in contradiction to his basic convictions about the true course the Convention should have taken.

v

Two tricky issues will serve to illustrate the later process of accommodation. The first was the institutional position of the Executive. Madison argued for an executive chosen by the National Legislature and on May 29 this had been adopted with a provision that after his seven-year term was concluded, the chief magistrate should not be eligible for re-election. In late July this was reopened and for a week the matter was argued from several different points of view. A good deal of desultory speech-making ensued, but the gist of the problem was the opposition from two sources to election by the legislature. One group felt that the states should have a hand in the process; another small but influential circle urged direct election by the people. There were a number of proposals: election by the people, election by state governers, by electors chosen by state legislatures, by the National Legislature (James Wilson, perhaps ironically, proposed at one point that an Electoral College be chosen by lot from the National Legislature!), and there was some resemblance to three-dimensional chess in the dispute because of the presence of two other variables, length of tenure and reeligibility. Finally, after opening, reopening, and re-reopening the debate, the thorny problem was consigned to a committee for absolution.

The Brearley Committee on Postponed Matters was a superb aggregation of talent and its compromise on the Executive was a masterpiece of political improvisation. (The Electoral College, its creation, however, had little in its favor as an *institution*—as the delegates well appreciated.) The point of departure for all discussion about the presidency in the Convention was that in immediate terms, the problem was non-existent; in other words, everybody present knew that under any system devised, George Washington would be President. Thus they were dealing in the future tense and to a body of working politicians the merits of the Brearley proposal were obvious: everybody got a piece of cake. (Or to put it more academically, each viewpoint could leave the Convention and argue to its constitutents that it had *really* won the day.) First, the state legislatures had the right to determine the mode of selection of the electors; second, the small states received a bonus in the Electoral College in the form of a guaranteed minimum of three votes while the big states got acceptance of the principle of proportional power; third, if the state legislatures agreed (as six did in the first presidential election), the people could be involved directly in the choice of electors; and finally, if no candidate received a majority in the College, the right of decision passed to the National Legislature with each state exercising equal strength. (In the Brearley recommendation, the election went to the Senate, but a motion from the floor substituted the House; this was accepted on the ground that the Senate already had enough authority over the executive in its treaty and appointment powers.)

This compromise was almost too good to be true, and the Framers snapped it up with little debate or controversy. No one seemed to think well of the College as an *institution;* indeed, what evidence there is suggests that there was an assumption that once Washington had finished his tenure as President, the electors would cease to produce majorities and the chief executive would usually be chosen in the House. George Mason observed casually that the selection would be made in the House nineteen times in twenty and no one seriously disputed this point. The vital aspect of the Electoral College was that it got the Convention over the hurdle and protected everybody's interests. The future was left to cope with the problem of what to do with this Rube Goldberg mechanism.

In short, the Framers did not in their wisdom endow the United States with a College of Cardinals—the Electoral College was neither an exercise in applied Platonism nor an experiment in indirect government based on elitist distrust of the masses. It was merely a jerry-rigged improvisation which has subsequently been endowed with a high theoretical content. When an elector from Oklahoma in 1960 refused to cast his vote for Nixon (naming Byrd and Goldwater instead) on the ground that the Founding Fathers intended him to exercise his great independent wisdom, he was indulging in historical fantasy. If one were to indulge in counter-fantasy, he would be tempted to suggest that the Fathers would be startled to find the College still in operation—and perhaps even dismayed at their descendants' lack of judgment or inventiveness.

The second issue on which some substantial practical bargaining took place was slavery. The morality of slavery was, by design, not at issue; but in its other concrete aspects, slavery colored the arguments over taxation, commerce, and representation. The "Three-Fifths Compromise," that three-fifths of the slaves would be counted both for representation and for purposes of direct taxation (which was drawn from the past—it was a formula of Madison's utilized by Congress in 1783 to establish the basis of state contributions to the Confederation treasury) had allayed some Northern fears about Southern over-representation (no one then foresaw the trivial role that direct taxation would play in alter federal financial policy), but doubts still remained. The Southerners, on the other hand, were afraid that Congressional control over commerce would lead to the exclusion of slaves or to their excessive taxation as imports. Moreover, the Southerners were disturbed over "navigation acts," *i.e.,* tariffs, or special legislation providing, for example, that exports be carried only in American ships; as a section depending upon exports, they wanted protection from the potential voracity of their commercial brethren of the Eastern states. To achieve this end, Mason and others urged that the Constitution include a proviso that navigation and commercial laws should require a two-thirds vote in Congress.

These problems came to a head in late August and, as usual, were handed to a committee in the hope that, in Gouverneur Morris' words, " . . . these things may form a bargain among the Northern and Southern states." The Committee reported its measures of reconciliation on August 25, and on August 29 the package was wrapped up and delivered. What

occurred can best be described in George Mason's dour version (he anticipated Calhoun in his conviction that permitting navigation acts to pass by
majority vote would put the South in economic bondage to the North—
it was mainly on this ground that he refused to sign the Constitution):

> The Constitution as agreed to till a fortnight before the Convention rose
> was such a one as he would have set his hand and heart to. . . . [Until
> that time] The 3 New England States were constantly with us in all
> questions . . . so that it was these three States with the 5 Southern ones
> against Pennsylvania, Jersey and Delaware. With respect to the importa-
> tion of slaves, [decision-making] was left to Congress. This disturbed the
> two Southernmost States who knew that Congress would immediately
> suppress the importation of slaves. Those two States therefore struck up
> a bargain with the three New England States. If they would join to admit
> slaves for some years, the two Southern-most States would join in chang-
> ing the clause which required the ⅔ of the Legislature in any vote [on
> navigation acts]. It was done.

On the floor of the Convention there was a virtual love-feast on this
happy occasion. Charles Pinckney of South Carolina attempted to overturn the committee's decision, when the compromise was reported to the
Convention, by insisting that the South needed protection from the imperialism of the Northern states. But his Southern colleagues were not
prepared to rock the boat and General C. C. Pinckney arose to spread
oil on the suddenly ruffled waters; he admitted that:

> It was in the true interest of the S[outhern] States to have no regulation
> of commerce; but considering the loss brought on the commerce of the
> Eastern States by the Revolution, their liberal conduct towards the views
> of South Carolina [on the regulation of the slave trade] and the interests
> the weak Southn. States had in being united with the strong Eastern
> states, he thought it proper that no fetters should be imposed on the
> power of making commercial regulations; *and that his constituents,*
> *though prejudiced against the Eastern States, would be reconciled to*
> *this liberality.* He had himself prejudices agst the Eastern States before
> he came here, but would acknowledge that he had found them as liberal
> and candid as any men whatever. (Italics added)

Pierce Butler took the same tack, essentially arguing that he was not too
happy about the possible consequences, but that a deal was a deal. Many
Southern leaders were later—in the wake of the "Tariff of Abominations"
—to rue this day of reconciliation; Calhoun's *Disquisition on Government*

was little more than an extension of the argument in the Convention against permitting a congressional majority to enact navigation acts.

VI

Drawing on their vast collective political experience, utilizing every weapon in the politician's arsenal, looking constantly over their shoulders at their constituents, the delegates put together a Constitution. It was a makeshift affair; some sticky issues (for example, the qualification of voters) they ducked entirely; others they mastered with that ancient instrument of political sagacity, studied ambiguity (for example, citizenship), and some they just overlooked. In this last category, I suspect, fell the matter of the power of the federal courts to determine the constitutionality of acts of Congress. When the judicial article was formulated (Article III of the Constitution), deliberations were still in the stage where the legislature was endowed with broad power under the Randolph formulation, authority which by its own terms was scarcely amenable to judicial review. In essence, courts could hardly determine when ". . . the separate States are incompetent or . . . the harmony of the United States may be interrupted"; the National Legislature, as critics pointed out, was free to define its own jurisdiction. Later the definition of legislative authority was changed into the form we know, a series of stipulated powers, *but the delegates never seriously reexamined the jurisdiction of the judiciary under this new limited formulation.* All arguments on the intention of the Framers in this matter are thus deductive and *a posteriori,* though some obviously make more sense than others.

The Framers were busy and distinguished men, anxious to get back to their families, their positions, and their constituents, not members of the French Academy devoting a lifetime to a dictionary. They were trying to do an important job, and do it in such a fashion that their handiwork would be acceptable to very diverse constituencies. No one was rhapsodic about the final document, but it was a beginning, a move in the right direction, and one they had reason to believe the people would endorse. In addition, since they had modified the impossible amendment provisions of the Articles (the requirement of unanimity which could always be frustrated by "Rogues Island") to one demanding approval by only three-quarters of the states, they seemed confident that gaps in the fabric which experience would reveal could be rewoven without undue difficulty.

So with a neat phrase introduced by Benjamin Franklin (but devised by Gouverneur Morris) which made their decision sound unanimous, and an inspired benediction by the Old Doctor urging doubters to doubt their own infallibility, the Constitution was accepted and signed. Curiously, Edmund Randolph, who had played so vital a role throughout, refused to sign, as did his fellow Virginian George Mason and Elbridge Gerry of Massachusetts. Randolph's behavior was eccentric, to say the least—his excuses for refusing his signature have a factitious ring even at this late date; the best explanation seems to be that he was afraid that the Constitution would prove to be a liability in Virginia politics, where Patrick Henry was burning up the countryside with impassioned denunciations. Presumably, Randolph wanted to check the temper of the populace before he risked his reputation, and perhaps his job, in a fight with both Henry and Richard Henry Lee. Events lend some justification to this speculation: after much temporizing and use of the conditional subjunctive tense, Randolph endorsed ratification in Virginia and ended up getting the best of both worlds.

Madison, despite his reservations about the Constitution, was the campaign manager in ratification. His first task was to get the Congress in New York to light its own funeral pyre by approving the "amendments" to the Articles and sending them on to the state legislatures. Above all, momentum had to be maintained. The anti-Constitutionalists, now thoroughly alarmed and no novices in politics, realized that their best tactic was attrition rather than direct opposition. Thus they settled on a position expressing qualified approval but calling for a second Convention to remedy various defects (the one with the most demagogic appeal was the lack of a Bill of Rights). Madison knew that to accede to this demand would be equivalent to losing the battle, nor would he agree to conditional approval (despite wavering even by Hamilton). This was an all-or-nothing proposition: national salvation or national impotence with no intermediate positions possible. Unable to get congressional approval, he settled for second best: a unanimous resolution of Congress transmitting the Constitution to the states for whatever action they saw fit to take. The opponents then moved from New York and the Congress, where they had attempted to attach amendments and conditions, to the states for the final battle.

At first the campaign for ratification went beautifully: within eight months after the delegates set their names to the document, eight states had ratified. Only in Massachusetts had the result been close (187–168). Theoretically, a ratification by one more state convention would set the new government in motion, but in fact until Virginia and New York acceded to the new Union, the latter was a fiction. New Hampshire was the next to ratify; Rhode Island was involved in its characteristic political convulsions (the Legislature there sent the Constitution out to the towns for decision by popular vote and it got lost among a series of local issues); North Carolina's convention did not meet until July and then postponed a final decision. This is hardly the place for an extensive analysis of the conventions of New York and Virginia. Suffice it to say that the Constitutionalists clearly outmaneuvered their opponents, forced them into impossible political positions, and won both states narrowly. The Virginia Convention could serve as a classic study in effective floor management: Patrick Henry had to be contained, and a reading of the debates discloses a standard two-stage technique. Henry would give a four- or five-hour speech denouncing some section of the Constitution on every conceivable ground (the federal district, he averred at one point, would become a haven for convicts escaping from state authority!); when Henry subsided, "Mr. Lee of Westmoreland" would rise and literally poleaxe him with sardonic invective (when Henry complained about the militia power, "Lighthorse Harry" really punched below the belt: observing that while the former Governor had been sitting in Richmond during the Revolution, *he* had been out in the trenches with the troops and thus felt better qualified to discuss military affairs). Then the gentlemanly Constitutionalists (Madison, Pendleton and Marshall) would pick up the matters at issue and examine them in the light of reason.

Indeed, modern Americans who tend to think of James Madison as a rather dessicated character should spend some time with this transcript. Probably Madison put on his most spectacular demonstration of nimble rhetoric in what might be called "The Battle of the Absent Authorities." Patrick Henry in the course of one of his harangues alleged that Jefferson was known to be opposed to Virginia's approving the Constitution. This was clever: Henry hated Jefferson, but was prepared to use any weapon that came to hand. Madison's riposte was superb: First, he said that with all due respect to the great reputation of Jefferson, he was not in the country and therefore could not formulate an adequate judgment; second, no one should utilize the reputation of an outsider—the Virginia Convention was there to think for itself; third, if there were to be recourse to outsiders, the opinions of George Washington should certainly be taken into consideration; and finally, he knew from privileged personal communications from Jefferson that in fact the latter *strongly favored* the Constitution. To devise an assault route into this rhetorical fortress was literally impossible.

VII

The fight was over; all that remained now was to establish the new frame of government in the spirit of its framers. And who were better qualified for this task than the Framers themselves? Thus victory for the Constitution meant simultaneous victory for the Constitutionalists; the anti-Constitutionalists either capitulated or vanished into limbo—soon Patrick Henry would be offered a seat on the Supreme Court and Luther Martin would be known as the Federalist "bull-dog." And irony of ironies, Alexander Hamilton and James Madison would shortly accumulate a reputation as the formulators of what is often alleged to be our political theory, the concept of "federalism." Also, on the other side of the ledger, the arguments would soon appear over what the Framers "really meant"; while these disputes have assumed the proportions of a big scholarly business in the last century, they began almost before the ink on the Constitution was dry. One of the best early ones featured Hamilton versus Madison on the scope of presidential power, and other Framers characteristically assumed positions in this and other disputes on the basis of their political convictions.

Probably our greatest difficulty is that we know so much more about what the Framers *should have meant* than they themselves did. We are intimately acquainted with the problems that their Constitution should have been designed to master; in short, we have read the mystery story backwards. If we are to get the right "feel" for their time and their circumstances, we must in Maitland's phrase, " . . . think ourselves back into a twilight." Obviously, no one can pretend completely to escape from the solipsistic web of his own environment, but if the effort is made, it is possible to appreciate the past roughly on its own terms. The first step in this process is to abandon the academic premise that because we can ask a question, there must be an answer.

Thus we can ask what the Framers meant when they gave Congress the power to regulate interstate and foreign commerce, and we emerge, reluctantly perhaps, with the reply that they may not have known what they meant, that there may not have been any semantic consensus. The Convention was not a seminar in analytic philosophy or linguistic analysis. Commerce was *commerce*—and if different interpretations of the word arose, later generations could worry about the problem of definition. The delegates were in a hurry to get a new government established; when definitional arguments arose, they characteristically took refuge in ambiguity. If different men voted for the same proposition for varying reasons, that was politics (and still is); if later generations were unsettled by this lack of precision, that would be their problem.

There was a good deal of definitional pluralism with respect to the problems the delegates did discuss, but when we move to the question of extrapolated intentions, we enter the realm of spiritualism. When men in our time, for instance, launch into elaborate talmudic exegesis to demonstrate that federal aid to parochial schools is (or is not) in accord with the intentions of the men who established the Republic and endorsed the Bill of Rights, they are engaging in historical Extra-Sensory Perception. (If one were to join this E. S. P. contingent for a minute, he might suggest that the hard-boiled politicians who wrote the Constitution and Bill of Rights would chuckle scornfully at such an invocation of authority: obviously a politician would chart his course on the intentions of the living, not of the dead, and count the number of Catholics in his constituency.)

The Constitution, then, was not an apotheosis of "constitutionalism," a triumph of architectonic genius; it was a patch-work sewn together under the pressure of both time and events by a group of extremely talented democratic politicians. They refused to attempt the establishment of a strong, centralized sovereignty on the principle of legislative supremacy for the excellent reason that the people would not accept it. They risked their political fortunes by opposing the established doctrines of state sovereignty because they were convinced that the existing system was leading to national impotence and probably foreign domination. For two years, they worked to get a convention established. For over three months, in what must have seemed to the faithful participants an endless process of give-and-take, they reasoned, cajoled, threatened, and bargained amongst themselves. The result was a Constitution which the people, in fact, by democratic processes, did accept, and a new and far better national government was established.

Beginning with the inspired propaganda of Hamilton, Madison and Jay, the ideological build-up got under way. *The Federalist* had little impact on the ratification of the Constitution, except perhaps in New York, but this volume had enormous influence on the image of the Constitution in the minds of future generations, particularly on historians and political scientists who have an innate fondness for theoretical symmetry. Yet, while the shades of Locke and Montesquieu *may* have been hovering in the background, and the delegates *may* have been unconscious instruments of a transcendent *telos,* the careful observer of the day-to-day work of the Convention finds no over-arching principles. The "separation of powers" to him seems to be a by-product of suspicion, and "federalism" he views as a *pis aller,* as the farthest point the delegates felt they could go in the destruction of state power without themselves inviting repudiation.

To conclude, the Constitution was neither a victory for abstract theory nor a great practical success. Well over half a million men had to die on the battlefields of the Civil War before certain constitutional principles could be defined—a baleful consideration which is somehow overlooked in our customary tributes to the farsighted genius of the Framers and to the supposed American talent for "constitutionalism." The Constitution was, however, a vivid demonstration of effective democratic political action, and of the forging of a national elite which literally persuaded its countrymen to hoist themselves by their own boot straps. American pro-consuls would be wise not to translate the Constitution into Japanese, or Swahili, or treat it as a work of semi-Divine origin; but when students of comparative politics examine the process of nation-building in countries newly freed from colonial rule, they may find the American experience instructive as a classic example of the potentialities of a democratic elite.

CHAPTER TWO

Federalism

American government utilizes a "federal" form in order to secure certain political and economic objectives. This chapter will devote itself to identifying both the traditional and modern goals of American federalism from the writings of important theorists who have concerned themselves with general and specific problems in the area of national-state relationships. Factors pertaining to the validity of federalism will also be analyzed.

4. Constitutional Background

No subject attracted greater attention or was more carefully analyzed at the time of the framing of the Constitution than that of federalism. *The Federalist* devoted a great deal of space to prove the advantages of a federal form of government relative to a confederacy, as the Constitution was going to take some of the power traditionally within the jurisdiction of state governments and give it to a newly constituted national government. Once again it is necessary to return to the Constitution and *The Federalist* to ascertain the basis for the establishment of a federal system of government, in which state governments as well as the national government receive independent constitutional grants of authority in defined areas.

FEDERALIST 16

Alexander Hamilton

The ... death of the confederacy ... is what we now seem to be on the point of experiencing, if the federal system be not speedily renovated in a more substantial form. It is not probable, considering the genius of this country, that the complying states would often be inclined to support the authority of the union, by engaging in a war against the non-complying states. They would always be more ready to pursue the milder course of putting themselves upon an equal footing with the delinquent members, by an imitation of their example. And the guilt of all would thus become the security of all. Our past experience has exhibited the operation of this spirit in its full light. There would, in fact, be an insuperable difficulty in ascertaining when force would with propriety be employed. In the article of pecuniary contribution, which would be the most usual source of delinquency, it would often be impossible to decide whether it had proceeded from disinclination, or inability. The pretense of the latter would always be at hand. And the case must be very flagrant in which its fallacy could be detected with sufficient certainty to justify the harsh expedient of compulsion. It is easy to see that this problem alone, as often as it should occur, would open a wide field to the majority that happened to prevail in the national council, for the exercise of factious views, of partiality, and of oppression.

It seems to require no pains to prove that the states ought not to prefer a national constitution, which could only be kept in motion by the instrumentality of a large army, continually on foot to execute the ordinary requisitions or decrees of the government. And yet this is the plain alternative involved by those who wish to deny it the power of extending its operations to individuals. Such a scheme, if practicable at all, would instantly degenerate into a military despotism; but it will be found in every light impracticable. The resources of the union would not be equal to the maintenance of any army considerable enough to confine the larger states within the limits of their duty; nor would the means ever be furnished of forming such an army in the first instance. Whoever considers the populousness and strength of several of these states singly at the present juncture, and looks forward to what they will become, even at the distance of half a century, will at once dismiss as idle and visionary any scheme which aims at regulating their movements by laws, to operate upon them in their collective capacities, and to be executed by a coercion applicable to them in the same capacities. A project of this kind is little less romantic than the monster-taming spirit attributed to the fabulous heroes and demigods of antiquity....

The result of these observations to an intelligent mind must clearly be this, that if it be possible at any rate to construct a federal government capable of regulating the common concerns, and preserving the general tranquillity, it must be founded, as to the objects committed to its case, upon the reverse of the principle contended for by the opponents of the proposed constitution [*i.e.,* a confederacy]. It must carry its agency to the persons of the citizens. It must stand in need of no intermediate legislations; but must itself be empowered to employ the arm of the ordinary magistrate to execute its own resolutions. The majesty of the national authority must be manifested through the medium of the courts of justice. The government of the union, like that of each state, must be able to address itself immediately to the hopes and fears of individuals; and to attract to its support, those passions which have the strongest influence upon the human heart. It must, in short, possess all the means, and have a right to resort to all the methods, of executing the powers with which it is entrusted, that are possessed and exercised by the governments of the particular states.

To this reasoning it may perhaps be objected, that if any state should be disaffected to the authority of the union, it could at any time obstruct the execution of its laws, and bring the matter to the same issue of force, with the necessity of which the opposite scheme is reproached.

The plausibility of this objection will vanish the moment we advert to the essential difference between a mere NON-COMPLIANCE and a DIRECT and ACTIVE RESISTANCE. If the interposition of the state legislatures be necessary to give effect to a measure of the union [as in a confederacy], they have only NOT TO ACT, or TO ACT EVASIVELY, and the measure is defeated. This neglect of duty may be disguised under affected but unsubstantial provisions so as not to appear, and of course not to excite any alarm in the people for the safety of the constitution. The state leaders may even make a merit of their surreptitious invasions of it, on the ground of some temporary convenience, exemption, or advantage.

But if the execution of the laws of the national government should not require the intervention of the state legislatures; if they were to pass into immediate operation upon the citizens themselves, the particular governments could not interrupt their progress without an open and violent exertion of an unconstitutional power. No omission, nor evasions, would answer the end. They would be obliged to act, and in such a manner, as would leave no doubt that they had encroached on the national rights.

An experiment of this nature would always be hazardous in the face of a constitution in any degree competent to its own defense, and of a people enlightened enough to distinguish between a legal exercise and an illegal usurpation of authority. The success of it would require not merely a factious majority in the legislature, but the concurrence of the courts of justice, and of the body of the people. . . . 🖋

FEDERALIST 17

Alexander Hamilton

A~N~ objection, of a nature different from that which has been stated and answered in my last address, may, perhaps, be urged against the principle of legislation for the individual citizens of America. It may be said, that it would tend to render the government of the union too powerful, and to enable it to absorb those residuary authorities, which it might be judged proper to leave with the states for local purposes. Allowing the utmost latitude to the love of power, which any reasonable man can require, I confess I am at a loss to discover what temptation the persons entrusted with the administration of the general government could ever feel to divest the states of the authorities of that description. The regulation of the mere domestic police of a state, appears to me to hold out slender allurements to ambition. Commerce, finance, negotiation, and war, seem to comprehend all the objects which have charms for minds governed by that passion; and all the powers necessary to those objects, ought, in the first instance, to be lodged in the national depository. The administration of private justice between the citizens of the same state; the supervision of agriculture, and of other concerns of a similar nature; all those things, in short, which are proper to be provided for by local legislation, can never be desirable cares of a general jurisdiction. It is therefore improbable, that there should exist a disposition in the federal councils, to usurp the powers with which they are connected; because the attempt to exercise them would be as troublesome as it would be nugatory; and the possession of them, for that reason, would contribute nothing to the dignity, to the importance, or to the splendor, of the national government.

But let it be admitted, for argument's sake, that mere wantonness, and lust of domination, would be sufficient to beget that disposition; still, it may be safely affirmed, that the sense of the constituent body of the national representatives, or in other words, of the people of the several states, would control the indulgence of so extravagant an appetite. It will always be far more easy for the state governments to encroach upon the national authorities, than for the national government to encroach upon the state authorities. The proof of this proposition turns upon the greater degree of influence which the state governments, if they administer their affairs with uprightness and prudence, will generally possess over the people; a circumstance which at the same time teaches us, that there is an inherent and intrinsic weakness in all federal constitutions; and that too much pains cannot be taken in their organization, to give them all the force which is compatible with the principles of liberty.

The superiority of influence in favor of the particular governments, would result partly from the diffusive construction of the national government; but chiefly from the nature of the objects to which the attention of the state administrations would be directed.

It is a known fact in human nature, that its affections are commonly weak in proportion to the distance of diffusiveness of the object. Upon the same principle that a man is more attached to his family than to his neighborhood, to his neighborhood than to the community at large, the people of each state would be apt to feel a stronger bias towards their local governments, than towards the government of the union, unless the force of that principle should be destroyed by a much better administration of the latter.

This strong propensity of the human heart, would find powerful auxiliaries in the objects of state regulation.

The variety of more minute interests, which will necessarily fall under the superintendence of the local administrations, and which will form so many rivulets of influence, running through every part of the society, cannot be particularized, without involving a detail too tedious and uninteresting to compensate for the instruction it might afford.

There is one transcendent advantage belonging to the province of the state governments, which alone suffices to place the matter in a clear and satisfactory light—I mean the ordinary administration of criminal and civil justice. This, of all others, is the most powerful, most universal and most attractive source of popular obedience and attachment. It is this, which, being the immediate and visible guardian of life and property; having its benefits and its terrors in constant activity before the public eye; regulating all those personal interests, and familiar concerns, to which the sensibility of individuals is more immediately awake; contributes, more than any other circumstance, to impress upon the minds of the people affection, esteem, and reverence towards the government. This great cement of society, which will diffuse itself almost wholly through the channels of the particular governments, independent of all other causes of influence, would insure them so decided an empire over their respective citizens, as to render them at all times a complete counterpoise, and not infrequently dangerous rivals to the power of the union. 🖎

5. The Doctrine of National Supremacy

As one traces the historical development of national–state relationships it will be found that there has been constant strife over the determination of the boundaries of national power in relation to the reserved powers of the states. The Civil War did not settle once and for all the difficult question of national versus state power. The Supreme Court has played an important role in the development of the federal system, and some of its most historic opinions have upheld national power at the expense of the states. In the early period of the Court, Chief Justice John Marshall in *McCulloch* v. *Maryland,* 4 Wheaton 316 (1819), stated two doctrines that have had a profound effect upon the federal system: (1) the doctrine of implied powers; (2) the doctrine of the supremacy of national law. The former enables Congress to expand its power into numerous areas affecting states directly. By utilizing the commerce clause, for example, Congress may now regulate what is essentially *intrastate* commerce, for the Court has held that this is implied in the original clause giving Congress the power to regulate commerce among the several states. The immediate issues in *McCulloch* v. *Maryland* were, first, whether or not Congress had the power to incorporate, or charter, a national bank; second, if Congress has such a power, although nowhere stated in the Constitution, does the existence of such a bank prevent state action that would interfere in its operation?

McCULLOCH v. MARYLAND

4 Wheaton 316 (1819)

Mr. Chief Justice Marshall delivered the opinion of the Court, saying in part:

In the case now to be determined, the defendant, a sovereign State, denies the obligation of a law enacted by the legislature of the Union; and the plaintiff, on his part, contests the validity of an Act which has been passed by the legislature of that State. The Constitution of our country, in its most interesting and vital parts, is to be considered; the conflicting powers of the government of the Union and of its members, as marked in that Constitution, are to be discussed; and an opinion given, which may essentially influence the great operations of the government. . . .

If any one proposition could command the universal assent of mankind, we might expect it would be this: that the government of the Union, though limited in its powers, is supreme within its sphere of action. This would seem to result necessarily from its nature. It is the government of all; its powers are delegated by all; it represents all, and acts for all. Though any one State may be willing to control its operations, no State is willing to allow others to control them. The nation, on those subjects on which it can act, must necessarily bind its component parts. But this question is not left to mere reason: the people have, in express terms, decided it, by saying, "this Constitution, and the laws of the United States, which shall be made in pursuance thereof," "shall be the supreme law of the land," and by requiring that the members of the State legislatures, and the officers of the executive and judicial departments of the States, shall take the oath of fidelity to it. . . .

A constitution, to contain an accurate detail of all the subdivisions of which its great powers will admit, and of all the means by which they may be carried into execution, would partake of the prolixity of a legal code, and could scarcely be embraced by the human mind. It would probably never be understood by the public. Its nature, therefore, requires that only its great outlines should be marked, its important objects designated, and the minor ingredients which compose those objects be deduced from the nature of the objects themselves. That this idea was entertained by the framers of the American Constitution, is not only to be inferred from the nature of the instrument, but from the language. . . .

Although, among the enumerated powers of government, we do not find the word "bank," or "incorporation," we find the great powers to lay and collect taxes; to borrow money; to regulate commerce; to declare and conduct a war; and to raise and support armies and navies. The sword and the purse, all the external relations, and no inconsiderable portion of the industry of the nation, are entrusted to its government. It can never be pretended that these vast powers draw after them others of inferior importance, merely because they are inferior. Such an idea can never be advanced. But it may, with great reason, be contended, that a government, entrusted with such ample powers, on the due execution of which the happiness and prosperity of the nation so vitally depends, must also be entrusted with ample means for their execution. The power being given, it is the interest of the nation to facilitate its execution. It can never be their interest, and cannot be presumed to have been their intention, to clog and embarrass its execution by withholding the most appropriate means. Throughout this vast republic, from the St. Croix to the Gulf of Mexico, from the Atlantic to the Pacific, revenue is to be collected and expended, armies are to be marched and supported. The exigencies of the nation may require, that the treasure raised in the North should be transported to the South, that raised in the East conveyed to the West, or that this order should be reversed. Is that construction of the Constitution to be preferred which would render these operations difficult, hazardous, and expensive? Can we adopt that construction (unless the words imperiously require it) which would impute to the framers of that instrument, when granting these powers for the public good, the intention of impeding their exercise by withholding a choice of means? If, indeed, such be the mandate of the Constitution, we have only to obey; but that instrument does not profess to enumerate the means by which the powers it confers may be executed; nor does it prohibit the creation of a corporation, if the existence of such a being be essential to the beneficial exercise of those powers. It is, then, the subject of fair inquiry, how far such means may be employed. . . .

We admit, as all must admit, that the powers of the government are limited, and that its limits are not to be transcended. But we think the sound construction of the Constitution must allow to the national legislature that discretion, with respect to the means by which the powers it confers are to be carried into execution, which will enable that body to perform the high duties assigned to it, in the manner most beneficial to the people. Let the end be legitimate, let it be within the scope of the Constitution, and all means which are appropriate, which are plainly adapted to that end, which are not prohibited, but consist with the letter and spirit of the Constitution, are constitutional. . . .

It being the opinion of the court that the act incorporating the bank is constitutional; and that the power of establishing a branch in the State of Maryland might be properly exercised by the bank itself, we proceed to inquire:

Whether the State of Maryland may, without violating the Constitution, tax that branch? . . .

That the power of taxation is one of vital importance; that it is retained by the States; that it is not abridged by the grant of a similar power to the government of the Union; that it is to be concurrently exercised by the two governments: are truths which have never been denied. But, such is the paramount character of the Constitution, that its capacity to withdraw any subject from the action of even this power, is admitted. The States are expressly forbidden to lay any duties on imports or exports, except what may be absolutely necessary for executing their inspection laws. If the obligation of this prohibition must be conceded—if it may restrain a State from the exercise of its taxing power on imports and exports; the same paramount character would seem to restrain, as it certainly may restrain, a State from such other exercise of this power, as is in its nature incompatible with, and repugnant to, the constitutional laws of the Union. A law, absolutely repugnant to another, as entirely repeals that other as if express terms of repeal were used.

On this ground the counsel for the bank place its claim to be exempted from the power of a State to tax its operations. There is no express provision for the case, but the claim has been sustained on a principle which so entirely pervades the Constitution, is so intermixed with the materials which compose it, so interwoven with its web, so blended with its texture, as to be incapable of being separated from it, without rending it into shreds.

This great principle is, that the Constitution and the laws made in pursuance thereof are supreme; that they control the Constitution and laws of the respective States, and cannot be controlled by them. From this, which may be almost termed an axiom, other propositions are deduced as corollaries, on the truth or error of which, and on their application to this case, the cause has been supposed to depend. These are, 1. That a power to create implies a power to preserve. 2. That a power to destroy, if wielded by a different hand, is hostile to, and incompatible with, these powers to create and preserve. 3. That where this repugnancy exists, that authority which is supreme must control, not yield to that over which it is supreme. . . .

If we apply the principle for which the State of Maryland contends, to the Constitution generally, we shall find it capable of changing totally the character of that instrument. We shall find it capable of arresting all the measures of the government, and of prostrating it at the foot of the States. The American people have declared their Constitution, and the laws made in pursuance thereof, to be supreme; but this principle would transfer the supremacy, in fact, to the States. . . .

The court has bestowed on this subject its most deliberate considera
tion. The result is a conviction that the States have no power, by taxation or otherwise, to retard, impede, burden, or in any manner control,
the operations of the constitutional laws enacted by Congress to carry
into execution the powers vested in the general government. That is,
we think, the unavoidable consequence of that supremacy which the
Constitution has declared.... ▚

6. National Power Over Commerce

Constitutional doctrine regarding the power of the national government
to regulate commerce among the states to promote general prosperity has
been clarified in a series of Supreme Court cases. At issue is the interpretation of the power to "regulate commerce with foreign nations, and
among the several States," granted to Congress in Article I. Some of these
cases emphasize the role of the national government as umpire, enforcing
certain rules of the game within which the free enterprise system functions; others have emphasized the positive role of the government in regulating the economy.

A key case supporting the supremacy of the national government in commercial regulation is *Gibbons* v. *Ogden,* 9 Wheaton 1 (1824). The New
York legislature, in 1798, had granted Robert R. Livingston the exclusive
privilege to navigate by steam the rivers and other waters of the state,
provided he could build a boat which would travel at four miles an hour
against the current of the Hudson River. A two-year time limitation was
imposed, and the conditions were not met; however, New York renewed
its grant for two years in 1803 and again in 1807. In 1807 Robert Fulton,
who now held the exclusive license with Livingston, completed and put
into operation a steamboat which met the legislative conditions. The New
York legislature now provided that a five-year extension of their monopoly
would be given to Livingston and Fulton for each new steamboat they
placed into operation on New York waters. The monopoly could not exceed thirty years, but during that period anyone wishing to navigate New
York waters by steam had first to obtain a license from Livingston and
Fulton, who were given the power to confiscate unlicensed boats. New
Jersey and Connecticut passed retaliatory laws, the former authorizing
confiscation of any New York ship for each ship confiscated by Livingston
and Fulton, the latter prohibiting boats licensed in New York from entering Connecticut waters. Ohio also passed retaliatory legislation. Open
commercial warfare seemed a possibility among the states of the union.

In 1793 Congress passed an act providing for the licensing of vessels engaged in the coasting trade, and Gibbons obtained under this statute a license to operate boats between New York and New Jersey. Ogden was engaged in a similar operation under an exclusive license issued by Livingston and Fulton, and thus sought to enjoin Gibbons from further operation. The New York court upheld the exclusive grants given to Livingston and Fulton, and Gibbons appealed to the Supreme Court. Chief Justice Marshall, in the following opinion, makes it quite clear that (1) states cannot interfere with a power granted to Congress by passing conflicting state legislation, and (2) the commerce power includes anything affecting "commerce among the states" and thus may include *intrastate* as well as interstate commerce. In this way the foundation was laid for broad national control over commercial activity.

GIBBONS v. OGDEN

9 Wheaton 1 (1824)

M R. Chief Justice Marshall delivered the opinion of the Court, saying in part:

The appellant contends that this decree [of the New York court enjoining Gibbons from further operation because of the exclusive nature of the New York law granting a monopoly to Fulton and Livingston] is erroneous, because the laws which purport to give the exclusive privilege it sustains, are repugnant to the Constitution and laws of the United States.

They are said to be repugnant—

1. To that clause in the Constitution which authorizes Congress to regulate commerce.

2. To that which authorizes Congress to promote the progress of science and useful arts. . . .

As preliminary to the very able discussions of the Constitution which we have heard from the bar, and as having some influence on its construction, reference has been made to the political situation of these States, anterior to its formation. It has been said that they were sovereign, were completely independent, and were connected with each other only by a league. This is true. But, when these allied sovereigns converted their league into a government, when they converted their congress of ambassadors, deputed to deliberate on their common concerns, and to recommend measures of general utility, into a legislature, empowered to enact laws on the most interesting subjects, the whole character in which the States appear underwent a change, the extent of which must be determined by a fair consideration of the instrument by which that change was effected.

This instrument contains an enumeration of powers expressly granted by the people to their government. It has been said that these powers ought to be construed strictly. By why ought they to be so construed? Is there one sentence in the Constitution which gives countenance to this rule? In the last of the enumerated powers, that which grants, expressly, the means for carrying all others into execution, Congress is authorized "to make all laws which shall be necessary and proper" for the purpose. But this limitation on the means which may be used, is not extended to the powers which are conferred; nor is there one sentence in the Constitution, which has been pointed out by the gentlemen of the bar, or which we have been able to discern, that prescribes this rule. We do not, therefore, think ourselves justified in adopting it. . . . If, from the imperfections of human language, there should be serious doubts respecting the extent of any given power, it is a well settled rule that the objects for which it was given, especially when those objects are expressed in the instrument itself, should have great influence in the construction. . . . We know of no rule for construing the extent of such powers, other than is given by the language of the instrument which confers them, taken in connection with the purposes for which they were conferred.

The words are: "Congress shall have power to regulate commerce with foreign nations, and among the several States, and with the Indian tribes."

The subject to be regulated is commerce; and our Constitution being, as was aptly said at the bar, one of enumeration, and not of definition, to ascertain the extent of the power, it becomes necessary to settle the meaning of the word. The counsel for the appellee would limit it to traffic, to buying and selling, or the interchange of commodities, and do not admit that it comprehends navigation. This would restrict a general term, applicable to many objects, to one of its significations. Commerce, undoubtedly, is traffic, but it is something more: it is intercourse. It describes the commercial intercourse between nations, and parts of nations, in all its branches, and is regulated by prescribing rules for carrying on that intercourse. The mind can scarcely conceive a system for regulating commerce between nations, which shall exclude all laws concerning navigation, which shall be silent on the admission of the vessels of the one nation into the ports of the other, and be confined to prescribing rules for the conduct of individuals, in the actual employment of buying and selling, or of barter.

If commerce does not include navigation, the government of the Union has no direct power over that subject, and can make no law prescribing what shall constitute American vessels, or requiring that they shall be navigated by American seamen. Yet this power has been exercised from the commencement of the government, has been exercised with the consent of all, and has been understood by all to be a commercial regulation. . . .

The word used in the Constitution, then, comprehends, and has been always understood to comprehend, navigation, within its meaning; and a power to regulate navigation is as expressly granted as if that term had been added to the word "commerce."

To what commerce does this power extend? The Constitution informs us, to commerce "with foreign nations, and among the several States, and with the Indian tribes."

It has, we believe, been universally admitted that these words comprehend every species of commercial intercourse between the United States and foreign nations. No sort of trade can be carried on between this country and any other, to which this power does not extend. It has been truly said that commerce, as the word is used in the Constitution, is a unit, every part of which is indicated by the term.

If this be the admitted meaning of the word, in its application to foreign nations, it must carry the same meaning throughout the sentence, and remain a unit, unless there be some plain intelligible cause which alters it.

The subject to which the power is next applied, is to commerce "among the several States." The word "among" means intermingled with. A thing which is among others, is intermingled with them. Commerce among the States, cannot stop at the external boundary line of each State, but may be introduced into the interior.

It is not intended to say that these words comprehend that commerce which is completely internal, which is carried on between man and man in a State, or between different parts of the same State, and which does not extend to or affect other States. Such a power would be inconvenient, and is certainly unnecessary.

Comprehensive as the word "among" is, it may very properly be restricted to that commerce which concerns more States than one. The phrase is not one which would probably have been selected to indicate the completely interior traffic of a State. . . . The completely internal commerce of a State, then, may be considered as reserved for the State itself.

But, in regulating commerce with foreign nations, the power of Congress does not stop at the jurisdictional lines of the several States. It would be a very useless power if it could not pass those lines. The commerce of the United States with foreign nations is that of the whole United States. Every district has a right to participate in it. The deep streams which penetrate our country in every direction pass through the interior of almost every State in the Union, and furnish the means of exercising this right. If Congress has the power to regulate it, that power must be exercised whenever the subject exists. If it exists within the States, if a foreign voyage may commence or terminate at a port within a State, then the power of Congress may be exercised within a State.

This principle is, if possible, still more clear when applied to commerce "among the several States." They either join each other, in which case they are separated by a mathematical line, or they are remote from each other, in which case other States lie between them. What is commerce "among" them; and how is it to be conducted? Can a trading expedition between two adjoining States commence and terminate outside of each? And if the trading intercourse be between two States remote from each other, must it not commence in one, terminate in the other, and probably pass through a third? Commerce among the States must, of necessity, be commerce with the States. In the regulation of trade with the Indian tribes, the action of the law, especially when the Constitution was made, was chiefly within a State. The power of Congress, then, whatever it may be, must be exercised within the territorial jurisdiction of the several States. . . .

We are now arrived at the inquiry, what is this power?

It is the power to regulate; that is, to prescribe the rule by which commerce is to be governed. This power, like all others vested in Congress, is complete in itself, may be exercised to its utmost extent, and acknowledges no limitations other than are prescribed in the Constitution. These are expressed in plain terms, and do not affect the questions which arise in this case, or which have been discussed at the bar. . . .

The power of Congress, then, comprehends navigation within the limits of every State in the Union, so far as that navigation may be, in any manner, connected with "commerce with foreign nations, or among the several States, or with the Indian tribes." It may, of consequence, pass the jurisdictional line of New York, and act upon the very waters to which the prohibition now under consideration applies.

But it has been urged with great earnestness that, although the power of Congress to regulate commerce with foreign nations, and among the several States, be coextensive with the subject itself, and have no other limits than are prescribed in the Constitution, yet the States may severally exercise the same power, within their respective jurisdictions. In support of this argument, it is said that they possessed it as an inseparable attribute of sovereignty, before the formation of the Constitution, and still retain it, except so far as they have surrendered it by that instrument; that this principle results from the nature of the government, and is secured by the Tenth Amendment; that an affirmative grant of power is not exclusive, unless in its own nature it be such that the continued exercise of it by the former possessor is inconsistent with the grant, and that this is not of that description.

The appellant, conceding these postulates, except the last, contends that full power to regulate a particular subject, implies the whole power, and leaves no *residuum;* that a grant of the whole is incompatible with the existence of a right in another to any part of it. . . .

. . . The sole question is, can a State regulate commerce with foreign nations and among the States, while Congress is regulating it? . . .

In our complex system, presenting the rare and difficult scheme of one general government, whose action extends over the whole, but which possesses only certain enumerated powers; and of numerous State governments, which retain and exercise all powers not delegated to the Union, contests respecting power must arise. Were it even otherwise, the measures taken by the respective governments to execute their acknowledged powers, would often be of the same description, and might, sometimes, interfere. This, however, does not prove that the one is exercising, or has a right to exercise, the powers of the other. . . .

It has been contended, by the counsel for the appellant, that, as the word to "regulate" implies in its nature full power over the thing to be regulated, it excludes, necessarily, the action of all others that would perform the same operation on the same thing. That regulation is designed for the entire result, applying to those parts which remain as they were, as well as to those which are altered. It produces a uniform whole, which is as much disturbed and deranged by changing what the regulating power designs to leave untouched, as that on which it has operated.

There is great force in this argument, and the Court is not satisfied that it has been refuted.

Since, however, in exercising the power of regulating their own purely internal affairs, whether of trading or police, the States may sometimes enact laws, the validity of which depends on their interfering with, and being contrary to, an act of Congress passed in pursuance of the Constitution, the Court will enter upon the inquiry, whether the laws of New York, as expounded by the highest tribunal of that State, have, in their application to this case, come into collision with an act of Congress, and deprived a citizen of a right to which that act entitles him. Should the collision exist, it will be immaterial whether those laws were passed in virtue of a concurrent power "to regulate commerce with foreign nations, or among the several States," or, in virtue of a power to regulate their domestic trade and police. In one case and the other, the acts of New York must yield to the law of Congress; and the decision sustaining the privilege they confer, against a right given by a law of the Union, must be erroneous.

This opinion has been frequently expressed in this Court, and is founded as well on the nature of the government as on the words of the Constitution. In argument, however, it has been contended that, if a law passed by a State, in the exercise of its acknowledged sovereignty, comes into conflict with a law passed by Congress in pursuance of the Constitution, they affect the subject, and each other, like equal opposing powers.

But the framers of our Constitution foresaw this state of things, and provided for it by declaring the supremacy not only of itself, but of the laws made in pursuance of it. The nullity of any act, inconsistent with the Constitution, is produced by the declaration that the Constitution is the supreme law. The appropriate application of that part of the clause which confers the same supremacy on laws and treaties, is to such acts of the State legislatures as do not transcend their powers, but, though enacted in the execution of acknowledged State powers, interfere with, or are contrary to the laws of Congress, made in pursuance of the Constitution, or some treaty made under the authority of the United States. In every such case, the act of Congress, or the treaty, is supreme; and the law of the State, though enacted in the exercise of powers not controverted, must yield to it. . . .

. . . The real and sole question seems to be, whether a steam machine, in actual use, deprives a vessel of the privileges conferred by a license. . . .

But all inquiry into this subject seems to the Court to be put completely at rest, by the act . . . entitled "An act for the enrolling and licensing of steam-boats." . . .

This act demonstrates the opinion of Congress, that steam-boats may be enrolled and licensed, in common with vessels using sails. They are, of course, entitled to the same privileges, and can no more be restrained from navigating waters, and entering ports which are free to such vessels, than if they were wafted on their voyage by the winds, instead of being propelled by the agency of fire. The one element may be as legitimately used as the other, for every commercial purpose authorized by the laws of the Union; and the act of a State inhibiting the use of either to any vessel having a license under the act of Congress, comes, we think, in direct collision with that act.

As this decides the cause, it is unnecessary to enter in an examination of that part of the Constitution which empowers Congress to promote the progress of science and the useful arts. . . . 🖋

Congress has used its constitutional power to regulate "commerce among the several States" to justify broad regulatory programs. In *Champion* v. *Ames,* 188 U.S. 321 (1903), the Court stated that Congress could bar objectionable articles from transportation in interstate commerce. This was in reference to an 1895 lottery law prohibiting lottery tickets from being sent through the channels of interstate commerce. After this decision Congress prohibited numerous other "objectionable" articles from transportation in interstate commerce, *e.g.,* impure food and drugs, uninspected meat, fabrics, and other things, stolen automobiles, kidnapped persons, women for immoral purposes, etc. In this way a national police power was developed similar to that of the states in intent, *i.e.,* the power to protect the health, welfare, and morals of the community, initially within the "reserved" powers of the states.

In 1916 Congress attempted to regulate child labor conditions within states by preventing the transportation in interstate commerce of goods produced by children under conditions which violated the standards of the Child Labor Act of 1916. Although the initial attempt was declared unconstitutional in *Hammer* v. *Dagenhart,* 247 U.S. 251 (1918), the device of regulation through controlling the transportation of goods in interstate commerce is now an accepted constitutional practice. Furthermore, the regulatory power of Congress extends to all economic areas—production, distribution, etc.—which in any way have an effect upon interstate commerce. Thus labor disputes that burden or obstruct interstate commerce are controlled under the Wagner Labor Relations Act of 1935 and the Taft-Hartley Act of 1947. The radio and television industry, because it uses the channels of interstate commerce, is regulated by the Federal Communications Act of 1934. The same is true of banks, securities dealers and exchanges, railroads, telephone companies, petroleum firms and natural gas companies, trucking firms, etc. The list of industries subject to national regulation through the use of the commerce clause could be extended indefinitely. Marshall's decision in *Gibbons* v. *Ogden* set the stage for extensive national regulation through its broad and flexible interpretation of the commerce clause.

Both *McCulloch* v. *Maryland* and *Gibbons* v. *Ogden* clearly held that the states cannot take action that will impinge upon the legitimate authority of Congress. These opinions reflected judicial acceptance of the fact that when the federal government acts, it generally pre-empts the field. But this does not mean that under no circumstances can the states legislate concurrently with the national government. It depends upon the circumstances. For example, in *Pennsylvania* v. *Nelson,* 350 U.S. 497 (1956), the Supreme Court found that the Smith Act superseded a Pennsylvania sedition statute under which Nelson had been convicted. The Pennsylvania law, like the Smith Act, made it a crime to advocate the violent overthrow of the government of the United States. It added that it was also a crime to make such advocacy regarding the government of Pennsylvania. The Supreme Court found that the Smith Act, in combination with a number of other federal subversive control statutes such as the Internal Security Act of 1950, and the Communist Control Act of 1954, proscribed advocacy to overthrow any government, whether federal, state, or local. On the basis of the aggregate of federal statutes in the sedition field, the Court concluded that "Congress had intended to occupy the field of sedition. Taken as a whole, they [the statutes] evince a Congressional plan which makes it reasonable to determine that no room has been left for the states to supplement it. Therefore, a state's sedition statute is superseded regardless of whether it purports to supplement the federal law. . . ." Although the *Nelson* case apparently nullified more than forty state sedition statutes, the issue has not been finally resolved. Several cases since the *Nelson* decision reflect a judicial hesitancy to prevent state and local authorities from enforcing statutes controlling subversive activities. In this regard see *Beilan* v. *Board of Education,* 357 U.S. 399 (1958); and *Lerner* v. *Casey,* 357 U.S. 468 (1958). The real problems that arise concerning the doctrine of national supremacy do not develop where there is clear state defiance of a federal law, or a federal court order, for in these situations the enforcement of the principle of the supremacy of the Constitution and of national law can easily and clearly be carried out. Thus in *Cooper* v. *Aaron,* 358 U.S. 1 (1958), a federal district court order to proceed with integration at Central High School in Little Rock was up-

held by the Supreme Court in the face of the defiance of the Governor of
Arkansas. The supremacy of the national government was clear, and the
opinion of the Court was not ambiguous.

A recent example of the problem of concurrent jurisdiction arose in the
case of *Colorado Anti-discrimination Commission* v. *Continental Air
Lines,* 372 U.S. 714 (1963). This case involved the constitutionality of the
Colorado Anti-discrimination Act, which made it an unfair employment
practice to refuse to hire qualified individuals because of race, creed, color,
national origin, or ancestry. Under the Act a commission was established
to investigate complaints. Marlon D. Green, a Negro, applied for a job as
a pilot with Continental Air Lines, a small interstate carrier whose route
passes through Colorado. He was refused a position, and he filed a complaint with the Anti-discrimination Commission, claiming that the only
reason he was not hired was because he was a Negro. The Commission
held extensive hearings to determine the validity of his charge, and finally
upheld it. Continental Air Lines was ordered to cease and desist from this
particular discrimination, and from any other discriminatory practices.
The Commission directed the Air Line to enroll the applicant for its first
opening in its pilot training school.

The validity of the Commission's cease and desist order was immediately attacked by Continental, which secured a judgment vacating the
order from a lower State District Court. On appeal, the Supreme Court
of Colorado affirmed the judgment. Both state courts held that the Colorado statute placed an undue burden upon interstate commerce, which
was within the exclusive jurisdiction of the national government. However, the Supreme Court found that the Colorado statute merely extended
the federal laws dealing with the same subject, rather than conflicting
with them.

7. Contemporary Federalism

The problems involved in determining the constitutional division of authority between the federal and the state governments reflect the more
formal aspects of our federal system. Contemporary federalism must be
viewed not only in this way, but also in relation to the broader political
and economic dimensions of the division of powers between the national
and state levels of government. Also, as the following selection points out,
there are many factors in addition to federalism that decentralize the
American political system. All kinds of interest groups, including state
and local governments, have numerous access points at the national level

through which they can influence policy making. Our decentralized political parties, a major cause of disunity, are controlled more by state organizations than by the national leaders. Federalism has not caused the disunity in the American system, although it has contributed to it. What kind of balance should exist between the federal and state levels in the exercise of governmental functions? In essence, this is part of a broader problem of centralization versus decentralization in government. The following selection deals with the many facets of this problem.

THE FEDERAL SYSTEM

Morton Grodzins*

Federalism is a device for dividing decisions and functions of government. As the constitutional fathers well understood, the federal structure is a means, not an end. The pages that follow are therefore not concerned with an exposition of American federalism as a formal, legal set of relationships. The focus, rather, is on the purpose of federalism, that is to say, on the distribution of power between central and peripheral units of government.

I. The Sharing of Functions

The American form of government is often, but erroneously, symbolized by a three-layer cake. A far more accurate image is the rainbow or marble cake, characterized by an inseparable mingling of differently colored ingredients, the colors appearing in vertical and diagonal strands and unexpected whirls. As colors are mixed in the marble cake, so functions are mixed in the American federal system. Consider the health officer, styled "sanitarian," of a rural county in a border state. He embodies the whole idea of the marble cake of government.

The sanitarian is appointed by the state under merit standards established by the federal government. His base salary comes jointly from state and federal funds, the county provides him with an office and office amenities and pays a portion of his expenses, and the largest city in the county also contributes to his salary and office by virtue of his appoint-

---

* "The Federal System" by Morton Grodzins, from *Goals for Americans.*
© 1960 by The American Assembly, Columbia University, New York City.
Reprinted by permission of Prentice-Hall, Inc., Englewood Cliffs, New Jersey.

ment as a city plumbing inspector. It is impossible from moment to moment to tell under which governmental hat the sanitarian operates. His work of inspecting the purity of food is carried out under federal standards; but he is enforcing state laws when inspecting commodities that have not been in interstate commerce; and somewhat perversely he also acts under state authority when inspecting milk coming into the county from producing areas across the state border. He is a federal officer when impounding impure drugs shipped from a neighboring state; a federal-state officer when distributing typhoid immunization serum; a state officer when enforcing standards of industrial hygiene; a state-local officer when inspecting the city's water supply; and (to complete the circle) a local officer when insisting that the city butchers adopt more hygienic methods of handling their garbage. But he cannot and does not think of himself as acting in these separate capacities. All business in the county that concerns public health and sanitation he considers his business. Paid largely from federal funds, he does not find it strange to attend meetings of the city council to give expert advice on matters ranging from rotten apples to rabies control. He is even deputized as a member of both the city and county police forces.

The sanitarian is an extreme case, but he accurately represents an important aspect of the whole range of governmental activities in the United States. Functions are not neatly parceled out among the many governments. They are shared functions. It is difficult to find any governmental activity which does not involve all three of the so-called "levels" of the federal system. In the most local of local functions—law enforcement or education, for example—the federal and state governments play important roles. In what, a priori, may be considered the purest central government activities—the conduct of foreign affairs, for example—the state and local governments have considerable responsibilities, directly and indirectly.

The federal grant programs are only the most obvious example of shared functions. They also most clearly exhibit how sharing serves to disperse governmental powers. The grants utilize the greater wealth-gathering abilities of the central government and establish nation-wide standards, yet they are "in aid" of functions carried out under state law, with considerable state and local discretion. The national supervision of such programs is largely a process of mutual accommodation. Leading state and local officials, acting through their professional organizations, are in considerable part responsible for the very standards that national officers try to persuade all state and local officers to accept.

Even in the absence of joint financing, federal-state-local collaboration is the characteristic mode of action. Federal expertise is available to aid in the building of a local jail (which may later be used to house federal prisoners), to improve a local water purification system, to step up building inspections, to provide standards for state and local personnel in protecting housewives against dishonest butchers' scales, to prevent gas explosions, or to produce a land use plan. States and localities, on the other hand, take important formal responsibilities in the development of national programs for atomic energy, civil defense, the regulation of commerce, and the protection of purity in foods and drugs; local political weight is always a factor in the operation of even a post office or a military establishment. From abattoirs and accounting through zoning and zoo administration, any governmental activity is almost certain to involve the influence, if not the formal administration, of all three planes of the federal system.

II. *Attempts to Unwind the Federal System*

Within the past dozen years there have been four major attempts to reform or reorganize the federal system: the first (1947–49) and second (1953–55) Hoover Commissions on Executive Organization; the Kestnbaum Commission on Intergovernmental Relations (1953–55); and the Joint Federal-State Action Committee (1957–59). All four of these groups have aimed to minimize federal activities. None of them has recognized the sharing of functions as the characteristic way American governments do things. Even when making recommendations for joint action, these official commissions take the view (as expressed in the Kestnbaum report) that "the main tradition of American federalism [is] the tradition of separateness." All four have, in varying degrees, worked to separate functions and tax sources.

The history of the Joint Federal-State Action Committee is especially instructive. The committee was established at the suggestion of President Eisenhower, who charged it, first of all, "to designate functions which the States are ready and willing to assume and finance that are now performed or financed wholly or in part by the Federal Government." He also gave the committee the task of recommending "Federal and State revenue adjustments required to enable the States to assume such functions."*

* The President's third suggestion was that the committee "identify functions and responsibilities likely to require state or federal attention in the future and . . . recommend the level of state effort, or federal effort, or

The committee subsequently established seemed most favorably situated to accomplish the task of functional separation. It was composed of distinguished and able men, including among its personnel three leading members of the President's cabinet, the director of the Bureau of the Budget, and ten state governors. It had the full support of the President at every point, and it worked hard and conscientiously. Excellent staff studies were supplied by the Bureau of the Budget, the White House, the Treasury Department, and, from the state side, the Council of State Governments. It had available to it a large mass of research data, including the sixteen recently completed volumes of the Kestnbaum Commission. There existed no disagreements on party lines within the committee and, of course, no constitutional impediments to its mission. The President, his cabinet members, and all the governors (with one possible exception) on the committee completely agreed on the desirability of decentralization-via-separation-of-functions-and-taxes. They were unanimous in wanting to justify the committee's name and to produce action, not just another report.

The committee worked for more than two years. It found exactly two programs to recommend for transfer from federal to state hands. One was the federal grant program for vocational education (including practical-nurse training and aid to fishery trades); the other was federal grants for municipal waste treatment plants. The programs together cost the federal government less than $80 million in 1957, slightly more than two per cent of the total federal grants for that year. To allow the states to pay for these programs, the committee recommended that they be allowed a credit against the federal tax on local telephone calls. Calculations showed that this offset device, plus an equalizing factor, would give every state at least 40 per cent more from the tax than it received from the federal government in vocational education and sewage disposal grants. Some states were "equalized" to receive twice as much.

The recommendations were modest enough, and the generous financing feature seemed calculated to gain state support. The President recommended to Congress that all points of the program be legislated. None of them was, none has been since, and none is likely to be.

---

both, that will be needed to assure effective action." The committee initially devoted little attention to this problem. Upon discovering the difficulty of making separatist recommendations, i.e., for turning over federal functions and taxes to the states, it developed a series of proposals looking to greater effectiveness in intergovernmental collaboration. The committee was succeeded by a legislatively-based, 26-member Advisory Commission on Intergovernmental Relations, established September 29, 1959.

III. *A Point of History*

The American federal system has never been a system of separated governmental activities. There has never been a time when it was possible to put neat labels on discrete "federal," "state," and "local" functions. Even before the Constitution, a statute of 1785, reinforced by the Northwest Ordinance of 1787, gave grants-in-land to the states for public schools. Thus the national government was a prime force in making possible what is now taken to be the most local function of all, primary and secondary education. More important, the nation, before it was fully organized, established by this action a first principle of American federalism: the national government would use its superior resources to initiate and support national programs, principally administered by the states and localities.

The essential unity of state and federal financial systems was again recognized in the earliest constitutional days with the assumption by the federal government of the Revolutionary War debts of the states. Other points of federal-state collaboration during the Federalist period concerned the militia, law enforcement, court practices, the administration of elections, public health measures, pilot laws, and many other matters.

The nineteenth century is widely believed to have been the preeminent period of duality in the American system. Lord Bryce at the end of the century described (in *The American Commonwealth*) the federal and state governments as "distinct and separate in their action." The system, he said, was "like a great factory wherein two sets of machinery are at work, their revolving wheels apparently intermixed, their bands crossing one another, yet each set doing its own work without touching or hampering the other." Great works may contain gross errors. Bryce was wrong. The nineteenth century, like the early days of the republic, was a period principally characterized by intergovernmental collaboration.

Decisions of the Supreme Court are often cited as evidence of nineteenth century duality. In the early part of the century the Court, heavily weighted with Federalists, was intent upon enlarging the sphere of national authority; in the later years (and to the 1930's) its actions were in the direction of paring down national powers and indeed all governmental authority. Decisions referred to "areas of exclusive competence" exercised by the federal government and the states; to their powers being "separated and distinct"; and to neither being able "to intrude within the jurisdiction of the other."

Judicial rhetoric is not always consistent with judicial action, and the Court did not always adhere to separatist doctrine. Indeed, its rhetoric sometimes indicated a positive view of cooperation. In any case, the Court was rarely, if ever, directly confronted with the issue of co-operation *vs.* separation as such. Rather it was concerned with defining permissible areas of action for the central government and the states; or with saying with respect to a point at issue whether any government could take action. The Marshall Court contributed to inter-governmental cooperation by the very act of permitting federal operations where they had not existed before. Furthermore, even Marshall was willing to allow interstate commerce to be affected by the states in their use of the police power. Later courts also upheld state laws that had an impact on inter-state commerce, just as they approved the expansion of the national com-merce power, as in statutes providing for the control of telegraphic communication or prohibiting the interstate transportation of lotteries, im-pure foods and drugs, and prostitutes. Similar room for cooperation was found outside the commerce field, notably in the Court's refusal to inter-fere with federal grants in land or cash to the states. Although research to clinch the point has not been completed, it is probably true that the Supreme Court from 1800 to 1936 allowed far more federal-state collab-oration than it blocked.

Political behavior and administrative action of the nineteenth cen-tury provide positive evidence that, throughout the entire era of so-called dual federalism, the many governments in the American federal system continued the close administrative and fiscal collaboration of the earlier period. Governmental activities were not extensive. But relative to what governments did, intergovernmental cooperation during the last century was comparable with that existing today.

Occasional presidential vetoes (from Madison to Buchanan) of cash and land grants are evidence of constitutional and ideological apprehen-sions about the extensive expansion of federal activities which produced widespread intergovernmental collaboration. In perspective, however, the vetoes are a more important evidence of the continuous search, not least by state officials, for ways and means to involve the central govern-ment in a wide variety of joint programs. The search was successful.

Grants-in-land and grants-in-services from the national government were of first importance in virtually all the principal functions undertaken by the states and their local subsidiaries. Land grants were made to the states for, among other purposes, elementary schools, colleges, and spe-cial educational institutions; roads, canals, rivers, harbors, and railroads; reclamation of desert and swamp lands; and veterans' welfare. In fact whatever was at the focus of state attention became the recipient of national grants. (Then, as today, national grants established state emphasis as well as followed it.) If Connecticut wished to establish a program for the care and education of the deaf and dumb, federal money in the form of a land grant was found to aid that program. If higher education relating to agriculture became a pressing need, Congress could dip into the public domain and make appropriate grants to states. If the need for swamp drainage and flood control appeared, the federal government could supply both grants-in-land and, from the Army's Corps of Engineers, the services of the only trained engineers then available.

Aid also went in the other direction. The federal government, theoretically in exclusive control of the Indian population, relied continuously (and not always wisely) on the experience and resources of state and local governments. State militias were an all-important ingredient in the nation's armed forces. State governments became unofficial but real partners in federal programs for homesteading, reclamation, tree culture, law enforcement, inland waterways, the nation's internal communications system (including highway and railroad routes), and veterans' aid of various sorts. Administrative contacts were voluminous, and the whole process of interaction was lubricated, then as today, by constituent-conscious members of Congress.

The essential continuity of the collaborative system is best demonstrated by the history of the grants. The land grant tended to become a cash grant based on the calculated disposable value of the land, and the cash grant tended to become an annual grant based upon the national government's superior tax powers. In 1887, only three years before the frontier was officially closed, thus signalizing the end of the disposable public domain, Congress enacted the first continuing cash grants.

A long, extensive, and continuous experience is therefore the foundation of the present system of shared functions characteristic of the American federal system, what we have called the marble cake of government. It is a misjudgment of our history and our present situation to believe that a neat separation of governmental functions could take place without drastic alterations in our society and system of government.

IV. *Dynamics of Sharing: The Politics of the Federal System*

Many causes contribute to dispersed power in the federal system. One is the simple historical fact that the states existed before the nation. A second is in the form of creed, the traditional opinion of Americans that expresses distrust of centralized power and places great value in the strength and vitality of local units of government. Another is pride in locality and state, nurtured by the naion's size and by variations of regional and state history. Still a fourth cause of decentralization is the sheer wealth of the nation. It allows all groups, including state and local governments, to partake of the central government's largesse, supplies room for experimentation and even waste, and makes unnecessary the tight organization of political power that must follow when the support of one program necessarily means the deprivation of another.

In one important respect, the Constitution no longer operates to impede centralized government. The Supreme Court since 1937 has given Congress a relatively free hand. The federal government can build substantive programs in many areas on the taxation and commerce powers. Limitations of such central programs based on the argument, "it's unconstitutional," are no longer possible as long as Congress (in the Court's view) acts reasonably in the interest of the whole nation. The Court is unlikely to reverse this permissive view in the foreseeable future.

Nevertheless, some constitutional restraints on centralization continue to operate. The strong constitutional position of the states—for example, the assignment of two senators to each state, the role given the states in administering even national elections, and the relatively few limitations on their law-making powers—establish the geographical units as natural centers of administrative and political strength. Many clauses of the Constitution are not subject to the same latitude of interpretation as the commerce and tax clauses. The simple, clearly stated, unambiguous phrases—for example, the President "shall hold his office during the term of four years"—are subject to change only through the formal amendment process. Similar provisions exist with respect to the terms of senators and congressmen and the amendment process. All of them have the effect of retarding or restraining centralizing action of the federal government. The fixed terms of the President and members of Congress, for example, greatly impede the development of nation-wide, disciplined political parties that almost certainly would have to precede continuous large-scale expansion of federal functions.

The constitutional restraints on the expansion of national authority are less important and less direct today than they were in 1879 or in 1936. But to say that they are less important is not to say that they are unimportant.

The nation's politics reflect these decentralizing causes and add some of their own. The political parties of the United States are unique. They seldom perform the function that parties traditionally perform in other countries, the function of gathering together diverse strands of power and welding them into one. Except during the period of nominating and electing a president and for the essential but non-substantive business of organizing the houses of Congress, the American parties rarely coalesce power at all. Characteristically they do the reverse, serving as a canopy under which special and local interests are represented with little regard for anything that can be called a party program. National leaders are elected on a party ticket, but in Congress they must seek cross-party support if their leadership is to be effective. It is a rare president during rare periods who can produce legislation without facing the defection of substantial numbers of his own party. (Wilson could do this in the first session of the sixty-third Congress; but Franklin D. Roosevelt could not, even during the famous hundred days of 1933.) Presidents whose parties form the majority of the congressional houses must still count heavily on support from the other party.

The parties provide the pivot on which the entire governmental system swings. Party operations, first of all, produce in legislation the basic division of functions between the federal government, on the one hand, and state and local governments, on the other. The Supreme Court's permissiveness with respect to the expansion of national powers has not in fact produced any considerable extension of exclusive federal functions. The body of federal law in all fields has remained, in the words of Henry M. Hart, Jr. and Herbert Wechsler, "interstitial in its nature," limited in objective and resting upon the principal body of legal relationships defined by state law. It is difficult to find any area of federal legislation that is not significantly affected by state law.

In areas of new or enlarged federal activity, legislation characteristically provides important roles for state and local governments. This is as true of Democratic as of Republican administrations and true even of functions for which arguments of efficiency would produce exclusive federal responsibility. Thus the unemployment compensation program of the New Deal and the airport program of President Truman's administration both provided important responsibilities for state governments. In both cases attempts to eliminate state participation were defeated by a cross-party coalition of pro-state votes and influence. A large fraction of the Senate is usually made up of ex-governors, and the membership of both houses is composed of men who know that their re-election depends less upon national leaders or national party organization than upon support from their home constituencies. State and local officials are key members of these constituencies, often central figures in selecting candidates and in turning out the vote. Under such circumstances, national legislation taking state and local views heavily into account is inevitable.

Second, the undisciplined parties affect the character of the federal system as a result of senatorial and congressional interference in federal administrative programs on behalf of local interests. Many aspects of the legislative involvement in administrative affairs are formalized. The Legislative Reorganization Act of 1946, to take only one example, provided that each of the standing committees "shall exercise continuous watchfulness" over administration of laws within its jurisdiction. But the formal system of controls, extensive as it is, does not compare in importance with the informal and extralegal network of relationships in producing continuous legislative involvement in administrative affairs.

Senators and congressmen spend a major fraction of their time representing problems of their constituents before administrative agencies. An even larger fraction of congressional staff time is devoted to the same task. The total magnitude of such "case work" operations is great. In one five-month period of 1943 the Office of Price Administration received a weekly average of 842 letters from members of Congress. If phone calls and personal contacts are added, each member of Congress on the average presented the OPA with a problem involving one of his constituents twice a day in each five-day work week. Data for less vulnerable agencies during less intensive periods are also impressive. In 1958, to take only one example, the Department of Agriculture estimated (and underestimated) that it received an average of 159 congressional letters per working day. Special congressional liaison staffs have been created to service this mass of business, though all higher officials meet it in one form or another. The Air Force in 1958 had, under the command of a major general, 137 people (55 officers and 82 civilians) working in its liaison office.

The widespread, consistent, and in many ways unpredictable character of legislative interference in administrative affairs has many consequences for the tone and character of American administrative behavior. From the perspective of this paper, the important consequence is the comprehensive, day-to-day, even hour-by-hour, impact of local views on national programs. No point of substance or procedure is immune from congressional scrutiny. A substantial portion of the entire weight of this impact is on behalf of the state and local governments. It is a weight that can alter procedures for screening immigration applications, divert the course of a national highway, change the tone of an international negotiation, and amend a social security law to accommodate local practices or fulfill local desires.

The party system compels administrators to take a political role. This is a third way in which the parties function to decentralize the American system. The administrator must play politics for the same reason that the politician is able to play in administration: the parties are without program and without discipline.

In response to the unprotected position in which the party situation places him, the administrator is forced to seek support where he can find it. One ever-present task is to nurse the Congress of the United States, that crucial constituency which ultimately controls his agency's budget and program. From the administrator's view, a sympathetic consideration of congressional requests (if not downright submission to them) is the surest way to build the political support without which the administrative job could not continue. Even the completely task-oriented administrator must be sensitive to the need for congressional support and to the relationship between case work requests, on one side, and budgetary and legislative support, on the other. "You do a good job handling the personal problems and requests of a Congressman," a White House officer said, "and you have an easier time convincing him to back your program." Thus there is an important link between the nursing of congressional requests, requests that largely concern local matters, and the most comprehensive national programs. The administrator must accommodate to the former as a price of gaining support for the latter.

One result of administrative politics is that the administrative agency may become the captive of the nation-wide interest group it serves or presumably regulates. In such cases no government may come out with effective authority: the winners are the interest groups themselves. But in a very large number of cases, states and localities also win influence. The politics of administration is a process of making peace with legislators who for the most part consider themselves the guardians of local interests. The political role of administrators therefore contributes to the power of states and localities in national programs.

Finally, the way the party system operates gives American politics their over-all distinctive tone. The lack of party discipline produces an openness in the system that allows individuals, groups, and institutions (including state and local governments) to attempt to influence national policy at every step of the legislative-administrative process. This is the "multiple-crack" attribute of the American government. "Crack" has two meanings. It means not only many fissures or access points; it also means, less statically, opportunities for wallops or smacks at government.

If the parties were more disciplined, the result would not be a cessation of the process by which individuals and groups impinge themselves upon the central government. But the present state of the parties clearly allows for a far greater operation of the multiple crack than would be possible under the conditions of centralized party control. American interest groups exploit literally uncountable access points in the legislative-administrative process. If legislative lobbying, from committee stages to the conference committee, does not produce results, a cabinet secretary is called. His immediate associates are petitioned. Bureau chiefs and their aides are hit. Field officers are put under pressure. Campaigns are instituted by which friends of the agency apply a secondary influence on behalf of the interested party. A conference with the President may be urged.

To these multiple points for bringing influence must be added the multiple voices of the influencers. Consider, for example, those in a small town who wish to have a federal action taken. The easy merging of public and private interest at the local level means that the influence attempt is made in the name of the whole community, thus removing it from political partisanship. The Rotary Club as well as the City Council, the Chamber of Commerce and the mayor, eminent citizens and political bosses—all are readily enlisted. If a conference in a senator's office will expedite matters, someone on the local scene can be found to make such a conference possible and effective. If technical information is needed, technicians will supply it. State or national professional organizations of local officials, individual congressmen and senators, and not infrequently whole state delegations will make the local cause their own. Federal field officers, who service localities, often assume local views. So may elected and appointed state officers. Friendships are exploited, and political mortgages called due. Under these circumstances, national policies are molded by local action.

In summary, then, the party system functions to devolve power. The American parties, unlike any other, are highly responsive when directives move from the bottom to the top, highly unresponsive from top to bottom. Congressmen and senators can rarely ignore concerted demands from their home constituencies; but no party leader can expect the same kind of response from those below, whether he be a President asking for congressional support or a congressman seeking aid from local or state leaders.

Any tightening of the party apparatus would have the effect of strengthening the central government. The four characteristics of the system, discussed above, would become less important. If control from the top were strictly applied, these hallmarks of American decentralization might entirely disappear. To be specific, if disciplined and program-oriented parties were achieved: (1) It would make far less likely legislation that takes heavily into account the desires and prejudices of the highly decentralized power groups and institutions of the country, including the state and local governments. (2) It would to a large extent prevent legislators, individually and collectively, from intruding themselves on behalf of non-national interests in national administrative programs. (3) It would put an end to the administrator's search for his own political support, a search that often results in fostering state, local, and other non-national powers. (4) It would dampen the process by which individuals and groups, including state and local political leaders, take advantage of multiple cracks to steer national legislation and administration in ways congenial to them and the institutions they represent.

Alterations of this sort could only accompany basic changes in the organization and style of politics which, in turn, presuppose fundamental changes at the parties' social base. The sharing of functions is, in fact, the sharing of power. To end this sharing process would mean the destruction of whatever measure of decentralization exists in the United States today.

V. Goals for the System of Sharing

The goal of understanding. Our structure of government is complex, and the politics operating that structure are mildly chaotic. Circumstances are ever-changing. Old institutions mask intricate procedures. The nation's history can be read with alternative glosses, and what is nearest at hand may be furthest from comprehension. Simply to understand the federal system is therefore a difficult task. Yet without understanding there is little possibility of producing desired changes in the system. Social structures and processes are relatively impervious to purposeful change. They also exhibit intricate interrelationships so that change induced at point "A" often produces unanticipated results at point "Z." Changes introduced into an imperfectly understood system are as likely to produce reverse consequences as the desired ones.

This is counsel of neither futility nor conservatism for those who seek to make our government a better servant of the people. It is only to say that the first goal for those setting goals with respect to the federal system is that of understanding it.

Two kinds of decentralization. The recent major efforts to reform the federal system have in large part been aimed at separating functions and tax sources, at dividing them between the federal government and the states. All of these attempts have failed. We can now add that their success would be undesirable.

It is easy to specify the conditions under which an ordered separation of functions could take place. What is principally needed is a majority political party, under firm leadership, in control of both Presidency and Congress, and, ideally but not necessarily, also in control of a number of states. The political discontinuities, or the absence of party links, (1) between the governors and their state legislatures, (2) between the President and the governors, and (3) between the President and Congress clearly account for both the picayune recommendations of the Federal-State Action Committee and for the failure of even those recommendations in Congress. If the President had been in control of Congress (that is, consistently able to direct a majority of House and Senate votes), this alone would have made possible some genuine separation and devolution of functions. The failure to decentralize by order is a measure of the decentralization of power in the political parties.

Stated positively, party centralization must precede governmental decentralization by order. But this is a slender reed on which to hang decentralization. It implies the power to centralize. A majority party powerful enough to bring about ordered decentralization is far more likely to choose in favor of ordered centralization. And a society that produced centralized national parties would, by that very fact, be a society prepared to accept centralized government.

Decentralization by order must be contrasted with the different kind of decentralization that exists today in the United States. It may be called the decentralization of mild chaos. It exists because of the existence of dispersed power centers. This form of decentralization is less visible and less neat. It rests on no discretion of central authorities. It produces at times specific acts that many citizens may consider undesirable or evil. But power sometimes wielded even for evil ends may be desirable power. To those who find value in the dispersion of power, decentralization by mild chaos is infinitely more desirable than decentralization by order. The preservation of mild chaos is an important goal for the American federal system.

Oiling the squeak points. In a governmental system of genuinely shared responsibilities, disagreements inevitably occur. Opinions clash over proximate ends, particular ways of doing things become the subject of public debate, innovations are contested. These are not basic defects in the system. Rather, they are the system's energy-reflecting life blood. There can be no permanent "solutions" short of changing the system itself by elevating one partner to absolute supremacy. What can be done is to attempt to produce conditions in which conflict will not fester but be turned to constructive solutions of particular problems.

A long list of specific points of difficulty in the federal system can be easily identified. No adequate congressional or administrative mechanism exists to review the patchwork of grants in terms of national needs. There is no procedure by which to judge, for example, whether the national government is justified in spending so much more for highways than for education. The working force in some states is inadequate for the effective performance of some nation-wide programs, while honest and not-so-honest graft frustrates efficiency in others. Some federal aid programs distort state budgets, and some are so closely supervised as to impede state action in meeting local needs. Grants are given for programs too narrowly defined, and over-all programs at the state level consequently suffer. Administrative, accounting and auditing difficulties are the consequence of the multiplicity of grant programs. City officials complain that the states are intrusive fifth wheels in housing, urban redevelopment, and airport building programs.

Some differences are so basic that only a demonstration of strength on one side or another can solve them. School desegregation illustrates such an issue. It also illustrates the correct solution (although not the most desirable method of reaching it): in policy conflicts of fundamental importance, touching the nature of democracy itself, the view of the whole nation must prevail. Such basic ends, however, are rarely at issue, and sides are rarely taken with such passion that loggerheads are reached. Modes of settlement can usually be found to lubricate the squeak points of the system.

A pressing and permanent state problem, general in its impact, is the difficulty of raising sufficient revenue without putting local industries at a competitive disadvantage or without an expansion of sales taxes that press hardest on the least wealthy. A possible way of meeting this problem is to establish a state-levied income tax that could be used as an offset for federal taxes. The maximum level of the tax which could be offset would be fixed by federal law. When levied by a state, the state collection would be deducted from federal taxes. But if a state did not levy the tax, the federal government would. An additional fraction of the total tax imposed by the states would be collected directly by the federal government and used as an equalization fund, that is, distributed among the less wealthy states. Such a tax would almost certainly be imposed by all states since not to levy it would give neither political advantage to its public leaders nor financial advantage to its citizens. The net effect would be an increase in the total personal and corporate income tax.

The offset has great promise for strengthening state governments. It would help produce a more economic distribution of industry. It would have obvious financial advantages for the vast majority of states. Since a large fraction of all state income is used to aid political subdivisions, the local governments would also profit, though not equally as long as cities are under-represented in state legislatures. On the other hand, such a scheme will appear disadvantageous to some low-tax states which profit from the in-migration of industry (though it would by no means end all state-by-state tax differentials). It will probably excite the opposition of those concerned over governmental centralization, and they will not be assuaged by methods that suggest themselves for making both state and central governments bear the psychological impact of the tax. Although the offset would probably produce an across-the-board tax increase, wealthier persons, who are affected more by an income tax than by other levies, can be expected to join forces with those whose fear is centralization. (This is a common alliance and, in the nature of things, the philosophical issue rather than financial advantage is kept foremost.)

Those opposing such a tax would gain additional ammunition from the certain knowledge that federal participation in the scheme would lead to some federal standards governing the use of the funds. Yet the political strength of the states would keep these from becoming onerous. Indeed, inauguration of the tax offset as a means of providing funds to the states might be an occasion for dropping some of the specifications for existing federal grants. One federal standard, however, might be possible because of the greater representation of urban areas in the constituency of Congress and the President than in the constituency of state legislatures: Congress might make a state's participation in the offset scheme dependent upon a periodic reapportionment of state legislatures.

The income tax offset is only one of many ideas that can be generated to meet serious problems of closely meshed governments. The fate of all such schemes ultimately rests, as it should, with the politics of a free people. But much can be done if the primary technical effort of those concerned with improving the federal system were directed not at separating its interrelated parts but at making them work together more effectively. Temporary commissions are relatively inefficient in this effort, though they may be useful for making general assessments and for generating new ideas. The professional organizations of government workers do part of the job of continuously scrutinizing programs and ways and means of improving them. A permanent staff, established in the President's office and working closely with state and local officials, could also perform a useful and perhaps important role.

The strength of the parts. Whatever governmental "strength" or "vitality" may be, it does not consist of independent decision-making in legislation and administration. Federal-state interpenetration here is extensive. Indeed, a judgment of the relative domestic strength of the two planes must take heavily into account the influence of one on the other's decisions. In such an analysis the strength of the states (and localities) does not weigh lightly. The nature of the nation's politics makes federal functions more vulnerable to state influence than state offices are to federal influence. Many states, as the Kestnbaum Commission noted, live with "self-imposed constitutional limitations" that make it difficult for them to "perform all of the services that their citizens require." If this has the result of adding to federal responsibilties, the states' importance in shaping and administering federal programs eliminates much of the sting.

The geography of state boundaries, as well as many aspects of state internal organization, are the products of history and cannot be justified on any grounds of rational efficiency. Who, today, would create major governmental subdivisions the size of Maryland, Delaware, New Jersey, or Rhode Island? Who would write into Oklahoma's fundamental law an absolute state debt limit of $500,000? Who would design (to cite only the most extreme cases) Georgia's and Florida's gross under-representation of urban areas in both houses of the legislature?

A complete catalogue of state political and administrative horrors would fill a sizeable volume. Yet exhortations to erase them have roughly the same effect as similar exhortations to erase sin. Some of the worst inanities—for example, the boundaries of the states, themselves—are fixed in the national constitution and defy alteration for all foreseeable time. Others, such as urban under-representation in state legislatures, serve the over-represented groups, including some urban ones, and the effective political organization of the deprived groups must precede reform.

Despite deficiencies of politics and organizations that are unchangeable or slowly changing, it is an error to look at the states as static anachronisms. Some of them—New York, Minnesota, and California, to take three examples spanning the country—have administrative organizations that compare favorably in many ways with the national establishment. Many more in recent years have moved rapidly towards integrated administrative departments, state-wide budgeting, and central leadership. The others have models-in-existence to follow, and active professional organizations (led by the Council of State Governments) promoting their development. Slow as this change may be, the states move in the direction of greater internal effectiveness.

The pace toward more effective performance at the state level is likely to increase. Urban leaders, who generally feel themselves disadvantaged in state affairs, and suburban and rural spokesmen, who are most concerned about national centralization, have a common interest in this task. The urban dwellers want greater equality in state affairs, including a more equitable share of state financial aid; non-urban dwellers are concerned that city dissatisfactions should not be met by exclusive federal, or federal-local, programs. Antagonistic, rather than amiable, cooperation may be the consequence. But it is a cooperation that can be turned to politically effective measures for a desirable upgrading of state institutions.

If one looks closely, there is scant evidence for the fear of the federal octopus, the fear that expansion of central programs and influence threatens to reduce the states and localities to compliant administrative arms of the central government. In fact, state and local governments are touching a larger proportion of the people in more ways than ever before; and they are spending a higher fraction of the total national product than ever before. Federal programs have increased, rather than diminished, the importance of the governors; stimulated professionalism in state agencies; increased citizen interest and participation in government; and, generally, enlarged and made more effective the scope of state action.* It may no longer be true in any significant sense that the states and localities are "closer" than the federal government to the people. It is true that the smaller governments remain active and powerful members of the federal system.

Central leadership: The need for balance. The chaos of party processes makes difficult the task of presidential leadership. It deprives the President of ready-made congressional majorities. It may produce, as in the chairmen of legislative committees, power-holders relatively hidden from

* See the valuable report, *The Impact of Federal Grants-in-Aid on the Structure and Functions of State and Local Governments,* submitted to the Commission on Intergovernmental Relations by the Governmental Affairs Institute (Washington, 1955).

public scrutiny and relatively protected from presidential direction. It allows the growth of administrative agencies which sometimes escape control by central officials. These are prices paid for a wide dispersion of political power. The cost is tolerable because the total results of dispersed power are themselves desirable and because, where clear national supremacy is essential, in foreign policy and military affairs, it is easiest to secure.

Moreover, in the balance of strength between the central and peripheral governments, the central government has on its side the whole secular drift towards the concentration of power. It has on its side technical developments that make central decisions easy and sometimes mandatory. It has on its side potent purse powers, the result of superior tax-gathering resources. It has potentially on its side the national leadership capacities of the presidential office. The last factor is the controlling one, and national strength in the federal system has shifted with the leadership desires and capacities of the chief executive. As these have varied, so there has been an almost rhythmic pattern: periods of central strength put to use alternating with periods of central strength dormant.

Following a high point of federal influence during the early and middle years of the New Deal, the post-war years have been, in the weighing of central-peripheral strength, a period of light federal activity. Excepting the Supreme Court's action in favor of school desegregation, national influence by design or default has not been strong in domestic affairs. The danger now is that the central government is doing too little rather than too much. National deficiencies in education and health require the renewed attention of the national government. Steepening population and urbanization trend lines have produced metropolitan area problems that can be effectively attacked only with the aid of federal resources. New definitions of old programs in housing and urban redevelopment, and new programs to deal with air pollution, water supply, and mass transportation are necessary. The federal government's essential role in the federal system is that of organizing, and helping to finance, such national-wide programs.

The American federal system exhibits many evidences of the dispersion of power not only because of formal federalism but more importantly because our politics reflect and reinforce the nation's diversities-within-unity. Those who value the virtues of decentralization, which writ large are virtues of freedom, need not scruple at recognizing the defects of those virtues. The defects are principally the danger that parochial and private interests may not coincide with, or give way to, the nation's interest. The necessary cure for these defects is effective national leadership. The centrifugal force of domestic politics needs to be balanced by the centripetal force of strong presidential leadership. Simultaneous strength at center and periphery exhibits the American system at its best, if also at its noisiest. The interests of both find effective spokesmen. States and localities (and private interest groups) do not lose their influence opportunities, but national policy becomes more than the simple consequence of successful, momentary concentrations of non-national pressures: it is guided by national leaders.

CHAPTER THREE

The Development of Civil Liberties and Civil Rights

The subject of civil liberties and civil rights covers a very broad area. Among the most fundamental civil liberties are those governing the extent to which individuals can speak, write, and read what they choose. The democratic process requires the free exchange of ideas. Constitutional government requires the protection of minority rights, and above all of the right to dissent.

8. Freedom of Speech and Press

There are many reasons to support freedom of speech and press. One of these is the impossibility of proving the existence of an Absolute Truth. No person nor group of men can be infallible. The "best" decisions are those that are made on the basis of the most widespread information available pertaining to the subject at hand. Freedom of information is an integral part of the democratic process. The following selection, from John Stuart Mill's famous essay *On Liberty,* published in 1859, discusses the justifications for permitting liberty of speech and press.

LIBERTY OF THOUGHT AND DISCUSSION
*John Stuart Mill**

THE TIME, it is to be hoped, is gone by when any defence would be necessary of the "liberty of the press" as one of the securities against

* Taken from Mill's famous essay *On Liberty* (1859).

corrupt or tyrannical government. No argument, we may suppose, can now be needed, against permitting a legislature or an executive, not identified in interest with the people, to prescribe opinions to them, and determine what doctrines or what arguments they shall be allowed to hear. This aspect of the question, besides, has been so often and so triumphantly enforced by preceding writers, that it needs not be specially insisted on in this place. Though the law of England, on the subject of the press, is as servile to this day as it was in the time of the Tudors, there is little danger of its being actually put in force against political discussion, except during some temporary panic, when fear of insurrection drives ministers and judges from their propriety; and, speaking generally, it is not, in constitutional countries, to be apprehended, that the government, whether completely responsible to the people or not, will often attempt to control the expression of opinion, except when in doing so it makes itself the organ of the general intolerance of the public. Let us suppose, therefore, that the government is entirely at one with the people, and never thinks of exerting any power of coercion unless in agreement with what it conceives to be their voice. But I deny the right of the people to exercise such coercion, either by themselves or by their government. The power itself is illegitimate. The best government has no more title to it than the worst. It is as noxious, or more noxious, when exerted in accordance with public opinion, than when in opposition to it. If all mankind minus one, were of one opinion, and only one person were of the contrary opinion, mankind would be no more justified in silencing that one person, than he, if he had the power, would be justified in silencing mankind. Were an opinion a personal possession of no value except to the owner; if to be obstructed in the enjoyment of it were simply a private injury, it would make some difference whether the injury was inflicted only on a few persons or on many. But the peculiar evil of silencing the expression of an opinion is, that it is robbing the human race; posterity as well as the existing generation; those who dissent from the opinion, still more than those who hold it. If the opinion is right, they are deprived of the opportunity of exchanging error for truth: if wrong, they lose, what is almost as great a benefit, the clearer perception and livelier impression of truth, produced by its collision with error.

It is necessary to consider separately these two hypotheses, each of which has a distinct branch of the argument corresponding to it. We can never be sure that the opinion we are endeavoring to stifle is a false opinion; and if we were sure, stifling it would be an evil still.

First: the opinion which it is attempted to suppress by authority may possibly be true. Those who desire to suppress it, of course deny its truth; but they are not infallible. They have no authority to decide the question for all mankind, and exclude every other person from the means of judging. To refuse a hearing to an opinion, because they are sure that it is false, is to assume that *their* certainty is the same thing as *absolute* certainty. All silencing of discussion is an assumption of infallibility. Its condemnation may be allowed to rest on this common argument, not the worse for being common.

Unfortunately for the good sense of mankind, the fact of their fallibility is far from carrying the weight in their practical judgment, which is always allowed to it in theory; for while every one well knows himself to be fallible, few think it necessary to take any precautions against their own fallibility, or admit the supposition that any opinion, of which they feel very certain, may be one of the examples of the error to which they acknowledge themselves to be liable. Absolute princes, or others who are accustomed to unlimited deference, usually feel this complete confidence in their own opinions on nearly all subjects. People more happily situated, who sometimes hear their opinions disputed, and are not wholly unused to be set right when they are wrong, place the same unbounded reliance only on such of their opinions as are shared by all who surround them, or to whom they habitually defer: for in proportion to a man's want of confidence in his own solitary judgment, does he usually repose, with implicit trust, on the infallibility of "the world" in general. And the world, to each individual, means the part of it with which he comes in contact; his party, his sect, his church, his class of society: the man may be called, by comparison, almost liberal and large-minded to whom it means anything so comprehensive as his own country or his own age. Nor is his faith in this collective authority at all shaken by his being aware that other ages, countries, sects, churches, classes, and parties have thought, and even now think, the exact reverse. He devolves upon his own world the responsibility of being in the right against the dissentient worlds of other people; and it never troubles him that mere accident has decided which of these numerous worlds is the object of his reliance, and that the same causes which make him a Churchman in London, would have made him a Buddhist or a Confucian in Pekin. Yet it is as evident in itself, as any amount of argument can make it, that ages are no more infallible than individuals; every age having held many opinions which subsequent ages have deemed not only false but absurd; and it is as certain that many opinions, now general, will be rejected by future ages, as it is that many, once general, are rejected by the present.

The objection likely to be made to this argument, would probably take some such form as the following. There is no greater assumption of infallibility in forbidding the propagation of error, than in any other thing which is done by public authority on its own judgment and responsibility. Judgment is given to men that they may use it. Because it may be used erroneously, are men to be told that they ought not to use it at all? To prohibit what they think pernicious, is not claiming exemption from error, but fulfilling the duty incumbent on them, although fallible, of acting on their conscientious conviction. If we were never to act on our opinions, because those opinions may be wrong, we should leave all our interests uncared for, and all our duties unperformed. An objection which applies to all conduct, can be no valid objection to any conduct in particular. It is the duty of governments, and of individuals, to form the truest opinions they can; to form them carefully, and never impose them upon others unless they are quite sure of being right. But when they are sure (such reasoners may say), it is not conscientiousness but cowardice to shrink from acting on their opinions, and allow doctrines which they honestly think dangerous to the welfare of mankind, either in this life or in another, to be scattered abroad without restraint, because other people, in less enlightened times, have persecuted opinions now believed to be true. Let us take care, it may be said, not to make the same mistake: but governments and nations have made mistakes in other things, which are not denied to be fit subjects for the exercise of authority: they have laid on bad taxes, made unjust wars. Ought we therefore to lay on no taxes, and, under whatever provocation, make no wars? Men, and governments, must act to the best of their ability. There is no such thing as absolute certainty, but there is assurance sufficient for the purposes of human life. We may, and must, assume our opinion to be true for the guidance of our own conduct: and it is assuming no more when we forbid bad men to pervert society by the propagation of opinions which we regard as false and pernicious.

I answer, that it is assuming very much more. There is the greatest difference between presuming an opinion to be true, because, with every opportunity for contesting it, it has not been refuted, and assuming its truth for the purpose of not permitting its refutation. Complete liberty of contradicting and disproving our opinion, is the very condition which justifies us in assuming its truth for purposes of action; and on no other terms can a being with human faculties have any rational assurance of being right.

When we consider either the history of opinion, or the ordinary conduct of human life, to what is it to be ascribed that the one and the other are no worse than they are? Not certainly to the inherent force of the human understanding; for, on any matter not self-evident, there are ninety-nine persons totally incapable of judging of it, for one who is capable; and the capacity of the hundredth person is only comparative; for the majority of the eminent men of every past generation held many opinions now known to be erroneous, and did or approved numerous things which no one will now justify. Why is it, then, that there is on the whole a preponderance among mankind of rational opinions and rational conduct? If there really is this preponderance—which there must be, unless human affairs are, and have always been, in an almost desperate state—it is owing to a quality of the human mind, the source of everything respectable in man either as an intellectual or as a moral being, namely, that his errors are corrigible. He is capable of rectifying his mistakes, by discussion and experience. Not by experience alone. There must be discussion, to show how experience is to be interpreted. Wrong opinions and practices gradually yield to fact and argument: but facts and arguments, to produce any effect on the mind, must be brought before it. Very few facts are able to tell their own story, without comments to bring out their meaning. The whole strength and value, then, of human judgment, depending on the one property, that it can be set right when it is wrong, reliance can be placed on it only when the means of setting it right are kept constantly at hand. In the case of any person whose judgment is really deserving of confidence, how has it become so? Because he has kept his mind open to criticism of his opinions and conduct. Because it has been his practice to listen to all that could be said against him; to profit by as much of it as was just, and expound to himself, and upon occasion to others, the fallacy of what was fallacious. Because he has felt, that the only way in which a human being can make some approach to knowing the whole of a subject, is by hearing what can be said about it by persons of every variety of opinion, and studying all modes in which it can be looked at by every character of mind. No wise man ever acquired his wisdom in any mode but this; nor is it in the nature of human intellect to become wise in any other manner. The steady habit of correcting and completing his own opinion by collating it with those of others, so far from causing doubt and hesitation in carrying it into practice, is the only stable foundation for a just reliance on it: for, being cognizant of all that can, at least obviously, be said against him, and having taken up his position against all gainsayers—knowing that he has sought for objections and difficulties, instead of avoiding them, and has shut out no light which can be thrown upon the subject from any quarter—he has a right to think his judgment better than that of any person, or any multitude, who have not gone through a similar process.

It is not too much to require that what the wisest of mankind, those who are best entitled to trust their own judgment, find necessary to warrant their relying on it, should be submitted to by that miscellaneous collection of a few wise and many foolish individuals, called the public. The most intolerant of churches, the Roman Catholic Church, even at the canonization of a saint, admits, and listens patiently to, a "devil's advocate." The holiest of men, it appears, cannot be admitted to posthumous honors, until all that the devil could say against him is known and weighed. If even the Newtonian philosophy were not permitted to be questioned, mankind could not feel as complete assurance of its truth as they now do. The beliefs which we have most warrant for, have no safeguard to rest on, but a standing invitation to the whole world to prove them unfounded. . . .

We have now recognized the necessity to the mental well-being of mankind (on which all their other well-being depends) of freedom of opinion, and freedom of the expression of opinion, on four distinct grounds; which we will now briefly recapitulate.

First, if any opinion is compelled to silence, that opinion may, for aught we can certainly know, be true. To deny this is to assume our own infallibility.

Secondly, though the silenced opinion be an error, it may, and very commonly does, contain a portion of truth; and since the general or prevailing opinion on any subject is rarely or never the whole truth, it is only by the collision of adverse opinions that the remainder of the truth has any chance of being supplied.

Thirdly, even if the received opinion be not only true, but the whole truth; unless it is suffered to be, and actually is, vigorously and earnestly contested, it will, by most of those who receive it, be held in the manner of a prejudice, with little comprehension or feeling of its rational grounds. And not only this, but, fourthly, the meaning of the doctrine itself will be in danger of being lost, or enfeebled, and deprived of its vital effect on the character and conduct: the dogma becoming a mere formal profession, inefficacious for good, but cumbering the ground, and preventing the growth of any real and heartfelt conviction from reason or personal experience.

Before quitting the subject of freedom of opinion, it is fit to take some notice of those who say, that the free expression of all opinions should be permitted, on condition that the manner be temperate, and do not pass the bounds of fair discussion. Much might be said on the impossibility of fixing where these supposed bounds are to be placed; for if the test be offence to those whose opinion is attacked, I think experience testifies that this offence is given whenever the attack is telling and powerful, and that every opponent who pushes them hard, and whom they find it difficult to answer, appears to them, if he shows any strong feeling on the subject, an intemperate opponent. But this, though an important consideration in a practical point of view, merges in a more fundamental objection. Undoubtedly the manner of asserting an opinion, even though it be a true one, may be very objectionable, and may justly incur severe censure. But the principal offences of the kind are such as it is mostly impossible, unless by accidental self-betrayal, to bring home to conviction. The gravest of them is, to argue sophistically, to suppress facts or arguments, to misstate the elements of the case, or misrepresent the opposite opinion. But all this, even to the most aggravated degree, is so continually done in perfect good faith, by persons who are not considered, and in many other respects may not deserve to be considered, ignorant or incompetent, that it is rarely possible on adequate grounds conscientiously to stamp the misrepresentation as morally culpable; and still less could law presume to interfere with this kind of controversial misconduct. With regard to what is commonly meant by intemperate discussion, namely, invective, sarcasm, personality, and the like, the denunciation of these weapons would deserve more sympathy if it were ever proposed to interdict them equally to both sides; but it is only desired to restrain the employment of them against the prevailing opinion: against the unprevailing they may not only be used without general disapproval, but will be likely to obtain for him who uses them the praise of honest zeal and righteous indignation. Yet whatever mischief arises from their use, is greatest when they are employed against the comparatively defenceless; and whatever unfair advantage can be derived by any opinion from this mode of asserting it, accrues almost exclusively to received opinions. The worst offence of this kind which can be committed by a polemic, is to stigmatize those who hold the contrary opinion as bad and immoral men. To calumny of this sort, those who hold any unpopular opinion are peculiarly exposed, because they are in general few and uninfluential, and nobody but themselves feels much interest in seeing justice done them; but this weapon is, from the nature of the case, denied to those who attack a prevailing opinion: they can neither use it with safety to themselves, nor, if they could, would it do anything but recoil on their own cause. In general, opinions contrary to those commonly received can only obtain a hearing by studied moderation of language, and the most cautious avoidance of unnecessary offence, from which they hardly ever deviate even in a slight degree without losing ground: while unmeasured vituperation employed on the side of the prevailing opinion, really does deter people from professing contrary opinions, and from listening to those who profess them. For the interest, therefore, of truth and justice, it is far more important to restrain this employment of vituperative language than the other; and, for example, if it were necessary to choose, there would be much more need to discourage offensive attacks on infidelity, than on religion. It is, however, obvious that law and authority have no business with restraining either, while opinion ought, in every instance, to determine its verdict by the circumstances of the individual case; condemning every one, on whichever side of the argument he places himself, in whose mode of advocacy either want of candor, or malignity, bigotry, or intolerance of feeling manifest themselves; but not inferring these vices from the side which a person takes, though it be the contrary side of the question to our own: and giving merited honor to every one, whatever opinion he may hold, who has calmness to see and honesty to state what his opponents and their opinions really are, exaggerating nothing to their discredit, keeping nothing back which tells, or can be supposed to tell, in their favor. This is the real morality of public discussion; and if often violated, I am happy to think that there are many controversialists who to a great extent observe it, and a still greater number who conscientiously strive towards it.

Mill does not justify absolute liberty of speech and press, but implies that there are boundaries to public debate. However, he also notes that there are extraordinary difficulties in determining where the boundaries are to be placed. Democratic governments have always had this dilemma. At what point can freedom of speech and press be curtailed? We shall see shortly that this problem is one of the most difficult that has faced the Supreme Court in areas involving censorship, and loyalty and security. Freedom of speech and press cannot be used to destroy the very government that protects these liberties. Abuses of freedom of speech and press may exist at many levels, which leads Carl Becker in the following selection to suggest that true freedom must be accompanied by responsibility. It cannot be enforced in all cases by the political system, but must be accepted by individuals indulging in their liberties to speak and publish freely.

FREEDOM AND RESPONSIBILITY IN THE AMERICAN WAY OF LIFE

*Carl L. Becker**

THE democratic doctrine of freedom of speech and of the press, whether we regard it as a natural and inalienable right or not, rests upon certain assumptions. One of these is that men desire to know the truth and will be disposed to be guided by it. Another is that the sole method of arriving at the truth in the long run is by the free competition of opinion in the open market. Another is that, since men will inevitably differ in their opinions, each man must be permitted to urge, freely and even strenuously, his own opinion, provided he accords to others the same right. And the final assumption is that from this mutual toleration and comparison of diverse opinions the one that seems the most rational will emerge and be generally accepted.

The classic expression of this procedure and this attitude of mind is the saying attributed, incorrectly it may be, to Voltaire: "I disagree absolutely with what you say, but I will defend to the death your right to say it." For me these famous words always call up, at first, an agreeable picture—the picture of two elderly gentlemen, in powdered wigs and buckled shoes, engaged over their toddy in an amiable if perhaps somewhat heated discussion about the existence of the deity. But when I try to fit the phrase into the free competition of opinion as it actually works out in our present democratic society, the picture fades out into certain other pictures, some even more agreeable, others much less so. The more agreeable picture might be that of Pierre and Marie Curie working day and night for four years in their leaky laboratory for the sole purpose of discovering the truth about pitchblende. The less agreeable picture might be that of some business tycoon placing self above service by purveying misinformation about the value of certain stocks which he wishes to palm off on the public. Or it might be the picture of a newspaper editor blue-penciling a story altogether true and needing to be known, because it does not have a sufficiently sensational "news value." Or it might be the picture of some fruity-throated radio announcer avail-

* Copyright, 1945 by Alfred A. Knopf, Inc. and by the University of Michigan. Reprinted from *Freedom and Responsibility in the American Way of Life* by C. I. Becker, Vintage Edition, by permission of Alfred A. Knopf, Inc.

ing himself every day of his inalienable right of misrepresenting the merits of a certain toothpaste. Or else the picture of a Congressional committee exercising its freedom of the press to denounce as Communists certain worthy men and women who are not Communists by any reasonable definition of Communism, because they have exercised their freedom of speech to say a good word for the labor unions or the Spanish Loyalists, or because they have subscribed for and read the *Nation,* the *New Republic,* or the *Daily Worker.*

These instances may serve to make vivid the fact that freedom of speech does not travel exclusively on a one-way street marked "Search for Truth." It often enough travels on a one-way street marked "Private Profit," or on another marked "Anything to Win the Election." Most often, no doubt, it travels every which way on the broad unmarked highway of diverse human activities. This is only to say that the right of free speech cannot be considered to any good purpose apart from the concrete situations in which it is exercised; and in all such situations the relevant questions are, who is exercising the right, by what means, and for what purposes? I have already quoted the Connecticut Constitution of 1818: "Every citizen may speak, write, and publish his sentiments on all subjects, being responsible for the abuse of that liberty." All of our constitutions recognize that there may be abuses of the liberty that need to be defined and prohibited by law. The relevant question always is, what abuses are sufficiently grave to be prohibited by law? And the most relevant and difficult question of all is, in limiting the right because it is abused, at what point precisely does the limitation of the right become a greater evil than the abuse because it threatens to destroy the right altogether?

The classic instance of this dilemma arises in connection with the Communists and the Fascists—a dilemma that may be stated in the following way:

Democratic government rests on the right of the people to govern themselves, and therefore on the right of all citizens to advocate freely in speech and writing a modification of the existing form of government —the right of advocating, let us say, the abolition of the House of Representatives, or the election of a president for life. Well, the Communists and the Fascists avail themselves of the right of free speech to advocate the abolition of the democratic form of government altogether, and they maintain that since it cannot be done by persuasion and voting it should be done by force. Is this an abuse of the right of free speech? Is the democratic right of free speech to be accorded to those whose avowed aim is to destroy democratic government and free speech as a part of it? Are we expected to be loyal to the principle of free speech to the point where, writhing in pain among its worshipers, it commits suicide? That is certainly asking a lot.

It is asking too much so long as we remain in the realm of logical discourse. The program of the Fascists, and of the Communists in so far at least as the preliminaries of political reform are concerned, is based on an appeal to force rather than to persuasion. Their own principles teach us that it is logical for them to resist suppression, but merely impudent for them to resent it. Very well, then, since that is their program, let us stop talking, appeal to force, and see which is the stronger. Freedom of speech is for those who are *for* it—for those who are willing to accept it and abide by it as a political method; and I can see no reason why a democratic government should not defend its existence by force against internal as well as against external enemies whose avowed aim is to destroy it.

But strict logic is a poor counselor of political policy, and I can see no practical virtue in a syllogistic solution of the problem of Communist or Fascist propaganda. Freedom of speech can neither be suppressed by argument nor supported by suppressing argument. The real danger is not that Communists and Fascists will destroy our democratic government by free speaking, but that our democratic government, through its own failure to cure social evils, will destroy itself by breeding Communists and Fascists. If we can by the democratic method sufficiently alleviate social injustice, freedom of speech will sufficiently justify itself; if not, freedom of speech will in any case be lost in the shuffle.

It is in connection with social injustices that the question of free speech raises practical rather than theoretical problems. These problems concern the abuses of free speech committed by those who employ freedom of speech, not to destroy democratic government, but to serve their own interests by distorting the truth or betraying the public interest. That such abuses exist no one denies, and that some of them should be prohibited by law no one has ever denied. No one believes in the freedom of speech that issues in libel and slander. The practical question is, are our laws against slander and libel well adapted to meet the modern ingenious methods of insidious within-the-law vilification?

Or, to take a different case, no one can deny that much of our modern advertising is essentially dishonest; and it can hardly be maintained that to lie freely and all the time for private profit is not to abuse the right of free speech, whether it be a violation of the law or not. But again the practical question is, how much lying for private profit is to be permitted by law? Vendors of toothpaste say every day that their particular brands will cure bad breath, restore to the teeth the original brilliance of the enamel, and thereby enable anyone to recover the lost affection of husband or wife or boy or girl friend. What to do about it? Well, better let it go. The law cannot do everything; it must assume that people have some intelligence; and if the toothpaste is harmless, and the people are so ignorant as not to know the obvious facts of life (one of which is that high-powered advertising is a kind of mental test of the gullibility factor of the people), well, it is too bad maybe, but it is not a responsibility that the law can wisely assume. Liberty is the right of anyone to do whatever does not injure others; and it does not injure anyone to use the permitted brands of toothpaste, even if salt water or powdered chalk would do him just as much good besides being much less expensive.

It is quite another matter, however, if the systematic lying for private profit or personal advantage does injure others. If the toothpaste destroys the enamel instead of leaving it as it was; if the cosmetic, instead of being harmless, poisons the skin; if published misinformation induces ignorant or gullible people to invest their money in worthless stocks—in such and many similar cases the freedom of the liar to "speak, write, and publish his sentiments" needs to be restrained by law. The number of such laws has increased, is increasing, and will undoubtedly continue to increase. There can be no natural and inalienable right to lie systematically for private profit or personal advantage; and if the individual will not assume the responsibility for being reasonably honest, the government must assume the responsibility of restraining his freedom of speaking and acting for dishonest purposes and to the injury of others. But this raises a question of fundamental importance for the maintenance of democracy and of the freedom of speech and action that are inseparable from it. The question is, how far will it be necessary to go in making laws for curbing the dishonest and protecting the ignorant and gullible? How much ignorance, gullibility, and dishonesty can there be without making it impossible, by any number of laws designed to protect the ignorant and curb the dishonest, to preserve anything that can rightly be called democracy?

Democratic government is self-government, and self-government, if it be more than an empty form, is something far more than the popular election of representatives to make laws regulating everything and thereby to relieve the people of the responsibility for what they do. Whatever the form of government may be, it is not self-government unless the people are mostly intelligent enough and honest enough to do of their own accord what is right and necessary with a minimum of legal compulsion and restraint. Self-government works best, of course, in a small community in which everyone knows everyone else and in which the relations of men are therefore mostly direct and personal. It works well enough in a new and sparsely settled community in which there is room enough for everyone, in which the people do not get in each other's way too much whatever they do, and in which there is a fair chance for every man to get on in life as well as his ability and industry permit.

But we no longer live in such a community. We live in a highly complex and economically integrated community in which the relations of men are largely indirect and impersonal, and the life and fortunes of every citizen are profoundly affected, in ways that are not apparent and cannot be foreseen or avoided, by what others unknown to him are doing or planning to do. In such a community it is increasingly difficult for the honest to be intelligent and informed about what is going on and who is getting away with it, and therefore increasingly easy for the intelligent and informed to push their interests dishonestly under cover of the general ignorance. In such a community, it is obvious, there must be more laws for curbing the dishonest and for protecting the ignorant and the gullible. But it is equally obvious that self-government cannot be maintained by laws alone, and that if there are too many ignorant and gullible and dishonest people in the community the process of curbing the dishonest and protecting the ignorant may easily reduce the sphere of individual responsibility, and therefore of individual freedom, to the point where self-government in any real sense of the word ceases to exist.

The dishonest, undercover promotion of selfish interests on the part of the intelligent and the informed few thrives on the ignorance and gullibility of the many, and both are intimately related to the means by which information and misinformation can be communicated. In the eighteenth century it was taken for granted by the prophets of liberal democracy that if all men were free to "speak, write, and publish" their sentiments, the means of doing so would be freely available. Any group of citizens could meet in public assembly and argue to their hearts' content. Any man could establish a newspaper and every week air his opinions on all questions. Any man could, in the spirit of Brutus or Publicola, write a piece and get it published in the newspaper, or at slight cost in a penny pamphlet. Any man, if sufficiently high-brow, could write and publish a book. And all intelligent citizens could without too much effort attend the public forums, read the newspapers and many of the most talked-of books and pamphlets, and thereby, such was the theory, keep well abreast of what was being thought and said about public affairs in his community, and so play his proper part in molding public opinion and legislation.

It was not, of course, even in the eighteenth century, quite so simple as that; but today it is far less simple than it was in the eighteenth century. The average citizen still enjoys the inestimable right of freedom of speech and of the press. Any man can express his sentiments without first looking furtively over his shoulder to see if a government spy is in the offing; any man can, so far as the law is concerned, print a newspaper or a book without first submitting it to an official censor. This is the fundamentally important privilege; and no cataloguing of incidental violations of the right can obscure the fact that through the press and the radio detailed information about events, and the most diverse opinions, are with little let or hindrance daily and hourly presented to the people.

Daily and hourly presented to the people—it is this submerging flood of information and misinformation that makes the situation today so much less simple than it was in the eighteenth century. The means of gathering and communicating information about all that is being said and done and thought all over the world have become so perfected that no man can possibly take in, much less assimilate, more than a very small part of it. No man, unless he makes a full-time job of it, can hope to keep abreast of what is being said and done in the world at large, or even in his own country. The average citizen, although free to form and express his opinion, therefore plays a minor role in molding public opinion. His role is not to initiate, but passively to receive information and misinformation and diverse opinions presented to him by those who have access to the means of communication.

The propagation of information and opinion, to be effective under modern conditions, must be organized; and its promoters will have an indifferent success unless they resort to mass production and mass distribution of their wares. The chief instruments of propaganda are the press and the broadcasting stations. No one who does not command a great deal of capital can establish a broadcasting station. Much less, but still a good deal, of capital is required to establish a publishing company or a newspaper. About fifty years ago William Allen White, borrowing a few thousand dollars, established the *Emporia Gazette*, and with the aid of one or two assistants was able to make a go of it—a very good go indeed! But William Allen White was not an average citizen. He was a genius and a Kansan; and even so he told me a few years ago that he could not now, starting from scratch, establish another *Emporia Gazette.* Any man can of course write a letter and get it published in a newspaper; but the chief instruments of propaganda are not readily available to the average citizen. They can be effectively used only by the Government, political parties, and party leaders, wealthy men and business corporations, associations organized for the promotion of specific causes, and the writers of books that publishers find it worth while to publish.

In our society free and impartial discussion, from which the truth is supposed to emerge, is permitted and does exist. But the thinking of the average citizen and his opinion about public affairs is in very great measure shaped by a wealth of unrelated information and by the most diverse ideas that the selective process of private economic enterprise presents to him for consideration—information the truth of which he cannot verify; ideas formulated by persons unknown to him, and too often inspired by economic, political, religious, or other interests that are never avowed.

As Jefferson and his contemporaries did, we still believe that self-government is the best form of government and that freedom of the mind is the most important of the rights that sustain it. We are less sure than they were that a beneficent intelligence designed the world on a rational plan for man's special convenience. We are aware that the laws of nature, and especially the laws of human nature, are less easily discovered and applied than they supposed. We have found it more difficult to define the essential rights of man and to secure them by simple institutional forms than they anticipated. We have learned that human reason is not the infallible instrument for recording the truth that they supposed it to be, and that men themselves are less amenable to rational persuasion. Above all we have learned that freedom of speech and of the press may be used to convey misinformation and distort the truth for personal advantage as well as to express and communicate it for the public good. But although we no longer have the unlimited and solvent backing of God or nature, we are still betting that freedom of the mind will never disprove the proposition that only through freedom of the mind can a reasonably just society ever be created.

We may win our bet, but we shall win it only on certain hard conditions. The conditions are that the people by and large be sufficiently informed to hold and express intelligent opinions on public affairs, and sufficiently honest and public-spirited to subordinate purely selfish interests to the general welfare. In so far as the intelligent and informed systematically employ freedom of speech and of the press for personal and antisocial ends, in so far as the mass of the people are so ignorant and ill-informed as to be capable of being fooled all of the time, freedom of speech and of the press loses its chief virtue and self-government is undermined. Self-government, and the freedom of speech and of the press that sustains it, can be maintained by law only in a formal sense; if they are to be maintained in fact the people must have sufficient intelligence and honesty to maintain them with a minimum of legal compulsion.

This heavy responsibility is the price of freedom, and it can be paid only by a people that has a high degree of integrity and intelligence. Neither intelligence nor integrity can be imposed by law. But the native intelligence, and perhaps the integrity of the people, can be reinforced by law, more especially by laws providing for schools and universities. This brings us to the consideration of another freedom and another responsibility, or rather to a special aspect of freedom and responsibility of the mind—that is to say, freedom of learning and teaching. ▰

9. The Problem of Loyalty and Security

Because the interpretation of the First Amendment freedoms by the Supreme Court is the same with reference to both the state and national levels of government, a distinction is rarely made in cases involving freedom of speech, press, or religion between application of standards under the due process clause of the Fourteenth Amendment with reference to states, and standards under the First Amendment with reference to the national government. Nevertheless one should always bear in mind the legal framework of a particular case, and note should always be taken of the jurisdiction in which the case initially falls; it is not inconsequential that before 1925 (*Gitlow* v. *New York,* 268 U.S. 652) the Supreme Court accepted the doctrine of *Prudential Insurance Co.* v. *Cheek,* 259 U.S. 530 (1922) that "neither the Fourteenth Amendment nor any other provision of the Constitution of the United States imposes upon the states any restrictions about 'freedom of speech.'" This was, of course, overruled in *Gitlow;* the new doctrine was put into effect in declaring a state statute unconstitutional in *Near* v. *Minnesota,* 283 U.S. 697 (1931).

At the national level Justice Holmes, in *Schenck* v. *United States,* 249 U.S. 47 (1919), stated his famous "clear and present danger" test, which subsequently was applied at both the national and state levels, for deciding whether or not Congress could abridge freedom of speech under the First Amendment: "The most stringent protection of free speech would not protect a man in falsely shouting fire in a theatre and causing a panic. It does not protect a man from an injunction against uttering words that may have all the effects of force. . . . The question in every case is whether the words used are used in such circumstances and are of such a nature as to create a clear and present danger that they will bring about the substantive evils that Congress has a right to prevent. It is a question of proximity and degree. When a nation is at war many things that might be said in time of peace are such a hindrance to its efforts that their utterance will not be endured so long as men fight and that no Court could regard them as protected by any constitutional right."

In 1940 Congress passed the Smith Act, Section 2 of which made it unlawful for any person: "(1) to knowingly or willfully advocate, abet, advise, or teach the duty, necessity, desirability, or propriety of overthrowing or destroying any government in the United States by force or violence . . .; (2) with intent to cause the overthrow or destruction of any government in the United States, to print, publish, edit, issue, circulate, sell, distribute, or publicly display any written or printed matter advocating, advising, or teaching the duty, necessity, desirability, or propriety of overthrowing or destroying any government in the United States by force or violence; (3) to organize or help to organize any society, group, or assembly of persons who teach, advocate, or encourage the overthrow or destruction of any government in the United States by force or violence; or to be or become a member of, or affiliate with, any such society . . ., knowing the purposes thereof."

The constitutionality of this act was tested in *Dennis* v. *United States,* 341 U.S. 494 (1951), which contained five opinions. Vinson spoke for the Court, with Frankfurter and Jackson concurring; Black and Douglas dissented.

DENNIS v. UNITED STATES

341 U.S. 494 (1951)

MR. Chief Justice Vinson announced the judgment of the Court, saying in part:

Petitioners were indicted in July, 1948, for violation of the conspiracy provisions of the Smith Act. . . . A verdict of guilty as to all the petitioners was returned by the jury on October 14, 1949. The Court of Appeals affirmed the convictions. . . . We granted certiorari. . . .

. . . Our limited grant of the writ of certiorari has removed from our consideration any question as to the sufficiency of the evidence to support the jury's determination that petitioners are guilty of the offense charged. Whether on this record petitioners did in fact advocate the overthrow of the Government by force and violence is not before us, and we must base any discussion of this point upon the conclusions stated in the opinion of the Court of Appeals, which treated the issue in great detail. That court held that the record in this case amply supports the necessary finding of the jury that petitioners, the leaders of the Communist Party in this country, were unwilling to work within our framework of democracy, but intended to initiate a violent revolution whenever the propitious occasion appeared. . . .

I

It will be helpful in clarifying the issues to treat next the contention that the trial judge improperly interpreted the statute by charging that the statute required an unlawful intent before the jury could convict. More specifically, he charged that the jury could not find the petitioners guilty under the indictment unless they found that petitioners had the intent to "overthrow . . . the Government of the United States by force and violence as speedily as circumstances would permit."

. . . The structure and purpose of the statute demand the inclusion of intent as an element of the crime. Congress was concerned with those who advocate and organize for the overthrow of the Government. Certainly those who recruit and combine for the purpose of advocating overthrow intend to bring about that overthrow. We hold that the statute requires as an essential element of the crime proof of the intent of those who are charged with its violation to overthrow the Government by force and violence. . . .

II

The obvious purpose of the statute is to protect existing Government, not from change by peaceable, lawful and constitutional means, but from change by violence, revolution and terrorism. That it is within the *power* of the Congress to protect the Government of the United States from armed rebellion is a proposition which requires little discussion. Whatever theoretical merit there may be to the argument that there is a "right" to rebellion against dictatorial governments is without force where the existing structure of the government provides for peaceful and orderly change. We reject any principle of governmental helplessness in the face of preparation for revolution, which principle, carried to its logical conclusion, must lead to anarchy. No one could conceive that it is within the power of Congress to prohibit acts intended to overthrow the Government by force and violence. The question with which we are concerned here is not whether Congress has such *power*, but whether the *means* that it has employed conflict with the First and Fifth Amendments to the Constitution.

One of the bases for the contention that the means which Congress has employed are invalid takes the form of an attack on the face of the statute on the grounds that by its terms it prohibits academic discussion of the merits of Marxism-Leninism, that it stifles ideas and is contrary to all concepts of a free speech and a free press. Although we do not agree that the language itself has that significance, we must bear in mind that it is the duty of the federal courts to interpret federal legislation in a manner not inconsistent with the demands of the Constitution. . . . This is a federal statute which we must interpret as well as judge. . . .

The very language of the Smith Act negates the interpretation which petitioners would have us impose on that Act. It is directed at advocacy, not discussion. Thus, the trial judge properly charged the jury that they could not convict if they found that petitioners did "no more than pursue peaceful studies and discussions or teaching and advocacy in the realm of ideas." He further charged that it was not unlawful "to conduct in an American college or university a course explaining the philosophical theories set forth in the books which have been placed in evidence." Such a charge is in strict accord with the statutory language, and illustrates the meaning to be placed on those words. Congress did not intend to eradicate the free discussion of political theories, to destroy the traditional rights of Americans to discuss and evaluate ideas without fear of governmental sanction. Rather Congress was concerned with the very kind of activity in which the evidence showed these petitioners engaged.

III

But although the statute is not directed at the hypothetical cases which petitioners have conjured, its application in this case has resulted in convictions for the teaching and advocacy of the overthrow of the Government by force and violence, which, even though coupled with the intent to accomplish that overthrow, contains an element of speech. For this reason, we must pay special heed to the demands of the First Amendment marking out the boundaries of speech.

We pointed out in *Douds, supra,* that the basis of the First Amendment is the hypothesis that speech can rebut speech, propaganda will answer propaganda, free debate of ideas will result in the wisest governmental policies. It is for this reason that this Court has recognized the inherent value of free discourse. An analysis of the leading cases in this Court which have involved direct limitations on speech, however, will demonstrate that both the majority of the Court and the dissenters in particular cases have recognized that this is not an unlimited, unqualified right, but that the societal value of speech must, on occasion, be subordinated to other values and considerations. . . .

The rule we deduce from these cases [*Schenck* and others] is that where an offense is specified by a statute in nonspeech or nonpress terms, a conviction relying upon speech or press as evidence of violation may be sustained only when the speech or publication created a "clear and present danger" of attempting or accomplishing the prohibited crime, *e.g.* interference with enlistment. The dissents . . . in emphasizing the value of speech, were addressed to the argument of the sufficiency of the evidence. . . .

In this case we are squarely presented with the application of the "clear and present danger" test, and must decide what that phrase imports. We first note that many of the cases in which this Court has reversed convictions by use of this or similar tests have been based on the fact that the interest which the State was attempting to protect was itself too insubstantial to warrant restriction of speech. . . . Overthrow of the Government by force and violence is certainly a substantial enough interest for the Government to limit speech. Indeed, this is the ultimate value of any society, for if a society cannot protect its structure from armed internal attack, it must follow that no subordinate value can be protected. If, then, this interest may be protected, the literal problem which is presented is what has been meant by the use of the phrase "clear and present danger" of the utterances bringing about the evil within the power of Congress to punish.

Obviously, the words cannot mean that before the Government may act, it must wait until the *putsch* is about to be executed, the plans have been laid and the signal is awaited. If Government is aware that a group aiming at its overthrow is attempting to indoctrinate its members and to commit them to a course whereby they will strike when the leaders feel the circumstances permit, action by the Government is required.

The argument that there is no need for Government to concern itself, for Government is strong, it possesses ample powers to put down a rebellion, it may defeat the revolution with ease needs no answer. For that is not the question. Certainly an attempt to overthrow the Government by force, even though doomed from the outset because of inadequate numbers or power of the revolutionists, is a sufficient evil for Congress to prevent. The damage which such attempts create both physically and politically to a nation makes it impossible to measure the validity in terms of the probability of success, or the immediacy of a successful attempt. In the instant case the trial judge charged the jury that they could not convict unless they found that petitioners intended to overthrow the Government "as speedily as circumstances would permit." This does not mean, and could not properly mean, that they would not strike until there was certainty of success. What was meant was that the revolutionists would strike when they thought the time was ripe. We must therefore reject the contention that success or probability of success is the criterion.

The situation with which Justices Holmes and Brandeis were concerned in *Gitlow* was a comparatively isolated event [involving a conviction for criminal anarchy in New York of one Gitlow for circulating Communist literature], bearing little relation in their minds to any substantial threat to the safety of the community. . . . They were not confronted with any situation comparable to the instant one—the development of an apparatus designed and dedicated to the overthrow of the Government, in the context of world crisis after crisis.

Chief Justice Learned Hand, writing for the majority below, interpreted the phrase as follows: "In each case [courts] must ask whether the gravity of the 'evil,' discounted by its improbability, justifies such invasion of free speech as is necessary to avoid the danger." 183 F. 2d at 212. We adopt this statement of the rule. . . .

Likewise, we are in accord with the court below, which affirmed the trial court's finding that the requisite danger existed. The mere fact that from the period 1945 to 1948 petitioners' activities did not result in an attempt to overthrow the Government by force and violence is of course no answer to the fact that there was a group that was ready to make the attempt. The formation by petitioners of such a highly organized conspiracy, with rigidly disciplined members subject to call when the leaders, these petitioners, felt that the time had come for action, coupled with the inflammable nature of world conditions, similar uprisings in other countries, and the touch-and-go nature of our relations with countries with whom petitioners were in the very least ideologically attuned, convince us that their convictions were justified on this score. And this analysis disposes of the contention that a conspiracy to advocate, as distinguished from the advocacy itself, cannot be constitutionally restrained, because it comprises only the preparation. It is the existence of the conspiracy which creates the danger. . . . If the ingredients of the reaction are present, we cannot bind the Government to wait until the catalyst is added. . . .

We hold that §§2(a) (1), 2(a) (2) and (3) of the Smith Act, do not inherently, or as construed or applied in the instant case, violate the First Amendment and other provisions of the Bill of Rights, or the First and Fifth Amendments because of indefiniteness. Petitioners intended to overthrow the Government of the United States as speedily as the circumstances would permit. Their conspiracy to organize the Communist Party and to teach and advocate the overthrow of the Government of the United States by force and violence created a "clear and present danger" of an attempt to overthrow the Government by force and violence. They were properly and constitutionally convicted for violation of the Smith Act. The judgments of conviction are affirmed. . . .

Mr. Justice Black, dissenting, said in part:

. . . At the outset I want to emphasize what the crime involved in this case is, and what it is not. These petitioners were not charged with an attempt to overthrow the Government. They were not charged with overt acts of any kind designed to overthrow the Government. They were not even charged with saying anything or writing anything designed to overthrow the Government. The charge was that they agreed to assemble and to talk and publish certain ideas at a later date: The indictment is that they conspired to organize the Communist Party and to use speech or newspapers and other publications in the future to teach and advocate the forcible overthrow of the Government. No matter how it is worded, this is a virulent form of prior censorship of speech and press, which I believe the First Amendment forbids. . . .

But let us assume, contrary to all constitutional ideas of fair criminal procedure, that petitioners although not indicted for the crime of actual advocacy, may be punished for it. Even on this radical assumption, the other opinions in this case show that the only way to affirm these convictions is to repudiate directly or indirectly the established "clear and present danger" rule. This the Court does in a way which greatly restricts the protections afforded by the First Amendment. The opinions for affirmance indicate that the chief reason for jettisoning the rule is the expressed fear that advocacy of Communist doctrine endangers the safety of the Republic. Undoubtedly, a governmental policy of unfettered communication of ideas does entail dangers. To the Founders of this Nation, however, the benefits derived from free expression were worth the risk. They embodied this philosophy in the First Amendment's command that "Congress shall make no law . . . abridging the freedom of speech, or of the press. . . ." I have always believed that the First Amendment is the keystone of our Government, that the freedoms it guarantees provide the best insurance against destruction of all freedom. At least as to speech in the realm of public matters, I believe that the "clear and present danger" test does not "mark the furthermost constitutional boundaries of protected expression" but does "no more than recognize a minimum compulsion of the Bill of Rights." . . .

So long as this Court exercises the power of judicial review of legislation, I cannot agree that the First Amendment permits us to sustain laws suppressing freedom of speech and press on the basis of Congress' or our own notions of mere "reasonableness." Such a doctrine waters down the First Amendment so that it amounts to little more than an admonition to Congress. The Amendment as so construed is not likely to protect any but those "safe" or orthodox views which rarely need its protection. I must also express my objection to the holding because, as Mr. Justice Douglas' dissent shows, it sanctions the determination of a crucial issue of fact by the judge rather than by the jury. Nor can I let this opportunity pass without expressing my objection to the severely limited grant of certiorari in this case which precluded consideration here of at least two other reasons for reversing these convictions: (1) the record shows a discriminatory selection of the jury panel which prevented trial before a representative cross-section of the community; (2) the record shows that one member of the trial jury was violently hostile to petitioners before and during the trial.

Public opinion being what it now is, few will protest the conviction of these Communist petitioners. There is hope, however, that in calmer times, when present pressures, passions and fears subside, this or some later Court will restore the First Amendment liberties to the high preferred place where they belong in a free society.

Mr. Justice Douglas, dissenting, said in part:

. . . [N]ever until today has anyone seriously thought that the ancient law of conspiracy could constitutionally be used to turn speech into seditious conduct. Yet that is precisely what is suggested. I repeat that we deal here with speech alone, not with speech *plus* acts of sabotage or unlawful conduct. Not a single seditious act is charged in the indictment. . . .

Free speech has occupied an exalted position because of the high service it has given our society. Its protection is essential to the very existence of a democracy. The airing of ideas releases pressures which otherwise might become destructive. When ideas compete in the market for acceptance, full and free discussion exposes the false and they gain few adherents. Full and free discussion even of ideas we hate encourages the testing of our own prejudices and preconceptions. Full and free discussion keeps a society from becoming stagnant and unprepared for the stresses and strains that work to tear all civilizations apart.

Full and free discussion has indeed been the first article of our faith. We have founded our political system on it. It has been the safeguard of every religious, political, philosophical, economic, and racial group amongst us. We have counted on it to keep us from embracing what is cheap and false; we have trusted the common sense of our people to choose the doctrine true to our genius and to reject the rest. This has been the one single outstanding tenet that has made our institutions the symbol of freedom and equality. We have deemed it more costly to liberty to suppress a despised minority than to let them vent their spleen. We have above all else feared the political censor. We have wanted a land where our people can be exposed to all the diverse creeds and cultures of the world.

There comes a time when even speech loses its constitutional immunity. Speech innocuous one year may at another time fan such destructive flames that it must be halted in the interest of the safety of the Republic. That is the meaning of the clear and present danger test. When conditions are so critical that there will be no time to avoid the evil that the speech threatens, it is time to call a halt. Otherwise, free speech which is the strength of the Nation will be the cause of its destruction.

Yet free speech is the rule, not the exception. The restraint to be constitutional must be based on more than fear, on more than passionate opposition against the speech, on more than a revolted dislike for its contents. There must be some immediate injury to society that is likely if speech is allowed. . . .

. . . This record . . . contains no evidence whatsoever showing that the acts charged, viz., the teaching of the Soviet theory of revolution with the hope that it will be realized, have created any clear and present danger to the Nation. The Court, however, rules to the contrary. . . .

The political impotence of the Communists in this country does not, of course, dispose of the problem. Their numbers; their positions in industry and government; the extent to which they have in fact infiltrated the police, the armed services, transportation, stevedoring, power plants, munitions works, and other critical places—these facts all bear on the likelihood that their advocacy of the Soviet theory of revolution will endanger the Republic. But the record is silent on these facts. If we are to proceed on the basis of judicial notice, it is impossible for me to say that the Communists in this country are so potent or so strategically deployed that they must be suppressed for their speech. I could not so hold unless I were willing to conclude that the activities in recent years of committees of Congress, of the Attorney General, of labor unions, of state legislatures, and of Loyalty Boards were so futile as to leave the country on the edge of grave peril. To believe that petitioners and their following are placed in such critical positions as to endanger the Nation is to believe the incredible. It is safe to say that the followers of the creed of Soviet Communism are known to the F.B.I.; that in case of war with Russia they will be picked up overnight as were all prospective saboteurs at the commencement of World War II; that the invisible army of petitioners is the best known, the most beset, and the least thriving of any fifth column in history. Only those held by fear and panic could think otherwise. . . .

. . . The political censor has no place in our public debates. Unless and until extreme and necessitous circumstances are shown, our aim should be to keep speech unfettered and to allow the processes of law to be invoked only when the provocateurs among us move from speech to action.

Vishinsky wrote in 1938 in the Law of the Soviet State, "In our state, naturally, there is and can be no place for freedom of speech, presss, and so on for the foes of socialism."

Our concern should be that we accept no such standard for the United States. Our faith should be that our people will never give support to these advocates of revolution, so long as we remain loyal to the purposes for which our Nation was founded. ▄

The *Dennis* case supported the concept that the Communist Party is a criminal conspiracy designed to overthrow the government by force and violence. Moreover, the Court stated that conspiracy to advocate the overthrow of the government can be constitutionally restrained: "It is the existence of the conspiracy which creates the danger. . . . If the ingredients of the reaction are present, we cannot bind the government to wait until the catalyst is added." From this it is possible to conclude that membership itself in the Communist Party constitutes unjustified *advocacy* because of the program of indoctrination carried out by the party—the ultimate end being to overthrow the government.

In *Yates* v. *United States,* 354 U.S. 298 (1957), the Court implied that mere membership in the Communist Party was not sufficient to warrant the conclusion that the member was advocating *action* to overthrow the government. The Court found that the Smith Act "reaches only advocacy of action for the overthrow of government by force and violence. The essential distinction is that those to whom the advocacy is addressed must be urged to *do* something, now or in the future, rather than merely to *believe* in something."

In *Scales* v. *United States,* 367 U.S. 203 (1961), the Court once again raised the issue of whether or not membership in the Communist Party implied an actual intention to overthrow the government by force and violence. The membership clause of the Smith Act makes a felony the acquisition or holding of *knowing* membership in any organization that advocates forcible overthrow of the government. In its opinion the Court distinguished between "active" and "passive" membership. Active, or knowing membership, means that the individual is fully aware of the purposes of the organization to which he belongs. If the organization seeks the violent overthrow of the government, then it can fairly be implied that an active member of that group also desires and is aiding the attainment of the same goal. Under such circumstances mere membership can imply illegal *action* under the Smith Act.

SCALES v. UNITED STATES
367 U.S. 203 (1961)

MR. Justice Harlan delivered the opinion of the Court, saying in part:
Our writ issued in this case to review a judgment of the Court of Appeals (260 F2d 21) affirming petitioner's conviction under the so-called membership clause of the Smith Act. 18 USC § 2385. The Act, among other things, makes a felony the acquisition or holding of knowing membership in any organization which advocates the overthrow of the Government of the United States by force or violence. The indictment charged that from January 1946 to the date of its filing (November 18, 1954) the Communist Party of the United States was such an organization, and that petitioner throughout that period was a member thereof, with knowledge of the Party's illegal purpose and a specific intent to accomplish overthrow "as speedily as circumstances would permit."

The validity of this conviction is challenged on statutory, constitutional, and evidentiary grounds, and further on the basis of certain alleged trial and procedural errors. We decide the issues raised upon the fullest consideration, the case having had an unusually long history in this Court. For reasons given in this opinion we affirm the Court of Appeals.

I. STATUTORY CHALLENGE

... The claim is that § 4 (f) of Internal Security Act of 1950, 64 Stat 987, constitutes a pro tanto repeal of the membership clause of the Smith Act by excluding from the reach of that clause membership in any Communist organization. Section 4 (f) provides:

"Neither the holding of office nor membership in any Communist organization by any person shall constitute per se a violation of subsection (a) or subsection (c) of this section or of any other criminal statute. ...

... Section 4 (f) provides that membership or office-holding in a Communist organization shall not constitute "per se a violation of subsection (a) or subsection (c) of this section or of any other criminal statute." Petitioner would most plainly be correct if the statute under which he was indicted purported to proscribe membership in Communist organizations, as such, and to punish membership per se in an organization engaging in proscribed advocacy. But the membership clause of the Smith Act on its face, much less as we construe it in this case, does not do this, for it neither proscribes membership in Communist organizations, as such, but only in organizations engaging in advocacy of violent overthrow, nor punishes membership in that kind of organization except as to one "knowing the purposes thereof," and, as we have interpreted the clause, with a specific intent to further those purposes. We have also held that the proscribed membership must be active, and not nominal, passive or theoretical. ...

... We hold that this prosecution is not barred by § 4 (f) of the Internal Security Act of 1950.

II. CONSTITUTIONAL CHALLENGE TO
THE MEMBERSHIP CLAUSE ON ITS FACE

Petitioner's constitutional attack goes both to the statute on its face and as applied. At this point we deal with the first aspect of the challenge and with one part of its second aspect. The balance of the latter, which essentially concerns the sufficiency of the evidence, is discussed in the next section of this opinion.

It will bring the constitutional issues into clearer focus to notice first the premises on which the case was submitted to the jury. The jury was instructed that in order to convict it must find that within the three-year limitations period (1) the Communist Party advocated the violent overthrow of the Government, in the sense of present "advocacy of action" to accomplish that end as soon as circumstances were propitious; and (2) petitioner was an "active" member of the Party, and not merely "a nominal, passive, inactive or purely technical" member, with knowledge of the Party's illegal advocacy and a specific intent to bring about violent overthrow "as speedily as circumstances would permit."

The constitutional attack upon the membership clause, as thus construed, is that the statute offends (1) the Fifth Amendment, in that it impermissibly imputes guilt to an individual merely on the basis of his associations and sympathies, rather than because of some concrete personal involvement in criminal conduct; and (2) the First Amendment, in that it infringes free political expression and association. Subsidiarily, it is argued that the statute cannot be interpreted as including a requirement of a specific intent to accomplish violent overthrow, or as requiring that membership in a proscribed organization must be "active" membership, in the absence of both or either of which it is said the statute becomes a fortiori unconstitutional. It is further contended that even if the adjective "active" may properly be implied as a qualification upon the term "member," petitioner's conviction would nonetheless be unconstitutional, because so construed the statute would be impermissibly vague under the Fifth and Sixth Amendments, and so applied would in any event infringe the Sixth Amendment, in that the indictment charged only that Scales was a "member," not an "active" member, of the Communist Party.

1. Statutory Construction

Before reaching petitioner's constitutional claims, we should first ascertain whether the membership clause permissibly bears the construction put upon it below. We think it does.

The trial court's definition of the kind of organizational advocacy that is proscribed was fully in accord with what was held in *Yates* v. *United States,* 354 US 298. And the statute itself requires that a defendant must have knowledge of the organization's illegal advocacy.

The only two elements of the crime, as defined below, about which there is controversy are therefore "specific intent" and "active" membership. As to the former, this Court held in *Dennis* v. *United States,* 341 US 494, 499, 500, that even though the "advocacy" and "organizing" provisions of the Smith Act, unlike the "literature" section, did not expressly contain such a specific intent element, such a requirement was fairly to be implied. We think that the reasoning of Dennis applies equally to the membership clause, and are left unpersuaded by the distinctions petitioner seeks to draw between this clause and the advocacy and organizing provisions of the Smith Act.

We find hardly greater difficulty in interpreting the membership clause to reach only "active" members. We decline to attribute to Congress a purpose to punish nominal membership, even though accompanied by "knowledge" and "intent," not merely because of the close constitutional questions that such a purpose would raise, but also for two other reasons: It is not to be lightly inferred that Congress intended to visit upon mere passive members the heavy penalties imposed by the Smith Act. Nor can we assume that it was Congress' purpose to allow the quality of the punishable membership to be measured solely by the varying standards of that relationship as subjectively viewed by different organizations. It is more reasonable to believe that Congress contemplated an objective standard fixed by the law itself, thereby assuring an evenhanded application of the statute.

This Court in passing on a similar provision requiring the deportation of aliens who have become members of the Communist Party—a provision which rested on Congress' far more plenary power over aliens, and hence did not press nearly so closely on the limits of constitutionality as this enactment—had no difficulty in interpreting "membership" there as meaning more than the mere voluntary listing of a person's name on Party rolls. *Galvan* v. *Press, 347* US 522. A similar construction is called for here.

Petitioner's particular constitutional objections to this construction are misconceived. The indictment was not defective in failing to charge that Scales was an "active" member of the Party, for that factor was not in itself a discrete element of the crime, but an inherent quality of the membership element. As such it was a matter not for the indictment, but for elucidating instructions to the jury on what the term "member" in the statute meant. Nor do we think that the objection on the score of vagueness is a tenable one. The distinction between "active" and "nominal" membership is well understood in common parlance, and the point at which one shades into the other is something that goes not to the sufficiency of the statute, but to the adequacy of the trial court's guidance to the jury by way of instructions in a particular case. Moreover, whatever abstract doubts might exist on the matter, this case presents no such problem. For petitioner's actions on behalf of the Communist Party most certainly amounted to active membership by whatever standards one could reasonably anticipate, and he can therefore hardly be considered to have acted unadvisedly on this score. . . .

2. Fifth Amendment

In our jurisprudence guilt is personal, and when the imposition of punishment on a status or on conduct can only be justified by reference to the relationship of that status or conduct to other concededly criminal activity (here advocacy of violent overthrow), that relationship must be sufficiently substantial to satisfy the concept of personal guilt in order to withstand attack under the Due Process Clause of the Fifth Amendment. Membership, without more, in an organization engaged in illegal advocacy, it is now said, has not heretofore been recognized by this Court to be such a relationship. This claim stands, and we shall examine it, independently of that made under the First Amendment.

Any thought that due process puts beyond the reach of the criminal law all individual associational relationships, unless accompanied by the commission of specific acts of criminality, is dispelled by familiar concepts of the law of conspiracy and complicity. While both are commonplace in the landscape of the criminal law, they are not natural features. Rather they are particular legal concepts manifesting the more general principle that society, having the power to punish dangerous behavior, cannot be powerless against those who work to bring about that behavior. The fact that Congress has not resorted to either of these familiar concepts means only that the enquiry here must direct itself to an analysis of the relationship between the fact of membership and the underlying substantive illegal conduct, in order to determine whether that relationship is indeed too tenuous to permit its use as the basis of criminal liability. In this instance it is an organization which engages in criminal activity, and we can perceive no reason why one who actively and knowingly works in the ranks of that organization, intending to contribute to the success of those specifically illegal activities, should be any more immune from prosecution than he to whom the organization has assigned the task of carrying out the substantive criminal act. Nor should the fact that Congress has focussed here on "membership," the characteristic relationship between an individual and the type of conspiratorial quasi-political associations with the criminal aspect of whose activities Congress was concerned, of itself require the conclusion that the legislature has traveled outside the familiar and permissible bounds of criminal imputability. In truth, the specificity of the proscribed relationship is not necessarily a vice; it provides instruction and warning.

What must be met, then, is the argument that membership, even when accompanied by the elements of knowledge and specific intent, affords an insufficient quantum of participation in the organization's alleged criminal activity, that is, an insufficiently significant form of aid and encouragement to permit the imposition of criminal sanctions on that basis. It must indeed be recognized that a person who merely becomes a member of an illegal organization, by that "act" alone need be doing nothing more than signifying his assent to its purposes and activities on one hand, and providing, on the other, only the sort of moral encouragement which comes from the knowledge that others believe in what the organization is doing. It may indeed be argued that such assent and encouragement do fall short of the concrete, practical impetus given to a criminal enterprise which is lent for instance by a commitment on the part of a conspirator to act in furtherance of that enterprise. A member, as distinguished from a conspirator, may indicate his approval of a criminal enterprise by the very fact of his membership without thereby necessarily committing himself to further it by any act or course of conduct whatever.

In an area of the criminal law which this Court has indicated more than once demands its watchful scrutiny (see Dennis, 341 US at 516; Yates, 354 US 328), these factors have weight and must be found to be overborne in a total constitutional assessment of the statute. We think, however, they are duly met when the statute is found to reach only "active" members having also a guilty knowledge and intent, and which therefore prevents a conviction on what otherwise might be regarded as merely an expression of sympathy with the alleged criminal enterprise, unaccompanied by any significant action in its support or any commitment to undertake such action.

Thus, given the construction of the membership clause already discussed, we think the factors called for in rendering members criminally responsible for the illegal advocacy of the organization fall within established, and therefore presumably constitutional standards of criminal imputability.

3. First Amendment

Little remains to be said concerning the claim that the statute infringes First Amendment freedoms. It was settled in Dennis that the advocacy with which we are here concerned is not constitutionally protected speech, and it was further established that a combination to promote such advocacy, albeit under the aegis of what purports to be a political party, is not such association as is protected by the First Amendment. We can discern no reason why membership, when it constitutes a purposeful form of complicity in a group engaging in this same forbidden advocacy, should receive any greater degree of protection from the guarantees of that Amendment.

If it is said that the mere existence of such an enactment tends to inhibit the exercise of constitutionally protected rights, in that it engenders an unhealthy fear that one may find himself unwittingly embroiled in criminal liability, the answer surely is that the statute provides that a defendant must be proven to have knowledge of the proscribed advocacy before he may be convicted. It is, of course, true that quasi-political parties or other groups that may embrace both legal and illegal aims differ from a technical conspiracy, which is defined by its criminal purpose, so that *all* knowing association with the conspiracy is a proper subject for criminal proscription as far as First Amendment liberties are concerned. If there were a similar blanket prohibition of association with a group having both legal and illegal aims, there would indeed be a real danger that legitimate political expression or association would be impaired, but the membership clause, as here construed, does not cut deeper into the freedom of association than is necessary to deal with "the substantive evils that Congress has a right to prevent." *Schenck* v. *United States,* 249 US 47, 52. The clause does not make criminal all association with an organization, which has been shown to engage in illegal advocacy. There must be clear proof that a defendant "specifically intend[s] to accomplish [the aims of the organization] by resort to violence." Thus the member for whom the organization is a vehicle for the advancement of legitimate aims and policies does not fall within the ban of the statute: he lacks the requisite specific intent "to bring about the overthrow of the government as speedily as circumstances would permit." Such a person may be foolish, deluded, or perhaps merely optimistic, but he is not by this statute made a criminal.

We conclude that petitioner's constitutional challenge must be overruled.

III. EVIDENTIARY CHALLENGE

Only in rare instances will this Court review the general sufficiency of the evidence to support a criminal conviction, for ordinarily that is a function which properly belongs to and ends with the Court of Appeals. We do so in this case . . . not only to make sure that substantive constitutional standards have not been thwarted, but also to provide guidance for the future to the lower courts in an area which borders so closely upon constitutionally protected rights.

On this phase of the case petitioner's principal contention is that the evidence was insufficient to establish that the Communist Party was engaged in present advocacy of violent overthrow of the Government in the sense required by the Smith Act, that is, in "advocacy of action" for the accomplishment of such overthrow either immediately or as soon as circumstances proved propitious, and uttered in terms reasonably calculated to "incite" to such action. . . . [Here the Court reviews the doctrines, organization, and procedures of the Communist Party, and Scales' role in it.]

We conclude that this evidence sufficed to make a case for the jury on the issue of illegal Party advocacy. Dennis and Yates have definitely laid at rest any doubt but that present advocacy of *future* action for violent overthrow satisfies statutory and constitutional requirements equally with advocacy of *immediate* action to that end. 341 US, at 509; 354 US, at 321. Hence this record cannot be considered deficient because it contains no evidence of advocacy for immediate overthrow.

Since the evidence amply showed that Party leaders were continuously preaching during the indictment period the inevitability of eventual forcible overthrow, the first and basic question is a narrow one: whether the jury could permissibly infer that such preaching, in whole or in part, "was aimed at building up a seditious group and maintaining it in readiness for action at a propitious time . . . the kind of indoctrination preparatory to action which was condemned in Dennis." On this score, we think that the jury, under instructions which fully satisfied the requirements of Yates, was entitled to infer from this systematic preaching that where the explicitness and concreteness, of the sort described previously, seemed necessary and prudent, the doctrine of violent revolution—elsewhere more a theory of historical predictability than a rule of conduct—was put forward as a guide to future action, in whatever tone, be it emotional or calculating that the audience and occasion required; in short, that "advocacy of action" was engaged in. . . .

We hold that this prosecution does not fail for insufficiency of the proof.

IV. ALLEGED TRIAL ERRORS

Petitioner contends that a number of errors were committed, having the effect of vitiating the fairness of his trial. . . . [W]e find that none of petitioner's contentions raise points meriting reversal.

1. *Admission of Remote or Prejudicial Evidence*

Petitioner complains as to the admission of certain evidence relating to the Party's general or specific purposes. In particular, he objects to the admission of evidence about the Party's program in the so-called "Black Belt" and especially to the admission of a pamphlet called "I Saw the Truth in Korea," which contained a very gruesome description of alleged American atrocities in Korea. There can be no doubt that this matter, and particularly the latter, would not have reflected well on the petitioner or the Party in the eyes of the jury, but if it was relevant to an element of the crime, then whether its asserted prejudicial effect so far outweighed its probative value as to require exclusion of the evidence, was a decision which rested in the sound discretion of the trial judge. Particularly in light of the fact that the most damaging of this material emanated from petitioner himself, we cannot say that its admission involved an abuse of discretion which would warrant our reversal of the conclusions of the trial judge and the Court of Appeals on this score.

We therefore need only consider whether the complained-of evidence was legally relevant and therefore admissible. As we have pointed out in our review of the record, the jury could have inferred that part of the Communist Party's program for violent revolution was the winning of favor with the Negro population in the South, which it thought was particularly susceptible to revolutionary propaganda and action. Surely, then, the evidence of the Party's teaching that the Negro population should be given the right to form a separate nation is not irrelevant to the issue of whether or not the Party's program as a whole constituted a call to stand in readiness for violent action, when this particular plank in the platform was intended as bait for one of the substantial battalions in the hoped-for revolutionary array. Of course, the preaching that the Negro population in the South has the right to form a separate nation does not of itself constitute illegal advocacy. But neither does the teaching of the abstract theory of Marxism-Leninism, which we have held cannot alone form the basis for a conviction for violation of the Smith Act, *Yates* v. *United States;* yet it cannot be seriously urged that evidence of such teaching is legally irrelevant to the charge. Similarly the evidence of the pamphlet on alleged American atrocities in Korea cannot be said to be irrelevant to the issue of illegal advocacy by the Party. Once again, the pamphlet may not in itself constitute such an incitement to violence as would justify a finding that the Party advocated violent overthrow, but it is possible to infer from it that it was the purpose of the Party to undermine the Government in the eyes of the people in time of war as a preparatory measure, albeit legal in itself, to the teaching and sympathetic reception of illegal advocacy to violent revolution.

Petitioner also argues that this and other evidence was not connected up with him or his activities. Whether it was or not, since it is necessary under the membership clause to prove the advocacy of the Party as an independent element of the offense, this renders admissible evidence not connected up with the defendant in the accepted conspiracy sense. Doubtless because of this there is a special need to make sure that the evidence establishing a defendant's personal knowledge of illegal Party advocacy and his intent in becoming or remaining a Party member to accomplish violent overthrow is cogent and adequately brought home to him. But, having said that, we have said all, in respect to petitioner's claim on this point. . . .

The judgment of the Court of Appeals must be
Affirmed.

Mr. Justice Black, dissenting.

Petitioner was convicted for violation of the "membership clause" of the Smith Act which imposes a penalty of up to twenty years' imprisonment together with a fine of $20,000 upon anyone who "becomes or is a member of, or affiliates with, any . . . society, group or assembly of persons [who teach, advocate, or encourage the overthrow of the existing government by force or violence], knowing the purposes thereof. . . ." Rejecting numerous contentions urged for reversal, the Court upholds a six-year sentence imposed upon petitioner. . . .

. . . I think it is important to point out the manner in which this case re-emphasizes the freedom-destroying nature of the "balancing test" presently in use by the Court to justify its refusal to apply specific constitutional protections of the Bill of Rights. In some of the recent cases in which it has "balanced" away the protections of the First Amendment, the Court has suggested that it was justified in the application of this "test" because no direct abridgment of First Amendment freedoms was involved, the abridgment in each of these cases being, in the Court's opinion, nothing more than "an incident of the informed exercise of a valid governmental function." A possible implication of that suggestion was that if the Court were confronted with what it would call a direct abridgment of speech, it would not apply the "balancing test" but would enforce the protections of the First Amendment according to its own terms. This case causes me to doubt that such an implication is justified.

Petitioner is being sent to jail for the express reason that he has associated with people who have entertained unlawful ideas and said unlawful things, and that of course is a *direct* abridgment of his freedoms of speech and assembly—under any definition that has ever been used for that term. Nevertheless, even as to this admittedly direct abridgment, the Court relies upon its prior decisions to the effect that the Government has power to abridge speech and assembly if its interest in doing so is sufficient to outweigh the interest in protecting these First Amendment freedoms.

This, I think, demonstrates the unlimited breadth and danger of the "balancing test" as it is currently being applied by a majority of this Court. Under that "test," the question in every case in which a First Amendment right is asserted is not whether there has been an abridgment of that right, not whether the abridgment of that right was intentional on the part of the Government, and not whether there is any other way in which the Government could accomplish a lawful aim without an invasion of the constitutionally guaranteed rights of the people. It is, rather, simply whether the Government has an interest in abridging the right involved and, if so, whether that interest is of sufficient importance, in the opinion of a majority of this Court, to justify the Government's action in doing so. This doctrine, to say the very least, is capable of being used to justify almost any action Government may wish to take to suppress First Amendment freedoms.

Mr. Justice Douglas, dissenting.

When we allow petitioner to be sentenced to prison for six years for being a "member" of the Communist Party, we make a sharp break with traditional concepts of First Amendment rights and make serious Mark Twain's lighthearted comment that "It is by the goodness of God that in our country we have those three unspeakably precious things: freedom of speech, freedom of conscience, and the prudence never to practice either of them."

Even the Alien and Sedition Laws—shameful reminders of an early chapter in intolerance—never went so far as we go today. They were aimed at conspiracy and advocacy of insurrection and at the publication of "false, scandalous, and malicious" writing against the Government. The Government then sought control over the press "in order to strike at one of the chief sources of disaffection and sedition." Miller, *Crisis in Freedom* (1951), p. 56. There is here no charge of conspiracy, no charge of any overt act to overthrow the Government by force and violence, no charge of any other criminal act. The charge is being a "member" of the

Communist Party, "well-knowing" that it advocated the overthrow of the Government by force and violence, "said defendant intending to bring about such overthrow by force and violence as speedily as circumstances would permit." That falls far short of a charge of conspiracy. Conspiracy rests not in intention alone but in an agreement with one or more others to promote an unlawful project. . . .

We legalize today guilt by association, sending a man to prison when he committed no unlawful act. Today's break with tradition is a serious one. It borrows from the totalitarian philosophy. . . .

The case is not saved by showing that petitioner was an active member. None of the activity constitutes a crime. The record contains evidence that Scales was the Chairman of the North and South Carolina Districts of the Communist Party. He recruited new members into the Party, and promoted the advanced education of selected young Party members in the theory of communism to be undertaken at secret schools. He was a director of one such school. He explained the principles of the Party to an FBI agent who posed as someone interested in joining the Party, and furnished him literature, including articles which criticized in vivid language the American "aggression" in Korea and described American "atrocities" committed on Korean citizens. He once remarked that the Party was setting up underground means of communication, and in 1951 he himself "went underground." At the school of which Scales was director, students were told (by someone else) that one of the Party's weaknesses was in failing to place people in key industrial positions. One witness told of a meeting arranged by Scales at which the staff of the school urged him to remain in his position in an industrial plant rather than return to college. In Scales' presence students at the school were once shown how to kill a person with a pencil, a device which, it was said, might come in handy on a picket line. Other evidence showed Scales to have made several statements or distributed literature containing implicating passages. Among them were comments to the effect that the Party line was that the Negroes in the South and the working classes should be used to foment a violent revolution; that a Communist government could not be voted into power in this country because the Government controlled communication media, newspapers, the military, and the educational systems, and that force was the only way to achieve the revolution; that if a depression were to come the Communist America would be closer at hand than predicted by William Z. Foster; that the revolution would come within a generation; that it would be easier in the United States than in Russia to effectuate the revolution because of assistance and advice from Russian

Communists. Petitioner at different times said or distributed literature which said that the goals of communism could only be achieved by violent revolution that would have to start internally with the working classes.

Not one single illegal act is charged to petitioner. That is why the essence of the crime covered by the indictment is merely belief—belief in the proletarian revolution, belief in Communist creed. . . .

What we lose by majority vote today may be reclaimed at a future time when the fear of advocacy, dissent, and non-conformity no longer cast a shadow over us.

Mr. Justice Brennan, joined by Chief Justice Warren and Justice Douglas, dissented in a separate opinion.

10. Freedom of Religion

The Establishment Clause of the First Amendment provides that: "Congress shall make no law respecting an establishment of religion, or prohibiting the free exercise thereof." What does this mean with regard to the rights of the individual? First, it means that every person is free to worship in his own way. In line with this meaning, the establishment of religion cannot be curtailed by government. That is, government cannot take action that would prevent religious groups from operating in accordance with their beliefs. There are, however, exceptions, and the meaning of the protection of religion in the First Amendment has varied from one case to another. In this area as in all others involving civil liberties and civil rights the Supreme Court has had to try to balance the needs of the state with the rights of the individual. Religious freedom is not absolute.

The Supreme Court has long held that there must be a wall of separation between church and state, which means that government cannot discriminate among religious creeds. At the present time this problem is manifested in the controversy over federal aid to parochial schools. It has been virtually impossible for Congress to reach an agreement upon the extent to which private schools with religious affiliations should receive federal aid. It is questionable how much aid can be given without affecting the separation of church and state.

At the state and local level the wall of separation between church and state has caused difficulties with respect to such issues as: Should bus transportation be given to private school students as well as those attending the public schools? Should released time be given for religious exercises in the public schools? And, perhaps the most controversial of all, should public schools have officially sanctioned prayers?

In the case of *Everson* v. *Board of Education,* 330 U.S. 1 (1947), the Supreme Court had to face the issue of how far local government could go in aiding Catholic parochial schools. New Jersey had authorized local boards of education to reimburse parents for money they spent on bus transportation without regard to the nature of the school attended. Both those going to public and private schools could receive reimbursement. When this statute was challenged as a violation of the wall of separation doctrine, the Supreme Court upheld it. In its opinion the Court pointed out that secular education serves a public purpose, and therefore tax money can be spent on private nonprofit schools as well as on public education. Although reimbursement for bus transportation to parochial schools constituted a degree of aid to religion, it was not in this case considered sufficient to justify a holding that it violated the First Amendment. The state was not acting as an agent of any religion, but remained neutral. It was providing a public service to all school children, in much the same way as it provides policemen and traffic control to assist children in reaching school safely.

Another issue that has developed concerning freedom of religion involves the "released time" program that public schools have instituted to permit religious instruction during the school day. In *McCollum* v. *Board of Education,* 333 U.S. 203 (1948), the Court held that a board of education could not use tax-supported property for religious instruction. This case involved an Illinois program that provided for released time for students while they received religious instruction on school property. In *Zorach* v. *Clauson,* 343 U.S. 306 (1952), the Court retreated slightly from its decision in *McCollum* when it upheld a New York program that permitted students to go to religious centers beyond school property for religious instruction during the school day.

The status of the wall of separation doctrine today is ambiguous. The Supreme Court has held that a religious oath for office requiring an expressed belief in God is unconstitutional. See *Torcaso* v. *Watkins,* 367 U.S. 488 (1961). But Sunday closing laws are not unconstitutional, for even though they may once have had a religious motivation, today they achieve secular goals. See *McGowan* v. *Maryland,* 366 U.S. 420 (1961). The most controversial decision of all made by the Supreme Court regarding the Establishment Clause was that in *Engel* v. *Vitale,* the famous school prayer case of 1962.

ENGEL v. VITALE
370 U.S. 421 (1962)

M<small>R</small>. Justice Black delivered the opinion of the Court, saying in part:
The respondent Board of Education of Union Free School District
No. 9, New Hyde Park, New York, acting in its official capacity under
state law, directed the School District's principal to cause the following
prayer to be said aloud by each class in the presence of a teacher at the
beginning of each school day:

> Almighty God, we acknowledge our dependence upon Thee, and
> we beg Thy blessings upon us, our parents, our teachers and our country.

This daily procedure was adopted on the recommendation of the
State Board of Regents, a governmental agency created by the State Constitution to which the New York Legislature has granted broad supervi-
sory, executive, and legislative powers over the State's public school system. These state officials composed the prayer which they recommended
and published as a part of their "Statement on Moral and Spiritual Training in the Schools," saying: "We believe that this Statement will be subscribed to by all men and women of good will, and we call upon all of
them to aid in giving life to our program."

Shortly after the practice of reciting the Regents' prayer was adopted
by the School District, the parents of ten pupils brought this action in a
New York State Court insisting that use of this official prayer in the public schools was contrary to the beliefs, religions, or religious practices of
both themselves and their children. Among other things, these parents
challenged the constitutionality of both the state law authorizing the
School District to direct the use of prayer in public schools and the School
District's regulation ordering the recitation of this particular prayer on the
ground that these actions of official governmental agencies violate that part
of the First Amendment of the Federal Constitution which commands
that "Congress shall make no law respecting an establishment of religion"
—a command which was "made applicable to the State of New York by
the Fourteenth Amendment of the said Constitution." The New York
Court of Appeals, over the dissents of Judges Dye and Fuld, sustained an
order of the lower state courts which had upheld the power of New York
to use the Regents' prayer as a part of the daily procedures of its public
schools so long as the schools did not compel any pupil to join in the

prayer over his or his parents' objection. We granted certiorari to review this important decision involving rights protected by the First and Fourteenth Amendments.

We think that by using its public school system to encourage recitation of the Regents' prayer, the State of New York has adopted a practice wholly inconsistent with the Establishment Clause. There can, of course, be no doubt that New York's program of daily classroom invocation of God's blessings as prescribed in the Regents' prayer is a religious activity. It is a solemn avowal of divine faith and supplication for the blessings of the Almighty. The nature of such a prayer has always been religious, none of the respondents has denied this and the trial court expressly so found....

The petitioners contend among other things that the state laws requiring or permitting use of the Regents' prayer must be struck down as a violation of the Establishment Clause because that prayer was composed by governmental officials as a part of a governmental program to further religious beliefs. For this reason, petitioners argue, the State's use of the Regents' prayer in its public school system breaches the constitutional wall of separation between Church and State. We agree with that contention since we think that the constitutional prohibition against laws respecting an establishment of religion must at least mean that in this country it is no part of the business of government to compose official prayers for any group of the American people to recite as a part of a religious program carried on by government.

It is a matter of history that this very practice of establishing governmentally composed prayers for religious services was one of the reasons which caused many of our early colonists to leave England and seek religious freedom in America. The Book of Common Prayer, which was created under governmental direction and which was approved by Acts of Parliament in 1548 and 1549, set out in minute detail the accepted form and content of prayer and other religious ceremonies to be used in the established, tax-supported Church of England. The controversies over the Book and what should be its content repeatedly threatened to disrupt the peace of that country as the accepted forms of prayer in the established church changed with the views of the particular ruler that happened to be in control at the time. Powerful groups representing some of the varying religious views of the people struggled among themselves to impress their particular views upon the Government and obtain amendments of the Book more suitable to their respective notions of how religious services should be conducted in order that the official religious establishment would advance their particular religious beliefs. Other groups, lacking the necessary political power to influence the Government on the matter, decided to leave England and its established church and seek freedom in America from England's governmentally ordained and supported religion.

It is an unfortunate fact of history that when some of the very groups which had most strenuously opposed the established Church of England found themselves sufficiently in control of colonial governments in this country to write their own prayers into law, they passed laws making their own religion the official religion of their respective colonies. Indeed, as late as the time of the Revolutionary War, there were established churches in at least eight of the thirteen former colonies and established religions in at least four of the other five. But the successful Revolution against English political domination was shortly followed by intense opposition to the practice of establishing religion by law. . . .

By the time of the adoption of the Constitution, our history shows that there was a widespread awareness among many Americans of the dangers of a union of Church and State. . . . The First Amendment was added to the Constitution to stand as a guarantee that neither the power nor the prestige of the Federal Government would be used to control, support or influence the kinds of prayer the American people can say— that the people's religions must not be subjected to the pressures of government for change each time a new political administration is elected to office. Under that Amendment's prohibition against governmental establishment of religion, as reinforced by the provisions of the Fourteenth Amendment, government in this country, be it state or federal, is without power to prescribe by law any particular form of prayer which is to be used as an official prayer in carrying on any program of governmentally sponsored religious activity.

There can be no doubt that New York's state prayer program officially establishes the religious beliefs embodied in the Regents' prayer. The respondents' argument to the contrary, which is largely based upon the contention that the Regents' prayer is "non-denominational" and the fact that the program, as modified and approved by state courts, does not require all pupils to recite the prayer but permits those who wish to do so to remain silent or be excused from the room, ignores the essential nature of the program's constitutional defects. Neither the fact that the prayer may be denominationally neutral, nor the fact that its observance on the part of the students is voluntary can serve to free it from the limitations of the Establishment Clause, as it might from the Free Exercise

Clause, of the First Amendment, both of which are operative against the States by virtue of the Fourteenth Amendment. Although these two clauses may in certain instances overlap, they forbid two quite different kinds of governmental encroachment upon religious freedom. The Establishment Clause, unlike the Free Exercise Clause, does not depend upon any showing of direct governmental compulsion and is violated by the enactment of laws which establish an official religion whether those laws operate directly to coerce nonobserving individuals or not. This is not to say, of course, that laws officially prescribing a particular form of religious worship do not involve coercion of such individuals. When the power, prestige and financial support of government is placed behind a particular religious belief, the indirect coercive pressure upon religious minorities to conform to the prevailing officially approved religion is plain. But the purposes underlying the Establishment Clause go much further than that. Its first and most immediate purpose rested on the belief that a union of government and religion tends to destroy government and to degrade religion. The history of governmentally established religion, both in England and in this country, showed that whenever government had allied itself with one particular form of religion, the inevitable result had been that it had incurred the hatred, disrespect and even contempt of those who held contrary beliefs. That same history showed that many people had lost their respect for any religion that had relied upon the support of government to spread its faith. The Establishment Clause thus stands as an expression of principle on the part of the Founders of our Constitution that religion is too personal, too sacred, too holy, to permit its "unhallowed perversion" by a civil magistrate. Another purpose of the Establishment Clause rested upon an awareness of the historical fact that governmentally established religions and religious persecutions go hand in hand. The Founders knew that only a few years after the Book of Common Prayer became the only accepted form of religious services in the established Church of England, an Act of Uniformity was passed to compel all Englishmen to attend those services and to make it a criminal offense to conduct or attend religious gatherings of any other kind—a law which was consistently flouted by dissenting religious groups in England and which contributed to widespread persecutions of people like John Bunyan who persisted in holding "unlawful [religious] meetings . . . to the great disturbance and distraction of the good subjects of this kingdom. . . ." And they knew that similar persecutions had received the sanction of law in several of the colonies in this country soon after the establishment of official religions in those colonies. It was in large part to get completely away from this sort of systematic religious persecution that the Founders brought into being our Nation, our Constitution, and our Bill of Rights with its prohibition against any governmental establishment of religion. The New York laws officially prescribing the Regents' prayer are inconsistent with both the purposes of the Establishment Clause and with the Establishment Clause itself.

It has been argued that to apply the Constitution in such a way as to prohibit state laws respecting an establishment of religious services in public schools is to indicate a hostility toward religion or toward prayer. Nothing, of course, could be more wrong. The history of man is inseparable from the history of religion. And perhaps it is not too much to say that since the beginning of that history many people have devoutly believed that "More things are wrought by prayer than this world dreams of." It was doubtless largely due to men who believed this that there grew up a sentiment that caused men to leave the cross-currents of officially established state religions and religious persecution in Europe and come to this country filled with the hope that they could find a place in which they could pray when they pleased to the God of their faith in the language they chose. And there were men of this same faith in the power of prayer who led the fight for adoption of our Constitution and also for our Bill of Rights with the very guarantees of religious freedom that forbid the sort of governmental activity which New York has attempted here. These men knew that the First Amendment, which tried to put an end to governmental control of religion and of prayer, was not written to destroy either. They knew rather that it was written to quiet well-justified fears which nearly all of them felt arising out of an awareness that governments of the past had shackled men's tongues to make them speak only the religious thoughts that government wanted them to speak and to pray only to the God that government wanted them to pray to. It is neither sacrilegious nor antireligious to say that each separate government in this country should stay out of the business of writing or sanctioning official prayers and leave that purely religious function to the people themselves and to those the people choose to look to for religious guidance.

It is true that New York's establishment of its Regents' prayer as an officially approved religious doctrine of that State does not amount to a total establishment of one particular religious sect to the exclusion of all others—that, indeed, the governmental endorsement of that prayer seems relatively insignificant when compared to the governmental encroachments upon religion which were commonplace 200 years ago. To those who may subscribe to the view that because the Regents' official prayer is so brief and general there can be no danger to religious freedom in its governmental establishment, however, it may be appropriate to say in the words of James Madison, the author of the First Amendment:

> [I]t is proper to take alarm at the first experiment on our liberties. . . . Who does not see that the same authority which can establish Christianity, in exclusion of all other Religions, may establish with the same ease any particular sect of Christians, in exclusion of all other Sects? That the same authority which can force a citizen to contribute three pence only of his property for the support of any one establishment, may force him to conform to any other establishment in all cases whatsoever?

The judgment of the Court of Appeals of New York is reversed and the cause remanded for further proceedings not inconsistent with this opinion.

Reversed and remanded.

Mr. Justice Frankfurter took no part in the decision of this case.

Mr. Justice White took no part in the consideration or decision of this case.

Mr. Justice Douglas concurred in a separate opinion.

Mr. Justice Stewart, dissenting.

A local school board in New York has provided that those pupils who wish to do so may join in a brief prayer at the beginning of each school day, acknowledging their dependence upon God and asking His blessing upon them and upon their parents, their teachers, and their country. The court today decides that in permitting this brief nondenominational prayer the school board has violated the Constitution of the United States. I think this decision is wrong.

The Court does not hold, nor could it, that New York has interfered with the free exercise of anybody's religion. For the state courts have made clear that those who object to reciting the prayer must be entirely free of any compulsion to do so, including any "embarrassments and pressures." Cf. *West Virginia State Board of Education* v. *Barnette,* 319 US 624. But the Court says that in permitting school children to say this simple prayer, the New York authorities have established "an official religion."

With all respect, I think the Court has misapplied a great constitutional principle. I cannot see how an "official religion" is established by letting those who want to say a prayer say it. On the contrary, I think that to deny the wish of these school children to join in reciting this prayer is to deny them the opportunity of sharing in the spiritual heritage of our Nation.

The Court's historical review of the quarrels over the Book of Common Prayer in England throws no light for me on the issue before us in this case. England had then and has now an established church. Equally unenlightening, I think, is the history of the early establishment and later rejection of an official church in our own States. For we deal here not with the establishment of a state church, which would, of course, be constitutionally impermissible, but with whether school children who want to begin their day by joining in prayer must be prohibited from doing so. Moreover, I think that the Court's task, in this as in all areas of constitutional adjudication, is not responsibly aided by the uncritical invocation of metaphors like the "wall of separation," a phrase nowhere to be found in the Constitution. What is relevant to the issue here is not the history of an established church in sixteenth century England or in eighteenth century America, but the history of the religious traditions of our people, reflected in countless practices of the institutions and officials of our government.

At the opening of each day's Session of this Court we stand, while one of our officials invokes the protection of God. Since the days of John Marshall our Crier has said, "God save the United States and this Honorable Court." Both the Senate and the House of Representatives open their daily Sessions with prayer. Each of our Presidents, from George Washington to John F. Kennedy, has upon assuming his office asked the protection and help of God.

The Court today says that the state and federal governments are without constitutional power to prescribe any particular form of words to be recited by any group of the American people on any subject touching religion. The third stanza of "The Star-Spangled Banner," made our National Anthem by Act of Congress in 1931, contains these verses:

"Blest with victory and peace, may the heav'n rescued land
Praise the Pow'r that hath made and preserved us a nation!
Then conquer we must, when our cause it is just,
And this be our motto 'In God is our Trust.' "

In 1954 Congress added a phrase to the Pledge of Allegiance to the Flag so that it now contains the words "one Nation *under God* indivisible, with liberty and justice for all." In 1952 Congress enacted legislation calling upon the President each year to proclaim a National Day of Prayer. Since 1865 the words "IN GOD WE TRUST" have been impressed on our coins.

Countless similar examples could be listed, but there is no need to belabor the obvious. It was all summed up by this Court just ten years ago in a single sentence: "We are a religious people whose institutions presuppose a Supreme Being." *Zorach* v. *Clauson,* 343 US 306, 313.

I do not believe that this Court, or the Congress, or the President has by the actions and practices I have mentioned established an "official religion" in violation of the Constitution. And I do not believe the State of New York has done so in this case. What each has done has been to recognize and to follow the deeply entrenched and highly cherished spiritual traditions of our Nation—traditions which come down to us from those who almost two hundred years ago avowed their "firm reliance on the Protection of Divine Providence" when they proclaimed the freedom and independence of this brave new world.

I dissent. 🖋

A storm of controversy arose over the Supreme Court's decision in *Engel* v. *Vitale*. Misunderstanding the intention of the Supreme Court, which was clearly to *increase* religious freedom rather than restrict it, opponents of the school prayer decision succeeded in having a proposed Constitutional Amendment introduced in Congress. Known as the Becker Amendment, it had the support of extremist groups throughout the country as well as many well-intentioned citizens who felt that the Court's decision unduly restricted their religious freedom and indeed implied a bias against religion. The proposed Amendment, which had virtually no chance of passing the first congressional hurdle, clearly overrules decisions of the Supreme Court that have prevented the use of public school facilities for religious exercises, as well as its opinion in the school prayer case.

THE BECKER AMENDMENT
"ARTICLE—

"SECTION 1. Nothing in this Constitution shall be deemed to prohibit the offering, reading from, or listening to prayers or biblical scriptures, if participation therein is on a voluntary basis, in any governmental or public school, institution, or place.

"SEC. 2. Nothing in this Constitution shall be deemed to prohibit making reference to belief in, reliance upon, or invoking the aid of God or a Supreme Being in any governmental or public document, proceeding, activity, ceremony, school, institution, or place, or upon any coinage, currency, or obligation of the United States.

"SEC. 3. Nothing in this article shall constitute an establishment of religion.

"SEC. 4. This article shall be inoperative unless it shall have been ratified as an amendment to the Constitution by the legislatures of three-fourths of the several States within seven years from the date of its submission to the States by the Congress." ☙

11. Equal Protection of the Laws

By now most students are thoroughly familiar with the evolution of the "separate but equal" doctrine first enunciated by the Supreme Court in *Plessy* v. *Ferguson,* 163 U.S. 537 (1896). Students should note that what is involved in cases in this area is legal interpretation of the provision in the Fourteenth Amendment which provides that no state may deny "to any person within its jurisdiction the equal protection of the laws." The *Plessy* case stated that separate but equal accommodations, required by state law to be established on railroads in Louisiana, did not violate the equal protection of the laws clause of the Fourteenth Amendment. The Court went on to say that the object of the Fourteenth Amendment "was undoubtedly to enforce the absolute equality of the two races before the law, but in the nature of things it could not have been intended to abolish distinctions based upon color, or to enforce social, as distinguished from political, equality, or a commingling of the two races upon terms unsatisfactory to either. Laws permitting, and even requiring, their separation in places where they are liable to be brought into contact do not necessarily imply the inferiority of either race to the other, and have been generally, if not universally, recognized as within the competency of the state legislatures in the exercise of their police power. The most common instance of this is connected with the establishment of separate schools for white and colored children, which has been held to be a valid exercise of the legislative power even by courts of States where the political rights of the colored race have been longest and most earnestly enforced." Both the police power and education are within the reserved powers of the states; they are reserved, however, only insofar as they do not conflict with provisions of the Constitution. The Supreme Court, in *Brown* v. *Board of Education,* 347 U.S. 483 (1954), finally crystallized its interpretation of the equal protection of the laws clause in a way that resulted in a significant decrease in state power in an area traditionally reserved to states, viz., education.

Further, a general principle was established which extended far beyond the field of education.

BROWN v. BOARD OF EDUCATION OF TOPEKA
347 U.S. 483 (1954)

MR. Chief Justice Warren delivered the opinion of the Court, saying in part:

These cases come to us from the States of Kansas, South Carolina, Virginia, and Delaware. They are premised on different facts and different local conditions, but a common legal question justifies their consideration together in this consolidated opinion.

In each of the cases, minors of the Negro race, through their legal representatives, seek the aid of the courts in obtaining admission to the public schools of their community on a nonsegregated basis. In each instance, they had been denied admission to schools attended by white children under laws requiring or permitting segregation according to race. This segregation was alleged to deprive the plaintiffs of the equal protection of the laws under the Fourteenth Amendment. In each of the cases other than the Delaware case, a three-judge federal district court denied relief to the plaintiffs on the so-called "separate but equal" doctrine announced by this Court in *Plessy* v. *Ferguson*. . . .

The plaintiffs contend that segregated public schools are not "equal" and cannot be made "equal," and that hence they are deprived of the equal protection of the laws. Because of the obvious importance of the question presented, the Court took jurisdiction. . . .

In the first cases in this Court construing the Fourteenth Amendment, decided shortly after its adoption, the Court interpreted it as proscribing all state-imposed discriminations against the Negro race. The doctrine of "separate but equal" did not make its appearance in this Court until 1896 in the case of *Plessy* v. *Ferguson, supra,* involving not education but transportation. American courts have since labored with the doctrine for over half a century. In this Court, there have been six cases involving the "separate but equal" doctrine in the field of public education. . . . In more recent cases, all on the graduate school level, inequality was found in that specific benefits enjoyed by white students were denied to Negro students of the same educational qualifications. . . . In none of these cases was it necessary to re-examine the doctrine to grant relief to the Negro plaintiff. And in *Sweatt* v. *Painter* [339 U.S. 629 (1950)], the Court expressly reserved decision on the question whether *Plessy* v. *Ferguson* should be held inapplicable to public education.

In the instant cases, that question is directly presented. Here, unlike *Sweatt* v. *Painter,* there are findings below that the Negro and white schools involved have been equalized, or are being equalized, with respect to buildings, curricula, qualifications and salaries of teachers, and other "tangible" factors. Our decision, therefore, cannot turn on merely a comparison of these tangible factors in the Negro and white schools involved in each of the cases. We must look instead to the effect of segregation itself on public education.

In approaching this problem, we cannot turn the clock back to 1868 when the Amendment was adopted, or even to 1896 when *Plessy* v. *Ferguson* was written. We must consider public education in the light of its full development and its present place in American life throughout the Nation. Only in this way can it be determined if segregation in public schools deprives these plaintiffs of the equal protection of the laws.

Today, education is perhaps the most important function of state and local governments. Compulsory school attendance laws and the great expenditures for education both demonstrate our recognition of the importance of education to our democratic society. It is required in the performance of our most basic public responsibilities, even service in the armed forces. It is the very foundation of good citizenship. Today it is a principal instrument in awakening the child to cultural values, in preparing him for later professional training, and in helping him to adjust normally to his environment. In these days, it is doubtful that any child may reasonably be expected to succeed in life if he is denied the opportunity of an education. Such an opportunity, where the state has undertaken to provide it, is a right which must be made available to all on equal terms.

We come then to the question presented: Does segregation of children in public schools solely on the basis of race, even though the physical facilities and other "tangible" factors may be equal, deprive the children of the minority group of equal educational opportunities? We believe that it does.

In *Sweatt* v. *Painter, supra,* in finding that a segregated law school for Negroes could not provide them equal educational opportunities, this Court relied in large part on "those qualities which are incapable of objective measurement but which make for greatness in a law school." In *McLaurin* v. *Oklahoma State Regents, supra* [339 U.S. 637 (1950)], the Court, in requiring that a Negro admitted to a white graduate school be treated like all other students, again resorted to intangible considerations: " . . . his ability to study, to engage in discussions and exchange views with other students, and, in general, to learn his profession." Such considerations apply with added force to children in grade and high schools. To separate them from others of similar age and qualifications solely because of their race generates a feeling of inferiority as to their status in the community that may affect their hearts and minds in a way unlikely ever to be undone. The effect of this separation of their educational opportunities was well stated by a finding in the Kansas case by a court which nevertheless felt compelled to rule against the Negro plaintiffs:

"Segregation of white and colored children in public schools has a detrimental effect upon the colored children. The impact is greater when it has the sanction of the law; for the policy of separating the races is usually interpreted as denoting the inferiority of the Negro group. A sense of inferiority affects the motivation of a child to learn. Segregation with the sanction of law, therefore, has a tendency to retard the educational and mental development of Negro children and to deprive them of some of the benefits they would receive in a racially integrated school system." Whatever may have been the extent of psychological knowledge at the time of *Plessy* v. *Ferguson,* this finding is amply supported by modern authority. Any language in *Plessy* v. *Ferguson* contrary to this finding is rejected.

We conclude that in the field of public education the doctrine of "separate but equal" has no place. Separate educational facilities are inherently unequal. Therefore, we hold that the plaintiffs and others similarly situated for whom the actions have been brought are, by reason of the segregation complained of, deprived of the equal protection of the laws guaranteed by the Fourteenth Amendment. This disposition makes unnecessary any discussion whether such segregation also violates the Due Process Clause of the Fourteenth Amendment.

Because these are class actions, because of the wide applicability of this decision, and because of the great variety of local conditions, the formulation of decrees in these cases presents problems of considerable complexity. On re-argument, the consideration of appropriate relief was necessarily subordinated to the primary question—the constitutionality of segregation in public education. We have now announced that such segregation is a denial of the equal protection of the laws. In order that we may have the full assistance of the parties in formulating decrees, the cases will be restored to the docket, and the parties are requested to present further argument on Questions 4 and 5 previously propounded by the Court for the re-argument this Term [which deal with the implementation of desegregation]. The Attorney General of the United States is again invited to participate. The Attorneys General of the states requiring or permitting segregation in public education will also be permitted to appear as *amici curiae* upon request to do so by September 15, 1954, and submission of briefs by October 1, 1954.

It is so ordered.

On the same day the decision was announced in the *Brown* case the Court held segregation in the District of Columbia unconstitutional on the basis of the due process clause of the Fifth Amendment. See *Bolling* v. *Sharpe*, 347 U.S. 497 (1954). This situation reversed the normal one in that a protection explicitly afforded citizens of states was not expressly applicable against the national government, and could be made so only through interpreting it into the concept of due process of law.

After hearing the views of all interested parties to the *Brown* case the Court, on May 31, 1955, announced its decision concerning the implementation of desegregation in public schools.

BROWN v. BOARD OF EDUCATION OF TOPEKA
349 U.S. 294 (1955)

M R. Chief Justice Warren delivered the opinion of the Court, saying in part:

These cases were decided on May 17, 1954. The opinions of that date, declaring the fundamental principle that racial discrimination in public education is unconstitutional, are incorporated herein by reference. All provisions of federal, state, or local law requiring or permitting such discrimination must yield to this principle. There remains for consideration the manner in which relief is to be accorded.

Because these cases arose under different local conditions and their disposition will involve a variety of local problems, we requested further argument on the question of relief. . . . The parties, the United States, and the States of Florida, North Carolina, Arkansas, Oklahoma, Maryland, and Texas filed briefs and participated in the oral argument.

These presentations were informative and helpful to the Court in its consideration of the complexities arising from the transition to a system of public education freed of racial discrimination. The presentations also demonstrated that substantial steps to eliminate racial discrimination in public schools have already been taken, not only in some of the communities in which these cases arose, but in some of the states appearing as *amici curiae,* and in other states as well. Substantial progress has been made in the District of Columbia and in the communities in Kansas and Delaware involved in this litigation. The defendants in the cases coming to us from South Carolina and Virginia are awaiting the decision of this Court concerning relief.

Full implementation of these constitutional principles may require solution of varied local school problems. School authorities have the primary responsibility for elucidating, assessing, and solving these problems; courts will have to consider whether the action of school authorities constitutes good faith implementation of the governing constitutional principles. Because of their proximity to local conditions and the possible need for further hearings, the courts which originally heard these cases can best perform this judicial appraisal. Accordingly, we believe it appropriate to remand the cases to those courts.

In fashioning and effectuating the decrees, the courts will be guided by equitable principles. Traditionally, equity has been characterized by a practical flexibility in shaping its remedies and by a facility for adjusting and reconciling public and private needs. These cases call for the exercise of these traditional attributes of equity power. At stake is the personal interest of the plaintiffs in admission to public schools as soon as practicable on a nondiscriminatory basis. To effectuate this interest may call for elimination of a variety of obstacles in making the transition to school systems operated in accordance with the constitutional principles set forth in our May 17, 1954, decision. Courts of equity may properly take into account the public interest in the elimination of such obstacles in a systematic and effective manner. But it should go without saying that the vitality of these constitutional principles cannot be allowed to yield simply because of disagreement with them.

While giving weight to these public and private considerations, the courts will require that the defendants make a prompt and reasonable start toward full compliance with our May 17, 1954, ruling. Once such a start has been made, the courts may find that additional time is necessary to carry out the ruling in an effective manner. The burden rests upon the defendants to establish that such time is necessary in the public interest and is consistent with good faith compliance at the earliest practicable date. To that end, the courts may consider problems related to administration, arising from the physical condition of the school plant, the school transportation system, personnel, revision of school districts and attendance areas into compact units to achieve a system of determining admission to the public schools on a nonracial basis, and revision of local laws and regulations which may be necessary in solving the foregoing problems. They will also consider the adequacy of any plans the defendants may propose to meet these problems and to effectuate a transition to a racially nondiscriminatory school system. During this period of transition, the courts will retain jurisdiction of these cases.

The judgments below, except that in the Delaware case, are accordingly reversed and the cases are remanded to the District Courts to take such proceedings and enter such orders and decrees consistent with this opinion as are necessary and proper to admit to public schools on a racially nondiscriminatory basis with all deliberate speed the parties to these cases. The judgment in the Delaware case—ordering the immediate admission of the plaintiffs to schools previously attended only by white children—is affirmed on the basis of the principles stated in our May 17, 1954, opinion, but the case is remanded to the Supreme Court of Delaware for such further proceedings as that Court may deem necessary in the light of this opinion.

It is so ordered. 🖾

After the second decision of the Supreme Court in *Brown* v. *Board of Education* in 1955, it soon became clear that many Southern states would proceed with deliberate speed not to implement the desegregation of public schools but to obstruct the intent of the Supreme Court. The Southern Manifesto, an excerpt from which is reprinted below, clearly indicated the line that would be taken by many Southern representatives and officials to justify defiance of the Supreme Court. The gist of the Manifesto was simply that the Supreme Court did not have the constitutional authority to interfere in an area such as education, which falls within the reserved powers of the states. The difficulty of changing the fabric of society by judicial decisions is illustrated in the area of desegregation of public schools. Ten years after the initial opinion of the Court less than 10 per cent of the Negro students in the 17 Southern states, including the border states and the District of Columbia, are attending integrated classrooms. Legal decisions alone cannot determine the course of events.

A Clear Abuse of Judicial Power*

The unwarranted decision of the Supreme Court in the public school cases is now bearing the fruit always produced when men substitute naked power for established law.

The Founding Fathers gave us a Constitution of checks and balances because they realized the inescapable lesson of history that no man or group of men can be safely entrusted with unlimited power. They framed this Constitution with its provision for change by amendment in order to secure the fundamentals of government against the dangers of temporary popular passion or the personal predilections of public officeholders.

We regard the decision of the Supreme Court in the school cases as a clear abuse of judicial power. It climaxes a trend in the Federal Judiciary undertaking to legislate, in derogation of the authority of Congress, and to encroach upon the reserved rights of the States and the people.

The original Constitution does not mention education. Neither does the 14th amendment nor any other amendment. The debates preceding the submission of the 14th amendment clearly show that there was no intent that it should affect the system of education maintained by the States. ✍

THE DESEGREGATION DECISION: TEN YEARS AFTER

Harry S. Ashmore**

On the morning of May 17, 1954, the laws of seventeen of the United States, and the federal statutes governing the District of Columbia, required racial segregation in public education. By noon this legal vestige of slavery was invalid, the Supreme Court having proclaimed that the public schools of the vast region must be opened to Negroes.

* From "The Southern Manifesto," a document signed by 101 Senators and Representatives from eleven Southern states and presented to Congress on March 12, 1956.

** Reprinted by permission of Willis Kingsley Wing. Copyright © 1964, by Saturday Review, Inc. (This article originally appeared in the *Saturday Review*, 16 May 1964.) [Mr. Ashmore and the *Arkansas Gazette* were awarded double Pulitzer Prizes in 1958 for distinguished reporting of the Little Rock integration controversy.]

Predictions were freely made on the day outraged Southern politicians promptly labeled Black Monday, and they ranged from roseate to dire. Perhaps the only prophecy that has stood the test of ten troubled years is that of a judicial expert who forecast that the *Brown* decision would launch a generation of litigation.

Cases before local, state and federal courts turning on the *Brown* precedent now number in the thousands, and the tide is still rising. The reason, of course, is that the landmark decision was far more than a directive to desegregate five local school districts. It was, as the nine justices in a rare display of unanimity clearly intended, the enunciation of a public policy intended to rid the nation of every manifestation of overt racial discrimination.

The structure of law erected upon the *Brown* precedent is largely judge-made. The Congress, hamstrung by Southern intransigence and a sharp national division of public opinion, only this year has seriously addressed itself to fundamental civil rights legislation. Still the cumulative reach of the court decisions is enormous, going far beyond the issue of segregation in education, which still remains central and unresolved.

In striking down the variety of legal devices by which Southern states have attempted to maintain their segregated schools, the Supreme Court has employed the Fourteenth Amendment as its constitutional instrument. In the process it has abrogated states rights to impose federal standards not only upon the organization of the schools but upon the conduct of a wide variety of public functions. Time after time the Court has affirmed the federal government's obligation to uphold the Bill of Rights, no matter where its guarantees are being violated, or by whom. In practice this has meant that the reluctant executive branch has had to exercise police powers in a fashion virtually unheard of before 1954. In three states the Justice Department has been pushed to the extreme of taking over law enforcement from local officials with a massive show of arms.

At the end of the decade the implications of these developments loom far larger than the actual results. The citadels of segregation still stand across much of the South. But they are under constant attack now by an increasingly militant Negro leadership, solidly supported by the Negro rank and file. And the Rights Movement itself is the direct product of the *Brown* precedent. Negroes everywhere read the 1954 school decision as a declaration that the essential neutrality of the federal government in racial matters had come to an end. The law of the land now did not merely permit but affirmatively supported the minority's crusade for equality, and in Arkansas, Mississippi, and Alabama Negroes would see the federal presence literally standing between them and the resistant white majority.

Even before the leading edge of the Negro crusade impatiently departed the courtroom in favor of the sidewalk, events were forcing the Supreme Court away from its initial narrow application of the anti-discrimination precedent to official institutions and actions. The end of legal segregation did not mean the end of *de facto* segregation, and here the pattern in the nation at large differed little from that in the South. Below the thin crust of the Negro middle class, the Negro mass was walled off from the white community as effectively, and in some ways more inhumanely, in the ghettoes of New York, Chicago, and San Francisco as it was in the "niggertowns" of Richmond, Atlanta, and Memphis.

It was in the private sector that the embattled Southern states proposed to erect their final defense against integrated education. The threatened last resort would be the total abandonment of the public system, with white children presumably attending white schools supported wholly by private funds. The obvious practical difficulties of the scheme have confined it largely to the oratorical level, but in Prince Edward County, Virginia, the attempt actually has been made. In its current session the Supreme Court will decide whether the Constitution can be read to require a once-sovereign state to provide a free education for all of its children, whether or not a majority of white voters wants to tax itself for the purpose.

The great sit-in campaign, aimed at forcing Negro admission to accommodations called public although privately owned, also has forced the Supreme Court to take a new look at one of the most revered of all American institutions, private property. The issue here is whether an entrepreneur who makes a general offer of goods or services, whether he is operating Mrs. Murphy's boardinghouse or Harry Truman's haberdashery, can arbitrarily choose his customers. If the Court holds that he cannot, it will write a significant new definition of private ownership, with implications that go well beyond the immediate issue of race.

It is quite clear that some of the Supreme Court Justices have not been easy in their own minds about the great expansion of federal authority inherent in this progression. The unanimous vote in *Brown* has dwindled to five-to-four in some recent applications of the precedent, and it is by no means improbable that the anti-discrimination majority may actually become a minority in the key public accommodations cases presently looming large on the docket.

If the Court should decide that it has, for the time being at least, reached the outer limits of the law, the *Brown* precedent will still stand as the great constitutional monument of our time. The Rights Movement, which it served as catalyst, is well past the point where it can be turned back by an adverse Supreme Court ruling. Indeed, it is being argued in a nervous Congress that the need for civil rights legislation is not to advance the Negro cause, but to control and contain it.

Underlying the surface tensions is a stern reality. The *Brown* precedent provides for, and the minority is avidly demanding, new relationships between whites and Negroes that are unacceptable under prevailing white attitudes. This is a national, not a uniquely Southern condition. Moreover the collision has come at a time when, in vital employment areas affecting most Negroes, the economic growth that could ameliorate the most immediate grievances has virtually come to a standstill.

Ten years ago, when the *Brown* decision came down, the shortage of manpower was such that the automobile manufacturers were sending teams south from Detroit to recruit Negro workers. This meant that an ambitious colored man at one stroke could escape the overt oppression of his Southern homeland, vastly improve his income and living standards and, perhaps most important of all, find a place in a skilled labor group where his status was equal to that of whites. This year the industry, harvesting the fruits of automation, will produce 25 per cent more automobiles with 80 per cent of the 1954 work force, and Detroit, with a restless mass of unemployed Negroes, is one of the tinderboxes of racial unrest.

Experience with the theoretically open school systems of non-Southern cities also has compounded Negro frustrations. With most child-bearing white families safely ensconced in solidly white neighborhoods, the effort to redistribute children to obtain an effective pattern of integration has required such drastic, essentially artificial devices as bussing children of both races long distances across crowded cities. Even where these experiments have been conscientiously supported by school and municipal officials, success has been limited and white dissatisfaction widespread. In enlightened New York, state court decisions handed down in Brooklyn and Malverne have sustained white parents protesting against having their children arbitrarily transferred across neighborhood boundaries to predominantly Negro schools. In these cases the anti-discrimination precedent has been held to mean that a white child cannot be denied the school of his choice on racial grounds, and this irony also is on its way to the Supreme Court.

Integrated neighborhoods would, of course, produce integrated schools, but the black and white patterns of housing have remained largely inviolate. The small Negro middle-class has gained significant new mobility even in suburbia, but the great majority of colored Americans remains ghetto-bound, and its efforts to break out are encountering retrograde action.

All of this is commonly cited as evidence of a widespread backlash of white public opinion brought on by the excesses of the Negro rights demonstrations. Rather, it seems to me, it is simply a belated revelation of prejudicial white attitudes that have always existed and can no longer be cloaked beneath Fourth-of-July pieties. Sensitive white Americans are discovering, with shock and dismay, what Negroes have long since learned by experience—that white tolerance dissipates rapidly when the abstractions of racial equality are translated into practices that threaten the established system of caste. At the extreme we see Northern communities reacting in the traditional pattern of the South, where fear is often translated into anger, and anger into brutal repression.

On the other side, we are nearing the end of the time when the Negro cause could advance from goal to clearly defined goal, making a record of steady, measurable progress that would sustain the tactical demands of the leadership for discipline and restraint. Principles of equality of treatment have been established, and written into law, but only in peripheral areas has practice been brought into conformity. Negroes have been guaranteed the right of admission to an integrated community, but nowhere in this fair land does an integrated community yet exist—and so the demands for freedom now echo a general frustration that often renders them as incoherent as they are passionate.

It is possible to read these manifestations as the harbingers of revolution, and it is fashionable to do so. In each of the past ten springs the approach of warm weather has brought forth predictions of massive racial violence, first in the South and now in the great cities outside the region. Certainly no one could deny that in the present state of tension a major race riot with widespread bloodshed is possible and may even be inevitable. But there remains the remarkable fact that we haven't had one yet, and with it the salient question: If the situation does get out of hand in a given city, or cities, what happens next?

No Negro leader can doubt that any outbreak of violence, whether spontaneous or organized, would be summarily put down by overwhelming white force. Thus the Negro revolution, if there is to be one, is practically denied the revolutionary's usual weapons—sustained campaigns of terror, sabotage, and guerrilla warfare. Nor does subversion offer any hope for the Negro revolutionary. While there is significant sympathy for his cause in the white power structure, nowhere is there any effective body of radical opinion that could be counted on to support the drastic remedies proposed by Black Muslims on the right, or the Freedom Now Party on the left.

We have, in fact, already had a reverse demonstration of the radical dilemma. In the South white activists have attempted to head off the Negro movement by mob violence, as in Little Rock and Oxford; by terror, as in the assassination of Medgar Evers; and by sabotage, as in the recurrent dynamiting of property owned by Negroes and sympathetic whites. Organized efforts on any significant scale have brought down the full weight of the federal government, in the person of armed U.S. troops. And so far at least those who have transgressed the red line of violence and have been caught have found themselves largely abandoned by respectable segregationists.

Finally, it seems to me the Negro movement is inherently devoid of true revolutionary character simply because its members do not seek to remake the community, only to join it. Social scientists, probing happily in the rich new territory of the Negro subconscious, turn up abundant evidence of alienation. Still the drive seems to be to obtain only what has been denied—a secure place in the larger commonalty whose standards, shabby though a moralist might find them, are those set by the white majority.

If I am correct in my view that a revolutionary resolution of the American racial issue is as unlikely as a sudden healing outburst of brotherly love, the prospect is for a protracted, wearing war of nerves. Most whites feel that they must give up something of value if Negroes are to gain their ordained place in society. I do not believe that this is so, but so long as it remains the conviction of the white community the drive for Negro rights will have the character of an adversary proceeding in which progress is possible but agreement in principle is not. This condition, inescapable now even for the white refugee in the most thoroughly restricted suburb, is ultimately intolerable and has its own force.

The ten abrasive years since *Brown* ought at least to have shucked us of the more debilitating of our national illusions. Chief among these was the happy notion that if we officially declared the Negro equal he automatically would become so—or at least would be able to stride briskly down the path that has led to effective accommodation of other racial minorities. It must be apparent by now that, morally and practically, the Negro's problem is special. If he is to get his just due he will need something more than the collected works of Horatio Alger and the support of a benevolent interracial committee.

Once we wear out the usual arguments over state and local responsibility, the primary burden is going to fall, inescapably, upon the central government. The immediate palliative must be more welfare services, already a federal preserve, and more jobs, which only the most addicted consumers of NAM propaganda now believe can be provided by the private sector in the range and quantity required by Negroes dispossessed by automation—three out of every five, according to the Urban League.

These unhappy facts belatedly have been noted in Washington. War on Poverty has become a slogan and inexorably will become a program. I do not know whether in the vagaries of a campaign year we can expect any more than warmed-over New Deal panaceas. But as Sargent Shriver's Poor Corps marches forth to battle, its intelligence reports clearly indicate that the mission is only incidentally to relieve resident and displaced white Appalachians. The primary attack must be upon the squalid Negro slums that stretch from sea to shining sea.

For the future, we still must look to the law to fulfill its historic role of preceptor.

In the ten years since *Brown* the courts have offered us much valuable instruction. The first lesson is that racial justice can no longer wait for a glacial change in the hearts and minds of men. The second is that the practice of racial equality can alter attitudes when argument and moral suasion cannot, a lesson to be read in the eyes of the rising generation of white and Negro children as they gaze with wonder upon their elders' seizures of racial prejudice.

So we will come back finally to the public schools, that battered, bureau-ridden, harassed, dispirited system of universal education that was once our national pride and remains our national hope. They did it once before, the red brick PS on the city street and the red schoolhouse on the village green. They made room for the frightened children with broken accents, peculiar religions, undernourished lunch boxes, and lice in their hair; contained the cruel curiosity of earlier settlers; taught the lessons of democracy and saw that they were put into practice.

It is a flaccid, morally disoriented society that now dumps a similar, even heavier burden upon our ill-prepared teachers. We ask them somehow to create a new melting pot in a dispersed educational system that operates without a national policy, leaving its professional practitioners exposed to meddling politicians and sustained only by the ministrations of local board members who often look upon education as a well-intentioned hobby.

Ten years after *Brown* the American race problem cannot be neatly defined as a moral, an economic, a social, or an educational issue. It is all of these at once, and it cannot be resolved by a society that no longer pays much attention to its preachers; is content with prosperity at the top even though the lower levels of its social and economic structure are in disarray; and cannot muster the will to put aside the petty religious, professional, and regional interests that stand in the way of an effective public school system.

By frightening a sometimes complacent citizenry, and always prodding an atrophied national conscience, marching Negroes may be offering a great gift to the society that has rejected them. The ugly manifestations of racial bitterness are an injunction to get back to the hard job to which we once professed dedication, the creation of one nation, under God. ✠

12. The Condition of Civil Rights Today

The varied dimensions of the problems of civil rights and equal protection of the laws are illustrated in the following selection from the Report of the United States Commission on Civil Rights. The *Brown* decisions dealt only with the problem of segregation in public education. Other significant problem areas include voting, the administration of justice, housing, employment, and generally the extent to which the Negro and members of other minority groups are treated equally in whatever endeavors they undertake. After a great deal of debate, and a lengthy Senate filibuster, the Civil Rights Act of 1964 was passed. This was the first major civil rights bill since Reconstruction days. The 1964 Act strengthened those of 1957 and 1960 by extending voting rights. Moreover, it bars discrimination on grounds of race, color, religion, or national origin in public accommodations, if the discrimination is supported by state laws or action, if the lodgings are provided to transient guests or interstate travelers, or if the firm involved is engaged in interstate commerce. Under this public accommodations section (Title II), restaurants, motion picture houses, theaters, hotels, and numerous other "public" establishments must provide equal facilities. The 1964 law also contains provisions strengthening the Civil Rights Commission, giving the Attorney General new authority to initiate suits to bring about desegregation, and provides for equal employment opportunity. The scope of the Act is extensive. Its passage illustrates the reluctance of civil rights groups to rely solely upon judicial doctrine to bring about desegregation. However, enforcement of the Civil Rights Bill is to take place primarily through the courts. This can be a slow and expensive process. *Potentially* the Act can remedy many of the deprivations of equal rights found throughout the United States. The dimensions of this problem are illustrated in the following selection.

REPORT OF THE UNITED STATES COMMISSION ON CIVIL RIGHTS*

VOTING

For most citizens of the United States, the exercise of the right to vote is the only personal participation they have in political self-government. Yet, for almost 100 years, this fundamental right has been denied to many Americans on the wholly arbitrary and irrelevant ground of race.

When Congress established the Commission on Civil Rights in 1957, it directed the Commission to investigate formal allegations that citizens were being denied the right to vote by reason of their color, race, religion, or national origin. In the 6 years since 1957, the Commission has conducted hearings, investigations, surveys, and related research. Its findings reveal clearly that the promise of the 14th and 15th amendments to the Constitution remains unfulfilled.

In its 1959 Report, the Commission noted the lack of vigorous enforcement of Federal laws designed to eliminate racial restrictions on voting. The Department of Justice since 1960, has initiated and sustained a determined attack on voter discrimination. The President, in public

---

* From the 1963 Report of the United States Commission on Civil Rights.

pronouncements, has made clear the immorality of denying the ballot to American citizens simply because of color. Yet, while few persons have sought to justify such discrimination on either moral or legal grounds, the right to vote is still denied many Americans solely because of their race.

After 5 years of Federal litigation, it is fair to conclude that case-by-case proceedings, helpful as they have been in isolated localities, have not provided a prompt or adequate remedy for widespread discriminatory denials of the right to vote. Two recent cases, as yet undecided, are aimed at discriminatory practices in the entire State of Mississippi and a large portion of Louisiana. If decided in favor of the Government, they will represent a major step forward. Even then, however, enforcement and registration will have to proceed on a county-by-county basis with many of the same difficulties manifested in the more limited suits.

In 1957, Congress enacted the first Civil Rights Act since 1875. One salient provision authorized the Federal Government to bring civil suits to end discriminatory voting practices. The Civil Rights Act of 1960 strengthened the earlier act by providing that States, as well as registrars, could be sued. It also required the preservation of voting records for 22 months and permitted the appointment of Federal referees to register voters. To implement the referee provisions, a judicial finding of a "pattern or practice" of discrimination by registration or election officials is required. Even where a "pattern or practice" is found, the court still has full discretion to leave the registration process in the hands of the officials who have discriminated in the past. If the court does appoint a referee, the local registrar would not be displaced, since the referee can only register applicants who have applied to the registrar and been rejected.

In 1961, this Commission found that substantial numbers of Negro citizens had been denied the right to vote in 100 counties of 8 Southern States. However, it was too early at that time to make a meaningful evaluation of what the new laws could accomplish in those counties.

That evaluation is the subject of this chapter of the 1963 Commission report. In 1956, the last year before the passage of legislation to secure the right to vote, about 5 percent of the voting-age Negroes in the 100 counties were registered to vote. Despite the subsequent passage of two civil rights acts, the institution of 36 voting rights suits by the Department of Justice, and the operation of several private registration drives, Negro registration in these counties has risen only to 8.3 percent.

The most recent reliable statistics indicate that only 55,711 of the 668,082 voting-age Negroes in the 100 counties have access to the ballot.

The reasons for the low rate of increase in Negro registration appear to include the high cost of litigation, the slowness of the judicial process on both the trial and appellate level, the inherent complexity of supervising the enforcement of decrees, intimidation and reprisals against Negroes who seek to vote, and the employment of diverse techniques by State and local officials to subvert the Constitution of the United States.

The 100 counties in which the Commission found voting denials in 1961 amounted to but 9 percent of the total number of counties in the 11 States of the former Confederacy. However, these 100 counties contained nearly a third of all Negroes of voting age in the 11 States. In view of the present evidence, the Commission was overly conservative in finding denials in only these areas. Eleven of the 40 counties in which the Department of Justice has filed suits alleging discrimination or intimidation by individual defendants are not within the 100. In addition, the broad-gage litigation in Louisiana and Mississippi challenges the application of certain State laws and regulations in all 82 counties in Mississippi and in 21 of Louisiana's 64 parishes. Proposed legislation authorizing the appointment of Federal voting referees where less than 15 percent of the Negro voting-age population is registered would cover 900,000 potential voters in over 250 counties.

Techniques of Discrimination

The practices used by voter registrars today to prevent Negro enfranchisement are the same as those described in the *1961 Voting Report*. An examination of voting complaints filed with the Commission during 1962 and 1963 demonstrates this, as do Justice Department voting suits filed during the intervening period.

Several methods were cited in 1961. One was the discriminatory application of legal qualifications, such as literacy tests, constitutional interpretation tests, calculation of age to the exact day, and requirements of good moral character. Others involved the use of plainly arbitrary procedures. These included requirement of vouchers or some other unduly technical method of identification, rejection for insignificant errors in filling out forms, failure to notify applicants of rejection, imposition of delaying tactics, and discrimination in giving assistance to applicants.

The Commission pointedly warned of a third possible form of discrimination. This has occurred in areas where virtually all the voting-age whites have been registered regardless of qualifications while Negroes have been systematically rejected. If litigation or a change in policy should result in the adoption of strict standards and procedures which would be equally applied to all applicants, the results of past discrimination would be perpetuated by virtue of the fact that the burden of the new requirements would fall on Negro applicants.

During 1962 and the first 7 months of 1963, the Commission received 104 voting complaints. No novel techniques of discrimination were involved. All of those cited in the *1961 Voting Report* were included except the requirement of calculating age to the precise day. The most common were the discriminatory application of legal standards, especially interpretations of "good moral character," and arbitrary procedures such as delay and refusing to notify applicants of their success or failure. Several complaints involved reprisals or intimidation by private citizens and public officials.

During 1962 and 1963, the Justice Department filed 22 voting suits. Of these, eight were directed at reprisals or intimidation. The remaining 14 were based on practices described in the *1961 Voting Report*. One challenged the registration laws as being inherently discriminatory in nature. The others alleged unequal application of standards to whites and Negroes and in some cases resort to delaying tactics.

The danger foreseen by the Commission that prior discrimination might be perpetuated where extremely strict standards are adopted has materialized. To counteract this "freezing" of the rolls, the Department has asked in every appropriate suit for decrees which would require registrars to apply the same standards to future Negro applicants that they had applied to whites in the past. Encountering a reluctance on the part of the district courts to issue such orders, the Department has appealed adverse rulings in three States to the Fifth Circuit Court of Appeals.

The constitutional argument for refusing to allow past discrimination to be permanently frozen into the rolls has been articulated by the Fifth Circuit Court of Appeals:

> Obviously a blanket requirement that all persons who have never paid the poll tax before, that being a relatively small percentage of white people and all Negroes, who now desire to pay their poll tax for the first time must see the Sheriff personally operates unequally and discriminatorily against Negroes. . . . Sheriff Dogan's new instructions by necessary result re-creates and perpetuates the very discrimination which prevailed under his former instructions and practices.*

* *United States* v. *Dogan*, 314 F. 2d 767, 772–73 (5th Cir. 1963).

EDUCATION

Nearly 10 years after the Supreme Court decision in the *School Segregation Cases,* Negro schoolchildren still attend segregated schools in all parts of the Nation.

In the South, most schools continue to be segregated by official policy, notwithstanding the Supreme Court's finding that segregation on the basis of race cannot constitutionally be enforced. But in the North and West, school segregation is widespread because of existing segregated housing patterns and the practice of assigning pupils to neighborhood schools. Whether this northern-style segregation is unconstitutional has yet to be considered by the Supreme Court, but the contention that it runs counter to the equal protection clause is being vigorously asserted.

Protests in the North and West

In the North and West, Negro protests until recently took the form of petition and personal appearance before school boards. However, segregated schools have now become targets of public demonstrations. The metropolitan area of New York City, which includes northern New Jersey, has been the center of demonstrations, picketing, sit-ins, and school boycotts since the summer of 1961. Englewood, N.J., has had periodic rallies featuring Negro celebrities, sit-ins in the school superintendent's office, picketing of the Governor's office in Trenton, school boycotts, and sit-ins in a white school by Negro children assigned to a nearby Negro school. Negroes have picketed in suburban Philadelphia and in Boston, Chicago, and St. Louis. In Boston, some 3,000 junior and senior high school students stayed out of school for a day and attended workshops in neighborhood churches and social centers where they were instructed in Negro history, U.S. Government and civil rights, and the principles of nonviolence. In St. Louis, 30 parents and ministers blocked the departure from a West End school of 12 buses containing about 500 children who were being transported to under-utilized white schools miles away, where they would attend all-Negro classes. Two weeks later, 2,000 Negroes marched on the board of education headquarters carrying signs saying "Freedom Now" and "Don't Teach Segregation."

The increase in the nonwhite population in the cities of the North and West since 1950 has had a severe impact on the public school systems. Besides a higher birth rate and the white exodus to the suburbs where housing is not generally available to Negroes, the factors creating school segregation include the arrival of nonwhite newcomers who tend to settle in those parts of the city where nonwhites already live. This is due partly to low economic status, partly to a desire to be near friends or relatives, and partly to their inability to find housing elsewhere. An additional factor in some places is the large and disproportionately white enrollment in private and parochial schools. All these factors make it difficult to achieve racial heterogeneity in the public schools even when a school board desires to do so.

In the 16 school systems in the North and West on which the Commission assembled data, the percentage of nonwhite pupils greatly exceeded the proportion of nonwhites in the total population. On the whole, the percentage of minority-group children in the public elementary schools is about double the percentage of nonwhites in the total population.

The proportionate size of the minority group enrollment does not entirely determine the percentage of segregated schools. At the elementary level, Chicago, with the same proportional minority group enrollment as New York, has over 60 percent more segregated schools. Chicago has tenaciously confined its Negro pupils to neighborhood schools, refused to rezone attendance areas on the fringes of the concentrated Negro residential areas, and declined to relax its rules forbidding transfers from area of residence. In contrast, New York City has made strenuous efforts to limit segregation in its schools. Its open enrollment program enables Negro and Puerto Rican pupils to transfer out of schools in which they are enrolled in excessive proportions to predominantly white schools. It also provides transportation for those electing to do so. . . .

Desegregation in the South

While housing patterns create segregation in the North and West, most schools in the South continue to be segregated by official policy. Even in ostensibly desegregated school districts, most schools are still segregated.

There are 6,196 school districts in the 17 Southern and Border States. Of these, 3,052 have both Negro and white students. A total of 979 or 32.1 percent of these biracial districts have policies or practices permitting the admission of Negroes to formerly all-white schools. Yet only 8 percent of the Negro pupils in the South attend schools with white children.

In the fall of 1962, 52 districts were desegregated for the first time. There were 31 in the previous year. Thirteen of the newly desegregated districts acted under court order, although, in many of the others, legal action was pending or threatened.

The Border States (Delaware, Kentucky, Maryland, Missouri, Oklahoma, and West Virginia) and the District of Columbia account for the bulk of desegregation to date. Of the 979 desegregated school districts,

702 lie in the border areas. Similarly, over 251,000 (94.7 percent) of the approximately 265,000 Negro students who attend school with whites in the South do so in the border areas. South Carolina, Alabama, and Mississippi, by contrast, have no Negroes attending school with white students below the college level.

Progress continues to be slow in the South. The Supreme Court's warning that a pace found acceptable for desegregation 9 years ago will not necessarily satisfy the Court today soon may be reflected in lower court rulings. Similar changes may flow from the Court's declaration of June 1963 that "no official transfer plan or provision of which racial segregation is the inevitable consequence may stand under the Fourteenth Amendment."

JUSTICE

The rights of citizens to speak freely, to assemble peaceably, and to petition government for the redress of grievances are guaranteed by the first amendment to the Constitution. These rights are protected against State encroachment by the 14th amendment. Official actions taken to stop recent civil rights protest demonstrations in the name of peace and order often have infringed upon these protected rights.

To determine the extent of these infringements, and to study the dilemma often caused by the need to guarantee private rights while maintaining public order the Commission focused its administration of justice study on five cities where protest demonstrations have taken place. They are Birmingham, Ala.; Cairo, Ill.; Baton Rouge, La.; Jackson, Miss.; and Memphis, Tenn. In its study, the Commission found that existing legal remedies for blocking official interference with legitimate demonstrations are insufficient and that protests against civil rights deprivations are being frustrated. The study also demonstrated that effective legal remedies must be fashioned if unwarranted official interference is not to result in the total suppression of constitutional rights to protest.

During its current term, the Commission also investigated the participation of Negroes in the administration of justice. The Commission found that in many places, Negroes have been discriminated against as lawyers; as law enforcement, court, and prison employees; and as prisoners. The results of this study also are presented in this chapter.

Civil Rights Protests and State Action

On February 1, 1960, four college students in Greensboro, North Carolina, entered a variety store, made several purchases, sat down at the lunch counter, ordered coffee, and were refused service because they were

Negroes. They remained in their seats until the store closed. In the spring and summer of 1960, young people, both white and Negro, participated in similar protests against segregation and discrimination wherever it was to be found. They sat in white libraries, waded at white beaches, and slept in the lobbies of white hotels. Many were arrested for trespassing, disturbing the peace, and disobeying police officers who ordered them off the premises. Thus began the sweeping protest movement against entrenched practices of segregation.

Since the equal protection clause of the 14th amendment prohibits State-enforced segregation, it is clear that convictions under a statute or ordinance requiring segregation cannot be sustained. In general, officials who acted to suppress demonstrations in the cities studied did not attempt to apply such laws directly. But any arrest, even without a conviction, operates as a sanction, since the imprisoned protester still must stay in jail or post bail, retain counsel, and defend himself.

The Supreme Court, following the *School Segregation Cases,* has consistently held that State and local governments may not segregate publicly owned or operated facilities. It has recently held that a municipality may not arrest and prosecute Negroes for peaceably seeking the use of city-owned and -operated facilities. But in both Jackson and Memphis, police arrested protesters seeking desegregated use of public facilities. The charge in most of these cases was breach of the peace or disorderly conduct. In finding the protesters guilty, a city judge in Jackson found that, while they had been orderly, their conduct could have provoked a breach of the peace by others. However, the mere "possibility of disorder by others cannot justify exclusion of persons from a place if they otherwise have a constitutional right (founded upon the Equal Protection Clause) to be present." The exercise of the first amendment freedoms of speech and assembly cannot be abridged "unless shown likely to produce a clear and present danger of a serious substantive evil that rises far above public inconvenience, annoyance, or unrest."

The right to use vehicles and terminal facilities in interstate commerce on a nonsegregated basis is another right that has been established by Federal court decisions and specific orders of the Interstate Commerce Commission. In Baton Rouge, Memphis, Jackson, and Birmingham, when protesters sought to use such facilities, they were arrested. They were charged, not with violation of segregation laws, but with breach of the peace. In Jackson, more than 300 demonstrators were arrested during the 1961 Freedom Rides. Local authorities claimed that they committed a breach of the peace by refusing to obey police commands to leave the interstate bus terminal's segregated waiting rooms. The riders claimed their Federal rights peaceably to seek and obtain unsegregated service as did protesters in the other cities. An early application to the Supreme Court for an injunction to stay the State criminal prosecutions in Jackson was denied. The lengthy route through the Mississippi courts is still being pursued some two and a half years later.

The constitutionality of arrests and prosecutions of those who seek desegregated service at privately owned facilities open to the public has also been questioned. These protests have included lunch counter sit-ins, which have occurred throughout the country and in four of the five cities studied by the Commission. While this type of demonstration has formed only a part of the total civil rights protest movement, it has presented one of the most difficult constitutional problems arising from protest activities. The question these cases raise is whether the arrest and conviction of protesters peacefully seeking such desegregated service represents unlawful "State action" under the 14th amendment.

Having disposed of the first sit-in cases on other grounds, the Supreme Court in May 1963 approached the question in a series of sit-in cases from Greenville, S.C.; New Orleans, Birmingham, and Durham. The protesters had been convicted, not for breach of the peace, but for trespass on the private property of those who operated restaurants and lunch counters. Confronted with an apparent conflict between the proprietors' property rights and the protesters' right to be free from State-enforced segregation, the Court found that State action was involved and reversed the convictions.

The Greenville and Birmingham cases involved ordinances requiring operators of eating places to segregate. Although not directly invoked, these ordinances were found to have left such operators no choice but to segregate. The Court held that the use of the State's criminal processes to arrest and convict the protesters had the effect of enforcing the segregation ordinances and was consequently prohibited State action in violation of the equal protection clause of the 14th amendment. In New Orleans, where there was no law requiring segregation in eating places, the Court ruled that city officials' public statements that attempts to secure desegregated service would not be permitted had the same effect as segregation ordinances.

These decisions have removed virtually all doubt about the validity of trespass convictions in situations such as Birmingham, where there are laws requiring segregated eating facilities. Moreover, the principle of the New Orleans case apparently applies to situations such as the Commission found in Baton Rouge and Jackson, where city officials were publicly committed to using State criminal processes to maintain segregation. But the applicability of the 1963 sit-in decisions to situations such as Cairo is not clear. Here, the voice of the State has clearly spoken for desegregation. The Mayor of Cairo has personally urged proprietors to obey the Illinois law prohibiting discrimination in places of public accommodation. Yet students were arrested for trespass when they sought service at a private restaurant.

Many cities either do not have or have repealed segregation ordinances. Many officials either have never made or have stopped making public statements committing the State to maintenance of segregation. This has brought to the Court the broad question of whether the State has any right to arrest and prosecute protesters for seeking equal access to places of public accommodation.

In these situations, the protesters acted to secure immediate desegregated use of a facility. But different problems may be presented when protesters engage in street demonstrations against discrimination in general. One such incident occurred in March 1961, when 187 Negro students marched on the South Carolina State House to make their grievances known to the public and the legislature, which was then in session. Refusing to disperse, they were arrested and convicted for breach of the peace. Their appeals were decided by the Supreme Court in February 1963. The Court found that the protesters had been orderly, that they had not obstructed pedestrian or vehicular traffic, and that there had been no clear and present threat of violence by bystanders which the police were unable to control. Reversing the convictions, the Court held that "in arresting, convicting, and punishing the petitioners under the circumstances disclosed by this record, South Carolina infringed the petitioners' constitutionally protected rights of free speech, free assembly, and freedom to petition for redress of grievances."

Application of this Supreme Court decision to events in the five cities is difficult because the material facts differ in each case. On many occasions Memphis and Cairo officials did not interfere with mass demonstrations on public streets. Cairo police arrested protesters under an ordinance requiring parade permits which was enacted after the demonstrations started. The Illinois attorney general joined in an NAACP suit challenging the constitutionality of the ordinance. State and local officials and protest leaders later consented to dismissal of the suit on the understanding that the charges against the arrested protesters would be dismissed and the ordinance would not again be invoked against peaceful street demonstrations. Baton Rouge officials did not interfere with mass street demonstrations during the 1960 protests. In 1961, official policy changed. Conduct that had been permitted in 1960 resulted in arrests.

The official policy in both Jackson and Birmingham, throughout the period covered by the Commission's study, was one of suppressing street demonstrations. While police action in each arrest may not have been improper, the total pattern of official action, as indicated by the public statements of city officials, was to maintain segregation and to suppress protests. The police followed that policy and they were usually supported by local prosecutors and courts.

Discrimination in Processes of Justice

Denials of equal protection may arise not only from attempts by officials to enforce segregation but also in the processes of justice when an official treats a person differently because of his color, race, religion, or national origin.

In civil rights demonstrations, the role of the policeman has been significant; his actions often speak for the community. When a policeman acts to deprive a person of his constitutional rights, he violates Federal law. Moreover, police inaction which results in a failure to provide adequate protection to persons asserting their constitutional rights may also constitute a violation of Federal law. When Montgomery police failed to provide protection for the Freedom Riders in 1961, a Federal district judge declared, "The failure of the defendant law enforcement officers to enforce the law in this case clearly amounts to unlawful State action in violation of the Equal Protection Clause of the Fourteenth Amendment."

Testimony at the Commission's Memphis hearings disclosed that none of the protesters there was subjected to physical mistreatment by the police. Nor were there any allegations of lack of police protection for demonstrators. On one occasion in Cairo, protesters complained of police beatings and the use of tear gas. They also charged that State police and sheriff's deputies failed in another instance to protect demonstrators against a crowd of violent whites. Commission investigations found some evidence to support these allegations; however, such instances were not part of a pattern of action by law enforcement officials in those cities.

There have been few complaints of police mistreatment of protesters in Baton Rouge. In fact, a leader of the 1960 protests praised the police for their conduct. But in 1961, students complained of police misconduct in dispersing a protest assembly and of mistreatment of arrested demonstrators by jail guards.

The situation was different in Jackson and Birmingham. There, the Commission found a pattern of police abuse of civil rights protesters. In Jackson, there were continuing police efforts to disperse by force many forms of demonstrations and there was evidence of mistreatment of students, both in the county jail and State penitentiary.

Evidence also showed there was continuing abuse of protesters by Birmingham police. In 1963, dogs, clubs, and firehoses were used to disperse mass demonstrations. Violent reaction by Negroes followed. The reaction was directed not against white bystanders, but against the city police.

Prosecutors claimed that Negro students received the same treatment in the criminal process as anyone else. But in October 1962 the district attorney in Baton Rouge told Commission investigators:

> I'm going to make it just as hard on these outside agitators as I can. And I don't know a judge or official [in Baton Rouge] who doesn't agree with me.

His statement was addressed primarily to the fixing of bail requirements for arrested demonstrators. Discriminatory use of bail requirements raises a question of denial of equal protection.

In neither Memphis nor Birmingham did bail requirements present a serious problem, although the aggregate bond cost was high when mass arrests were made. In Cairo, most students were released on their own recognizance. The 1961 mass arrests of Freedom Riders in Jackson presented a serious bail problem. Surety bonds were required, and exhaustive efforts by protest leaders were unsuccessful in finding a company anywhere in the country to write the bonds. The result was that most of the riders spent extended periods in the county jail and State penitentiary....

Participation in Agencies of Justice

Participation by Negroes in the agencies of justice as police officers, prosecutors, judges, jurors, and other officials and employees has often been prohibited or limited. This exclusion raises equal protection issues; so does segregation of Negroes in justice facilities such as police stations, court houses, jails, and prisons. Such segregation has been widely practiced in many parts of the country. Concerning such practices, the Commission pointed out in its *1961 Report:* "This can hardly contribute to impartiality in the administration of justice or to respect for the agencies of law on the part of those who are excluded."

The Negro protest movement also has highlighted the inequalities suffered by Negro lawyers in the administration of justice. Thousands of demonstrators have required the services of legal counsel. The greatest burden of providing these services has fallen upon local Negro lawyers.

In order to determine whether counsel was available to civil rights protesters and whether their counsel suffered any special difficulties because of involvement in civil rights litigation, the Commission conducted a study based upon a questionnaire survey of 17 Southern and Border States and upon field investigations in the five cities where large-scale protest demonstrations had occurred. Questionnaires were sent to 3,555 lawyers, of whom about one-eighth were Negroes. There were 242 responses from Negro lawyers and 1,081 responses from whites, constituting a total return of 37.2 percent. Among the respondents, only 14 percent (184 lawyers) answered that they had represented Negro clients in civil rights cases within the preceding 8 years. One-third of this group reported having suffered threats of physical violence, loss of clients, or social ostracism as a result.

The Commission's study shows that Negro lawyers have played an active role far out of proportion to their numbers in handling civil rights cases in the South in recent years. Many have suffered reprisals as a result.

In those same States, Negro lawyers have faced difficulty in gaining admission to law schools, impediments to admission to the bar, and severe limitations on their professional association and contacts.

In the five cities where the Commission conducted field investigations, protesters who were arrested and prosecuted were in most cases represented by Negro lawyers. The Commission's survey disclosed that, among the respondents who had taken civil rights cases, 86 percent were Negroes.

Between 1940 and 1960, the number of Negro lawyers in the Southern and Border States increased by 75 percent. Yet, in proportion to the total Negro population, the number is still very small. Several factors appear to contribute to this situation. Until World War II, nearly all of these States not only excluded Negroes from publicly supported law schools, but also failed to establish segregated institutions. They provided funds for a limited number of qualified Negroes to receive their legal education elsewhere, mainly in the North.

Twenty-seven percent of the questionnaire responses from Negro lawyers claimed that "occasionally" or "infrequently" Negroes were excluded from admission to the bar on racial grounds. Most complaints referred to the discriminatory screening of bar examination applicants or to examination grading based upon a racial quota. However, only 6 percent of the white respondents indicated that racial discrimination has been a factor in limiting Negro admissions to the bar. Most of these answers cited inadequate educational and economic backgrounds as the underlying factor.

Most of the Negro lawyers are almost entirely dependent on Negro clientele. The economic position of the rural Negro is such that it is often impossible for a Negro lawyer to subsist professionally in smaller southern towns. Added to this is the problem, related by many of the Negro respondents, that Negro clients often seek out white lawyers because they feel them to be more capable, or because they feel that Negro lawyers are at a disadvantage against a white adversary and before a white judge and jury.

The opportunities for professional contacts and continuing legal education that attend bar association membership appear to be severely limited for Negro lawyers. Except where State bar association membership is a prerequisite to practice, exclusion of Negroes from State and local associations seems to be common throughout the Southern and Border States. Even where Negroes are admitted to membership, they are usually excluded or discouraged from participation in social and educational programs sponsored by the associations.

Negro Employment by Agencies of Justice

To determine the extent of Negro employment in agencies of justice, the Commission sent questionnaires to the chief justice of the State's highest court, to the attorney general, to the superintendent of State police and to the administrators of the State's prison and parole agencies in every State in the Nation. Questionnaires were sent to the court of original criminal jurisdiction, the prosecutor, and the sheriff in each county in the United States with a Negro population of over 5,000. Questionnaires also were sent to police departments in all cities with a Negro population of over 5,000.

Police departments of 124 Southern and Border State cities responded, as did 106 departments in Northern and Western States. The responses show that, on the basis of population proportion, relatively few Negroes are employed in northern and western departments. In southern and border departments, their participation is generally token.

In its study of Negro employment by the county sheriffs' departments the Commission received questionnaire responses from 170 departments in Southern and Border States and from 102 departments in the North and West. The questionnaires disclosed a common practice in the South of assigning Negro sheriff's deputies, as was the case with Negro police officers, to law enforcement duties in segregated areas. Many departments also place limitations on the Negro deputy's authority to apprehend white suspects. Such limitations were found to be almost nonexistent in the North and West.

State police and highway patrols employed almost no Negroes. One Negro officer was reported in the 12 Southern and Border States which responded. There were 33 Negro officers found in 19 Northern and Western States.

The Commission's survey disclosed that Negro employment in county prosecutors' offices throughout the country was extremely limited. In 289 counties in Southern and Border States, only 7 Negro lawyers, 3 investigators, and 2 stenographers were reported. Among the Northern and Western States, 103 prosecutors responded. Their offices employed 35 Negro investigators and 88 secretaries. Twenty-seven counties employed Negro lawyers. Many with substantial Negro populations employed no Negroes in any professional or administrative capacity.

The Department of Justice serves the Federal Government as prosecuting agency. There are U.S. attorneys' offices in each Federal judicial district. Three Negroes were serving as U.S. attorneys. At the close of 1962, 35 of 778 assistant U.S. attorneys were Negroes. Other offices in the Department employed 1,372 attorneys, of whom 34 were Negro. While Negro participation is low, it has increased substantially since 1960.

Negro employment in State courts was rare in the Southern and Border States. No Negro judges or court clerks were reported. Among the positions of jury commissioner, bailiff, and secretary, Negroes occupied 3 percent or fewer of the jobs. For probation officers, the percentage was slightly higher.

In the North and West, Negro employment in State courts was considerably higher. This was especially so in California, Indiana, Iowa, Minnesota, and New Mexico. In probation positions, Negro representation was particularly high.

The Commission also surveyed Negro employment in Federal courts. The Administrative Office of the United States Courts advised that "each court has its own employment practices." In all Federal courts responding from Southern and Border States, no Negro judges or Negro court employees were found with the exceptions of one probation officer in the

Southern District of West Virginia and a few court criers. In courts in the District of Columbia, Negroes served as judges, clerks, secretaries and clerical workers, bailiffs, and probation officers. However, among Federal courts reporting from the North and West, little Negro employment was found.

At State adult correctional institutions in Southern and Border States, Negro employment was rare. Two-thirds of the small number reported served in Maryland. In Arkansas, Alabama, Georgia, Kentucky, Louisiana, Mississippi, Oklahoma, and Tennessee, no Negroes were found in administrative, professional, or clerical positions or as correctional officers. At juvenile institutions—where separate facilities are more often established for each race—Negro employment was considerably higher. Among adult institutions reporting from Northern and Western States, about one-thirtieth of the administrative, professional, clerical, and correctional officer positions were filled by Negroes. Negro employment at juvenile institutions accounted for about 12 percent of the positions tabulated.

Token employment of Negroes also was found at Federal correctional institutions in Southern and Border States. The Commission received data from 15 facilities with 2,390 employees, of whom only 70 were Negro. At 18 Federal institutions in the North and West, Negro employment was slightly lower. Only at the facilities operated by the Bureau of Prisons, the Department of Correction, and the Department of Public Welfare in the District of Columbia was there substantial Negro employment.

Segregation in Facilities

While discrimination exists in employment, segregation occurs in the facilities of justice. Criminal suspects are usually first detained in police department jails or lockups. Of 114 departments in Southern and Border States responding to the Commission survey, 83 percent reported racial segregation in these facilities. In contrast to this were the responses of 105 northern and western departments, 95 percent of which reported no segregation.

Comparable figures were received on segregation in county jails, which are customarily used for the detention of persons awaiting trial or serving short sentences. Of 152 responses from Southern and Border States, 87 percent reported segregated facilities; 83 percent of the respondents in the North and West (99 counties) reported no segregation.

Responses also were received from State adult and juvenile correctional institutions throughout the country. These included reception and assignment centers, prisons, work farms and camps, reformatories and training schools. A total of 145 institutions reported from Southern and Border States. Of these, 93 were completely segregated. Forty-one institutions maintained partial segregation in housing and in one or more other areas such as dining facilities and work details. Only 13 institutions reported no segregation. All of these are in the States of Delaware, Kentucky, Maryland, Missouri, Virginia, and West Virginia. Of 236 institutions reporting from Northern and Western States, 220 were totally desegregated. The remainder segregated living quarters.

As late as 1954, inmates were segregated throughout the Federal correctional system, particularly in the use of living quarters, dining areas, and auditoriums. Today, all Federal institutions are completely desegregated with the exception of a single cell block at the U.S. Penitentiary in Atlanta, where desegregation is underway. Administrators of Federal facilities in the South reported that very few problems attended desegregation and that the process has assisted in rehabilitation.

Clerks of criminal courts of original jurisdiction in the counties surveyed reported on racial segregation in courthouse facilities. In Southern and Border States, courtroom segregation was reported in 17 percent of the returns, waiting room segregation in 14 percent, segregation in jury boxes in 5 percent, and segregation of rest rooms in 63 percent. In responses from counties in the North and West, no racial segregation in any courthouse facilities was reported.

In April 1963, the Supreme Court reversed the conviction of a Negro found guilty of contempt in a Richmond, Va., traffic court for refusing to sit on the side of the courtroom reserved for Negroes. The Court said:

> Such a conviction cannot stand, for it is no longer open to question that a State may not constitutionally require segregation of public facilities. . . . State-compelled segregation in a court of justice is a manifest violation of the State's duty to deny no one the equal protection of its laws.

CHAPTER FOUR

Political Parties
and the Electorate

The political process involves the sources, distribution, and use of power in the state. Needless to say all of the institutions and processes of government relate to this area. This chapter will devote itself to a consideration of the role of political parties and the electoral system in the determination and control of political power.

13. Constitutional Background

Political parties and interest groups have developed outside of the original constitutional framework to channel political power in the community, and as such they deserve special consideration from students of American government. The Constitution was designed to structure power relationships in such a way that the arbitrary exercise of political power would be prevented by any one group or individual. One of the most important concepts held by the framers of the Constitution was that faction, *i.e.*, parties and interest groups, is inherently dangerous to political freedom and stable government. This is evident from *Federalist 10*.

FEDERALIST 10
James Madison

AMONG the numerous advantages promised by a well constructed Union, none deserves to be more accurately developed than its tendency to break and control the violence of faction. The friend of popular governments, never finds himself so much alarmed for their character and fate, as when he contemplates their propensity to this dangerous vice. He will not fail, therefore, to set a due value on any plan which, without violating the principles to which he is attached, provides a proper cure for it. The instability, injustice, and confusion, introduced into the public councils, have, in truth, been the mortal diseases under which popular governments have everywhere perished; as they continue to be the favorite and fruitful topics from which the adversaries to liberty derive their most specious declamations. The valuable improvements made by the American constitutions on the popular models, both ancient and modern, cannot certainly be too much admired; but it would be an unwarrantable partiality, to contend that they have as effectually obviated the danger on this side, as was wished and expected. Complaints are everywhere heard from our most considerate and virtuous citizens, equally the friends of public and private faith, and of public and personal liberty, that our governments are too unstable; that the public good is disregarded in the conflicts of rival parties; and that measures are too often decided, not according to the rules of justice, and the rights of the minor party, but by the superior force of an interested and overbearing majority. However anxiously we may wish that these complaints had no foundation, the evidence of known facts will not permit us to deny that they are in some degree true. It will be found, indeed, on a candid review of our situation, that some of the distresses under which we labor, have been erroneously charged on the operation of our governments; but it will be found, at the same time, that other causes will not alone account for many of our heaviest misfortunes; and, particularly, for that prevailing and increasing distrust of public engagements, and alarm for private rights, which are echoed from one end of the continent to the other. These must be chiefly, if not wholly, effects of the unsteadiness and injustice, with which a factious spirit has tainted our public administrations.

By a faction, I understand a number of citizens, whether amounting to a majority or minority of the whole, who are united and actuated by some common impulse of passion, or of interest, adverse to the rights of other citizens, or to the permanent and aggregate interest of the community.

There are two methods of curing the mischiefs of faction: The one, by removing its causes; the other, by controlling its effects.

There are again two methods of removing the causes of faction: the one, by destroying the liberty which is essential to its existence; the other, by giving to every citizen the same opinions, the same passions, and the same interests.

It could never be more truly said, that of the first remedy, that it was worse than the disease. Liberty is to faction what air is to fire, an aliment, without which it instantly expires. But it could not be a less folly to abolish liberty, which is essential to political life because it nourishes faction, than it would be to wish the annihilation of air, which is essential to animal life, because it imparts to fire its destructive agency.

The second expedient is as impracticable, as the first would be unwise. As long as the reason of man continues fallible, and he is at liberty to exercise it, different opinions will be formed. As long as the connection subsists between his reason and his self-love, his opinions and his passions will have a reciprocal influence on each other; and the former will be objects to which the latter will attach themselves. The diversity in the faculties of men, from which the rights of property originate, is not less an insuperable obstacle to a uniformity of interests. The protection of those faculties is the first object of government. From the protection of different and unequal faculties of acquiring property, the possession of different degrees and kinds of property immediately results; and from the influence of these on the sentiments and views of the respective proprietors, ensues a division of the society into different interests and parties.

The latent causes of faction are thus sown in the nature of man; and we see them everywhere brought into different degrees of activity, according to the different circumstances of civil society. A zeal for different opinions concerning religion, concerning government, and many other points, as well of speculation as of practice; an attachment to different leaders, ambitiously contending for pre-eminence and power; or to persons of other descriptions, whose fortunes have been interesting to the human passions, have, in turn, divided mankind into parties, inflamed them with mutual animosity, and rendered them much more disposed to vex and oppress each other, than to co-operate for their common good. So strong is this propensity of mankind, to fall into mutual animosities, that where no substantial occasion presents itself, the most frivolous and fanciful distinctions have been sufficient to kindle their unfriendly passions, and excite their most violent conflicts. But the most common and durable source of factions has been the various and unequal distribution of property. Those who hold, and those who are without property, have ever formed distinct interests in society. Those who are creditors, and those who are debtors, fall under a like discrimination. A landed interest, a manufacturing interest, a mercantile interest, a moneyed interest, with many lesser interests, grow up of necessity in civilized nations, and divide them into different classes, actuated by different sentiments and views.

The regulation of these various and interfering interests forms the principal task of modern legislation, and involves the spirit of party and faction in the necessary and ordinary operations of government.

No man is allowed to be a judge in his own cause; because his interest will certainly bias his judgment, and, not improbably, corrupt his integrity. With equal, nay, with greater reason, a body of men are unfit to be both judges and parties at the same time; yet what are many of the most important acts of legislation, but so many judicial determinations, not indeed concerning the rights of single persons, but concerning the rights of large bodies of citizens? And what are the different classes of legislators, but advocates and parties to the causes which they determine? Is a law proposed concerning private debts? It is a question to which the creditors are parties on one side, and the debtors on the other. Justice ought to hold the balance between them. Yet the parties are, and must be, themselves the judges; and the most numerous party, or, in other words, the most powerful faction, must be expected to prevail. Shall domestic manufactures be encouraged, and in what degree, by restrictions on foreign manufactures? are questions which would be differently decided by the landed and the manufacturing classes; and probably by neither with a sole regard to justice and the public good. . . .

It is in vain to say, that enlightened statesmen will be able to adjust these clashing interests, and render them all subservient to the public good. Enlightened statesmen will not always be at the helm; nor, in many cases, can such an adjustment be made at all, without taking into view indirect and remote considerations, which will rarely prevail over the immediate interest which one party may find in disregarding the rights of another, or the good of the whole.

The inference to which we are brought is, that the *causes* of faction cannot be removed; and that relief is only to be sought in the means of controlling its *effects*.

If a faction consists of less than a majority, relief is supplied by the republican principle, which enables the majority to defeat its sinister views, by regular vote. It may clog the administration, it may convulse the society; but it will be unable to execute and mask its violence under the forms of the constitution. When a majority is included in a faction, the form of popular government, on the other hand, enables it to sacrifice to its ruling passion or interest, both the public good and the rights of other citizens. To secure the public good, and private rights, against the danger of such a faction, and at the same time to preserve the spirit and the form of popular government, is then the great object to which our inquiries are directed. Let me add, that it is the great desideratum, by which alone this form of government can be rescued from the opprobrium under which it has so long labored, and be recommended to the esteem and adoption of mankind.

By what means is this object attainable? Evidently by one of two only. Either the existence of the same passion or interest in a majority, at the same time must be prevented; or the majority, having such coexistent passion or interest, must be rendered, by their number and local situation, unable to concert and carry into effect schemes of oppression. If the impulse and the opportunity be suffered to coincide, we well know, that neither moral nor religious motives can be relied on as an adequate control. They are not found to be such on the injustice and violence of individuals, and lose their efficacy in proportion to the number combined together; that is, in proportion as their efficacy becomes needful.

From this view of the subject, it may be concluded, that a pure democracy, by which I mean a society consisting of a small number of citizens, who assemble and administer the government in person, can admit of no cure from the mischiefs of faction. A common passion or interest will, in almost every case, be felt by a majority of the whole; a communication and concert, results from the form of government itself; and there is nothing to check the inducements to sacrifice the weaker party, or an obnoxious individual. Hence it is, that such democracies have ever been spectacles of turbulence and contention; have ever been found incompatible with personal security, or the rights of property; and have, in general, been as short in their lives, as they have been violent in their deaths. Theoretic politicians, who have patronized this species of government, have erroneously supposed that by reducing mankind to a perfect equality in their political rights, they would, at the same time, be perfectly equalized and assimilated in their possessions, their opinions, and their passions.

A republic, by which I mean a government in which the scheme of representation takes place, opens a different prospect, and promises the cure for which we are seeking. Let us examine the points in which it varies from pure democracy, and we shall comprehend both the nature of the cure and the efficacy which it must derive from the union.

The two great points of difference, between a democracy and a republic, are, first, the delegation of the government, in the latter, to a small number of citizens elected by the rest; secondly, the greater number of citizens, and greater sphere of country, over which the latter may be extended.

The effect of the first difference is, on the one hand, to refine and enlarge the public views, by passing them through the medium of a chosen body of citizens, whose wisdom may best discern the true interest of their country, and whose patriotism and love of justice, will be least likely to sacrifice it to temporary or partial considerations. Under such a regulation, it may well happen, that the public voice, pronounced by the representatives of the people, will be more consonant to the public good, than if pronounced by the people themselves, convened for the purpose. On the other hand, the effect may be inverted. Men of factious tempers, of local prejudices, or of sinister designs, may by intrigue, by corruption, or by other means, first obtain the suffrages, and then betray the interests of the people. The question resulting is, whether small or extensive republics are most favorable to the election of proper guardians of the public weal; and it is clearly decided in favor of the latter by two obvious considerations.

In the first place, it is to be remarked, that however small the republic may be, the representatives must be raised to a certain number, in order to guard against the cabals of a few; and that however large it may be, they must be limited to a certain number, in order to guard against the confusion of a multitude. Hence, the number of representatives in the two cases not being in proportion to that of the constituents, and being proportionally greatest in the small republic, it follows that if the proportion of fit characters be not less in the large than in the small republic, the former will present a greater option, and consequently a greater probability of a fit choice.

In the next place, as each representative will be chosen by a greater number of citizens in the large than in the small republic, it will be more difficult for unworthy candidates to practice with success the vicious arts, by which elections are too often carried; and the suffrages of the people being more free, will be more likely to center in men who possess the most attractive merit, and the most diffusive and established characters. . . .

The other point of difference is, the greater number of citizens, and extent of territory, which may be brought within the compass of republican, than of democratic government; and it is this circumstance principally which renders factious combinations less to be dreaded in the former, than in the latter. The smaller the society, the fewer probably will be the distinct parties and interests composing it; the fewer the distinct parties and interests, the more frequently will a majority be found of the same party; and the smaller the number of individuals composing a majority, and the smaller the compass within which they are placed, the more easily will they concert and execute their plans of oppression. Extend the sphere, and you take in a greater variety of parties and interests; you make it less probable that a majority of the whole will have a common motive to invade the rights of other citizens; or if such a common motive exists, it will be more difficult for all who feel it to discover their own strength, and to act in unison with each other. . . .

Hence, it clearly appears, that the same advantage, which a republic has over a democracy, in controlling the effects of faction, is enjoyed by a large over a small republic—is enjoyed by the union over the states composing it. Does this advantage consist in the substitution of representatives, whose enlightened views and virtuous sentiments render them superior to local prejudices, and to schemes of injustice? It will not be denied, that the representation of the union will be most likely to possess these requisite endowments. Does it consist in the greater security afforded by a greater variety of parties, against the event of any one party being able to outnumber and oppress the rest? In an equal degree does the increased variety of parties, comprised within the union, increase this security? Does it, in fine, consist in the greater obstacles opposed to the concert and accomplishment of the secret wishes of an unjust and interested majority? Here, again, the extent of the union gives it the most palpable advantage.

The influence of factious leaders may kindle a flame within their particular states, but will be unable to spread a general conflagration through the other states; a religious sect may degenerate into a political faction in a part of the confederacy; but the variety of sects dispersed over the entire face of it, must secure the national councils against any danger from that source; a rage for paper money, for an abolition of debts, for an equal division of property, or for any other improper or wicked project, will be less apt to pervade the whole body of the union, than a particular member of it; in the same proportion as such a malady is more likely to taint a particular county or district, than an entire state.

In the extent and proper structure of the union, therefore, we behold a republican remedy for the diseases most incident to republican government. And according to the degree of pleasure and pride we feel in being republicans, ought to be our zeal in cherishing the spirit, and supporting the character of Federalists.

The following selection is taken from E. E. Schattschneider's well-known treatise, *Party Government*. In this material he examines the implications of *Federalist 10* and counter-arguments to the propositions stated by Madison, both with respect to political parties and with regard to interest groups.

PARTY GOVERNMENT
E. E. Schattschneider*

THE Convention at Philadelphia produced a constitution with a dual attitude: it was proparty in one sense and antiparty in another. The authors of the Constitution refused to suppress the parties by destroying the fundamental liberties in which parties originate. They or their immediate successors accepted amendments that guaranteed civil rights and thus established a system of party tolerance, *i.e.,* the right to agitate and to organize. This is the proparty aspect of the system. On the other hand, the authors of the Constitution set up an elaborate division and balance of powers within an intricate governmental structure designed to make parties ineffective. It was hoped that the parties would lose and exhaust themselves in futile attempts to fight their way through the labyrinthine framework of the government, much as an attacking army is expected to spend itself against the defensive works of a fortress. This is the antiparty part of the constitutional scheme. To quote Madison, the "great object" of the Constitution was "to preserve the public good and private rights against the danger of such a faction [party] and at the same time to preserve the spirit and form of popular government."

In Madison's mind the difference between an autocracy and a free republic seems to have been largely a matter of the precise point at which parties are stopped by the government. In an autocracy parties are controlled (suppressed) at the source; in a republic parties are tolerated but are invited to strangle themselves in the machinery of government. The result in either case is much the same, sooner or later the government checks the parties but *never do the parties control the government.* Madison was perfectly definite and unmistakable in his disapproval of party government as distinguished from party tolerance. In the opinion

---

* From *Party Government,* by E. E. Schattschneider. Copyright © 1942, by E. E. Schattschneider. Quoted with the permission of Holt, Rinehart and Winston, Inc., publishers.

of Madison, parties were intrinsically bad, and the sole issue for discussion was the means by which bad parties might be prevented from becoming dangerous. What never seems to have occurred to the authors of the Constitution, however, is that parties might be *used* as beneficent instruments of popular government. It is at this point that the distinction between the modern and the antique attitude is made.

The offspring of this combination of ideas was a constitutional system having conflicting tendencies. The Constitution made the rise of parties inevitable yet was incompatible with party government. This scheme, in spite of its subtlety, involved a miscalculation. Political parties refused to be content with the role assigned to them. The vigor and enterprise of the parties have therefore made American political history the story of the unhappy marriage of the parties and the Constitution, a remarkable variation of the case of the irresistible force and the immovable object, which in this instance have been compelled to live together in a permanent partnership. . . .

The Raw Materials of Politics

People who write about interests sometimes seem to assume that all interests are special and exclusive, setting up as a result of this assumption a dichotomy in which the interests on the one side are perpetually opposed to the public welfare on the other side. But there are common interests as well as special interests, and common interests resemble special interests in that they are apt to influence political behavior. The raw materials of politics are not all antisocial. Alongside of Madison's statement that differences in wealth are the most durable causes of faction there should be placed a corollary that the common possessions of the people are the most durable cause of unity. To assume that people have merely conflicting interests and nothing else is to invent a political nightmare that has only a superficial relation to reality. The body of agreement underlying the conflicts of a modern society ought to be sufficient to sustain the social order provided only that the common interests supporting this unity are mobilized. Moreover, not all differences of interests are durable causes of conflict. Nothing is apt to be more perishable than a political issue. In the democratic process, the nation moves from controversy to agreement to forgetfulness; politics is not a futile exercise like football, forever played back and forth over the same ground. The government creates and destroys interests at every turn.

There are, in addition, powerful factors inhibiting the unlimited pursuit of special aims by any organized minority. To assume that minorities will stop at nothing to get what they want is to postulate a degree of unanimity and concentration within these groups that does not often exist in real life. If every individual were capable of having only one interest to the exclusion of all others, it might be possible to form dangerous unions of monomaniacs who would go to great extremes to attain their objectives. In fact, however, people have many interests leading to a dispersion of drives certain to destroy some of the unanimity and concentration of any group. How many interests can an individual have? Enough to make it extremely unlikely that any two individuals will have the same combination of interests. Anyone who has ever tried to promote an association of people having some special interest in common will realize, first, that there are marked differences of enthusiasm within the group and, second, that interests compete with interests for the attention and enthusiasm of every individual. Every organized special interest consists of a group of busy, distracted individuals held together by the efforts of a handful of specialists and enthusiasts who sacrifice other matters in order to concentrate on one. The notion of resolute and unanimous minorities on the point of violence is largely the invention of paid lobbyists and press agents.

The result of the fact that every individual is torn by the diversity of his own interests, the fact that he is a member of many groups, is *the law of the imperfect political mobilization of interests*. That is, it has never been possible to mobilize any interest 100 per cent. . . .

It is only another way of saying the same thing to state that conflicts of interests are not cumulative. If it were true that the dividing line in every conflict (or in all major conflicts) split the community identically in each case so that individuals who are opposed on one issue would be opposed to each other on all other issues also, while individuals who joined hands on one occasion would find themselves on the same side on all issues, always opposed to the same combination of antagonists, the cleavage created by the cumulative effect of these divisions would be fatal. But actually conflicts are not cumulative in this way. In real life the divisions are not so clearly marked, and the alignment of people according to interests requires an enormous shuffling back and forth from one side to the other, tending to dissipate the tensions created.

In view of the fact, therefore, (1) that there are many interests, including a great body of common interests, (2) that the government pursues a multiplicity of policies and creates and destroys interests in the process, (3) that each individual is capable of having many interests, (4) that interests cannot be mobilized perfectly, and (5) that conflicts

among interests are not cumulative, it seems reasonable to suppose that
the government is not the captive of blind forces from which there is no
escape. There is nothing wrong about the raw materials of politics. ✑

14. The Function and Organization of Parties

The preceding material provides a useful introduction both to parties and
to interest groups. It is indicative, in part, of the constitutional and political frame of reference within which these institutions should be examined.

In the following selection Clinton Rossiter, a distinguished commen-
tator on the American scene, discusses the functions of American political
parties. It will become evident to the student that although the Constitution was framed in an atmosphere of distrust of parties they are an integral
part of the democratic process.

THE FUNCTIONS OF AMERICAN PARTIES

*Clinton Rossiter**

Parties, it could be argued, exist primarily to serve the interests of the
men who lead or support them. They are justified by their fruits, by
which I mean the fruits that are showered on the leaders in the form
of power and on the supporters in the form of favors. This, however, is
a crude and narrow view of the role of parties in our society; for whatever they may have been in their beginnings, parties are now public institutions rather than private preserves. They stand closer to Congress
and the courts than they do, say, to the American Legion or General
Motors or the A.F.L.–C.I.O. on the spectrum of social organization that
runs from the very private to the totally official. They are justified by
their functions, by which I mean functions that are performed as services
to the entire nation. We tolerate and even celebrate their existence because they do things for us in the public realm that would otherwise be
done poorly or not at all.

Let us turn now to look at our parties in this light. Let us describe
the political and social functions of any party in any democracy, and see

* From *Parties and Politics in America,* by Clinton Rossiter. Copyright ©
1960, by Cornell University. Reprinted with the permission of the author
and the publisher, Cornell University Press.

how well our particular parties have performed each of these functions in our peculiar democracy. Let us see, too, if there are any special "characteristically American" functions that they have been called upon to perform or, more accurately, have performed without knowing it. . . .

The primary function of a political party in a democracy such as ours is to control and direct the struggle for power. From this function all others derive naturally. I trust that no apologies need be made for calling attention to the fact that the political process in a free country is essentially a conflict, limited and regularized but nonetheless relentless, among groups of men who have contradictory interests and more or less mutually exclusive hopes of securing them. . . .

It is one of the aspirations of democracy to bring this struggle as much as possible into the open. It is the great purpose of political parties, the handmaidens of democracy, to bring the struggle under control: to institutionalize it with organization, to channel it through nominations and elections, to publicize it by means of platforms and appeals, above all to stabilize it in the form of that traditional quadrille in which the Ins and the Outs change places from time to time on a signal from the voters. The parties did not create the struggle for power; it would go on merrily without them. It would go on, however, much less purposefully and effectively and openly, and we might well be more grateful to our own parties for their modest efforts to bring under benevolent control the eternal conflict of interests described by Madison in *The Federalist*, no. 10. . . .

The first of what we might call the subsidiary functions of a party in a democracy (subsidiary, that is, to the great, inclusive function we have just noted) is to act as an immense personnel agency. Constitutions make frugal provision for the election or appointment of persons to high office, but they extend no aid at all to those persons in and out of government who must act as recruiters. Statutes and ordinances bloom in profusion to create the rules and rewards of a civil service, but they offer no guaranty that the men on top of the permanent bureaucracy will be like-minded enough to give it a sense of cohesion or alert enough to the needs of the public to give it a sense of direction.

This is exactly where parties enter the picture decisively and why, all things considered, we could hardly do without them. Willingly and indeed eagerly they set up and operate the machinery that places men and women in public office, and they do it at four key points: *nominations,* for they are organized to do the preliminary sifting of aspirants to elective office, or, if necessary, to go out and recruit them actively;

campaigns, for they make known to the voting public the credentials and promises of the narrowed list of candidates; *elections,* for they can provide (in bulk and at small cost) the swarm of citizens needed to man the polls and count the votes; and *appointments,* for they are no less eager to assist in the selective process than they are in the elective process. Indeed, they can come up even more quickly with a reasonably qualified candidate for appointment as Secretary of State or district attorney or recorder of deeds than with an equally qualified candidate for election as President or assemblyman or county coroner. . . .

How would we ever get through the process of electing a Congress if the parties did not take over the primaries and elections? How would the President ever find candidates for several thousand offices a year if his party's informal patronage machinery were not quick with suggestions? How would we go about filling the 750,000 (give or take 100,000) elective offices in the United States if we were a strictly nonpartisan people? If we do not get as many first-rate men as we should in Congress and the administration, in state legislatures and school boards, the blame must be laid at the doors of the people with their antipolitical mores and not of the politicians with their vulgar methods. The latter, after all, stay in business by pleasing the former, and up to now they seem to have pleased us well enough. . . .

Parties can also serve as important sources of public policy. They have no monopoly of this function, to be sure, nor should they in the kind of pluralistic society we identify with democracy. The great and small policies by which we live emerged first as special pleadings of an infinite variety of groups and persons, and we should be happy to live in a society in which organizations like N.A.M. or N.A.A.C.P. and men like Walter Lippmann or Bernard Baruch come up constantly with new proposals for our consideration. Yet the parties—and in this instance I include third parties—are perhaps best fitted of all agencies to convert formless hopes or frustrations into proposals that can be understood, debated, and, if found appealing, approved by the people. Because they are the only truly national, multi-interest, broadly based organizations active in our society (the only ones, indeed, that we can permit to be active), they are uniquely situated to originate policies themselves or to broaden the special pleadings of other men and groups. Their policies, moreover, are likely to be a little more realistic than those that emerge from the paid researches of interest groups, for any one policy must be fitted with dozens of others into a full program for governing the nation.

Thanks to the fuzzy nature of our political system, the major parties have not been especially effective in performing this function. In the words of the Committee on Political Parties of the American Political Science Association, "the American two-party system has shown little propensity for evolving original or creative ideas about public policy; it has even been rather sluggish in responding to such ideas in the public interest." The platforms of the parties, which are presumably the most eloquent statements they can make of their current intentions, have never been noted for originality or clarity. One cannot fail to be impressed by some of the reports of the Democratic Advisory Council or by the Report of the Republican Committee on Program and Progress, *Decisions for a Better America,* issued in September 1959, yet one is struck by the scarcity of concrete proposals in all these reports and bound to wonder if the members of these committees really speak with the voice of authority. Yet the remembrance of Wilson's New Freedom and Roosevelt's New Deal should be enough to convince us that parties can originate policies, and that their policies, unlike those of most interest groups, can cut a broad swath through American life....

The point at which our parties may indeed have failed us in this matter of policies is not in originating or formulating or advertising them, but in converting them into the hard coin of purposeful law and skillful administration. Before we go into that problem, however, we must take note of the function that makes it possible and even mandatory for parties in a democracy to put their policies into effect: the organization and operation of government. Within every true party there exists . . . a governmental party, a hard core of office-holders whose duty to the community goes beyond mere electioneering or even formulating policies. If this party has been victorious in the most recent election, it is expected to organize the legislative and executive branches and to run them with the aid of the appeals and disciplines of party loyalty. . . . A political organization unwilling to govern is not, by any definition, a party. . . .

If we have few complaints about the technical competence with which our majority parties organize and operate the agencies of government, we have many, probably more than any other people in the democratic world, about the skill and dedication they bring to the process of making their own policies the policies of city or state or nation; and that, as I have already indicated, is one of the basic functions of a party in a democracy: to make concrete promises to the electorate and then, if invited by the electorate to govern, to make good on those promises. . . . If parties

are not expected or encouraged to make good on their reasonable promises, then other groups less open in operation and accountable in fact—
blocs and interest groups and loose coalitions of lobby-ridden legislators
—will assume the authority to make public policy.

The last of what we might call the political functions of parties in
a democracy is one that a party does not choose happily yet must accept
willingly if the burden is thrust upon it. This is the delicate function,
so necessary to democracy and so incomprehensible to autocracy, of "loyal
opposition." . . . They must oppose the proposals of the majority, develop alternative proposals for the electorate to consider at the next
election, and keep a close watch on those who are executing the laws
under the direction of the majority party. . . .

American parties have had perhaps more success in opposition than in
governing, which is a revealing commentary on the nature of our political system. In fact, it often seems that American politicians are happier
out of power than in it. Like the great Constitution under which we live
serenely, our political instinct seems to prefer restraint to power and
delay to action. . . .

To this list of the political functions of parties in a democracy we
can add three others that might more accurately be described as social,
since in performing them parties serve men in their roles as social rather
than political animals. First, parties are important agencies in the educational process. The citizens of a free country must be instructed in the
practices of democracy and kept informed on the issues of their times,
not merely to become more forceful agents of public opinion and more
skillful voters, but also to live more satisfying lives. Once they have
finished the last stage of their formal education, they must rely on a bat-
tery of informal instruments ranging from Sunday afternoon television
to word of mouth. Political parties are at best crude instruments of adult
education, yet they can do much to compel study and discussion of important problems. . . .

Next, the parties serve a useful social purpose in acting as buffers
and adjusters between individuals and society, especially as the latter in-
trudes into the lives of ordinary persons in the shape of impersonal political authority. . . .

. . . [T]he parties are still important dispensers of those aids, favors,
and immunities (for example, from prosecution of father for peddling
without a license or son for breaking windows) that make it possible
for men and women to live reasonably confident lives in a harsh environment. If poor Negroes in Atlantic City no longer need to be given

coal, they do need help in obtaining unemployment compensation with which to buy coal. The more penetrating and complicated the power of government becomes, the more demand there is for skilled "adjusters," who might as well be politicians as priests or social workers. There is, of course, a seamy side to this function; politicians contribute more than their fair share to the corruptions and injustices of American life, in the country as well as in the city. Yet the fact that a function is performed corruptly is no decisive argument against its being performed in the first place. . . . The lives of millions of Americans would have been much harder to bear if the parties had not done their work as agencies of social welfare.

Finally, parties serve a symbolic function—or should we start from the other direction and call it psychological?—by providing an object, large and friendly and often exciting, to which men can extend allegiance. Graham Wallas, in his memorable study of *Human Nature in Politics,* was perhaps the first observer to isolate and examine this function. Having taken note of the multitude of voters and of the physical inability of any one voter to deal with more than a few men and ideas, he went on: "Something is required simpler and more permanent, something which can be loved and trusted, and which can be recognized at successive elections as being the same thing that was loved and trusted before; and a party is such a thing." . . .

Although parties perform, as Rossiter suggests, many functions apart from that of formulating and implementing public policy, many political scientists insist that the policy function is of overriding significance. These observers feel that in a two-party system (and they all support the concept of a two-party system as the only effective democratic party system) each party should present clear-cut alternative policies to the electorate, and to make such alternatives meaningful these parties must have the power, once elected, to implement their programs. In this way parties bridge the gap between the people and their government, and they become the principal democratic instruments in a political system by enabling the people, albeit in a limited way, to participate in governmental policy formulation through exercising the power of choice at the polls. The constitutional framework is one factor which has prevented the achievement of effective party government in this sense while limiting the "evils" of faction in accordance with Madison's predictions in *Federalist 10.* Stephen K. Bailey addresses himself to this area of concern in the following selection.

THE CONDITION OF OUR NATIONAL POLITICAL PARTIES

*Stephen K. Bailey**

THE American government today suffers from three weaknesses:

1. Its difficulty in generating sustained political power.

2. Its difficulty in developing a flow of imaginative, informed, consistent and power-related responses to pressing national and world issues.

3. Its difficulty in making policy truly accountable to a national popular majority.

These are serious defects, not only because they interfere with wise and coherent governing in these dangerous days, but because they undermine the faith of the citizen in the reality or even the possibility of responsible government.

The temptation to blame all this on the President, the 22nd Amendment, the split election of 1956 . . . is easy—and perhaps justified. But the defects are not new. Occasionally, in the past, they have been masked by brilliant presidential leadership in times of crisis or by the virtuosity of congressional leaders in times of presidential ineptitude. But the underlying defects have not disappeared. Nor, in spite of the hopes of a few recent writers, are they going to be overcome by countervailing pressure groups or by the expertness, decency, and continuity in office of civilian and military career officials, important as these factors are in the conduct of free and effective government.

V. O. Key sounds not a hopeful but an ominous note when he writes: "Representative bodies, the institutional embodiment of democratic ideology, have by the compelling force of events lost both power and prestige. Their role in the initiation of public policy has been diminished by losses to pressure groups and administrative agencies; their authority to decide many issues has, of necessity, been delegated to the administrative services. They have been driven towards a role of futile and uninformed criticism, at its worst motivated either by partisan or picayune considerations."

Even if we assume that the work of modern government is so technical and complex that enormous discretion must be lodged in the hands of experts, their capacity to act steadily in the public interest depends upon the effectiveness of the very institutions whose influence is threatened

* Publication sponsored by the Fund for the Republic, 1959.

by the expert mind. This dilemma will continue until we recognize that our representative institutions invite disuse and denigration because their structure is inadequate to perform the functions required of them. It is increasingly obvious that there are innovative, integrative, and perhaps sacrificial tasks ahead for which our government is not institutionally equipped.

Is Leadership the Basic Issue?

To say that we need a new kind of political leadership may be true, but it begs the question. Where and how does political leadership arise in the United States? Who selects presidential and congressional candidates? How can the process of selection be improved? How can leadership be sustained? How can first-class political executives be found to run our great public departments? Why is their present tenure so ephemeral? By what means can presidential and congressional purposes be brought into a working relationship? And why cannot leadership be held more fully accountable to the desires of popular majorities?

All of these questions are related to the structural handicaps under which the American government now operates. At first glance, the problem seems to be constitutional—and in part it is. But the only two structural faults of the Constitution which really get in the way of responsible power in the national government are the 22nd Amendment, which limits the President to two terms, and the provisions for staggered elections. The only two constitutional reforms that this paper will suggest are the repeal of the 22nd Amendment and changes in the term of Members of the House from two to four years and of United States Senators from six to eight years (half the Senate coming up every four years at the same time as the presidential elections). The real problem is *political*. If our *political* institutions can be modernized by certain changes in statutory law and in political party rules, the old problems associated with separation of powers, checks and balances, and federalism would, it seems probable, largely disappear.

The root of the weakness is that while the two national parties for years have genuinely competed for the Presidency they have not made a similar effort in the election of United States Senators and Members of the House of Representatives. Nor have they been of sufficient help to the President and the Congress in providing candidates of high quality for the grand patronage of departmental and agency direction. So long as we lack strong national parties operating as catalysts in the Congress, the executive branch, and the national government as a whole, and between the national government and state and local governments, power will continue to be dangerously diffused or, perhaps what is worse, will whipsaw between diffusion and presidential dictatorship.

The Natural Party Distinctions

Contrary to the view of many writers, the parties do not need to be strongly ideological or even strongly programmatic—that is, beholden to comprehensive and distinct sets of policies—in order to accomplish the kind of re-alignment of the party system that would stabilize the national power and help to make it responsible. There are vast areas of overlap in the rather vague programmatic shadows that our two great parties cast over the nation—and this is as it should be if consensus is to continue in the making of public policy and in the administration of foreign policy.

But the centers of gravity of the two parties are quite distinct. The Democratic party basically is a party of innovation, with a "pro-government" bias. The Republican party is an essentially "consolidating" party with a limited-government bias. The distinction has become blurred in the last two generations, largely because of the extreme economic and social conservatism of one-party areas in the South—a conservatism which has been reflected in the Congress through its seniority rules and some other carefully contrived rules and myths. But now, the peculiar condition which has smudged party images for so long is on its way out. The economic base of the solid South has shifted monumentally in the past fifteen years; one-party areas across the land are on the wane; the northern migration of the Negro is having vast political consequences.

Political reform does not include making the parties any more ideological than they are now. It does include making them competitive across the nation, allowing them to appeal to the natural ideological divisions within the population and within us as individuals. The stumbling block in this task is that neither party has a sufficiently unified structure to enable it to dramatize its program around its ideology; neither has the power, even if it had the right structure, to carry out the program; neither has sufficiently clear and unambiguous lines of political accountability running to the voters.

The Results of Party Diffusion

The structural limitations of the parties have grave consequences. First, they virtually insure a government by fits-and-starts. Some historians claim that the United States was wise in having rejected the League of

Nations; but few would claim that the *process* by which the League was rejected was a rational way of arriving at a major foreign policy decision. In more recent times presidential requests for an adequate United States Information Agency budget have been listened to one year and ignored the next by the House Appropriations Committee. As a result, cultural officers abroad have had to spend much of their time hiring and firing—inflating and deflating programs like an accordion. This has made us look ridiculous as a nation, and has also made it extremely difficult for a coherent information program to develop as a vital element in our foreign policy. The some is true of foreign economic aid.

Spasms in domestic policy have been equally obvious and equally unsettling. The executive department and the Congress have been unable to agree on any coordinated methods of applying the kind of devices needed to stabilize the economy and promote the goals of the Employment Act of 1946. Similar fits and starts have been noticeable in defense policy, atomic energy policy, welfare policy, and conservation policy. They have been quite as apparent when the Presidency and both Houses of Congress have been in one party as when the control of the government has been divided.

The second consequence of the structural limitations of the parties has been the lack of rationality and consistency in the substance of much public policy. In Paul Appleby's phrase, in this day and age someone or something has to "make a mesh of things." In a world in which, for example, the indiscriminate dumping of rice on the world market in order to ease a temporary glut in Louisiana could cost us the friendship of Burma, there are huge dangers in having unlinked centers of power making their own policy for the nation. And yet, parochial groups in the Congress (often in league with sections of the executive branch and with outside pressure groups) still carry on an inordinate amount of power.

The third consequence of the absence of coherent party machinery truly responsive to popular majorities is that congressional compromise tends to fall with considerable regularity on the side of minority rather than majority interests. Committee chairmen from "safe," and often sparsely populated, one-party states and districts; the minority-weighted bipartisan rules committee; and the myths, rules, and influence structure which enable congressional leaders to ignore demands for greater majority representation in policy decisions—all these combine to inflate the power of minority interests at the expense of the national popular majority. . . . The bills and policies introduced or supported by Senators and Congressmen from the areas of greatest popular concentration in America have almost without exception been substantially watered down according to the predilections and petitions of powerful minority interests in and out of the Congress.

This is government by tollgate. It leads directly to consequence four: the increasing danger of public cynicism and apathy toward the Congress, partly because its power is too diffuse or too subtle to comprehend; partly because when the power *is* clearly identifiable it seems to work more consistently for minorities than for the majority.

The last and by no means the least important consequence stemming from the absence of a unified party structure is that desperately needed criticism of both domestic and foreign policy is dissipated and discouraged. There is no effective vehicle for responsible opposition criticism of programs; there is no machinery for anticipating the implications of social changes and their effects on policy. With the help of a huge and in part brilliant staff, Members of Congress may fill the air and the *Congressional Record* with daring solutions to our dilemmas. But without some sort of party sanction, these ideas are worth little more than an inch or two in *The New York Times.*

In sum, the absence of effective party machinery in each House, and in the government generally, means that policy is frequently developed by an infinitely intricate system of barter and legerdemain.

Some defenders of America's traditional disorder have discounted the dangers to policy-making of these intermittencies and irresponsibilities. They argue that our survival suggests that presidential leadership and a congressional desire to cooperate during periods of crisis can save us in the future as they have in the past; that the thermidor between crises allows the divergences in our society to have their day without being subject to the tyranny of a transient numerical majority; and that the accepted American tradition of government by extraordinary or "concurrent" majorities has not stopped innovation or social criticism, it has only slowed change, and in the process has insured a healthy unity behind public policy.

In relation to the past, these may be strong arguments. But are they addressed to a world of big bureaucracies, sustained cold wars, and chronic international and domestic crises? Are there any longer identifiable periods between crises? As long as the frontier was open and the spirit of laissez faire encouraged political parties to be barriers against government action, anarchy in program and uncontrolled shifts in power within the national government were of little consequence. For many years the parties were anti-governmental vehicles, so to speak, minimizing public policy and fencing off large sections of the population and of the domain for private exploitation and private dreams. But we are now in a different world....

The Prophets

For three quarters of a century America has heard warnings from a variety of distinguished political prophets about its governmental weaknesses. Whether their solution has been constitutional revision or political revision, they have all agreed about the limitations of our governing instruments. Starting with Woodrow Wilson ... criticism has been directed at a single issue: the difficulties of achieving sustained and responsible political power adequate to contemporary necessities.

All seem to accept one proposition: such power can be achieved through a greater synthesis of presidential and congressional purposes. Some say the synthesis is impossible without broad constitutional revisions along the lines of the British parliamentary system, including provision for the executive dissolution of the legislature in case of loggerheads and provision for concurrent terms for President and Congress. Others believe that the catalytic effect of a reformed party system, together with certain changes in congressional organization and procedure, will make drastic constitutional reform as unnecessary as they believe it to be improbable.

Two statements—one from Woodrow Wilson and one from Thomas K. Finletter—sum up seventy-five years of prophetic writing on this subject. In the 1880's, Wilson wrote:

> The Constitution is not honored by blind worship. The more open-eyed we become, as a nation, to its defects, and the prompter we grow in applying with the unhesitating courage of conviction all thoroughly tested or well-considered expedients necessary to make self-government among us a straight-forward thing of a simple method, single, unstinted power, and clear responsibility, the nearer will we approach to the sound sense and practical genius of the great and honorable statesmen of 1787. [From *Congressional Government*, pp. 332–333.]

Two generations later, Thomas Finletter wrote:

> The question thus is whether means, that is the procedures of our government, are adequate in relation to its objectives, or its ends. The usual pattern has been long periods of negative government interlarded with short periods of strong action. . . . The irregular flow of power endangers repre-

sentative government in the United States. . . . You cannot have a government capable of handling the most difficult problems that peacetime democracy has ever faced with the two main parts of it at each other's throats. . . . A government of fits and starts is no longer good enough for our purposes. [From *Can Representative Government Do the Job?* pp. 2, 7, 8, 9, and 64.] 🖎

15. Democrats and Republicans—Are They Different?

One often hears that the American party system presents no meaningful choice to the electorate because of the lack of significant differences between the two major parties. Admittedly, there are many similarities between the presidential wings of the two parties and also between the leadership of the congressional Republicans and their Democratic counterparts. But which party occupies the White House does seem to make a difference, regardless of the fact that the presidential candidates of the two parties often agree on many important issues of public policy, particularly in foreign affairs. The following selection presents the results of a systematic study designed to determine the nature and extent of divergence in attitudes among the leaders and the followers of the Democrats and Republicans.

ISSUE CONFLICT AND CONSENSUS AMONG PARTY
LEADERS AND FOLLOWERS

*Herbert McClosky, Paul J. Hoffmann,
and Rosemary O'Hara**

AMERICAN political parties are often regarded as "brokerage" organizations, weak in principle, devoid of ideology, and inclined to differ chiefly over unimportant questions. In contrast to the "ideological" parties of Europe—which supposedly appeal to their followers through sharply defined, coherent, and logically related doctrines—the American parties are thought to fit their convictions to the changing demands of the political contest. According to this view, each set of American party leaders is satisfied to play Tweedledee to the other's Tweedledum.

* Reprinted from *The American Political Science Review* (June 1960) by permission of The American Political Science Association and the authors.

I. Pressures Toward Uniformity and Cleavage

Although these "conclusions" are mainly derived from *a priori* analysis or from casual observations of "anecdotal" data (little systematic effort having been made so far to verify or refute them), they are often taken as confirmed—largely, one imagines, because they are compatible with certain conspicuous features of American politics. Among these features is the entrenchment of a two-party system which, by affording both parties a genuine opportunity to win elections, tempts them to appeal to as many diverse elements in the electorate as are needed to put together a majority. Since both parties want to attract support from the centrist and moderate segments of the electorate, their views on basic issues will, it is thought, tend to converge. Like giant business enterprises competing for the same market, they will be led to offer commodities that are in many respects identical. It is one thing for a small party in a multi-party system to preserve its ideological purity, quite another for a mass party in a two-party system to do so. The one has little hope of becoming a majority, and can most easily survive by remaining identified with the narrow audience from which it draws its chief supporters; the other can succeed only by accommodating the conflicting claims of many diverse groups—only, in short, by blunting ideological distinctions.

Constraints against enlarging intellectual differences also spring from the loosely confederated nature of the American party system, and from each national party's need to adjust its policies to the competing interests of the locality, the state, and the nation. Many party units are more concerned with local than with national elections, and prefer not to be handicapped by clear-cut national programs. Every ambitious politician, moreover, hopes to achieve a *modus vivendi* tailored to the particular and often idiosyncratic complex of forces prevailing in his constituency, an objective rarely compatible with doctrinal purity. Often, too, local politics are largely non-partisan or are partisan in ways that scarcely affect the great national issues around which ideologies might be expected to form. The development and enforcement of a sharply delineated ideology is also hindered by the absence in either party of a firmly established, authoritative, and continuing organizational center empowered to decide questions of doctrine and discipline. Party affiliation is loosely defined, responsibility is weak or non-existent, and organs for indoctrinating or communicating with party members are at best rudimentary.

Cultural and historical differences may also contribute to the weaker ideological emphasis among American, as compared with European, parties. Many of the great historical cleavages that have divided European nations for centuries—monarchism *vs.* republicanism; clericalism *vs.* anti-clericalism; democracy *vs.* autocracy, etc.—have never taken root in this country. Apart from the slavery (and subsequently the race) issue, the United States has not experienced the intense class or caste conflict often found abroad, and contests of the capitalism *vs.* socialism variety have never achieved an important role in American politics. In addition, never having known a titled nobility, we have largely been freed from the conflicts found elsewhere between the classes of inherited and acquired privilege.

Consider, too, the progress made in the United States toward neutralizing the forces which ordinarily lead to sharp social, and hence intellectual and political, differentiation. The class and status structure of American society has attained a rate of mobility equalling or exceeding that of any other long established society. Popular education, and other facilities for the creation of common attitudes, have been developed on a scale unequalled elsewhere. Improvements in transportation and communication, and rapid shifts in population and industry have weakened even sectionalism as a source of political cleavage. Rural-urban differences continue to exist, of course, but they too have been diminishing in force and have become less salient for American politics than the differences prevailing, for example, between a French peasant proprietor and a Parisian *boulevardier.* In short, a great many Americans have been subjected in their public lives to identical stimuli—a condition unlikely to generate strong, competing ideologies.

The research reported here was designed not to refute these observations but to test the accuracy of the claim that they are sufficient to prevent differences in outlook from taking root in the American party system. We believed that the homogenizing tendencies referred to are strongly offset by contrary influences, and that voters are preponderantly led to support the party whose opinions they share. We further thought that the competition for office, though giving rise to similarities between the parties, also impels them to diverge from each other in order to sharpen their respective appeals. For this and other reasons, we expected to find that the leaders of the two parties, instead of ignoring differences alleged to exist within the electorate, would differ on issues more sharply than their followers would. We believed further that even in a brokerage system the parties would serve as independent reference groups, developing norms, values, and self-images to which their supporters could readily respond. Their influence, we felt, would frequently exceed that of ethnic, occupational, residential and other reference groups. In sum, we proceeded on the belief that the parties are not simply spokesmen for other interest groups, but are in their own right agencies for formulating, transmitting, and anchoring political opinions, that they attract adherents who in general share those opinions, and that through a feedback process of mutual reinforcement between the organization and its typical supporters, the parties develop integrated and stable political tendencies. Other hypotheses will be specified as we present and analyze our findings.

II. Procedures

The questions considered in this paper were part of a large field study made in 1957–1958 on the nature, sources, and correlates of political affiliation, activity, and belief in the American party system (hereafter referred to as the PAB study). Pilot studies on Minnesota samples had led us to suspect that many "settled" notions about party affiliation and belief in America would not stand up under careful empirical scrutiny; further, we felt that little progress would be made in the exploration of this subject until a comprehensive portrait of party membership in America has been drawn. Accordingly, a nationwide study was launched to acquire a detailed description of party leaders and supporters, gathering data on their backgrounds, political experiences, personality characteristics, values, motivations, social and political attitudes, outlooks on key issues, and related matters.

For our samples of party "leaders" we turned to the Democratic and Republican national conventions, largely because they are the leading and most representative of the party organs, their delegates coming from every part of the United States and from every level of party and government activity. Our samples ranged from governors, senators, and national committeemen at the one end to precinct workers and local officials at the other. In the absence of comprehensive information about the characteristics of the party elites in America, no one can say how closely the convention delegates mirror the total party leadership. We felt it fair to assume, nevertheless, that the delegates represented as faithful a cross section of American party leadership as could be had without an extraordinary expenditure of money and labor. Using convention delegates as our universe of leaders also held some obvious advantages for research, since the composition of this universe (by name, address, party, state, sex, place of residence, and party or public office) can usually be ascertained from the convention calls. Of the 6,848 delegates and alternates available to be sampled, 3,193 actually participated; 3,020 (1,788 Democrats and 1,232 Republicans) completed and returned questionnaires that were usable in all respects. The proportion of returns was roughly equivalent for both sets of party leaders.

The rank and file sample, which we wanted both for its intrinsic value and for its utility as a control group, was obtained by special arrangement with the American Institute of Public Opinion. In January 1958, Gallup interviewers personally distributed our questionnaire to 2,917 adult voters in two successive national cross-section surveys. Some 1,610 questionnaires were filled out and returned, of which 1,484 were completely usable. This sample closely matched the national population on such characteristics as sex, age, region, size of city, and party affiliation, and, though it somewhat oversampled the upper educational levels, we considered it sufficiently large and representative for most of our purposes. Of the 1,484 respondents, 821 were Democratic supporters (629 "pure" Democrats, plus 192 whom we classified as "independent" Democrats) and 623 were Republican supporters (479 "pure" Republicans, plus 144 "independent" Republicans). Forty respondents could not be identified as adherents of either party. . . .

The questions most relevant for the present article were those which asked each respondent to express his attitudes toward twenty-four important national issues, and to state whether he believed support for each issue should be "increased," "decreased," or "remain as is." The list of issues and the responses of each sample will be found in Tables II-a through II-e, where for convenience of analysis, the issues have been grouped under five broad headings: Public Ownership, Government Regulation of the Economy, Equalitarianism and Human Welfare, Tax Policy and Foreign Policy.

In tabulating the results, we first scored each individual on each issue and then computed aggregate scores for all the members of a given sample. To begin with, percentages were used to show the proportion who favored increasing, decreasing, or retaining the existing level of support on each issue. But as it was clumsy to handle three figures for each issue, we constructed a single index or "ratio of support" which would simultaneously take account of all three scores. The index was built by assigning a weight of 1.0 to each "increase" response in the sample, of 0 to each "decrease" response, and of .50 to each "remain as is" (or "same") response. Thus the ratio-of-support score shown for any given sample is in effect a mean score with a possible range of 0 to 1.0, in which support for an issue increases as the scores approach 1.0 and decreases as they approach 0. In general, the scores can be taken to approximate the following over-all positions: .o to .25—strongly wish to reduce support; .26 to .45—wish to reduce support; .46 to .55—satisfied with the *status quo;* .56 to .75—wish to increase support; and .76 to 1.00—strongly wish to increase support. Note that the differences in degree suggested by these categories refer not to the *strength of feeling* exhibited by individuals toward an issue but rather to the *numbers of people* in a sample who hold points of view favoring or opposing that issue. . . .

One may wonder about the value of opinions stated on a questionnaire compared with the worth of views formally expressed by an organization or implicit in the actions of its leaders. Advantages can be cited on both sides. The beliefs expressed in official party statements or in legislative roll calls, it might be claimed, represent the *operating* beliefs of the organization by virtue of having been tested in the marketplace or in the competition of legislative struggle. Positions taken on issues on which a party stakes its future may be more valid evidence of what the party truly

TABLE I. Average Differences in the Ratio-of-Support Scores Among Party Leaders and Followers for Five Categories of Issues

Category of Issues	Democratic Leaders vs. Republican Leaders	Democratic Followers vs. Republican Followers	Democratic Leaders vs. Democratic Followers	Republican Leaders vs. Republican Followers	Democratic Leaders vs. Republican Followers	Republican Leaders vs. Democratic Followers
a. Public Ownership of Resources	.28	.04	.06	.18	.10	.22
b. Government Regulation of the Economy	.22	.06	.08	.10	.12	.16
c. Equalitarianism, Human Welfare	.22	.05	.08	.21	.06	.25
d. Tax Policy	.20	.06	.06	.20	.04	.26
e. Foreign Policy	.15	.02	.05	.08	.07	.10
Average Differences in Ratio Scores for all Categories	.21	.04	.07	.15	.08	.20

Sample Sizes: Democratic Leaders, 1,788; Republican Leaders, 1,232; Democratic Followers, 821; Republican Followers, 623.

believes than are the opinions expressed by individual members under conditions of maximum safety. On the other hand, the responses to the issue and attitude questions in the PAB study represent the anonymous private opinions of party leaders and followers, uncomplicated by any need to make political capital, to proselytize, to conciliate critics, or to find grounds for embarrassing the opposition at the next election. Hence they may for some purposes represent the most accurate possible reflection of the "actual" state of party opinion. The controversy over the value of the two approaches is to some extent spurious, however, for they offer different perspectives on the same thing. In addition, considerable correspondence exists between the party positions evident in congressional roll calls and the privately expressed opinions of the party leaders in our study.

III. Findings: Comparisons Between Leaders

No more conclusive findings emerge from our study of party issues than those growing out of the comparisons between the two sets of party leaders. Despite the brokerage tendency of the American parties, their active members are obviously separated by large and important differences. The differences, moreover, conform with the popular image in which the Democratic party is seen as the more "progressive" or "radical," the Republican as the more "moderate" or "conservative" of the two. In addition, the disagreements are remarkably consistent, a function not of chance but of systematic points of view, whereby the responses to any one of the issues could reasonably have been predicted from knowledge of the responses to the other issues.

Examination of Tables II-a–e . . . shows that the leaders differ significantly on 23 of the 24 issues listed and that they are separated on 15 of these issues by .18 or more ratio points—in short, by differences that are in absolute magnitude very large. The two samples are further apart in their attitudes toward public ownership and are especially divided on the question of government ownership of natural resources, the Democrats strongly favoring it, the Republicans just as strongly wanting it cut back. The difference of .39 in the ratio scores is the largest for any of the issues tested. In percentages, the differences are 58 per cent (D) vs. 13 per cent (R) in favor of increasing support, and 19 per cent (D) vs. 52 per cent (R) in favor of decreasing support. Both parties preponderantly support public control and development of atomic energy, but the Democrats do so more uniformly.

V. O. Key, among others, has observed that the Republican party is especially responsive to the "financial and manufacturing community,"

TABLE II-A. Comparison of Party Leaders and Followers on "Public Ownership" Issues, by Percentages and Ratios of Support

	Leaders		Followers	
Issues	Dem. N = 1,788	Repub. N = 1,232	Dem. N = 821	Repub. N = 623
		(%s down)		
Public Ownership of Natural Resources				
% favoring: Increase	57.5	12.9	35.3	31.1
Decrease	18.6	51.9	15.0	19.9
Same, n.c.*	23.8	35.2	49.7	49.0
Support Ratio	.69	.30	.60	.56
Public Control of Atomic Energy				
% favoring: Increase	73.2	45.0	64.2	59.4
Decrease	7.2	15.3	7.1	10.0
Same, n.c.*	19.6	39.7	28.7	30.6
Support Ratio	.83	.65	.79	.75
Mean Support Ratios for the Public Ownership Category	.76	.48	.70	.66

* n.c. = no code.

reflecting the view that government should intervene as little as possible to burden or restrain prevailing business interests. The validity of this observation is evident throughout all our data, and is most clearly seen in the responses to the issues listed under Government Regulation of the Economy, Equalitarianism and Human Welfare, Tax Policy. Democratic leaders are far more eager than Republican leaders to strengthen enforcement of anti-monopoly laws and to increase regulation of public utilities and business. Indeed, the solidarity of Republican opposition to the regulation of business is rather overwhelming: 84 per cent want to decrease such regulation and fewer than .01 per cent say they want to increase it. Although the Democrats, on balance, also feel that government

TABLE II-B. Comparison of Party Leaders and Followers on "Government Regulation of the Economy" Issues, by Percentages and Ratios of Support

	Leaders		Followers	
Issues	Dem. N = 1,788	Repub. N = 1,232	Dem. N = 821	Repub. N = 623
		(%s down)		
Level of Farm Price Supports				
% favoring: Increase	43.4	6.7	39.0	23.0
Decrease	28.1	67.4	27.6	40.3
Same, n.c.	28.5	25.8	33.4	36.7
Support Ratio	.58	.20	.56	.41
Government Regulation of Business				
% favoring: Increase	20.2	0.6	18.6	7.4
Decrease	38.5	84.1	33.4	46.2
Same, n.c.	41.3	15.3	48.0	46.4
Support Ratio	.41	.08	.43	.31
Regulation of Public Utilities				
% favoring: Increase	59.0	17.9	39.3	26.0
Decrease	6.4	17.6	11.1	12.0
Same, n.c.	34.6	64.5	49.6	62.0
Support Ratio	.76	.50	.64	.57
Enforcement of Anti-Monopoly Laws				
% favoring: Increase	78.0	44.9	53.2	51.0
Decrease	2.9	9.0	7.9	6.6
Same, n.c.	19.1	46.1	38.9	42.4
Support Ratio	.88	.68	.73	.72

TABLE II-B. (continued)

Issues	Leaders		Followers	
	Dem. N = 1,788	Repub. N = 1,232	Dem. N = 821	Repub. N = 623
		(%s down)		
Regulation of Trade Unions				
% favoring: Increase	59.3	86.4	46.6	57.8
Decrease	12.4	4.5	8.9	10.6
Same, n.c.	28.3	9.2	44.5	31.6
Support Ratio	.73	.91	.69	.74
Level of Tariffs				
% favoring: Increase	13.0	19.2	16.6	15.2
Decrease	43.0	26.3	25.3	21.3
Same, n.c.	43.9	54.5	58.1	63.4
Support Ratio	.35	.46	.46	.47
Restrictions on Credit				
% favoring: Increase	24.8	20.6	26.1	25.7
Decrease	39.3	20.6	22.2	23.8
Same, n.c.	35.9	58.8	51.8	50.5
Support Ratio	.43	.50	.52	.51
Mean Support Ratios for "Government Regulation of the Economy" Category	.59	.48	.58	.53

controls on business should not be expanded further, the differences between the two samples on this issue are nevertheless substantial.

The two sets of leaders are also far apart on the farm issue, the Democrats preferring slightly to increase farm supports, the Republicans wanting strongly to reduce them. The Republican ratio score of .20 on

TABLE II-C. Comparison of Party Leaders and Followers on "Equalitarian and Human Welfare" Issues, by Percentages and Ratios of Support

Issues	Leaders		Followers	
	Dem. N = 1,788	Repub. N = 1,232	Dem. N = 821	Repub. N = 623
		(%s down)		
Federal Aid to Education				
% favoring: Increase	66.2	22.3	74.9	64.8
Decrease	13.4	43.2	5.6	8.3
Same, n.c.	20.4	34.5	19.5	26.8
Support Ratio	.76	.40	.85	.78
Slum Clearance and Public Housing				
% favoring: Increase	78.4	40.1	79.5	72.5
Decrease	5.6	21.6	5.8	7.9
Same, n.c.	16.0	38.3	14.6	19.6
Support Ratio	.86	.59	.87	.82
Social Security Benefits				
% favoring: Increase	60.0	22.5	69.4	57.0
Decrease	3.9	13.1	3.0	3.8
Same, n.c.	36.1	64.4	27.5	39.2
Support Ratio	.78	.55	.83	.77
Minimum Wages				
% favoring: Increase	50.0	15.5	59.0	43.5
Decrease	4.7	12.5	2.9	5.0
Same, n.c.	45.2	72.0	38.1	51.5
Support Ratio	.73	.52	.78	.69
Enforcement of Integration				
% favoring: Increase	43.8	25.5	41.9	40.8
Decrease	26.6	31.7	27.4	23.6
Same, n.c.	29.5	42.8	30.7	35.6
Support Ratio	.59	.47	.57	.59

TABLE II-C. (continued)

Issues	Leaders		Followers	
	Dem.	Repub.	Dem.	Repub.
	N = 1,788	N = 1,232	N = 821	N = 623
		(%s down)		
Immigration into United States				
% favoring: Increase	36.1	18.4	10.4	8.0
Decrease	27.0	29.9	52.0	44.6
Same, n.c.	36.9	51.7	37.6	47.4
Support Ratio	.54	.44	.29	.32
Mean Support Ratios for "Equalitarian and Human Welfare" Category	.71	.50	.70	.66

this issue is among the lowest in the entire set of scores. The magnitude of these scores somewhat surprised us, for while opposition to agricultural subsidies is consistent with Republican dislike for state intervention, we had expected the leaders to conform more closely to the familiar image of the Republican as the more "rural" of the two parties. It appears, however, that the party's connection with business is far more compelling than its association with agriculture. The Republican desire to reduce government expenditures and to promote independence from "government handouts" prevails on the farm question as it does on other issues, while the Democratic preference for a more regulated economy in which government intervenes to reduce economic risk and to stabilize prosperity is equally evident on the other side. Party attitudes on this issue appear to be determined as much by ideological tendencies as by deliberate calculation of the political advantages to be gained by favoring or opposing subsidies to farmers.

Having implied that agricultural policies partly result from principle, we must note that on three other issues in this category (trade unions, credit, and tariffs), principle seems to be overweighed by old-fashioned economic considerations. In spite of their distaste for government interference in economic affairs, the Republicans almost unanimously favor greater regulation of trade unions and they are more strongly disposed than

TABLE II-D. Comparison of Party Leaders and Followers on "Tax Policy" Issues, by Percentages and Ratios of Support

	Leaders		Followers	
Issues	*Dem.* N = 1,788	*Repub.* N = 1,232	*Dem.* N = 821	*Repub.* N = 623
		(%s down)		
Corporate Income Tax				
% favoring: Increase	32.3	4.0	32.0	23.3
Decrease	23.3	61.5	20.5	25.7
Same, n.c.	44.4	34.5	47.5	51.0
Support Ratio	.54	.21	.56	.49
Tax on Large Incomes				
% favoring: Increase	27.0	5.4	46.6	34.7
Decrease	23.1	56.9	13.8	21.7
Same, n.c.	49.9	37.7	39.6	43.6
Support Ratio	.52	.24	.66	.56
Tax on Business				
% favoring: Increase	12.6	1.0	24.6	15.9
Decrease	38.3	71.1	24.1	32.6
Same, n.c.	49.1	27.8	51.3	51.5
Support Ratio	.37	.15	.50	.42
Tax on Middle Incomes				
% favoring: Increase	2.7	0.8	4.5	3.0
Decrease	50.2	63.9	49.3	44.3
Same, n.c.	47.1	35.3	46.2	52.6
Support Ratio	.26	.18	.28	.29
Tax on Small Incomes				
% favoring: Increase	1.4	2.9	1.6	2.1
Decrease	79.2	65.0	77.5	69.6
Same, n.c.	19.4	32.1	20.9	28.3
Support Ratio	.11	.19	.12	.16
Mean Support Ratios for "Tax Policy" Category	.36	.19	.42	.38

TABLE II-E. Comparison of Party Leaders and Followers on "Foreign Policy" Issues, by Percentages and Ratios of Support

Issues	Leaders		Followers	
	Dem. N = 1,788	Repub. N = 1,232	Dem. N = 821	Repub. N = 623
	(%s down)			
Reliance on the United Nations				
% favoring: Increase	48.9	24.4	34.7	33.4
Decrease	17.6	34.8	17.3	19.3
Same, n.c.	33.5	40.7	48.0	47.3
Support Ratio	.66	.45	.59	.57
American Participation in Military Alliances				
% favoring: Increase	41.5	22.7	39.1	32.3
Decrease	17.6	25.7	14.0	15.4
Same, n.c.	40.9	51.6	46.9	52.3
Support Ratio	.62	.48	.62	.58
Foreign Aid				
% favoring: Increase	17.8	7.6	10.1	10.1
Decrease	51.0	61.7	58.6	57.3
Same, n.c.	31.1	30.7	31.3	32.6
Support Ratio	.33	.23	.26	.26
Defense Spending*				
% favoring: Increase	20.7	13.6	50.5	45.7
Decrease	34.4	33.6	16.4	15.4
Same, n.c.	44.8	52.8	33.0	38.8
Support Ratio	.43	.40	.67	.65
Mean Support Ratios for "Foreign Policy" Category (excl. Defense Spending)	.54	.39	.49	.47

the Democrats toward government intervention to restrict credit and to raise tariffs. Of course, party cleavages over the credit and tariff issues have a long history, which may by now have endowed them with ideological force beyond immediate economic considerations. The preponderant Democratic preference for greater regulation of trade unions is doubtless a response to recent "exposures" of corrupt labor practices, though it may also signify that the party's perspective toward the trade unions is shifting somewhat.

The closer Republican identification with business, free enterprise, and economic conservatism in general, and the friendlier Democratic attitude toward labor and toward government regulation of the economy, are easily observed in the data from other parts of our questionnaire. Republican leaders score very much higher than Democratic leaders on, for example, such scales as economic conservatism, independence of government, and business attitudes. On a question asking respondents to indicate the groups from which they would be most and least likely to take advice, 41 per cent of the Democratic leaders but only 3.8 per cent of the Republican leaders list trade unions as groups from which they would seek advice. Trade unions are scored in the "least likely" category by 25 per cent of the Democrats and 63 per cent of the Republicans. Similarly, more than 94 per cent of the Republican leaders, but 56 per cent of the Democratic leaders, name trade unions as groups that have "too much power." These differences, it should be noted, cannot be accounted for by reference to the greater number of trade union members among the Democratic party leadership, for in the 1956 conventions only 14 per cent of the Democrats belonged to trade unions, and while an even smaller percentage (4 per cent) of the Republicans were trade unionists, this disparity is hardly great enough to explain the large differences in outlook. The key to the explanation has to be sought in the symbolic and reference group identifications of the two parties, and in their underlying values.

Nowhere do we see this more clearly than in the responses to the Equalitarian and Human Welfare issues. The mean difference in the ratio scores for the category as a whole is .22, a very large difference and one that results from differences in the expected direction on all six issues that make up the category. On four of these issues—federal aid to education, slum clearance and public housing, social security, and minimum wages—the leaders of the two parties are widely separated, the differences in their ratio scores ranging from .36 to .21. The percentages showing the proportions who favor increased support for these issues are even more striking. In every instance the Democratic percentages are considerably higher: 66 *vs.* 22 per cent (education); 78 *vs.* 40 per cent (slum clearance and housing); 60 *vs.* 23 per cent (social security); and 50 *vs.* 16 per cent (minimum wages). The Democratic leaders also are better disposed than the Republican leaders toward immigration: twice as many of them (36 per cent *vs.* 18 per cent) favor a change in policy to permit more immigrants to enter. The over-all inclination of both party élites, however, is to accept the present levels of immigration, the Democratic ratio score falling slightly above, and the Republican slightly below, the midpoint.

More surprising are the differences on the segregation issue, for, despite strong Southern influence, the Democratic leaders express significantly more support for enforcing integration than the Republicans do. Moreover, the difference between the two parties rises from .12 for the national samples as a whole to a difference of .18 when the southern leaders are excluded. . . .

Examination of the actual magnitude of the ratio scores in this category reveals that the Republicans want not so much to abrogate existing social welfare or equalitarian measures as to keep them from being broadened. The Democrats, by comparison, are shown to be the party of social equality and reform, more willing than their opponents to employ legislation for the benefit of the underprivileged. . . .

The self-images and reference group identifications of the two parties also should be noted in this connection. For example, many more Democratic than Republican leaders call themselves liberal and state that they would be most likely to take advice from liberal reform organizations, the Farmers' Union, and (as we have seen) from the trade unions; only a small number consider themselves conservative or would seek advice from conservative reform organizations, the National Association of Manufacturers, or the Farm Bureau Federation. The Republicans have in almost all instances the reverse identifications: only a handful regard themselves as liberal or would seek counsel from liberal organizations, while more than 42 per cent call themselves conservative and would look to the NAM or to conservative reform organizations for advice. Almost two-thirds of the Republicans (compared with 29 per cent of the Democrats) regard the Chamber of Commerce as an important source of advice. Businessmen are listed as having "too much power" by 42 per cent of the Democrats but by only 9 per cent of the Republicans. The Democrats are also significantly more inclined than the Republicans to consider Catholics, Jews, and the foreign born as having "too little power." While self-descriptions and reference group identifications often correspond poorly with actual beliefs—among the general population they scarcely correspond at all, in fact—we are dealing, in the case of the leaders, with a politically informed and highly articulate set of people who have little difficulty connecting the beliefs they hold and the groups that promote or obstruct those beliefs.

Our fourth category, Tax Policy, divides the parties almost as severely as do the other categories. The mean difference for the category as a whole is .20, and it would doubtless have been larger but for the universal unpopularity of proposals to increase taxes on small and middle income groups. Table II-d shows that the differences between the parties on the tax issues follow the patterns previously observed and that tax policy is for the Democrats a device for redistributing income and promoting social equality. Neither party, however, is keen about raising taxes for *any* group: even the Democrats have little enthusiasm for new taxes on upper income groups or on business and corporate enterprises. The Republican leaders are overwhelmingly opposed to increased taxes for *any* group, rich *or* poor. This can be seen in their low ratio scores on the tax issues, which range from only .15 to .24. But while they are far more eager than the Democratic leaders to cut taxes on corporate and private wealth, they are less willing to reduce taxes on the lower income groups. These differences, it should be remarked, are not primarily a function of differences in the income of the two samples. Although there are more people with high incomes among the Republican leaders, the disproportion between the two samples is not nearly great enough to account for the dissimilarities in their tax views.

Of the five categories considered, Foreign Policy shows the smallest average difference, but even on these issues the divergence between Democratic and Republican leader attitudes is significant. Except for defense spending the Democrats turn out to be more internationalist than the Republicans, as evidenced in their greater commitment to the United Nations and to American participation in international military alliances like NATO. Twice as many Democrats as Republicans want the United States to rely more heavily upon such organizations, while many more Republicans want to reduce our international involvements. Both parties are predominantly in favor of cutting back foreign aid—a somewhat surprising finding in light of Democratic public pronouncements on this subject—but more Republicans feel strongly on the subject. Our data thus furnish little support for the claim that the parties hold the same views on foreign policy or that their seeming differences are merely a response to the demands of political competition.

Nevertheless, it would be incorrect to conclude that one party believes in internationalism and the other in isolationism. The differences are far too small to warrant any such inference. Traces of isolationism, to be sure, remain stronger in the Republican party than in the Democratic party—an observation buttressed by the finding that twice as many Republicans as Democrats score high on the isolationism scale. The pattern of Republican responses on both the issue and scale items signifies, however, that the leaders of that party generally accept the degree of "internationalism" now in effect, but shrink from extending it further. Consider too, the similarities in the leaders' scores on defense spending, for despite their greater leaning toward isolationism, the Republicans are no more inclined than the Democrats to leave the country defenseless. . . .

IV. Comparisons Between Followers

So far we have addressed ourselves to the differences between Democratic and Republican *leaders*. In each of the tables presented, however, data are included from which the two sets of party *followers* may also be compared.

The observation most clearly warranted from these data is that the rank and file members of the two parties are far less divided than their leaders. Not only do they diverge significantly on fewer issues—seven as compared with 23 for the leader samples—but the magnitudes of the differences in their ratio scores are substantially smaller for every one of the 24 issues. . . .

. . . Even on business attitudes, independence of government, and economic conservatism, the differences are small and barely significant. No differences were found on such scales as tolerance, faith in democracy, procedural rights, conservatism-liberalism (classical), . . . and isolationism. The average Democrat is slightly more willing than the average Republican to label himself a liberal or to seek advice from liberal organizations; the contrary is true when it comes to adopting conservative identifications. Only in the differential trust they express toward business and labor are the two sets of followers widely separated.

These findings give little support to the claim that the "natural divisions" of the electorate are being smothered by party leaders. Not only do the leaders disagree more sharply than their respective followers, but the level of consensus among the electorate (with or without regard to party) is fairly high. . . . Of course, voters may divide more sharply on issues at election time, since campaigns intensify party feeling and may also intensify opinions on issues. . . . But even the party-linked differences found among voters during elections may largely be echoes of the opinions announced by the candidates—transient sentiments developed for the occasion and quickly forgotten.

V. Leader Conflict and Follower Consensus: Explanations

Considering the nature of the differences between the leader and follower samples, the interesting question is not why the parties fail to represent the "natural division" in the electorate (for that question rests on an unwarranted assumption) but why the party élites disagree at all, and why they divide so much more sharply than their followers.

Despite the great pressures toward uniformity we have noted in American society, many forces also divide the population culturally, economically, and politically. The United States is, after all, a miscellany of ethnic and religious strains set down in a geographically large and diverse country. Many of these groups brought old conflicts and ideologies with them, and some have tried to act out in the new world the hopes and frustrations nurtured in the old. Then, too, despite rapid social mobility, social classes have by no means been eliminated. No special political insight is needed to perceive that the two parties characteristically draw from different strata of the society, the Republicans from the managerial, proprietary, and to some extent professional classes, the Democrats from labor, minorities, low income groups, and a large proportion of the intellectuals. Partly because the leaders of the two parties tend to overrespond to the modal values of the groups with which they are principally identified, they gradually grow further apart on the key questions which separate their respective supporters. The Republican emphasis on business ideology is both a cause and a consequence of its managerial and proprietary support; the greater Democratic emphasis on social justice, and on economic and social levelling, is both the occasion and the product of the support the party enjoys among intellectuals and the lower strata. These interrelationships are strengthened, moreover, by the tendency for a party's dominant supporters to gain a disproportionate number of positions in its leadership ranks.

The differences which typically separate Democratic from Republican leaders seem also to reflect a deep-seated ideological cleavage often found among Western parties. One side of this cleavage is marked by a strong belief in the power of collective action to promote social justice, equality, humanitarianism, and economic planning, while preserving freedom; the other is distinguished by faith in the wisdom of the natural competitive process and in the supreme virtue of individualism, "character," self-reliance, frugality, and independence from government. To this cleavage is added another frequent source of political division, namely, a difference in attitude toward change between "radicals" and "moderates," between those who prefer to move quickly or slowly, to reform or to conserve. These differences in social philosophy and posture do not always coincide with the divisions in the social structure, and their elements do not, in all contexts, combine in the same way. But, however crudely, the American parties do tend to embody these competing points of view and to serve as reference groups for those who hold them.

Party cleavage in America was no doubt intensified by the advent of the New Deal, and by its immense electoral and intellectual success. Not only did it weld into a firm alliance the diverse forces that were to be crucial to all subsequent Democratic majorities, but it also made explicit the doctrines of the "welfare state" with which the party was henceforth to be inseparably identified. Because of the novelty of its program and its apparently radical threat to the familiar patterns of American political and economic life, it probably deepened the fervor of its Republican adversaries and drove into the opposition the staunchest defenders of business ideology. The conflict was further sharpened by the decline of left-wing politics after the war, and by the transfer of loyalties of former and potential radicals to the Democratic party. Once launched, the cleavage has been sustained by the tendency for each party to attract into its active ranks a disproportionate number of voters who recognize and share its point of view.

Why, however, are the leaders so much more sharply divided than their followers? The reasons are not hard to understand and are consistent with several of the hypotheses that underlie the present study.

(1) Consider, to begin with, that the leaders come from the more articulate segments of society and, on the average, are politically more aware than their followers and far better informed about issues. For them, political issues and opinions are the everyday currency of party competition, not esoteric matters that surpass understanding. With their greater awareness and responsibility, and their greater need to defend their party's stands, they have more interest in developing a consistent set of attitudes —perhaps even an ideology. The followers of each party, often ignorant of the issues and their consequences, find it difficult to distinguish their beliefs from those of the opposition and have little reason to be concerned with the consistency of their attitudes. Furthermore, the American parties make only a feeble effort to educate the rank and file politically, and since

no central source exists for the authoritative pronouncement of party policy, the followers often do not know what their leaders believe or on what issues the parties chiefly divide. In short, if we mean by ideology a coherent body of informed social doctrine, it is possessed mainly by the articulate leadership, rarely by the masses.

(2) Differences in the degree of partisan involvement parallel the differences in knowledge and have similar consequences. The leaders, of course, have more party spirit than the followers and, as the election studies make plain, the stronger the partisanship, the larger the differences on issues. The leaders are more highly motivated not only to belong to a party appropriate to their beliefs, but to accept its doctrines and to learn how it differs from the opposition party. Since politics is more salient for leaders than for followers, they develop a greater stake in the outcome of the political contest and are more eager to discover the intellectual grounds by which they hope to make victory possible. Through a process of circular reinforcement, those for whom politics is most important are likely to become the most zealous participants, succeeding to the posts that deal in the formation of opinion. Ideology serves the instrumental purpose, in addition, of justifying the heavy investment that party leaders make in political activity. While politics offers many rewards, it also makes great demands on the time, money, and energies of its practitioners —sacrifices which they can more easily justify if they believe they are serving worthwhile social goals. The followers, in contrast, are intellectually far less involved, have less personal stake in the outcome of the competition, have little need to be concerned with the "correctness" of their views on public questions, and have even less reason to learn in precisely what ways their opinions differ from their opponents'. Hence, the party élites recruit members from a population stratified in some measure by ideology, while the rank and file renews itself by more random recruitment and is thus more likely to mirror the opinions of a cross section of the population.

(3) Part of the explanation for the greater consensus among followers than leaders resides in the nature and size of the two types of groups. Whereas the leader groups are comparatively small and selective, each of the follower groups number in the millions and, by their very size and unwieldiness, are predisposed to duplicate the characteristics of the population as a whole. Even if the Republicans draw disproportionately from the business-managerial classes and the Democrats from the trade union movement, neither interest group has enough influence to shape distinctively the aggregate opinions of so large a mass of supporters. Size also affects the nature and frequency of interaction within the two types of

groups. Because they comprise a smaller, more selectively chosen, organized, and articulate élite, the leaders are apt to associate with people of their own political persuasion more frequently and consistently than the followers do. They are not only less cross-pressured than the rank and file but they are also subjected to strong party group efforts to induce them to conform. Because their political values are continually renewed through frequent communication with people of like opinions, and because they acquire intense reference group identifications, they develop an extraordinary ability to resist the force of the opposition's arguments. While the followers, too, are thrown together and shielded to some extent, they are likely to mingle more freely with people of hostile political persuasions, to receive fewer partisan communications, and to hold views that are only intermittently and inconsistently reinforced. Since, by comparison with the leaders, they possess little interest in or information about politics, they can more easily embrace "deviant" attitudes without discomfort and without challenge from their associates. Nor are they likely to be strongly rewarded for troubling to have "correct" opinions. The followers, in short, are less often and less effectively indoctrinated than their leaders. The group processes described here would function even more powerfully in small, sectarian, tightly organized parties of the European type, but they are also present in the American party system, where they yield similar though less potent consequences.

(4) Political competition itself operates to divide the leaders more than the followers. If the parties are impelled to present a common face to the electorate, they are also strongly influenced to distinguish themselves from each other. For one thing, they have a more heightened sense of the "national interest" than the followers do, even if they do not all conceive it in the same way. For another, they hope to improve their chances at the polls by offering the electorate a recognizable and attractive commodity. In addition, they seek emotional gratification in the heightened sense of brotherhood brought on by the struggle against an "outgroup" whose claim to office seems always, somehow, to border upon usurpation. As with many ingroup-outgroup distinctions, the participants search for moral grounds to justify their antagonisms toward each other, and ideologies help to furnish such grounds. Among the followers, on the other hand, these needs exist, if at all, in much weaker form. . . .

VI. The Homogeneity of Support for Leaders and Followers

So far we have only considered conflict and agreement *between* groups. We should now turn to the question of consensus *within* groups. To what extent is each of our samples united on fundamental issues?

In order to assess homogeneity of opinion within party groups, standard deviation scores were computed on each issue for each of the four samples. The higher the standard deviation, of course, the greater the disagreement. The range of possible sigma scores is from 0 (signifying that every member of the sample has selected the same response) to .500 (signifying that all responses are equally divided between the "increase" and "decrease" alternatives). If we assume that the three alternative responses had been randomly (and therefore equally) selected, the standard deviations for the four samples would fall by chance alone around .410. Scores at or above this level may be taken to denote extreme dispersion among the members of a sample while scores in the neighborhood of .300 or below suggest that unanimity within the sample is fairly high. By these somewhat arbitrary criteria we can observe immediately (Table IV) that

TABLE IV. Consensus Within Party Groups: Rank Order of . Homogeneity of Support on Twenty-Four Issues

Average Rank Order*	Issue	Democratic Leaders		Republican Leaders		Democratic Followers		Republican Followers	
		Rank Order	Sigma	Rank Order	Sigma	Rank Order	Sigma	Rank Order	Sigma
1	Tax on Small Incomes	1	.220	6	.270	1	.224	1	.250
2	Tax on Middle Incomes	3	.276	4	.248	6	.292	2	.278
3	Social Security Benefits	5	.282	8	.296	2	.266	3	.286
4	Minimum Wages	6	.292	5	.268	4	.276	4	.294
5	Enforcement of Anti-Monopoly	2	.246	13	.321	8	.324	7	.314
6	Regulation of Public Utilities	8	.307	10	.300	10	.336	5.5	.310
7	Slum Clearance	4	.276	23	.386	3	.274	5.5	.310
8	Regulation of Trade Unions	12	.356	3	.240	9	.331	15	.345
9	Government Regulation of Business	17	.376	1	.192	20	.363	8	.315
10	Tax on Business	9	.338	2	.236	19	.362	16	.348
11	Level of Tariffs	10	.350	16	.344	11	.338	9	.316
12	Public Control of Atomic Energy	7	.302	20	.362	7	.312	13	.340

consensus within groups is greater on most issues than we would expect by chance alone, but that it is extremely high in only a few instances. Although the Republican leaders appear on the average to be the most united and the Democratic leaders the least united of the four groups, the difference between their homogeneity scores (.340 vs. .310) is too small to be taken as conclusive. The grounds are somewhat better for rejecting the belief that leaders are more homogeneous in their outlooks than their followers, since the hypothesis holds only for one party and not for the other.

While generalizations about the relative unity of the four samples seem risky, we can speak more confidently about the rank order of agreement *within* samples. In Table IV we have ranked the issues according to the degree of consensus exhibited toward them by the members of each

TABLE IV. (continued)

Average Rank Order*	Issue	Democratic Leaders		Republican Leaders		Democratic Followers		Republican Followers	
		Rank Order	Sigma	Rank Order	Sigma	Rank Order	Sigma	Rank Order	Sigma
13	Federal Aid to Education	13	.360	24	.394	5	.283	11	.322
14	Foreign Aid	19	.383	12	.317	12.5	.340	12	.340
15	Tax on Large Incomes	11	.356	9	.298	17	.358	22	.379
16	American Participa- in Military Alliances, NATO	14	.370	18	.351	14	.350	14	.344
17	Immigration into U.S.	21	.399	17	.345	12.5	.340	10	.318
18	Corporate Income Tax	16	.375	7	.284	21	.371	17	.361
19	Restrictions on Credit	22	.400	14	.324	16	.358	18	.362
20	Defense Spending	15	.371	15	.334	22	.380	21	.366
21	Public Ownership of Natural Resources	20	.393	19	.354	15	.352	19	.362
22	Reliance on U.N.	18	.380	22	.384	18	.359	20	.365
23	Level of Farm Supports	24	.421	11	.306	23	.414	23	.397
24	Enforce Integration	23	.416	21	.382	24	.418	24	.399

* The range of sigma scores is from .192 to .421, out of a possible range of .000 (most united) to .500 (least united). Hence, the lower the rank order the greater the unity on the issue named.

of the four party groups. There we see that the leaders of the Republican party are most united on the issues that stem from its connections with business—government regulation of business, taxes (especially on business), regulation of trade unions, and minimum wages. The Democratic leaders are most united on those issues which bear upon the support the party receives from the lower and middle income groups—taxes on small and middle incomes, anti-monopoly, slum clearance, social security, and minimum wages. The Republican leaders divide most severely on federal aid to education, slum clearance, U.N. support, segregation, and public control of atomic energy and natural resources; the Democratic leaders are most divided on farm prices, segregation, credit restrictions, immigration, and the natural resources issue. Among the followers the patterns of unity and division are very similar, as attested by the high correlation of .83 between the rank orders of their homogeneity scores. Both Republican and Democratic followers exhibit great cohesion, for example, on taxes on small and middle incomes, social security, slum clearance, and minimum wages. Both divide rather sharply on segregation, farm price supports, defense spending, U.N. support, and taxes on large incomes. The two sets of followers, in short, are alike not only in their opinions on issues but in the degree of unanimity they exhibit toward them. . . .

Summary and Conclusions

The research described in this paper—an outgrowth of a nationwide inquiry into the nature and sources of political affiliation, activity, and belief—was principally designed to test a number of hypotheses about the relation of ideology to party membership. Responses from large samples of Democratic and Republican leaders and followers were compared on twenty-four key issues and on a number of attitude questions and scales. Statistical operations were carried out to assess conflict and consensus among party groups and to estimate the size and significance of differences. From the data yielded by this inquiry, the following inferences seem most warranted:

1. Although it has received wide currency, especially among Europeans, the belief that the two American parties are identical in principle and doctrine has little foundation in fact. Examination of the opinions of Democratic and Republican leaders show them to be distinct communities of co-believers who diverge sharply on many important issues. Their disagreements, furthermore, conform to an image familiar to many observers and are generally consistent with differences turned up by studies of Congressional roll calls. The unpopularity of many of the positions held by Republican leaders suggests also that the parties

submit to the demands of their constituents less slavishly than is commonly supposed.

2. Republican and Democratic leaders stand furthest apart on the issues that grow out of their group identification and support—out of the managerial, proprietary, and high-status connections of the one, and the labor, minority, low-status, and intellectual connections of the other. The opinions of each party élite are linked less by chance than by membership in a common ideological domain. Democratic leaders typically display the stronger urge to elevate the lowborn, the uneducated, the deprived minorities, and the poor in general; they are also more disposed to employ the nation's collective power to advance humanitarian and social welfare goals (*e.g.,* social security, immigration, racial integration, a higher minimum wage, and public education). They are more critical of wealth and big business and more eager to bring them under regulation. Theirs is the greater faith in the wisdom of using legislation for redistributing the national product and for furnishing social services on a wide scale. Of the two groups of leaders, the Democrats are the more "progressively" oriented toward social reform and experimentation. The Republican leaders, while not uniformly differentiated from their opponents, subscribe in greater measure to the symbols and practices of individualism, *laissez-faire,* and national independence. They prefer to overcome humanity's misfortunes by relying upon personal effort, private incentives, frugality, hard work, responsibility, self-denial (for both men and government), and the strengthening rather than the diminution of the economic and status distinctions that are the "natural" rewards of the differences in human character and fortunes. Were it not for the hackneyed nature of the designation and the danger of forcing traits into a mold they fit only imperfectly, we might be tempted to describe the Republicans as the chief upholders of what Max Weber has called the "Protestant Ethic." Not that the Democrats are insensible to the "virtues" of the Protestant-capitalistic ethos, but they embrace them less firmly or uniformly. The differences between the two élites have probably been intensified by the rise of the New Deal and by the shift of former radicals into the Democratic party following the decline of socialist and other left-wing movements during and after the war.

3. Whereas the leaders of the two parties diverge strongly, their followers differ only moderately in their attitudes toward issues. The hypothesis that party beliefs unite adherents and bring them into the party ranks may hold for the more active members of a mass party but not for its rank and file supporters. Republican followers, in fact, dis-

agree far more with their own leaders than with the leaders of the
Democratic party. Little support was found for the belief that deep
cleavages exist among the electorate but are ignored by the leaders.
One might, indeed, more accurately assert the contrary, to wit: that the
natural cleavages between the leaders are largely ignored by the voters.
However, we cannot presently conclude that ideology exerts no influence over the habits of party support, for the followers do differ significantly and in the predicted directions on some issues. Furthermore,
we do not know how many followers may previously have been led by
doctrinal considerations to shift their party allegiances.

4. Except for their desire to ingratiate themselves with as many
voters as possible, the leaders of the two parties have more reason than
their followers to hold sharply opposing views on the important political
questions of the day. Compared with the great mass of supporters, they
are articulate, informed, highly partisan, and involved; they comprise a
smaller and more tightly knit group which is closer to the well-springs
of party opinion, more accessible for indoctrination, more easily rewarded or punished for conformity or deviation, and far more affected,
politically and psychologically, by engagement in the party struggle for
office. If the leaders of the two parties are not always candid about their
disagreements, the reason may well be that they sense the great measure
of consensus to be found among the electorate.

5. Finding that party leaders hold contrary beliefs does not prove
that they *act* upon those beliefs or that the two parties are, in practice,
governed by different outlooks. In a subsequent paper we shall consider
these questions more directly by comparing platform and other official
party pronouncements with the private opinions revealed in this study.
Until further inquiries are conducted, however, it seems reasonable to
assume that the views held privately by party leaders can never be
entirely suppressed but are bound to crop out in hundreds of large and
small ways—in campaign speeches, discussions at party meetings, private
communications to friends and sympathizers, statements to the press by
party officials and candidates, legislative debates, and public discussions
on innumerable national, state, and local questions. If, in other words,
the opinions of party leaders are as we have described them, there is
every chance that they are expressed and acted upon to some extent.
Whether this makes our parties "ideological" depends, of course, on how
narrowly we define that term. Some may prefer to reserve that designation for parties that are more obviously preoccupied with doctrine, more
intent upon the achievement of a systematic political program, and

more willing to enforce a common set of beliefs upon their members and spokesmen.

6. The parties are internally united on some issues, divided on others. In general, Republican leaders achieve greatest homogeneity on issues that grow out of their party's identification with business, Democratic leaders on issues that reflect their connection with liberal and lower-income groups. We find no support for the hypothesis that the parties achieve greatest internal consensus on the issues which principally divide them from their opponents.

In a sequel to this paper we shall offer data on the demographic correlates of issue support, which show that most of the differences presented here exist independently of factors like education, occupation, age, religion, and sectionalism. Controlling for these influences furnishes much additional information and many new insights but does not upset our present conclusions in any important respect. Thus, the parties must be considered not merely as spokesmen for other interest groups but as reference groups in their own right, helping to formulate, to sustain, and to speak for a recognizable point of view. ▨

16. The Electoral System

Functional aspects and organizational problems of American political parties have been examined in the preceding section. It is now necessary to analyze some aspects of elections and electoral behavior that bear upon the role of political parties in the governmental system. Parties are supposed to bridge the gap between people and their government. Theoretically they are primary vehicles for translating the wishes of the electorate into public policy, sharing this role with interest groups and other governmental instrumentalities in varying degrees. If parties are to perform this aspect of their job properly the party system must be conducive to securing meaningful debate and action. The organizational aspects of parties themselves and the party system profoundly affect the ability of parties to act in a democratically responsible manner. It should also be pointed out, however, that the *electorate* has a responsibility in a political process, and presumably that responsibility is to act rationally, debate the issues of importance, and record a vote for one party or the other at election time. These, at least, are electoral norms traditionally discussed. But can the electorate act in this manner? Is it desirable to have 100 per cent electoral participation considering the characteristics of voting behavior? What are the determinants of electoral behavior? Do all elections have similar characteristics and fulfill identical purposes, or are there significant differences among elections? These questions will be discussed in the following readings.

A THEORY OF CRITICAL ELECTIONS
V. O. Key, Jr.*

Pᴇʀʜᴀᴘs the basic differentiating characteristic of democratic orders consists in the expression of effective choice by the mass of the people in elections. The electorate occupies, at least in the mystique of such orders, the position of the principal organ of governance; it acts through elections. An election itself is a formal act of collective decision that occurs in a stream of connected antecedent and subsequent behavior. Among democratic orders elections, so broadly defined, differ enormously in their nature, their meaning, and their consequences. Even within a single nation the reality of election differs greatly from time to time. A systematic comparative approach, with a focus on variations in the nature of elections would doubtless be fruitful in advancing understanding of the democratic governing process. In behavior antecedent to voting, elections differ in the proportions of the electorate psychologically involved, in the intensity of attitudes associated with campaign cleavages, in the nature of expectations about the consequences of the voting, in the impact of objective events relevant to individual political choice, in individual sense of effective connection with community decision, and in other ways. These and other antecedent variations affect the act of voting itself as well as subsequent behavior. An understanding of elections and, in turn, of the democratic process as a whole must rest partially on broad differentiations of the complexes of behavior that we call elections.

While this is not the occasion to develop a comprehensive typology of elections, the foregoing remarks provide an orientation for an attempt to formulate a concept of one type of election—based on American experience—which might be built into a more general theory of elections. Even the most fleeting inspection of American elections suggests the existence of a category of elections in which voters are, at least from impressionistic evidence, unusually deeply concerned, in which the extent of electoral involvement is relatively quite high, and in which the decisive results of the voting reveal a sharp alteration of the pre-existing cleavage within the electorate. Moreover, and perhaps this is the truly

* Reprinted from *The Journal of Politics* (February 1955) by permission.

differentiating characteristic of this sort of election, the realignment made manifest in the voting in such elections seems to persist for several succeeding elections. All these characteristics cumulate to the conception of an election type in which the depth and intensity of electoral involvement are high, in which more or less profound readjustments occur in the relations of power within the community, and in which new and durable electoral groupings are formed. These comments suppose, of course, the existence of other types of complexes of behavior centering about formal elections, the systematic isolation and identification of which, fortunately, are not essential for the present discussion.

I

The presidential election of 1928 in the New England states provides a specific case of the type of critical election that has been described in general terms. In that year Alfred E. Smith, the Democratic Presidential candidate, made gains in all the New England states. The rise in Democratic strength was especially notable in Massachusetts and Rhode Island. When one probes below the surface of the gross election figures it becomes apparent that a sharp and durable realignment also occurred within the electorate, a fact reflective of the activation by the Democratic candidate of low-income, Catholic, urban voters of recent immigrant stock. In New England, at least, the Roosevelt revolution of 1932 was in large measure an Al Smith revolution of 1928, a characterization less applicable to the remainder of the country.

The intensity and extent of electoral concern before the voting of 1928 can only be surmised, but the durability of the realignment formed at the election can be determined by simple analyses of election statistics. An illustration of the new division thrust through the electorate by the campaign of 1928 is provided by the graphs in Figure A, which show the Democratic percentages of the presidential vote from 1916 through 1952 for the city of Somerville and the town of Ashfield in Massachusetts. Somerville, adjacent to Boston, had a population in 1930 of 104,000 of which 28 per cent was foreign born and 41 per cent was of foreign-born or mixed parentage. Roman Catholics constituted a large proportion of its relatively low-income population. Ashfield, a farming community in western Massachusetts with a 1930 population of 860, was predominantly native born (8.6 per cent foreign born), chiefly rural-farm (66 per cent), and principally Protestant.

The impressiveness of the differential impact of the election of 1928 on Somerville and Ashfield may be read from the graphs in Figure A.

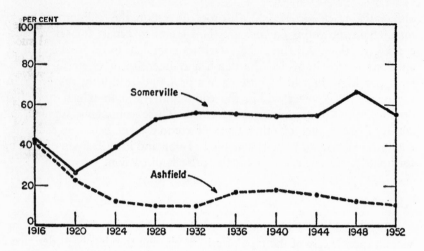

Figure A. Democratic percentages of major-party Presidential vote, Somerville and Ashfield, Massachusetts, 1916–1952

From 1920 the Democratic percentage in Somerville ascended steeply while the Democrats in Ashfield, few in 1920, became even less numerous in 1928. Inspection of the graphs also suggests that the great reshuffling of voters that occurred in 1928 was perhaps the final and decisive stage in a process that had been under way for some time. That antecedent process involved a relatively heavy support in 1924 for La Follette in those towns in which Smith was subsequently to find special favor. Hence, in Figure A, as in all the other charts, the 1924 figure is the percentage of the total accounted for by the votes of both the Democratic and Progressive candidates rather than the Democratic percentage of the two-party vote. This usage conveys a minimum impression of the size of the 1924–1928 Democratic gain but probably depicts the nature of the 1920–1928 trend.

For present purposes, the voting behavior of the two communities shown in Figure A after 1928 is of central relevance. The differences established between them in 1928 persisted even through 1952, although the two series fluctuated slightly in response to the particular influences of individual campaigns. The nature of the process of maintenance of the cleavage is, of course, not manifest from these data. Conceivably the impress of the events of 1928 on individual attitudes and loyalties formed partisan attachments of lasting nature. Yet it is doubtful that the new crystallization of 1928 projected itself through a quarter of a century solely from the momentum given it by such factors. More probably subsequent events operated to re-enforce and to maintain the 1928 cleavage. Whatever the mechanism of its maintenance, the durability of the realignment is impressive.

Somerville and Ashfield may be regarded more or less as samples of major population groups within the electorate of Massachusetts. Since no sample survey data are available for 1928, about the only analysis feasible is inspection of election returns for geographic units contrasting in their population composition. Lest it be supposed, however, that the good citizens of Somerville and Ashfield were aberrants simply unlike the remainder of the people of the Commonwealth, examination of a large number of towns and cities is in order. In the interest of both compression and comprehensibility, a mass of data is telescoped into Figure B. The graphs in that figure compare over the period 1916–1952 the voting behavior of the 29 Massachusetts towns and cities having the sharpest Democratic increases, 1920–1928, with that of the 30 towns and cities having the most marked Democratic loss, 1920–1928. In other words, the figure averages out a great many Ashfields and Somervilles. The data

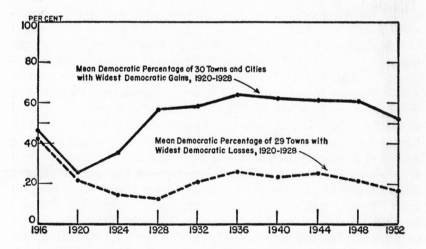

Figure B. Persistence of electoral cleavage of 1928 in Massachusetts: Mean Democratic percentage of Presidential vote in towns with sharpest Democratic gains, 1920–1928, and in towns of widest Democratic losses, 1920–1928

of Figure B confirm the expectation that the pattern exhibited by the pair of voting units in Figure A represented only a single case of a much more general phenomenon. Yet by virtue of the coverage of the data in the figure, one gains a stronger impression of the difference in the character of the election of 1928 and the other elections recorded there. The cleavage confirmed by the 1928 returns persisted. At subsequent elections the voters shifted to and fro within the outlines of the broad division fixed in 1928.

Examination of the characteristics of the two groups of cities and towns of Figure B—those with the most marked Democratic gains, 1920–1928, and those with the widest movement in the opposite direction —reveals the expected sorts of differences. Urban, industrial, foreign-born, Catholic areas made up the bulk of the first group of towns, although an occasional rural Catholic community increased its Democratic vote markedly. The towns with a contrary movement tended to be rural, Protestant, native-born. The new Democratic vote correlated quite closely with a 1930 vote on state enforcement of the national prohibition law.

Melancholy experience with the eccentricities of data, be they quantitative or otherwise, suggests the prudence of a check on the interpretation of 1928. Would the same method applied to any other election yield a similar result, *i.e.,* the appearance of a more or less durable realignment? Perhaps there can be no doubt that the impact of the events of any election on many individuals forms lasting party loyalties; yet not often is the number so affected so great as to create a sharp realignment. On the other hand, some elections are characterized by a large-scale transfer of party affection that is quite short-term, a different sort of phenomenon from that which occurs in elections marked by broad and durable shifts in party strength. The difference is illustrated by the data on the election of 1932 in New Hampshire in Figure C. The voting records of the twenty-five towns with the widest Democratic gains from 1928 to 1932 are there traced from 1916 to 1952. Observe that Democratic strength in these towns shot up in 1932 but fairly quickly resumed about the same position in relation to other towns that it had occupied in 1928. It is also evident from the graph that this group of towns had on the whole been especially strongly repelled by the Democratic appeal of 1928. Probably the depression drove an appreciable number of hardened Republicans of these towns to vote for a change in 1932, but they gradually found their way back to the party of their fathers. In any case, the figure reflects a type of behavior differing markedly from that of 1928. To the extent that 1932 resembled 1928 in the recrystallization of party lines, the proportions of new Democrats did not differ significantly

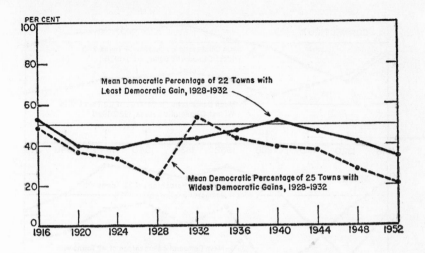

Figure C. Impact of election of 1932 in New Hampshire: Mean Democratic percentage of Presidential vote of towns with sharpest Democratic gain, 1928–1932, compared with mean vote of towns at opposite extreme of 1928–1932 change

among the groups of towns examined. In fact, what probably happened to a considerable extent in New England was that the 1928 election broke the electorate into two new groups that would have been formed in 1932 had there been no realignment in 1928.

The Massachusetts material has served both to explain the method of analysis and to present the case of a single state. Examinations of the election of 1928 in other New England states indicates that in each a pattern prevailed similar to that of Massachusetts. The total effect of the realignment differed, of course, from state to state. In Massachusetts and Rhode Island the number of people affected by the upheaval of 1928 was sufficient to form a new majority coalition. In Maine, New Hampshire, and Vermont the same sort of reshuffling of electors occurred, but the proportions affected were not sufficient to overturn the Republican combination, although the basis was laid in Maine and New Hampshire for later limited Democratic successes. To underpin these remarks the materials on Connecticut, Maine, New Hampshire, and Rhode Island are presented in Figure D. The data on Vermont, excluded for lack of space, form a pattern similar to that emerging from the analysis of the other states.

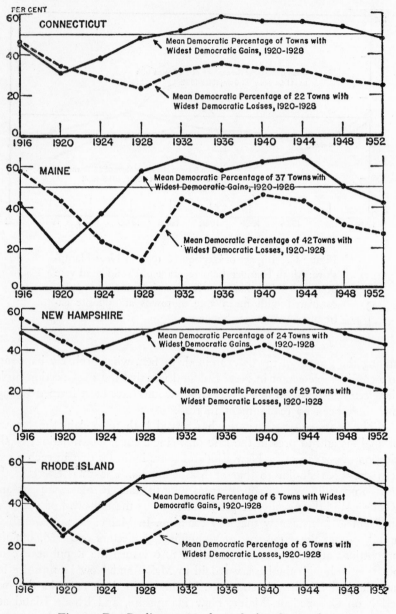

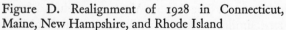

Figure D. Realignment of 1928 in Connecticut,
Maine, New Hampshire, and Rhode Island

In the interpretation of all these 1928 analyses certain limitations of the technique need to be kept in mind. The data and the technique most clearly reveal a shift when voters of different areas move in opposite directions. From 1928 to 1936 apparently a good deal of Democratic growth occurred in virtually all geographic units, a shift not shown up sharply by the technique. Hence, the discussion may fail adequately to indicate the place of 1928 as the crucial stage in a process of electoral change that began before and concluded after that year.

II

One of the difficulties with an ideal type is that no single actual case fits exactly its specifications. Moreover, in any system of categorization the greater the number of differentiating criteria for classes, the more nearly one tends to create a separate class for each instance. If taxonomic systems are to be of analytical utility, they must almost inevitably group together instances that are unlike at least in peripheral characteristics irrelevant to the purpose of the system. All of which serves to warn that an election is about to be classified as critical even though in some respects the behavior involved differed from that of the 1928 polling.

Central to our concept of critical elections is a realignment within the electorate both sharp and durable. With respect to these basic criteria the election of 1896 falls within the same category as that of 1928, although it differed in other respects. The persistence of the new division of 1896 was perhaps not so notable as that of 1928; yet the Democratic defeat was so demoralizing and so thorough that the party could make little headway in regrouping its forces until 1916. Perhaps the significant feature of the 1896 contest was that, at least in New England, it did not form a new division in which partisan lines became more nearly congruent with lines separating classes, religions, or other such social groups. Instead, the Republicans succeeded in drawing new support, in about the same degree, from all sorts of economic and social classes. The result was an electoral coalition formidable in its mass but which required both good fortune and skill in political management for its maintenance, given its latent internal contradictions.

If the 1896 election is described in our terms as a complex of behavior preceding and following the formal voting, an account of the action must include the panic of 1893. Bank failures, railroad receiverships, unemployment, strikes, Democratic championship of deflation and of the gold standard, and related matters created the setting for a Democratic setback in 1894. Only one of the eight New England Democratic Representatives survived the elections of 1894. The two 1892 Democratic governors fell by the wayside and in all the states the Democratic share of the gubernatorial vote fell sharply in 1894. The luckless William Jennings Bryan and the free-silver heresy perhaps did not contribute as much as is generally supposed to the 1892–1896 decline in New England Democratic strength; New England Democrats moved in large numbers over to the Republican ranks in 1894.

The character of the 1892–1896 electoral shift is suggested by the data of Figure E, which presents an analysis of Connecticut and New Hampshire made by the technique used earlier in examining the election of 1928. The graphs make plain that in these states (and the other New England states show the same pattern) the rout of 1896 produced a basic realignment that persisted at least until 1916. The graphs in Figure E also make equally plain that the 1892–1896 realignment differed radically from that of 1928 in certain respects. In 1896 the net movement

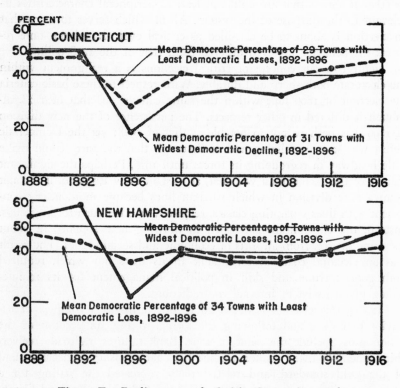

Figure E. Realignment of 1896 in Connecticut and New Hampshire

in all sorts of geographic units was toward the Republicans; towns differed not in the direction of their movement but only in the extent. Moreover, the persistence of the realignment of 1896 was about the same in those towns with the least Democratic loss from 1892 to 1896 as it was in those with the most marked decline in Democratic strength. Hence, the graphs differ from those on 1928 which took the form of opening scissors. Instead, the 1896 realignment appears as a parallel movement of both groups to a lower plateau of Democratic strength.

If the election of 1896 had had a notable differential impact on geographically segregated social groups, the graphs in Figure E of towns at the extremes of the greatest and least 1892-96 change would have taken the form of opening scissors as they did in 1928. While the election of 1896 is often pictured as a last-ditch fight between the haves and the have-nots, that understanding of the contest was, at least in New England, evidently restricted to planes of leadership and oratory. It did not extend to the voting actions of the electorate. These observations merit some buttressing, although the inference emerges clearly enough from Figure E.

Unfortunately the census authorities have ignored the opportunity to advance demographic inquiry by publishing data of consequence about New England towns. Not much information is available on the characteristics of the populations of these small geographic areas. Nevertheless, size of total population alone is a fair separator of towns according to politically significant characteristics. Classification of towns according to that criterion groups them roughly according to industrialization and probably generally also according to religion and national origin. Hence, with size of population of towns and cities as a basis, Table 1 contrasts the elections of 1896 and 1928 for different types of towns. Observe from the table that the mean shift between 1892 and 1896 was about the same for varying size groups of towns. Contrast this lack of association between size and political movement with the radically different 1920-28 pattern which also appears in the table.

Table 1 makes clear that in 1896 the industrial cities, in their aggregate vote at least, moved toward the Republicans in about the same degree as did the rural farming communities. Some of the misinterpretations of the election of 1896 flow from a focus on that election in isolation rather than in comparison with the preceding election. In 1896, even in New England cities, the Democrats tended to be strongest in the poor, working-class, immigrant sections. Yet the same relation had existed, in a sharper form, in 1892. In 1896 the Republicans gained in the working-class wards, just as they did in the silk-stocking wards, over their 1892

TABLE I. Contrasts Between Elections of 1896 and 1928 in Massachusetts: Shifts in Democratic Strength, 1892–1896 and 1920–1928, in Relation to Population Size of Towns

Population Size Group	Mean Democratic Percentage		Mean Change 1892–96	Mean Democratic Percentage		Mean Change 1920–28
	1892	1896		1920	1928	
1–999	34.0	14.7	−19.3	16.5	18.6	+2.1
2000–2999	38.8	18.3	−20.5	21.0	33.1	+12.1
10,000–14,999	46.7	26.9	−19.8	25.8	43.7	+17.9
50,000+	47.7	30.1	−17.6	29.5	55.7	+26.2

vote. They were able to place the blame for unemployment upon the Democrats and to propagate successfully the doctrine that the Republican Party was the party of prosperity and the "full dinner pail." On the whole, the effect apparently was to reduce the degree of coincidence of class affiliation and partisan inclination. Nor was the election of 1896, in New England at least, a matter of heightened tension between city and country. Both city and country voters shifted in the same direction. Neither urban employers nor industrial workers could generate much enthusiasm for inflation and free trade; rather they joined in common cause. Instead of a sharpening of class cleavages within New England the voting apparently reflected more a sectional antagonism and anxiety, shared by all classes, expressed in opposition to the dangers supposed to be threatening from the West.

Other contrasts between the patterns of electoral behavior of 1896 and 1928 could be cited but in terms of sharpness and durability of realignment both elections were of roughly the same type, at least in New England. In these respects they seem to differ from most other elections over a period of a half century, although it may well be that each round at the ballot boxes involves realignment within the electorate similar in kind but radically different in extent.

III

The discussion points toward the analytical utility of a system for the differentiation of elections. A concept of critical elections has been developed to cover a type of election in which there occurs a sharp and durable electoral realignment between parties, although the techniques employed do not yield any information of consequences about the mechanisms for the maintenance of a new alignment, once it is formed. Obviously any sort of system for the gross characterization of elections presents difficulties in application. The actual election rarely presents in pure form a case fitting completely any particular concept. Especially in a large and diverse electorate a single polling may encompass radically varying types of behavior among different categories of voters; yet a dominant characteristic often makes itself apparent. Despite such difficulties, the attempt to move toward a better understanding of elections in the terms here employed could provide a means for better integrating the study of electoral behavior with the analysis of political systems. In truth, a considerable proportion of the study of electoral behavior has only a tenuous relation to politics.

The sorts of questions here raised, when applied sufficiently broadly on a comparative basis and carried far enough, could lead to a consideration of basic problems of the nature of democratic orders. A question occurs, for example, about the character of the consequences for the political system of the temporal frequency of critical elections. What are the consequences for public administration, for the legislative process, for the operation of the economy of frequent serious upheavals within the electorate? What are the correlates of that pattern of behavior? And, for those disposed to raise such questions, what underlying changes might alter the situation? Or, when viewed from the contrary position, what consequences flow from an electorate which is disposed, in effect, to remain largely quiescent over considerable periods? Does a state of moving equilibrium reflect a pervasive satisfaction with the course of public policy? An indifference about matters political? In any case, what are the consequences for the public order? Further, what are the consequences when an electorate builds up habits and attachments, or faces situations, that make it impossible for it to render a decisive and clearcut popular verdict that promises not to be upset by caprice at the next round of polling? What are the consequences of a situation that creates recurring, evenly balanced conflict over long periods? On the other hand, what characteristics of an electorate or what conditions permit sharp and decisive changes in the power structure from time to time? Such directions of speculation are suggested by a single criterion for the differentiation of elections. Further development of an electoral typology would probably point to useful speculation in a variety of directions.

DEMOCRATIC PRACTICE AND DEMOCRATIC THEORY

*Bernard R. Berelson, Paul F. Lazarsfeld, William N. McPhee**

REQUIREMENTS FOR THE INDIVIDUAL

PERHAPS the main impact of realistic research on contemporary politics has been to temper some of the requirements set by our traditional normative theory for the typical citizen. "Out of all this literature of political observation and analysis, which is relatively new," says Max Beloff, "there has come to exist a picture in our minds of the political scene which differs very considerably from that familiar to us from the classical texts of democratic politics."

Experienced observers have long known, of course, that the individual voter was not all that the theory of democracy requires of him. As Bryce put it:

> How little solidity and substance there is in the political or social beliefs of nineteen persons out of every twenty. These beliefs, when examined, mostly resolve themselves into two or three prejudices and aversions, two or three prepossessions for a particular party or section of a party, two or three phrases or catch-words suggesting or embodying arguments which the man who repeats them has not analyzed.

While our data [from the Elmira study] do not support such an extreme statement, they do reveal that certain requirements commonly assumed for the successful operation of democracy are not met by the behavior of the "average" citizen. The requirements, and our conclusions concerning them, are quickly reviewed.

Interest, discussion, motivation. The democratic citizen is expected to be interested and to participate in political affairs. His interest and participation can take such various forms as reading and listening to campaign materials, working for the candidate or the party, arguing politics, donating money, and voting. In Elmira the majority of the people vote, but in general they do not give evidence of sustained interest. Many vote without real involvement in the election, and even the party workers are not typically motivated by ideological concerns or plain civic duty.

* From *Voting*, Chapter 14, by Bernard R. Berelson, Paul F. Lazarsfeld, and William N. McPhee. Reprinted by permission of the University of Chicago Press. Copyright © 1954 by the University of Chicago.

If there is one characteristic for a democratic system (besides the ballot itself) that is theoretically required, it is the capacity for and the practice of discussion. "It is as true of the large as of the small society," says Lindsay, "that its health depends on the mutual understanding which discussion makes possible; and that discussion is the only possible instrument of its democratic government." How much participation in political discussion there is in the community, what it is, and among whom—these questions have been given answers . . . earlier. . . . In this instance there was little true discussion between the candidates, little in the newspaper commentary, little between the voters and the official party representatives, some within the electorate. On the grass-roots level there was more talk than debate, and, at least inferentially, the talk had important effects upon voting, in reinforcing or activating the partisans if not in converting the opposition.

An assumption underlying the theory of democracy is that the citizenry has a strong motivation for participation in political life. But it is a curious quality of voting behavior that for large numbers of people motivation is weak if not almost absent. It is assumed that this motivation would gain its strength from the citizen's perception of the difference that alternative decisions made to him. Now when a person buys something or makes other decisions of daily life, there are direct and immediate consequences for him. But for the bulk of the American people the voting decision is not followed by any direct, immediate, visible personal consequences. Most voters, organized or unorganized, are not in a position to foresee the distant and indirect consequences for themselves, let alone the society. The ballot is cast, and for most people that is the end of it. If their side is defeated, "it doesn't really matter."

Knowledge. The democratic citizen is expected to be well informed about political affairs. He is supposed to know what the issues are, what their history is, what the relevant facts are, what alternatives are proposed, what the party stands for, what the likely consequences are. By such standards the voter falls short. Even when he has the motivation, he finds it difficult to make decisions on the basis of full information when the subject is relatively simple and proximate; how can he do so when it is complex and remote? The citizen is not highly informed on details of the campaign, nor does he avoid a certain misperception of the political situation when it is to his psychological advantage to do so. The electorate's perception of what goes on in the campaign is colored by emotional feeling toward one or the other issue, candidate, party, or social group.

Principle. The democratic citizen is supposed to cast his vote on the basis of principle—not fortuitously or frivolously or impulsively or habitually, but with reference to standards not only of his own interest but of the common good as well. Here, again, if this requirement is pushed at all strongly, it becomes an impossible demand on the democratic electorate.

Many voters vote not for principle in the usual sense but "for" a group to which they are attached—their group. The Catholic vote or the hereditary vote is explainable less as principle than as a traditional social allegiance. The ordinary voter, bewildered by the complexity of modern political problems, unable to determine clearly what the consequences are of alternative lines of action, remote from the arena, and incapable of bringing information to bear on principle, votes the way trusted people around him are voting. . . .

On the issues of the campaign there is a considerable amount of "don't know"—sometimes reflecting genuine indecision, more often meaning "don't care." Among those with opinions the partisans *agree* on most issues, criteria, expectations, and rules of the game. The supporters of the different sides disagree on only a few issues. Nor, for that matter, do the candidates themselves always join the issue sharply and clearly. The partisans do not agree overwhelmingly with their own party's position, or, rather, only the small minority of highly partisan do; the rest take a rather moderate position on the political consideration involved in an election.

Rationality. The democratic citizen is expected to exercise rational judgment in coming to his voting decision. He is expected to have arrived at his principles by reason and to have considered rationally the implications and alleged consequences of the alternative proposals of the contending parties. Political theorists and commentators have always exclaimed over the seeming contrast here between requirement and fulfillment. . . . The upshot of this is that the usual analogy between the voting "decision" and the more or less carefully calculated decisions of consumers or businessmen or courts, incidentally, may be quite incorrect. For many voters political preferences may better be considered analogous to cultural tastes—in music, literature, recreational activities, dress, ethics, speech, social behavior. Consider the parallels between political preferences and general cultural tastes. Both have their origin in ethnic, sectional, class, and family traditions. Both exhibit stability and resistance to change for individuals but flexibility and adjustment over generations for the society as a whole. Both seem to be matters of sentiment and disposition rather than "reasoned preferences." While both are responsive to changed conditions and unusual stimuli, they are relatively invulnerable to direct argumentation and vulnerable to indirect social influences. Both are characterized more by faith than by conviction and by wishful expectation rather than careful prediction or consequences. The preference for one party rather than another must be highly similar to the preference for one kind of literature or music rather than another, and the choice of the same political party every four years may be parallel to the choice of the same old standards of conduct in new social situations. In short, it appears that a sense of fitness is a more striking feature of political preference than reason and calculation.

REQUIREMENTS FOR THE SYSTEM

If the democratic system depended solely on the qualifications of the individual voter, then it seems remarkable that democracies have survived through the centuries. After examining the detailed data on how individuals misperceive political reality or respond to irrelevant social influences, one wonders how a democracy ever solves its political problems. But when one considers the data in a broader perspective—how huge segments of the society adapt to political conditions affecting them or how the political system adjusts itself to changing conditions over long periods of time—he cannot fail to be impressed with the total result. Where the rational citizen seems to abdicate, nevertheless angels seem to tread....

That is the paradox. *Individual voters* today seem unable to satisfy the requirements for a democratic system of government outlined by political theorists. But the *system of democracy* does meet certain requirements for a going political organization. The individual members may not meet all the standards, but the whole nevertheless survives and grows. This suggests that where the classic theory is defective is in its concentration on the *individual citizen*. What are undervalued are certain collective properties that reside in the electorate as a whole and in the political and social system in which it functions.

The political philosophy we have inherited, then, has given more consideration to the virtues of the typical citizen of the democracy than to the working of the *system* as a whole. Moreover, when it dealt with the system, it mainly considered the single constitutive institutions of the system, not those general features necessary if the institutions are to work as required. For example, the rule of law, representative government, periodic elections, the party system, and the several freedoms of discussion, press, association, and assembly have all been examined by political philosophers seeking to clarify and to justify the idea of political democracy. But liberal democracy is more than a political system in which individual voters and political institutions operate. For political democracy to survive, other features are required: the intensity of conflict must be limited, the rate of change must be restrained, stability in the social and economic structure must be maintained, a pluralistic social organization must exist, and a basic consensus must bind together the contending parties.

Such features of the system of political democracy belong neither to the constitutive institutions nor to the individual voter. It might be said that they form the atmosphere or the environment in which both operate. In any case, such features have not been carefully considered by political philosophers, and it is on these broader properties of the democratic political system that more reflection and study by political theory is called for. In the most tentative fashion let us explore the values of the political system, as they involve the electorate, in the light of the foregoing considerations.

Underlying the paradox is an assumption that the population is homogeneous socially and should be homogeneous politically: that everybody is about the same in relevant social characteristics; that, if something is a political virtue (like interest in the election), then everyone should have it; that there is such a thing as "the" typical citizen on whom uniform requirements can be imposed. The tendency of classic democratic literature to work with an image of "the" voter was never justified. For, as we will attempt to illustrate here, some of the most important requirements that democratic values impose on a system require a voting population that is not homogeneous but heterogeneous in its political qualities.

The need for heterogeneity arises from the contradictory functions we expect our voting system to serve. We expect the political system to adjust itself and our affairs to changing conditions; yet we demand too that it display a high degree of stability. We expect the contending interests and parties to pursue their ends vigorously and the voters to care; yet, after the election is over, we expect reconciliation. We expect the voting outcome to serve what is best for the community; yet we do not want disinterested voting unattached to the purposes and interests of different segments of that community. We want voters to express their own free and self-determined choices; yet, for the good of the community, we would like voters to avail themselves of the best information and guidance available from the groups and leaders around them. We expect a high degree of rationality to prevail in the decision; but were all irrationality and mythology absent, and all ends pursued by the most coldly rational selection of political means, it is doubtful if the system would hold together.

In short, our electoral system calls for apparently incompatible properties—which, although they cannot all reside in each individual voter, can (and do) reside in a heterogeneous electorate. What seems to be required of the electorate as a whole is a *distribution* of qualities along important dimensions. We need some people who are active in a certain respect, others in the middle, and still others passive. The contradictory things we want from the total require that the parts be different. This can be illustrated by taking up a number of important dimensions by which an electorate might be characterized.

Involvement and indifference. How could a mass democracy work if all the people were deeply involved in politics? Lack of interest by some people is not without its benefits, too. True, the highly interested voters vote more, and know more about the campaign, and read and listen more, and participate more; however, they are also less open to persuasion and less likely to change. Extreme interest goes with extreme partisanship and might culminate in rigid fanaticism that could destroy democratic processes if generalized throughout the community. Low affect toward the election—not caring much—underlies the resolution of many political problems; votes can be resolved into a two-party split instead of fragmented into many parties (the splinter parties of the left, for example, splinter because their advocates are *too* interested in politics). Low interest provides maneuvering room for political shifts necessary for a complex society in a period of rapid change. Compromise might be based upon sophisticated awareness of costs and returns—perhaps impossible to demand of a mass society—but it is more often induced by indifference. Some people are and should be highly interested in politics, but not everyone is or needs to be. Only the doctrinaire would deprecate the moderate indifference that facilitates compromise.

Hence, an important balance between action motivated by strong sentiments and action with little passion behind it is obtained by heterogeneity within the electorate. Balance of this sort is, in practice, met by a distribution of voters rather than by a homogeneous collection of "ideal" citizens.

Stability and flexibility. A similar dimension along which an electorate might be characterized is stability-flexibility. The need for change and adaptation is clear, and the need for stability ought equally to be (especially from observation of current democratic practice in, say, certain Latin-American countries). . . . [I]t may be that the very people who are most sensitive to changing social conditions are those most susceptible to political change. For, in either case, the people exposed to membership in overlapping strata, those whose former life-patterns are being broken up, those who are moving about socially or physically, those who are forming new families and new friendships—it is they who are open to adjustments of attitudes and tastes. They may be the least partisan and the least interested voters, but they perform a valuable function for the entire system. Here again is an instance in which an individual "inadequacy" provides a positive service for society: The campaign can be a reaffirming force for the settled majority and a creative force for the unsettled minority. There is stability on both sides and flexibility in the middle.

Progress and conservation. Closely related to the question of stability is the question of past versus future orientation of the system. In America a progressive outlook is highly valued, but, at the same time, so is a conservative one. Here a balance between the two is easily found in the party system and in the distribution of voters themselves from extreme conservatives to extreme liberals. But a balance between the two is also achieved by a distribution of political dispositions through time. There are periods of great political agitation (*i.e.*, campaigns) alternating with periods of political dormancy. Paradoxically, the former—the campaign period—is likely to be an instrument of conservatism, often even of historical regression. . . .

Again, then, a balance (between preservation of the past and receptivity to the future) seems to be required of a democratic electorate. The heterogeneous electorate in itself provides a balance between liberalism and conservatism; and so does the sequence of political events from periods of drifting change to abrupt rallies back to the loyalties of earlier years.

Consensus and cleavage. . . . [T]here are required *social* consensus and cleavage—in effect pluralism—in politics. Such pluralism makes for enough consensus to hold the system together and enough cleavage to make it move. Too much consensus would be deadening and restrictive of liberty; too much cleavage would be destructive of the society as a whole. . . . Thus again a requirement we might place on an electoral system—balance between total political war between segments of the society and total political indifference to group interests of that society—translates into varied requirements for different individuals. With respect to group or bloc voting, as with other aspects of political behavior, it is perhaps not unfortunate that "some do and some do not."

Individualism and collectivism. Lord Bryce pointed out the difficulties in a theory of democracy that assumes that each citizen must himself be capable of voting intelligently:

> Orthodox democratic theory assumes that every citizen has, or ought to have, thought out for himself certain opinions, *i.e.,* ought to have a definite view, defensible by argument, of what the country needs, of what principles ought to be applied in governing it, of the man to whose hands the government ought to be entrusted. There are persons who talk, though certainly very few who act, as if they believed this theory, which may be compared to the theory of some ultra-Protestants that every good Christian has or ought to have . . . worked out for himself from the Bible a system of theology.

In the first place, however, the information available to the individual voter is not limited to that directly possessed by him. True, the individual casts his own personal ballot. But, as we have tried to indicate . . . , that is perhaps the most individualized action he takes in an election. His vote is formed in the midst of his fellows in a sort of group decision —if, indeed, it may be called a decision at all—and the total information and knowledge possessed in the group's present and past generations can be made available for the group's choice. Here is where opinion-leading relationships, for example, play an active role.

Second, and probably more important, the individual voter may not have a great deal of detailed information, but he usually has picked up the crucial *general* information as part of his social learning itself. He may not know the parties' positions on the tariff, or who is for reciprocal trade treaties, or what are the differences on Asiatic policy, or how the parties split on civil rights, or how many security risks were exposed by whom. But he cannot live in an American community without knowing broadly where the parties stand. He has learned that the Republicans are more conservative and the Democrats more liberal—and he can locate his own sentiments and cast his vote accordingly. After all, he must vote for one or the other party, and, if he knows the big thing about the parties, he does not need to know all the little things. The basic role a party plays as an institution in American life is more important to his voting than a particular stand on a particular issue.

It would be unthinkable to try to maintain our present economic style of life without a complex system of delegating to others what we are not competent to do ourselves, without accepting and giving training to each other about what each is expected to do, without accepting our dependence on others in many spheres and taking responsibility for their dependence on us in some spheres. And, like it or not, to maintain our present political style of life, we may have to accept much the same interdependence with others in collective behavior. We have learned slowly in economic life that it is useful not to have everyone a butcher or a baker, any more than it is useful to have no one skilled in such activities. The same kind of division of labor—as repugnant as it may be in some respects to our individualistic tradition—is serving us well today in mass politics. There is an implicit division of political labor within the electorate. 📭

17. Electoral Reapportionment

A development of profound significance to the political process has been the entrance of the federal judiciary into the sphere of legislative reapportionment. The Court has always attempted to avoid "political questions" that are highly controversial. Judicial intervention into the arena of electoral reapportionment accompanied a shift on the Supreme Court from a majority emphasizing self-restraint in such matters to one desiring positive judicial action.

What does the Constitution say about electoral apportionment? There is no explicit provision pertaining to representation in *state* legislatures, and regarding congressional districts, Article I provides only that each state shall have a number of representatives in proportion to its population, and that every ten years this number may be changed in accordance with whatever directives Congress makes. Thus the matter of congressional districting seemed to be solely within the jurisdiction of Congress, and by implication, the apportionment of state legislative districts would be the exclusive concern of state governments.

Gradually it became evident that leaving the problem of redistricting up to Congress and state legislatures would not bring about equality of representation. In *Colegrove* v. *Green,* 328 U.S. 549 (1946), a strong appeal was made to the Supreme Court to change congressional districting in Illinois that had resulted in giving a very unfair advantage to rural interests. For example, a congressional district in Chicago with a population of close to a million voters had the same representation in the House of Representatives as a southern Illinois rural district with a population of only about 100,000 voters. Regardless of such disparities, the Supreme Court ruled that the issue of equal representation was not a matter of judicial concern. It was a political question that should be left up to Congress to resolve. After holding in the *Colegrove* case that congressional districting was beyond judicial scrutiny the Court later refused to intervene in the districting for elections to state legislatures. See *South* v. *Peters*, 339 U.S. 276 (1950).

In 1962 the judicial doctrine of self-restraint in the field of legislative reapportionment changed completely in the historic case of *Baker* v. *Carr*, 369 U.S. 186 (1962). A civil action had been brought against the state of Tennessee to prohibit it from holding further elections under the provisions of a 1901 apportioning statute that based apportionment upon a census taken in the year 1900. All efforts to change the method of apportionment as the population of the state grew and shifted failed, resulting in what the Court called a "crazy-quilt" of representation. For example, a relatively urban county with a population of approximately 37,000 voters had only twice as much representation as a rural county with a population of less than 3,000. There seemed to be no logic whatsoever in the patterns of representation from county to county. Counties with almost exactly the same number of voters had substantially different numbers of representatives in the state legislature. When the *Baker* case was initially brought before the Federal District Court of Tennessee, the action was dismissed for lack of jurisdiction on the basis of the *Colegrove* doctrine. The appellants had claimed that their rights under the Fourteenth Amendment, Equal Protection of the Laws Clause had been violated by the lack of equal representation in the state. In the opinion printed below the Supreme Court overruled the District Court decision, holding that apportionment of the Tennessee State Legislature was a proper matter for judicial concern.

BAKER v. CARR

369 U.S. 186 (1962)

M R. Justice Brennan delivered the opinion of the Court, saying in part:

This civil action was brought under 42 USC §§ 1983 and 1988 to redress the alleged deprivation of federal constitutional rights. The complaint, alleging that by means of a 1901 statute of Tennessee apportioning the members of the General Assembly among the State's 95 counties, "these plaintiffs and others similarly situated, are denied the equal protection of the laws accorded them by the Fourteenth Amendment to the

Constitution of the United States by virtue of the debasement of their votes," was dismissed by a three-judge court. . . . The court held that it lacked jurisdiction of the subject matter and also that no claim was stated upon which relief could be granted. . . . We hold that the dismissal was in error, and remand the cause to the District Court for trial and further proceedings consistent with this opinion.

The General Assembly of Tennessee consists of the Senate with 33 members and the House of Representatives with 99 members. . . .

. . . Tennessee's standard for allocating legislative representation among her counties is the total number of qualified voters resident in the respective counties, subject only to minor qualifications. Decennial reapportionment in compliance with the constitutional scheme was effected by the General Assembly each decade from 1871 to 1901. . . . In 1901 the General Assembly abandoned separate enumeration in favor of reliance upon the Federal Census and passed the Apportionment Act here in controversy. In the more than 60 years since that action, all proposals in both Houses of the General Assembly for reapportionment have failed to pass.

Between 1901 and 1961, Tennessee has experienced substantial growth and redistribution of her population. In 1901 the population was 2,020,616, of whom 487,380 were eligible to vote. The 1960 Federal Census reports the State's population at 3,567,089, of whom 2,092,891 are eligible to vote. The relative standings of the counties in terms of qualified voters have changed significantly. It is primarily the continued application of the 1901 Apportionment Act to this shifted and enlarged voting population which gives rise to the present controversy.

Indeed, the complaint alleges that the 1901 statute, even as of the time of its passage, "made no apportionment of Representatives and Senators in accordance with the constitutional formula . . . , but instead arbitrarily and capriciously apportioned representatives in the Senate and House without reference . . . to any logical or reasonable formula whatever." It is further alleged that "because of the population changes since 1900, and the failure of the legislature to reapportion itself since 1901," the 1901 statute became "unconstitutional and obsolete." Appellants also argue that, because of the composition of the legislature effected by the 1901 apportionment act, redress in the form of a state constitutional amendment to change the entire mechanism for reapportioning, or any other change short of that, is difficult or impossible. The complaint concludes that "these plaintiffs and others similarly situated, are denied the equal protection of the laws accorded them by the Fourteenth Amendment to the Constitution of the United States by virtue of the debasement of their votes." They seek a declaration that the 1901 statute is unconstitutional and an injunction restraining the appellees from acting to conduct any further elections under it. They also pray that unless and until the General Assembly enacts a valid reapportionment, the District Court should either decree a reapportionment by mathematical application of the Tennessee constitutional formulae to the most recent Federal Census figures, or direct the appellees to conduct legislative elections, primary and general, at large. They also pray for such other and further relief as may be appropriate.

I. The District Court's Opinion and Order of Dismissal

Because we deal with this case on appeal from an order of dismissal granted on appellees' motions, precise identification of the issues presently confronting us demands clear exposition of the grounds upon which the District Court rested in dismissing the case. The dismissal order recited that the court sustained the appellees' grounds "(1) that the Court lacks jurisdiction of the subject matter, and (2) that the complaint fails to state a claim upon which relief can be granted, ..." ...

The court proceeded to explain its action as turning on the case's presenting a "question of the distribution of political strength for legislative purposes." For, "from a review of [numerous Supreme Court] . . . decisions there can be no doubt that the federal rule, as enunciated and applied by the Supreme Court, is that the federal courts, whether from a lack of jurisdiction or from the inappropriateness of the subject matter for judicial consideration, will not intervene in cases of this type to compel legislative reapportionment."

The court went on to express doubts as to the feasibility of the various possible remedies sought by the plaintiffs. Then it made clear that its dismissal reflected a view not of doubt that violation of constitutional rights was alleged, but of a court's impotence to correct that violation:

"With the plaintiff's argument that the legislature of Tennessee is guilty of a clear violation of the state constitution and of the rights of the plaintiffs the Court entirely agrees. It also agrees that the evil is a serious one which should be corrected without further delay. But even so the remedy in this situation clearly does not lie with the courts. It has long been recognized and is accepted doctrine that there are indeed some rights guaranteed by the Constitution for the violation of which the courts cannot give redress."

In light of the District Court's treatment of the case, we hold today only (a) that the court possessed jurisdiction of the subject matter; (b) that a justiciable cause of actions is stated upon which appellants would be entitled to appropriate relief; and (c) because appellees raise the issue before this Court, that the appellants have standing to challenge the Tennessee apportionment statutes. Beyond noting that we have no cause at this stage to doubt the District Court will be able to fashion relief if violations of constitutional rights are found, it is improper now to consider what remedy would be most appropriate if appellants prevail at the trial.

II. Jurisdiction of the Subject Matter

. . . Our conclusion, . . . that this cause presents no nonjusticiable "political question" settles the only possible doubt that it is a case or controversy [under Article 3].

Article 3 § 2 of the Federal Constitution provides that "the judicial Power shall extend to all Cases, in Law and Equity, arising under this Constitution, the Laws of the United States, and Treaties made, or which shall be made, under their Authority; . . ." It is clear that the cause of action is one which "arises under" the Federal Constitution. The complaint alleges that the 1901 statute effects an apportionment that deprives the appellants of the equal protection of the laws in violation of the Fourteenth Amendment. Dismissal of the complaint upon the ground of lack of jurisdiction of the subject matter would, therefore, be justified only if that claim were "so attenuated and unsubstantial as to be absolutely devoid of merit." . . . Since the District Court obviously and correctly did not deem the asserted federal constitutional claim unsubstantial and frivolous, it should not have dismissed the complaint for want of jurisdiction of the subject matter. And of course no further consideration of the merits of the claim is relevant to a determination of the court's jurisdiction of the subject matter.

An unbroken line of our precedents sustains the federal courts' jurisdiction of the subject matter of federal constitutional claims of this nature. . . .

The appellees refer to *Colegrove* v. *Green,* 328 US 549, as authority that the District Court lacked jurisdiction of the subject matter. Appellees misconceive the holding of that case. The holding was precisely contrary to their reading of it. Seven members of the Court participated in the decision. Unlike many other cases in this field which have assumed without discussion that there was jurisdiction, all three opinions filed in Colegrove discussed the question. Two of the opinions expressing the views of four of the Justices, a majority, flatly held that there was jurisdiction of the subject matter. . . .

We hold that the District Court has jurisdiction of the subject matter of the federal constitutional claim asserted in the complaint.

III. Standing

A federal court cannot "pronounce any statute, either of a State or of the United States, void, because irreconcilable with the Constitution, except as it is called upon to adjudge the legal rights of litigants in actual controversies." Have the appellants alleged such a personal stake in the outcome of the controversy as to assure that concrete adverseness which sharpens the presentation of issues upon which the court so largely depends for illumination of difficult constitutional questions? This is the gist of the question of standing. . . .

We hold that the appellants do have standing to maintain this suit. . . .

These appellants seek relief in order to protect or vindicate an interest of their own, and of those similarly situated. Their constitutional claim is, in substance, that the 1901 statute constitutes arbitrary and capricious state action, offensive to the Fourteenth Amendment in its irrational disregard of the standard of apportionment prescribed by the State's Constitution or of any standard, effecting a gross disproportion of representation to voting population. The injury which appellants assert is that this classification disfavors the voters in the counties in which they reside, placing them in a position of constitutionally unjustifiable inequality vis-à-vis voters in irrationally favored counties. A citizen's right to a vote free of arbitrary impairment by state action has been judicially recognized as a right secured by the Constitution, when such impairment resulted from dilution by a false tally, or by a refusal to count votes from arbitrarily selected precincts, or by a stuffing of the ballot box.

It would not be necessary to decide whether appellants' allegations of impairment of their votes by the 1901 apportionment will, ultimately, entitle them to any relief, in order to hold that they have standing to seek it. If such impairment does produce a legally cognizable injury, they are among those who have sustained it. They are entitled to a hearing and to the District Court's decision on their claims. "The very essence of civil liberty certainly consists in the right of every individual to claim the protection of the laws, whenever he receives an injury."

IV. Justiciability

In holding that the subject matter of this suit was not justiciable, the District Court relied on *Colegrove* v. *Green,* and subsequent per curiam cases. The court stated: "From a review of these decisions there can be no doubt that the federal rule . . . is that the federal courts . . . will not intervene in cases of this type to compel legislative reapportionment." We understand the District Court to have read the cited cases as compelling the conclusion that since the appellants sought to have a legislative apportionment held unconstitutional, their suit presented a "political question" and was therefore nonjusticiable. We hold that this challenge to an apportionment presents no nonjusticiable "political question." The cited cases do not hold the contrary.

Of course the mere fact that the suit seeks protection of a political right does not mean it presents a political question. Such an objection "is little more than a play upon words." Rather, it is argued that apportionment cases, whatever the actual wording of the complaint, can involve no federal constitutional right except one resting on the guaranty of a republican form of government, and that complaints based on that clause have been held to present political questions which are nonjusticiable.

We hold that the claim pleaded here neither rests upon nor implicates the Guaranty Clause and that its justiciability is therefore not foreclosed by our decisions of cases involving that clause. The District Court misinterpreted *Colegrove* v. *Green* and other decisions of this Court on which it relied. Appellants' claim that they are being denied equal protection is justiciable, and if "discrimination is sufficiently shown, the right to relief under the equal protection clause is not diminished by the fact that the discrimination relates to political rights." To show why we reject the argument based on the Guaranty Clause, we must examine the authorities under it. But because there appears to be some uncertainty as to why those cases did present political questions, and specifically as to whether this apportionment case is like those cases, we deem it necessary first to consider the contours of the "political question" doctrine.

Our discussion, even at the price of extending this opinion, requires review of a number of political question cases, in order to expose the attributes of the doctrine—attributes which, in various settings, diverge, combine, appear, and disappear in seeming disorderliness. Since that review is undertaken solely to demonstrate that neither singly nor collectively do these cases support a conclusion that this apportionment case is nonjusticiable, we of course do not explore their implications in other contexts. That review reveals that in the Guaranty Clause cases and in the other "political question" cases, it is the relationship between the judiciary and the coordinate branches of the Federal Government, and not the federal judiciary's relationship to the States, which gives rise to the "political question."

We have said that "in determining whether a question falls within [the political question] category, the appropriateness under our system of government of attributing finality to the action of the political departments and also the lack of satisfactory criteria for a judicial determination are dominant considerations." The nonjusticiability of a political question is primarily a function of the separation of powers. Much confusion results from the capacity of the "political question" label to obscure the need for case-by-case inquiry. Deciding whether a matter has in any measure been committed by the Constitution to another branch of government, or whether the action of that branch exceeds whatever authority has been committed, is itself a delicate exercise in constitutional interpretation, and is a responsibility of this Court as ultimate interpreter of the Constitution. To demonstrate this requires no less than to analyze representative cases and to infer from them the analytical threads that make up the political question doctrine. We shall then show that none of those threads catches this case....

We come, finally to the ultimate inquiry whether our precedents as to what constitutes a nonjusticiable "political question" bring the case before us under the umbrella of that doctrine. A natural beginning is to note whether any of the common characteristics which we have been able to identify and label descriptively are present. We find none: The question here is the consistency of state action with the Federal Constitution. We have no question decided, or to be decided, by a political branch of government coequal with this Court. Nor do we risk embarrassment of our government abroad, or grave disturbance at home if we take issue with Tennessee as to the constitutionality of her action here challenged. Nor need the appellants, in order to succeed in this action, ask the Court to enter upon policy determinations for which judicially manageable standards are lacking. Judicial standards under the Equal Protection Clause are well developed and familiar, and it has been open to courts since the enactment of the Fourteenth Amendment to determine, if on the particular facts they must, that a discrimination reflects *no* policy, but simply arbitrary and capricious action....

We conclude that the complaint's allegations of a denial of equal protection present a justiciable constitutional cause of action upon which appellants are entitled to a trial and a decision. The right asserted is within the reach of judicial protection under the Fourteenth Amendment.

The judgment of the District Court is reversed and the cause is remanded for further proceedings consistent with this opinion.

Reversed and remanded.

Mr. Justice Whittaker did not participate in the decision of this case.

Mr. Justice Douglas, concurring.

While I join the opinion of the Court and, like the Court, do not reach the merits, a word of explanation is necessary. I put to one side the

problems of "political" questions involving the distribution of power between this Court, the Congress, and the Chief Executive. We have here
a phase of the recurring problem of the relation of the federal courts to
state agencies. More particularly, the question is the extent to which a
State may weight one person's vote more heavily than it does another's....

It is . . . clear that by reason of the commands of the Constitution
there are several qualifications that a State may not require.

Race, color, or previous condition of servitude are impermissible standards by reason of the Fifteenth Amendment....

Sex is another impermissible standard by reason of the Nineteenth
Amendment.

There is a third barrier to a State's freedom in prescribing qualifications of voters and that is the Equal Protection Clause of the Fourteenth
Amendment, the provision invoked here. And so the question is, may a
State weight the vote of one county or one district more heavily than it
weights the vote in another?

The traditional test under the Equal Protection Clause has been
whether a State has made "an invidious discrimination," as it does when
it selects "a particular race or nationality for oppressive treatment."

I agree with my Brother Clark that if the allegations in the complaint
can be sustained a case for relief is established. We are told that a single
vote in Moore County, Tennessee, is worth 19 votes in Hamilton County,
that one vote in Stewart or in Chester County is worth nearly eight times
a single vote in Shelby or Knox County. The opportunity to prove that
an "invidious discrimination" exists should therefore be given the appellants....

With the exceptions of *Colegrove* v. *Green,* 328 US 549, *MacDougall*
v. *Green,* 335 US 281, *South* v. *Peters,* 339 US 276, and the decisions they
spawned, the Court has never thought that protection of voting rights was
beyond judicial cognizance. Today's treatment of those cases removes the
only impediment to judicial cognizance of the claims stated in the present
complaint.

The justiciability of the present claims being established, any relief
accorded can be fashioned in the light of well-known principles of equity.

Mr. Justice Clark, concurring.

One emerging from the rash of opinions with their accompanying
clashing of views may well find himself suffering a mental blindness.
The Court holds that the appellants have alleged a cause of action. How-

ever, it refuses to award relief here—although the facts are undisputed—and fails to give the District Court any guidance whatever. One dissenting opinion, bursting with words that go through so much and conclude with so little, condemns the majority action as "a massive repudiation of the experience of our whole past." Another describes the complaint as merely asserting conclusory allegations that Tennessee's apportionment is "incorrect," "arbitrary," "obsolete," and "unconstitutional." I believe it can be shown that this case is distinguishable from earlier cases dealing with the distribution of political power by a State, that a patent violation of the Equal Protection Clause of the United States Constitution has been shown, and that an appropriate remedy may be formulated. . . .

Although I find the Tennessee apportionment statute offends the Equal Protection Clause, I would not consider intervention by this Court into so delicate a field if there were any other relief available to the people of Tennessee. But the majority of the people of Tennessee have no "practical opportunities for exerting their political weight at the polls" to correct the existing "invidious discrimination." Tennessee has no initiative and referendum. I have searched diligently for other "practical opportunities" present under the law. I find none other than through the federal courts. The majority of the voters have been caught up in a legislative strait jacket. Tennessee has an "informed, civically militant electorate" and "an aroused popular conscience," but it does not sear "the conscience of the people's representatives." This is because the legislative policy has riveted the present seats in the Assembly to their respective constituencies, and by the votes of their incumbents a reapportionment of any kind is prevented. The people have been rebuffed at the hands of the Assembly; they have tried the constitutional convention route, but since the call must originate in the Assembly it, too, has been fruitless. They have tried Tennessee courts with the same result, and Governors have fought the tide only to flounder. It is said that there is recourse in Congress and perhaps that may be, but from a practical standpoint this is without substance. To date Congress has never undertaken such a task in any State. We therefore must conclude that the people of Tennessee are stymied and without judicial intervention will be saddled with the present discrimination in the affairs of their state government.

Finally, we must consider if there are any appropriate modes of effective judicial relief. The federal courts are, of course, not forums for political debate, nor should they resolve themselves into state constitutional conventions or legislative assemblies. Nor should their jurisdiction be exercised in the hope that such a declaration, as is made today, may have the direct effect of bringing on legislative action and relieving the courts of the problem of fashioning relief. To my mind this would be nothing less than blackjacking the Assembly into reapportioning the State. If judicial competence were lacking to fashion an effective decree, I would dismiss this appeal. However, like the Solicitor General of the United States, I see no such difficulty in the position of this case. One plan might be to start with the existing assembly districts, consolidate some of them, and award the seats thus released to those counties suffering the most egregious discrimination. Other possibilities are present and might be more effective. But the plan here suggested would at least release the strangle hold now on the Assembly and permit it to redistrict itself. . . .

In view of the detailed study that the Court has given this problem, it is unfortunate that a decision is not reached on the merits. The majority appears to hold, at least sub silentio, that an invidious discrimination is present, but it remands to the three-judge court for it to make what is certain to be that formal determination. It is true that Tennessee has not filed a formal answer. However, it has filed voluminous papers and made extended arguments supporting its position. At no time has it been able to contradict the appellants' factual claims; it has offered no rational explanation for the present apportionment; indeed, it has indicated that there are none known to it. As I have emphasized, the case proceeded to the point before the three-judge court that it was able to find an invidious discrimination factually present, and the State has not contested that holding here. In view of all this background I doubt if anything more can be offered or will be gained by the State on remand, other than time. Nevertheless, not being able to muster a court to dispose of the case on the merits, I concur in the opinion of the majority and acquiesce in the decision to remand. However, in fairness I do think that Tennessee is entitled to have my idea of what it faces on the record before us and the trial court some light as to how it might proceed.

As John Rutledge (later Chief Justice) said 175 years ago in the course of the Constitutional Convention, a chief function of the Court is to secure the national rights. Its decision today supports the proposition for which our forebears fought and many died, namely that "to be fully conformable to the principle of right, the form of government must be representative." That is the keystone upon which our government was founded and lacking which no republic can survive. It is well for this Court to practice self-restraint and discipline in constitutional adjudication, but never in its history have those principles received sanction where the national rights of so many have been so clearly infringed for so long a time. National respect for the courts is more enhanced through the forthright enforcement of those rights rather than by rendering them nugatory through the interposition of subterfuges. In my view the ultimate decision today is in the greatest tradition of this Court.

Mr. Justice Frankfurter, whom Mr. Justice Harlan joins, dissenting.

The Court today reverses a uniform course of decision established by a dozen cases, including one by which the very claim now sustained was unanimously rejected only five years ago. The impressive body of rulings thus cast aside reflected the equally uniform course of our political history regarding the relationship between population and legislative representation—a wholly different matter from denial of the franchise to individuals because of race, color, religion or sex. Such a massive repudiation of the experience of our whole past in asserting destructively novel judicial power demands a detailed analysis of the role of this Court in our constitutional scheme. Disregard of inherent limits in the effective exercise of the Court's "judicial Power" not only presages the futility of judicial intervention in the essentially political conflict of forces by which the relation between population and representation has time out of mind been and now is determined. It may well impair the Court's position as the ultimate organ of "the supreme Law of the Land" in that vast range of legal problems, often strongly entangled in popular feeling, on which this Court must pronounce. The Court's authority—possessed neither of the purse nor the sword—ultimately rests on sustained public confidence in its moral sanction. Such feeling must be nourished by the Court's complete detachment, in fact and in appearance, from political entanglements and by abstention from injecting itself into the clash of political forces in political settlements.

A hypothetical claim resting on abstract assumptions is now for the first time made the basis for affording illusory relief for a particular evil even though it foreshadows deeper and more pervasive difficulties in consequence. The claim is hypothetical and the assumptions are abstract because the Court does not vouchsafe the lower courts—state and federal—guide-lines for formulating specific, definite, wholly unprecedented remedies for the inevitable litigations that today's unbrageous disposition is bound to stimulate in connection with politically motivated reapportionments in so many States. In such a setting, to promulgate jurisdiction in the abstract is meaningless. It is devoid of reality as "a brooding omnipresence in the sky" for it conveys no intimation what relief, if any, a District Court is capable of affording that would not invite legislatures to play ducks and drakes with the judiciary. For this Court to direct the District Court to enforce a claim to which the Court has over the years consistently found itself required to deny legal enforcement and at the same time to find it necessary to withhold any guidance to the lower court how to enforce this turnabout, new legal claim, manifests an odd—indeed an esoteric—conception of judicial propriety. One of the Court's supporting opinions, as elucidated by commentary, unwittingly affords a disheartening preview of the mathematical quagmire (apart from divers judicially inappropriate and elusive determinants), into which this Court today catapults the lower courts of the country without so much as adumbrating the basis for a legal calculus as a means of extrication. Even assuming the indispensable intellectual disinterestedness on the part of judges in such matters, they do not have accepted legal standards or criteria or even reliable analogies to draw upon for making judicial judgments. To charge courts with the task of accommodating the incommensurable factors of policy that underlie these mathematical puzzles is to attribute, however flatteringly, omnicompetence to judges. The Framers of the Constitution persistently rejected a proposal that embodied this assumption and Thomas Jefferson never entertained it.

Recent legislation, creating a district appropriately described as "an atrocity of ingenuity," is not unique. Considering the gross inequality among legislative electoral units within almost every State, the Court naturally shrinks from asserting that in districting at least substantial equality is a constitutional requirement enforceable by courts. Room continues to be allowed for weighting. This of course implies that geography, economics, urban-rural conflict, and all the other nonlegal factors which have throughout our history entered into political districting are to some extent not to be ruled out in the undefined vista now opened up by review in the federal courts of state reapportionments. To some extent —aye, there's the rub. In effect, today's decision empowers the courts of the country to devise what should constitute the proper composition of the legislatures of the fifty States. If state courts should for one reason or another find themselves unable to discharge this task, the duty of doing so is put on the federal courts or on this Court, if State views do not satisfy this Court's notion of what is proper districting.

We were soothingly told at the bar of this Court that we need not worry about the kind of remedy a court could effectively fashion once the abstract constitutional right to have courts pass on a state-wide system of electoral districting is recognized as a matter of judicial rhetoric, because legislatures would heed the Court's admonition. This is not only an euphoric hope. It implies a sorry confession of judicial impotence in place of a frank acknowledgment that there is not under our Constitution a judicial remedy for every political mischief, for every undesirable exercise of legislative power. The Framers carefully and with deliberate fore-thought refused so to enthrone the judiciary. In this situation, as in others of like nature, appeal for relief does not belong here. Appeal must be to an informed, civically militant electorate. In a democratic society like ours, relief must come through an aroused popular conscience that sears the conscience of the people's representatives. In any event there is nothing judicially more unseemly nor more self-defeating than for this Court to make in terrorem pronouncements, to indulge in merely empty rhetoric, sounding a word of promise to the ear, sure to be disappointing to the hope. . . .

Dissenting opinion of Mr. Justice Harlan, whom Mr. Justice Frank-furter joins.

The dissenting opinion of Mr. Justice Frankfurter, in which I join, demonstrates the abrupt departure the majority makes from judicial history by putting the federal courts into this area of state concerns—an area which, in this instance, the Tennessee state courts themselves have refused to enter.

It does not detract from his opinion to say that the panorama of judicial history it unfolds, though evincing a steadfast underlying principle of keeping the federal courts out of these domains, has a tendency, because of variants in expression, to becloud analysis in a given case. With due respect to the majority, I think that has happened here.

Once one cuts through the thicket of discussion devoted to "jurisdiction," "standing," "justiciability" and "political question," there emerges a straightforward issue which, in my view, is determinative of this case. Does the complaint disclose a violation of a federal constitutional right, in other words, a claim over which a United States District Court would have jurisdiction . . . ? The majority opinion does not actually discuss this basic question, but, as one concurring Justice observes, seems to decide it "sub silentio." However, in my opinion, appellants' allegations, accepting all of them as true, do not, parsed down or as a whole, show an infringement by Tennessee of any rights assured by the Fourteenth Amendment. Accordingly, I believe the complaint should have been dismissed for "failure to state a claim upon which relief can be granted."

It is at once essential to recognize this case for what it is. The issue here relates not to a method of state electoral apportionment by which seats in the *federal* House of Representatives are allocated, but solely to the right of a State to fix the basis of representation in its *own* legislature. Until it is first decided to what extent that right is limited by the Federal Constitution, and whether what Tennessee has done or failed to do in this instance runs afoul of any such limitation, we need not reach the issues of "justiciability" or "political question" or any of the other considerations which in such cases as *Colegrove* v. *Green,* 328 US 549, led the Court to decline to adjudicate a challenge to a state apportionment affecting seats in the federal House of Representatives, in the absence of a controlling Act of Congress.

The appellants' claim in this case ultimately rests entirely on the Equal Protection Clause of the Fourteenth Amendment. It is asserted that Tennessee has violated the Equal Protection Clause by maintaining in effect a system of apportionment that grossly favors in legislative representation the rural sections of the State as against its urban communities. . . .

I can find nothing in the Equal Protection Clause or elsewhere in the Federal Constitution which expressly or impliedly supports the view that state legislatures must be so structured as to reflect with approximate equality the voice of every voter. Not only is that proposition refuted by history, as shown by my Brother Frankfurter, but it strikes deep into the heart of our federal system. Its acceptance would require us to turn our backs on the regard which this Court has always shown for the judgment of state legislatures and courts on matters of basically local concern.

In the last analysis, what lies at the core of this controversy is a difference of opinion as to the function of representative government. It is surely beyond argument that those who have the responsibility for devising a system of representation may permissibly consider that factors other than bare numbers should be taken into account. The existence of the United States Senate is proof enough of that. To consider that we may ignore the Tennessee Legislature's judgment in this instance because that body was the product of an asymmetrical electoral apportionment would in effect be to assume the very conclusion here disputed. Hence we must accept the present form of the Tennessee Legislature as the embodiment of the State's choice, or, more realistically, its compromise, between competing political philosophies. The federal courts have not been empowered by the Equal Protection Clause to judge whether this resolution of the State's internal political conflict is desirable or undesirable, wise or unwise. . . .

. . . [R]educed to its essentials, the charge of arbitrariness and capriciousness rests entirely on the consistent refusal of the Tennessee Legislature over the past 60 years to alter a pattern of apportionment that was reasonable when conceived.

A Federal District Court is asked to say that the passage of time has rendered the 1901 apportionment obsolete to the point where its continuance becomes vulnerable under the Fourteenth Amendment. But is not this matter one that involves a classic legislative judgment? Surely it lies within the province of a state legislature to conclude that an existing allocation of senators and representatives constitutes a desirable balance of geographical and demographical representation, or that in the interest of stability of government it would be best to defer for some further time the redistribution of seats in the state legislature.

Indeed, I would hardly think it unconstitutional if a state legislature's expressed reason for establishing or maintaining an electoral imbalance between its rural and urban population were to protect the State's agricultural interests from the sheer weight of numbers of those residing in its cities....

In conclusion, it is appropriate to say that one need not agree, as a citizen, with what Tennessee has done or failed to do, in order to deprecate, as a judge, what the majority is doing today. Those observers of the Court who see it primarily as the last refuge for the correction of all inequality or injustice, no matter what its nature or source, will no doubt applaud this decision and its break with the past. Those who consider that continuing national respect for the Court's authority depends in large measure upon its wise exercise of self-restraint and discipline in constitutional adjudication, will view the decision with deep concern.

I would affirm. 🖋

After the *Baker* decision the Supreme Court on February 17, 1964 rendered additional decisions affecting *congressional* apportionment. In *Wesberry* v. *Sanders,* 376 U.S. 1 (1964) the Court relied on Article I, Section 2, of the Constitution, which provides that congressmen must be chosen "by the people of the several states," as a basis for holding that congressional districts must be as nearly as possible equal in population. The *Baker* case was used as precedent.

WESBERRY v. SANDERS

376 *U.S.* 1 (1964)

Mr. Justice Black delivered the opinion of the Court, saying in part:
Appellants are citizens and qualified voters of Fulton County, Georgia, and as such are entitled to vote in congressional elections in Georgia's Fifth Congressional District. That district, one of ten created by a 1931 Georgia statute, includes Fulton, DeKalb, and Rockdale Coun-

ties and has a population according to the 1960 census of 823,680. The average population of the ten districts is 394,312, less than half that of the Fifth. One district, the Ninth, has only 272,154 people, less than one-third as many as the Fifth. Since there is only one Congressman for each district, this inequality of population means that the Fifth District's Congressman has to represent from two to three times as many people as do Congressmen from some of the other Georgia districts.

Claiming that these population disparities deprived them and voters similarly situated of a right under the Federal Constitution to have their votes for Congressmen given the same weight as the votes of other Georgians, the appellants brought this action . . . asking that the Georgia statute be declared invalid and that the appellees, the Governor and Secretary of the State of Georgia, be enjoined from conducting elections under it. The complaint alleged that appellants were deprived of the full benefit of their right to vote, in violation of (1) Art. I, § 2 of the Constitution of the United States, which provides that "The House of Representatives shall be composed of Members chosen every second year by the People of the several States . . ."; (2) the Due Process, Equal Protection, and Privileges and Immunities Clauses of the Fourteenth Amendment; and (3) that part of Section 2 of the Fourteenth Amendment which provides that "Representatives shall be apportioned among the several States according to their respective numbers. . . ."

The case was heard by a three-judge District Court, which found unanimously, from facts not disputed, that:

"It is clear by any standard . . . that the population of the Fifth District is grossly out of balance with that of the other nine congressional districts of Georgia and in fact, so much so that the removal of DeKalb and Rockdale Counties from the District, leaving only Fulton with a population of 556,326, would leave it exceeding the average by slightly more than forty per cent."

Notwithstanding these findings, a majority of the court dismissed the complaint, citing as their guide Mr. Justice Frankfurter's minority opinion in *Colegrove* v. *Green,* an opinion stating that challenges to apportionment of congressional districts raised only "political" questions, which were not justiciable. Although the majority below said that the dismissal here was based on "want of equity" and not on justiciability, they relied on no circumstances which were peculiar to the present case; instead, they adopted the language and reasoning of Mr. Justice Frankfurter's Colegrove opinion in concluding that the appellants had presented a wholly "political" question. Judge Tuttle, disagreeing with the court's reliance on that opinion, dissented from the dismissal, though he would have denied an injunction at that time in order to give the Georgia Legislature ample opportunity to correct the "abuses" in the apportionment. He relied on *Baker* v. *Carr,* which, after full discussion of Colegrove and all the opinions in it, held that allegations of disparities of population in state legislative districts raise justiciable claims on which courts may grant relief. We noted probable jurisdiction. 374 US 802. We agree with Judge Tuttle that in debasing the weight of appellants' votes the State has abridged the right to vote for members of Congress guaranteed them by the United States Constitution, that the District Court should have entered a declaratory judgment to that effect, and that it was therefore error to dismiss this suit. The question of what relief should be given we leave for further consideration and decision by the District Court in light of existing circumstances. . . .

This statement in Baker, which referred to our past decisions holding congressional apportionment cases to be justiciable, we believe was wholly correct and we adhere to it. Mr. Justice Franfurter's Colegrove opinion contended that Art. I, § 4, of the Constitution had given Congress "exclusive authority" to protect the right of citizens to vote for Congressmen, but we made it clear in Baker that nothing in the language of that article gives support to a construction that would immunize state congressional apportionment laws which debase a citizen's right to vote from the power of courts to protect the constitutional rights of individuals from legislative destruction. . . . The right to vote is too important in our free society to be stripped of judicial protection by such an interpretation of Article I. This dismissal can no more be justified on the ground of "want of equity" than on the ground of "nonjusticiability." We therefore hold that the District Court erred in dismissing the complaint.

This brings us to the merits. We agree with the District Court that the 1931 Georgia apportionment grossly discriminates against voters in the Fifth Congressional District. A single Congressman represents from two to three times as many Fifth District voters as are represented by each of the Congressmen from the other Georgia congressional districts. The apportionment statute thus contracts the value of some votes and expands that of others. If the Federal Constitution intends that when qualified voters elect members of Congress each vote be given as much weight as any other vote, then this statute cannot stand.

We hold that, construed in its historical context, the command of Art. I, § 2, that Representatives be chosen "by the People of the several States" means that as nearly as is practicable one man's vote in a congressional election is to be worth as much as another's. This rule is followed automatically, of course, when Representatives are chosen as a group on a statewide basis, as was a widespread practice in the first 50 years of our Nation's history. It would be extraordinary to suggest that in such statewide elections the votes of inhabitants of some parts of a State, for example, Georgia's thinly populated Ninth District, could be weighed at two or three times the value of the votes of people living in more populous parts of the State, for example, the Fifth District around Atlanta. We do not believe that the Framers of the Constitution intended to permit the same vote-diluting discrimination to be accomplished through the device of districts containing widely varied numbers of inhabitants. To say that a vote is worth more in one district than in another would not only run counter to our fundamental ideas of democratic government, it would cast aside the principle of a House of Representatives elected "by the People," a principle tenaciously fought for and established at the Constitutional Convention. The history of the Constitution, particularly that part of it relating to the adoption of Art I, § 2, reveals that those who framed the Constitution meant that, no matter what the mechanics of an election, whether statewide or by districts, it was population which was to be the basis of the House of Representatives. . . .

The debates at the Convention make at least one fact abundantly clear: that when the delegates agreed that the House should represent "people" they intended that in allocating Congressmen the number assigned to each State should be determined solely by the number of the State's inhabitants. The Constitution embodied Edmund Randolph's proposal for a periodic census to ensure "fair representation of the people," an idea endorsed by Mason as assuring that "numbers of inhabitants" should always be the measure of representation in the House of Representatives. The Convention also overwhelmingly agreed to a resolution offered by Randolph to base future apportionment squarely on numbers and to delete any reference to wealth. And the delegates defeated a motion made by Elbridge Gerry to limit the number of Representatives from newer Western States so that it would never exceed the number from the original States.

It would defeat the principle solemnly embodied in the Great Compromise—equal representation in the House of equal numbers of people —for us to hold that, within the States, legislatures may draw the lines of congressional districts in such a way as to give some voters a greater voice in choosing a Congressman than others. The House of Representatives, the Convention agreed, was to represent the people as individuals, and on a basis of complete equality for each voter. The delegates were quite aware of what Madison called the "vicious representation" in Great Britain whereby "rotten boroughs" with few inhabitants were represented in Parliament on or almost on a par with cities of greater population. Wilson urged that people must be represented as individuals, so that America would escape the evils of the English system under which one man could send two members to Parliament to represent the borough of Old Sarum while London's million people sent but four. The delegates referred to rotten borough apportionments in some of the state legislatures as the kind of objectionable governmental action that the Constitution should not tolerate in the election of congressional representatives. . . .

It is in the light of such history that we must construe Art I, § 2, of the Constitution, which, carrying out the ideas of Madison and those of like views, provides that Representatives shall be chosen "by the People of the several States" and shall be "apportioned among the several States . . . according to their respective numbers." It is not surprising that our Court has held that this Article gives persons qualified to vote a constitutional right to vote and to have their votes counted. *United States* v. *Mosley,* 238 US 383; *Ex parte Yarbrough,* 110 US 651. Not only can this right to vote not be denied outright, it cannot, consistently with Article I, be destroyed by alteration of ballots, see *United States* v. *Classic,* 313 US 299, or diluted by stuffing of the ballot box, see *United States* v. *Saylor,* 322 US 385. No right is more precious in a free country than that of having a voice in the election of those who make the laws under which, as good citizens, we must live. Other rights, even the most basic, are illusory if the right to vote is undermined. Our Constitution leaves no room for classification of people in a way that unnecessarily abridges this right. In urging the people to adopt the Constitution, Madison said in No. 57 of *The Federalist:*

"Who are to be the electors of the Federal Representatives? Not the rich more than the poor; not the learned more than the ignorant; not the haughty heirs of distinguished names, more than the humble sons of obscure and unpropitious fortune. The electors are to be the great body of the people of the United States. . . ."

Readers surely could have fairly taken this to mean, "one person, one vote."

While it may not be possible to draw congressional districts with mathematical precision, that is no excuse for ignoring our Constitution's plain objective of making equal representation for equal numbers of people the fundamental goal for the House of Representatives. That is the high standard of justice and common sense which the Founders set for us. Reversed and remanded.

Mr. Justice Clark wrote a separate opinion, concurring in part and dissenting in part;

Mr. Justice Harlan dissented, saying in part:

I had not expected to witness the day when the Supreme Court of the United States would render a decision which cast grave doubt on the constitutionality of the composition of the House of Representatives. It is not an exaggeration to say that such is the effect of today's decision. The Court's holding that the Constitution requires States to select Representatives either by elections at large or by elections in districts composed "as nearly as is practicable" of equal population places in jeopardy the seats of almost all the members of the present House of Representatives.

In the last congressional election, in 1962, Representatives from 42 States were elected from congressional districts. In all but five of those States, the difference between the populations of the largest and smallest districts exceeded 100,000 persons. A difference of this magnitude in the size of districts the average population of which in each State is less than 500,000 is presumably not equality among districts "as nearly as is practicable," although the Court does not reveal its definition of that phrase. Thus, today's decision impugns the validity of the election of 398 Representatives from 37 States, leaving a "constitutional" House of 37 members now sitting.

Only a demonstration which could not be avoided would justify this Court in rendering a decision the effect of which, inescapably as I see it, is to declare constitutionally defective the very composition of a coordinate branch of the Federal Government. The Court's opinion not only fails to make such a demonstration. It is unsound logically on its face and demonstrably unsound historically. . . .

. . . [T]he language of Art. I, §§ 2 and 4, the surrounding text, and the relevant history are all in strong and consistent direct contradiction of the Court's holding. The constitutional scheme vests in the States plenary power to regulate the conduct of elections for Representatives, and, in order to protect the Federal Government, provides for congressional supervision of the States' exercise of their power. Within this scheme, the appellants do not have the right which they assert, in the absence of provision for equal districts by the Georgia Legislature or the Congress. The constitutional right which the Court creates is manufactured out of whole cloth.

The unstated premise of the Court's conclusion quite obviously is that the Congress has not dealt, and the Court believes it will not deal, with the problem of congressional apportionment in accordance with what the Court believes to be sound political principles. Laying aside for the moment the validity of such a consideration as a factor in constitutional interpretation, it becomes relevant to examine the history of congressional action under Art. I, § 4. This history reveals that the Court is not simply undertaking to exercise a power which the Constitution reserves to the Congress; it is also overruling congressional judgment. . . .

Today's decision has portents for our society and the Court itself which should be recognized. This is not a case in which the Court vindicates the kind of individual rights that are assured by the Due Process Clause of the Fourteenth Amendment, whose "vague contours," *Rochin* v. *California,* 342 US 165, of course leave much room for constitutional developments necessitated by changing conditions in a dynamic society. Nor is this a case in which an emergent set of facts requires the Court to frame new principles to protect recognized constitutional rights. The claim for judicial relief in this case strikes at one of the fundamental doctrines of our system of government, the separation of powers. In upholding that claim, the Court attempts to effect reforms in a field which the Constitution, as plainly as can be, has committed exclusively to the political process.

This Court, no less than all other branches of the Government, is bound by the Constitution. The Constitution does not confer on the Court blanket authority to step into every situation where the political branch may be thought to have fallen short. The stability of this institution ultimately depends not only upon its being alert to keep the other branches of government within constitutional bounds but equally upon recognition of the limitations on the Court's own functions in the constitutional system.

What is done today saps the political process. The promise of judicial intervention in matters of this sort cannot but encourage popular inertia in efforts for political reform through the political process, with the inevitable result that the process is itself weakened. By yielding to the demand for a judicial remedy in this instance, the Court in my view does a disservice both to itself and to the broader values of our system of government.

Believing that the complaint fails to disclose a constitutional claim, I would affirm the judgment below dismissing the complaint.

APPENDIX[1]

State and number of representatives[2]	Largest district	Smallest district	Difference between largest and smallest districts
Alabama (8)	....	....	....
Alaska (1)	....	....	....
Arizona (3)	663,510	198,236	465,274
Arkansas (4)	575,385	332,844	242,541
California (38)	588,933	301,872	287,061
Colorado (4)	653,954	195,551	458,403
Connecticut (6)	689,555	318,942	370,613
Delaware (1)	....	....	....
Florida (12)	660,345	237,235	423,110
Georgia (10)	823,680	272,154	551,526
Hawaii (2)	....	....	....
Idaho (2)	409,949	257,242	152,707
Illinois (24)	552,582	278,703	273,879
Indiana (11)	697,567	290,596	406,971
Iowa (7)	442,406	353,156	89,250
Kansas (5)	539,592	373,583	166,009
Kentucky (7)	610,947	350,839	260,108
Louisiana (8)	536,029	263,850	272,179
Maine (2)	505,465	463,800	41,665
Maryland (8)	711,045	243,570	467,475
Massachusetts (12)	478,962	376,336	102,626
Michigan (19)	802,994	177,431	625,563
Minnesota (8)	482,872	375,475	107,397
Mississippi (5)	608,441	295,072	313,369
Missouri (10)	506,854	378,499	128,355
Montana (2)	400,573	274,194	126,379
Nebraska (3)	530,507	404,695	125,812
Nevada (1)	....	....	....
New Hampshire (2)	331,818	275,103	56,715
New Jersey (15)	585,586	255,165	330,421
New Mexico (2)	....	....	....
New York (41)	471,001	350,186	120,815
North Carolina (11)	491,461	277,861	213,600
North Dakota (2)	333,290	299,156	34,134

APPENDIX[1] (continued)

State and number of representatives[2]	Largest district	Smallest district	Difference between largest and smallest districts
Ohio (24)	726,156	236,288	489,868
Oklahoma (6)	552,863	227,692	325,171
Oregon (4)	522,813	265,164	257,649
Pennsylvania (27)	553,154	303,026	250,128
Rhode Island (2)	459,706	399,782	59,924
South Carolina (6)	531,555	302,235	229,320
South Dakota (2)	497,669	182,845	314,824
Tennessee (9)	627,019	223,387	403,632
Texas (23)	951,527	216,371	735,156
Utah (2)	572,654	317,973	254,681
Vermont (1)	....	....	....
Virginia (10)	539,618	312,890	226,728
Washington (7)	510,512	342,540	167,972
West Virginia (5)	422,046	303,098	118,948
Wisconsin (10)	530,316	236,870	293,446
Wyoming (1)	....	....	....

[1] The populations of the districts are based on the 1960 Census. The districts are those used in the election of the current 88th Congress. The populations of the districts are available in the biographical section of the Congressional Directory, 88th Cong., 2d Sess.
[2] 435 in all.

Mr. Justice Stewart.

I think it is established that "this Court has power to afford relief in a case of this type as against the objection that the issues are not justiciable," and I cannot subscribe to any possible implication to the contrary which may lurk in Mr. Justice Harlan's dissenting opinion. With this single qualification I join the dissent because I think Mr. Justice Harlan has unanswerably demonstrated that Art. I, § 2, of the Constitution gives no mandate to this Court or to any court to ordain that congressional districts within each State must be equal in population.

After the *Wesberry* decision the Supreme Court held, in a series of decisions in June of 1964, that the Equal Protection Clause of the Fourteenth

Amendment requires the equal apportionment of *both* houses of state legislatures. Obviously such a decision could not be made regarding Congress because of constitutional specifications requiring that the Senate represent states as units, with two Senators for each state, regardless of population. The precedent-setting decision in June of 1964 was *Reynolds* v. *Sims*. In holding that both houses of bicameral state legislatures must now be apportioned on a population basis, the Court nevertheless provided that some deviations might be permissible. In what can only be described as a mystical statement the Court held that "so long as the divergencies from a strict population standard are based on legitimate considerations incident to the effectuation of a rational state policy, some deviations from the equal-population principle are constitutionally permissible with respect to the apportionment of seats in either or both of the two houses of a bicameral state legislature." Thus political subdivisions of a state may be given some representation that is not directly related to population. But the Court made it abundantly clear that the states would not be permitted to stray very far from the equal-population principle.

As a result of the *Baker* and *Reynolds* decisions substantial changes are being made throughout the country in the basis of representation in state legislatures. Already Federal District Courts have required the reapportionment of many state legislatures. There is little doubt that the Supreme Court's decisions affecting state legislatures, as well as the requirement for equal population in congressional districts, will have a profound effect upon the pattern of American politics. The long-felt power of the rural sections of the country will begin to fade. If the present trend toward the increment of *suburban* populations continues, these areas may begin to exercise important political power. In the final analysis the suburbs may be the biggest beneficiaries of equal apportionment. Therefore, although the reapportioned state legislatures may be more sympathetic to urban problems than their predecessors, there is no guarantee that urban issues will be emphasized unless a community of interest develops between the suburbs and the urban centers. Reapportionment will thus not necessarily bring about renewed emphasis upon the problems of the city hoped for by those who feel urban interests have been submerged in the face of rural legislatures.

Are there any arguments that can be advanced against equal apportionment? Certainly it is important for any political system to take into account varied interests. The representation of equal numbers of people in different electoral districts may not by itself bring about this equality. As the suburbs grow in population it is entirely possible that with the advent of equal apportionment both the center city and the rural areas of the country will be underrepresented in relation to their importance. Public policy formulated by elected officials who are chosen from constituencies whose boundaries are determined solely on the basis of equal population may not balance the interests of all sections of the country. The following selection illustrates one aspect of this problem.

TWO AMERICAS: RURAL AND SUBURBAN

Andrew Hacker*

EXPERIENCE with congressional districting during the fifties made clear that rural voters were overrepresented and that, for the most part, their extra seats were secured by depriving suburban citizens of equitable representation. Outside the South, large-city districts were roughly proportionate to population; and while mid-urban seats were underrepresented, they were far less so than the suburbs. The conflict, therefore, is essentially between two groups of Americans. On the one side are those living in small towns and rural areas; on the other are those inhabiting the fringes of large cities.

Actually, these two groups of Americans are minorities within the total population. According to the 1960 Census, there were approximately 36 million people in the districts classified as "rural" . . . , and only 29 million in those under the "suburban" heading.** This may explain, in part at least, why congressional districting has not become a vivid national issue. Most Americans feel neither sufficiently underrepresented to become exercised over their muted legislative voice nor so overrepresented as to want

---

* Reprinted from *Congressional Redistricting* by Andrew Hacker, by permission of The Brookings Institution. Copyright 1963 by The Brookings Institution.

** These are, of course, conservative estimates. In an early 1962 analysis of population composition, the *Congressional Quarterly*, February 2, 1962, counted 91 million Americans in districts it classified as "rural" and 33 million in those it called "suburban." In terms of population and regardless of district, there were 84 million rural Americans and 36 million suburbanites. The reason why these figures are so high is that the *Congressional Quarterly* breakdown of districts and population into urban-suburban-rural failed to make provision for what has been called here "mid-urban" America. Most of the Americans classified by the *Congressional Quarterly* as "rural" are actually "mid-urban," as are many of the suburbanites—especially those on the fringes of medium-sized cities. No hard and fast definitions are possible in this area, but the evidence still suggests that those who inhabit the countryside and suburbia are distinct minorities.

to preserve an entrenched position of advantage. But among those who are most affected, many in varying degrees are conscious of the maldistribution of power and the benefits to be gained or lost by moves in the direction of equitable districting. That those who stand to gain or lose are minorities does not lessen the principles involved. Indeed, the theoretical question has always been one of "minority rights" and the extent to which they are to be safeguarded. In this instance, instead of the opposing force being "majority rule" as is usually the case, two minorities are posed against each other.

Rural America now has disproportionate legislative power and will not willingly part with its extra congressional seats. On its side is the simple possession of this advantage and its inclination to fight to preserve the status quo. Suburban Americans, on the other hand, would prefer more equitable representation in the Congress. When two minority groups clash, majority opinion may be the referee, but it is clear that a greater intensity of feeling on one side can contribute to the outcome. It is, therefore, in order to examine the ideology and interests of what has been called rural America. For these are the underlying currents in the debate over representation.*

The Case for Overrepresentation of Rural America

There is no denying that the population of rural America is on the decline. Approximately half of the country's 3,000 counties lost population between 1950 and 1960, and virtually all of these were in the countryside. The rural community has not been sharing in the prosperity that supposedly characterizes America's affluent society. The median family income for rural farm population was less than $3,000 per year in 1960, and that for rural nonfarm families was only a little more than $1,000 higher. Despite pleas and inducements, industry is not moving to the hinterland to the extent needed to blot up chronic underemployment, and the small businesses of small towns are suffering from declining patronage and the competition of national corporations. Young people are tending to leave —especially those with skills, education, and ambition. The outlook is hardly encouraging for this still-proud heartland of the nation.

* It should be emphasized that the following paragraphs attempt to give a sympathetic rendering of the case for rural overrepresentation. The ultimate conclusion, as will be made clear, is that this case is not sufficiently persuasive to warrant the perpetuation of existing inequities. At the same time, I should add that I have lived for almost a decade in provincial America and have some personal familiarity with sentiment on this subject.

Those who remain in rural America are aware that they have been losing status and power over the past several decades. They realize that decisions once made locally are now handed down from Washington, New York, and other centers beyond their influence. These decisions, often uniform and impersonal, seem to have little concern for the preservation of the rural and small-town way of life. Thus, there arises the conviction that if this way of life is to be safeguarded it can only be by political means. Economic power and social prestige may have gravitated to metropolitan America, but the rural areas can hold their own if they retain disproportionate influence in the political arena. This view was apparently accepted by Associate Justice John Marshall Harlan who, in his dissenting opinion in *Baker* v. *Carr,* said: "I would hardly think it unconstitutional if a state legislature's express reason for establishing or maintaining an electoral imbalance between its rural and urban population were to protect the state's agricultural interests from the sheer weight of numbers of those residing in the cities."

The problem is not simply the "weight of numbers" said to characterize urban electorates. There is also the belief that the cities and suburbs have the economic and social resources to solve their own problems. Rural areas, in contrast, are said to be underprivileged, to need aid and support that can only be drawn from outside resources. And, to their inhabitants, it seems apparent that this help will not come voluntarily; hence, the need for additional legislative representation to ensure that rural America is not forgotten. The argument for added weight to the rural voice is that an increment of political power is required if the economic and social advantages of the cities and suburbs are to be balanced. From this point of view, the dictum of "one man, one vote" is appropriate when all sections of the country are equal in economic and social resources. But when one area is in a depressed state, it must have disproportionate political influence if its right to continued existence is to be guaranteed. The rural minority senses—no doubt, correctly—that its treatment at the hands of government would be far less generous had it not legislative power in excess of its numbers.

Those differing with the point of view of rural America might argue that there is a price for progress, that it is an abuse of the principle of minority rights to ask that one section of the community be shored up after it has outlived its social usefulness. For example, they might ask, why must the nation be taxed to purchase agricultural commodities that are not needed but nevertheless continue to be produced? A customary answer to this and similar questions is that the rural minority is a special minority, one deserving consideration that may not easily be claimed by others.

There is another reason why voters in rural areas and small towns believe they should have relatively more representatives than urban voters. This is the rural ideology which assumes that those who live on, or close to, the land are superior people. America has espoused the rhetoric of democracy, but there have always been occasions when the suggestion is made that some citizens are superior to others in character and virtue. Even Thomas Jefferson, for all his talk of human equality, could say:

> Those who labor in the earth are the chosen people of God, if ever He had a chosen people, whose breasts He has made His peculiar deposit for substantial and genuine virtue. . . . The mobs of great cities add just so much to the support of pure government, as sores do to the strength of the human body.

It would appear that the Jeffersonian principle of majority rule and its corollary of equal votes for equal citizens applied only when and where the political constituency was comprised wholly of yeomen farmers. From this point of view, when citizens are of superior moral character, then all may be treated as equals. But, once a new and less virtuous element emerges in the population, lines of discrimination must be drawn and political power cannot be a function simply of numbers. Quantity, in this view, ought not to be permitted to outvote quality.

The assumption of the superior character of the rural life is by no means dead. Not many years ago an official of a national trade association could proclaim:

> Today the greatest threat to democratic institutions, to the republican form of government, and ultimately to freedom itself, lies in our big cities. They are populated for the most part with the massman, devoid of intelligence, and devoid of civic responsibility. He talks only about rights and has no conception of responsibilities. He will vote for anyone who offers him something for nothing. Whether it be subway fares at half-price or public housing at one-third price. . . . Our one hope of survival as a free country is that rural and semi-rural areas still dominate most of the state legislatures through their representatives and still dominate the House of Representatives at Washington. Our best hope for the future is to keep it that way.

Rural legislators seem willing to apply the same description to the suburbs as they do to the cities. Indeed, if the allocation of representation to suburban voters is any index, the countryside regards them with somewhat more disdain than it does those who reside in the cities. As noted earlier, state legislatures dominated by rural Republicans have been less than enthusiastic about giving a full political voice to their fellow Republicans in the suburbs. For the suburbs are, in many ways, more modern than the cities, and often appear no less willing to embark on extravagant programs of expenditure. At all events, there is little community of interest between rural areas and the suburbs, and the former have few scruples about being overrepresented at the expense of the latter.

There are, then, two strands to the argument for disproportionate power for rural America. The first is that the countryside needs an added increment of votes if it is to be raised to a parity with sections of the nation that have been moving ahead at a more accelerated rate. If it is countered that there are other depressed groups in the population that might call for additional legislative strength on the same grounds, the reply is that rural America differs from all of them by virtue of its superior character and heritage. This second, ideological, strand is of interest, if only because it makes the plea for minority rights on a different plane. On the one hand, the rural minority sees itself as having been bypassed in terms of material prosperity and social influence and, therefore, asks for political power as a form of compensation. On the other hand, it regards itself as possessed of a moral excellence deserving power beyond its numbers, perhaps even to a degree where it may thwart measures initiated by groups less sterling in motive and quality.

It is difficult to argue with ideology, for discourse in this realm is based on interest and emotion rather than reason and logic. What can be said is that the sentiments expressed here, whether true or false by any objective evaluation, are deeply felt in the countryside. This depth of feeling means that a rearguard action inevitably will be fought in defense of rural overrepresentation on both the state and congressional levels. There will be dilatory tactics and judicial appeals—to be sure, not to the extent witnessed in the desegregation cases—in an attempt to preserve the status quo. For the stakes, whether material or ideological, are real; and if a minority feels it is being threatened it is difficult to argue it out of its own definition of reality.

The Suburban Minority

Political experience in the United States seems to suggest that significant steps will not be taken to aid a minority unless the minority itself is exercised over its plight and its members are prepared to organize efforts for improving their condition. It has been indicated that suburbanites suffer from a greater degree of underrepresentation in the Congress than the other segments of the population. The question, however, is the extent to which this deprivation of influence is felt and the degree to which suburbanites are willing to expend energy to achieve redress.

The suburbs of America's large cities are, of course, symbolic of the nation's era of affluence. The median family income of the urban-fringe areas was over $7,000 in 1960, and almost a quarter of the families had incomes of over $10,000. In the Chicago suburbs, for example, the median family income was $8,388 and 34.8 percent of the families earned over $10,000. These citizens are faring quite well under existing arrangements. Many of them have come up in the world, in both economic and social terms, and they can be counted as successful by prevailing standards. Suburban America has its problems, but they are the growing pains of a healthy child. The suburbs naturally have a political life and their residents turn out to vote in predictably high proportions. Nevertheless, there is a widespread attitude that most problems are personal in the sense that they can be solved by a raise in salary, a change of job, or rising to a new social circle. Whereas rural America tends to keep its eye fixed on Congress for agricultural price supports, a new military installation, or the dredging of a local river, most suburbs are relatively unconcerned with the federal government's role in their continued existence. For these reasons, plus the fact that suburban party organizations are only beginning to take on coherent form, comparatively little grumbling is heard from suburbanites over the fact that so many of them are crowded into a single congressional district. If this American minority is currently being deprived of its right to equal representation, the deprivation does not appear to be causing it untoward pain.

This does not mean that there are not notable exceptions to these generalizations. Suburban suits asking for redistricting along more equitable lines have been directed against the legislatures of several states, and others concerning congressional districts are bound to follow. Indeed, there need not be a groundswell of public opinion behind a complainant to ensure a decision on his behalf, and it may well be that the suburbs will receive more congressional seats despite the indifference of most of their residents to underrepresentation. After all, one of the tenets of democracy is that citizens should be given the blessings of equality whether they want them or not.

Equal Representation: Pro and Con

Legal principles and practical justice are not easily reconciled. The question may be raised as to who most needs the congressional seats at issue. The rural demand is not simply for equal representation, but for overrepresentation on the ground that the problems and character of its constituents call for a stronger than average voice in the chambers where laws are made. Spokesmen for the suburbs ask only for equal status with everyone else. From the rural point of view, therefore, the argument is that rural America has a greater need for preserving its admittedly disproportionate share of power than suburban America has for even an equitable share. The rural claim is that changes in districts to provide equal representation for the suburbs would be a gratuitous gift to a section of the community already in a favored economic and social position; such a transfer of seats would be at the expense of a part of the country that could not easily absorb the loss.

One drawback to accepting this reasoning is that rural areas are only in a position to make their argument because they already possess more seats than they are entitled to as a minority. There are other underprivileged minority groups that could logically make claims for additional representation, but theirs would have to be for a change in the status quo rather than its preservation. It has been suggested that Negroes could use far more legislative influence than they now have, and their demand for extra seats would be no less reasonable than that now heard from the countryside. Other deprived minorities such as migrant workers, the mentally ill, and the indigent aged might request added electoral weight, if only to reach a parity with their more fortunate neighbors. But if there are many minorities experiencing difficulties in our society, the assumption of the American political system has been that they must accept the principle of majority rule and try to persuade the majority of the merits of their case. Only the rural minority has been able to circumvent this principle. Its defense rests more on possession than on logic, and if there is to be a claim for the defense of minority rights it should be achieved by means other than distorting the districts of the House of Representatives.

The alleged superiority of rural Americans and their way of life, of course, cannot be either proved or disproved. It may be noted in passing that the small town merchant and the farmer of today are not exactly the aristocrats that the framers of the Constitution had in mind when they suggested added influence for people of quality. Nor is it clear that congressmen from rural areas embody more statesmanlike virtues than those elected by other kinds of constituencies. Even so, it must be reiterated that the House of Representatives has never served the function of an aristocratic chamber but, rather, has been to reflect the views of all Americans. In the final analysis, it is best to ignore all pretexts of superior character and a superior way of life, for there comes a point when such rhetoric is obviously a rationalization of vested interests which cannot be taken seriously.

The case for rural overrepresentation will continue to be made, if only because man is a rationalizing animal and feels compelled to give reasons whenever he seeks to gain or maintain a position of power. Instead of simply admitting that he likes things as they are because they redound to his benefit, he waxes philosophical and seeks to persuade others that such a state of affairs is in the general interest. If anything, these outpourings serve as an index of the intensity with which a group feels attached to its advantageous position. And there is reason to believe that on the subject of political representation rural sentiment runs deep.

Nevertheless, the principle of equal votes for all Americans is the overriding consideration. The development of democratic institutions in this country has been undeviating in its movement in that direction. Complete equality will not be secured rapidly or without struggles in both legislative and judicial arenas. Those who seek to defend existing inequities are clearly on the defensive, and it is plain that the principle of equal representation in the nation's legislatures is closer to achievement than ever before.

CHAPTER FIVE

Interest Groups

Interest groups are vital cogs in the wheel of the democratic process. Although *Federalist 10* suggested that one of the major purposes of the separation of powers system was to break and control the "evil effects" of faction, modern political theorists take a much more sanguine view of the role that political interest groups as well as parties play in government. No longer are interest groups defined as being opposed to the "public interest." They are vital channels through which particular publics participate in the governmental process. This chapter will examine the origin and nature of contemporary interest group theory, and illustrate the way in which interest groups function.

18. Interest Groups and Constitutional Government: The Theory of Concurrent Majority

It is very useful to discuss the operation of interest groups within the framework of what can best be described as a concurrent majority system. In contemporary usage the phrase "concurrent majority" means a system in which major government policy decisions must be approved by the dominant interest groups directly affected. The word "concurrent" refers to the fact that each group involved must give its consent before policy can be enacted. Thus a concurrent majority is a majority of each group considered separately. Perhaps the best way of visualizing this idea would be to take an area such as agricultural policy, in which three or four major private interest groups can be identified. The concurrent majority is reached when each group affected gives its approval before agricultural policy is passed. The extent to which such a system of concurrent majority is actually functioning is a matter that has not been fully clarified by empirical research. Nevertheless, it does seem tenable to conclude that in many major areas of public policy it is necessary at least to achieve a concurrent majority of the *major* or *dominant* interests affected.

The *theory* of concurrent majority originated with John C. Calhoun. Calhoun, born in 1781, had a distinguished career in public service at both the national and state levels. The idea of concurrent majority evolved from the concept of state nullification of federal law. Under this states' rights doctrine, states would be able to veto any national action. The purpose of this procedure was theoretically to protect states in a minority from encroachment by a national majority that could act through Congress, the President, and even the Supreme Court. Those who favored this procedure had little faith in the separation of powers doctrine as an effective device to prevent the arbitrary exercise of national power. At the end of his career Calhoun decided to incorporate his earlier views on state nullification into a more substantial theoretical treatise in political science; thus he wrote his famous *Disquisition on Government* in the decade between 1840 and 1850. He attempted to develop a general theory of constitutional (limited) government, the primary mechanism of which would be the ability of the major interest groups (states in Calhoun's time) to veto legislation adverse to their interests. Students should overlook some of the theoretical inconsistencies in Calhoun and concentrate upon the basic justification he advances for substituting his system of concurrent majority for the separation of powers device. Under the latter, group interests are not necessarily taken into account, for national laws can be passed on the basis of a numerical majority. And even though this majority may reflect the interests of some groups it will not necessarily take into account the interests of all groups affected. Thus, Calhoun is arguing that a system in which the major interest groups can dominate the policy process is really more in accord with constitutional democracy than that established in our Constitution and supported in *Federalist 10*.

A DISQUISITION ON GOVERNMENT

John C. Calhoun

... W<small>HAT</small> I propose is ... to explain on what principles government must be formed in order to resist by its own interior structure—or to use a single term, *organism*—the tendency to abuse of power. This structure ... is what is meant by constitution, in its strict and more usual sense; and it is this which distinguishes what are called "constitutional" governments from "absolute." ...

How government, then, must be constructed in order to counteract, through its organism, this tendency on the part of those who make and execute the laws to oppress those subject to their operation is the next question which claims attention.

There is but one way in which this can possibly be done, and that is by such an organism as will furnish the ruled with the means of resisting successfully this tendency on the part of the rulers to oppression and abuse. Power can only be resisted by power—and tendency by tendency. Those who exercise power and those subject to its exercise—the rulers and the ruled—stand in antagonistic relations to each other. The same constitution of our nature which leads rulers to oppress the ruled —regardless of the object for which government is ordained—will, with equal strength, lead the ruled to resist when possessed of the means of making peaceable and effective resistance. Such an organism, then, as will furnish the means by which resistance may be systematically and peaceably made on the part of the ruled to oppression and abuse of power on the part of the rulers is the first and indispensable step toward *forming* a constitutional government. And as this can only be effected by or through the right of suffrage—the right on the part of the ruled to choose their rulers at proper intervals and to hold them thereby responsible for their conduct—the responsibility of the rulers to the ruled, through the right of suffrage, is the indispensable and primary principle in the foundation of a constitutional government. When this right is properly guarded, and the people sufficiently enlightened to understand their own rights and the interests of the community and duly to appreciate the motives and conduct of those appointed to make and execute the laws, it is all-sufficient to give to those who elect effective control over those they have elected.

I call the right of suffrage the indispensable and primary principle, for it would be a great and dangerous mistake to suppose, as many do, that it is, of itself, sufficient to form constitutional governments. To this erroneous opinion may be traced one of the causes why so few attempts to form constitutional governments have succeeded, and why of the few which have, so small a number have had durable existence. It has led not only to mistakes in the attempts to form such governments, but to their overthrow when they have, by some good fortune, been correctly formed. So far from being, of itself, sufficient—however well guarded it might be and however enlightened the people—it would, unaided by other provisions, leave the government as absolute as it would be in the hands of irresponsible rulers; and with a tendency, at least as strong, toward oppression and abuse of its power, as I shall next proceed to explain.

. . . The right of suffrage . . . transfers, in reality, the actual control over the government from those who make and execute the laws to the body of the community and thereby places the powers of the government as fully in the mass of the community as they would be if they, in fact, had assembled, made, and executed the laws themselves without the intervention of representatives or agents. The more perfectly it does this, the more perfectly it accomplishes its ends; but in doing so, it only changes the seat of authority without counteracting, in the least, the tendency of the government to oppression and abuse of its powers.

If the whole community had the same interests so that the interests of each and every portion would be so affected by the action of the government that the laws which oppressed or impoverished one portion would necessarily oppress and impoverish all others—or the reverse—then the right of suffrage, of itself, would be all-sufficient to counteract the tendency of the government to oppression and abuse of its powers, and, of course, would form, of itself, a perfect constitutional government. . . .

But such is not the case. On the contrary, nothing is more difficult than to equalize the action of the government in reference to the various and diversified interests of the community; and nothing more easy than to pervert its powers into instruments to aggrandize and enrich one or more interests by oppressing and impoverishing the others. . . . The more extensive and populous the country, the more diversified the condition and pursuits of its population; and the richer, more luxurious, and dissimilar the people, the more difficult is it to equalize the action of the government, and the more easy for one portion of the community to pervert its powers to oppress and plunder the other.

Such being the case, it necessarily results that the right of suffrage, by placing the control of the government in the community, must, from the same constitution of our nature which makes government necessary to preserve society, lead to conflict among its different interests—each striving to obtain possession of its powers as the means of protecting itself against the others or of advancing its respective interests regardless of the interests of others. For this purpose, a struggle will take place between the various interests to obtain a majority in order to control the government. If no one interest be strong enough, of itself, to obtain it, a combination will be formed between those whose interests are most alike—each conceding something to the others until a sufficient number is obtained to make a majority. The process may be slow and much time may be required before a compact, organized majority can be thus formed, but formed it will be in time, even without preconcert or design, by the sure workings of that principle or constitution of our nature in which government itself originates. When once formed, the community will be divided into two great parties—a major and minor—between which there will be incessant struggles on the one side to retain, and on the other to obtain the majority and, thereby, the control of the government and the advantages it confers. . . .

Nor is it less certain . . . that the dominant majority . . . would have the same tendency to oppression and abuse of power which, without the right of suffrage, irresponsible rulers would have. No reason, indeed, can be assigned why the latter would abuse their power, which would not apply, with equal force, to the former. The dominant majority, for the time, would in reality, through the right of suffrage, be the rulers —the controlling, governing, and irresponsible power; and those who make and execute the laws would, for the time, be in reality but *their* representatives and agents.

Nor would the fact that the former would constitute a majority of the community counteract a tendency originating in the constitution of man and which, as such, cannot depend on the number by whom the powers of the government may be wielded. . . . Be it which it may, the minority, for the time, will be as much the governed or subject portion as are the people in an aristocracy or the subjects in a monarchy. The only difference in this respect is that in the government of a majority the minority may become the majority, and the majority the minority, through the right of suffrage, and thereby change their relative positions without the intervention of force and revolution. But the duration or

uncertainty of the tenure by which power is held cannot, of itself, counteract the tendency inherent in government to oppression and abuse of
power. On the contrary, the very uncertainty of the tenure, combined
with the violent party warfare which must ever precede a change of
parties under such governments, would rather tend to increase than
diminish the tendency to oppression.

As, then, the right of suffrage, without some other provision, cannot counteract this tendency of government, the next question for consideration is, What is that other provision? . . .

From what has been said, it is manifest that this provision must be
of a character calculated to prevent any one interest or combination of
interests from using the powers of government to aggrandize itself at
the expense of the others. . . . There is but one certain mode in which
this result can be secured, and that is by the adoption of some restriction
or limitation which shall so effectually prevent any one interest or combination of interests from obtaining the exclusive control of the government as to render hopeless all attempts directed to that end. There is,
again, but one mode in which this can be effected, and that is by taking
the sense of each interest or portion of the community which may be
unequally and injuriously affected by the action of the government separately, through its own majority or in some other way by which its
voice may be fairly expressed, and to require the consent of each interest
either to put or to keep the government in action. This, too, can be accomplished only . . . by dividing and distributing the powers of government, giv[ing] to each division or interest, through its appropriate organ,
either a concurrent voice in making and executing the laws or a veto on
their execution. It is only by such an organism that the assent of each
can be made necessary to put the government in motion, or the power
made effectual to arrest its action when put in motion; and it is only by
the one or the other that the different interests, orders, classes, or portions
into which the community may be divided can be protected, and all conflict and struggle between them prevented—by rendering it impossible
to put or to keep it in action without the concurrent consent of all.

Such an organism as this, combined with the right of suffrage, constitutes, in fact, the elements of constitutional government. The one, by
rendering those who make and execute the laws responsible to those on
whom they operate, prevents the rulers from oppressing the ruled; and
the other, by making it impossible for any one interest or combination
of interests, or class, or order, or portion of the community to obtain exclusive control, prevents any one of them from oppressing the other. It is

clear that oppression and abuse of power must come, if at all, from the one or the other quarter. . . . It follows that the two, suffrage and proper organism combined, are sufficient to counteract the tendency of government to oppression and abuse of power and to restrict it to the fulfillment of the great ends for which it is ordained.

In coming to this conclusion I have assumed the organism to be perfect and the different interests, portions, or classes of the community to be sufficiently enlightened to understand its character and object, and to exercise, with due intelligence, the right of suffrage. . . . Where the organism is perfect, every interest will be truly and fully represented, and of course the whole community must be so. It may be difficult, or even impossible, to make a perfect organism—but, although this be true, yet even when, instead of the sense of each and of all, *it takes that of a few great and prominent interests only,* it would still, in a great measure, if not altogether, fulfill the end intended by a constitution. For in such case it would require so large a portion of the community, compared with the whole, to concur or acquiesce in the action of the government that the number to be plundered would be too few and the number to be aggrandized too many to afford adequate notices to oppression and the abuse of its powers. . . .

It results, from what has been said, that there are two different modes in which the sense of the community may be taken: one, simply by the right of suffrage, unaided; the other, by the right through a proper organism. Each collects the sense of the majority. But one regards numbers only and considers the whole community as a unit having but one common interest throughout, and collects the sense of the greater number of the whole as that of the community. The other, on the contrary, regards interests as well as numbers—considering the community as made up of different and conflicting interests, as far as the action of the government is concerned—and takes the sense of each through its majority or appropriate organ, and the united sense of all as the sense of the entire community. The former of these I shall call the numerical or absolute majority, and the latter, the concurrent or constitutional majority. . . .

19. The Nature and Functions of Interest Groups

What is an "interest group"? The typical picture painted of interest or "pressure" groups involves an evil-minded, crooked-nosed lobbyist attempting to corner a Congressman to get him to vote for some "selfish" proposal which is, of course, against the "public interest." Lobbyists and interest groups are generally considered to be bad, working for their own ends against a higher national purpose.

The following selection, taken from David Truman's *The Governmental Process* (1951), contains (1) a definition of the term "interest group" and (2) a brief outline of a frame of reference within which the operations of interest groups should be considered. There is a fairly articulate interest group theory of the governmental process, and this is sketched by Truman in the following material. It will become evident to the student of American government that interest groups, like political parties, form an integral part of our political system. Further, interest group theory involves an entirely new way of looking at government.

THE GOVERNMENTAL PROCESS

*David Truman**

Interest Groups

INTEREST GROUP refers to any group that, on the basis of one or more shared attitudes, makes certain claims upon other groups in the society for the establishment, maintenance, or enhancement of forms of behavior that are implied by the shared attitudes. . . . [F]rom interaction in groups arise certain common habits of response, which may be called norms, or shared attitudes. These afford the participants frames of reference for interpreting and evaluating events and behaviors. In this respect all groups are interest groups because they are shared-attitude groups. In some groups at various points in time, however, a second kind of common response emerges, in addition to the frame of reference. These are shared attitudes toward what is needed or wanted in a given situation, as demands or claims upon other groups in the society. The term "interest group" will be reserved here for those groups that exhibit both aspects of the shared attitudes. . . .

Definition of the interest group in this fashion . . . permits the identification of various potential as well as existing interest groups. That is, it invites examination of an interest whether or not it is found at the moment as one of the characteristics of a particular organized group. Although no group that makes claims upon other groups in the society will be found without an interest or interests, it is possible to examine

* From *The Governmental Process,* by David Truman, by permission of Alfred A. Knopf, Inc. Copyright © 1952, by Regents of U. of Mich.

interests that are not at a particular point in time the basis of interactions among individuals, but that may become such. . . .

Groups and Government:
Difficulties in a Group Interpretation of Politics

Since we are engaged in an effort to develop a conception of the political process in the United States that will account adequately for the role of groups, particularly interest groups, it will be appropriate to take account of some of the factors that have been regarded as obstacles to such a conception and that have caused such groups to be neglected in many explanations of the dynamics of government. Perhaps the most important practical reason for this neglect is that the significance of groups has only fairly recently been forced to the attention of political scientists by the tremendous growth in the number of formally organized groups in the United States within the last few decades. It is difficult and unnecessary to attempt to date the beginning of such attention, but Herring in 1929, in his ground-breaking book, *Group Representation Before Congress*, testified to the novelty of the observations he reported when he stated: "There has developed in this government an extra-legal machinery of as integral and of as influential a nature as the system of party government that has long been an essential part of the government. . . ." Some implications of this development are not wholly compatible with some of the proverbial notions about representative government held by specialists as well as laymen. . . . This apparent incompatibility has obstructed the inclusion of group behaviors in an objective description of the governmental process.

More specifically, it is usually argued that any attempt at the interpretation of politics in terms of group patterns inevitably "leaves something out" or "destroys something essential" about the processes of "our" government. On closer examination, we find this argument suggesting that two "things" are certain to be ignored: the individual, and a sort of totally inclusive unity designated by such terms as "society" and "the state."

The argument that the individual is ignored in any interpretation of politics as based upon groups seems to assume a differentiation or conflict between "the individual" and some such collectivity as the group. . . .

Such assumptions need not present any difficulties in the development of a group interpretation of politics, because they are essentially unwarranted. They simply do not square with . . . evidence concerning group affiliations and individual behavior. . . . We do not, in fact, find individuals otherwise than in groups; complete isolation in space and time is so rare as to be an almost hypothetical situation. It is equally demonstrable that the characteristics of any interest group, including the activities by which we identify it, are governed by the attitudes and the circumstances that gave rise to the interactions of which it consists. These are variable factors, and, although the role played by a particular individual may be quite different in a lynch mob from that of the same individual in a meeting of the church deacons, the attitudes and behaviors involved in both are as much a part of his personality as is his treatment of his family. "The individual" and "the group" are at most merely convenient ways of classifying behavior, two ways of approaching the same phenomena, not different things.

The persistence among nonspecialists of the notion of an inherent conflict between "the individual" and "the group" or "society" is understandable in view of the doctrines of individualism that have underlain various political and economic conflicts over the past three centuries. The notion persists also because it harmonizes with a view of the isolated and independent individual as the "cause" of complicated human events. The personification of events, quite apart from any ethical considerations, is a kind of shorthand convenient in everyday speech and, like supernatural explanations of natural phenomena, has a comforting simplicity. Explanations that take into account multiple causes, including group affiliations, are difficult. The "explanation" of a national complex like the Soviet Union wholly in terms of a Stalin or the "description" of the intricacies of the American government entirely in terms of a Roosevelt is quick and easy. . . .

The second major difficulty allegedly inherent in any attempt at a group interpretation of the political process is that such an explanation inevitably must ignore some greater unity designated as society or the state. . . .

Many of those who place particular emphasis upon this difficulty assume explicitly or implicitly that there is an interest of the nation as a whole, universally and invariably held and standing apart from and superior to those of the various groups included within it. This assumption is close to the popular dogmas of democratic government based on the familiar notion that if only people are free and have access to "the facts," they will all want the same thing in any political situation. It is no derogation of democratic preferences to state that such an assertion flies in the face of all that we know of the behavior of men in a complex society. Were it in fact true, not only the interest group but even the political party should properly be viewed as an abnormality. The differing experiences and perceptions of men not only encourage individuality but also . . . inevitably result in differing attitudes and conflicting group affiliations. "There are," says Bentley in his discussion of this error of the social whole, "always some parts of the nation to be found arrayed against other parts." [From *The Process of Government* (1908).] Even in war, when a totally inclusive interest should be apparent if it is ever going to be, we always find pacifists, conscientious objectors, spies, and subversives, who reflect interests opposed to those of "the nation as a whole."

There is a political significance in assertions of a totally inclusive interest within a nation. Particularly in times of crisis, such as an international war, such claims are a tremendously useful promotional device by means of which a particularly extensive group or league of groups tries to reduce or eliminate opposing interests. Such is the pain attendant upon not "belonging" to one's "own" group that if a normal person can be convinced that he is the lone dissenter to an otherwise universally accepted agreement, he usually will conform. This pressure accounts at least in part for the number of prewar pacifists who, when the United States entered World War II, accepted the draft or volunteered. Assertion of an inclusive "national" or "public interest" is an effective device in many less critical situations as well. In themselves, these claims are part of the data of politics. However, they do not describe any actual or possible political situation within a complex modern nation. In developing a group interpretation of politics, therefore, we do not need to account for a totally inclusive interest, because one does not exist.

Denying the existence of an interest of the nation as a whole does not completely dispose of the difficulty raised by those who insist that a group interpretation must omit "the state." We cannot deny the obvious fact that we are examining a going political system that is supported or at least accepted by a large proportion of the society. We cannot account for such a system by adding up in some fashion the National Association of Manufacturers, the Congress of Industrial Organizations, the American Farm Bureau Federation, the American Legion, and other groups that come to mind when "lobbies" and "pressure groups" are mentioned. Even if the political parties are added to the list, the result could properly be designated as "a view which seems hardly compatible with the relative stability of the political system. . . ." Were such the exclusive ingredients of the political process in the United States, the entire system would have torn itself apart long since.

If these various organized interest groups more or less consistently reconcile their differences, adjust, and accept compromises, we must acknowledge that we are dealing with a system that is not accounted for by the "sum" of the organized interest groups in the society. We must go farther to explain the operation of such ideals or traditions as constitutionalism, civil liberties, representative responsibility, and the like. These are not, however, a sort of disembodied metaphysical influence, like Mr. Justice Holmes's "brooding omnipresence." We know of the existence of such factors only from the behavior and the habitual interactions of men. If they exist in this fashion, they are interests. We can account for their operation and for the system by recognizing such interests as representing what . . . we called potential interest groups in the "becoming" stage of activity. "It is certainly true," as Bentley has made clear, "that we must accept a . . . group of this kind as an interest group itself." It makes no difference that we cannot find the home office and the executive secretary of such a group. Organization in this formal sense, as we have seen, represents merely a stage or degree of interaction that may or may not be significant at any particular point in time. Its absence does not mean that these interests do not exist, that the familiar "pressure groups" do not operate as if such potential groups were organized and active, or that these interests may not move from the potential to the organized stage of activity.

It thus appears that the two major difficulties supposedly obstacles to a group interpretation of the political process are not insuperable. We can employ the fact of individuality and we can account for the existence of the state without doing violence to the evidence available from the observed behaviors of men and groups. . . .

Interest Groups and the Nature of the State

Men, wherever they are observed, are creatures participating in those established patterns of interaction that we call groups. Excepting perhaps the most casual and transitory, these continuing interactions, like all such interpersonal relationships, involve power. This power is exhibited in two closely interdependent ways. In the first place, the group exerts power over its members; an individual's group affiliations largely determine his attitudes, values, and the frames of reference in terms of which he interprets his experiences. For a measure of conformity to the norms of the group is the price of acceptance within it. . . . In the second place, the group, if it is or becomes an interest group, which any group in a society may be, exerts power over other groups in the society when it successfully imposes claims upon them.

Many interest groups, probably an increasing proportion in the United States, are politicized. That is, either from the outset or from time to time in the course of their development they make their claims through or upon the institutions of government. Both the forms and functions of government in turn are a reflection of the activities and claims of such groups. . . .

The institutions of government are centers of interest-based power; their connections with interest groups may be latent or overt and their activities range in political character from the routinized and widely accepted to the unstable and highly controversial. In order to make claims, political interest groups will seek access to the key points of decision within these institutions. Such points are scattered throughout the structure, including not only the formally established branches of government but also the political parties in their various forms and the relationships between governmental units and other interest groups.

The extent to which a group achieves effective access to the institutions of government is the resultant of a complex of interdependent factors. For the sake of simplicity these may be classified in three somewhat overlapping categories: (1) factors relating to a group's strategic position in the society; (2) factors associated with the internal characteristics of the group; and (3) factors peculiar to the governmental institutions themselves. In the first category are: the group's status or prestige in the society, affecting the ease with which it commands deference from those outside its bounds; the standing it and its activities have when measured against the widely held but largely unorganized interests or "rules of the game"; the extent to which government officials are formally or informally "members" of the group; and the usefulness of the group as a source of technical and political knowledge. The second category includes: the degree and appropriateness of the group's organization; the degree of cohesion it can achieve in a given situation, especially in the light of competing group demands upon its membership; the skills of the leadership; and the group's resources in numbers and money. In the third category are: the operating structure of the government institutions, since such established features involve relatively fixed advantages and handicaps; and the effects of the group life of particular units or branches of the government. . . .

A characteristic feature of the governmental system in the United States is that it contains a multiplicity of points of access. The federal system establishes decentralized and more or less independent centers of power, vantage points from which to secure privileged access to the national government. Both a sign and a cause of the strength of the constituent units in the federal scheme is the peculiar character of our party system, which has strengthened parochial relationships, especially those of national legislators. National parties, and to a lesser degree those in the States, tend to be poorly cohesive leagues of locally based organizations rather than unified and inclusive structures. Staggered terms for executive officials and various types of legislators accentuate differences in the effective electorates that participate in choosing these officers. Each of these different, often opposite, localized patterns (constituencies) is a channel of independent access to the larger party aggregation and to the formal government. Thus, especially at the national level, the party is an electing-device and only in limited measure an integrated means of policy determination. Within the Congress, furthermore, controls are diffused among committee chairmen and other leaders in both chambers. The variety of these points of access is further supported by relationships stemming from the constitutional doctrine of separation of powers, from related checks and balances, and at the State and local level from the common practice of choosing an array of executive officials by popular election. At the Federal level the formal simplicity of the executive branch has been complicated by a Supreme Court decision that has placed a number of administrative agencies beyond the removal power of the president. The position of these units, however, differs only in degree from that of many that are constitutionally within the executive branch. In consequence of alternative lines of access available through the legislature and the executive and of divided channels for the control of administrative policy, many nominally executive agencies are at various times virtually independent of the chief executive. . . . Within limits, therefore, organized interest groups, gravitating toward responsive points of decision, may play one segment of the structure against another as circumstances and strategic considerations permit. The total pattern of government over a period of time thus presents a protean complex of crisscrossing relationships that change in strength and direction with alternations in the power and standing of interests, organized and unorganized. 🔖

From Truman's definition *any* group, organized or unorganized, which has a shared attitude toward goals and methods for achieving them should be classified as an "interest group." Truman is essentially saying that since people generally function as members of groups it is more useful and accurate for the political observer to view the governmental process as the interaction of political interest groups. If one accepts the sociologist's assumption that men act and interact only as members of groups, then it is imperative that the governmental process be viewed as one of interest group interaction.

Within the framework of Truman's definition it is possible to identify both *public* and *private* interest groups. In the political process governmental groups sometimes act as interest groups in the same sense as private organizations. In many public policies, governmental groups may have more at stake than private organizations. Thus administrative agencies, for example, may "lobby" as vigorously as their private counterparts to advance their own interests.

The following selection concentrates upon private pressure groups, and discusses the extent to which they are links between public opinion and government. One of the most interesting conclusions of Key is that the elites of interest groups are not able to influence the attitudes of their members to anywhere near the degree commonly thought possible. Pressure group participation in government more often than not reflects highly limited participation by the active elements of the groups. Public policy is often hammered out by very small numbers of individuals both in the government and the private sphere. Political leaders can never stray too far beyond the boundaries of consent, but these are often very broad.

PRESSURE GROUPS*

*V. O. Key, Jr.**

Pʀᴇssuʀᴇ ɢʀᴏᴜᴘs occupy a prominent place in analyses of American politics. In a regime characterized by official deference to public opinion and by adherence to the doctrine of freedom of association, private organizations may be regarded as links that connect the citizen and government. They are differentiated in both composition and function from political parties. Ordinarily they concern themselves with only a narrow range of policies, those related to the peculiar interests of the group membership. Their aim is primarily to influence the content of public policy rather than the results of elections. Those groups with a mass membership, though, may oppose or support particular candidates; in that case they are treated as groups with power to affect election results and, thereby, with the capacity to pressure party leaders, legislators, and others in official position to act in accord with their wishes. . . .

. . . [There are] a series of puzzles as we seek to describe the role of pressure groups as links between opinion and government. Clearly the model of the lobbyist who speaks for a united following, determined in its aims and prepared to reward its friends and punish its enemies at the polls, does not often fit reality. Nor is it probable that the unassisted effort of pressure organizations to mold public opinion in support of their position has a large effect upon mass opinion. Yet legislators listen respectfully to the representations of the spokesmen of private groups, which in turn spend millions of dollars every year in propagandizing the public. Leaders of private groups articulate the concerns of substantial numbers of persons, even though they may not have succeeded in indoctrinating completely the members of their own groups. All this activity must have some functional significance in the political system. The problem is to identify its functions in a manner that seems to make sense. In this endeavor a distinction of utility is that made . . . between mass-membership organizations and nonmass organizations, which far outnumber the former.

Representation of Mass-Membership Groups. Only the spokesmen for mass-membership organizations can give the appearance of representing voters in sufficient numbers to impress (or intimidate) government. The influence of nonmass groups, which often have only a few hundred or a few thousand members, must rest upon something other than the threat of electoral retribution. As has been seen, the reality of the behavior of members of mass organizations is that in the short run they are not manipulable in large numbers by their leaders. Their party identification anchors many of them to a partisan position, and over the longer run they seem to be moved from party to party in presidential elections by the influences that affect all types and classes of people.

The spokesmen of mass-membership groups also labor under the handicap that they may be made to appear to be unrepresentative of the opinions of their members. When the president of an organization announces to a congressional committee that he speaks for several million people, the odds are that a substantial proportion of his members can be shown to have no opinion or even to express views contrary to those voiced by their spokesmen. This divergency is often explained as a wicked betrayal of the membership or as a deliberate departure from the mass mandate. Yet it is not unlikely that another type of explanation more often fits the facts. Opinions, as we have seen in many contexts, do not fall into blacks and whites. It may be the nature of mass groups that attachment to the positions voiced by the peak spokesmen varies with attachment to and involvement in the group. At the leadership level the group position is voiced in its purest and most uncompromising form. A substantial layer of group activists subscribes to the official line, but among those with less involvement the faith wins less general acceptance. At the periphery of the group, though, the departure from the official line may be more a matter of indifference than of dissent. Leadership policy is often pictured as the consequence of interaction between leadership and group membership, which may be only partially true. Leaders may be more accurately regarded as dedicated souls who bid for group support of their position. Almost invariably they receive something less than universal acquiescence. This may be especially true in mass organizations in which political endeavor is to a degree a side issue—as, for example, in trade unions and farm organizations. As one traces attitudes and opinions across the strata of group membership, the clarity of position and the extremeness of position become more marked at the level of high involvement and activism.

If it is more or less the nature of mass organizations to encompass a spectrum of opinion rather than a single hue, much of the discussion of the representativeness of group leadership may be beside the point. However that may be, circumstances surrounding the leadership elements of mass organizations place them, in their work of influencing government, in a position not entirely dissimilar to that of leaders of nonmass groups. They must rely in large measure on means not unlike those that must be employed by groups with only the smallest membership. The world of pressure politics becomes more a politics among the activists than a politics that involves many people. Yet politics among the activists occurs in a context of concern about public opinion, a concern that colors the mode of action if not invariably its substance.

Arenas of Decision and Norms of Action. The maneuvers of pressure-group politics thus come ordinarily to occur among those highly involved and immediately concerned about public policy; the connection of these maneuvers with public opinion and even with the opinions of mass-membership organizations tends to be tenuous. Many questions of policy are fought out within vaguely bounded arenas in which the activists concerned are clustered. A major factor in the determination of the balance of forces within each arena is party control of the relevant governmental apparatus. Included among the participants in each issue-cluster of activists are the spokesmen for the pressure groups concerned, the members of the House and Senate committees with jurisdiction, and the officials of the administrative departments and agencies concerned. In the alliances of pressure politics those between administrative agencies and private groups are often extremely significant in the determination of courses of action. The cluster of concerned activists may include highly interested persons, firms, and organizations scattered over the country, though the boundaries delimiting those concerned vary from question to question, from arena to arena. In short, pressure politics among the activists takes something of the form that it would take if there were no elections or no concern about the nature of public opinion; that is, those immediately concerned make themselves heard in the process of decision.

In the give and take among the activists, norms and values with foundations in public opinion are conditioning factors. The broad values of the society determine to a degree who will be heard, who can play the game. Those who claim to speak for groups that advocate causes outside the range of consensus may be given short shrift. Some groups advocating perfectly respectable causes may be heard with less deference than others. Subtle standards define what David Truman calls "access" to the decisionmakers. To some extent this is a party matter: an AFL-CIO delegation does not expect to be heard with much sympathy by a committee dominated by right-wing Republicans. The reality of access, too, may provide an index to the tacit standards in definition of those interests regarded as having a legitimate concern about public policy. The spokesmen of groups both large and small are often heard with respect, not because they wield power, but because they are perceived as the representatives of interests entitled to be heard and to be accorded consideration as a matter of right.

Within the range of the permissible, the process of politics among the activists is governed to some extent by the expectation that all entitled to play the game shall get a fair deal (or at least a fair hearing before their noses are rubbed in the dirt). Doubtless these practices parallel a fairly widespread set of attitudes within the population generally. Probably those attitudes could be characterized as a disposition to let every group—big business and labor unions as well—have its say, but that such groups should not be permitted to dominate the government. In the implementation of these attitudes the legalism of American legislators plays a role. Frequently congressional committeemen regard themselves as engaged in a judicial role of hearing the evidence and of arriving at decisions based on some sort of standards of equity.

Rituals of the Activists. The maneuvers of group spokesmen, be they spokesmen for mass or nonmass organizations, are often accompanied by rituals in obeisance to the doctrine that public opinion governs. The belief often seems to be that congressmen will be impressed by a demonstration that public opinion demands the proposed line of action or inaction. Hence, groups organize publicity campaigns and turn up sheaves of editorials in support of their position. They stimulate people to write or to wire their congressmen; if the labor of stimulation is too arduous, they begin to sign to telegrams names chosen at random from the telephone directory. They solicit the endorsement of other organizations for their position. They lobby the American Legion and the General Federation of Women's Clubs for allies willing to permit their names to be used. On occasion they buy the support of individuals who happen to hold official positions in other organizations. They form fraudulent organizations with impressive letterheads to advance the cause. They attempt to anticipate and to soften the opposition of organizations that might be opposed to their position. Groups of similar ideological orientation tend to "run" together or to form constellations in confederation for mutual advantage.

All these maneuvers we have labelled "rituals"; that is, they are on the order of the dance of the rainmakers. That may be too brutal a characterization, for sometimes these campaigns have their effects—just as rain sometimes follows the rainmakers' dance. Yet the data make it fairly clear that most of these campaigns do not affect the opinion of many people and even clearer that they have small effect by way of punitive or approbative feedback in the vote. Their function in the political process is difficult to divine. The fact that organizations engage in these practices, though, is in itself a tribute to the importance of public opinion. To some extent, too, these opinion campaigns are not so much directed to mass opinion as to other activists who do not speak for many people either but have access to the arena of decision-making and perhaps have a viewpoint entitled to consideration. In another direction widespread publicity, by its creation of the illusion of mass support, may legitimize a position taken by a legislator. If a legislator votes for a measure that seems to arouse diverse support, his vote is not so likely to appear to be a concession to a special interest.

Barnums among the Businessmen. An additional explanation that apparently accounts for a good deal of group activity is simply that businessmen (who finance most of the campaigns of public education by pressure groups) are soft touches for publicity men. The advertising and public-relations men have demonstrated that they can sell goods; they proceed on the assumption that the business of obtaining changes in public policy is analogous to selling soap. They succeed in separating businessmen from large sums of money to propagate causes, often in a manner that sooner or later produces a boomerang effect.

Professional bureaucrats of the continuing and well-established organizations practice restraint in their public-relations campaigns. They need to gain the confidence of congressmen and other officials with whom they also need to be able to speak the next time they meet. The fly-by-night organization or the business group that falls into the clutches of an unscrupulous public-relations firm is more likely to indulge in the fantastic public relations and pressure campaign. Thus the National Tax Equality Association raised some $600,000 to finance a campaign against the tax exemptions of cooperatives, the most important of which are farm coops. Contributions came from concerns as scattered as the Central Power & Light Co., of Corpus Christi, Texas; Fairmont Foods Co., of Omaha, Nebraska; Central Hudson Gas and Electric Corporation, of Poughkeepsie, New York; and the Rheem Manufacturing Co., of San Francisco. The late Representative Reed, of New York, who was not one to attack business lightly, declared:

> Mr. Speaker, an unscrupulous racket, known as the National Tax Equality Association, has been in operation for some time, directing its vicious propaganda against the farm co-operatives. To get contributions from businessmen, this racketeering organization has propagandized businessmen with false statements to the effect that if farm co-operatives were taxed and not exempted the revenue to the government would mount annually to over $800,000,000. [The treasury estimate was in the neighborhood of $20,000,000.] This is, of course, absolutely false and nothing more nor less than getting money under false pretenses. . . . This outfit of racketeers known as the Tax Equality Association has led honest businessmen to believe that their contributions were deductible from gross income as ordinary and necessary business expense with reference to their Federal income-tax return.

The Tax Equality Association provided its subscribers with the following form letter to send to their Congressmen:

> Dear Mr. Congressman: You raised my income taxes. Now I hear you are going to do it again. But you still let billions in business and profits escape. How come you raise my taxes, but let co-ops, mutuals, and other profit-making corporations get off scot free, or nearly so? I want a straight answer—and I want these businesses fully taxed before you increase my or anyone else's income taxes again.

Letters so phrased are not well designed to produce favorable congressional response. The ineptness of this sort of campaign creates no little curiosity about the political judgment of solvent businessmen who put their money or their corporation's money into the support of obviously stupidly managed endeavors.

Autonomous Actors or Links? This review of the activities of pressure groups may raise doubts about the validity of the conception of these groups as links between public opinion and government. The reality seems to be that the conception applies with greater accuracy to some groups than to others. Certainly group spokesmen may represent a shade of opinion to government even though not all their own members share the views they express. Yet to a considerable degree the work of the spokesmen of private groups, both large and small, proceeds without extensive involvement of either the membership or a wider public. Their operations as they seek to influence legislation and administration, though, occur in a milieu of concern about opinion, either actual or latent. That concern also disposes decision-makers to attend to shades of opinion and preference relevant to decision though not necessarily of great electoral strength—a disposition of no mean importance in the promotion of the equitable treatment of people in a democratic order. The chances are that the effects of organized groups on public opinion occur mainly over the long run rather than in short-run maneuvers concerned with particular congressional votes. Moreover, group success may be governed more by the general balance of partisan strength than by the results of group endeavors to win friends in the mass public. An industry reputed to be led by swindlers may not expect the most cordial reception from legislative committees, especially at times when the balance of strength is not friendly to any kind of business. If the industry can modify its public image, a task that requires time, its position as it maneuvers on particulars (about which few of the public can ever know anything) may be less unhappy. That modification may be better attained by performance than by propaganda. 🦜

20. Case Studies in Pressure Group Politics

Administrative agencies often are the focal point of government policy making, and therefore pressure groups concentrate upon the bureaucracy in order to achieve their objectives. Public policy often emerges from administrative agency–pressure group interaction, for together such an alliance of public and private interest is very difficult to overcome. The following selection illustrates the way in which such a combination of interests has developed in the defense policy field, causing concern to proponents of greater presidential and congressional control independent of the Pentagon and private contractors' interests.

THE "MILITARY LOBBY":
ITS IMPACT ON CONGRESS AND THE NATION
Congressional Quarterly*

WHAT led President Eisenhower, on the eve of his retirement, to warn the Nation of "unwarranted influence" by what he called "the military-industrial complex"?

What is this complex, what is the nature and extent of its influence, and how is it exercised?

What dangers—if any—are implicit in the situation described by the former President?

These were the principal questions raised by the President's parting words (for text, see below). In an attempt to answer them, *Congressional Quarterly* culled the record of Presidential press conferences, Congressional hearings, and other public documents. In addition, extensive off-the-record interviews were conducted with Members of Congress, representatives of defense contractors, former Government officials, and other persons with pertinent information. Results of this survey of fact and opinion are summarized on the following pages.

* From the *Congressional Quarterly*, March 24, 1961, copyright © 1961 by the Congressional Quarterly Service. Reprinted by permission. This article appeared in the *Congressional Record*, March 27, 1961, p. 4557 ff.

EISENHOWER'S WARNING

In his final address to the Nation on January 17, President Eisenhower noted that the United States has been compelled to "create a permanent armaments industry of vast proportions" and to maintain a defense establishment employing 3.5 million persons and spending huge sums. He continued as follows:

"This conjunction of an immense military establishment and a large arms industry is new in American experience. The total influence—economic, political, even spiritual—is felt in every city, every State house, every office of the Federal government. We recognize the imperative need for this development. Yet we must not fail to comprehend its grave implications. Our toil, resources and livelihood are all involved; so is the very structure of our society.

"In the councils of government, we must guard against the acquisition of unwarranted influence, whether sought or unsought, by the military-industrial complex. The potential for the disastrous rise of misplaced power exists and will persist. We must never let the weight of this combination endanger our liberties or democratic processes. We should take nothing for granted. Only an alert and knowledgeable citizenry can compel the proper meshing of the huge industrial and military machinery of defense with our peaceful methods and goals, so that security and liberty may prosper together."

EISENHOWER'S VIEWS

The President's warning of January 17 was his first public reference to a "military-industrial complex." But the concept was in the making for 8 years, during which the President had touched on most of the major components of his final declaration. These were the principal elements of his thinking, as seen by his associates and partially reflected in the record:

National survival, he stated in 1953 and repeatedly thereafter, rested on "security with solvency." To achieve this required maximum effort to counter the inherent tendency of Federal expenditures in general, and defense spending in particular, to rise. The key to success lay in "balance" —not, as he said April 25, 1958, during his battle with Congress over reorganization, in "overindulging sentimental attachments to outmoded military machines and concepts," nor, as he put it January 27, 1960, in heeding the "noisy trumpeting about dazzling military schemes or untrustworthy programs."

Ranged against this view, the President realized, was a host of special interests—the armed services and their civilian allies in business and in Congress. Beginning in 1953, when he cut the Air Force budget by $5 billion, the services had repeatedly carried their fight for more funds to Congress and the press. (More than one Member had called him to say that they were changing their votes in response to local pressures generated by the Pentagon.) "Obviously political and financial considerations" rather than "strict military needs" were influencing the situation, he said June 3, 1959. If such forces were allowed to prevail, he said March 11, 1959, "everybody with any sense knows that we are finally going to a garrison state."

Revered by the Nation as its chief military hero, and respected as its Commander in Chief, the President was confident of his ability to "put need above pressure-group inducement, before local argument, before every kind of any pressure except that that America needs," as he put it February 11, 1960. The star-studded brass of the Pentagon awed him not a bit; "there are too many of these generals who have all sorts of ideas," he said February 3, 1960. Knowing how they "operated," however, he feared that his successor—whether Nixon or Kennedy—would be unable to withstand their pressures.

This, according to a close associate, was what impelled the President to speak out as he prepared to leave office. Deeply committed to the goal of disarmament, he was sensitive to the counterinfluence of the "military-industrial complex." The extent of his concern was indicated when, at his final press conference, January 18, he described the impact of widespread advertising by missile manufacturers as "almost an insidious penetration of our own minds that the only thing this country is engaged in is weaponry and missiles." This, he said, was something "we just can't afford."

BACKGROUND

Defense spending reached its postwar low of $11.1 billion in fiscal 1948. By 1953, the cold war and a hot war in Korea had boosted spending to its postwar high of $43.7 billion. President Eisenhower cut that to $35.5 billion in 1955; thereafter, defense outlays climbed each year, to reach a projected $42.9 billion in fiscal 1962. At no time during his 8 years in office did military spending amount to less than one-half of the Federal budget or less than 8 per cent of the Nation's gross national product. All told, the armed services spent $313 billion during the 8 years, fiscal 1954–61; when the costs of military aid, atomic energy, and stockpiling are added, that total mounts to $354 billion.

There is no yardstick by which to measure with precision the economic impact of these expenditures, but there is no question that it has been considerable. According to a 1960 study by the Defense Procurement Subcommittee of the Joint Economic Committee, there were 38 million procurement transactions with a dollar volume of $228 billion from 1950 through 1959. Few areas of the economy were untouched by these purchases of goods and services.

The largest portion of defense spending, however, is allocated to the development, production, and deployment of major weapons systems. In fiscal 1960, when military prime contract awards of $10,000 or more totaled $21 billion, $15.4 billion or 73.4 per cent of the total went to 100 companies (or their subsidiaries) of which 65 were engaged primarily in "research, development, test or production of aircraft, missiles, or electronics." . . .

Despite the heavy concentration of prime contract awards among a small number of companies (in 1960 five companies accounted for 25 per cent of the dollar volume, 21 companies for 50 per cent), extensive subcontracting helps to spread procurement expenditures, employment and profits throughout the country—although not as evenly as some States would like it. In addition, some 1.5 million members of the armed services and almost 1 million civilian employees of the Defense Department are spread throughout the 50 States, with payrolls that totaled $11.4 billion in fiscal 1960. Another $650 million was paid to more than 1 million members of the National Guard and other Reserve groups. . . .

A further indication of the extent of defense-related activities is the wide distribution of facilities. From lists furnished by the military services, Atomic Energy Commission, and National Aeronautics and Space Administration, CQ determined the location of 738 separate installations by Congressional district. According to this list, there are one or more installations in 282 of the country's 437 districts. . . .

Taken together, these data suggest the sweeping extent of the defense establishment and its economic impact, and provide the background against which to examine the concept of a "military-industrial complex."

HÉBERT PROBE

In mid-1959, the House Armed Services Special Investigations Subcommittee, headed by Representative F. Edward Hébert, Democrat of Louisiana, questioned 75 witnesses over 25 days regarding the employment of retired officers by defense industries. The public, and Hébert as the hearings began, was alarmed by reports "about the alleged conduct of some military men who depart the ranks of defense for lush places on the payrolls of defense contractors." As it turned out, no real evidence of misconduct was produced. But the hearings shed considerable light on the ramifications of military-industrial relations.

Retired officers. More than 1,400 retired officers in the rank of major or higher—including 261 of general or flag rank—were found to be employed by the top 100 defense contractors. The company employing the largest number (187, including 27 retired generals and admirals) was General Dynamics Corp., headed by former Secretary of the Army Frank Pace, which also received the biggest defense orders of any company in 1960. Duties of these officers, according to the testimony of their employers, encompassed a wide range of technical, management, and "representation" functions. But in no case, it appeared, was the officer involved in "selling" or the negotiation of defense contracts.

"Influence." With little variation, retired officers told the Hébert subcommittee that they were "has-beens" without influence upon the decisions of their former colleagues still on active duty. None had experienced "pressure" of this kind while still in the service; if any retired officers had asked him for a favor, "I would throw them out on their ear," said Lt. Gen. C. S. Irvine (retired), director of planning for Avco Corp. No one, however, took issue with the statement of Vice Adm. H. G. Rickover that the former jobs of retired officers often were filled "by people who are their dear friends, or even by people whom they have been influential in appointing, and naturally they will be listened to."

Illustrative of this point was the testimony of Adm. William M. Fechteler, retired, former Chief of Naval Operations and a consultant to General Electric Atomic Products Division. He told of arranging appointments for a GE vice president: "I took him in to see Mr. Gates, the Secretary of the Navy. I took him in to see Admiral Burke. He had not met Admiral Burke before. And then I made appointments with him with the Chief of the Bureau of Ships. But I did not accompany him there, because those are materiel bureaus which make contracts. And I studiously avoid even being in the room when anybody talks about a contract."

Entertainment. Two instances of entertainment by defense contractors came before the Hébert subcommittee. George Bunker, chairman of the Martin Co., acknowledged that his firm had entertained at least 26 active-duty officers at a weekend retreat in the Bahamas. Bunker denied there was any impropriety involved, saying "a man could neither operate nor compete effectively unless he had a close personal relationship." But spokesmen for the Secretaries of the three services agreed that such chumminess "doesn't look well" and could not be condoned.

The second case concerned an invitation to a "small off-the-record party" to discuss the plans and problems of the Air Research and Development Command with its newly promoted chief, Lt. Gen. Bernard S. Schriever. The invitation, sent to Representative Hébert and nine other Members of Congress (all but two of whom were members of the Armed Services or Appropriations Committees), was issued by three Air Force contractors: Aerojet-General President Dan A. Kimball (onetime Secretary of the Navy), General Dynamics' Pace, and Martin's Bunker. All three men defended the propriety of the proposed party (which was called off because of the "publicity") as being in Pace's words, "a means of advancing the interests of the United States of America."

Advertising. Shortly before the Hébert hearings began, a major controversy developed in and out of Congress over the respective merits of two competing antiaircraft missile systems—the Army's Nike-Hercules and the Air Force's Bomarc. Advertisements extolling the virtues of the two systems were inserted in Washington, D.C., newspapers by their prime contractors—Western Electric Co. and Boeing Airplane Co., respectively —while the issue was before Congress. Questioned by the Hébert subcommittee about the timing and purpose of the ads, spokesmen for the companies insisted that they were parts of long-term "information" programs.

However, Boeing's Harold Mansfield acknowledged that his company was fighting against a "campaign" of "misinformation" about the Bomarc, while Western Electric's W. M. Reynolds said the Nike ads had been suggested to the company by the Army. Both companies also acknowledged discussing proposed cutbacks in the Nike and Bomarc programs with Members of Congress from areas where employment would be affected. Said Mansfield: "Many of the most important decisions in the defense of our country are not made by military technicians. They are made in the Congress of the United States. And the Bomarc-Nike decision is one such decision."

Associations. Also questioned by the Hébert subcommittee were representatives of six organizations engaged in promoting the mutual interests of the armed services and their contractors in national security matters. All headquartered in Washington, they are the—

Association of the U.S. Army, with about 63,000 members (including military personnel on active duty) and 1958 income of $290,000, of which $143,000 was revenue from advertising in *Army* magazine. One of its aims: "To foster public understanding and support of the U.S. Army." Executive vice president: Lt. Gen. W. L. Weible, USA (retired). Among those on its advisory board: Donald Douglas, Jr., president of Douglas Aircraft Co.; Frank Pace, chairman of General Dynamics Corp.; Senators John J. Sparkman, Democrat, of Alabama, and Strom Thurmond, Democrat, of South Carolina.

Navy League, with about 38,000 members (no active duty personnel) and 1958 income of $179,000 plus $32,000 from advertising in *Navy—The Magazine of Sea Power*. Self-description: "The civilian arm of the Navy." President: Frank Gard Jameson. Among those on its advisory council: Dan Kimball, president of Aerojet-General and former Secretary of the Navy; Adm. Robert B. Carney (retired), chairman of Bath Iron Works Shipbuilding Corp., and former Chief of Naval Operations.

Air Force Association, with about 60,000 members (including about 30,000 Air Force personnel) and 1958 income of $1.2 million, including $527,000 from advertising in *Air Force and Space Digest*. Its aim: "To support the achievement of such airpower as is necessary" for national security. Executive director: James H. Straubel. Among its directors: 14 employees of defense contractors, including Lt. Gen. James H. Doolittle, USAF (retired) of Space Technology Laboratories.

American Ordnance Association, formerly the Army Ordnance Association, with about 42,000 members and 1958 income of $474,000, of which subscriptions and advertisements in the magazine *Ordnance* furnished $253,000. Its aim: "Armament preparedness." Executive vice president: Col. Leo A. Codd, USAR (retired).

Aerospace Industries Association, formerly the Aircraft Industries Association, a trade association with 79 member companies and 1958 income of $1.4 million in dues ranging up to $75,000 per member. Its aim: To promote the manufacture and sale of "aircraft and astronautical vehicles of every nature and description." President: Gen. Orval R. Cook, USAF (retired).

National Security Industrial Association, formerly the Navy Industrial Association, with 502 member companies and 1958 income $238,000, mostly from dues. Its aim: "To establish a close working relationship between industrial concerns" and national security agencies. Executive director: Capt. R. N. McFarlane, USN (retired).

According to the testimony of their representatives, none of these groups had anything to do with procurement; all were ignorant of any "pressure" in behalf of one or another manufacturer. The three service groups acknowledged their interest in building up grassroots support for the respective branches of the Armed Forces; they also maintained that they were fully independent of the services they represented, although the testimony showed that, for the most part, Army, Navy, and Air Force doctrines and weapon systems received enthusiastic support in their respective publications.

All of the groups insisted that their primary function was to inform and educate. Only the Aerospace Industries Association has registered under the lobby law, but General Cook said "we believe we do not operate according to the classic definition of a lobbyist. . . . We don't even dream of buying any influence of any kind." Asked whether the best interests of the industry would be served by an increase or decrease in defense spending, Cook said: "From a selfish point of view, the best interest of the industry would be served by an increase, of course, but from a patriotic and national point of view, it might not be."

Peter J. Schenck, then president of the Air Force Association and an official of Raytheon Corp., described the basis for close military-industrial relations as follows: "The day is past when the military requirements for a major weapons system is set up by the military and passed on to industry to build the hardware. Today it is more likely that the military requirement is the result of joint participation of military and industrial personnel, and it is not unusual for industry's contribution to be a key factor. Indeed there are highly placed military men who sincerely feel that industry currently is setting the pace in the research and development of new weapons systems."

Conclusion. In its report filed January 18, 1960, the Hébert subcommittee said it was "impressed by several obvious inconsistencies in testimony" relating to the influence enjoyed by retired officers in the employment of defense contractors. Said the report: "The better grade and more expensive influence is a very subtle thing when being successfully applied. . . . The 'coincidence' of contract and personal contacts with firms represented by retired officers and retired civilian officials sometimes raises serious doubts as to the complete objectivity of some of these decisions." The subcommittee proposed, among other steps, a much tighter law regarding "sales" to the Government by retired personnel; the House later passed a watered-down version of the proposal. (1959 Almanac, p. 727; 1960 Almanac, p. 279.)

ROLE OF CONGRESS

Charged with the responsibility of appropriating more than $40 billion each year for defense—and in the process deciding how to meet the conflicting claims of competing services for a larger share of the pie—Congress is up to its ears in the military-industrial issue. Collectively, the record shows, the Members strive to sift fact from fancy, and to point up and root out instances of waste and duplication in the defense program. The record also shows that, individually, the Members are zealous in representing the interests of their districts and States. Here are some examples:

"Fair share." Documenting his case with facts and figures, Representative Hechler, Democrat, of West Virginia, told the House of June 1, 1959: "I am firmly against the kind of logrolling which would subject our defense program to narrowly sectional or selfish pulling and hauling. But I am getting pretty hot under the collar about the way my State of West Virginia is shortchanged in Army, Navy, and Air Force installations. I am going to stand up on my hind legs and roar until West Virgina gets the fair treatment she deserves." (Hechler plans to resume his campaign shortly.)

In the same vein, Members of the New York delegation, led by Senators Kenneth B. Keating, Republican, and Jacob K. Javits, Republican, have long complained about the overconcentration of prime contract awards placed with California firms. Asking only for a "fair share," they want defense procurement officials to consider "the strategic and economic desirability of allocating purchases to different geographic areas" of the country. . . .

Installations. The opening, expansion, cutback, or closing of any military installation is of vital interest to the Member whose area is affected. In recent years, with reductions in the size of the Army and other changes in the composition of defense forces, there have been more closings than openings, and the affected Members have been quick to take issue. Some recent instances: Senator Albert Gore, Democrat, of Tennessee, said February 15 that he had written Secretary of the Air Force Eugene M. Zuckert about reports that Sewart Air Force Base at Smyrna, Tenn., might be closed, and had been assured that "as of now no change is contemplated which should cause any concern."

Senator Olin D. Johnston, Democrat, of South Carolina, after calling on President Kennedy February 20, said he had been assured that careful consideration would be given to the future of Fort Jackson at Columbia, S.C., and Donaldson Air Force Base at Greenville, S.C.

Representative Samuel S. Stratton, Democrat, of New York, said March 3 that he had wired Secretary Zuckert about reports of a plan to transfer certain operations from Griffiss Air Force Base at Rome, N.Y. Said Stratton: "It is fantastic to learn that one more defense department is considering recommendations which would have the effect of increasing unemployment in upstate New York, already hard hit by layoffs."

Representative Emanuel Celler, Democrat, of New York, said March 6 that Secretary of Defense Robert S. McNamara had assured him he had no knowledge "of any plans or proposals to shut down the operations" at the Brooklyn Navy Yard.

Procurement. Decisions to begin, accelerate, reduce, or stop production of various weapons and weapon systems are also of major interest to Members in whose districts or States the manufacturers involved are located. Here are examples of Representatives at work:

When the House Appropriations Committee chopped the Air Force's 1959 request for the Bomarc by $162.7 million, Representative Don Magnuson, Democrat, of Washington, charged that few Members were aware of "the incredible lengths to which the adherents of the Nike defense system have gone in their attempt to discredit the Bomarc. . . . Of course, this is Army inspired." (Contractor for Bomarc was Boeing Airplane Co., headquartered in Seattle, Wash.)

Also in 1959, Representative John R. Foley, Democrat, of Maryland, offered an amendment to the defense bill to add $10 million to Air Force funds to buy 10 F-27 transports from the Fairchild Aircraft Co. of Hagerstown, Md., in Foley's district. This failed, but the Senate obliged with $11 million. When House conferees refused to go along, Senator J. Glenn Beall, Republican, of Maryland, begged the Senate to insist, saying that, of the $4 billion to be spent on aircraft, "all we ask for Fairchild is $11 million."

Recent reports that the Pentagon was thinking of cutting back the B-70 program led Representative Edgar W. Hiestand, Republican, of California, to write Secretary McNamara February 27 to assure him of "the strong congressional support for this valued program." North American Aviation, Inc., prime contractor for the B-70, is located in Hiestand's district.

Reserves. The well-known solicitude shown by Congress for the National Guard and other Reserve forces reflects to some degree a widespread local interest in the payrolls, armories, and other benefits involved, as well as effective work by the National Guard Association and the Reserve Officers Association. Among the 40 Reserve officers in Congress are . . . [four] generals: Howard W. Cannon, Democrat, of Nevada, brigadier general, USAFR; Strom Thurmond, Democrat, of South Carolina, major general, USAR; and Representatives James Roosevelt, Democrat, of California, brigadier general, USMCR; and Robert L. F. Sikes, Democrat, of Florida, brigadier general, USAR; Cannon and Thurmond are members of the Armed Services Committee; Sikes, of the Defense Appropriations Subcommittee. . . .

President Eisenhower made no headway whatsoever in his 3-year campaign to reduce National Guard and Army Reserve manpower levels to "conform to the changing character and missions" of the active forces; Congress responded with a mandatory floor of 400,000 for the Guard, and funds to maintain both the Guard and the Reserve at full strength. These actions, said the President in his final budget message, "are unnecessarily costing the American people over $80 million annually and have been too long based on other than strictly military needs." Even at the lower strengths he again proposed, the Reserves would cost "well over $1 billion in 1962," he said.

Summing up the cumulative impact of these varied expressions of Congressional interest, Representative Jamie L. Whitten, Democrat, of Mississippi, a member of the House Appropriations Defense Subcommittee, testified as follows Jan. 29, 1960, before the Joint Economic Committee's Defense Procurement Subcommittee:

"I am convinced defense is only one of the factors that enter into our determinations for defense spending. The others are pump priming, spreading the immediate benefits of defense spending, taking care of all services, giving all defense contractors a fair share, spreading the military bases to include all sections, etc. There is no State in the Union and hardly a district in a State which doesn't have defense spending, contracting, or a defense establishment. We see the effect in public and Congressional insistence on continuing contracts, or operating military bases, though the need has expired."

CASE OF THE ZEUS

The confluence of service, contractor, and Congressional pressures is illustrated by the current revival of a campaign to launch production of the Army's Nike-Zeus anti-missile system, although final tests are more than a year away. Congress added $137 million to the budget in 1958 to start production, but the President refused to spend it; in his final budget, providing about $287 million for further development of Nike-Zeus, he said, "funds should not be committed to production until development tests are satisfactorily completed." Subsequently, these things happened.

On February 1 the magazine *Army* appeared with seven articles lauding the Nike-Zeus—four of them by Army commanders on active duty. Also in the issue: full-page advertisements by Western Electric Co., prime contractor for Nike-Zeus, and 8 of its major subcontractors, together with a map showing how much of the $410 million contract was being spent in each of 37 States (but $111 million in California, $110 million in New Jersey). The general message: It's time to start production.

On February 2, Senator Thurmond told the Senate that "we must start production of the Nike-Zeus now." Extolling the "experienced Army-industry team" that developed the system, he argued that "by spending money now to provide a capability for the production of components in quantity, we will save money in the long run." Rising to support his arguments were Senators B. Everett Jordan, Democrat, of North Carolina, and Frank Carlson, Republican, of Kansas. (*Army's* map showed spending of $36 million in North Carolina and $8.5 million in Kansas.)

On February 7, Representative George P. Miller, Democrat, of California, urged every Member of the House to "read the current issue of *Army* magazine" and to "support immediate action for limited component production of the Nike-Zeus system." Miller, a member of the Science and Astronautics Committee, said this could be done "with the addition of less than $175 million to the present Army budget."

On February 13, Representative Daniel J. Flood, Democrat, of Pennsylvania, gave the House substantially the same speech delivered February 2 by Senator Thurmond, and also concluded that "we must start production of the Nike-Zeus now." Flood appended an article on the subject published by the Sperry Rand Corp., a subcontractor for Nike-Zeus. (*Army's* figure for spending in Pennsylvania: $10 million.)

On February 23, Representative John W. McCormack, Democrat, of Massachusetts, House majority leader, asked every Member to read Flood's "prescient address" of February 13. McCormack's conclusion: "Close the gap in our military posture; muzzle the mad-dog missile threat of the Soviet Union; loose the Zeus through America's magnificent production lines now." (*Army's* figure for Massachusetts: $1.5 million.)

On March 6, the press reported that President Kennedy was expected to approve a Defense Department compromise plan calling for an additional $100 million to $200 million to start tooling up. Eventual costs were estimated at from $5 billion to $20 billion.

EXTENT OF INFLUENCE

Proponents of the Nike-Zeus, it should be noted, base their case squarely on the national interest—the touchstone of debate, pro and con, concerning the merits of every proposal made in the name of defense. It is never clear, however, where the national interest begins and self-interest leaves off.

All of the persons questioned by CQ agreed that an element of self-interest pervades relationships among the services, their contractors and Members of Congress. There was no consensus, however, regarding the extent to which decisions affecting the national interest are influenced by the self-interest of persons and organizations involved. Here is the gist of these views.

The Services. Locked in competition for larger shares of a defense budget that has not kept pace with the soaring costs of new weapon systems, the services toil constantly to "sell" their particular doctrines, programs, and requirements to the public, industry, and Congress. Recent examples: television programs on the Navy's Polaris and "The New Marine," an Army-Industry Liaison Seminar in New Orleans, an Air Force tour of Strategic Air Command headquarters in Omaha for 35 new Members of Congress.

The services are especially careful of their relations with Congress, particularly with members of the Armed Services and Appropriations Committees. When a senior member of the House Armed Services Committee complained of rumors that a Marine Corps installation might be removed from his district, the Commandant came in person to assure him that no change would be made "so long as I am in the job." A junior committee member, on learning that an unsolicited Army training center was to be located in his district, concluded that "someone" in the Pentagon was looking out for his interests.

There is some truth, all agree, in Representative Whitten's statement to the Defense Procurement Subcommittee that "you can look at some of our key people in the key places in Congress and go see how many military establishments are in their districts." One oft-cited example: the state of Georgia, home of the chairmen of both Senate and House Armed Services Committees. (To the proposal that a new Air Force installation be placed in Georgia, one brave General is credited with replying that "one more base would sink the State.")

But Congressmen accustomed to the prevalence of "logrolling" in many other areas see nothing sinister in this situation. The services are generally credited with being "correct" in their dealings with Members; none of those questioned by CQ complained of "pressure" by the services.

The Contractors. For many of the major defense contractors, their only client of any importance is the U.S. Government and the bulk of their business is obtained through negotiated contracts with one or more of the armed services. It is a highly competitive field, by all accounts, in which a considerable premium is placed on "good personal relations" with the client. Even those companies doing business exclusively with one service will be found supporting all three service sounding-boards: the Air Force Association, Navy League, and Association of the U.S. Army. Entertainment practices vary widely throughout the industry, but no one denies that personal friendships play an important part in shaping working relationships between client and vendor. Two episodes serve to illustrate the point.

In one "competition" for a new weapon system, Navy technicians decided to throw out one proposal on grounds it was based on faulty data. Warned by a Navy friend of the impending decision, the contractor promptly went to the admiral in charge and persuaded him to order a 30-day delay to permit all bidders to submit additional data. (The well-informed contractor failed to win in the end, however.)

An Air Force "competition" for a new missile ended with a top-level decision to award the contract to Company A. Learning of this, the president of Company B went straight to the Secretary and persuaded him to order a complete review of the decision. Result: the contract went to Company B.

Sometimes helped and sometimes hurt by such manifestations of "influence," contractors generally accept it as "part of the game," recognizing that to some degree the outcome reflects a tendency on the part of all three services to take care of companies with whom they have been doing business for some time, before admitting any "outsiders." (Some companies have nevertheless managed to secure important prime contracts from all three services.)

Defense contractors vary in their attitudes toward relations with Congress. Small, new companies, trying to gain a foothold in the defense business, are quick to seek the aid of their Congressmen; established contractors recognize that such intercession may backfire, especially in an attempt to reverse an essentially technical decision by the services. As the Hébert hearings demonstrated, however, contractors are not at all reluctant to solicit the aid of interested Members when (as in the Nike-Bomarc dispute) it is in the mutual interest of all concerned.

Congress. As the elected representatives of their States and districts, Members of Congress take a keen political interest in the economic impact of defense activities in their areas, and are the first to admit it. But few believe that such considerations exert any significant influence over the course of defense spending or the shape of national strategy. The major complaint of some Members is their lack of influence!

Certain members of the Armed Services Committees admit seeking the assignment because of large military installations and defense industries in their states or districts. Others consider themselves fortunate that they do not have such activities—and the local pressures that go along with them—in their own areas. Recognizing that changing military requirements may produce a "boom and bust" effect on any given community, they try to dissuade local enthusiasts who clamor for a new installation.

Outsiders detect a Navy bias in the makeup of the House Armed Services Committee and to a lesser extent, the Senate Armed Services Committee. (Of the former's 37 members, 25 come from coastal states.) Committee members acknowledge that some of their colleagues reflect a service point of view (10 members of the House Committee are active reservists) and that the Navy's position is amply represented; they also contend, however, that there is a minimum of service-oriented partisanship in the work of the Committees.

As for dealings with contractors, most Members express doubt concerning both the desirability and feasibility of intervening in procurement decisions. One Senator who did go to bat for one of his constituents (to no avail) found himself under fire from a competitor in the same state. His conclusion: it doesn't pay to get involved.

PROS AND CONS

Does the evidence support President Eisenhower's warning against "the acquisition of unwarranted influence, whether sought or unsought, by the military-industrial complex"? The answer varies with the individual.

"There is no question that the services and their contractors have an interest in maintaining a high degree of tension in the country," says a senior member of the House Defense Appropriations Subcommittee. But he foresees no threat to the democratic process, although admitting the need to guard against overly intimate relations between soldier, salesman, and legislator.

"There is a real danger that we may go the way of prewar Japan and Germany," says one member of the House Armed Services Committee, who objects to the presence of reserve officers on the Committee and sees the appointment of industrialists to top Defense Department posts as a bad practice.

"I don't know what Eisenhower was talking about," says a former Defense Department official. Strong civilian control over the military services can be maintained, he believes, by the selection of a sufficient number of able Presidential appointees, regardless of their industrial background.

"The trouble is that national security has become popular—and the record of Congressional appropriations proves it," says a former Eisenhower associate. He sees the military-industrial complex as a "floating power" largely free of any restraint.

Several of those questioned by CQ ascribed the President's concern to over-preoccupation with the budget. Believing that the nation needs and can afford an even larger defense effort, they were inclined to dismiss his warning as misdirected. This point of view was reflected in *Air Force* magazine, which characterized reaction to the President's statement as a "flap" and deplored the "small wave of learned essays rehashing all of the irresponsible charges and insinuations that have been bandied around in Congressional hearings for the past few years." The great danger, it concluded, was that "an exercise of misdirected caution . . . could menace national security."

The first moves of the Kennedy administration suggest little sympathy with the Eisenhower viewpoint. Orders have been placed for large numbers of additional transport planes. Steps have been taken to speed up defense purchases and "spread the business" in the interests of stimulating the lagging economy. Other proposals under consideration would add substantially to defense spending in the future.

At the same time, the new administration stands pledged to seek an agreement with the Soviets on banning nuclear tests and to pursue the goal of arms control. As yet, the chances of achieving either appear to be so remote as to preclude serious consideration of the possible opposition to any agreement by a "military-industrial complex." It may be worth noting, however, that the American Ordnance Assn. is calling for the "immediate resumption . . . of nuclear tests for both small and large weapons," and that *Ordnance* magazine argues that until the Communist "goal of world dominion . . . is abandoned, there can be no lessening of our armament preparedness." ▶

The kind of amalgamation of interests that has created the "military-industrial complex" is not unique. The following selection adds additional empirical evidence to support the view that a concurrent majority system often operates in contemporary American politics. That is, major public policy is not usually made without the consent of the dominant private interest groups concerned, whose views are more often than not directly represented in the administrative agency that has policy responsibility in their area.

HOW THE FARMERS GET WHAT THEY WANT

Theodore Lowi*

In his Farm Message of January 31 [1964], President Johnson proposed that Congress establish a bipartisan commission to investigate the concentration of power in the food industry. In the same message the President called for new legislation to strengthen farmer co-operatives, to encourage their expansion through merger and acquisition, and to provide them with further exemptions from the anti-trust laws.

This was the beginning of the "Johnson round" in agriculture. It is part of a familiar pattern. An attack on the food industry's market power, coupled with proposals for expanded and stronger farm co-operatives, is obviously not an attack on concentration itself. Rather it is an attack on the intervention of nonagricultural groups into strictly agricultural affairs.

That agricultural affairs should be handled strictly within the agricultural community is a basic political principle established before the turn of the century and maintained since then without serious re-examination. As a result, agriculture has become neither public nor private enterprise. It is a system of self-government in which each leading farm interest controls a segment of agriculture through a delegation of national sovereignty. Agriculture has emerged as a largely self-governing federal estate within the Federal structure of the United States.

President Johnson recognized these facts within three weeks of his accession when he summoned a conference of agricultural leaders to formulate a program by which agriculture should be served and regulated. The most recent concession to agriculture's self-government was the wheat-cotton bill. Because cotton supports were too high, the cotton interests wrote a bill providing for a subsidy of six to eight cents a pound to mills in order to keep them competitive with foreign cotton and domestic rayon without touching the price supports. On the other hand, wheat supports were too low because wheat farmers last year in referendum overwhelmingly rejected President Kennedy's plan to provide some Federal regulation along with supports. The wheat section of the new act calls for a program whereby wheat farmers may voluntarily comply with acreage reduction for subsidies of up to seventy cents a bushel but

* Reprinted from *The Reporter* (May 21, 1964) by permission of the author and *The Reporter*. Copyright 1964 by The Reporter Magazine Company.

without the Federal supply regulations. The press called this a major legislative victory for Mr. Johnson, but the credit is not his. That the press could see this as a victory for anyone but organized cotton and wheat is a testimonial to the total acceptance by President, press, and public of the principle that private agricultural interests alone govern agriculture and should do so.

The reasons for agriculture's self-government are deep-rooted, and the lessons to be drawn are important to the future of American politics. For a century agriculture has been out of step with American economic development. Occasional fat years have only created unreal expectations, to be undercut by the more typical lean years.

Quite early, farmers discovered the value of politics as a counterweight to industry's growth and concentration. Land-grant and homesteading acts were followed by governmental services in research and education. Continuing distress led to bolder demands. First there were efforts to effect a redistribution of wealth in favor of agriculture. As a debtor class, farmers saw inflation as the solution, and Bryan was their spokesman for cheaper money and cheaper credit. The monopolies, the railroads, the grain merchants and other processors, the banks, and the brokers were to be deprived of power over the market by dissolution or by severe restraints. Next, farmers sought solutions by emulating the business system: the co-operative to restrain domestic trade and international dumping over high tariff walls to restrain international trade. Yet all these mechanisms either were not enacted or did not live up to expectations.

With the coming of the New Deal and with its help, organized agriculture turned to self-regulation. The system created during the 1930's has endured to this day, and with only a few marginal additions and alterations is accepted almost unanimously by farm leaders. Self-regulation might have taken several forms, the most likely one being a national system of farm-leader representation within a farmers' NRA. Instead, a more complicated system of highly decentralized and highly autonomous subgovernments developed, largely for Constitutional reasons. Agriculture was the most "local" of the manufacturing groups the Federal government was trying to reach. The appearance if not the reality of decentralizing Federal programs through farmer-elected local committees helped avoid strains on the interstate commerce clause of the Constitution. But this avoidance of Constitutional troubles created very special political difficulties.

The Local Committees

The Federal Extension Service shows how the system works. It is "co-operative" in that it shares the job of farm improvement with the states, the land-grant colleges, the county governments, and the local associations of farmers. The county agent is actually employed by the local associations. In the formative years, the aid of local chambers of commerce was enlisted, the local association being the "farm bureau" of the chamber. In order to co-ordinate local activities and to make more effective claims for additional outside assistance, these farm bureaus were organized into state farm bureau federations. The American Farm Bureau Federation, formed at the Agriculture College of Cornell University in 1919, was used as a further step toward amalgamation. To this day there is a close relationship between the farm bureaus, the land-grant colleges, and the Extension Service. This transformation of an administrative arrangement into a political system has been repeated in nearly all the agricultural programs during recent decades. The Extension Service exercises few controls from the top. There are cries of "Federal encroachment" at the mere suggestion in Washington that the Department of Agriculture should increase its supervision of the extension programs or co-ordinate them with other Federal activities.

As the financial stakes have grown larger, the pattern of local self-government remains the same. Price support—the "parity program"—is run by the thousands of farmer-elected county committees that function alongside but quite independently of the other local committees. Acreage allotments to bring supply down and prices up are apportioned among the states by the Agricultural Stabilization and Conservation Service. State committees of farmers apportion the allotment among the counties. The farmer-elected county Stabilization and Conservation Committees receive the county allotment.

These committees made the original acreage allotments among individual farmers back in the 1930's; today, they make new allotments, work out adjustments and review complaints regarding allotments, determine whether quotas have been complied with, inspect and approve storage facilities; and perform as the court of original jurisdiction on violations of price-support rules and on eligibility for parity payments. The committees are also vitally important in the campaigns for the two-thirds vote required to fix high price supports. Congress determines the general level of supports, and the Secretary of Agriculture proclaims the national acreage quotas for adjusting the supply to the guaranteed price. But the locally elected committees stand between the farmer and Washington.

Most other agricultural programs have evolved similarly. Each is independent of the others, and any conflicts or overlapping mandates have been treated as nonexistent or beyond the jurisdiction of any one agency. The Soil Conservation Service operates through its independent soil-conservation districts, of which there were 2,936 in 1963, involving ninety-six per cent of the nation's farms. Each district's farmer-elected committee is considered a unit of local government. The Farmer Cooperative Service operates through the member-elected boards of directors of the farm co-ops. In agricultural credit, local self-government is found in even greater complexity. The Farm Credit Administration exists outside the Department of Agriculture and is made up of not one but three separate bodies politic, a triangular system mostly farmer-owned and totally farmer-controlled.

Ten Systems and Politics

The ten principal self-governing systems in agriculture, in fiscal 1962 disposed of $5.6 billion of the total of $6.7 billion in expenditures passing through the Department of Agriculture. During the calendar year 1962, $5.8 billion in loans was handled similarly. This combined amount represents a large portion of the total of Federal activity outside national defense.

Each of the ten systems has become a powerful political instrumentality. The self-governing local units become one important force in a system that administers a program and maintains the autonomy of that program against political forces emanating from other agricultural programs, from antagonistic farm and nonfarm interests, from Congress, from the Secretary of Agriculture, and from the President. To many a farmer, the local outpost of one or another of these systems *is* the government.

The politics within each system is built upon a triangular trading pattern involving the central agency, a Congressional committee or subcommittee, and the local district farmer committees (usually federated in some national or regional organization). Each side of the triangle complements and supports the other two.

The Extension Service, for example, is one side of the triangle completed by the long-tenure "farm bureau" members of the Agriculture Committees in Congress and, at the local level, the American Farm

Bureau Federation with its local committees. Further group support is provided by two intimately related groups, the Association of Land Grant Colleges and Universities and the National Association of County Agricultural Agents.

Another such triangle unites the Soil Conservation Service, the Agriculture subcommittee of the House Appropriations Committee, and the local districts organized in the energetic National Association of Soil Conservation Districts. Further support comes from the Soil Conservation Society of America (mainly professionals) and the former Friends of the Land, now the Izaak Walton League of America.

Probably the most complex of the systems embraces the parity program. It connects the Agricultural Stabilization and Conservation Service with the eight (formerly ten) commodity subcommittees of the House Agriculture Committee and the dozens of separately organized groups representing the various commodities. (Examples: National Cotton Council, American Wool Growers Association, American Cranberry Growers Association.) These groups and congressmen draw support from the local price-support committees wherever a particular commodity is grown.

The Farmer Had His Way

These systems have a vigorous capacity to maintain themselves and to resist encroachment. They have such institutional legitimacy that they have become practically insulated from the three central sources of democratic political responsibility. Thus, within the Executive branch, they are autonomous. Secretaries of Agriculture have tried and failed to consolidate or even to co-ordinate related programs. Within Congress, they are sufficiently powerful to be able to exercise an effective veto or create a stalemate. And they are almost totally removed from the view, not to mention the control, of the general public. (Throughout the 1950's, Victor Anfuso of Brooklyn was the only member of the House Agriculture Committee from a non-farm constituency.)

Important cases illustrate their power:

In 1947, Secretary of Agriculture Clinton P. Anderson proposed a consolidation of all soil-conservation, price-support, and FHA programs into one committee system with a direct line from the committees to the Secretary. Bills were prepared providing for consolidation within the price-support committees. Contrary bills provided for consolidation under soil conservation districts. The result: stalemate. In 1948, a leading farm senator proposed consolidation of the programs under the local associa-

tions of the Extension Service. Immediately a House farm leader introduced a contrary bill. The result: continuing stalemate.

In Waco, Texas, on October 14, 1952, Presidential candidate Eisenhower said: "I would like to see in every county all Federal farm agencies
under the same roof." Pursuant to this promise, Secretary Ezra Taft
Benson issued a series of orders during early 1953 attempting to bring
about consolidation of local units as well as unification at the top. Finally,
amid cries of "sneak attack" and "agricrat," Benson proclaimed that "any
work on the further consolidation of county and state offices . . . shall
be suspended."

From the very beginning, Secretary Benson sought to abandon rigid
price supports and bring actual supports closer to market prices. In 1954,
as he was beginning to succeed, Congress enacted a "commodity set-
aside" by which $2.5 billion of surplus commodities already held by the
government were declared to be a "frozen reserve" for national defense.
Since the Secretary's power to cut price supports depends heavily upon
the amount of government-owned surplus carried over from previous
years, the commodity set-aside was a way of freezing parity as well as
reserves. Benson eventually succeeded in reducing supports on the few
commodities over which he had authority. But thanks to the set-aside,
Congress, between fiscal 1952 and 1957, helped increase the value of
commodities held by the government from $1.1 billion to $5.3 billion.
What appeared, therefore, to be a real Republican policy shift amounted
to no more than giving back with one hand what had been taken away
by the other.

President Eisenhower's first budget sought to abolish farm home-
building and improvement loans by eliminating the budgetary request
and by further requesting that the 1949 authorization law be allowed to
expire. Congress overrode his request in 1953 and each succeeding year,
and the President answered Congress with a year-by-year refusal to
implement the farm housing program. In 1956, when the President asked
again explicitly for elimination of the program, he was rebuffed. The
Housing subcommittee of the House Banking and Currency Committee
added to the President's omnibus housing bill a renewal of the farm
housing program, plus an authorization for $500 million in loans over
a five-year period, and the bill passed with a Congressional mandate to
use the funds. They were used thereafter at a rate of about $75 million
a year.

On March 16, 1961, President Kennedy produced a "radically different" farm program in a special message to Congress. For the first time

in the history of price supports, the bill called for surplus control through quotas placed on bushels, tons, or other units, rather than on acreage. An acreage allotment allows the farmer to produce as much as he can on the reduced acreage in cultivation. For example, in the first ten years or so of acreage control, acreage under cultivation dropped by about four per cent while actual production rose by fifteen per cent. The Kennedy proposal called for national committees of farmers to be elected to work out the actual program. This more stringent type of control was eliminated from the omnibus bill in the Agriculture Committees of both chambers and there were no attempts to restore them during floor debate. Last-minute efforts by Secretary Orville L. Freeman to up the ante, offering to raise wheat supports from $1.79 to $2.00, were useless. Persistence by the administration led eventually to rejection by wheat farmers in 1963 of all high price supports and acreage controls.

The politics of this rejected referendum is of general significance. Despite all the blandishments and inducements of the administration, the farmer had his way. The local price-support committees usually campaign in these referendums for the Department of Agriculture, but this time they did not. And thousands of small farmers, eligible to vote for the first time, joined with the local leadership to help defeat the referendum. It is not so odd that wheat farmers would reject a proposal that aims to regulate them more strictly than before. What is odd is that only wheat farmers are allowed to decide the matter. It seems that in agriculture, as in many other fields, the regulators are powerless without the consent of the regulated.

Agriculture is the field where the distinction between public and private has been almost completely eliminated, not by public expropriation of private domain but by private expropriation of public domain. For more than a generation, Americans have succeeded in expanding the public sphere without giving thought to the essential democratic question of how each expansion is to be effected. The creation of private governments has profoundly limited the capacity of the public government to govern responsibly and flexibly. 🏴

The techniques employed by interest groups are many and varied, depending upon their nature and objectives. The following selection is a case study dealing with the methods employed by the American Medical Association to defeat the adoption of a national health insurance program.

It illustrates the different interest groups that become involved in hotly contested political and economic issues, and the kinds of devices used to achieve various goals.

MEDICAL ECONOMICS AND DOCTOR POLITICS
*Stanley Kelley, Jr.**

THE story of the American Medical Association's National Education Campaign begins in December of 1948. On December 2, the leaders of the AMA announced that the association would assess its 140,000 members twenty-five dollars each in order to sponsor ". . . a nationwide plan of education on the progress of American medicine, the importance of the conservation of health and the advantage of the American system in securing a wide distribution of a high quality of medical care." For a professional organization that had never required any form of dues from its membership, this was an unprecedented action. The immediate stimulus was the Democratic administration's advocacy of a system of national health insurance, suddenly given new authority by the unexpected re-election of President Harry S. Truman. On December 16, Major General George F. Lull, Secretary and General Manager of the AMA, announced that California's Whitaker and Baxter had been retained to direct this education drive. [W. & B. is a political public relations firm.]

National health insurance was a kind of legislative left-over of the social welfare program and reform *élan* of the New Deal. President Franklin D. Roosevelt's Technical Committee on Medical Care had called for measures to "lighten the burden of sickness costs" in 1938. . . .

After 1946 the health insurance movement had as a center of publicity and educational activities the Committee for the Nation's Health, with which were associated such nationally prominent persons as Mrs. Franklin D. Roosevelt, Phillip Murray, and William Green. In the movement's support had been enlisted a substantial number of influential legislators. The American Federation of Labor, the American Jewish Congress, Americans for Democratic Action, the American Veterans Committee, the Brotherhood of Railroad Trainmen, the Congress of Industrial Organizations, the National Association for the Advancement

* From *Professional Public Relations and Political Power,* by Stanley Kelley, Jr. Copyright © 1956, by The Johns Hopkins Press. Reprinted with the permission of the publisher.

of Colored People, and the National Farmers Union had given it their endorsement. After a survey of the officers of 1500 civic organizations, the *American Druggist* concluded, ". . . national health insurance is regarded with favor by a majority of citizen organization leaders in the United States . . . it foreshadows the possibility of broad grass roots support for the Truman program."

In May of 1948, President Truman convened a National Health Assembly which was attended by 800 professional and community leaders. Using the assembly as a publicity springboard, Federal Security Administrator Oscar Ewing prepared a report to the President entitled *The Nation's Health: A Ten Year Program*, outlining a plan for comprehensive, federally sponsored, compulsory health insurance. This report was regarded as a signal of danger by the leaders of the AMA. They were frightened by its attractive format almost as much as by its content. They decided that the danger had arrived, and arrived for good, when Truman won his second term.

During all this time, government health insurance had been consistently opposed by organized medicine, whose public relations and lobbying arm, the National Physicians Committee, spent some one million dollars in a seven-year period after 1938 to prevent its enactment. Under Whitaker and Baxter guidance, however, the AMA's efforts began to take on new force. During 1949 and 1950, the AMA supported the nation's best financed lobby, and health insurance never came to a Congressional test. As a direct outgrowth of the education campaign, the issues of medical economics achieved a surprising prominence in a large number of the political contests that were fought out between the Dewey defeat of 1948 and the Eisenhower victory of 1952. . . .

. . . The AMA's earlier hostility to voluntary health insurance had been gradually overcome as the movement for a government sponsored program grew in strength. Said Whitaker, "We will offer a positive program, because we realize that you can't beat something with nothing. . . . We believe that anything the government can do for the people, the people can do better for themselves. . . ."

Three proposals were designed as compromises. Two . . . provided for federal appropriations for the purpose of extending medical service to persons unable to pay for it fully. Senator Hill's measure called for government sponsored membership for needy persons in private health plans and Senator Taft's for a grant-in-aid program. Both assumed a "means" test. The third bill, backed by Senators Ralph E. Flanders and Irving M. Ives, would have given aid directly to voluntary medical care plans, provided that they would charge their subscribers a percentage of income rather than the customary flat-rate premium.

Education by Whitaker and Baxter

These were the kinds of problems and proposals on which Whitaker and Baxter were to educate the public. When they came to the AMA, they had already frustrated a proposal for compulsory health insurance in California, sponsored by Governor Earl Warren. Asking for such legislation in January, 1945, the popular Governor had so timed his action that the firm and its California Medical Association employers had had only three months in which to work. Warren's bill failed by only one vote in the Legislature after Whitaker and Baxter had staged a fast paced campaign, in which they pre-tested the tactics they were later to use on a much larger scale. When the AMA began to look for someone to manage its educational efforts, California doctors knew whom to suggest.

Whitaker and Baxter opened their National Education Campaign headquarters on February 10, 1949. A co-ordinating committee, responsible only to the AMA's House of Delegates and headed by Dr. Elmer Henderson, was set up as the campaign's policy-forming board; and Whitaker and Baxter, directing a staff of thirty-seven, were in turn responsible to this committee. The AMA's Washington lobby was made responsible for keeping an eye on Congress and stopping so-called "fringe-bills." Its public relations department was to occupy itself "with many local and general problems beyond the broader issues of the present Campaign." But the campaign, and Whitaker and Baxter, were to meet the challenge of the Democratic Administration.

They designed it to effect a maximum reiteration of the same themes from as many apparently independent sources as possible. For themselves and their headquarters, they reserved the task of producing all basic campaign literature and materials: posters; pamphlets; leaflets; reprints; form resolutions and form speeches; cartoons and mats; and publicity adaptable for local use. The job of local and state medical societies became primarily one of distribution—to serve as the media through which the themes could reach the public.

Their argument was to be presented free of encumbrance by opposing or distracting appeals. . . . Whitaker and Baxter took for themselves the responsibility for giving the arguments, both pro and con. For not only did they hesitate to subject the public to the opposition point of view, they set out further to destroy the credibility of its spokesmen. They asked, "Does the *Report on the Nation's Health* give a factual picture of the people's health in America?" They answered: "No. This widely publicized Report is a hoax. It is a propagandist treatment of a subject far too important for such loose handling by political experimenters." They asked, "Who is for Compulsory Health Insurance?" and answered, "The Federal Security Administration. The President. All who seriously believe in a Socialistic State. Every left-wing organization in America. . . . The Communist Party."

Substantively, the position which they presented for the AMA went somewhat as follows: The United States had the highest standards of medical care the world has ever known. It is true that there are many health problems that need to be solved, but this has been exaggerated by advocates of national health insurance. National health insurance does not really meet the problem. As in England, the AMA charged, government medicine would mean assembly-line service. It would bring grave personal hardships—staggering taxes, patients assigned to doctors and doctors to patients, destruction of the privacy of medical records. It is a part of the trend toward complete socialization of American life: "The Government proposes to assume control not only of the medical profession, but of hospitals—both public and private—the drug and appliance industries, dentistry, pharmacy, nursing and allied professions."

The alternative is protection under a voluntary medical care plan. . . .

Thus, national health policy was debated in terms of compulsory *versus* voluntary health insurance or, rather, as "Socialized Medicine" *versus* "The Voluntary Way." . . .

Further, they tried to present their case in a way that would have meaning to the individual citizen, to translate public issues into private emotions. They asked their average man if he wanted to face ". . . a nameless, unknown man on the desk-end of a long pill line." They told him that "In America, We Don't Like Compulsion!" They asked, "When You're Sick, Do You Want Doctors—or Clerks?"—"Your Own Doctor, or Doctor X?" They told him again and again that "Political Medicine is Bad Medicine!" and that "The Voluntary Way is the American Way!" In these instances, words have become the charge which the public relations man aims at social atoms.

If the typical exigencies of mass communication conditioned the style which Whitaker and Baxter used in their literature, so did the peculiar qualities of a highly specialized medium at their disposal: the doctor. The doctor enjoys the authority of the expert and has previously had his greatest political influence in that role. . . . Whitaker and Baxter were . . . able to counter Federal Security Administration statistics with the opinions of those prominent in the medical profession, with all that implied.

They carried the analysis of their medium well beyond this point, however. Students of mass communication have been aware of the importance of "opinion leaders" in the formation of public attitudes. . . . Whitaker and Baxter recognized that the social role of the doctor made him both an opinion leader and an instrument capable of organizing other opinion leaders. How they made use of this fact will be apparent from the record of their activities.

In waiting rooms during the National Education Campaign, patients found the theme-piece of the campaign, a poster with a color reproduction of Sir Luke Fildes' painting of the doctor at the bedside of a sick child. Underneath, the text read:

KEEP POLITICS OUT OF THIS PICTURE

When the life—or health of a loved one is at stake, hope lies in the devoted service of your Doctor. Would you change this picture?

Compulsory health insurance is political medicine.

It would bring a third party—a politician—between you and your Doctor. It would bind up your family's health in red tape. It would result in heavy payroll taxes—and inferior medical care for you and your family. Don't let that happen here!

You have a right to prepaid medical care—of your own choice. Ask your Doctor, or your insurance man, about budget-basis health protection.

This poster would indicate that Whitaker and Baxter had carried their analysis of the doctor's social role still another step. It showed recognition that ties of peculiar emotional force can bind the patient to his doctor. . . . By putting their message in the waiting room, they could suggest the destruction of the relationship on which the patient even then might be placing all his hope—and write a prescription for the resulting anxiety. . . .

In accordance with their standard practice, Whitaker and Baxter developed a Plan of Campaign. . . . [T]hey outlined four principal campaign projects: a drive for the endorsement of the AMA stand by national, state, and local organizations; a publicity campaign; a speakers' bureau operation; and the preparation and distribution of pamphlets. . . .

By the end of 1949, Whitaker and Baxter had succeeded in getting 1829 organizations on record as opposed to compulsory health insurance. By the end of their campaign in 1952, they had secured supporting action by some 8000 more. . . .

The drive for endorsements was, of course, an integral part of the Whitaker and Baxter publicity campaign for organized medicine. Once they had been adopted by a major organization, their form resolutions were reported as news by press and radio throughout the country. But there were other approaches to publicity as well. Following the strategy of their work against health insurance in California, press committees were organized to "call on every newspaper and get the real facts . . . before the editor." An attempt was made to maintain contact with editors through doctors personally known to them. . . . Whitaker claimed that editorial support of the AMA position jumped from 74 per cent to almost 90 per cent in two years' time.

In terms of money spent, the heart of the AMA's National Education Campaign was the production and distribution of pamphlets. Literature was produced by the national office and distributed through the doctors, through co-operating organizations, and by direct mail. It was designed both for special population groups and for a general audience. By the end of 1950, the AMA was distributing some 43 different publications. In the first year of the campaign, Whitaker and Baxter reported a total distribution of literature which ran to 54,233,915 pieces, and which cost $1,045,614.52. In 1950, 43,150,682 pieces were printed and distributed. Although the principal distribution agents were doctors and organizations of doctors, other groups made a substantial contribution. Dentists took 851,935 pieces of campaign literature; druggists, 2,131,839; the insurance industry, 1,153,926; and miscellaneous lay groups, 7,248,288.

The preceding selection illustrates the entry of the professional public relations man into politics. It is difficult to gauge the effectiveness of propaganda activities. One point that should be especially noted is that a basic technique of modern organized groups in fighting for or against particular policies is to enlist the aid of *potential* groups that might be persuaded to join the campaign. This technique requires a keen awareness of potential interests in unorganized as well as organized groups. The campaign of Whitaker and Baxter for the American Medical Association was very shrewd in this respect. They recognized that medical patients, an unorganized group, might have a common interest with doctors regarding national policy involving health insurance, and they attempted to mobilize this interest to help in defeating the legislation.

CHAPTER SIX

The Presidency

The American Presidency is the only unique political institution that the United States has contributed to the world. It developed first in this country, and later was imitated, usually unsuccessfully, in many nations. In no country, and at no time, has the institution of the Presidency achieved the status and power that it possesses in the United States. This chapter will analyze the basis, nature, and implications of the power of this great American institution.

21. Constitutional Background

Undoubtedly the change that has taken place in the Presidency since the office was established in 1789 is dramatic and significant. The framers of the Constitution were primarily concerned with the control of the arbitrary exercise of power by the legislature; thus, they were willing to give the President broad power since he was not to be popularly elected and would be constantly under attack by the coordinate legislative branch. Although the framers were not afraid of establishing a vigorous Presidency, there was a great deal of opposition to a potentially strong executive at the time the Constitution was drafted. In the following selection Alexander Hamilton attempts to persuade the people of the desirability of a strong presidential office. In the process of persuasion he sets forth the essential constitutional basis of the office.

FEDERALIST 70
Alexander Hamilton

THERE is an idea, which is not without its advocates, that a vigorous executive is inconsistent with the genius of republican government. The enlightened well-wishers to this species of government must at least hope that the supposition is destitute of foundation; since they can never admit its truth, without, at the same time, admitting the condemnation of their own principles. Energy in the executive is a leading character in the definition of good government. It is essential to the protection of the community against foreign attacks; it is not less essential to the steady administration of the laws, to the protection of property against those irregular and high-handed combinations, which sometimes interrupt the ordinary course of justice, to the security of liberty against the enterprises and assaults of ambition, of faction, and of anarchy. Every man, the least conversant in Roman story, knows how often that republic was obliged to take refuge in the absolute power of a single man, under the formidable title of dictator, as well as against the intrigues of ambitious individuals, who aspired to the tyranny, and the seditions of whole classes of the community, whose conduct threatened the existence of all government, as against the invasions of external enemies, who menaced the conquest and destruction of Rome.

There can be no need, however, to multiply arguments or examples on this head. A feeble executive implies a feeble execution of the government. A feeble execution is but another phrase for a bad execution; and a government ill executed, whatever it may be in theory, must be, in practice, a bad government.

Taking it for granted, therefore, that all men of sense will agree in the necessity of an energetic executive, it will only remain to inquire, what are the ingredients which constitute this energy? How far can they be combined with those other ingredients, which constitute safety in the republican sense? And how far does this combination characterize the plan which has been reported by the convention?

The ingredients which constitute energy in the executive are, unity; duration; an adequate provision for its support; competent powers.

The ingredients which constitute safety in the republican sense are, a due dependence on the people; a due responsibility.

Those politicians and statesmen, who have been the most celebrated for the soundness of their principles, and for the justness of their views, have declared in favor of a single executive, and a numerous legislature. They have, with great propriety, considered energy as the most necessary qualification of the former, and have regarded this as most applicable to power in a single hand; while they have, with equal propriety, considered the latter as best adapted to deliberation and wisdom, and best calculated to conciliate the confidence of the people, and to secure their privileges and interests.

That unity is conducive to energy will not be disputed. Decision, activity, secrecy, and dispatch, will generally characterize the proceedings of one man, in a much more eminent degree than the proceedings of any greater number; and in proportion as the number is increased, these qualities will be diminished.

This unity may be destroyed in two ways; either by vesting the power in two or more magistrates, of equal dignity and authority; or by vesting it ostensibly in one man, subject, in whole or in part, to the control and co-operation of others, in the capacity of counsellors to him. . . .

The experience of other nations will afford little instruction on this head. As far, however, as it teaches anything, it teaches us not to be enamoured of plurality in the executive. . . .

Wherever two or more persons are engaged in any common enterprise or pursuit, there is always danger of difference of opinion. If it be a public trust of office, in which they are clothed with equal dignity and authority, there is peculiar danger of personal emulation and even animosity. From either, and especially from all these causes, the most bitter dissentions are apt to spring. Whenever these happen, they lessen the respectability, weaken the authority, and distract the plans and operations of those whom they divide. If they should unfortunately assail the supreme executive magistracy of a country, consisting of a plurality of persons, they might impede or frustrate the most important measures of the government, in the most critical emergencies of the state. And what is still worse, they might split the community into violent and irreconcilable factions, adhering differently to the different individuals who composed the magistracy. . . .

Upon the principles of a free government, inconveniences from the source just mentioned, must necessarily be submitted to in the formation of the legislature; but it is unnecessary, and therefore unwise, to introduce them into the constitution of the executive. It is here, too, that they may be most pernicious. In the legislature, promptitude of decision is oftener an evil than a benefit. The differences of opinion, and the jarrings of parties in that department of the government, though they may sometimes obstruct salutary plans, yet often promote deliberation and circumspection;

and serve to check excesses in the majority. When a resolution, too, is once taken, the opposition must be at an end. That resolution is a law, and resistance to it punishable. But no favorable circumstances palliate, or atone for the disadvantages of dissention in the executive department. Here they are pure and unmixed. There is no point at which they cease to operate. They serve to embarrass and weaken the execution of the plan or measure to which they relate, from the first step to the final conclusion of it. They constantly counteract those qualities in the executive, which are the most necessary ingredients in its composition—vigor and expedition; and this without any counterbalancing good. In the conduct of war, in which the energy of the executive is the bulwark of the national security, everything would be to be apprehended from its plurality.

It must be confessed, that these observations apply with principal weight to the first case supposed, that is, to a plurality of magistrates of equal dignity and authority, a scheme, the advocates for which are not likely to form a numerous sect; but they apply, though not with equal, yet with considerable weight, to the project of a council, whose concurrence is made constitutionally necessary to the operations of the ostensible executive. An artful cabal in that council would be able to distract and to enervate the whole system of administration. If no such cabal should exist, the mere diversity of views and opinions would alone be sufficient to tincture the exercise of the executive authority with the spirit of habitual feebleness and dilatoriness.

But one of the weightiest objections to a plurality in the executive, and which lies as much against the last as the first plan, is, that it tends to conceal faults, and destroy responsibility. . . . It often becomes impossible, amidst mutual accusations, to determine on whom the blame or the punishment of a pernicious measure . . . ought really to fall. It is shifted from one to another with so much dexterity, and under such plausible appearances, that the public opinion is left in suspense about the real author. . . .

A little consideration will satisfy us, that the species of security sought for in the multiplication of the executive, is unattainable. Numbers must be so great as to render combination difficult; or they are rather a source of danger than of security. The united credit and influence of several individuals must be more formidable to liberty than the credit and influence of either of them separately. When power, therefore, is placed in the hands of so small a number of men, as to admit of their interests and views being easily combined in a common enterprise, by an artful leader, it becomes more liable to abuse, and more dangerous when abused, than if it be lodged in the hands of one man; who, from the very circumstance of his being alone, will be more narrowly watched and more readily suspected, and who cannot unite so great a mass of influence as when he is associated with others. . . .

I will only add, that prior to the appearance of the constitution, I rarely met with an intelligent man from any of the states, who did not admit as the result of experience, that the unity of the executive of this state was one of the best of the distinguishing features of our constitution. ▰

22. The Nature of the Presidency

What is the position of the presidential office today? There is little doubt that it has expanded far beyond the expectations of the framers of the Constitution. The Presidency is the only governmental branch with the necessary unity and energy to meet many of the most crucial problems of twentieth-century government in the United States; people have turned to the President in times of crisis to supply the central direction necessary for survival. In the following selection Clinton Rossiter, one of the leading American scholars of the Presidency, discusses the present-day role of the office.

THE PRESIDENCY—FOCUS OF LEADERSHIP

*Clinton Rossiter**

No American can contemplate the Presidency . . . without a feeling of solemnity and humility—solemnity in the face of a historically unique concentration of power and prestige, humility in the thought that he has had a part in the choice of a man to wield the power and enjoy the prestige.

Perhaps the most rewarding way to grasp the significance of this great office is to consider it as a focus of democratic leadership. Free men, too, have need of leaders. Indeed, it may well be argued that one of the decisive forces in the shaping of American democracy has been the extraordinary capacity of the Presidency for strong, able, popular leadership. If this has been true of our past, it will certainly be true of our

* From *The New York Times Magazine,* Nov. 11, 1956. Reprinted by permission of *The New York Times* and the author.

future, and we should therefore do our best to grasp the quality of this leadership. Let us do this by answering the essential question: For what men and groups does the President provide leadership?

First, the President is *leader of the Executive Branch*. To the extent that our Federal civil servants have need of common guidance, he alone is in a position to provide it. We cannot savor the fullness of the President's duties unless we recall that he is held primarily accountable for the ethics, loyalty, efficiency, frugality and responsiveness to the public's wishes of the two and one-third million Americans in the national administration.

Both the Constitution and Congress have recognized his power to guide the day-to-day activities of the Executive Branch, strained and restrained though his leadership may often be in practice. From the Constitution, explicitly or implicitly, he receives the twin powers of appointment and removal, as well as the primary duty, which no law or plan or circumstances can ever take away from him, to "take care that the laws be faithfully executed."

From Congress, through such legislative mandates as the Budget and Accounting Act of 1921 and the succession of Reorganization Acts, the President has received further acknowledgment of his administrative leadership. Although independent agencies such as the Interstate Commerce Commission and the National Labor Relations Board operate by design outside his immediate area of responsibility, most of the Government's administrative tasks are still carried on within the fuzzy-edged pyramid that has the President at its lonely peak; the laws that are executed daily in his name and under his general supervision are numbered in the hundreds.

Many observers, to be sure, have argued strenuously that we should not ask too much of the President as administrative leader, lest we burden him with impossible detail, or give too much to him, lest we inject political considerations too forcefully into the steady business of the civil service. Still, he cannot ignore the blunt mandate of the Constitution, and we should not forget the wisdom that lies behind it. The President has no more important tasks than to set a high personal example of integrity and industry for all who serve the nation, and to transmit a clear lead downward through his chief lieutenants to all who help shape the policies by which we live.

Next, the President is *leader of the forces of peace and war*. Although authority in the field of foreign relations is shared constitutionally among three organs—President, Congress, and, for two special purposes, the Senate—his position is paramount, if not indeed dominant. Constitution, laws, customs, the practice of other nations and the logic of history have combined to place the President in a dominant position. Secrecy, dispatch, unity, continuity and access to information—the ingredients of successful diplomacy—are properties of his office, and Congress, needless to add, possesses none of them. Leadership in foreign affairs flows today from the President—or it does not flow at all.

The Constitution designates him specifically as "Commander in Chief of the Army and Navy of the United States." In peace and war he is the supreme commander of the armed forces, the living guarantee of the American belief in "the supremacy of the civil over military authority."

In time of peace he raises, trains, supervises and deploys the forces that Congress is willing to maintain. With the aid of the Secretary of Defense, the Joint Chiefs of Staff and the National Security Council—all of whom are his personal choices—he looks constantly to the state of the nation's defenses. He is never for one day allowed to forget that he will be held accountable by the people, Congress and history for the nation's readiness to meet an enemy assault.

In time of war his power to command the forces swells out of all proportion to his other powers. All major decisions of strategy, and many of tactics as well, are his alone to make or to approve. Lincoln and Franklin Roosevelt, each in his own way and time, showed how far the power of military command can be driven by a President anxious to have his generals and admirals get on with the war.

But this, the power of command, is only a fraction of the vast responsibility the modern President draws from the Commander in Chief clause. We need only think back to three of Franklin D. Roosevelt's actions in World War II—the creation and staffing of a whole array of emergency boards and offices, the seizure and operation of more than sixty strike-bound or strike-threatened plants and industries and the forced evacuation of 70,000 American citizens of Japanese descent from the West Coast—to understand how deeply the President's authority can cut into the lives and liberties of the American people in time of war. We may well tremble in contemplation of the kind of leadership he would be forced to exert in a total war with the absolute weapon.

The President's duties are not all purely executive in nature. He is also intimately associated, by Constitution and custom, with the legislative process, and we may therefore consider him as *leader of Congress*. Congress has its full share of strong men, but the complexity of the problems it is asked to solve by a people who still assume that all problems are solvable has made external leadership a requisite of effective operation.

The President alone is in a political, constitutional and practical position to provide such leadership, and he is therefore expected, within

the limits of propriety, to guide Congress in much of its law-making
activity. Indeed, since Congress is no longer minded or organized to
guide itself, the refusal or inability of the President to serve as a kind of
prime minister results in weak and disorganized government. His tasks
as leader of Congress are difficult and delicate, yet he must bend to them
steadily or be judged a failure. The President who will not give his best
thoughts to leading Congress, more so the President who is tempera-
mentally or politically unfitted to "get along with Congress," is now
rightly considered a national liability.

The lives of Jackson, Lincoln, Wilson and the two Roosevelts should
be enough to remind us that the President draws much of his real power
from his position as *leader of his party*. By playing the grand politician
with unashamed zest, the first of these men gave his epic administration a
unique sense of cohesion, the second rallied doubting Republican leaders
and their followings to the cause of the Union, and the other three
achieved genuine triumphs as catalysts of Congressional action. That
gifted amateur, Dwight D. Eisenhower, has also played the role for every
drop of drama and power in it. He has demonstrated repeatedly what
close observers of the Presidency know well: that its incumbent must
devote an hour or two of every working day to the profession of Chief
Democrat or Chief Republican.

It troubles many good people, not entirely without reason, to watch
the President dabbling in politics, distributing loaves and fishes, smiling on
party hacks, and endorsing candidates he knows to be unfit for anything
but immediate delivery to the county jail. Yet if he is to persaude Congress, if he is to achieve a loyal and cohesive administration, if he is to
be elected in the first place (and re-elected in the second), he must put
his hand firmly to the plow of politics. The President is inevitably the
nation's No. 1 political boss.

Yet he is, at the same time, if not in the same breath, *leader of public
opinion*. While he acts as political chieftain of some, he serves as moral
spokesman for all. It took the line of Presidents some time to sense the
nation's need of a clear voice, but since the day when Andrew Jackson
thundered against the Nullifiers of South Carolina, no effective President
has doubted his prerogative to speak the people's mind on the great issues
of his time, to serve, in Wilson's words, as "the spokesman for the real
sentiment and purpose of the country."

Sometimes, of course, it is no easy thing, even for the most sensitive
and large-minded Presidents, to know the real sentiment of the people or
to be bold enough to state it in defiance of loudly voiced contrary opinion.
Yet the President who senses the popular mood and spots new tides even

before they start to run, who practices shrewd economy in his appearances as spokesman for the nation, who is conscious of his unique power to compel discussion on his own terms and who talks the language of Christian morality and the American tradition, can shout down any other voice or chorus of voices in the land. The President is the American people's one authentic trumpet, and he has no higher duty than to give a clear and certain sound.

The President is easily the most influential leader of opinion in this country principally because he is, among all his other jobs, our Chief of State. He is, that is to say, the ceremonial head of the Government of the United States, the *leader of the rituals of American democracy*. The long catalogue of public duties that the Queen discharges in England and the Governor General in Canada is the President's responsibility in this country, and the catalogue is even longer because he is not a king, or even the agent of one, and is therefore expected to go through some rather undignified paces by a people who think of him as a combination of scoutmaster, Delphic oracle, hero of the silver screen and father of the multitudes.

The role of Chief of State may often seem trivial, yet it cannot be neglected by a President who proposes to stay in favor and, more to the point, in touch with the people, the ultimate support of all his claims to leadership. And whether or not he enjoys this role, no President can fail to realize that his many powers are invigorated, indeed are given a new dimension of authority, because he is the symbol of our sovereignty, continuity and grandeur as a people.

When he asks a Senator to lunch in order to enlist his support for a pet project, when he thumps his desk and reminds the antagonists in a labor dispute of the larger interests of the American people, when he orders a general to cease caviling or else be removed from his command, the Senator and the disputants and the general are well aware—especially if the scene is laid in the White House—that they are dealing with no ordinary head of Government. The framers of the Constitution took a momentous step when they fused the dignity of a king and the power of a Prime Minister in one elective office—when they made the President a national leader in the mystical as well as the practical sense.

Finally, the President has been endowed—whether we or our friends abroad like it or not—with a global role as *a leader of the free nations*. His leadership in this area is not that of a dominant executive. The power he exercises is in a way comparable to that which he holds as a leader of Congress. Senators and Congressmen can, if they choose, ignore the President's leadership with relative impunity. So, too, can our friends abroad; the action of Britain and France in the Middle East is a case in point. But so long as the United States remains the richest and most powerful member of any coalition it may enter, then its President's words and deeds will have a direct bearing on the freedom and stability of a great many other countries.

Having engaged in this piecemeal analysis of the categories of Presidential leadership, we must now fit the pieces back together into a seamless unity. For that, after all, is what the Presidency is, and I hope this exercise in political taxonomy has not obscured the paramount fact that this focus of democratic leadership is a single office filled by a single man.

The President is not one kind of leader one part of the day, another kind in another part—leader of the bureaucracy in the morning, of the armed forces at lunch, of Congress in the afternoon, of the people in the evening. He exerts every kind of leadership every moment of the day, and every kind feeds upon and into all the others. He is a more exalted leader of ritual because he can guide opinion, a more forceful leader in diplomacy because he commands the armed forces personally, a more effective leader of Congress because he sits at the top of his party. The conflicting demands of these categories of leadership give him trouble at times, but in the end all unite to make him a leader without any equal in the history of democracy.

I think it important to note the qualification: "the history of democracy" For what I have been talking about here is not the Fuehrerprinzip of Hitler or the "cult of personality," but the leadership of free men. The Presidency, like every other instrument of power we have created for our use, operates within a grand and durable pattern of private liberty and public morality, which means that the President can lead successfully only when he honors the pattern—by working toward ends to which a "persistent and undoubted" majority of the people has given support, and by selecting means that are fair, dignified and familiar.

The President, that is to say, can lead us only in the direction we are accustomed to travel. He cannot lead the gentlemen of Congress to abdicate their functions; he cannot order our civil servants to be corrupt and slothful; he cannot even command our generals to bring off a *coup d'état*. And surely he cannot lead public opinion in a direction for which public opinion is not prepared—a truth to which our strongest Presidents would make the most convincing witnesses. The leadership of free men must honor their freedom. The power of the Presidency can move as a mighty host only with the grain of liberty and morality.

The President, then, must provide a steady focus of leadership—of administrators, Ambassadors, generals, Congressmen, party chieftains,

people and men of good will everywhere. In a constitutional system compounded of diversity and antagonism, the Presidency looms up as the
countervailing force of unity and harmony. In a society ridden by
centrifugal forces, it is the only point of reference we all have in common.
The relentless progress of this continental republic has made the Presidency our one truly national political institution.

There are those, to be sure, who would reserve this role to Congress,
but, as the least aggressive of our Presidents, Calvin Coolidge, once testified, "It is because in their hours of timidity the Congress becomes subservient to the importunities of organized minorities that the President
comes more and more to stand as the champion of the rights of the whole
country." The more Congress becomes, in Burke's phrase, "a confused and
scuffling bustle of local agency" the more the Presidency must become a
clear beacon of national purpose.

It has been such a beacon at most great moments in our history. In
this great moment, too, we may be confident it will burn brightly. ◢

The constitutional and statutory *authority* of the President is indeed
extraordinary. Before discussing the way in which the Supreme Court has
interpreted this authority, however, it is important to point out that the
actual power of the President depends upon his political abilities. The
President must act within the framework of a complex and diversified
political constituency. There is little doubt that he can use the authority
of his office to buttress his strength, but this alone is not sufficient. Somehow he must be able to persuade those with whom he deals to follow
him; otherwise, he will be weak and ineffective. The following selection
deals with the nature of presidential power with these facts in mind.

PRESIDENTIAL POWER
*Richard E. Neustadt**

IN THE United States we like to "rate" a President. We measure him
as "weak" or "strong" and call what we are measuring his "leadership."
We do not wait until a man is dead; we rate him from the moment he

* Reprinted from *Presidential Power* by Richard Neustadt by permission
of John Wiley & Sons, Inc. Copyright © 1960 by John Wiley & Sons, Inc.

takes office. We are quite right to do so. His office has become the focal
point of politics and policy in our political system. Our commentators
and our politicians make a specialty of taking the man's measurements.
The rest of us join in when we feel "government" impinging on our
private lives. In the third quarter of the twentieth century millions of
us have that feeling often.

. . . Although we all make judgments about presidential leadership,
we often base our judgments upon images of office that are far removed
from the reality. We also use those images when we tell one another
whom to choose as President. But it is risky to appraise a man in office
or to choose a man for office on false premises about the nature of his
job. When the job is the Presidency of the United States the risk becomes
excessive. . . .

We deal here with the President himself and with his influence
on governmental action. In institutional terms the Presidency now
includes 2000 men and women. The President is only one of them. But
his performance scarcely can be measured without focusing on *him*.
In terms of party, or of country, or the West, so-called, his leadership
involves far more than governmental action. But the sharpening of spirit
and of values and of purposes is not done in a vacuum. Although governmental action may not be the whole of leadership, all else is nurtured
by it and gains meaning from it. Yet if we treat the Presidency as the
President, we cannot measure him as though he were the government.
Not action as an outcome but his impact on the outcome is the measure
of the man. His strength or weakness, then, turns on his personal capacity
to influence the conduct of the men who make up government. His
influence becomes the mark of leadership. To rate a President according
to these rules, one looks into the man's own capabilities as seeker and as
wielder of effective influence upon the other men involved in governing
the country. . . .

"Presidential" . . . means nothing but the President. "Power" means
his influence. It helps to have these meanings settled at the start.

There are two ways to study "presidential power." One way is
to focus on the tactics, so to speak, of influencing certain men in given
situations: how to get a bill through Congress, how to settle strikes, how
to quiet Cabinet feuds, or how to stop a Suez. The other way is to step
back from tactics on those "givens" and to deal with influence in more
strategic terms: what is its nature and what are its sources? What can *this*
man accomplish to improve the prospect that he will have influence when
he wants it? Strategically, the question is not how he masters Congress

in a peculiar instance, but what he does to boost his chance for mastery in any instance, looking toward tomorrow from today. The second of these two ways has been chosen for this [selection]. . . .

In form all Presidents are leaders, nowadays. In fact this guarantees no more than that they will be clerks. Everybody now expects the man inside the White House to do something about everything. Laws and customs now reflect acceptance of him as the Great Initiator, an acceptance quite as widespread at the Capitol as at his end of Pennsylvania Avenue. But such acceptance does not signify that all the rest of government is at his feet. It merely signifies that other men have found it practically impossible to do *their* jobs without assurance of initiatives from him. Service for themselves, not power for the President, has brought them to accept his leadership in form. They find his actions useful in their business. The transformation of his routine obligations testifies to their dependence on an active White House. A President, these days, is an invaluable clerk. His services are in demand all over Washington. His influence, however, is a very different matter. Laws and customs tell us little about leadership in fact.

Why have our Presidents been honored with this clerkship? The answer is that no one else's services suffice. Our Constitution, our traditions, and our politics provide no better source for the initiatives a President can take. Executive officials need decisions, and political protection, and a referee for fights. Where are these to come from but the White House? Congressmen need an agenda from outside, something with high status to respond to or react against. What provides it better than the program of the President? Party politicians need a record to defend in the next national campaign. How can it be made except by "their" Administration? Private persons with a public axe to grind may need a helping hand or they may need a grinding stone. In either case who gives more satisfaction than a President? And outside the United States, in every country where our policies and postures influence home politics, there will be people needing just the "right" thing said and done or just the "wrong" thing stopped *in Washington*. What symbolizes Washington more nearly than the White House?

A modern President is bound to face demands for aid and service from five more or less distinguishable sources: from Executive officialdom, from Congress, from his partisans, from citizens at large, and from abroad. The Presidency's clerkship is expressive of these pressures. In effect they are constituency pressures and each President has five sets of constituents. The five are not distinguished by their membership; membership is obviously an overlapping matter. And taken one by one they do not match the man's electorate; one of them, indeed, is outside his electorate. They are distinguished, rather, by their different claims upon him. Initiatives are what they want, for five distinctive reasons. Since government and politics have offered no alternative, our laws and customs turn those wants into his obligations.

Why, then, is the President not guaranteed an influence commensurate with services performed? Constituent relations are relations of dependence. Everyone with any share in governing this country will belong to one (or two, or three) of his "constituencies." Since everyone depends on him why is he not assured of everyone's support? The answer is that no one else sits where he sits, or sees quite as he sees; no one else feels the full weight of his obligations. Those obligations are a tribute to his unique place in our political system. But just because it is unique they fall on him alone. *The same conditions that promote his leadership in form preclude a guarantee of leadership in fact.* No man or group at either end of Pennsylvania Avenue shares his peculiar status in our government and politics. That is why his services are in demand. By the same token, though, the obligations of all other men are different from his own. His Cabinet officers have departmental duties and constituents. His legislative leaders head *congressional* parties, one in either House. His national party organization stands apart from his official family. His political allies in the States need not face Washington, or one another. The private groups that seek him out are not compelled to govern. And friends abroad are not compelled to run in our elections. Lacking his position and prerogatives, these men cannot regard his obligations as their own. They have their jobs to do; none is the same as his. As they perceive their duty they may find it right to follow him, in fact, or they may not. Whether they will feel obliged *on their responsibility* to do what he wants done remains an open question. . . .

There is reason to suppose that in the years immediately ahead the power problems of a President will remain what they have been in the decades just behind us. If so there will be equal need for presidential expertise of the peculiar sort . . . that has [been] stressed [i.e., political skill]. Indeed, the need is likely to be greater. The President himself and with him the whole government are likely to be more than ever at the mercy of his personal approach.

What may the Sixties do to politics and policy and to the place of Presidents in our political system? The Sixties may destroy them as we know them; that goes without saying. But barring deep depression or unlimited war, a total transformation is the least of likelihoods. Without catastrophes of those dimensions nothing in our past experience suggests that we shall see either consensus of the sort available to F.D.R. in 1933 and 1942, or popular demand for institutional adjustments likely to assist a President. Lacking popular demand, the natural conservatism of established institutions will keep Congress and the party organizations quite resistant to reforms that could give him a clear advantage over them. Four-year terms for congressmen and senators might do it, if the new terms ran with his. What will occasion a demand for that? As for crisis consensus it is probably beyond the reach of the next President. We may have priced ourselves out of the market for "productive" crises on the pattern Roosevelt knew—productive in the sense of strengthening his chances for sustained support *within* the system. Judging from the Fifties, neither limited war nor limited depression is productive in those terms. Anything unlimited will probably break the system.

In the absence of productive crises, and assuming that we manage to avoid destructive ones, nothing now foreseeable suggests that our next President will have assured support from any quarter. There is no use expecting it from the bureaucracy unless it is displayed on Capitol Hill. Assured support will not be found in Congress unless contemplation of their own electorates keeps a majority of members constantly aligned with him. In the Sixties it is to be doubted . . . that pressure from electorates will move the same majority of men in either House toward consistent backing for the President. Instead the chances are that he will gain majorities, when and if he does so, by *ad hoc* coalition-building, issue after issue. In that respect the Sixties will be reminiscent of the Fifties; indeed, a closer parallel may well be the late Forties. As for "party discipline" in English terms—the favorite cure-all of political scientists since Woodrow Wilson was a youth—the first preliminary is a party link between the White House and the leadership on both sides of the Capitol. But even this preliminary has been lacking in eight of the fifteen years since the Second World War. If ballot-splitting should continue through the Sixties it will soon be "un-American" for President and Congress to belong to the same party.

Even if the trend were now reversed, there is no short-run prospect that behind each party label we would find assembled a sufficiently likeminded bloc of voters, similarly aligned in states and districts all across the country, to negate the massive barriers our institutions and traditions have erected against "discipline" on anything like the British scale. This does not mean that a reversal of the ballot-splitting trend would be without significance. If the White House and the legislative leadership were linked by party ties again, a real advantage would accrue to both. Their opportunities for mutually productive bargaining would be enhanced. The policy results might surprise critics of our system. Bargaining "within the family" has a rather different quality than bargaining with members of the rival clan. But we would still be a long way from "party government." Bargaining, not "discipline," would still remain the key to congressional action on a President's behalf. The critical distinctions between presidential party and congressional party are not likely to be lost in the term of the next President. ✍

23. The President and His Cabinet

The Cabinet may enhance or detract from presidential power. Previous selections have pointed out the multiple responsibilities of the President, which require leadership of the public, his party, Congress, and the bureaucracy. The Cabinet may affect the leadership capacities of the President in these various areas in many ways. These are discussed in the following selection.

THE CABINET AND POLITICS

Richard F. Fenno, Jr.*

Face-to-face contact between the President and his Cabinet is occasional and limited. Both parties make their greatest expenditure of time and energy in activities beyond the immediate President-Cabinet nexus. For the Chief Executive, there are the multiple tasks of leadership—formal and informal, legal or extra-legal. For the Cabinet member, there are a host of involvements arising out of his departmental, constituency, partisan, and legislative relationships. What is the effect of these extensive extra-Cabinet activities on the President-Cabinet relationship? Do they help to account for the group behavior we have observed in the Cabinet meeting? Will the individual member's other involvements affect his position as adviser and "chief lieutenant" to the President? The answer to these questions must be sought by moving beyond the immediate President-Cabinet nexus and into the political system as a whole.

* Reprinted by permission of the publishers from Richard F. Fenno, Jr., *The President's Cabinet* (Cambridge, Mass.: Harvard University Press), copyright, 1959, by the President and Fellows of Harvard College.

The President, it is commonly said, is "many men." He plays at least four distinguishable yet overlapping and frequently conflicting roles—as Chief Representative of the Nation, Chief of his Party, Chief Legislator, and Chief Executive. His leadership, like all leadership, can be understood in terms of the interrelation of personal and situational phenomena. In playing his variety of roles, singly or in juxtaposition, the President will be required to demonstrate many different personal abilities, involving intelligence, skill, and temperament. He will be required, also, to function in different contexts, with regard for the limitations imposed upon him, the social constituencies to which he speaks, the degree of support he wishes to get, the goals he seeks to achieve. In performing his tasks, the President needs assistance that is definable in terms of personal traits and assistance that is related to particular situations. The Cabinet member is a source of both of these types. Most Presidents display an awareness of their needs during the appointment process. If they should not, however, the search for diverse kinds of assistance will be pressed upon them by the necessities of survival.

The Cabinet member has built-in features which recommend him to the President as an extra-Cabinet-meeting source of assistance, for he, too, must be "many men." He, too, is cast in a diversity of roles, which require a corresponding diversity of personal talents and capabilities. The locus of his activities within the political system is similar to that of the Chief Executive. The Cabinet member, too, acts as the representative spokesman for the interests of large segments of the population. He, too, must reach out into a constituency to win and consolidate group support. As a member of a political party more or less committed to certain actions in the realm of policy or patronage, he is rarely free from the obligations and pressures of that relationship. Every Cabinet official is a chief executive in his own right—the head of a great administrative establishment. He is, next to the President, a top-level executive of the national government. In the conduct of the business of his department and in advocating its policies he is thrown into constant contact with the legislature. His usefulness to the President must be judged not just by what he does in the Cabinet meeting, but by his performance elsewhere in the political system. The ultimate question is, of course, how well suited the variety of Cabinet-member relationships is to the variety of presidential needs.

For the purposes of examination, the extra-Cabinet relationships of the Cabinet member have been divided into categories of public prestige, party, Congress, and departmental administration. They are designed to correspond roughly to the four presidential leadership roles mentioned earlier. The inclusion of a section on departmental administration under the rubric of "politics" is largely a matter of convenience, but it does indicate that it is the politics of administration with which that section is mainly concerned, and that no support is given here to a dichotomous view of politics and administration.

The President as Chief Representative

As Chief Representative of the Nation the President plays the most general of all his leadership roles. It transcends his position as leader of a party or as a legislative leader, involving as it does more than the task of mobilizing electoral and congressional majorities. As Chief Representative, the President speaks for the entire nation whenever a single voice is required, be it a time of crisis or of national ceremony. The Presidency in its unity can symbolize the nation as a whole; and as a human being, the President personalizes that symbol. He cannot avoid the role of preeminence in the public mind, though some individuals will make much more of it than others. Whenever he speaks or acts he commands nationwide attention. He can fix national goals, alter national morale, and raise national standards. In representing the nation the President finds his broadest basis of support in the population. He represents the most fundamental and most widely shared ideals of the community. He becomes a political leader in the highest sense of the term.

If the President's function as Chief Representative be construed in its purest sense, the Cabinet can be of little help. It is no match for the President, in terms of public relations. At the Republican National Convention of 1956, the members of the Eisenhower Cabinet were scheduled to make an unprecedented appearance before that body and before the American public via television. They were going to take turns reading the party platform. But scarcely had the first man opened his mouth when all television coverage abruptly switched to the San Francisco airport in anticipation of the President's forthcoming arrival. And while the members of the Cabinet spoke to the convention on the crucial policies of the Eisenhower administration, millions of Americans followed the presidential plane Columbine as it flew around in circles over the airfield. By the time the viewer was returned to the convention hall, the Cabinet members had long since disappeared in the crowd. The lesson, which the communications media understood, is obvious. There is only one President, and the gap in prestige between him and his closest subordinate is unbridgeable in the public eye. Even though, as in this case, it is the President's intention to publicize his Cabinet, he can, almost by moving a muscle, defeat that purpose.

His role as Chief Representative, however, is not exhausted by a single act performed at a moment when only he commands attention. He can fulfill the role only on the basis of the confidence he inspires and the prestige he commands in the nation as a whole. Confidence and prestige are intangible assets, accumulated over a period of time and amassed by actions in many areas of activity. Here, perhaps, the Cabinet member can be of assistance. By virtue of his performance in certain areas, he may bring to the administration as a whole an increment of prestige which can be banked or traded upon by the President. The net result may increase the President's success as Chief Representative of the Nation.

Cabinet and Prestige: Possibilities and Limitations

Taken as a group, the Cabinet may add to or subtract from the public's estimation of the President. "I should not fear to predict the result of your administration," wrote James Buchanan to Franklin Pierce, "as soon as I learn who are members of your Cabinet." The selection of the Cabinet is a symbolic act for the interested public, and they hasten to judge the extent to which the appointments as a whole will bring him overall public support. The Cabinet is the show window of the administration, and a favorable reception for the group will be an asset which the President can use to augment his own public prestige.

Group prestige is, however, a highly perishable commodity. It may give the President a lift in the early days of his administration, while the concept of "the team" is uppermost in the public mind. There is usually a Cabinet honeymoon period while a partly-sympathetic and partly-apprehensive public waits for the Secretaries to act in their respective fields. The first Cabinet meeting is usually publicized with pictures and front page coverage. Quickly, however, "the team" and the Cabinet meeting vanish from sight. Departmental policies are the subject of attention. Praise and blame are allocated individually. Some members are constantly in the public eye and others hardly at all. The Cabinet group which had looked so "balanced" in the newspapers becomes less balanced in action. . . . Although the Cabinet group is periodically resurrected for public display, it rarely receives consideration as a whole.

If the Cabinet as a group, therefore, provides only minimal assistance by way of accumulating public prestige and confidence for the President, can the individual member do any more? The answer is probably yes—subject, however, to some very severe limitations of the political system in which the President-Cabinet relationship is placed. The appointment of a nationally known figure with an established reputation of his own can undoubtedly be of assistance to the Chief Executive. . . .

Cabinet and Party: Possibilities and Limitations

The Cabinet as a group has no institutionalized relationship with the political party. A few traditions have grown up by which it is made susceptible to party influences, but in no sense do they make it a party organ. Cabinet members are usually taken from the same party as the President, and customarily one or more members are party managers dealing with such partisan matters as the distribution of patronage. Otherwise, the party impact on the Cabinet and the Cabinet's effect on the party are not regularized. The President's actions will be influential in settling the nature and extent of party-Cabinet relationships, if and when he tries to turn the Cabinet to some advantage in performing his functions as Party Chief.

The appointment of the Cabinet may symbolize some of the President's own notions about party leadership, and it may provoke some kind of response among the interested public. He could alienate large numbers of his party followers by its composition, and thus with one stroke undermine his party position. Ordinarily no President does this, however, and while each of his appointments does not please everyone, taken as a whole they do not threaten his leadership. On the other hand, his selection may do something by way of consolidating the party behind him. He may try to consolidate his party-in-the-electorate by bringing into the Cabinet representatives of those groups in the country which helped form his majority coalition—as when Roosevelt appointed independent Republican Harold Ickes and Eisenhower selected southerner Oveta Culp Hobby. He may choose to accentuate his own leadership within the party by selecting for representation only such individuals or factions as supported his original nomination—as Roosevelt did. He may, in an extreme case, wish to symbolize his independence of both his "parties" with a bipartisan selection—such as that of Martin Durkin.

The best known of all the types of Cabinet-party relationships is produced by the attempt to weld together the various factions within the party-in-the-government by bringing them into the President's advisory group. Such a move will be taken as a definite bid for party unity, looking toward harmonious relationships between its leader, the President, and the rest of the party. The President may seek out the leaders of the various factions or merely seek representatives of each. The most radical experiment of this sort on record was made by Lincoln, who invited and obtained for his Cabinet all of his major rivals for the Presidency. Warren Harding tried to get his two major opponents and failed, but he then selected representatives of various factions. . . . Eisenhower solicited suggestions from his major rival, Senator Taft, and selected at least one and possibly two of them. One cannot say, however, that the future role which the President will assume vis-à-vis the party is forecast by his quest for harmony. He may be, in effect, abdicating his leadership of the party-in-the-government as Harding was; he may be able to harness the group under his own leadership as Lincoln was; or he may be feeling his way along in a new situation as Eisenhower was, caught between the desire to be above party and the fear of isolating himself from it.

The symbolic appeal for party unity may, in itself, be a helpful gesture in keeping the party intact. Probably the best it can do, as in the case of the Cabinet's group prestige, is to postpone party splits long enough to get the new administration off on the right foot. Its net effect upon the party will be distinctly minor. Depending upon the condition of the party and the President's own self-confidence, however, it is a move which many Presidents cannot afford not to make. . . .

PRESIDENT, CABINET, AND CONGRESS

The Cabinet Member in the Legislative-Executive Context

The executive and legislative branches of the government interact within a constitutional framework, which provides for independent bases of power but a sharing of decision-making authority. The President is given the constitutional authority to send messages to Congress, to "recommend to their consideration such measures as he shall judge necessary and expedient," to call special sessions, to exercise a veto power over legislation, and to control certain aspects of our foreign relations. The Congress, on the other hand, has the legal authority to set up executive departments and agencies, to appropriate money for the executive branch, to confirm presidential appointments, to conduct investigations in the executive branch, and to share with the President the control and the conduct of foreign relations. This is by no means a complete catalogue of the points of formal contact, but it is sufficient to show the basis of the President's role as Chief Legislator and the basis of congressional control over the executive branch.

Threaded through and around the formal legal structure are a whole set of informal, less visible relationships which help to shape the character of the President's legislative relations. The subtle threat of a veto, a well-timed distribution of patronage, personal confidence or hostility—all these may be decisive in the making of a legislative decision favorable to the Chief Legislator. Interpersonal contact between the President and legislative leaders or between members of the executive branch and Congressmen may be most effective in winning cooperation. Nor is the continual interplay of the legislature and the executive branch through interest groups recorded in formal documents. The President needs help in both formal and informal legislative activities, and since the Cabinet member is constantly involved in both, he has the opportunity to furnish it.

The Cabinet member's position in the context of executive-legislative relations is by no means a consistent one. He will find himself playing two roles at once when he faces Congress—he is a presidential adviser, but he is also a department head. In the first role, he is bound tightly by the power-responsibility relationship to the Chief Executive. According to the hierarchical or vertical conception of authority, he acts as the agent of the President helping him to carry out his ultimate responsibility. But as a department head, the lines of responsibility are not quite so distinct. His department is subject to *both* presidential direction and legislative control—to both vertical and horizontal lines of responsibility. This conception of the Cabinet member's activity is not an internally harmonious one, and opportunities to help the President may also be opportunities to harm. . . .

Theoretical ambiguities become reinforced by ambiguities in the realm of informal power relationships, and the upshot is that the President-Cabinet member, power-responsibility relationship will not suffice as an explanation of the extra-Cabinet activity of the Cabinet member. The legislative branch is found to be competing with the President for control over the department head's activities. The clientele publics from which the Cabinet member draws so much of his support may have easy access to the legislature and may work through it to establish a proprietary relationship with the department. The department head, for his part, knows that from the President alone he cannot get all of the power that he needs to operate his department as he wishes. He frequently responds favorably to legislative control in return for the power which he draws from it. It may be of mutual benefit to the Cabinet member and "the legislature," i.e., a committee or a Congressman, to develop horizontal relationships. In formally institutionalized ways, in informal contact, or in combinations of both, department head-legislative-interest group relations develop and become counterweights to presidential control.

Depending on the circumstances, the Cabinet member will probably have alternatives of action when he confronts Congress. He may play his role as presidential adviser and department head in such a way that they mutually reinforce one another—in which case he may not only help the President but himself as well. Or, at the other extreme, he may be able to divorce one role from the other. If he appears as the President's man, he may aid his superior and may or may not (probably not) improve his own departmental position. If he operates independently of the President, he may aid his own future and may or may not (probably not) help the President. Between these extremes lie the intermediary positions most often taken—positions which accommodate, with shifting emphasis, one role to the other. The context in which this accommodation goes on is filled with sources of difficulty, as well as help, for the Chief Legislator....

PRESIDENT, CABINET, AND DEPARTMENTAL ADMINISTRATION

The President as Chief Executive

"The executive power shall be vested in a President of the United States," who shall "take care that the laws are faithfully executed," and who "shall nominate, and by and with the consent of the Senate shall appoint" thousands of public officials. Such are the broad, vague lines of the President's mandate to function as the nation's Chief Executive. By following them, and by assuming responsibility for the effective management of the executive branch of the government, he performs his role as *Chief Executive-Administrator*. In 1848, President James K. Polk entered a pair of comments in his diary which may stand as one high-water mark in the performance of this leadership role:

I have not had my full Cabinet together in council since the adjournment of Congress on the 14th of August last. I have conducted the government without their aid. Indeed, I have become so familiar with the duties and workings of the government, not only upon general principles, but in most of its minute details, that I find but little difficulty in doing this. I have made myself acquainted with the duties of my subordinate officers, and have probably given more attention to details than any of my predecessors.

No president who performs his duty faithfully and conscientiously can have any leisure. If he entrusts the details and smaller matters to subor-

dinates, constant errors will occur. I prefer to supervise the whole operations of the government myself than entrust the public business to subordinates, and this makes my duties very great.

The first comment that comes to mind *apropos* of such a feverish
expenditure of energy is this: Polk died a few months later, surviving his
tenure of office by only one month. But the essential point to be made
involves the extraordinary primitiveness of Polk's prescription for presidential administration of governmental activity. In the twentieth century,
no President can treat his department heads as superfluous.

The trenchant statement of the President's Committee on Administrative Management that "the President needs help" is well enough
known. Quite apart from the specific context in which it was written,
the sentiment has always been a valid one. It was George Washington
who first recognized "the impossibility that one man should be able to
perform all the great business of the state," and who found the solution
to his problem by "instituting the great departments." From that day to
this, the executive departments of the national government have been,
formally speaking, "the major organizational and crucial elements in the
administrative structure of the executive branch below the presidency."
The department head becomes an "outpost of the President in an assigned
field of administrative activities." He helps to implement the broad policy
views of the President within his department, provides a responsible line
of communication between the department and the President, and functions in general as a link in the hierarchical chain of command running
from top to bottom within the executive branch. In addition to his
functions as a presidential lieutenant, the department head is a chief
executive in his own right, "the administrative leader of the agency to
which he is assigned." He has an immense organization whose activities
he must direct, coordinate, and keep on an even keel. He is positioned
at the peak of one distinct pyramid of authority, concerned with the
particular interests and problems of those groups of people subordinate
to him. Administratively, then, the department head is cast in two interrelated yet distinguishable roles—one President-oriented, the other depart-
ment-oriented. His formal responsibilities extend both upward toward
the President and downward toward his own department.

In the frictionless world of organization-chart hierarchies, this double-
jointed job presents no analytical problem. The department head takes
his marching orders from the President and transmits them to his organization. He accepts political responsibility for day-to-day administration

according to the standards established by his superior. Thus does he help the administrator-in-chief increase his own effectiveness. The political universe inhabited by the department head is, however, not so simply understood. Just as his possibilities of helping the Chief Legislator in Congress are complicated by the impingement of non-presidential forces upon him, so too are his possibilities of helping the Chief Executive-Administrator in the departments. There is, to begin with, the personality factor, the set of attitudes and abilities which the department head brings to his job. Furthermore, within his department he operates according to formal organizational prescription and under the influence of less formalized group interests, all of which set limits on his activity. As for the environment outside of his department, it is one of conflicting responsibilities and institutional rivalries, certain to involve him in problems of role conflict. . . .

THE CABINET AND POLITICS: SOME CONCLUSIONS

The investigations which we have made into Cabinet-member activity in the areas of public prestige, party, Congress, and departmental administration lead to a few conclusions about the Cabinet and the political system in which it operates. One striking circumstance is the extent to which the Cabinet concept breaks down in the course of the members' activities outside the Cabinet meeting. In matters of prestige, partisan politics, and legislative relations alike, the Cabinet as a collectivity has only a symbolic value, a value which readily disappears when the need for action supersedes the need for a show window. In the day-to-day work of the Cabinet member, each man fends for himself without much consideration for Cabinet unity. His survival, his support, and his success do not depend on his fellow members. His performance is judged separately from theirs. This condition is but another result of the combination of the centrifugal tendencies in our political system with the low degree of institutionalization which characterizes the Cabinet.

The political help which the President receives comes not from the group but from individual Cabinet members, who can and do augment the President's effectiveness in his leadership roles. It would be a serious mistake not to emphasize the possibilities for crucial assistance by individuals. But probably most striking is the fact that the possibilities for such assistance are very frequently negated by the number of limitations which surround them. There are pervasive limitations of a personal or a situational nature, and there are limitations inherent in the political system—all of which make it neither easy for a Cabinet member to help the President nor axiomatic that he should do so. In the final reckoning, the President receives much less assistance of a positive, non-preventive type from his individual Cabinet members than one might expect. This fact serves to accent the high degree of success which is represented by preventive assistance. It also helps to underline the tremendous gap which separates the presidential level of responsibility from that of his subordinates. It demonstrates, too, the extent to which the two levels are subject to the pulls of different political forces.

The President-Cabinet power-responsibility relationship is, according to the analysis of this chapter, inadequate as a total explanation for the extra-Cabinet performance of the individual member. As a group the Cabinet draws its life breath from the President, but as individuals the Cabinet members are by no means so dependent on him. In many instances, we are presented with the paradox that in order for the Cabinet member to be of real help to the President in one of his leadership roles, the member must have non-presidential "public" prestige, party following, legislative support, or roots of influence in his department. And in any case, the problems of his own success and survival will encourage him to consolidate his own nexus of power and will compel him to operate with some degree of independence from the President. For his part, the President's influence over the Cabinet member becomes splintered and eroded as the member responds to political forces not presidential in origin or direction. From the beginnings of his involvement in the appointment process, the President's power is subject to the pervasive limitations of the pluralistic system in which he seeks to furnish political leadership.

One final conclusion takes the form of a restatement of the pluralism of American politics. In every area we have noted the diffusion, the decentralization, and the volatility of political power. The same kaleidoscopic variety which characterized the factors influential in the appointment process is evident in the political processes which engulf the Cabinet member. Each member interacts with a great variety of political units, interest groups, party groups, and legislative groups, and each has his own pattern of action and his own constellation of power. The feudal analogy is an apt one. It frequently makes more sense to describe the Cabinet member as part of a "feudal pattern of fiefs, baronies, and dukedoms than . . . an orderly and symmetrical pyramid of authority."

Here, then, is an underlying explanation for Cabinet-meeting behavior. Departmentalism is a condition whose roots are grounded in the basic diversity of forces which play upon the individual member. By the same token, this pluralism generates centrifugal influences which help to keep the Cabinet in its relatively non-institutionalized state. The greatest problems for Cabinet and President, like the greatest problems in American politics, are those which center around the persistent dilemmas of unity and diversity. ▨

24. Presidential Transition

As the Presidency assumes greater importance the problem of presidential transition becomes more critical. Although the Presidency is an institution it is at the same time highly personal in many significant respects. The flavor of a presidential administration is often transferred to the bureaucracy, and sometimes remains long after the new President has assumed office. In order for a new President to carry out his programs he must have a high degree of cooperation from many parts of the administrative branch. He must be informed about the current problems of foreign and domestic policy even before he assumes office. Transition is more easily brought about when there is no change in the party of the President. A change in administration from one party to another can involve many difficulties. When Eisenhower came into office in 1952 he confronted a bureaucracy that was largely dedicated to the New Deal and Fair Deal of the prior Democratic administrations. His selection of new Cabinet officers took place in an atmosphere of entrenched bureaucratic hostility. The following selection discusses the problem of Presidential transition generally, with special emphasis upon the Eisenhower–Kennedy changeover in 1960–1961.

THE PROBLEM OF PRESIDENTIAL TRANSITION

*Laurin L. Henry**

IN A SENSE, it is misleading to speak, as we sometimes carelessly do, of "transferring the Presidency." *Presidential responsibility* is essentially transferred on inauguration day, although even this may not be as simple as it appears. But the *Presidency*, except in its most formal aspects, is not a tangible thing that can be passed along intact from one man to another. Each new President must re-create the Presidency in unique form—starting with the materials at hand, but guided by his own concepts

* Reprinted from *The Presidential Election and Transition 1960–1961* by Paul T. David (editor), by permission of The Brookings Institution. Copyright 1961, The Brookings Institution.

and limited by what events and his own skills permit him to make of the formal office. In the same sense, he may inherit a bureaucracy, but he cannot inherit an administration. He must build his own.

The *presidential transition*, then, consists of those critical decisions, acts, or events by which the new Presidency and new administration are given their characteristic shape, style, and content. Presidencies and administrations are, of course, ever-evolving, and it is impossible to say— at least not until they are over—at precisely what moment the outlines began to be stable. Usually, different aspects stabilize at different times. But certainly the first three months, or the first 100 days, to use the period of measure favored by journalists, are the most critical; by the end of the first six months the essential characteristics of style and approach, if not of continuing substantive policies, are likely to be apparent. . . .

The 1960–1961 transition can be identified as the one in which the "transition problem" came of age and received appropriate recognition. The unsatisfactory experience of 1952–1953 was remembered, and during 1960 scholars, journalists, and conscientious public servants called attention to the lessons of history and the facts of the current situation. In the resulting climate of public concern, political leaders responded with efforts to guard the public interest during the change of leadership made mandatory by the Twenty-second Amendment. The transfer of responsibility from Eisenhower to Kennedy, although by no means flawlessly executed, was the smoothest such transition in recent times. The gubernatorial transitions being carried out at the same time also benefited, for almost the first time, from specific attention to problems of transition at the state level.

An Improving Record

The "presidential common law" covering such events was confirmed and further developed by the Eisenhower-Kennedy transition. Both the incoming and outgoing administrations recognized the obligation to make suitable preparations and to cooperate with each other in achieving a smooth transition. The necessity of starting some of these preparations before the election was accepted, although, unlike 1952, pre-election preparations were more prominent in the out-party than the in-party. However, Eisenhower followed unquestioningly the precedent of giving intelligence briefings to the candidates and, against his own political instincts, permitted some of the most essential staff preparations to go on within the administration. He was probably unduly sensitive on this point; in the future there should be a sufficient public understanding of the problem to permit overt preparations and pre-election communication between the administration and the candidates to the extent necessary.

The designation of Clifford and Persons as top-level liaison officers between the incoming and outgoing administrations was an innovation that proved useful and is likely to be used again. The need for such formalization presumably depends in part on the personalities involved and the circumstances. It might become less necessary if the President-elect is ready for early designation of key members of his administration.

Relations between Eisenhower and Kennedy were conducted at a level of dignity and responsibility that their successors will do well to emulate. Eisenhower's offers of assistance to Kennedy were up to the norm for an outgoing President. Kennedy's consideration for Eisenhower, which was especially noteworthy in an incoming President, set an example for other incoming officials and proved its utility soon after inauguration when he was able to consult Eisenhower in the Cuban crisis. Taking their cues from Kennedy, other members of the incoming administration overcame much of the suspicion usually shown by men in their positions and took advantage of the advance information and aid offered by their predecessors.

This transition was notable for the quick assertion of policy leadership by the new President, particularly in relation to Congress. Consciously guided by a tradition and theory of strong presidential leadership, Kennedy took early action to prepare himself, and he and his associates made skillful use of the resources at hand, both inside and outside of the government. The bureaucracy was regarded not as an obstacle but as an instrument through which the new administration could achieve its purposes.

Some Continuing Problems

Despite these and other advances, the transition experience of 1960–1961 revealed the survival of old problems, some of which took on new or more acute forms. One was the problem of recruiting political executives on short notice and in a party system that does not clearly designate a cadre from which top appointees will be selected when the party next achieves power. In this case, Kennedy's creative cabinet-making achieved a result that might be envied in any parliamentary system, and the early "talent search" for lesser appointees was unusually effective for such an operation. The success of the Kennedy approach, in fact, suggests the desirability of continuing a high-level recruiting operation, on a smaller scale, in the White House. Nevertheless, the Kennedy staffing was done with a degree of haste that occasionally appalled even those most intimately involved. There were some costly mistakes and serious delays in filling several of the most important posts; and the work of completing the administration's personnel began to drag soon after inauguration.

This raises the question, which is not new, of pre-election staff work on personnel for presidential candidates. It is probably both impractical and undesirable for a candidate to attempt to reach firm decisions on cabinet and subcabinet appointments before he is elected. But would not a preliminary search for potential appointees of high caliber, and an assembly of dossiers on the obvious prospects, put the personnel operation that much ahead and permit faster and more rational decisions after election?

The obstacle usually cited is that such an operation, if it is to be useful, must be conducted by people in whom the candidate has special confidence, and such people cannot be spared from campaign assignments. This argument has great force. Yet, much of the preliminary spadework in the Kennedy talent search was done by individuals who had been given only minor roles in the campaign, and it appears in retrospect that this would have been a good investment of the time of even one or two who were relatively close to Kennedy during the campaign. Despite the difficulties and the danger of wasted effort, a greater realization of the stakes and the potential benefits may well bring future presidential candidates to the point of authorizing pre-election search for and investigation of potential appointees. A more organized approach to the appointment problems of a future administration might even prove helpful in relation to the problems of campaign strategy.

The scale of the Kennedy post-election preparations magnified what had hitherto been a problem of minor proportions: financing the activities of the President-elect and his staff, including consultants and persons designated for office in the executive agencies. Since it is clearly in the public interest to have the next administration ready to operate as completely as possible on inauguration day, the essential expenses of preparatory work after the election should be covered by a regular appropriation for that purpose. Establishing a proper amount and appropriate limitations on what can be considered reimbursable expenses would be debatable but not insoluble problems.

Although no grave difficulties arose in this turnover, the problem of reconciling policy control and career continuity along the upper edge of the civil service structure is still far from solved. Civil service Schedule C, which has evolved in a way probably unforeseen by either its original founders or critics, seems to have done part of the job of institutionalizing a zone of flexibility in which career and noncareer appointees mingle and in which adjustments can be made at the pleasure of the administration as situations change. Fortunately, the Democrats tended to regard Schedule C as a list of positions in which they could make changes and put in their own appointees if necessary but did not feel compelled to clear out all the incumbents who bore Schedule C labels. Thus many career men who had in one way or another got into Schedule C jobs were retained— at the pleasure of the Secretary, as before. Whether there should be more or less positions in Schedule C is a debatable issue, but it is more than a transition problem.

The important problem yet remaining is that there is no established system or practice giving protection to career men, either in Schedule C or regular civil service positions, who become casualties of policy or leadership changes. In this transition most such displaced persons were picked up and used elsewhere, partly through the efforts of the career executive placement service operated by the Civil Service Commission. However, most such reassignments resulted from personal arrangements and were possible because of the low level of partisan feeling that characterized the period. This might not be possible in a new administration that was reducing the total level of government activities amid suspicions of the bureaucracy in general. Despite the rejection of the Second Hoover Commission's proposal for a Senior Civil Service with rank-in-the-person, we may yet see some arrangement by which high ranking career men can be temporarily assigned to some central pool or reassigned without immediate loss of pay or status.

Shortly before he left the White House, President Eisenhower characterized as "silly" the present requirement that the outgoing President submit a State of the Union message, economic report, and budget to the new Congress. He suggested that these presentations be made the responsibility of the new President in years of presidential change, and that the date of inauguration be advanced to give the incoming President time to prepare them. Embedded in a "package" of reforms proposed by Senator Mansfield is a provision seeking to accomplish this objective. The Mansfield proposals . . . would abolish the electoral college and elect the President by direct popular vote, provide for federally financed and supervised presidential preference primaries in the states, provide federal financial assistance to the campaigns of major party candidates *if nominated after September* 1, and (making no change in the present election date) change presidential inauguration day to December 1.

Such proposals raise questions that go far beyond the scope of this chapter, but three brief comments from the viewpoint of transition problems are in order.

First, the present assignment of responsibility for the messages, although anomalous in form, raises no overwhelming difficulties in practice. New messages and appropriate budgetary revisions were prepared and presented in timely fashion by the new President in both 1953 and 1961. The existing arrangement burdens the outgoing administration with work that may be unnecessary but it may be better than a schedule that would give the incoming President full responsibility for the budget but insufficient time to take charge of preparing it. The present untidiness about the budget could be modified either by advancing inauguration day or by delaying the budget submission deadline. But in either course, small changes will not do. A new President should have at least 60 days, and preferably more, before having to assume responsibility for presenting the complete annual budget, for the budget has to be more or less built up from the bottom on the basis of given policies or assumptions.

Second, a strong case can be made for some shortening of the election-inauguration interval because of the inevitable uncertainties of leadership and paralysis of high level policy making in such periods. The relative obligations of the President and President-elect have been greatly clarified since the days when Hoover and Roosevelt engaged in futile maneuvering over the 1932–1933 depression crisis. But, as we have seen in the case of Eisenhower and Kennedy, there are stubborn ambiguities in the relationship that are dangerous under present-day requirements for quick decisions.

Third, there is a limit to how much the election-inauguration interval can be shortened without running the equal danger of having a new administration legally installed and responsible but actually disorganized and unready to function. Those who have participated in the process of organizing a new administration under the present schedule shudder at the thought of having to do it any faster. Any advance in inauguration day will require corresponding intensification of pre-election preparations by the candidates, in the realms both of personnel and of policy. There is room for some progress in this direction, but how much room is not clear, especially if, as in the Mansfield proposal, the campaign period itself is to be shortened. Shortening the election-inauguration interval will also require a strengthening and more effective use of the career service, and perhaps a change from the present custom of simultaneous replacement of so large a number of important executive officers on inauguration day. Even under the most optimistic assumptions about earlier preparations by candidates and improvement in relationships between incoming and outgoing administrations, a preparatory period of 30 to 45 days after election seems essential.

In summary, the Eisenhower-Kennedy transition was, from the viewpoint of the public interest, a considerable improvement over other party turnovers of recent times. It established some useful precedents and suggested some lines of improvement for the future. It also suggested some of the inherent limitations on ability to achieve smooth transitions within the framework of the present constitutional and party system. Fundamental constitutional changes from the presidential system seem out of the question, but there is some possibility of useful adjustments in scheduling along lines indicated by the Mansfield proposals. Reforms in the party system tending toward more doctrinal coherence and leadership stability, should they occur, would make a significant contribution to minimizing transitional difficulties. But in the transitions of the foreseeable future we shall be greatly dependent, as in the past, on the quality of the political leadership of the moment, plus an element of sheer luck in regard to the circumstances of the times.

25. Presidential Style

When all is said and done presidential decision-making often depends upon the style of the occupant of the White House. Perhaps positions of such great leadership should not depend so completely upon the personal characteristics of one man. But in the case of the American Presidency it is unavoidable. In our political system candidates for the Presidency are sifted by the political parties and the electorate very carefully. Presidents often reflect the times in which they live. Times of crisis have in the past tended to produce strong presidential leadership, whereas those of calm have supported less vigorous Presidents. The nature of presidential responsibilities today requires strong leadership. This subject is discussed in the following selection.

HOW TO PICK A PRESIDENT

*Sidney Warren**

Is THERE any way for the American people to determine whether a
potential President will provide effective leadership? What standards
should be applied in selecting a candidate for the highest office in the
land? When a business organization seeks a man for a top job, the applicant's background, training, and experience are major factors in evaluating his competence. But how useful are these criteria for judging the
future head of state?

In his incisive commentary on American political institutions published toward the end of the nineteenth century, *The American Commonwealth*, James Bryce entitled one of his chapters "Why Great Men Are
Not Chosen President." With some notable exceptions, the Presidents
during the era he was discussing were a mediocre lot selected for reasons
that had nothing to do with their capacity to fill the office with distinction.
During the bitter controversy over slavery, for example, both parties
sought innocuous candidates who could be depended upon to dodge the
issue. In 1840 the Whigs turned away from men of towering stature like
Henry Clay and Daniel Webster in favor of a nonentity like William
Henry Harrison, who, having been unable to earn a living as a farmer,
turned to running a whiskey distillery and then became a clerk of a
county court.

About fifty years later, when the nation was racked by agrarian discontent and the social consequences of urbanization and industrialization,
the political parties still selected their candidates in what was sometimes
the most haphazard manner. An indifferent Republican convention in
1888 gave the nomination to Benjamin Harrison, a man whose only distinction was a brief service in the Senate, who had been defeated for
re-election and frankly described himself as "a dead duck," because James
G. Blaine, too ill to run, cabled from Scotland, "Take Harrison." A contemporary observer, commenting on the political conventions of the time,
declared that they functioned like "the exquisite economy of Nature,
which ever strives to get into each place the smallest man that can fill it."

Nevertheless, feeble as the leadership frequently was, the Republic
prospered—the nation could afford the luxury of mediocrity. In our era,

---

* Reprinted from the *Saturday Review* (July 4, 1964) by permission of the
author and the *Saturday Review*.

however, when the President plays so strategic a role in promoting the nation's welfare at home and safeguarding its position of world leadership abroad, a Grant or Harding in the White House would be an unmitigated disaster. Today his preparation must be such as to fully prepare him to cope with the unprecedented problems not only at home but throughout the world.

Yet no school exists to prepare an aspirant for the unique and complex roles the Chief Executive is required to fill. Years spent in public service, whether in Congress, administration, or a governorship, may be helpful but do not necessarily prepare a man for greatness, or even for competence. If the Presidential office were merely administrative, involving technical proficiency in details and procedure, the requisite skills could be acquired. But as Franklin D. Roosevelt once said, the Presidency is pre-eminently a place of moral leadership. It therefore requires the ability to adapt the national purpose to the continually changing requirements of a dynamic society, to preserve and transmit to posterity the nation's heritage of humane and liberal values.

An impressive record of administrative competency may be misleading when assessing the potential of a candidate, as William Howard Taft sadly illustrates. Taft's distinguished career as judge, Governor-General of the Philippine Islands, and Secretary of War greatly impressed the party leaders. The judicial mind, however, is likely to hobble rather than encourage vigorous executive leadership. In a crisis, the President must often rely on his instincts and intuition. If he stops too long to prepare an opinion by chewing over evidence and consulting precedents, the race may be finished before he enters the lists. Moreover, emphasis on the machinery of government and official routine can thwart the kind of initiative that thrusts a country forward. Franklin D. Roosevelt, who lacked both interest in or talent for administration, injected vitality and dynamism into the councils of government.

A professional career in politics or a record of achievement in Congress is not necessarily a factor in the preparation of a President. Abraham Lincoln's experience was confined to a single term as a member of the House of Representatives a dozen years before his election. Woodrow Wilson spent a lifetime as an academician and had only two years as governor of New Jersey before entering the White House, yet he exercised a vigorous, commanding leadership of Congress, scoring triumphs that seasoned politicians could envy. Even before the electorate had digested the significance of Wilson's "New Freedom," with its tariff reform act, Federal Reserve Law, and Clayton antitrust legislation, it concluded that the scholar-turned-politician had proved a consummate master in the great game of politics. The failure that climaxed Wilson's administration was not caused by his lack of political experience but was the result of a tragic flaw of personality.

By contrast, Calvin Coolidge was hardly an amateur in politics. He reached the heights of political power after serving as city councilman, a member of both houses of the state legislature, mayor, lieutenant-governor, governor, and Vice President. Yet during his six years in the White House all he offered the American people was a steady stream of platitudes and banalities, encouraging a perilous blindness to the stirrings at home and abroad that were portents of debacle. As his biographer said, Coolidge believed his task "was to keep the Ship of State on an even keel before a favoring wind—not to reconstruct the hull or install motive power or alter the course. . . . He won no battles, challenged no traditions, instituted few reforms" Coolidge was completely inept as a party leader and a legislative leader. His bills were defeated and his vetoes overridden by Congress.

Whether a President will have the capacity to meet the demands made upon him by crises cannot be predicted solely on the basis of past achievement and service. If judged in terms of his background, James Buchanan should have been ideally suited for effective Presidential leadership. Few men came to office with a longer official training—forty years in the legislative, executive, and diplomatic service. Yet at a critical juncture in the nation's history, with the Union on a disaster course toward dissolution, he was tragically indecisive when the imperatives of the hour called for vigor and resolution.

Although Harry S. Truman had been in political life for a fairly substantial period, his nomination for the Vice Presidency in 1944 was agreed to by Democratic party leaders mainly because he was an ideal compromise candidate—he was acceptable to both North and South, to organized labor, and to the machine bosses. No premature termination of Roosevelt's leadership was anticipated, and when it occurred the nation as a whole was appalled that its fate during such a precarious period was in the hands of this unassuming man. One journalist characterized the new President as "a sedative in a double-breasted suit," and most informed observers were prepared to write off his administration. Truman had not been a member of the inner war council or made privy to the negotiations at the various wartime conferences, or been informed about the progress of atomic development. But the years that followed were decision-packed, with Truman demonstrating a creative and imaginative approach to foreign relations as striking as the feeling in the spring of 1943 that the man was not suited for his prodigious tasks.

To a great extent the Cabinet or parliamentary form of government in Great Britain solves the problem of unpredictability. The Prime Minister is the product of the House of Commons, steeped in its traditions, habituated to its ways, and is required to have been the leader of his party in that body before he can be chosen the Queen's First Minister. From leader of the loyal opposition to Prime Minister may involve a transition in power, but not a transition in leadership. As head of his party, he has been displaying leadership for years in the law-making body of a kind that the electorate has endorsed. There are no "Johnny-come-latelys" or dark horses. By contrast, the President's preparation is largely a random affair. Still, ours is a Presidential system, and, that being so, what are the criteria that ultimately determine Presidential success if the traditional yardsticks are largely irrelevant? Is there a common pattern displayed by "strong" Presidents that might provide clues to whether a candidate is adequately prepared?

Perhaps most important is a broad, expansive view of the office that would permit the occupant of the White House to extend the potentialities of executive prerogative to its outermost limits whenever the public necessity requires it. Theodore Roosevelt was better prepared for leadership by virtue of his approach to the Presidency than he was by the years he spent as police commissioner of New York, member of the federal Civil Service Commission, Assistant Secretary of the Navy, governor of New York, or even Vice President. As he once said: "The most important factor in getting the right spirit in my administration was my insistence upon the theory that the executive power was limited only by specific restrictions and prohibitions appearing in the Constitution or imposed by Congress under its constitutional power. . . . I declined to adopt the view that what was imperatively necessary for the nation could not be done by the President unless he could find some specific authorization to do it."

John Fitzgerald Kennedy regarded the Presidency as the repository of political and moral leadership, believing that the occupant of the office must be willing to use the powerful tools available to him. The choice, he felt, was either to emulate Roosevelt and Wilson or Taft and Harding. In an address before the National Press Club a year before his inauguration he left no room for doubt as to which of the previous Presidents he would use as models. "Whatever the political affiliation of our next President," he said, "whatever his views may be on all the issues and problems that rush in upon us, he must above all be the Chief Executive in every sense of the word. He must be prepared to exercise the fullest powers of his office, all that are specified and some that are not. He must master complex problems as well as receive one-page memoranda. He must originate action as well as study groups. He must reopen the channels of communication between the world of thought and the seat of power."

It is no coincidence that throughout our history the Presidents who have been most ineffectual were those like Taylor, Taft, Harding, and Coolidge who were firmly committed to the concept that the Chief Executive could exercise only that authority specifically granted him by the Constitution. Taft could be considered their spokesman with his declaration that "the President can exercise no power which cannot be fairly and reasonably traced to some specific grant of power or justly implied and included within such express grant as proper and necessary to its exercise."

However rich and varied the aspirant's career, he comes ill-prepared to discharge the duties and responsibilities of the Presidential office if his theoretical position would inhibit rather than encourage bold, assertive leadership. In less tempestuous and complex times this element in the preparation of a President was of no great significance. As a matter of fact, the relatively untroubled periods in our history produced the textbook image of the Presidency as an equal and coordinate branch operating strictly within its own sphere and never trespassing beyond certain specified boundary lines. Today, however, it must encompass party and legislative leadership, providing direction in economic matters and initiative in world affairs.

Significantly, with the exception of George Washington, all the Presidents who made a lasting impact on the nation were men who eagerly sought the office and were avid for leadership in public affairs. To reach the White House would be the ultimate fulfilment of their profoundest ambitions. Once in office, they approached their tasks with driving zest and enthusiasm. Theodore Roosevelt, who was elevated to the Presidency through an accident of fate, probably would have achieved it eventually on his own. He reveled in the opportunity to occupy the seat of power. For him the Presidency was a glorious adventure and he enjoyed every minute of it; for his successor, whom he had hand-picked, it was an ordeal that he endured with outward stoicism but inward wretchedness. William Howard Taft was persuaded to take a job he never wanted and for which, realistically, he felt ill-suited. "Politics, when I am in it, makes me sick," he once said. His private letters offer pathetic evidence of his lack of self-confidence. Several months after his inauguration he wrote to Roosevelt:

If I followed my impulse, I should still say "My dear Mr. President." I cannot overcome the habit. When I am addressed as "Mr. President," I turn to see whether you are not at my elbow. . . .

I want you to know that I do nothing in the Executive Office without considering what you would do under the circumstances and without having in a sense a mental talk with you over the pros and cons of the situation. I have not the facility for educating the public as you had. . . .

The Presidency is a lonely place—that "splendid misery" as Thomas Jefferson once called it—especially in times of crisis when the occupant of the office must repeatedly make vital decisions for which he and he alone is responsible. No one can share the burden with him, and only a man who has confidence in his own judgment is adequately prepared for White House leadership. Harry S. Truman's initial response to the news of President Roosevelt's sudden death was certainly understandable. "I don't know whether you fellows ever had a load of hay or a bull fall on you," he told reporters, "but last night the stars and all the planets fell on me. . . . I've got the most terribly responsible job any man ever had." But Truman's inner core was sound and firm. Within weeks he began to demonstrate the inner security that enabled him to deal with the many grave problems that beset the nation.

Woodrow Wilson's self-confidence was of another caliber. Lacking humility, tinged with mysticism, this trait was to prove his undoing. "God ordained that I should be the next President of the United States," he announced as he was about to enter the White House. On another occasion he said, "I am sorry for those who disagree with me because I know I am right." While the President must be firmly convinced that the course he has chosen *is* the right one, he must at the same time be flexible enough to bend when circumstances require resilient behavior.

A significant element in a President's preparation is that he have a plan that embodies his view of the country's future. It should reflect his talent for creative innovation and demonstrate a sense of the direction in which the times are moving, diagnose contemporary maladies, and offer possible means for their solution. Today that plan must embrace Ghana and Ceylon as well as Georgia and Oregon. In Franklin D. Roosevelt's campaign speeches in 1932, he presented a plan for the economic future of the nation that was as bold in outline as it was imaginative. Although containing no specific blueprint, it articulated goals that were the basis for the "New Deal" program.

While campaign rhetoric and political oratory can be discounted to a large extent, they provide some means for discerning the quality of a candidate. What could have been expected from Warren G. Harding on the basis of the hackneyed speeches delivered from the front porch of his home? As William G. McAdoo colorfully put it, his addresses "leave the impression of an army of pompous phrases moving over the landscape in search of an idea; sometimes these meandering words would actually capture a straggling thought and bear it triumphantly, a prisoner in their midst, until it died of servitude and overwork!" The nation at the time was not aware of the machinations that gave Harding the nomination, but Americans recklessly voted for a man whose only claim to the highest office in the land was that he *looked* like a President.

A leading contemporary journal in all seriousness declared that whatever might be the defects of the nominee as a world statesman, Harding was "an exceedingly courteous gentleman." If he were elected, "good nature, both to political friends and to political enemies," would once again prevail in the White House. "The Senator's speeches may be properly criticized for their vagueness, for their lack of original thought, for their occasionally conflicting character . . . but they are certainly not lacking in the decencies of political controversy. And this is another case where style is the man."

Style is indeed the man. The last sentence, which succinctly and accurately summed up the matter, was a portent. The character of the nation is influenced by the "style" of its chosen head. With "normalcy" enthroned in the White House, the nation drifted, devitalized, without standards and without goals.

Leadership in our democratic society performs a strategic role above and beyond the functions mapped out by our constitutional system. An essential component is the President's capacity and will to influence public opinion so that necessary programs are carried out. Those men who were strong Presidents had both an intellectual and intuitive comprehension of this ingredient. As Theodore Roosevelt put it, "Our prime necessity is that public opinion should be properly educated." And again, "I do not desire to act unless I can get the bulk of our people to understand the situation and to back up the action; and to do that I have to get the facts vividly before them. The ineffectual Presidents were either indifferent about shaping public opinion or believed, with Calvin Coolidge, that "the people have their own affairs to look after and cannot give much attention to what Congress is doing."

The preparation of a President, then, is compounded of many intangibles. Attributes for which there is no specific training—character, convictions, and style—appear to be more basic for successful leadership than background, training, and experience. Political skill taken for granted, the effective leader captures the public imagination because he possesses moral and physical stamina, because he has a humanitarian outlook and the determination to alleviate the ills that plague our society, and because when he speaks and acts he does so not only for the moment but for the age. He has the capacity to inspire the people, to elevate them above the commonplace, to set a tone for the nation so that the vision of the future becomes the objective for the present. Such a President is a total President, both a politician and a statesman. ✍

The Cuban crisis of 1962 was perhaps the greatest since World War II. The following case study illustrates the manner in which President Kennedy dealt with that problem. Students should note in particular the personal involvement of the President in the decisions that were made, but at the same time should take into account the participation of presidential staff and agency officials. The selection emphasizes the complexity and dimensions of presidential decision-making.

THE CUBAN CRISIS OF 1962—A CASE STUDY

*E. W. Kenworthy**

THE Cuban crisis began in the whirring cameras of a single Air Force U–2 reconnaissance plane high above San Cristobal on Sunday afternoon, Oct. 14.

By 5:30 P.M. the next day intelligence officers in Washington had completed their preliminary analysis of the developed film and had made up their minds:

Soviet medium-range missiles, the mobile type used by the Red Army, were in place near San Cristobal, 100 miles west of Havana.

Before the night was over, the incontrovertible evidence had hit the Administration with terrific impact.

* From *The New York Times,* November 3, 1962. © 1962 by The New York Times Company. Reprinted by permission.

"Remember," said an official later, "we had had a posture we'd all signed on to—that this (Soviet build-up) was not an offensive build-up."

Those first reconnaissance pictures set off two weeks of diplomatic thrust and parry, of military build-up and alert, and of strident propaganda activity that were perhaps without precedent in the peacetime history of the United States. . . .

The Soviet military build-up in Cuba started in the second half of July. At that time American intelligence sources reported suspicious movements of Soviet ships apparently laden with war materiel destined for Cuba.

All through August, according to intelligence reports, the build-up continued. More than 30 ships unloaded 2,000 Soviet technicians and instructors and such war materiel as surface-to-air missiles, patrol boats with missiles and MIG–21 fighters.

But photographic reconnaissance, which had been going on secretly for some time, showed nothing of an offensive character. The President said publicly on Sept. 4 that as far as was known the Soviet arms in Cuba were defensive.

"Were it to be otherwise," he added, "the gravest issues would arise."

Possibility Studied

Within the Administration the possibility that some of the build-up was offensive was not being overlooked. The intelligence community—the Central Intelligence Agency, military intelligence and others—specifically raised the question whether there might be surface-to-surface missiles in Cuba with nuclear warheads.

Reports of such missiles were coming from Cuban refugees in Florida, who are regularly screened by intelligence agents. And refugee organizations published claims that Cuba had offensive missiles.

As a result of the persistent reports and intelligence concern, President Kennedy approved an order—apparently at the beginning of September—that the entire island of Cuba be photographed.

The Soviet ships heading for Cuba in increasing numbers also gave concern, and they were photographed. A picture taken on Sept. 28 showed crates on a freighter's deck that could hold fuselages of the Ilyushin 28, a twin-engine Soviet jet bomber.

In early October the pictures gave what a high official said was "clear evidence" of IL–28's in Cuba. This may have been the reason for the secret dispatch of a squadron of Phantoms, a Navy fighter-bomber, to Florida Oct. 6 and a sizable build-up of antiaircraft and other air defense equipment there.

Hard evidence of missiles was another matter.

As late as Sept. 5, high-altitude photographs of the San Cristobal area showed an unmarred landscape. For the rest of the month the planes concentrated on the rest of the island, to the east.

But by the beginning of October, agents' reports had convinced officials in Washington that something suspicious was going on around San Cristobal. On Oct. 3 orders were accordingly issued to go back for more photographs.

Weather Intervenes

The weather intervened. Hurricane Ella delayed flights for a week, and then a cloud cover blocked high-altitude surveillance.

It was during this interval, on Oct. 10, that Senator Kenneth B. Keating, Republican, of New York, said he had confirmed reports of intermediate-range missile sites under construction in Cuba.

At last, on the sunny Sunday afternoon of Oct. 14, the cameras of the U-2 provided confirmation.

Looking back with all the evidence available later, officials estimated that the first medium-range missiles—or parts of them—began arriving in Cuba about Sept. 10. Sections started moving to the launching sites about the middle of September.

It takes only 24 hours from the time photographs are taken over Cuba until they are processed and analyzed in Washington.

General Carter Informed

At 3 P.M. Monday, John A. McCone, Director of the C.I.A., left Washington to take the body of a stepson who had been killed in Los Angeles to Seattle. The reconnaissance findings, therefore, were first communicated to his deputy, Lieut. Gen. Marshall S. Carter.

To make sure no mistake had been made, specialists analyzed the photos through the early evening hours. At about 9:30 a C.I.A. official telephoned Mr. McGeorge Bundy, the President's Special Adviser on National Security Affairs, at home.

In security parlance, he informed Mr. Bundy of the incontrovertible evidence of offensive missiles. Mr. Bundy immediately set in motion plans already made for limited distribution of the evidence.

After the past caution, why did that telephone call so swiftly and completely persuade Mr. Bundy that there were offensive missiles in Cuba? This explanation is given:

"The difference was conviction on the part of the experts."

Word Goes to Gilpatric

Other telephone calls began to spread the word that evening. Lieut. Gen. Joseph F. Carroll, director of the Defense Intelligence Agency, made the calls at the Defense Department.

Even before the guarded call to Mr. Bundy, General Carroll had telephoned the news to Roswell L. Gilpatric, Deputy Secretary of Defense.

Then General Carroll took two civilian photo-analysts of his agency to dinner at the home of the Chairman of the Joint Chiefs of Staff, Gen. Maxwell D. Taylor. At General Taylor's home—and joining in the briefing—were Mr. Gilpatric, General Carter of the C.I.A. and U. Alexis Johnson, Deputy Under Secretary of State for Political Affairs.

Defense Secretary Robert S. McNamara was not told that night. He happened to have left the Pentagon unusually early, at 7 P.M., because he was host that night to "Hickory Hill University"—the intellectual gathering usually held at the home of Attorney General Robert F. Kennedy.

At the State Department it was Roger Hilsman, Director of Intelligence and Research. Mr. Hilsman got Secretary of State Rusk out of a dinner he was giving for Gerhard Schröder, the West German Foreign Minister. Mr. Rusk took the call in the pantry.

TUESDAY, OCT. 16

The First Decisions

A team of intelligence experts had worked through the night on a report. At 8 A.M. an intelligence officer accompanied by two photo analysts took the report and the pictures to Mr. Bundy at the White House.

At about 8:45 Mr. Bundy went to the President's bedroom. Mr. Kennedy was still in pajamas and robe, reading the papers.

Straightaway the President began indicating who should be called in. After 10 minutes with the President, Mr. Bundy left to start the machinery.

At the State Department, at 9 A.M., Secretary Rusk was briefed by the Under Secretary, George W. Ball, and Messrs. Hilsman, Johnson and Edward M. Martin, Assistant Secretary for Inter-American Affairs. At 10

Mr. Rusk had to leave to meet the Crown Prince of Libya at the airport.

The President kept a 9:30 date at the White House with Cmdr. Walter M. Schirra, the astronaut, his wife and two children. The President took them all out to see his daughter Caroline's ponies.

General Carter Arrives

While this was going on, General Carter arrived at the White House with other analysts and photographic enlargements. At 11:45 the group later known as the Executive Committee of the National Security Council assembled in the Cabinet room.

The President presided. Also present were Vice President Johnson, Secretary Rusk, Secretary of Defense McNamara, Secretary of the Treasury Douglas Dillon, Attorney General Kennedy, Under Secretary Ball, Deputy Secretary of Defense Gilpatric, General Carter, Assistant Secretary of State Martin, General Taylor, Mr. Bundy and Theodore C. Sorenson, Special Counsel and principal speech writer.

General Carter spoke briefly about the new evidence that he had brought with him, and then one of his photo interpreters gave the group a "reading" of the prints.

To those in the Cabinet room, it now seems in retrospect that the issues that dominated the weeks' deliberations were already visible, "in a sketchy way," at this meeting.

Air of Challenge

An air of challenge hung over the room. There was an awareness that any United States response might worsen the world situation. But not challenging the Soviet move would surely be the worst course of all.

In first analysis of what Premier Khrushchev was up to, Berlin bulked very large.

The first reading, as one official put it, was: "This is a left hook designed to make him tougher when he comes at us in November, presumably on Berlin." Premier Khrushchev, they were convinced, planned to present the United States with a nasty set of alternatives.

If the United States did nothing, the credibility of its pledges would be destroyed. The Soviet Union would have made a military gain vis-a-vis this score in Latin America. One official said: "Latin-American affairs would never have been the same. The Latins "go with a winner."

If the United States bombed the bases or invaded Cuba, its moral position in the world would be tarnished. A great cry would go up from the neutral nations, and the North Atlantic Treaty Organization alliance would be thrown into disarray. The Russians would have an excuse for counteraction in Berlin or some other spot.

Third Possibility

The third possibility that began to be considered at that first meeting was some sort of blockade. It might irritate our North Atlantic Treaty allies because many of them are maritime powers sensitive to freedom of the seas. And it might not get at the missiles already in Cuba.

At this first meeting the President and his advisers were not yet clear on what was to be their objective—to get the missiles out of Cuba. Some talked, rather, about getting Premier Castro out.

The meeting produced two immediate decisions. One was to intensify air surveillance of Cuba. The second was that the President should disclose the news about the bases at the time he put in motion the United States response.

The decision to time the announcement with the response necessarily put a tight time framework on the enterprise. To gain as much time as possible in traditionally loose-lipped Washington, the President ordered everyone at the meeting to keep the tightest security. Intelligence data would go only to those with a "need to know." Secretaries and friends would not be told.

Size of Problems Evident

By the end of the first meeting some of the enormous problems of staff work were evident.

The Pentagon had to produce estimates of the cost of various military alternatives—in time and men.

The State Department would begin exploring the chances of support from Latin America and from our European allies, who had often said Cuba was our problem and who had themselves lived for years under the shadow of Soviet bases.

That afternoon at the State Department the "demonologists"—Federal language for Russian experts—were brought into the picture.

Ambassador-at-Large Llewellyn E. Thompson Jr. and Charles E. Bohlen, who was about to leave for Paris to take up the duties of Ambassador there, conferred with Mr. Rusk. Both were former Ambassadors to Moscow.

Adlai E. Stevenson, United States representative at the United Nations, was also brought into the discussions. He was in Washington to talk to a private session of newspaper editors at the State Department. In a similar session the day before, high officials had told the editors that the Government knew of no offensive missiles in Cuba.

Messrs. Thompson, Bohlen and Stevenson joined the earlier conferees at another White House session early in the evening. At 8 P.M. Secretary Rusk went off for a dinner for the Crown Prince of Libya. He met with his aides again at 11:10 P.M.

WED., THURS., Oct. 17, 18

Blockade or Air Strike?

Weeks before, the President had promised Connecticut Democrats to campaign for them Wednesday, Oct. 17. After a meeting with Mr. McCone and Mr. Bundy he took off for speaking dates in Stratford, New Haven and Waterbury. He was gone until about midnight.

In his absence the top-level planning group met at the State Department, in Mr. Ball's conference room, most of the day and night. The meetings were neither formal nor orderly. Men would wander in and out doing jobs. Sandwiches were brought in when needed.

There was much discussion that day of a "surgical operation"—an air strike to take the missiles out of Cuba by force.

Invasion was not considered as a possible first action. It would take too long to mount. Surprise would be impossible. The effect on world opinion was certain to be unfavorable. The Soviet response might rapidly "escalate" the affair.

But the air strike did win significant support. So did a blockade.

Photos Add to Urgency

New photographs coming in from the U-2's added to the urgency of the situation. They provided more evidence of the medium-range missiles at San Cristobal and also showed intermediate (longer) range sites under construction in the Guanajay area between San Cristobal and Havana. It was estimated that intermediate-range sites would be ready for missiles by Dec. 1. Later other intermediate sites were found at Remedios in eastern Cuba.

Dean Acheson, the former Secretary of State, joined in the meetings most of that day. He had been called in that morning by Mr. Rusk.

Mr. Rusk took time out for a dinner at the German Embassy for Foreign Minister Schröder, returning to the meeting afterward. Robert Kennedy and Mr. Sorensen were at the airport to meet the President when he returned.

On Thursday morning the newspapers carried a report that the Defense Department had begun a buildup of air power in the southeastern United States. A Pentagon spokesman called this "an ordinary thing to do" in light of Cuban possession of jet fighters.

Actually, a considerable military deployment was under way—ostensibly under previous orders not connected with the Cuban crisis.

The Navy had long scheduled a Navy-Marine amphibious exercise called Philbriglex-62. By the middle of the week there were 5,000 marines at sea and 40 ships converging on the Caribbean.

The purpose of the exercise was to liberate the mythical "Republican of Vieques" from the rule of a tyrant named Ortsac—Castro spelled backwards.

Eventually, of course, the exercise was canceled, and the ships and planes were used for blockade duty. But it was important to maintain the myth of the exercise as long as possible. Newsmen scheduled to board the ships in Puerto Rico were told that they could not because bad weather had dispersed the fleet.

President Kennedy's official schedule Thursday was an ordinary mixture of the serious and the ceremonial.

Regular Activities Continue

At 9:30 he presented some aviation trophies. At 10 he met with the Cabinet on domestic affairs. At noon he met with a former Japanese Finance Minister, Eifaku Sato. At 5 P.M. he was to meet Soviet Foreign Minister Andrei A. Gromyko. This meeting had been set before the crisis.

Unannounced sessions with the planners in the Cuba crisis were sandwiched into the President's schedule at 11 A.M. and 3 P.M. During the rest of the daylight hours they met without him, again at the State Department.

The absence of the President from these meetings was deliberate. During the whole week he, and sometimes Mr. Rusk and Mr. McNamara, stayed away at times so that their subordinates could speak their minds more freely on the ideas of both "the boss" and their own colleagues.

But at the decision-time meetings, in the White House, it was the President who gave the orders.

"He held everyone under tight control," one official said. "He issued orders like a military officer expecting to be obeyed immediately and to be challenged only on grounds of overriding disagreement."

The meeting of the planners that afternoon was in Secretary Rusk's conference room. It moved the thinking of the group more clearly toward a blockade as opposed to a strike.

Consequences Weighed

The tendency had been in that direction anyway. Those who had spoken for a strike were weighing the consequences of the almost certain casualties among Soviet military personnel.

At 5 P.M. Secretary Rusk and Mr. Thompson left for the White House to join the President's session with Foreign Secretary Gromyko. The meeting lasted 2 hours 15 minutes—and was a strange affair.

Mr. Gromyko repeated the public assurance of Soviet officials that the Soviet effort in Cuba was defensive—and to his warning that any change in that estimate would have grave consequences.

They May Not Have Known

There is still some doubt in the minds of officials whether Mr. Gromyko knew that day the full extent of the Soviet commitment in Cuba. Officials are virtually certain that Soviet Ambassador Anatoly F. Dobrynin, who accompanied him to the White House, did not know.

Why did the President not confront Mr. Gromyko with what he knew? A number of critics of United States policy have suggested that this should have been done, that the Russians should have been given a last chance to draw back.

One reason for not telling Mr. Gromyko, according to the President's advisers, was that the Administration had not yet decided what action to take. Another was the fear that, in the face of a warning, the Russians would not really back off, but would take some evasive action to blunt the effect of the eventual decision.

Mr. Gromyko was jovial with reporters as he came out of the meeting. He said the talk had been "useful, very useful."

The President had asked to see Robert A. Lovett, former Secretary of Defense, the only outsider brought in except for Mr. Acheson. He was briefed by Mr. Bundy during the Gromyko call, then brought upstairs to the President.

Gromyko Comes to Dinner

At 8 o'clock Mr. Gromyko joined Secretary Rusk, Mr. Thompson and others for dinner on the eighth floor of the State Department Building. One floor below—unknown to Mr. Gromyko—the planning group continued its crisis discussions.

When Mr. McCone and Mr. McNamara arrived at the State Department reporters happened to see them and asked whether they were going to the Gromyko dinner. The two said they were.

There was one further security scare that evening, when someone remarked on the vast number of Government limousines parked outside the State Department. Mr. Ball sent all but one into the department's underground garage.

At 9 P.M. nine members of the planning group (they called it "The Think Tank" among themselves at that time, or sometimes "the War Council"; went over to the White House. They all piled into one limousine.

From there Attorney General Kennedy called his deputy, Nicholas deB. Katzenbach, at home and asked him to get to work on the legal basis for a blockade of Cuba.

Emphasis on Legality

Ambassador Thompson had emphasized in the meetings the need for a solid legal basis for any action taken. He said the Russians had a feeling for "legality," and there was general agreement that a good legal case would help with world reaction.

Mr. Katzenbach, a former professor of international law, met at the Justice Department with three department lawyers: Harold F. Reis, Leon Ulman and Richard K. Berg. He did not tell them precisely why they were there; he just said that the situation in Cuba was deteriorating, and that the possibility of a blockade had to be researched.

There was already some legal material in the files on a possible Cuban blockade, done on Attorney General Kennedy's orders. Mr. Katzenbach and the others worked over it until 4 A.M. Saturday.

At the State Department, meanwhile, the Deputy Legal Adviser, Leonard C. Meeker, was doing his own research on blockade law. The Legal Adviser, Abram J. Chayes, was in Paris on a mission to halt Western shipping to Cuba.

The Gromyko dinner ended shortly after midnight. Half a dozen State Department members of the "war council" then had one more meeting on Cuba Friday, Oct. 19.

FRIDAY, OCT. 19

The President had scheduled Friday for political campaigning. He and the "Think Tank" had decided he should stick to the plans, for one thing to avoid arousing suspicions.

The secret had been well kept despite the presence of some clues. It was announced this day, for example, that Secretary McNamara had asked the Joint Chiefs of Staff to stay in Washington for six weeks to consult on "budget planning."

The President was a few minutes late to his plane. His press secretary, Pierre Salinger, explained that he had had a last-minute briefing session with Messrs. Rusk, McNamara and Taylor. The subject was not specified.

Before leaving, the President indicated his approval of the trend of decision toward blockade. All along, the planners spoke of "blockade." The President himself came up later with the word "quarantine."

First Stop is Cleveland

Cleveland was the first campaign stop. The President appeared relaxed. He even told some jokes. He started in Public Square with a greeting to "fellow Democrats, and Republicans who are passing through the square for lunch."

At 10 A.M. in Washington the planners met again at the State Department. Mr. Katzenbach and Mr. Meeker were included for the first time. Each gave a brief statement of his legal views.

They agreed that a resolution by the Organization of American States would provide strong legal support for a blockade. Mr. Katzenbach thought a unilateral order for a blockade could be justified legally if necessary. Mr. Meeker was less certain.

During that meeting there were some second thoughts about the blockade, some renewed interest in an air attack.

The reason was the reading of what the group called a "scenario"— a paper indicating in detail the possible consequences of an action—for the blockade.

Monday Speech Set

One decision was pretty well tied down that morning: the President would speak Monday night. That was the earliest time possible if all necessary steps were to be taken first.

The meeting broke up at noon. Most of the officials stayed at the State Department to do the jobs assigned to them—drafting telegrams, making calls.

Secretary Rusk telephoned Roger Blough of the United States Steel Corporation to cancel a scheduled talk to the Business Council in Hot Springs, Va., that evening. His explanation was "the press of business."

Mr. Bohlen sailed on schedule for Paris at noon. It had been decided that postponing his departure would arouse too much suspicion.

The President left Cleveland just before 2 P.M. He stopped at Springfield, Ill., to lay flowers on Lincoln's tomb.

In Mr. Ball's conference room that afternoon there was a critical session of the "War Council." The issue, again, was strike or blockade.

Attorney General Kennedy argued against a strike on moral grounds. He reminded the group of Pearl Harbor. For the United States to attack a small country like Cuba without warning, he said, would irreparably hurt our reputation in the world—and our own conscience.

The moral argument won general assent. As one official put it later: "A surprise attack would violate our deepest traditions and aspirations. What kind of a country would this be after such an action? What kind of a world."

As had been true all week, there was no pitched battle between opposing groups within the council. All had considered every alternative; they were talking out the merits and demerits with no argumentative commitment to a particular solution on anyone's part.

The blockade proposal was recognized as the one raising the most serious dangers. As recently as Oct. 6 Vice President Johnson had warned that "stopping a Russian ship is an act of war."

Alternatives Kept Alive

By the end of the afternoon meeting the blockade was clearly the indicated answer. But it was decided to do thorough staff work on alternatives, so the President could have everything before him when he decided. Mr. Bundy made it his special duty to keep the alternatives alive.

The President reached Chicago late in the afternoon and went to the Sheraton Blackstone, seemingly enjoying the crowds. One man held a sign about Cuba: "Less profile—More courage."

From Chicago Mr. Kennedy checked with the "War Council" by telephone. It was indicated that he probably should break off campaigning the next day and come home. But the final decision was put off until the next morning.

That evening Mr. Katzenbach called to his office the Defense Department's General Counsel, John T. McNaughton, and Mr. McNamara's Special Assistant, Adam Yarmolinsky. He asked them to start drafting a blockade proclamation.

Mr. Ball kept a speaking date with the board of the Chamber of Commerce.

SATURDAY, OCT. 20

Blockade It Is

At 9:35 A.M. (Central Daylight Time) on Saturday, in the Sheraton Blackstone, Pierre Salinger announced that the President was canceling the rest of his trip and flying back to Washington.

Mr. Salinger had gotten the word from Kenneth O'Donnell, the White House appointments secretary. He explained that Rear Adm. George Burkley, assistant White House physician had found that the President had a slight infection of the upper respiratory tract, with one degree of fever.

The story was true as far as it went—although the cold was not the real reason for the President's return. The newsmen accepted it, and so did Mr. Salinger, who was not at this time in the "need-to-know" group.

Robert Kennedy had stepped out of a "Think Tank" meeting that morning to return a call from the President. It was felt that, once the news broke Monday, it would look strange for the President to have campaigned for two days just before. Besides, the secrecy that was the purpose of fulfilling the campaign plans was already crumbling.

There was tension in Washington. Reporters were beginning to ask questions. One called Mr. Salinger immediately after the President's return and asked point-blank whether there was an emergency. Mr. Salinger said he knew of none.

Mr. Kennedy reached the White House at 1:37 P.M., supposedly to go to bed. Mr. Bundy briefed him. He read a first draft of the proposed speech for Monday evening prepared overnight by Mr. Sorensen. Eventually the speech went through five drafts.

That afternoon upstairs in the Oval Room, the President all but clinched the decision for blockade. He ordered operations to proceed, subject only to a final word from him the next day.

The smell of crisis hung over Washington that evening like the smell of burning leaves. Too many trips had been canceled, too many announcements made for what seemed "good" rather than real reasons.

All over town high officials failed to turn up for dinner parties or else left suddenly, murmuring apologies. Reporters used all their numbers and succeeded only in alerting half the diplomatic corps. After midnight, when they finally reached knowledgeable officials they got: "I can't say anything about anything."

At the Pentagon Mr. Katzenbach, Mr. Chayes, Mr. McNaughton and Mr. Yarmolinsky buttoned up the main points of the blockade proclamation. Just before midnight Mr. Yarmolinsky left for a party he had arranged for his wife's birthday.

At the State Department officials were preparing such things as the approach to the Organization of American States. Mr. Acheson was asked to take the news of the blockade to General de Gaulle and to the North Atlantic Treaty Organization Council.

Alexis Johnson turned out a "master scenario" for the whole government, laying out everything that would have to be done before the President's speech—orders to embassies, ship movements and briefings.

The scheduled hour of the speech, 7 P.M. Monday, was called P hour. The scenario began with 7 P.M. Saturday—"P minus 48."

SUNDAY, OCT. 21

Diplomatic Orchestration

Sunday was a golden fall day in Washington. It was also a day of tremendous activity.

The State Department went on a 24-hour schedule. The Operations Center was alerted for traffic. The communications officers brought in code clerks and telegraphers. All were warned about the need for the tightest security.

Early in the morning secretary Rusk went to see Mr. Sorensen, probably to check on the evolving speech and to make a plea that his people needed it soon to draft other papers.

At 11 A.M. there was a meeting of key officials with the President in the Executive Mansion. The President had wanted certain specific information from certain people. The information confirmed his view on the blockade, and the all-clear signal was given about noon. Early in the afternoon there was a big meeting at the State Department with all the important officials present.

At 2:30 P.M. in the White House the real, statutory National Security Council, with the Office of Emergency Planning represented for the first time, met formally.

Back in Washington, Livingston T. Merchant, former Ambassador to Canada, was called away from a Princeton football weekend. Because his successor had not yet been accredited, he was to go to Ottawa to inform the Canadian Government.

In the State Department 43 letters were drafted for the President's signature to the heads of government of all the alliances around the globe, as well as to Willy Brandt, Mayor of West Berlin. Also drafted was the letter from the President to Premier Khrushchev to be delivered with a copy of his speech.

Instructions to Embassies

In addition, instructions were drafted to 60 embassies concerning delivery of the letters or of the speech itself. All embassies and consulates were warned to take precautions against demonstrations and riots.

The Latin-American nations were to be informed of the plan for a meeting of the Organization of American States Tuesday and given copies of the United States resolution to be introduced. This required work late into the night.

At 9 A.M. the "Think Tank," including Messrs. Rusk, McNamara, Robert Kennedy, Ball, and Alexis Johnson, met in the White House. The National Security Council formally transformed the "tank" group into its own executive committee.

While the meeting was going on, Lawrence F. O'Brien, the President's Congressional liaison, began telephoning 20 leaders of both parties. The President wanted them back in Washington today, Mr. O'Brien told them.

Some could make it by commercial aircraft. Those who couldn't were fetched by Air Force planes. A few got the ride of their lives in jet fighters.

Message to Boggs

Representative Hale Boggs, Democrat of Louisiana, who was fishing in the Gulf of Mexico, got an "mss. in a bottle" dropped from an Air Force plane. Following its instructions, his boat came alongside an off-shore oil rig, and Representative Boggs climbed up to the towering platform. There a helicopter picked him up and took him to the nearest Air Force field.

At noon Mr. Salinger announced that the President would make a speech of the greatest urgency by radio and television at 7 P.M.

At 1 P.M. the President took a quick swim in the White House pool, then lunched in the family dining room and returned to his office at about 2.

There were two moments of consternation:

First, Foreign Secretary Gromyko's departure for Moscow had been held by bad weather in New York. Around noon, the Soviet United Nations mission announced it would soon have an important statement. There was fear the Russians had got wind of the United States plans. A plan was quickly formed to issue a short announcement of the blockade, which would be followed later by the speech. Mr. Salinger called in the microphones and cameras. But the Soviet statement turned out to be Mr. Gromyko's farewell. He took off early in the afternoon.

Second, at one point during the day a Soviet Ilyushin-18, a four-engine turboprop, was spotted heading for Cuba. There was a great to-do over whether it should be ordered away. Only at the last moment, Washington got word that it was headed for Brazil to pick up the remains of the Soviet Ambassador who had drowned the week before.

During the afternoon the State Department called Ambassador Dobrynin, who was in New York to see Mr. Gromyko off, and asked him to come to Mr. Rusk's office at 6 P.M.

MONDAY, OCT. 22

There was frantic activity in the State Department to make sure all embassies had received Sunday's messages. It was discovered that a radio relay station in Nicosia, Cyprus, had blacked out, and that some of the embassies in Africa had not received the message. It was too late to do anything about it, and word was given to the African nations through their embassies here.

McCloy Flies Home

Last-minute changes in the speech were radioed, and then instructions for delivery of the speech and letters to all the foreign governments.

A message went to Gen. Lauris E. Norstad, as NATO Commander in Chief, warning him to be alert for possible trouble in the NATO area.

In Frankfurt John J. McCloy was about to go into a big private business conference when he got a call from Mr. Kennedy. He told the waiting businessmen, "Sorry, boys, I hate to drop names, but the Secretary needs me." He took the next plane home.

In Paris, Mr. Acheson called on President de Gaulle in the afternoon at the Elysee Palace and told him of the President's plans. President de Gaulle, Mr. Acheson reported later, was "splendid." If he resented the unilateral action being taken without prior consultation he did not show it. He listened to Mr. Acheson courteously, asked some pertinent questions and expressed his support of the United States.

At 3 P.M. in Washington, the National Security Council met at the White House. Then the Cabinet met. At 4 P.M., the President greeted the Prime Minister of Uganda, Milton Obote. Forty-five minutes later, when the President escorted Mr. Obote through the swarming news room to his waiting limosine, reporters crowded about him.

"It has been a very interesting day," the President said with the air of a man whose mind was elsewhere.

In front of the White House hundreds of pickets paraded with advice—"Don't chicken this time, Jack," "Cuba can be negotiated," "Peace, Mr. President."

Time for Briefings

It was P-minus two hours and time for the briefings. At 5 P.M. the President and Secretary Rusk laid the photos before the Congressional leaders.

"We have decided to take action," the President told them.

Senator Richard B. Russell, Democrat of Georgia and chairman of the Senate Armed Services Committee, spoke his mind. He thought invasion was the only solution. Blockade was too slow and therefore carried the greater risk. He found support in Senator J. W. Fulbright who, in April, 1961, had unavailingly urged the President not to support an invasion by Cuban refugees.

The President listened without anger, but was not to be dissuaded.

At 6 P.M. Ambassador Dobrynin was affable with newsmen as he entered Mr. Rusk's office.

With Mr. Rusk were Mr. Martin John C. Guthrie, head of the Office of Soviet Affairs, and Helmut Sonnenfeld, a Russian-speaking expert on the Soviet Union.

When Mr. Dobrynin emerged 25 minutes later, the President's speech and letter clutched in his hand, he looked grim and shaken.

"Ask the Secretary," he said when a reporter asked whether there was a crisis. When he was asked to appraise the situation he snapped, "You can judge for yourself."

At 6:15 Under Secretary Ball and Mr. Hilsman, Director of the department's Bureau of Intelligence and Research, briefed 46 allied ambassadors in the State Department's International Conference Room.

In the President's study, as the minute hand moved toward the hour, Mr. Kennedy cast an eye over his speech. A sound of voices came through an open door at one side. The President looked around as if startled. The door was hastily closed. His secretary, Evelyn Lincoln, came in with a brush for a final swipe at his hair. The technicians gave the signal. He was on the air.

The President began with the evidence of the missile sites. He did not blame Cuba for the crisis, but the Soviet Union which, he said, had violated the most solemn assurances of its leaders that only defensive weapons were being sent to Cuba.

And he drew the line with the Soviet Union.

"This secret, swift and extraordinary build-up of Communist missiles —in an area well known to have a special and historical relationship to the United States and the nations of the Western hemisphere is a deliberately provocative and unjustified change in the status quo which cannot be accepted by this country, if our courage and our commitments are ever again to be trusted by either friend or foe."

The President said that he had ordered a quarantine on all such offensive weapons for Cuba and that ships carrying them would be turned back.

Furthermore, he said, the preparation of the missile sites must cease, and if it did not, "further action" would be taken. He was ordering the surveillance continued. Finally, he called upon Chairman Khrushchev to withdraw the weapons already there.

In the State Department the 46 allied ambassadors who had been briefed watched the speech on a large screen.

At 7:30 Mr. Martin gave a further private briefing for the Latin-American Ambassadors in Mr. Ball's office.

At 8 Secretary Rusk and Mr. Hilsman briefed the ambassadors of the so-called neutral nations, including Yugoslavia, in the International Conference room.

At the same hour Mr. Ball and Mr. Chayes, the State Department Legal Adviser, held a large briefing for diplomatic correspondents, and in the Pentagon Secretary McNamara briefed military correspondents. The Secretary of Defense made very clear that "whatever force is required"—even sinking—would be used to prevent ships from trying to run the blockade.

O.A.S. Meeting Requested

Meanwhile the United States had called for the O.A.S. to meet the next day in its highest capacity—as an organ of consultation.

And in New York, Mr. Stevenson delivered a letter to Valerian A. Zorin, head of the Soviet delegation to the United Nations, who was the October President of the Security Council, calling on him to summon an urgent meeting of the Council.

With the letter went a draft resolution calling on the Soviet Union to dismantle and withdraw the missiles under United Nations verification, after which the United States would end the quarantine and the two nations could confer "on measures to remove the existing threat to the security of the Western Hemisphere and the peace of the world."

During the evening Mr. Acheson in Paris had laid before the North Atlantic Treaty Organization Council the reasons for the United States action. He got a courteous, considered hearing. A few questions were asked and general support was expressed by the allies.

TUESDAY, OCT. 23

U.S. Wins Support

Thirteen hours after the President's speech came Moscow's first reaction. On Tuesday at 3 P.M. Moscow time—8 A.M. Eastern daylight time—Tass, the Soviet press agency, began sending out a Government statement. At the same time Foy D. Kohler, the United States Ambassador, was handed the statement at the Foreign Office, together with a letter from Chairman Khrushchev to President Kennedy.

The statement was long and discursive. Accusations against the United States of "unheard of violation of international law," commission of "piracy," and "provocative" acts that might lead to thermonuclear war alternated with tributes to peace, professions of the most humanitarian motives toward Cuba and indignant denials that the missiles were intended for offensive purposes.

Altogether it was interpreted in Washington as betraying an uncertainty that convinced the experts that the Kremlin had been caught off guard and was playing for time to think out its next move. There was an almost immediate feeling that Soviet strategy, whatever its intended thrust, had been checked by the President's challenge.

This feeling grew as reaction came in from European capitals and the drama unfolded at the Organization of American States.

Acheson Flies to Bonn

Prime Minister Macmillan, in the first of what were to become daily calls to the President, gave Mr. Kennedy full support. The Foreign Office straightway issued a statement charging the Soviet Union with "deliberately" threatening the United States and Latin Amercia.

In the morning Mr. Acheson left Paris for Bonn. He and Chancellor Adenauer are old and warm friends, and they had a long session. Later Mr. Acheson talked with Defense Minister Franz Josef Strauss. German support was wholehearted.

In New York, representatives of the other NATO nations said they had instructions to vote for the United States resolution.

The meeting of the Organization of American States began at 9 A.M. and ran into the early evening. Secretary Rusk represented the United States. He offered the resolution to authorize the use of force, individually or collectively, to enforce the blockade. He cited the Rio Pact of 1947.

Although the necessary two-thirds majority was assured, some delegates had not yet received detailed instructions from their governments.

Priorities Arranged

To speed communications, Assistant Secretary Martin made arrangements with the telephone company to get top Government priorities for the Latin-American embassies.

As the meeting progressed, delegates darted back and forth between their seats and the telephones.

A few minutes before 5 P.M. the Council approved the resolution 19 to 0. Emilio Oribe, of Uruguay never got his instructions and abstained. Emilio Sarmiente Carruncho of Bolivia got through to La Paz, but could hear nothing over the bad connection. He took his political life in his hands and voted "Si."

The unanimity of the council, together with the solid support of the NATO allies for the blockade decision, is believed by officials to have surprised the Soviet Union and to have accounted for much of her diplomatic confusion during the week.

During the planning state, no one expected such overwhelming support. Why did the United States get it? In part, officials said, because the reality of missiles that could reach their own countries enabled some Latin American presidents to defy the leftist opinion that had cowed them before.

But in large measure the outcome was credited to Assistant Secretary of State Martin who had organized, drafted, and argued all day and most of the night to round up the vote that would hit Moscow with staggering impact.

The President was prepared to act alone, but he wanted the support of the Organization of American States before issuing the proclamation of a blockade legally based on the Rio Pact. Therefore, the proclamation was held up until after the vote.

In it he declared contraband and prohibited—offensive missiles, their warheads and electronic equipment, and bomber aircraft. He authorized the Navy to stop and search any vessel believed to be carrying contraband to Cuba, to take it into custody if it refused to sail to another port and to use force if necessary.

The blockade would become effective at 10 A.M. the next morning.

At the Pentagon the same evening, Secretary McNamara said 25 Soviet merchant ships were heading toward Cuba, their course unchanged in the last 24 hours. He had sent orders to interdict these and all other ships headed for Cuba the next day.

Under authority granted the President by Congress Oct. 3, Mr. McNamara ordered the tours of duty of all Navy and Marine Corps personnel extended until further notice.

In New York the first round at the Security Council followed a familiar script. Ambassador Zorin countered the American resolution with one calling upon the United States to withdraw the blockade, stop interfering in Cuba's domestic affairs and enter talks with the Soviet Union to normalize the situation.

Mr. Stevenson said the Soviet Union had presented the "world of the Charter" with the most fateful challenge since World War II.

At the White House during the morning, the Executive Committee met with the President, and at the State Department the British, French and West German Ambassadors conferred with United States officials on a possible Soviet countermove against Berlin.

WEDNESDAY, OCT. 24

Soviet Still Hesitates

The blockade went into effect at 10 A.M. Wednesday.

From Moscow that morning came word that the Soviet Government had returned the President's proclamation of a blockade as unacceptable. Soon after the news agencies carried bulletins that Premier Khrushchev had proposed a summit meeting.

The proposal turned out to be a somewhat vague suggestion in a message to Bertrand Russell, the British philosopher and pacifist.

Mr. Khrushchev told Lord Russell—who once advocated dropping nuclear bombs on the Soviet Union if it refused international control of the atom—that he would take no "reckless decision."

The Premier's suggestion brought no response from the President, for officials here looked on it as only another delaying move that offered no real clue to Soviet intentions.

U Thant Offers Proposal

But a proposal that could not be ignored came from an unexpected quarter: U Thant, the Acting Secretary General of the United Nations. He acted largely on his own, but with the urging of the large group of nonaligned nations, whose thought was to draw the nuclear powers apart.

Mr. Thant sent letters to Mr. Kennedy and Mr. Khrushchev urging the suspension for two or three weeks of both the blockade and the arms shipments to Cuba while negotiations were held.

Mr. Khrushchev hastily accepted the proposal, but Washington was displeased and annoyed.

Washington thought the proposal would surely disarm its powerful diplomatic and military initiative and doubted that it could ever regain momentum if negotiations failed, as it was expected they would. The path of negotiation already had been rejected until the Russians agreed to undo their move, until they had dismantled the Cuban bases.

Mr. Thant's proposal was not much sweetened in Washington's view by his subsequent expression that it would be helpful if work on "major military installations" in Cuba were also suspended during negotiations.

Campaigning Dropped

The President met with the Executive Committee during the day and with Congressional leaders who were leaving for home, subject to return on eight hours' notice from the White House. Mr. Kennedy ordered the Cabinet to follow his and the Vice President's example by cancelling all campaigning.

At the State Department, Secretary Rusk met at 3 P.M. with the British, French and West German Ambassadors to keep them posted. In the afternoon, intelligence officials, at Britain's request, reviewed some passages in the speech that Prime Minister Macmillan was to deliver in the House of Commons the next day.

What about work on the missile bases?

To get that information accurately and speedily, the President authorized special low-level reconnaissance missions by Navy P–8U's, flying in groups of four to eight planes, to supplement the high-level photograph of the U–2's. The Navy planes found the work at the bases was continuing unabated.

And what about the blockade?

At about noon, Secretary McNamara said the Communist ship nearest Cuba should make contact with the blockade by about 7:30 P.M. But later in the afternoon, assistant Secretary Arthur Sylvester, the Pentagon press chief, announced that some of the Soviet ships had apparently altered course.

In the first day of the blockade, no contact was made. And that was the day's biggest news.

THURSDAY, OCT. 25

Kennedy's Tough Line

At 8 A.M.—20 hours after the imposition of the blockade—a Navy ship made the first interception of a Soviet ship. It was the oil tanker Bucharest, and it was allowed to proceed to Cuba without search because the Navy was satisfied it carried only petroleum.

Although the day had begun rather auspiciously in low key, tension rapidly mounted as rumors began to circulate that the United States would invade Cuba, or at least bomb the missile sites, if the Soviet Union did not quickly stop construction.

In part this talk was set off by a statement of Representative Boggs to his constituents. "Believe me," he said, "if these missiles are not dismantled, the United States has the power to destroy them, and I assure you this will be done."

The rumors gained impetus with reports of the arrival of Marine contingents in the Florida keys and a continued military build-up there.

Challenge Shown on TV

At the dinner hour and all through the evening, millions of Americans viewed on television the melodramatic challenge of Ambassador Zorin by Mr. Stevenson in the Security Council that afternoon.

Leaning forward and looking directly at the Russian, Mr. Stevenson challenged him to say "yes or no" whether the Soviet Union was placing medium and intermediate range missiles and sites in Cuba.

"I am prepared to wait for my answer until hell freezes over if that is your decision," said Mr. Stevenson. Then: "And I am also prepared to present the evidence in this room."

With that he turned to the blown-up photographs of the missile sites waiting on easels behind him.

While this was great spectator sport, the significant developments of the day were the replies of Chairman Khrushchev and President Kennedy to the Thant appeal for a moratorium and the interpretation of the United States position which Washington officials supplied reporters for guidance.

Thant Gets Replies

Mr. Khrushchev wrote U Thant: "I agree with your proposal, which meets the interests of peace."

The President wrote: "The existing threat was created by the secret introduction of offensive weapons into Cuba, and the answer lies in the removal of such weapons."

But the word from American intelligence sources was that work on the missile bases was continuing at full speed.

In Washington, officials made clear that Mr. Thant's proposal as it stood was unacceptable, even temporarily. The ultimate objective was the removal of the missiles. Nothing else would suffice. And there must be absolute verification. There would be no reliance on relaxation of surveillance. The United States was always willing to talk, but without limitation on its freedom of action.

After the Executive Committee meeting at the White House, all the top State Department officials gathered in Mr. Rusk's office. The mood all around was grim and tough. The next move was up to Moscow.

In his speech to Commons, Prime Minister Macmillan made no concession to criticism of the United States by many Labor party members. He said the Soviet Union had launched "a deliberate adventure designed to test the ability and determination of the United States." In any negotiations, the word of the Soviet Union must be verified, he said.

FRIDAY, OCT. 26

This was the day, with the Kremlin still stalling, that the United States Government began to step up the psychological pressure.

Once again the prelude was deceptive, giving little hint of "the act coming on." Just before 8 A.M. two destroyers that had been tailing a Soviet-chartered freighter of Lebanese registry all night put search parties aboard her without incident. When the search disclosed no contraband, the ship was cleared to proceed to Cuba.

At the usual morning Executive Committee meeting at the White House, Mr. Stevenson was understood to have been instructed to make it unmistakably clear to Mr. Thant that the United States was immovable in its determination to get the missiles out of Cuba. One high official said: "Adlai was down to pick up his Oscar."

In the regular noon briefing, the State Department press officer, Lincoln White, called attention to a sentence in the President's Monday night speech declaring that if the Soviet's offensive military preparations continued, "further action will be justified."

In the afternoon Mr. Salinger said at a White House news conference that the Russians "are rapidly continuing" work on the sites, and showed no intention "to dismantle or discontinue work" on them.

New Intelligence Report

Early in the evening, the White House issued a new intelligence report. In detail it reported the activities of bulldozers and cranes at the intermediate-range missile bases and the refinements over the past few days at the medium-range sites. The Russians, the White House said, were obviously trying to achieve "full operational capability as soon as possible."

The Army moved antiaircraft missiles into Key West. The commander of the Atlantic Fleet, Adm. Robert L. Dennison, said the strengthened Guantanamo Naval Base was now defensible against attack.

Amid reports of imminent military action newsmen asked: "Tomorrow or Monday?" The Pentagon spokesman declined to comment on a statement by Rep. Clement Zablocki, Democrat of Wisconsin, that the United States might soon have to resort to "pinpoint bombing" of the missile bases.

At the Organization of American States headquarters, Latin diplomats were reported in agreement that the resolution authorized the United States to dismantle the bases by force if necessary.

That evening, after talks with Mr. Stevenson and Mr. Zorin, the United Nations chief made public the replies of the President and Mr. Khrushchev to a new appeal. Mr. Thant had asked the Premier to keep Soviet vessels away from the blockade zone for a few days and Mr. Kennedy to order the Navy to avoid confrontation with Soviet ships.

President Presses Point

The two leaders agreed, but the President said that the withdrawal of the military systems was "a matter of great urgency," and he reminded Mr. Thant that the work still went on.

The late editions of many evening newspapers had headlines on possible invasion or bombing.

At the White House officials later had made plain to newsmen that any next step would almost certainly have been an expansion of the blockade rather than an attack.

"Invasion was hardly ever seriously considered," one official stated. Another said that the air-strike possibility did not disappear after the President's first decision, but that considerations of decency and caution had deferred it until a time when it might have been necessary and no longer a surprise.

That time, officials agree, had not arrived Friday night.

But the Kremlin might well have wondered if the time was fast approaching.

At about 9 P.M.—4 A.M. Moscow time—a letter from Premier Khrushchev to the President began to come into the State Department message center from Moscow.

It came in bit by bit as it was translated by the embassy in Moscow. In the department, officials read it eagerly. It was rambling, but the tone seemed conciliatory.

Secretary Rusk was called, and he convened a meeting at about 10 P.M.

Officials waited for a "catch." But it did not come. When the letter was all assembled, officials agreed that Mr. Khrushchev had "climbed down."

Never explicity stated, but embedded in the letter was an offer to withdraw the offensive weapons under United Nations supervision in return for a guarantee that the United States would not invade Cuba.

The letter reached the President at 11 P.M.

He read it with relief. The next morning, after officials had given it further study, a reply would go off.

SATURDAY, OCT. 27

Saturday brought the climax of the crisis, but not the peaceful climax that the Executive Committee expected as it convened to draft a reply to the strange Khrushchev letter.

Suddenly there clattered over the wires a second Khrushchev letter, with the long-awaited catch: The Premier offered to trade his bases in Cuba for the North Atlantic Treaty missile base in Turkey.

It was to be hours before the diplomatic copy of the letter about the Turkey base was actually received at the White House. Which proposal was genuine and which merited a reply?

The second letter was markedly different in tone and style from the previous Khrushchev communications. Had the Premier been overruled? Was he raising the ante? Or was he applying pressure by demanding a higher price if his private proposal was rejected?

These were the questions before the committee as it received news of favorable reaction in many parts of the world to the Turkey-Cuba trade proposal. Such a proposal had already been rejected as unacceptable; though the Turkey missile base had no great military value, it was of great symbolic importance to a stout ally. To bargain Turkey's safety for the greater security of the United States would have meant shocking, and perhaps shaking, the Western alliance.

Conflict Is Disclosed

The conferees drafted a terse White House statement revealing that there now were conflicting Soviet proposals and that there could be no sensible negotiation until work on the missile sites in Cuba had stopped.

Without formally rejecting the Turkey-Cuba deal, the statement made clear that Cuba was a special problem that had to be settled first.

Perhaps time would clear up some of the apparent confusion in Moscow, the conferees decided, but by the time they reconvened at 2:30 P.M. in Mr. Ball's office at the State Department the news was alarming.

Not only had Mr. Khrushchev's diplomacy changed, but his Cuban allies' action also had changed. A U-2 plane was missing off Cuba and presumed lost. Another reconnaissance plane had drawn antiaircraft fire. Premier Fidel Castro was shouting defiance on Cuban television, vowing to shoot down the intruders.

The committee went back to the White House at 4 P.M. so that the President could weigh the evidence of "a widening of Cuban activity." United States surveillance had to continue, the meeting agreed, and if the shooting went on, fighter escorts would have to be provided.

Perhaps the antiaircraft batteries would have to be attacked directly; most were known to be in Cuban hands, but was the President prepared to run the risk of killing Russians?

The group decided to give the Russians a little more time—to gain control over Premier Castro if he had acted alone, to change their minds if they had ordered the shooting.

But there was to be no mistaking United States reaction: The Pentagon warned that it would resist interference with reconnaissance and it called up more than 14,000 air reservists to support the warning.

World Opinion Viewed

The Turkey note had been parried early in the day, but Washington realized that too much of the world's attitude seemed negative. Indirectly, at least, Mr. Khrushchev had admitted now that there were missiles in Cuba, allegedly for the same reason the West had missiles in Turkey. But with the secret Khrushchev letter still before it, the group now tried a diplomatic gamble.

It drafted a new letter to Moscow, all but ignoring the Turkey proposal. The letter tried to make sense of the secret Khrushchev offer and said that if the President had understood the Premier correctly—if he was offering to remove the offensive weapons from Cuba in return for an end of the blockade and a promise that the United States would not invade the island—then it was a deal.

The letter was published and delivered to the Russians at about the same time, 7 P.M. The conferees took an hour's break, from 8 to 9, then reconvened until 10.

One participant recalled that the group sat that evening with a "strong sense that we were coming right down to the wire of another decision—probably more than the public realized." It had no explanation for the conflicting letters from Moscow. Shooting had begun.

No decision was made on the next step, "but we were pretty close," one official reported. The decision might have been to expand the embargo, to keep Soviet petroleum from Cuba. But the possibility of having to knock out hostile antiaircraft batteries on the island was very real and there was doubt about how much longer the crisis could be carefully controlled.

Even that night, none of the officials expected the Cuban showdown to "turn nuclear," as they put it. But they felt that large-scale fighting would probably force Moscow into counteraction elsewhere.

They sat with an over-all confidence in the nation's nuclear superiority over the Soviet Union, but this was little comfort if the Russians chose to go to a war that neither side could win.

The President gravely remarked that evening that it seemed to him to be touch and go, that it could now go "either way."

The return to standard time that night brought the promise of an extra hour's sleep. But it was a troubled sleep.

SUNDAY, OCT. 28

Air of Gloom Lifts

Official Washington awoke to a glorious morning in a dismal mood. But the mood did not last.

A few minutes before 9 A.M., the Moscow radio announced that it would have an important announcement on the hour.

It was another letter from the chairman, a response to the President's letter of the night before. All told, the two men had now exchanged 10 letters—five each way—in seven days. In addition, there had been verbal contact between the sides, at least one meeting between Robert Kennedy and Ambassador Dobrynin, at least one telephone conversation between Mr. Thompson and Mr. Dobrynin. It was almost impossible to keep track of who was telling whom what and when.

The last letter from Mr. Khrushchev said the Premier had ordered work on the bases stopped, the missiles crated and returned to the Soviet Union. Representatives of the United Nations, he promised, would "verify the dismantling."

Accepts Kennedy Pledge

In return, Mr. Khrushchev trusted the President's assurance that there would be no attack, no invasion of Cuba. Going beyond the President's pledge, he added, "not only on the part of the United States, but also on the part of other nations of the Western hemisphere."

At 11 A.M., Secretary Rusk, and presumably some other officials, came to the White House. They stayed an hour. A quick statement was composed. It was to be released immediately while the letter was being transmitted by the embassy in Moscow.

The statement was released at noon and directed at Moscow over Voice of America facilities.

The President welcomed Premier Khrushchev's "statesman-like decision" to dismantle the bases in Cuba and return the offensive weapons to the Soviet Union under verification. This was a "welcome and constructive contribution to peace."

In the afternoon a fuller reply to the Khrushchev letter was drafted. When all of the Khrushchev letter had not arrived by 5 P.M., it was decided to broadcast the reply.

The President said he considered his letter of Saturday and Premier Khrushchev's reply as "firm undertakings" which should be "promptly" carried out. He hoped the necessary measures for United Nations inspection would be taken "at once" so that the United States could lift the quarantine.

There was immense relief in Washington but no sense of jubilation. An armed clash had been avoided. The Premier had agreed to meet United States terms. The immediate crisis had been surmounted. But officials knew that a long road lay ahead full of pitfalls and dangers and arduous negotiation. Time would tell whether the last 15 days would prove to be the great, fortunate turning point in the cold war that the United States hoped for. ✊

26. Boundaries of Presidential Authority

When the President or any other governmental department acts, the legal and constitutional authority necessary to justify the action must be present. The President may derive such authority (1) directly from provisions in the Constitution, such as his power to function as Commander in Chief of the armed forces; or (2) from a congressional law delegating power to him. Important presidential actions have been challenged in the courts in both of these areas on the basis that (1) the President acted beyond powers granted to him by the Constitution or Congress; (2) Congress delegated to the President too much legislative power, which is an incidental, not a primary, function of the executive branch under the Constitution. In adjudicating these cases the courts have been inclined to give to the President greater discretion in the field of foreign affairs than in domestic affairs.

In the following case the issue is whether or not Congress may delegate an essentially legislative power to the President to establish an embargo preventing the sale of arms and munitions in the United States to countries at war in the Chaco (Paraguay and Bolivia) if he finds that such action "may contribute to the reestablishment of peace between those countries." Such an embargo was to be established by proclamation after consultation with other American Republics, and violation was made a crime punishable "by a fine not exceeding $10,000 or by imprisonment not exceeding two years, or both." Such broad delegations of power had been held unconstitutional by the Supreme Court in the past in internal affairs. Would the same rule apply to the President in foreign affairs?

UNITED STATES v. CURTISS-WRIGHT CORP.

299 U.S. 304 (1936)

M<small>R.</small> Justice Sutherland delivered the opinion of the Court, saying in part:

On January 27, 1936, an indictment was returned in the court below, the first count of which charges that appellees, beginning with the 29th day of May, 1934, conspired to sell in the United States certain arms of war, namely fifteen machine guns, to Bolivia, a country then engaged in armed conflict in the Chaco, in violation of the Joint Resolution of Congress approved May 28, 1934, and the provisions of a proclamation issued on the same day by the President of the United States pursuant to authority conferred by #1 of the resolution. . . .

. . . [The appellees, Curtiss-Wright Corp., urge] that the joint resolution effects an invalid delegation of legislative power to the executive. . . .

First. It is contended that by the Joint Resolution, the going into effect and continued operation of the resolution was conditioned (a) upon the President's judgment as to its beneficial effect upon the reestablishment of peace between the countries engaged in armed conflict in the Chaco; (b) upon the making of a proclamation, which was left to his unfettered discretion, thus constituting an attempted substitution of the President's will for that of Congress; (c) upon the making of a proclamation putting an end to the operation of the resolution, which again was left to the President's unfettered discretion; and (d) further, that the extent of its operation in particular cases was subject to limitation and exception by the President, controlled by no standard. In each of these particulars, appellees urge that Congress abdicated its essential functions and delegated them to the Executive.

Whether, if the Joint Resolution had related solely to internal affairs it would be open to the challenge that it constituted an unlawful delegation of legislative power to the Executive, we find it unnecessary to determine. The whole aim of the resolution is to affect a situation entirely external to the United States, and falling within the category of foreign affairs. The determination which we are called to make, therefore, is whether the Joint Resolution, as applied to that situation, is vulnerable to attack under the rule that forbids a delegation of the law-making power. In other words, assuming (but not deciding) that the challenged delegation, if it were confined to internal affairs, would be invalid, may it nevertheless be sustained on the ground that its exclusive aim is to afford a remedy for a hurtful condition within foreign territory?

It will contribute to the elucidation of the question if we first consider the differences between the powers of the federal government in respect of foreign or external affairs and those in respect of domestic or internal affairs. That there are differences between them, and that these differences are fundamental, may not be doubted.

The two classes of powers are different, both in respect of their origin and their nature. The broad statement that the federal government can exercise no powers except those specifically enumerated in the Constitution, and such implied powers as are necessary and proper to carry into effect the enumerated power, is categorically true only in respect of our internal affairs. In that field, the primary purpose of the Constitution was to carve from the general mass of legislative powers *then possessed by the states* such portions as it was thought desirable to vest in the federal government, leaving those not included in the enumeration still in the states. . . . That this doctrine applies only to powers which the states had, is self evident. And since the states severally never possessed international powers, such powers could not have been carved from the mass of state powers but obviously were transmitted to the United States from some other source. During the colonial period, those powers were possessed exclusively by and were entirely under the control of the Crown. . . .

It results that the investment of the federal government with the powers of external sovereignty did not depend upon the affirmative grants of the Constitution. The powers to declare and wage war, to conclude peace, to make treaties, to maintain diplomatic relations with other sovereignties, if they had never been mentioned in the Constitution, would have vested in the federal government as necessary concomitants of nationality. . . .

Not only, as we have shown, is the federal power over external affairs in origin and essential character different from that over internal affairs, but participation in the exercise of the power is significantly limited. In this vast external realm, with its important, complicated, delicate and manifold problems, the President alone has the power to speak or listen as a representative of the nation. He *makes* treaties with the advice and consent of the Senate; but he alone negotiates. Into the field of negotiation the Senate cannot intrude; and Congress itself is powerless to invade it. As Marshall said in his great argument of March 7, 1800, in the House of Representatives, "The President is the sole organ of the nation in its external relations, and its sole representative with foreign nations." . . . The Senate Committee on Foreign Relations at a very early day in our history (February 15, 1816), reported to the Senate, among other things, as follows:

"The President is the constitutional representative of the United States with regard to foreign nations. He manages our concerns with foreign nations and must necessarily be most competent to determine when, how, and upon what subjects negotiation may be urged with the greatest prospect of success. For his conduct he is responsible to the Constitution. The committee consider this responsibility the surest pledge for the faithful discharge of his duty. They think the interference of the Senate in the direction of foreign negotiations calculated to diminish that responsibility and thereby to impair the best security for the national safety. The nature of transactions with foreign nations, moreover, requires caution and unity of design, and their success frequently depends on secrecy and dispatch." . . .

It is important to bear in mind that we are here dealing not alone with an authority vested in the President by an exertion of legislative power, but with such an authority plus the very delicate, plenary and exclusive power of the President as the sole organ of the federal government in the field of international relations—a power which does not require as a basis for its exercise an act of Congress, but which, of course, like every other governmental power, must be exercised in subordination to the applicable provisions of the Constitution. It is quite apparent that if, in the maintenance of our international relations, embarrassment—perhaps serious embarrassment—is to be avoided and success for our aims achieved, congressional legislation which is to be made effective through negotiation and inquiry within the international field must often accord to the President a degree of discretion and freedom from statutory restriction which would not be admissible were domestic affairs alone involved. Moreover, he, not Congress has the better opportunity of knowing the conditions which prevail in foreign countries, and especially is this true in time of war. He has his confidential sources of information. He has his agents in the form of diplomatic, consular and other officials. Secrecy in respect of information gathered by them may be highly necessary, and the premature disclosure of it productive of harmful results. Indeed, so clearly is this true that the first President refused to accede to a request to lay before the House of Representatives the instructions, correspondence and documents relating to the negotiation of the Jay Treaty—a refusal the wisdom of which was recognized by the House itself and has never since been doubted. . . .

When the President is to be authorized by legislation to act in respect of a matter intended to affect a situation in foreign territory, the legislator properly bears in mind the important consideration that the form of the President's action—or, indeed, whether he shall act at all—may well depend, among other things, upon the nature of the confidential information which he has or may thereafter receive, or upon the effect which his action may have upon our foreign relations. This consideration, in connection with what we have already said on the subject, discloses the unwisdom of requiring Congress in this field of governmental power to lay down narrowly defined standards by which the President is to be governed. . . .

In light of the foregoing observations, it is evident that this court should not be in haste to apply a general rule which will have the effect of condemning legislation like that under review as constituting an unlawful delegation of legislative power. The principles which justify such legislation find overwhelming support in the unbroken legislative practice which has prevailed almost from the inception of the national government to the present day. . . .

We deem it unnecessary to consider, seriatim, the several clauses which are said to evidence the unconstitutionality of the joint resolution as involving an unlawful delegation of legislative power. It is enough to summarize by saying that, both upon principle and in accordance with precedent, we conclude there is sufficient warrant for the broad discretion vested in the President to determine whether the enforcement of the statute will have a beneficial effect upon the reestablishment of peace in the affected countries; whether he shall make proclamation to bring the resolution into operation; whether and when the resolution shall cease to operate and to make proclamation accordingly; and to prescribe limitations and exceptions to which the enforcement of the resolution shall be subject. . . .

Reversed. [The District Court had sustained the appellees' contention regarding an unlawful delegation of legislative power.]

Mr. Justice McReynolds dissented.

Although presidential supremacy in foreign affairs is universally acknowledged, his prerogatives in the domestic field are not so clearly defined. There is little doubt that during global war the President can become, to use Rossiter's phrase, a "constitutional dictator." This may be accomplished through direct reliance upon his powers as Commander in Chief or through extensive congressional delegation of power to the President. On the other hand during time of peace or limited war the extent of presidential prerogatives is limited and debatable.

During the Korean war President Truman, having failed to bring about an agreement between the steel companies and the steel workers through reference of their dispute to the Federal Wage Stabilization Board on December 22, 1951, decided to frustrate the announced intentions of the union to strike on April 9 through issuance of Executive Order 10340, which directed the Secretary of Commerce (Sawyer) to take possession of most of the steel mills through government seizure and to operate them. Sawyer issued the necessary orders and the seizure was accomplished. The companies involved sought an immediate temporary injunction to restrain government action in the District Court of the District of Columbia. The District Court issued the preliminary injunction, which was stayed on the same day by the Court of Appeals. On May

3 the Supreme Court, by-passing the Court of Appeals, granted certiorari, and heard argument on May 12. The case was decided June 2, which indicates the speed with which the Supreme Court can act when it considers it necessary. The question to be decided by the Court was whether or not the President, as Commander in Chief and Chief Executive, could constitutionally justify his seizure on the basis that a national defense emergency would be created by a work stoppage in the steel industry.

YOUNGSTOWN SHEET & TUBE CO. v. SAWYER
343 U.S. 579 (1952)

Mr. Justice Black delivered the opinion of the Court, saying in part:

We are asked to decide whether the President was acting within his constitutional power when he issued an order directing the Secretary of Commerce to take possession of and operate most of the Nation's steel mills. The mill owners argue that the President's order amounts to lawmaking, a legislative function which the Constitution has expressly confided to the Congress and not to the President. The Government's position is that the order was made on findings of the President that his action was necessary to avert a national catastrophe which would inevitably result from a stoppage of steel production, and that in meeting this grave emergency the President was acting within the aggregate of his constitutional powers as the Nation's Chief Executive and the Commander in Chief of the Armed Forces of the United States. . . .

The President's power, if any, to issue the order must stem either from an act of Congress or from the Constitution itself. There is no statute that expressly authorizes the President to take possession of property as he did here. Nor is there any act of Congress to which our attention has been directed from which such a power can fairly be implied. Indeed, we do not understand the Government to rely on statutory authorization for this seizure. There are two statutes which do authorize the President to take both personal and real property under certain conditions [the Selective Service Act of 1948 and the Defense Production Act of 1950]. However, the Government admits that these conditions were not met and that the President's order was not rooted in either of the statutes. . . .

Moreover, the use of the seizure technique to solve labor disputes in order to prevent work stoppages was not only unauthorized by any congressional enactment; prior to this controversy, Congress has refused to adopt that method of settling labor disputes. When the Taft-Hartley Act was under consideration in 1947, Congress rejected an amendment which would have authorized such governmental seizures in case of emergency. Apparently it was thought that the technique of seizure, like that of compulsory arbitration, would interfere with the process of collective bargaining. Consequently, the plan Congress adopted in that Act did not provide for seizure under any circumstances. Instead, the plan sought to bring about settlements by use of the customary devices of mediation, conciliation, investigation by boards of inquiry, and public reports. In some instances temporary injunctions were authorized to provide cooling-off periods. All this failing, unions were left free to strike after a secret vote by employees as to whether they wished to accept their employers' final settlement offer.

It is clear that if the President had authority to issue the order he did, it must be found in some provision of the Constitution. And it is not claimed that express constitutional language grants this power to the President. The contention is that presidential power should be implied from the aggregate of his powers under the Constitution. Particular reliance is placed on provisions in Article II which say that "The executive Power shall be vested in a President . . ."; that "he shall take Care that the Laws be faithfully executed"; and that he "shall be Commander in Chief of the Army and Navy of the United States."

The order cannot properly be sustained as an exercise of the President's military power as Commander in Chief of the Armed Forces. The Government attempts to do so by citing a number of cases upholding broad powers in military commanders engaged in day-to-day fighting in a theater of war. Such cases need not concern us here. Even though "theater of war" be an expanding concept, we cannot with faithfulness to our constitutional system hold that the Commander in Chief of the Armed Forces has the ultimate power as such to take possession of private property in order to keep labor disputes from stopping production. This is a job for the Nation's lawmakers, not for its military authorities.

Nor can the seizure order be sustained because of the several constitutional provisions that grant executive power to the President. In the framework of our Constitution, the President's power to see that the laws are faithfully executed refutes the idea that he is to be a lawmaker. The Constitution limits his functions in the lawmaking process to the recommending of laws he thinks wise and the vetoing of laws he thinks bad. And the Constitution is neither silent nor equivocal about who shall make laws which the President is to execute. The first section of the first article says that "All legislative Powers herein granted shall be vested in a Congress of the United States." . . .

The President's order does not direct that a congressional policy be executed in a manner prescribed by Congress—it directs that a presidential policy be executed in a manner prescribed by the President. The preamble of the order itself, like that of many statutes, sets out reasons why the President believes certain policies should be adopted, proclaims these policies as rules of conduct to be followed, and again, like a statute, authorizes a government official to promulgate additional rules and regulations consistent with the policy proclaimed and needed to carry that policy into execution. The power of Congress to adopt such public policies as those proclaimed by the order is beyond question. It can authorize the taking of private property for public use. It can make laws regulating the relationships between employers and employees, prescribing rules designed to settle labor disputes, and fixing wages and working conditions in certain fields of our economy. The Constitution does not subject this lawmaking power of Congress to presidential or military supervision or control.

It is said that other Presidents without congressional authority have taken possession of private business enterprises in order to settle labor disputes. But even if this be true, Congress has not thereby lost its exclusive constitutional authority to make laws necessary and proper to carry out the powers vested by the Constitution "in the Government of the United States, or any Department or Officer thereof."

The Founders of this Nation entrusted the lawmaking power to the Congress alone in both good and bad times. It would do no good to recall the historical event, the fears of power and the hopes for freedom that lay behind their choice. Such a review would but confirm our holding that this seizure order cannot stand.

The judgment of the District Court is affirmed.

Justices Frankfurter, Douglas, Jackson, Burton and Clark wrote separate concurring opinions.

Mr. Chief Justice Vinson, with whom Justices Reed and Minton joined, dissented, saying in part:

The President of the United States directed the Secretary of Commerce to take temporary possession of the Nation's steel mills during the existing emergency because "a work stoppage would immediately jeopardize and imperil our national defense and the defense of those joined

with us in resisting aggression, and would add to the continuing danger
of our soldiers, sailors, and airmen engaged in combat in the field." The
District Court ordered the mills returned to their private owners on the
ground that the President's action was beyond his powers under the
Constitution.

This Court affirms. Some members of the Court are of the view that
the President is without power to act in time of crisis in the absence of
express statutory authorization. Other members of the Court affirm on the
basis of their reading of certain statutes. Because we cannot agree that
affirmation is proper on any ground, and because of the transcending
importance of the questions presented not only in this critical litigation
but also to the powers of the President and of future Presidents to act in
time of crisis, we are compelled to register this dissent.

In passing upon the question of Presidential powers in this case, we
must first consider the context in which those powers were exercised.

Those who suggest that this is a case involving extraordinary powers
should be mindful that these are extraordinary times. A world not yet
recovered from the devastation of World War II has been forced to face
the threat of another and more terrifying global conflict. . . .

A review of executive action demonstrates that our Presidents have
on many occasions exhibited the leadership contemplated by the Framers
when they made the President Commander in Chief, and imposed upon
him the trust to "take Care that the Laws be faithfully executed." With
or without explicit statutory authorization, Presidents have at such times
dealt with national emergencies by acting promptly and resolutely to
enforce legislative programs, at least to save those programs until Congress could act. Congress and the courts have responded to such executive
initiative with consistent approval. . . . [Numerous illustrations of Presidents exercising independent authority to meet national emergencies follow. A few are cited below as examples.]

Without declaration of war, President Lincoln took energetic action
with the outbreak of the War Between the States. He summoned troops
and paid them out of the Treasury without appropriation therefor. He
proclaimed a naval blockade of the Confederacy and seized ships violating
that blockade. Congress, far from denying the validity of these acts, gave
them express approval. The most striking action of President Lincoln
was the Emancipation Proclamation, issued in aid of the successful prosecution of the War Between the States, but wholly without statutory
authority.

In an action furnishing a most apt precedent for this case, President Lincoln without statutory authority directed the seizure of rail and telegraph lines leading to Washington. Many months later, Congress recognized and confirmed the power of the President to seize railroads and telegraph lines and provided criminal penalties for interference with Government operation. This Act did not confer on the President any additional powers of seizure. Congress plainly rejected the view that the President's acts had been without legal sanction until ratified by the legislature. Sponsors of the bill declared that its purpose was only to confirm power which the President already possessed. Opponents insisted a statute authorizing seizure was unnecessary and might even be construed as limiting existing Presidential powers. . . .

During World War I, President Wilson established a War Labor Board without awaiting specific direction by Congress. With William Howard Taft and Frank P. Walsh as co-chairmen, the Board had as its purpose the prevention of strikes and lockouts interfering with the production of goods needed to meet the emergency. Effectiveness of the War Labor Board decision was accomplished by Presidential action, including seizure of industrial plants. Seizure of the Nation's railroads was also ordered by President Wilson [under authority granted by Congress].

Beginning with the Bank Holiday Proclamation and continuing through World War II, executive leadership and initiative were characteristic of President Franklin D. Roosevelt's administration. In 1939, upon the outbreak of war in Europe, the President proclaimed a limited national emergency for the purpose of strengthening our national defense. In May of 1941, the danger from the Axis belligerents having become clear, the President proclaimed "an unlimited national emergency" calling for mobilization of the Nation's defenses to repel aggression. The President took the initiative in strengthening our defenses by acquiring rights from the British Government to establish air bases in exchange for overage destroyers.

In 1941, President Roosevelt acted to protect Iceland from attack by Axis powers, when British forces were withdrawn, by sending our forces to occupy Iceland. Congress was informed of this action on the same day that our forces reached Iceland. The occupation of Iceland was but one of "at least 125 incidents" in our history in which Presidents, "without congressional authorization, and in the absence of a declaration of war, [have] ordered the Armed Forces to take action or maintain positions abroad."

Some six months before Pearl Harbor, a dispute at a single aviation plant at Inglewood, California, interrupted a segment of the production of military aircraft. In spite of the comparative insignificance of this work stoppage to total defense production as contrasted with the complete paralysis now threatened by a shutdown of the entire basic steel industry, and even though our armed forces were not then engaged in combat, President Roosevelt ordered the seizure of the plant "pursuant to the powers vested in [him] by the Constitution and laws of the United States, as President of the United States of America and Commander in Chief of the Army and Navy of the United States." The Attorney General (Jackson) vigorously proclaimed that the President had the moral duty to keep this Nation's defense effort a "going concern." His ringing moral justification was coupled with a legal justification equally well stated:

> "The Presidential proclamation rests upon the aggregate of the Presidential powers derived from the Constitution itself and from statutes enacted by Congress.
>
> "The Constitution lays upon the President the duty 'to take care that the laws be faithfully executed.' Among the laws which he is required to find means to execute are those which direct him to equip an enlarged army, to provide for a strengthened navy, and to protect Government property, to protect those who are engaged in carrying out the business of the Government, and to carry out the provisions of the Lend-Lease Act. For the faithful execution of such laws the President has back of him not only each general law-enforcement power conferred by the various acts of Congress but the aggregate of all such laws plus that wide discretion as to method vested in him by the Constitution for the purpose of executing the laws.
>
> "The Constitution also places on the President the responsibility and vests in him the powers of Commander in Chief of the Army and the Navy. These weapons for the protection of the continued existence of the Nation are placed in his sole command and the implication is clear that he should not allow them to become paralyzed by failure to obtain supplies for which Congress has appropriated the money and which it has directed the President to obtain."

At this time, Senator Connally proposed amending the Selective Training and Service Act to authorize the President to seize any plant where an interruption of production would unduly impede the defense effort. Proponents of the measure in no way implied that the legislation would add to the powers already possessed by the President and the amendment was opposed as unnecessary since the President already had the power. . . .

Meanwhile, and also prior to Pearl Harbor, the President ordered the seizure of a shipbuilding company and an aircraft parts plant. Following the declaration of war, but prior to the Smith-Connally Act of 1943 [similar to the Connally amendment, *supra,* which was not adopted], five additional industrial concerns were seized to avert interruption of needed production. During the same period, the President directed seizure of the Nation's coal mines to remove an obstruction to the effective prosecution of the war. . . .

More recently, President Truman acted to repel aggression by employing our armed forces in Korea. Upon the intervention of the Chinese Communists, the President proclaimed the existence of an unlimited national emergency requiring the speedy build-up of our defense establishment. . . .

This is but a cursory summary of executive leadership. But it amply demonstrates that Presidents have taken prompt action to enforce the laws and protect the country whether or not Congress happened to provide in advance for the particular method of execution. At the minimum, the executive actions reviewed herein sustain the action of the President in this case. And many of the cited examples of Presidential practice go far beyond the extent of power necessary to sustain the President's order to seize the steel mills. The fact that temporary executive seizures of industrial plants to meet an emergency have not been directly tested in this Court furnishes not the slightest suggestion that such actions have been illegal. Rather, the fact that Congress and the Courts have consistently recognized and given their support to such executive action indicates that such a power of seizure has been accepted throughout our history.

History bears out the genius of the Founding Fathers, who created a Government subject to law but not left subject to inertia when vigor and initiative are required.

Focusing now on the situation confronting the President on the night of April 8, 1953, we cannot but conclude that the President was performing his duty under the Constitution to "take Care that the Laws be faithfully executed"—a duty described by President Benjamin Harrison as "the central idea of the office."

The President reported to Congress the morning after the seizure that he acted because a work stoppage in steel production would immediately imperil the safety of the Nation by preventing execution of the legislative programs for procurement of military equipment. And, while a shutdown could be averted by granting the price concessions requested by plaintiffs, granting such concessions would disrupt the price stabilization program also enacted by Congress. Rather than fail to execute either legislative program, the President acted to execute both.

Much of the argument in this case has been directed at straw men. We do not now have before us the case of a President acting solely on the basis of his own notions of the public welfare. Nor is there any question of unlimited executive power in this case. The President himself closed the door to any such claim when he sent his Message to Congress stating his purpose to abide by any action of Congress, whether approving or disapproving his seizure action. Here, the President immediately made sure that Congress was fully informed of the temporary action he had taken only to preserve the legislative programs from destruction until Congress could act.

The absence of a specific statute authorizing seizure of the steel mills as a mode of executing the laws—both the military procurement program and the anti-inflation program—has not until today been thought to prevent the President from executing the laws. Unlike an administrative commission confined to the enforcement of the statute under which it was created, or the head of a department when administering a particular statute, the President is a constitutional officer charged with taking care that a "mass of legislation" be executed. Flexibility as to mode of execution to meet critical situations is a matter of practical necessity. . . .

The diversity of views expressed in the six opinions of the majority, the lack of reference to authoritative precedent, the repeated reliance upon prior dissenting opinions, the complete disregard of the uncontroverted facts showing the gravity of the emergency and the temporary nature of the taking all serve to demonstrate how far afield one must go to affirm the order of the District Court.

The broad executive power granted by Article II to an officer on duty 365 days a year cannot, it is said, be invoked to avert disaster. Instead, the President must confine himself to sending a message to Congress recommending action. Under this messenger-boy concept of the Office, the President cannot even act to preserve legislative programs from destruction so that Congress will have something left to act upon. . . .

Seizure of plaintiff's property is not a pleasant undertaking. Similarly unpleasant to a free country are the draft which disrupts the home and military procurement which causes economic dislocation and compels adoption of price controls, wage stabilization and allocation of materials. The President informed Congress that even a temporary Government operation of plaintiffs' properties was "thoroughly distasteful" to him, but was necessary to prevent immediate paralysis of the mobilization program. Presidents have been in the past, and any man worthy of the Office should be in the future, free to take at least interim action necessary to execute legislative programs essential to survival of the Nation.

As the District Judge stated, this is no time for "timorous" judicial action. But neither is this a time for timorous executive action. Faced with the duty of executing the defense programs which Congress had enacted and the disastrous effects that any stoppage in steel production would have on these programs, the President acted to preserve those programs by seizing the steel mills. There is no question that the possession was other than temporary in character and subject to congressional direction —either approving, disapproving or regulating the manner in which the mills were to be administered and returned to the owners. The President immediately informed Congress of his action and clearly stated his intention to abide by the legislative will. No basis for claims of arbitrary action, unlimited powers or dictatorial usurpation of congressional power appears from the facts of this case. On the contrary, judicial, legislative and executive precedents throughout our history demonstrate that in this case the President acted in full conformity with his duties under the Constitution. Accordingly, we would reverse the order of the District Court. ⚑

CHAPTER SEVEN

Congress

The United States Congress, exercising supreme legislative power, was at the beginning of the nineteenth century the most powerful political institution in the national government. It was feared by the framers of the Constitution, who felt that unless it was closely guarded and limited it would easily dominate both the Presidency and the Supreme Court. Its powers were carefully enumerated, and it was made a bicameral body. This latter provision was not only to secure representation of different interests, but also to limit the power of the legislature, which could not act as swiftly and with such force when hobbled by two houses often working against each other. Congress is still of major importance; however, there is little doubt that its power and prestige have suffered a decline relative to the powers of the President and the Supreme Court, not to mention the increasing power of the vast governmental bureaucracy. This chapter illustrates the basis and nature of congressional power, and the factors influencing the current position of Congress *vis à vis* coordinate government departments.

27. Constitutional Background

Article I, section 1 of the Constitution states that "all legislative powers herein granted shall be vested in a Congress of the United States, which shall consist of a Senate and House of Representatives." Section 8 specifically enumerates congressional powers, and provides that Congress shall nave power "to make all laws which shall be necessary and proper for carrying into execution the foregoing powers, and all other powers vested by this Constitution in the government of the United States, or in any department or officer thereof."

Apart from delineating the powers of Congress Article I provides that the House shall represent the people, and the Senate the states through appointment of members by the state legislatures. The representative function of Congress is written into the Constitution, and at the time of the framing of the Constitution a great deal of discussion was centered upon the question of the nature of representation and what constitutes adequate representation in a national legislative body. Further, relating in part to the question of representation, the framers of the Constitution had to determine what constitutes appropriate tasks for each branch of the legislature, and to what extent certain legislative activities should be within the exclusive or initial jurisdiction of the House or the Senate. All of these questions depended to some extent upon the conceptualization the framers had of the House as representative of popular interests on a short-term basis, and the Senate as a reflection of conservative interests on a long-term basis. The following selection from *The Federalist* indicates the thinking of the framers with regard to the nature and functions of the House of Representatives and the Senate.

FEDERALIST 53

Hamilton or Madison

.. No man can be a competent legislator who does not add to an upright intention and a sound judgment a certain degree of knowledge of the subjects on which he is to legislate. A part of this knowledge may be acquired by means of information, which lie within the compass of men in private, as well as public stations. Another part can only be attained, or at least thoroughly attained, by actual experience in the station which requires the use of it. The period of service ought, therefore, in all such cases, to bear some proportion to the extent of practical knowledge requisite to the due performance of the service. . . .

In a single state the requisite knowledge relates to the existing laws, which are uniform throughout the state, and with which all the citizens are more or less conversant. . . . The great theatre of the United States presents a very different scene. The laws are so far from being uniform that they vary in every state; whilst the public affairs of the union are spread throughout a very extensive region, and are extremely diversified by the local affairs connected with them, and can with difficulty be correctly learnt in any other place than in the central councils, to which a knowledge of them will be brought by the representatives of every part of the empire. Yet some knowledge of the affairs, and even of the laws of all the states, ought to be possessed by the members from each of the states. . . .

A branch of knowledge which belongs to the acquirements of a federal representative, and which has not been mentioned, is that of foreign affairs. In regulating our own commerce he ought to be not only acquainted with the treaties between the United States and other nations, but also with the commercial policy and laws of other nations. He ought not to be altogether ignorant of the law of nations; for that, as far as it is a proper object of municipal legislation, is submitted to the federal government. And although the House of Representatives is not immediately to participate in foreign negotiations and arrangements, yet from the necessary connection between the several branches of public affairs, those particular subjects will frequently deserve attention in the ordinary course of legislation, and will sometimes demand particular legislative sanction and co-operation. Some portion of this knowledge may, no doubt, be acquired in a man's closet; but some of it also can only be acquired to best effect, by a practical attention to the subject, during the period of actual service in the legislature. . . . 📝

FEDERALIST 56

Hamilton or Madison

THE . . . charge against the House of Representatives is, that it will be too small to possess a due knowledge of the interests of its constituents.

As this objection evidently proceeds from a comparison of the proposed number of representatives, with the great extent of the United States, the number of their inhabitants, and the diversity of their interests, without taking into view, at the same time, the circumstances which will distinguish the Congress from other legislative bodies, the best answer that can be given to it, will be a brief explanation of these peculiarities.

It is a sound and important principle that the representative ought to be acquainted with the interests and circumstances of his constituents. But this principle can extend no farther than to those circumstances and interests to which the authority and care of the representative relate. An ignorance of a variety of minute and particular objects, which do not lie within the compass of legislation, is consistent with every attribute necessary to a due performance of the legislative trust. In determining the extent of information required in the exercise of a particular authority, recourse then must be had to the objects within the purview of that authority.

What are to be the objects of federal legislation? Those which are of most importance, and which seem most to require knowledge, are commerce, taxation, and the militia.

A proper regulation of commerce requires much information, as has been elsewhere remarked; but as far as this information relates to the laws, and local situation of each individual state, a very few representatives would be sufficient vehicles of it to the federal councils.

Taxation will consist, in great measure, of duties which will be involved in the regulation of commerce. So far the preceding remark is applicable to this object. As far as it may consist of internal collections, a more diffusive knowledge of the circumstances of the state may be necessary. But will not this also be possessed in sufficient degree by a very few intelligent men, diffusively elected within the state? . . .

With regard to the regulation of the militia there are scarcely any circumstances in reference to which local knowledge can be said to be necessary. . . . The art of war teaches general principles of organization, movement, and discipline, which apply universally.

The attentive reader will discern that the reasoning here used, to prove the sufficiency of a moderate number of representatives, does not, in any respect, contradict what was urged on another occasion, with regard to the extensive information which the representatives ought to possess, and the time that might be necessary for acquiring it. . . . 🖾

FEDERALIST 57

Hamilton or Madison

. . . THE House of Representatives is so constituted as to support in the members an habitual recollection of their dependence on the people. Before the sentiments impressed on their minds by the mode of their elevation, can be effaced by the exercise of power, they will be compelled to anticipate the moment when their power is to cease, when their exercise of it is to be reviewed, and when they must descend to the level from which they were raised; there for ever to remain unless a faithful discharge of their trust shall have established their title to a renewal of it.

I will add, as a . . . circumstance in the situation of the House of Representatives, restraining them from oppressive measures, that they can make no law which will not have its full operation on themselves and their friends, as well as on the great mass of the society. This has always been deemed one of the strongest bonds by which human policy can connect the rulers and the people together. It creates between them that communion of interest, and sympathy of sentiments, of which few governments have furnished examples; but without which every government degenerates into tyranny. If it be asked, what is to restrain the House of Representatives from making legal discriminations in favor of themselves, and a particular class of the society? I answer, the genius of the whole system; the nature of just and constitutional laws; and, above all, the vigilant and manly spirit which actuates the people of America; a spirit which nourishes freedom, and in return is nourished by it.

If this spirit shall ever be so far debased as to tolerate a law not obligatory on the legislature, as well as on the people, the people will be prepared to tolerate anything but liberty.

Such will be the relation between the House of Representatives and their constituents. Duty, gratitude, interest, ambition itself, are the cords by which they will be bound to fidelity and sympathy with the great mass of the people. It is possible that these may all be insufficient to control the caprice and wickedness of men. But are they not all that government will admit, and that human prudence can devise? Are they not the genuine, and the characteristic means, by which republican government provides for the liberty and happiness of the people? . . .

FEDERALIST 58

Hamilton or Madison

. . . In this review of the constitution of the House of Representatives . . . one observation . . . I must be permitted to add . . . as claiming, in my judgment, a very serious attention. It is, that in all legislative assemblies, the greater the number composing them may be, the fewer will be the men who will in fact direct their proceedings. In the first place, the more numerous any assembly may be, of whatever characters composed, the greater is known to be the ascendancy of passion over reason. In the next place, the larger the number, the greater will be the proportion of members of limited information and of weak capacities. Now it is precisely on characters of this description that the eloquence and address of the few are known to act with all their force. In the ancient republics, where the whole body of the people assembled in person, a single orator, or an artful statesman, was generally seen to rule with as complete a sway as if a sceptre had been placed in his single hands. On the same principle, the more multitudinous a representative assembly may be rendered, the more it will partake of the infirmities incident to collective meetings of the people. Ignorance will be the dupe of cunning; and passion the slave of sophistry and declamation. The people can never err more than in supposing, that by multiplying their representatives beyond a certain list, they strengthen the barrier against the government of a few. Experience will for ever admonish them, that, on the contrary, after securing a sufficient number for the purposes of safety, of local information, and of diffusive sympathy with the whole society, they will counteract their own views by every addition to their representatives. The countenance of the government may become more democratic; but the soul that animates it will be more oligarchic. The machine will be enlarged, but the fewer, and often the more secret, will be the springs by which its motions are directed.... ▨

FEDERALIST 62

Hamilton or Madison

Having examined the constitution of the House of Representatives ... I enter next on the examination of the Senate.

The heads under which this member of the government may be considered are—I. The qualifications of senators; II. The appointment of them by the state legislatures; III. The equality of represenation in the Senate; IV. The number of senators, and the term for which they are to be elected; V. The powers vested in the Senate.

I. The qualifications proposed for senators, as distinguished from those of representatives, consist in a more advanced age and a longer period of citizenship. A senator must be thirty years of age at least; as a representative must be twenty-five. And the former must have been a citizen nine years; as seven years are required for the latter. The propriety of these distinctions is explained by the nature of the senatorial trust; which, requiring greater extent of information and stability of character, requires at the same time, that the senator should have reached a period of life most likely to supply these advantages. . . .

II. It is equally unnecessary to dilate on the appointment of senators by the state legislators. Among the various modes which might have been devised for constituting this branch of the government, that which has been proposed by the convention is probably the most congenial with the public opinion. It is recommended by the double advantage of favoring a select appointment, and of giving to the state governments such an agency in the formation of the federal government, as must secure the authority of the former, and may form a convenient link between the two systems.

III. The equality of representation in the Senate is another point, which, being evidently the result of compromise between the opposite pretensions of the large and the small states, does not call for much discussion. If indeed it be right, that among a people thoroughly incorporated into one nation, every district ought to have a *proportional* share in the government: and that among independent and sovereign states bound together by a simple league, the parties, however unequal in size, ought to have an *equal* share in the common councils, it does not appear to be without some reason, that in a compound republic, partaking both of the national and federal character, the government ought to be founded on a mixture of the principles of proportional [as found in the House of Representatives] and equal representation [in the Senate]. . . .

. . . [T]he equal vote allowed to each state, is at once a constitutional recognition of the portion of sovereignty remaining in the individual states, and an instrument for preserving that residuary sovereignty. So far the equality ought to be no less acceptable to the large than to the small states; since they are not less solicitous to guard by every possible expedient against an improper consolidation of the states into one simple republic.

Another advantage accruing from this ingredient in the constitution of the Senate is, the additional impediment it must prove against improper acts of legislation. No law or resolution can now be passed without the concurrence, first, of a majority of the people, and then, of a majority of the states. It must be acknowledged that this complicated check on legislation may, in some instances, be injurious as well as beneficial; and that the peculiar defense which it involves in favor of the smaller states, would be more rational, if any interests common to them, and distinct from those of the other states, would otherwise be exposed to peculiar danger. But as the larger states will always be able, by their power over the supplies, to defeat unreasonable exertions of this prerogative of the lesser states; and as the facility and excess of law-making seem to be the diseases to which our governments are most liable, it is not impossible, that this part of the constitution may be more convenient in practice than it appears to many in contemplation.

IV. The number of senators, and the duration of their appointment, come next to be considered. In order to form an accurate judgment on both these points, it will be proper to inquire into the purposes which are to be answered by the Senate; and, in order to ascertain these, it will be necessary to review the inconveniences which a republic must suffer from the want of such an institution.

First. It is a misfortune incident to republican government, though in a less degree than to other governments, that those who administer it may forget their obligations to their constituents, and prove unfaithful to their important trust. In this point of view, a senate, as a second branch of the legislative assembly, distinct from, and dividing the power with, a first, must be in all cases a salutary check on the government. It doubles the security to the people by requiring the concurrence of two distinct bodies in schemes of usurpation or perfidy, where the ambition or corruption of one would otherwise be sufficient. . . . [A]s the improbability of sinister combinations will be in proportion to the dissimilarity in the genius of the two bodies, it must be politic to distinguish them from each other by every circumstance which will consist with a due harmony in all proper measures, and with the genuine principles of republican government.

Second. The necessity of a senate is not less indicated by the propensity of all single and numerous assemblies, to yield to the impulse of sudden and violent passions, and to be seduced by factious leaders into intemperate and pernicious resolutions. Examples on this subject might be cited without number; and from proceedings within the United States, as well as from the history of other nations. But a position that will not be contradicted need not be proved. All that need be remarked is, that a body which is to correct this infirmity ought itself to be free from it, and consequently ought to be less numerous. It ought, moreover, to possess great firmness, and consequently ought to hold its authority by a tenure of considerable duration.

Third. Another defect to be supplied by a senate lies in a want of due acquaintance with the objects and principles of legislation. It is not possible that an assembly of men, called, for the most part, from pursuits of a private nature, continued in appointments for a short time, and led by no permanent motive to devote the intervals of public occupation to a study of the laws, the affairs, and the comprehensive interests of their country, should, if left wholly to themselves, escape a variety of important errors in the exercise of their legislative trust. . . .

Fourth. The mutability in the public councils, arising from a rapid succession of new members, however qualified they may be, points out, in the strongest manner, the necessity of some stable institution in the government. Every new election in the states is found to change one-half of the representatives. From this change of men must proceed a change of opinions; and from a change of opinions, a change of measures. But a continual change even of good measures is inconsistent with every rule of prudence, and every prospect of success. . . . ✹

FEDERALIST 63

Hamilton or Madison

A *fifth* desideratum, illustrating the utility of a senate, is the want of a due sense of national character. Without a select and stable member of the government, the esteem of foreign powers will not only be forfeited by an unenlightened and variable policy . . . ; but the national councils will not possess that sensibility to the opinion of the world, which is perhaps not less necessary in order to merit, than it is to obtain, its respect and confidence. . . .

I add, as a *sixth* defect, the want in some important cases of a due responsibility in the government to the people, arising from that frequency of elections, which in other cases produces this responsibility. . . .

Responsibility, in order to be reasonable, must be limited to objects within the power of the responsible party, and in order to be effectual, must relate to operations of that power, of which a ready and proper judgment can be formed by the constituents. The objects of government may be divided into two general classes; the one depending on measures, which have singly an immediate and sensible operation; the other depending on a succession of well chosen and well connected measures, which have a gradual and perhaps unobserved operation. The importance of the latter description to the collective and permanent welfare of every country, needs no explanation. And yet it is evident that an assembly elected for so short a term as to be unable to provide more than one or two links in a chain of measures, on which the general welfare may essentially depend, ought not to be answerable for the final result, any more than a steward or tenant, engaged for one year, could be justly made to answer for plans or improvements, which could not be accomplished in less than half a dozen years. Nor is it possible for the people to estimate the *share* of influence, which their annual assemblies may respectively have on events resulting from the mixed transactions of several years. It is sufficiently difficult, at any rate, to preserve a personal responsibility in the members of a *numerous* body, for such acts of the body as have an immediate, detached, and palpable operation on its constituents.

The proper remedy for this defect must be an additional body in the legislative department, which, having sufficient permanency to provide for such objects as require a continued attention, and a train of measures, may be justly and effectually answerable for the attainment of those objects.

Thus far I have considered the circumstances, which point out the necessity of a well constructed senate, only as they relate to the representatives of the people. To a people as little blinded by prejudice, or corrupted by flattery, as those whom I address, I shall not scruple to add, that such an institution may be sometimes necessary, as a defense to the people against their own temporary errors and delusions. As the cool and deliberate sense of the community ought, in all governments, and actually will, in all free governments, ultimately prevail over the views of its rulers; so there are particular moments in public affairs, when the people, stimulated by some irregular passion, or some illicit advantage, or misled by the artful misrepresentations of interested men, may call for measures which they themselves will afterwards be the most ready to lament and condemn. In these critical moments, how salutary will be the interference of some temperate and respectable body of citizens, in order to check the misguided career, and to suspend the blow meditated by the people against themselves, until reason, justice and truth can regain their authority over the public mind? What bitter anguish would not the people of Athens have often avoided, if their government had contained so provident a safeguard against the tyranny of their own passions? Popular liberty might then have escaped the indelible reproach of decreeing to the same citizens the hemlock on one day, and statues on the next.

It may be suggested that a people spread over an extensive region cannot, like the crowded inhabitants of a small district, be subject to the infection of violent passions; or to the danger of combining in the pursuit of unjust measures. I am far from denying that this is a distinction of peculiar importance. I have, on the contrary, endeavored in a former paper to show that it is one of the principal recommendations of a confederated republic. At the same time this advantage ought not to be considered as superseding the use of auxiliary precautions. It may even be remarked that the same extended situation, which will exempt the people of America from some of the dangers incident to lesser republics, will expose them to the inconveniency of remaining for a longer time under the influence of those misrepresentations which the combined industry of interested men may succeed in distributing among them. . . .

28. The Environment of Congressional Decision Making

In *Federalist 51* Madison noted that "A dependence on the people is, no doubt, the primary control on the government." Congress was to respond to local interests in the House of Representatives, and to a broader state-based constituency in the Senate. Congress was to be the primary law-making body. Presumably the views of constituents concerning matters of public policy were to be transmitted through the electoral process to members of Congress. These were to be taken into account by legislators, who would be held responsible at the polls. Congress was to legislate in an environment that would balance the interests of the community. The two-year term of office for members of the House in combination with election by the people was to make them directly and continuously responsive to popular wishes. The passage of the 17th Amendment brought the Senate into this arena of popular control, although its six-year term of office makes it less responsive than the House.

Does Congress today fulfill its constitutional purpose? Is it a deliberative and responsive law-making body? The operation of Congress depends on the forces acting upon it. The following selections deal with the environment of congressional decision making, and in particular the nature of the relationship between Congressmen and their constituents.

OBSERVATIONS OF A FRESHMAN CONGRESSMAN

*Clarence D. Long**

A LETTER from PRAY (Paul Revere Association, Yeomen, Inc.) predicts that the nuclear test ban will end up with "the Russians and Zionists ruling the world, all Christianity wiped out, and all wives, mothers, and daughters in the brothels of Asia, China and India."

George W. ("Wake Up Humanity") Adams demands that I "banish organized religion damned quick lest organized religion banish the world a hell of a lot quicker."

A neighbor wants to know "What are you clowns doing in Washington?" A 13-year-old boy asks me if I have ever taken a bribe. A tired-looking woman timidly seeks help in getting veterans' benefits, since she just learned that her husband, who years ago abandoned her with 10 children, had recently died after living with another woman in Brazil.

This is a tiny sample of the requests, problems and comments that have come to me since January when, after a quarter of a century as a professor, I found myself a freshman again—in the United States Congress.

I was no stranger to Washington. The center of my Maryland seat—Baltimore, Carroll and Hartford Counties—is only one hour from the Capitol City. While professor of economics at the Johns Hopkins University in Baltimore, I had served in advisory capacities in the Administrations of three Presidents and testified before numerous Congressional committees. I had read—and written—books on the operation of government.

Judging Congress

Now, taking inventory, I am impressed at how much I had to learn and what a gap in attitude and experience separates the "Hill" from the rest of Washington. Nowhere is this gap greater than between the attitudes I once had, and now have, concerning the effectiveness of Congress.

Is Congress doing its job? What is its job? How are we to judge its performance? These questions are especially pertinent as a new Administration takes over.

*From *The New York Times,* December 1, 1963. © 1963 by The New York Times Company. Reprinted by permission of the author and The New York Times.

Surely the job of Congress is not just to pass a lot of laws. Many acts suppressing freedom of speech and religion, or giving fat pensions to all over 55, would not entitle Congress to praise for accomplishing a lot. Nor would a law limiting civilian control of the military—passed without hearing or debate—entitle it to credit for getting things done quickly.

Whether Congress is effective depends really on how well it does its job—how many witnesses it hears, how carefully it questions them and listens to them, how responsibly it debates the issues and how wisely it makes up its mind and votes.

On this question of quality there will necessarily be many verdicts. The fact is, there is plenty of everything in the record: brashness, ponderous emptiness, cheapness, stale humor, twisted logic.

But you can also find the classical oratory of George Mahon, the calm judgment of Wilbur Mills, the verbal time-bombs of Wayne Hays, and the good-humored sagacity of the gently powerful Carl Vinson, chairman of my Armed Services Committee.

In the late afternoon, when the quorum calls have brought the members together, and when minds are alerted by parliamentary maneuvering and the approaching vote, the House of Representatives is at its most impressive. Its occasional flashes of wit, of homely erudition, of adroitness, of eloquence to penetrate the mind and move the heart, I have seldom heard surpassed.

But the Congress should be judged neither by its best nor by its worst; it would be a poor service to the truth to maintain that it is as effective as it could be. Few observers, including members, would dispute that Congress could be doing a better job. Why doesn't it?

Rules Held Secondary

Many explanations are offered. Criticism has been directed at the seniority and staffing systems of the committees, at the parliamentary rules and procedures on the floor, at the appropriations process, at conflicts of interest, nepotism, and junketing, at disproportionate representation, campaign financing, and the poll tax.

My own feeling now is that procedures are secondary. If Americans value good Congressmen they can get them under any election procedures. If Congressmen are competent and well-intentioned, they can be effective with any set of rules.

My short stay in Congress has impressed me with three closely related factors that may hamper Congressmen from doing a better job:

The two-year term of House members, which forces them to campaign continually for re-election;

The vast amount of time Congressmen and their staffs must spend on service for their districts;

The modest net salary of Congressmen, which forces many of them to practice law or run businesses on the side, in order to support dual residences and educate their children.

The two-year term of Representatives is one of the briefest in American politics. The Constitutional Convention made it brief deliberately to keep it responsive to the people, and it has certainly had that effect. But has it not overshot its mark?

It was instituted at a time when the average Congressman represented only a few thousand instead of hundreds of thousands of constituents; when Congress met a month or two instead of nearly all year; and when the Federal Government confined its activities to national defense, the excise tax, and a few internal improvements, instead of pervading every aspect of personal and business life and spending a quarter to a third of all the income of the economy.

Considering and voting on laws was in those early days a very part-time job. It is now a very full-time job—actually too big for the most brilliant and well-informed legislator—even if he had full time to devote to it. Yet the two-year term requires that most Congressmen campaign, not just every other year, but literally all the time. The essence of campaigning is personal contact in the home district.

7 Days a Week

My "rubber-chicken" calendar for a not untypical week included the following: Addressed students of three high schools visiting the House floor, veterans groups in two counties, officers club in Army Chemical Center, and civil-defense officials of seven states; attended meeting of 13th District Community Council, and various meetings on urban renewal, alcoholism, and relocation of a post office; attended a bar mitzvah, two bull roasts, and dedication of a school; went to a Democratic club dinner, a political cocktail party and dinner for a visiting Indian industrialist.

This routine—on top of legislative and administrative work—goes on seven days and five nights a week, except in July and August. Holidays are busiest. On July 4, I marched in four parades, smiled at 200,000 people, spoke to 5,000 more in the evening, attended a party, drove 100 miles.

I have discovered—or think I have!—that a Congressman is judged by the overwhelming mass of his constituents on the personal service he gives the home folks and the contracts he brings to his area.

Immigration Trouble

Four times a young constituent tried to enlist in the Army and had been turned down for high blood pressure; yet the Selective Service Board would not reclassify him, and no employer would hire him while he was subject to draft. I arranged for one more physical exam—by this time his blood pressure was *really* high!—and got his classification changed. He just wrote to tell me that he is employed and happy.

A Naval officer fell in love with a girl in South Africa and, having been informed he could bring his fiance to the United States, paid her way to Niagara Falls, Canada. There she was given the sad news that it was all a mistake, no admittance. At my request the State Department cut the red tape and let her in. Shortly afterward I received their wedding announcement.

An elderly woman, ill and living on $25 a week, was pressed for $1,000 arrears in income taxes. I convinced the Internal Revenue Service that squeezing blood out of a turnip was a cinch compared to getting $1,000 from a sick old lady existing on a pittance. Now she can live, if not in luxury, at least at peace.

Not all cases are desperate. A constituent complains that post office trucks wake the neighborhood at 4:30 every morning. A lady begs me to investigate why her young son in Vietnam could get "plenty of whisky but no soap."

And not long ago a 7-year-old girl asked for some dirt from the White House lawn. I sent an assistant across town, instructing him not to knock on the front door—that the President was busy with Alabama! —but to reach through the back fence and dig some dirt into an envelope.

Many requests are important to more than one person, for most Congressmen run for office on an implied pledge to get business and jobs. Although my counties are in sound health, certain key firms in space, electronics and shipbuilding have lost employment. Small firms there, as everywhere, complain of increasing difficulties.

During recent months I have toured plants and offices and talked extensively with management, workers and union leaders. I visited the Government procurement agencies, including Defense, General Services, Space, and Small Business.

These explorations led me in June to set up a Business Desk, to serve as a center of information on defense business and how to obtain it and to put firms and individuals in touch with Government agencies. Major accomplishments have included getting a contract for radiosondes against the opposition of the entire Pennsylvania delegation and successfully upholding the low bidder on a contract for paper butter dishes.

Salary Called Low

This service has brought an enthusiastic response from firms, as well as from workers who benefit from the fuller employment. But this service—and time spent listening to pleas for personal help—is what takes up half of my own energies and two-thirds of those of my excellent staff.

The salary of a Congressman is $22,500 [now $30,000] a year. This will seem ample to many readers; yet I am less well off than I was as a professor.

To begin with, my election left me with bills I had not even known about. (An Alabama Congressman told me his entire first year's salary went to debts from his campaign.) In addition, my salary, before being available to pay those bills, feed my family, and keep two children in college, must first cover a myriad of expenses, partly political and partly Congressional.

There is a durable myth that a Congressman is reimbursed for trips from Washington to home. In actual fact, he is paid for one round trip a year, at 20 cents a mile, and under a law just passed, two additional round trips, at actual expenses, up to 12 cents a mile.

In my case, the total reimbursement amounts to $53 for the year. Since I commute daily my annual expense for car, trains and taxis is a very considerable item.

Expenses Mount

Even Congressmen from distant states commute weekly by train or plane to their districts. A Congressman from Michigan confided that he spent $3,000 for trips last year. Within my district, I drove 3,000 miles a month at my own expense.

A Congressman is allowed $2,400 a year for stationery and supplies. For two offices and ten persons, this covers writing paper, desk supplies, radio tapes, flags donated to schools and patriotic organizations, the telephone in the Congressman's district office, and most expensive, his newsletter.

This year is not over; yet I have spent my entire year's allowance and am in debt to the stationers by $800. As I expand my newsletter circulation—one of the best ways to keep in touch with my large constituency—I shall have to dip further into my own pocket.

Most Congressmen maintain residences in Washington, as well as at home. For this, they get no allowance—only an income tax deduction on what they spend up to $3,000.

A Congressman is under daily pressure to spend on miscellaneous items: luncheons for visitors; chances on "baskets-of-cheer," space in program books of clubs and churches, tickets to dances, dinners and barbecues.

Outside Jobs

Balanced against all these expenses are a few fringe benefits: haircuts at $1.00 including tip, free parking, and a free footlocker valued officially at $21.57 but worth perhaps $12 in downtown Washington stores. Total value, under $200.

As a result of this financial strain, most Congressmen—used to a far higher living standard than I, a former professor—keep a hand in their law practices and businesses. This time and energy they spend on these activities can only be at the expense of what they should be spending on the complicated issues that face them in committee or on the floor. These other commitments account for the substantial membership in the Tuesday–Thursday Club—Congressmen who get to Washington on Tuesday morning and leave Thursday night.

Higher salaries would possibly attract better men to Congress—although I know of nobody who has resigned because of salary. They would certainly reduce moonlighting and give the voter a higher degree of full-time representation. They would also enable us more effectively to eliminate conflict of interest.

If these are some of the rules of practical politics which keep legislators too busy to legislate, what are the prospects of changing them?

So far as the two-year term is concerned; the main obstacle may not be the public—which seems startlingly sympathetic to a longer term—but Congress itself. Between 1789 and 1960 about 120 resolutions introduced in Congress proposed a term longer than two years. Only two of these were reported out of committee; only one was debated on the floor of the House where it was defeated during the 59th Congress—over half a century ago. And if the longer term ever survived the House it would probably lose in the Senate for the very practical reason that Senators would prefer to retain the present system under which a House member can never run for the Senate without losing his job!

As for cutting down on the service function of Congressmen, a far-reaching proposal to delegate service chores has been made by the alert and fertile-minded Rep. Henry Reuss of Wisconsin, who believes Congress should adapt the Scandinavian institution of the *ombudsman*. This special administrator is appointed by the legislature to handle constituent complaints concerning the executive branch. Germany took up the idea in 1957 as a channel for complaints by members of the armed forces and Great Britain has considered its establishment.

Would this system work in the United States? I somehow doubt it.

Power of a Vote

First, Congressmen would scarcely abandon the one function which has been demonstrated to be the most effective means of getting re-elected.

Second, the main reason a Congressman can get things done is that he has a vote. The Defense Department will listen to me when I ask for justice for an enlisted man or an access road for Aberdeen Proving Ground, because my vote may someday be critical on a $2-billion military construction bill or a $1-billion pay raise. I can't picture an appointed bureaucrat getting that kind of attention.

Third, what might work for a small, closely knit nation will scarcely fit the needs of a continent of 200 million, composed of widely diverse economic, geographic and ethnic interests. People write their Congressmen because they want special attention to their peculiar needs which a huge, complex, indifferent bureaucracy never seems to give.

A Congressman can do a lot for the ordinary fellow because he is a Congressman. Separate the service from the office and I suspect it won't get done.

Lips vs. Heart

What are the prospects for raising salaries high enough to sustain full-time legislating? Congress can set its pay scales at anything it likes, subject to Presidential veto. Yet, currently, the President, the American Bar Association, and many others are urging Congress to raise its pay by at least $10,000 to $32,500; a bill to accomplish this is in the hands of the House Rules Committee, but still Congress drags its feet!

Every Congressman I have talked to wants the raise—some desperately. But many will hesitate to vote for it, and some are committed to vote against it. As one Congressman told the President when the subject came up: "My lips say 'No, No,' but my heart says 'Yes, Yes'!"

Most such Congressmen have rural constituencies unacquainted with the dis-economies of large-city living in general and of Washington in particular. And every Congressman hears from letter-writers who hold firmly to the philosophy that the only good Congressman is a broke one.

Function of Congress

This Congressman, it is plain, sees no real prospect of lasting mitigation of the working conditions that may reduce the effectiveness of Congress.

But do they have such a deleterious effect?

The answer to this depends on your views as to what is the function of a Congressman. On this there are two extreme views. One view—mine in my days of innocence!—is that it is to pass good laws. The other view—held by the old-time politician—is that it is to survive, by representing constituents, giving them what they want, and staying out of trouble.

Both views are unsound. The first is naive, the second cynical. Neither would require very special skill. If our problem were to pass a logically consistent legislative program without reference to popular consent, it would be easy to assemble half a thousand experts many times as learned as any Congress ever elected. But this would be the Platonian rule of "philosopher-kings," not a democracy which rules with public consent.

Role of Congressman

In an oligarchy of experts, wisdom is ultimately corrupted by power. On the other hand, in a crude democracy, power is dispersed, to the endless frustration of the expert.

Here seems to be the ideal role of the Congressman: To represent his constituency, by knowing its needs and aspirations—at the same time inspiring it to something better. Both functions—to represent and to lead —are indispensable if a democracy of ordinary humans is to survive scientific revolutions every decade.

The one requires the Congressman to keep close to his constituency. The other requires him to know what goes on, in economics, in science, and in law. No Congressman is capable of all this, but a surprising number attempt it and a few come amazingly close.

This small band could be enlarged if the public would support better working conditions for Congressmen. Since it is not likely to do this very soon or very materially, Congress will continue to be less than fully effective as a purely legislative body.

In adding up the score, however, let us put some of the blame on the public which makes the rules of practical politics, not entirely on the Congressman who has to live with them. And why shouldn't the critics of Congress-as-an-institution add the vital service function of Congress to its legislative one in deciding whether it gets a passing mark? ▨

The preceding selection illustrates the extent to which Congressmen must involve themselves in activities that do not relate directly to lawmaking. In fact, service to constituents in the alleviation of individual grievances is one of the most important functions of Congress today. Re-election does not depend so much upon the legislative activities of the Congressman, but upon his actions in behalf of constituents. In the legislative field, the question remains: To what extent do constituents influence Congressmen in the legislative process? The following selection presents the findings of an empirical study dealing with this question.

CONSTITUENCY INFLUENCE IN CONGRESS

*Warren E. Miller and Donald E. Stokes**

Substantial constituency influence over the lower house of Congress is commonly thought to be both a normative principle and a factual truth of American government. From their draft constitution we may assume the Founding Fathers expected it, and many political scientists feel, regretfully, that the Framers' wish has come all too true. Nevertheless, much of the evidence of constituency control rests on inference. The fact that our House of Representatives, especially by comparison with the House of Commons, has irregular party voting does not of itself indicate that Congressmen deviate from party in response to local pressure. And even more, the fact that many Congressmen *feel* pressure from home does not of itself establish that the local constituency is performing any of the acts that a reasonable definition of control would imply.

I. Constituency Control in the Normative Theory of Representation

Control by the local constituency is at one pole of *both* the great normative controversies about representation that have arisen in modern times. It is generally recognized that constituency control is opposite to

* Reprinted from *The American Political Science Review* (March 1963) by permission of The American Political Science Association and the authors.

the conception of representation associated with Edmund Burke. Burke wanted the representative to serve the constituency's *interest* but not its *will*, and the extent to which the representative should be compelled by electoral sanctions to follow the "mandate" of his constituents has been at the heart of the ensuing controversy as it has continued for a century and a half.

Constituency control also is opposite to the conception of government by responsible national parties. This is widely seen, yet the point is rarely connected with normative discussions of representation. Indeed, it is remarkable how little attention has been given to the model of representation implicit in the doctrine of a "responsible two-party system." When the subject of representation is broached among political scientists the classical argument between Burke and his opponents is likely to come at once to mind. So great is Burke's influence that the antithesis he proposed still provides the categories of thought used in contemporary treatments of representation despite the fact that many students of politics today would advocate a relationship between representative and constituency that fits *neither* position of the mandate-independence controversy.

The conception of representation implicit in the doctrine of responsible parties shares the idea of popular control with the instructed-delegate model. Both are versions of popular sovereignty. But "the people" of the responsible two-party system are conceived in terms of a national rather than a local constituency. Candidates for legislative office appeal to the electorate in terms of a *national* party program and leadership, to which, if elected, they will be committed. Expressions of policy preference by the local district are reduced to endorsements of one or another of these programs, and the local district retains only the arithmetical significance that whichever party can rally to its program the greater number of supporters in the district will control its legislative seat.

No one tradition of representation has entirely dominated American practice. Elements of the Burkean, instructed-delegate, and responsible party models can all be found in our political life. Yet if the American system has elements of all three, a good deal depends on how they are combined. Especially critical is the question whether different models of representation apply to different public issues. Is the saliency of legislative action to the public so different in quality and degree on different issues that the legislator is subject to very different constraints from his constituency? Does the legislator have a single generalized mode of response to his constituency that is rooted in a normative belief about the representative's role or does the same legislator respond to his constituency differently on different issues? More evidence is needed on matters so fundamental to our system.

II. An Empirical Study of Representation

To extend what we know of representation in the American Congress the Survey Research Center of The University of Michigan interviewed the incumbent Congressman, his nonincumbent opponent (if any), and a sample of constituents in each of 116 congressional districts, which were themselves a probability sample of all districts. These interviews, conducted immediately after the congressional election of 1958, explored a wide range of attitudes and perceptions held by the individuals who play the reciprocal roles of the representative relation in national government. The distinguishing feature of this research is, of course, that it sought direct information from both constituent and legislator (actual and aspiring). To this fund of comparative interview data has been added information about the roll call votes of our sample of Congressmen and the political and social characteristics of the districts they represent.

Many students of politics, with excellent reason, have been sensitive to possible ties between representative and constituent that have little to do with issues of public policy. For example, ethnic identifications may cement a legislator in the affections of his district, whatever (within limits) his stands on issues. And many Congressmen keep their tenure of office secure by skillful provision of district benefits ranging from free literature to major federal projects. In the full study of which this analysis is part we have explored several bases of constituency support that have little to do with policy issues. Nevertheless, the question how the representative should make up his mind on legislative issues is what the classical arguments over representation are all about, and we have given a central place to a comparison of the policy preferences of constituents and Representatives and to a causal analysis of the relation between the two.

In view of the electorate's scanty information about government it was not at all clear in advance that such a comparison could be made. Some of the more buoyant advocates of popular sovereignty have regarded the citizen as a kind of kibitzer who looks over the shoulder of his representative at the legislative game. Kibitzer and player may disagree as to which card should be played, but they were at least thought to share a common understanding of what the alternatives are.

No one familiar with the findings of research on mass electorates could accept this view of the citizen. Far from looking over the shoulder of their Congressmen at the legislative game, most Americans are almost totally uninformed about legislative issues in Washington. At best the average citizen may be said to have some general ideas about how the country should be run, which he is able to use in responding to particular questions about what the government ought to do. For example, survey studies have shown that most people have a general (though differing) conception of how far government should go to achieve social and economic welfare objectives and that these convictions fix their response to various particular questions about actions government might take.

What makes it possible to compare the policy preferences of constituents and Representatives despite the public's low awareness of legislative affairs is the fact that Congressmen themselves respond to many issues in terms of fairly broad evaluative dimensions. Undoubtedly policy alternatives are judged in the executive agencies and the specialized committees of the Congress by criteria that are relatively complex and specific to the policies at issue. But a good deal of evidence goes to show that when proposals come before the House as a whole they are judged on the basis of more general evaluative dimensions. For example, most Congressmen, too, seem to have a general conception of how far government should go in the area of domestic social and economic welfare, and these general positions apparently orient their roll call votes on a number of particular social welfare issues.

It follows that such a broad evaluative dimension can be used to compare the policy preferences of constituents and Representatives despite the low state of the public's information about politics. In this study three such dimensions have been drawn from our voter interviews and from congressional interviews and roll call records. As suggested above, one of these has to do with approval of government action in the social welfare field, the primary domestic issue of the New Deal-Fair Deal (and New Frontier) eras. A second dimension has to do with support for American involvement in foreign affairs, a latter-day version of the isolationist-internationalist continuum. A third dimension has to do with approval of federal action to protect the civil rights of Negroes.

Because our research focused on these three dimensions, our analysis of constituency influence is limited to these areas of policy. No point has been more energetically or usefully made by those who have sought to clarify the concepts of power and influence than the necessity of specifying the acts *with respect to which* one actor has power or influence or control over another. Therefore, the scope or range of influence for our analysis is the collection of legislative issues falling within our three policy domains. We are not able to say how much control the local constituency may or may not have over *all* actions of its Representative, and there may well be pork-barrel issues or other matters of peculiar relevance to the district on which the relation of Congressman to constituency is quite distinctive. However, few observers of contemporary politics would regard the issues of government provision of social and economic welfare, of American involvement in world affairs, and of federal action in behalf of the Negro as constituting a trivial range of action. Indeed, these domains together include most of the great issues that have come before Congress in recent years. . . .

III. The Conditions of Constituency Influence

Broadly speaking, the constituency can control the policy actions of the Representative in two alternative ways. The first of these is for the district to choose a Representative who so shares its views that in following his own convictions he does his constituents' will. In this case district opinion and the Congressman's actions are connected through the Representative's own policy attitudes. The second means of constituency control is for the Congressman to follow his (at least tolerably accurate) perceptions of district attitude in order to win re-election. In this case constituency opinion and the Congressman's actions are connected through his perception of what the district wants.

These two paths of constituency control are presented schematically in Figure I. As the figure suggests, each path has two steps, one connecting the constituency's attitude with an "intervening" attitude or perception, the other connecting this attitude or perception with the Representative's roll call behavior. Out of respect for the processes by which the human actor achieves cognitive congruence we have also drawn arrows between

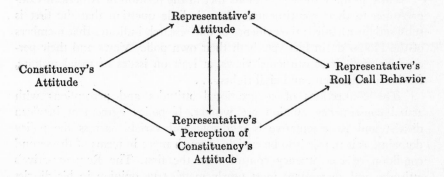

FIGURE I. Connections between a constituency's attitude and its Representative's roll call behavior

the two intervening factors, since the Congressman probably tends to see his district as having the same opinion as his own and also tends, over time, to bring his own opinion into line with the district's. The inclusion of these arrows calls attention to two other possible influence paths, each consisting of *three* steps, although these additional paths will turn out to be of relatively slight importance empirically.

Neither of the main influence paths of Figure I will connect the final roll call vote to the constituency's views if either of its steps is blocked. From this, two necessary conditions of constituency influence can be stated: *first*, the Representative's votes in the House must agree substantially with his own policy views or his perceptions of the district's views, and not be determined entirely by other influences to which the Congressman is exposed; and, *second*, the attitudes or perceptions governing the Representative's acts must correspond, at least imperfectly, to the district's actual opinions. It would be difficult to describe the relation of constituency to Representative as one of control unless these conditions are met.

Yet these two requirements are not sufficient to assure control. A *third* condition must also be satisfied: the constituency must in some measure take the policy views of candidates into account in choosing a Representative. If it does not, agreement between district and Congressman may arise for reasons that cannot rationally be brought within the idea of control. For example, such agreement may simply reflect the fact that a Representative drawn from a given area is likely, by pure statistical probability, to share its dominant values, without his acceptance or rejection of these ever having been a matter of consequence to his electors.

IV. Evidence of Control: Congressional Attitudes and Perceptions

How well are these conditions met in the relation of American Congressmen to their constituents? There is little question that the first is substantially satisfied; the evidence of our research indicates that members of the House do in fact vote both their own policy views and their perceptions of their constituents' views, at least on issues of social welfare, foreign involvement, and civil rights. . . .

The connections of congressional attitudes and perceptions with actual constituency opinion are weaker. If policy agreement between district and Representative is moderate and variable across the policy domains, as it is, this is to be explained much more in terms of the second condition of constituency control than the first. The Representative's attitudes and perceptions most nearly match true opinion in his district on the issues of Negro rights. . . . [See Table I]

TABLE I. Correlations of Constituency Attitudes

Policy domain	Correlation of constituency attitude with	
	Representative's perception of constituency attitude	Representative's own attitude
Social welfare	.17	.21
Foreign involvement	.19	.06
Civil rights	.63	.39

V. Evidence of Control: Electoral Behavior

Of the three conditions of constituency influence, the requirement that the electorate take account of the policy positions of the candidates is the hardest to match with empirical evidence. Indeed, given the limited information the average voter carries to the polls, the public might be thought incompetent to perform any task of appraisal. Of constituents living in congressional districts where there was a contest between a Republican and a Democrat in 1958, less than one in five said they had read or heard something about both candidates, and well over half conceded they had read or heard nothing about either. And these proportions are not much better when they are based only on the part of the sample, not much more than half, that reported voting for Congress in 1958. The extent of awareness of the candidates among voters is indicated in Table II. As the table shows, even of the portion of the public that was sufficiently interested to vote, almost half had read or heard nothing about either candidate.

Just how low a hurdle our respondents had to clear in saying they had read or heard something about a candidate is indicated by detailed qualitative analysis of the information constituents *were* able to associate with congressional candidates. Except in rare cases, what the voters "knew" was confined to diffuse evaluative judgments about the candidate: "he's a good man," "he understands the problems," and so forth. Of detailed information about policy stands not more than a chemical trace was found. Among the comments about the candidates given in

TABLE II. Awareness of Congressional Candidates Among Voters, 1958

		Read or heard something about incumbent[a]		
		Yes	No	
Read or heard	Yes	24	5	29
something about				
non-incumbent	No	25	46	71
		49	51	100%

[a] In order to include all districts where the House seat was contested in 1958 this table retains ten constituencies in which the incumbent Congressman did not seek re-election. Candidates of the retiring incumbent's party in these districts are treated here as if they were incumbents. Were these figures to be calculated only for constituencies in which an incumbent sought re-election, no entry in this four-fold table would differ from that given by more than two percent.

response to an extended series of free-answer questions, less than two percent had to do with stands in our three policy domains; indeed, only about three comments in every hundred had to do with legislative issues of *any* description.

This evidence that the behavior of the electorate is largely unaffected by knowledge of the policy positions of the candidates is complemented by evidence about the forces that *do* shape the voters' choices among congressional candidates. The primary basis of voting in American congressional elections is identification with party. In 1958 only one vote in twenty was cast by persons without any sort of party loyalty. And among those who did have a party identification, only one in ten voted against their party. As a result, something like 84 percent of the vote that year was cast by party identifiers voting their usual party line. What is more, traditional party voting is seldom connected with current legislative issues. As the party loyalists in a nationwide sample of voters told us what they liked and disliked about the parties in 1958, only a small fraction of the comments (about 15 per cent) dealt with current issues of public policy.

Yet the idea of reward or punishment at the polls for legislative stands is familiar to members of Congress, who feel that they and their records are quite visible to their constituents. Of our sample of Congressmen who were opposed for re-election in 1958, more than four-fifths said the outcome in their districts had been strongly influenced by the electorate's response to their records and personal standing. Indeed, this belief is clear enough to present a notable contradiction: Congressmen feel that their individual legislative actions may have considerable impact on the electorate, yet some simple facts about the Representative's salience to his constituents imply that this could hardly be true.

In some measure this contradiction is to be explained by the tendency of Congressmen to overestimate their visibility to the local public, a tendency that reflects the difficulties of the Representative in forming a correct judgment of constituent opinion. The communication most Congressmen have with their districts inevitably puts them in touch with organized groups and with individuals who are relatively well informed about politics. The Representative knows his constituents mostly from dealing with people who *do* write letters, who *will* attend meetings, who *have* an interest in his legislative stands. As a result, his sample of contacts with a constituency of several hundred thousand people is heavily biased: even the contacts he apparently makes at random are likely to be with people who grossly over-represent the degree of political information and interest in the constituency as a whole.

But the contradiction is also to be explained by several aspects of the Representative's electoral situation that are of great importance to the question of constituency influence. The first of these is implicit in what has already been said. Because of the pervasive effects of party loyalties, no candidate for Congress starts from scratch in putting together an electoral majority. The Congressman is a dealer in increments and margins. He starts with a stratum of hardened party voters, and if the stratum is broad enough he can have a measurable influence on his chance of survival simply by attracting a small additional element of the electorate—or by not losing a larger one. Therefore, his record may have a very real bearing on his electoral success or failure without most of his constituents ever knowing what that record is.

Second, the relation of Congressman to voter is not a simple bilateral one but is complicated by the presence of all manner of intermediaries: the local party, economic interests, the news media, racial and nationality organizations, and so forth. Such is the lore of American politics, as it is known to any political scientist. Very often the Representative reaches the mass public through these mediating agencies, and the information about himself and his record may be considerably transformed as it diffuses out to the electorate in two or more stages. As a result, the public

—or parts of it—may get simple positive or negative cues about the Congressman which were provoked by his legislative actions but which no longer have a recognizable issue content.

Third, for most Congressmen most of the time the electorate's sanctions are potential rather than actual. Particularly the Representative from a safe district may feel his proper legislative strategy is to avoid giving opponents in his own party or outside of it material they can use against him. As the Congressman pursues this strategy he may write a legislative record that never becomes very well known to his constituents; if it doesn't win votes, neither will it lose any. This is clearly the situation of most southern Congressmen in dealing with the issue of Negro rights. By voting correctly on this issue they are unlikely to increase their visibility to constituents. Nevertheless, the fact of constituency influence, backed by potential sanctions at the polls, is real enough.

That these potential sanctions are all too real is best illustrated in the election of 1958 by the reprisal against Representative Brooks Hays in Arkansas' Fifth District. Although the perception of Congressman Hays as too moderate on civil rights resulted more from his service as intermediary between the White House and Governor Faubus in the Little Rock school crisis than from his record in the House, the victory of Dale Alford as a write-in candidate was a striking reminder of what can happen to a Congressman who gives his foes a powerful issue to use against him. The extraordinary involvement of the public in this race can be seen by comparing how well the candidates were known in this constituency with the awareness of the candidates shown by Table II above for the country as a whole. As Table III indicates, not a single voter in our sample of Arkansas' Fifth District was unaware of either candi-

TABLE III.   Awareness of Congressional Candidates Among Voters in
Arkansas Fifth District, 1958

		Read or heard something about Hays		
		Yes	No	
Read or heard	Yes	100	0	100
something about				
Alford	No	0	0	0
		100	0	100%

date. What is more, these interviews show that Hays was regarded both by his supporters and his opponents as more moderate than Alford on civil rights and that this perception brought his defeat. In some measure, what happened in Little Rock in 1958 can happen anywhere, and our Congressmen ought not to be entirely disbelieved in what they say about their impact at the polls. Indeed, they may be under genuine pressure from the voters even while they are the forgotten men of national elections.

VI. Conclusion

Therefore, although the conditions of constituency influence are not equally satisfied, they are met well enough to give the local constituency a measure of control over the actions of its Representatives. Best satisfied is the requirement about motivational influences on the Congressman: our evidence shows that the Representative's roll call behavior is strongly influenced by his own policy preferences and by his perception of preferences held by the constituency. However, the conditions of influence that presuppose effective communication between Congressman and district are much less well met. The Representative has very imperfect information about the issue preferences of his constituency, and the constituency's awareness of the policy stands of the Representative ordinarily is slight.

The findings of this analysis heavily underscore the fact that no single tradition of representation fully accords with the realities of American legislative politics. The American system *is* a mixture, to which the Burkean, instructed-delegate, and responsible-party models all can be said to have contributed elements. Moreover, variations in the representative relation are most likely to occur as we move from one policy domain to another. No single, generalized configuration of attitudes and perceptions links Representative with constituency but rather several distinct patterns, and which of them is invoked depends very much on the issue involved.

The issue domain in which the relation of Congressman to constituency most nearly conforms to the instructed-delegate model is that of civil rights. This conclusion is supported by the importance of the influence-path passing through the Representative's perception of district opinion, although even in this domain the sense in which the constituency may be said to take the position of the candidate into account in reaching its electoral judgment should be carefully qualified.

The representative relation conforms most closely to the responsible-party model in the domain of social welfare. In this issue area, the arena of partisan conflict for a generation, the party symbol helps both constituency and Representative in the difficult process of communication between them. On the one hand, because Republican and Democrat voters tend to differ in what they would have government do, the Representative has some guide to district opinion simply by looking at the partisan division of the vote. On the other hand, because the two parties tend to recruit candidates who differ on the social welfare role of government, the constituency can infer the candidates' position with more than random accuracy from their party affiliation, even though what the constituency has learned directly about these stands is almost nothing. How faithful the representation of social welfare views is to the responsible-party model should not be exaggerated. Even in this policy domain, American practice departs widely from an ideal conception of party government. But in this domain, more than any other, political conflict has become a conflict of national parties in which constituency and Representative are known to each other primarily by their party association.

It would be too pat to say that the domain of foreign involvement conforms to the third model of representation, the conception promoted by Edmund Burke. Clearly it does in the sense that the Congressman looks elsewhere than to his district in making up his mind on foreign issues. However, the reliance he puts on the President and the Administration suggests that the calculation of where the public interest lies is often passed to the Executive on matters of foreign policy. Ironically, legislative initiative in foreign affairs has fallen victim to the very difficulties of gathering and appraising information that led Burke to argue that Parliament rather than the public ought to hold the power of decision. The background information and predictive skills that Burke thought the people lacked are held primarily by the modern Executive. As a result, the present role of the legislature in foreign affairs bears some resemblance to the role that Burke had in mind for the elitist, highly restricted *electorate* of his own day. 🢒

29. Congress and the Committee System

In 1885 Woodrow Wilson was able to state categorically, in his famous work *Congressional Government,* that "the leaders of the House are the chairmen of the principal Standing Committees. Indeed, to be exactly accurate, the House has as many leaders as there are subjects of legislation; for there are as many Standing Committees as there are leading classes of legislation, and in the consideration of every topic of business the House is guided by a special leader in the person of the chairman of the Standing Committee, charged with the superintendence of measures of the particular class to which that topic belongs. It is this multiplicity of leaders, this many-headed leadership, which makes the organization of the House too complex to afford uninformed people and unskilled observers any easy clue to its methods of rule. For the chairmen of the Standing Committees do not constitute a cooperative body like a ministry. They do not consult and concur in the adoption of homogeneous and mutually helpful measures; there is no thought of acting in concert. Each Committee goes its own way at its own pace. It is impossible to discover any unity or method in the disconnected and therefore unsystematic, confused, and desultory action of the House, or any common purpose in the measures which its Committees from time to time recommend." With regard to the Senate he noted that "it has those same radical defects of organization which weaken the House. Its functions also, like those of the House, are segregated in the prerogatives of numerous Standing Committees. In this regard Congress is all of a piece. There is in the Senate no more opportunity than exists in the House for gaining such recognized party leadership as would be likely to enlarge a man by giving him a sense of power, and to steady and sober him by filling him with a grave sense of responsibility. So far as its organization controls it, the Senate . . . proceedings bear most of the characteristic features of committee rule."

The Legislative Reorganization Act of 1946 was designed to streamline congressional committee structure and provide committees and individual Congressmen with increased expert staff; however, although the number of standing committees was reduced, subcommittees have increased so that the net numerical reduction is not as great as was originally intended. Further, Congress still conducts its business through committees, which means that: (1) the senior members of the party with the majority in Congress dominate the formulation of public policy through the seniority rule; (2) policy formulation is fragmented with each committee maintaining relative dominance over policy areas within its jurisdiction; (3) stemming from this fragmentation party control is weakened, especially when the President attempts to assume legislative dominance.

The following selection discusses the nature of the committee system in Congress. It is based upon the perspectives of Congressmen themselves as they were expressed at a round-table conference conducted under the auspices of the Brookings Institution in Washington.

THE CONGRESSMAN: HIS WORK AS HE SEES IT

*Charles L. Clapp**

"No one will be able to understand Congress unless he understands the committee system and how it functions," said one congressman at the opening session of the Brookings round table conference. The House and Senate must, of course, work their will on legislative proposals that are cleared by committees, but it is in the committee rooms that the real work is done. There, choices are made between alternative proposals and decisions are reached to pigeonhole or kill outright other bills. The latter actions virtually eliminate the possibility of further consideration by the House or Senate; the former involve determinations that generally govern the reception of the measure in the parent body. By weighting a measure with unpalatable items though reporting it, a committee can hasten its demise. By amending a bill so as to weaken the opposition it can almost guarantee success. By endorsing a measure strongly, a committee increases significantly the likelihood that it will be accepted. Close House and Senate adherence to committee recommendations is the practice although recommended legislation in controversial fields, such as agricultural policy, may face defeat on the floor. Normally, few substantive changes are made during floor debate. The volume and complexity of legislative proposals, the strong tradition of deferring to the "specialist," the search for ways to reconcile often conflicting pressures on congressmen, the very size of Congress—all conspire to enhance the authority of committee action. According to a congressional committee study, 90 percent of all the work of the Congress on legislative matters is carried out in committee.

The influence of committees in the legislative process is bolstered by the practice, particularly prevalent in the Appropriations Committee, of confining efforts to defeat or modify a proposal to activities within the committee itself. Once the battle has been fought and resolved there, those in the committee minority often do not press their case on the House floor. If they do intend to press it, they are careful, at the time of the committee vote, to "reserve" the right to do so. But the emphasis is on closing ranks and presenting a united front.

Committee pre-eminence and the difficulties involved in setting aside measures receiving committee endorsement have led party leaders on

---

* Reprinted from *The Congressman: His Work as He Sees It* by Charles L. Clapp, by permission of The Brookings Institution. Copyright © 1963 by The Brookings Institution.

occasion to ignore seniority in making assignments to committees handling crucial or controversial legislation, as has been illustrated in Chapter 5. They also have led the Executive and the interest groups to concern themselves with the assignment process.

The central role of committees in the legislative process has also underscored the importance of strategic referral of bills to committee: by careful attention to the wording, a congressman may have his bill sent to a committee more favorably disposed to it than the one to which it might otherwise have been referred.

POWERS AND PROCEDURES

Committees are virtually autonomous bodies, hiring their own staffs, establishing their own rules of procedure, proceeding at their own pace for the most part, and resisting on occasion the urgings of the party. Chairmen may openly and successfully flaunt the party leadership, or they may have such stature that they are seldom requested to follow specific courses of action. And the reports of committees or their subcommittees may become as binding on executive departments as if they were law.

Committees differ tremendously in composition and method of operation, and may change significantly from one year to the next. As one congressman said, "Each committee tends to be unique in its unwritten rules—an organism in itself. The character changes with different chairmen and with different congresses." Some rely heavily on staff, interest groups, or the executive; others are relatively free from all such influences. Some are characterized by a lack of partisanship and generally report measures to the House floor by unanimous or nearly unanimous vote; strong partisanship is typical of others. In view of the central role of committees in the legislative process, an understanding of the working relationships that exist within the various committees is very helpful—often indispensable—to those who desire to influence legislation.

Just as different personalities alter procedures, the impact of a committee on the outlook of its members may be perceptible also. For example, service on the Appropriations Committee seems to make members more conservative. This is true in part because the membership is recruited carefully from the ranks of representatives likely to be susceptible to the socialization process. Although their attitudes toward issues vary, they are considered "reasonable" and "responsible," capable of adjusting easily to committee procedures and committee thinking. The fact that there is little turnover in committee membership tends to promote a group identity that is unusual and that aids in the assimilation of new members. Explained one liberal who sits on the committee:

The Appropriations Committee develops a strange sort of breed. As soon as you get on the committee somehow you become more responsible as a member of Congress. You find you have to justify expenditures and you cannot pass over any situation very lightly. As a result you become more conservative. I think it is fair to say that on the whole the members of the Appropriations Committee are more conservative than most members of Congress. Committee members pause long before they support various programs. They are always thinking of what additional taxes are necessary to carry these programs out. Most congressmen, on the other hand, are just thinking how worthwhile the program would be, neglecting the point of how much additional taxes would be required.

The important work of committees takes place in closed rather than open sessions. It has been estimated that in recent years from 30 percent to 40 percent of committee meetings have been held in executive session. While House committees dealing with money matters and unusually technical or sensitive legislation, such as the Appropriations, Ways and Means, and Foreign Affairs committtees are concerned with, are more disposed to meet in private than most other groups, nearly every committee makes fairly extensive use of this procedure. Closed sessions facilitate compromise, promote candor and serious discussion, and eliminate the temptation to "play to the spectators," which occasionally overcomes members of Congress. Party representatives may have met together prior to a "mark-up" session in order to determine strategy and the party stand on a bill. But partisan stances are often sublimated and an atmosphere conducive to thoughtful consideration of legislation is more likely to prevail. Here representatives whose names the general public would not recognize may develop reputations among their colleagues based on their insights and their capacity for hard work. Despite the obvious advantages of holding executive sessions on many kinds of problems, there are persistent complaints, particularly from the press, that too many committee sessions are conducted behind closed doors. Far from promoting better legislation, these critics assert, closed sessions are often detrimental since, there, decisions are reached that would not be tolerated were the proceedings conducted in public. . . .

The Rules Committee. The Rules Committee possesses important powers, and its actions can go far to determine the nature of the legislation passed by the House. Thus control of the committee is eagerly sought by legislative leaders, and its resistance to suggestions of the Speaker and his allies inevitably leads to demands for reform of the group.

A center of controversy in recent years because of its occasional defiance of the wishes of the majority leadership, the Rules Committee was once a central element in the centralization of party responsibility in the House. It represented an important source of the Speaker's power; it was, in effect, *his* committee. He chaired it, determined its membership, and it bent to his will. Curtailment in 1910 of the Speaker's power of appointment has made the committee more independent of the leadership, despite the fact that in recent years the majority party has maintained a two to one edge in its membership. Since 1937 occasional coalitions of its Republican and conservative Southern Democratic members have functioned to thwart certain programs of the Democratic leadership when that party has controlled the House.

Most bills of any importance that are reported out of the legislative committees reach the House floor by means of a "rule" presented to the House by the Rules Committee. This resolution establishes the condition of debate on the bill: it specifies the time allocated for discussion and may stipulate the number and kind of amendments that can be offered. A rule from the committee does not guarantee House consideration of a measure—the leadership occasionally fails to schedule measures so reported—but it makes consideration likely. Committee refusal to grant a rule, on the other hand, usually means the bill will not be considered at all. The power of the committee to determine when to report out a bill is not an inconsiderable one either: timing is an important element of legislative strategy and delaying or expediting a bill can do much to affect its fate.

Measures are reported from the Rules Committee under an "open" rule, which places no limitation on the number or kind of amendments permitted during floor debate, or a "closed" rule. The latter is used less frequently and either permits no amendment or specifies those that are permissible. Closed rules are confined largely to complicated, technical measures, generally fiscal in nature, which come from the Appropriations or the Ways and Means Committee. Proponents of a bill may seek a closed rule to prevent the possibility that crippling amendments will be added; when they can get one, they gain an important initial advantage. Additionally, the committee may provide for waivers against points of order which could normally be raised against inclusion of non-privileged matters in privileged bills, such as legislation in an appropriations bill.

Generally, the Rules Committee cooperates with the legislative committees and the House leadership both in scheduling hearings on bills and in reporting them to the floor for House action. Seldom will a rule be granted for a measure opposed by the leadership, for example. But a bill it supports may occasionally either not be reported out or will be given a rule not favorable to the position of the majority party. In other instances, bills may be delayed in the Rules Committee until agreement is reached with the legislative committee regarding the nature of its activity on the floor: the Rules unit may elicit a promise to seek to amend the bill to conform more closely to Rules Committee preferences, or it may demand assurances that the committee will oppose amendments designed to disturb certain features of the bill. If the legislative committee declines to make the desired commitment, the bill may languish in the Rules Committee.

Few rules reported to the House are defeated. When they are rejected, the reason is more often opposition to the bill itself than a belief that the rule is unsatisfactory or unfair. The special orders under which measures proceed from the Rules Committee to the floor require only a majority vote; in effect they constitute suspension of the House rules, an action that ordinarily requires a two-thirds vote. Thus Rules Committee support eases the way of a measure.

Defenders of the Rules Committee maintain that while the committee has not always been responsive to the entreaties of the leadership, it has almost always been an accurate reflector of House opinion. Where it has clashed with the leadership, it has often expressed the judgment of the House. To charges that the committee flouts the will of the House, it is said that no committee that flagrantly ignored House opinion could maintain its power for long. And, it is asserted, the committee renders a valuable service to congressmen by refusing to act on bills on which the House does not wish to be recorded or in drafting rules so as to protect colleagues from difficult votes. The committee, it is said, often serves as a convenient whipping boy for the leadership or even the rank and file when in fact the latter groups privately applaud the actions taken. Stated one representative:

> There are many House members who spend time excoriating institutions like the Rules Committee, yet in their heart they thank Providence that the Rules Committee exists. They can't wait to get back home to make the Rules Committee a scapegoat. We could have done this or that, they say, if the reactionary Rules Committee hadn't bottled things up and prevented us from working our will. These people are secretly pleased that organizations like the committee exist to slow down the process and prevent bad legislation from developing. In a sense the Rules Committee takes them off the hook.

Explained another congressman, "Members are always going around to the Rules Committee and asking them to let a bill die there. Then they turn around and berate the committee for not reporting the bill out."

Although the values of the committee are appreciated, there is recognition that with respect to certain legislative proposals deemed important, if not crucial, to the program of the House leadership the Rules Committee has proved uncooperative and obstinate. It is often charged that the committee exceeds its "traffic manager" functions to perform a policy-making role rather than leaving determination of policy to the House itself. Undeniably the committee leaves its imprint on major legislation. As its chairman, Howard Smith, says: "My people did not elect me to Congress to be a traffic cop." One Democrat is particularly outraged that in certain circumstances a rule must be obtained to send a bill to conference. Said he: "After a bill has passed both houses, to let a half dozen men prevent the will of the majority of each house from being carried out is just outrageous."

While critics assert that the committee has denied the House the opportunity to vote on good legislation, friends of the Rules Committee unit retort that if a majority of the House desire action on a measure, there are sufficient means available to get it before the House despite lack of cooperation by the committee. Stated one House leader, "The Rules Committee which is nothing more than a committee on agenda has been unfairly used as a whipping boy. It never has had the power to bottle up legislation the majority really wanted." The main ways in which the Rules Committee can be circumvented are by (1) unanimous consent; (2) suspension of the rules; (3) Calendar Wednesday; and (4) discharge. All of them are difficult ways by which to attain enactment of major legislation.*

* A single objection can prevent consideration of a bill by unanimous consent, making it unlikely that controversial measures can be disposed of in that manner. Under suspension procedures the Speaker may, on the first and third Mondays of each month, recognize a member to move suspension of the rules and immediate consideration of a bill. But the Speaker has absolute power of recognition and may entertain or refuse to entertain such a motion. And, even if the Speaker is cooperative, suspension requires a two-thirds vote, which may be difficult to obtain. Calendar Wednesday provides that on Wednesdays the Speaker may call on committee chairmen (in alphabetical order by committee) who may call up for a vote any bill that has previously been reported out of their committee. But the measure must be disposed of in the same legislative day, and dilatory tactics may make this difficult. Further, hostile chairmen heading committees

The occasional reluctance of the Rules Committee to respond to leadership requests and its assumption of policy-making roles, combined with the difficulties inherent in seeking to bypass the committee by resorting to any of the procedures mentioned above, have led proponents of party responsibility to seek to return the committee to its earlier status as an instrument of the majority party. Failing that, they have sought to provide a more satisfactory means of circumventing the committee.

In recent years, critics of the committee have been successful on two occasions in imposing restrictions on the independence of the group. In 1949 they secured adoption of the "21 day rule." This provided that the chairman of a legislative committee could bring directly to the House floor any bill reported out of his committee for which the Rules Committee had failed to grant a rule within twenty-one calendar days of a request for action. The twenty-one day rule lasted only two years, falling victim to reduced majority party strength in the succeeding Congress. In 1961, the Democratic House majority sought to make the committee more responsive to its leadership by enlarging the membership of the committee from twelve to fifteen, maintaining the two to one party division. Explained one Democrat closely allied with the leadership: "The Rules Committee is a bit too powerful. If what we really want is to have a representative body and to have the majority will prevail, then it is clear something should be done to modify the Rules Committee."

And some Democrats who felt the need for an effective party policy committee believed the Rules Committee might be reconstituted to meet that need: "We need some kind of effective party instrument such as the policy committee. The Rules Committee might perform this function provided it is increased to make it more representative of the party point of view. As it stands now, it is not an effective instrument of Democratic party policy."

Although the 1961 changes did not make the committee a potential policy committee, they clearly made it more responsive to majority party leadership, for the time being at least. Even so, despite the increased majority, the leadership was not able to dislodge from the committee some measures in which it was interested. In 1963, the House voted to make permanent the larger committee size. The importance of the committee

---

further up the list may prevent consideration of the bill in question by bringing up a bill from their own committee. The discharge petition is a difficult procedure since a majority of the membership must sign the petition to bring about action, and many legislators refuse to sign any discharge petition as a matter of policy.

in the legislative process soon was emphasized by the intra-party struggle which developed when it was announced that a member of the committee from Texas could leave Congress to accept a judgeship. A tentative agreement between the Speaker and the Texas delegation as to a successor was quickly challenged by liberal Democrats, who feared the views of the designee would lead him to be less cooperative with the leadership than the congressman leaving the committee. Whether the move by the liberals was designed to substitute another congressman as the successor to the seat or merely to wrest concessions from the member designated was not immediately apparent. 🔖

The use of the committee system helps Congress in many ways. It provides a basis for doing business in an orderly fashion in the absence of a disciplined party system. It helps Congress to develop specialized knowledge in an age in which lawmaking is generally highly technical. One of the most vital functions fulfilled by the committee system is that of representation. The following selection illustrates this point in relation to the House Agriculture Committee.

REPRESENTATION IN CONGRESS: THE CASE OF THE HOUSE AGRICULTURE COMMITTEE

*Charles O. Jones**

STUDENTS of American politics are told that our political system is fundamentally a *representative* democracy. Concepts of representation, since Burke, have commonly employed his distinction between action taken in response to instructions from constituents and action based on an independent appraisal of the national interest. A very recent analysis has offered a refinement of this, by distinguishing three types: "delegate," "trustee" and "politico." Theory and history alike tell us, however, that a representative does not invariably act in only one of these roles. There have been a number of empirical studies of representatives, few of which concentrate on specific policy fields; and studies also of the play of interests

* Reprinted from *The American Political Science Review* (June 1961) by permission of The American Political Science Association and the author.

in the enactment of specific legislation, but without a systematic account of the legislative committee members involved, acting in their representative capacities as they saw them. How then can we tell when to expect a representative to view his role in one way rather than another? The aim of this article is to shed a little light on some aspects of this broad question by means of a case study.

The subjects of the study were the members of the House Agriculture Committee and their action on the omnibus farm legislation (H. R. 12954 and S. 4071) in 1958 (85th Congress, second session). . . .

For analytical purposes the most useful concept I developed, to account for the behavior of a representative, was one I shall call his "policy constituency." This may be defined as those interests within his geographical or legal constituency which he perceives to be affected by the policy under consideration. When he regards these interests as actively and homogeneously concerned, they are ordinarily sufficient to determine his public stand. When he sees them as weak, indifferent or divided, other factors come into play. But he is affected too by the nature of the committee institution within which the policy is being formed.

I. THE HOUSE AGRICULTURE COMMITTEE AND ITS WORK

Organization. In 1958 a Republican President was again faced with a Democratic Congress in a congressional campaign year. The margin of control for Democrats in the House Agriculture Committee was a less-than-comfortable four votes; the split was 19 to 15. The margin in sub-committees was one vote in most cases. . . .

The principal work units in the House Agriculture Committee are the subcommittees. In 1958 there were 18 subcommittees of two kinds—ten commodity subcommittees and eight special-action subcommittees. The former are more important since they consider legislation designed to solve the many crises for specific commodities. Usually a member is assigned to at least one commodity subcommittee of his choice. The chairman consults the ranking minority leader but has the last word on appointments. Actually few decisions have to be made, since most commodity subcommittees are permanent and their membership is continuing; only the new members need assignments. The size of subcommittees varies considerably (from 12 for tobacco to five for rice), giving the chairman some flexibility in case several members are interested in one commodity. . . .

Representing Agriculture. As might be expected, congressmen from constituencies with significant interests in farm policy make up the membership of the House Agriculture Committee. In 1958 there was but one exception to this rule—Victor Anfuso, Democrat from Brooklyn. Thirteen of the 19 Democrats came from areas where tobacco, cotton, peanuts, and rice are the principal commodities. Republican Committee members came from areas producing corn, hogs, small grain, wheat, and areas where the farming is diversified.

Committee members may be classified by commodities of greatest interest to their constituencies, as in Table II. Commodities receiving price supports are grown in the constituencies of members of all six groups there listed. The *basic* commodities, so labeled by the Agricultural

TABLE II. Committee Members and Their Constituencies' Commodities*

1. *Corn and Livestock*
   Harrison (R-Nebraska)
   Harvey (R-Indiana)
   Hill (R-Colorado)†
   Hoeven (R-Iowa)
   Polk (D-Ohio)
   Simpson (R-Illinois)†
2. *Cotton and Rice*
   Abernethy (D-Mississippi)
   Albert (D-Oklahoma)
   Gathings (D-Arkansas)
   Grant (D-Alabama)
   Jones (D-Missouri)
   Poage (D-Texas)
   Thompson (D-Texas)
3. *Dairy, Livestock, Small Grains*
   Johnson (D-Wisconsin)
   Knutson (D-Minnesota)
   Quie (R-Minnesota)
   Tewes (R-Wisconsin)
   Williams (R-New York)†

4. *Diversified* (non-basics)
   Anfuso (D-New York)
   Dague (R-Pennsylvania)
   Dixon (R-Utah)
   Hagen (D-California)
   McIntire (R-Maine)
   Teague (R-California)
5. *Tobacco*
   Abbitt (D-Virginia)
   Bass (D-Tennessee)
   Cooley (D-North Carolina)
   Jennings (D-Virginia)
   McMillan (D-South Carolina)
   Matthews (D-Florida)
   Watts (D-Kentucky)
6. *Wheat*
   Belcher (R-Oklahoma)
   Krueger (R-North Dakota)†
   Smith (R-Kansas)

* Members were classified on the basis of their constituencies' principal commodities, as listed in the *Census of Agriculture,* Vol. I, 1956, and interviews with the members.

† These members were not interviewed. Simpson, Williams and Krueger clearly belong to the groups to which they have been assigned. Hill might also have been included in the wheat group.

Adjustment Act of 1938, are corn, cotton, tobacco, rice, wheat, and peanuts; price supports have been mandatory for them. An increasing number of *non-basics* have also received price supports, *e.g.,* milk and wool. The "diversified" (mainly non-basics) group often find their interests conflicting with those of representatives in the other groups. They complain that their farmers are at a disadvantage since their non-basics either do not receive price supports or receive less support than the basics; the price supports for the few basics grown do not make up for the deprivation of profits attributable to acreage and marketing controls (the complaint of California cotton farmers); and they must pay higher prices for the basics as well as pay higher taxes.

Almost without exception the six groups show an alignment between commodity interests and party allegiance. The corn and livestock group has five Republicans and one Democrat; the cotton and rice group, seven Democrats; the dairy, livestock, small grains group, two Democrats and three Republicans; the diversified group, four Republicans and two Democrats; the tobacco group, seven Democrats; and the wheat group, three or four Republicans. Consequently, different commodities will ordinarily be favored when different parties are in control. For example, cotton, rice, and tobacco usually receive more attention when the Democrats are a majority in the Committee.

Committee organization has been strongly influenced by the commodity problems in agriculture. First, subcommittees are established to deal with currently critical commodity problems. Second, members are assigned to commodity subcommittees on the basis of their constituency interests. Table III shows the high correlation prevailing. Only one Democrat (Anfuso) was assigned to no commodity subcommittee representing producers in his constituency and he has no agricultural production at all

TABLE III.   Constituency Interests and Commodity Subcommittee Assignments*

Member†	Major agricultural interests in constituency	Commodity subcommittees
Democrats		
Poage	Cotton, Livestock, Peanuts	Cotton; Livestock & Feed Grains (C)
Grant	Cotton, Peanuts, Wood Products	Forests (C); Peanuts
Gathings	Cotton, Rice, Soybeans	Cotton (C); Rice; Soybeans-Oil-seeds
McMillan	Cotton, Tobacco, Peanuts	Forests; Peanuts (C); Tobacco
Abernethy	Cotton	Cotton; Dairy Products (C); Soybeans-Oilseeds

Albert	Cotton, Livestock	Livestock and Feed Grains; Peanuts; Wheat (C)
Abbitt	Tobacco, Peanuts	Tobacco (C); Peanuts
Polk	Feed Grains, Livestock, Dairy	Dairy Products; Tobacco
Thompson	Rice, Cotton, Peanuts	Rice (C); Poultry-Eggs
Jones	Cotton, Livestock, Soybeans	Rice; Soybeans-Oilseeds (C); Wheat
Watts	Tobacco, Feed Grains, Seeds	Tobacco; Wheat
Hagen	Cotton, Alfalfa Seed, Potatoes, Fruit	Cotton; Soybeans-Oilseeds
Johnson	Dairy, Forests, Livestock	Dairy Products; Forests; Poultry-Eggs
Anfuso	None	Poultry-Eggs
Bass	Tobacco, Cotton	Tobacco; Wheat
Knutson	Wheat, Dairy, Feed Grains	Dairy Products
Jennings	Tobacco, Livestock	Livestock and Feed Grains; Tobacco; Wheat
Matthews	Tobacco, Peanuts, Vegetables	Livestock and Feed Grains; Tobacco

Republicans

Hoeven	Feed Grains, Livestock	Livestock and Feed Grains; Soybeans-Oilseeds
Simpson	Feed Grains, Livestock	Cotton; Livestock and Feed Grains; Soybeans-Oilseeds; Tobacco
Dague	Tobacco, Truck Farming, Poultry, Dairy	Tobacco; Wheat
Harvey	Feed Grains, Livestock	Livestock and Feed Grains; Soybeans-Oilseeds
Belcher	Wheat	Cotton; Peanuts; Wheat
McIntire	Forests, Poultry, Potatoes	Forests; Poultry-Eggs; Tobacco
Williams	Dairy, Truck Farming	Dairy Products; Rice
Harrison	Feed Grains, Livestock	Peanuts; Poultry-Eggs
Dixon	Wheat, Potatoes, Small Grain, Sugar Beets	Forests; Poultry-Eggs
Smith	Wheat	Peanuts; Wheat
Krueger	Wheat, Small Grains	Rice; Wheat
Teague	Vegetables, Fruit, Small Grains, Cotton	Cotton; Forests
Tewes	Dairy, Tobacco, Livestock	Dairy Products; Tobacco
Quie	Dairy, Feed Grains, Livestock	Dairy Products; Tobacco

* The major interests were deduced from the *Census of Agriculture, 1954,* Vol. 1, 1956, and from interviews with members.

† Members listed according to committee rank. Chairman Cooley, whose principal interests were tobacco, cotton and poultry, and William Hill, whose principal interests were wheat, feed grains, and sugar beets, were *ex officio* members of all subcommittees by virtue of their positions as chairman and ranking minority member, respectively.

in his Brooklyn district, though the poultry trade is important there. Two Republicans (Harrison and Dixon) found themselves on subcommittees of little or no concern to their constituencies. Significantly both of these members were identified by other members as being supporters of Secretary Benson's recommendations.

Party considerations dictate that some members must be on subcommittees of no concern to their constituencies: there must be Republicans on the cotton subcommittee and Democrats on the wheat subcommittee. For the most part, members who have little interest in the proceedings are expected either to remain silent during hearings or not to attend. . . . [Here the author discusses the legislation introduced in 1958 and the modifications made to secure its passage.]

III. CONCLUSIONS

The conclusions suggested by this case study can be set forth . . . as follows:

1. If a policy measure is seen to affect substantial interests in a representative's legal constituency, then he will rely on his perception of the interests affected (his "policy constituency") when he acts at the working level (usually the subcommittee) in regard to this measure.

A. Institutional arrangements affect his ability to represent his policy constituency. The House Agriculture Committee is organized to allow a maximum of constituency-oriented representation.

B. The representative has a "sense" of constituency interests drawn from first-hand experience in the "legal" constituency and this "sense" influences his perception of a policy constituency.

C. Party allegiance is an important modifying factor.

(1) The legislative majority party may demand a vote in support of its policies. The legislative minority party may demand a vote in opposition to the majority's policies. The Administration may press for support for its stands.

(2) Representatives, whether or not affected by the legislation, tend to support their party's position more as the action moves beyond the basic working level, and most at the final vote.

2. If a measure is seen to have little or no direct effect on interests in a representative's legal constituency, then he will tend more readily to look to his political party for a cue when he acts in regard to this measure.

A. The representative will tend the more to suggest that he relies on "independent judgment," the less his constituency's interests are seen to be directly or positively affected by a policy.

B. He will vote in support of his political party but will not actively support the policy in other ways if his constituency interests are not perceived to be affected. . . .

An adequate concept of representation should account for a total action pattern, not merely a final vote. The representative on the House Agriculture Committee can view his composite role retrospectively as one in which he has taken several separate actions to make up a total pattern in regard to the omnibus farm legislation. He also can recognize that on different occasions he felt differing demands upon him in his several capacities, as a member of a party, a representative of a constituency, a member of a committee, of a Congress, of interest groups, etc. He was able to reconcile, compromise or avoid some of the inherent conflicts in these demands, at least in part, because of the multiple action points. Examples of such reconciliations in this case study justify a final hypothesis which merits separate study:

3. If a representative has a multiplicity of conflicting demands upon him in any series of actions on policy, he can satisfy many of them, over a period of time, because of the multiplicity of action points at successive stages in the legislative process.

30. The Senate: The South's Revenge on the North?

From reading *The Federalist* students can see that the framers of the Constitution expected the Senate to be the most important conservative force in our government. To some extent the Seventeenth Amendment, which provided for the popular election of Senators, modified conservative expectations regarding the Senate; however, the basic provisions of the Constitution designed to render this a conservative branch of the government remained, the most important being the long term of office. Proportionately, of course, the less populous states are better represented in the Senate than in the House. This fact, combined with the seniority system, reliance upon committees, and Southern solidarity renders the Senate, in the words of William S. White, an "old Southern home." Its essential conservatism remains, and regardless of the Seventeenth Amendment it is still an institution in which state and regional influence is dominant. Perhaps the best way for the student to grasp the fundamental nature of the Senate is to become aware of its informal atmosphere and the typical "Senate type." The following selection is directed to this end.

THE SENATE AND THE CLUB
*William S. White**

WHEN one unexpectedly needs a room in a good, and crowded, hotel in New York like the Pierre, which is not so very long on tradition, his best course is to approach the clerk in masterful determination, allowing no other assumption at all than that he will be accommodated. When such a need arises in a traditional hotel abroad, say Brown's in London, the wiser attitude is precisely the reverse. There it is better to approach the subject wearily and a bit hopelessly and to say to the clerk, of course I know it is hardly possible that you could find a place for me.

When one enters the House of Representatives, or becomes an official in the Executive Department, the sound attitude is not simply to put the best foot forward, but to stamp it for emphasis—in front of the photographers if any are present, and if official superiors are not. But when one enters the Senate he comes into a different place altogether. The long custom of the place impels him, if he is at all wise, to walk with a soft foot and to speak with a soft voice, and infrequently. Men who have reached national fame in less than two years in powerful non-Senatorial office— Saltonstall as Governor of Massachusetts, Duff as Governor of Pennsylvania for recent examples—have found four years and more not to be long enough to feel free to speak up loudly in the Institution. All the newcomer needs, if he is able and strong, is the passage of time—but this he needs indispensably, save in those rare cases where the authentic geniuses among Senate types are involved.

The old definition of the Senate as "the most exclusive club in the world" is no longer altogether applicable, as perhaps it never was. It *is*, however, both a club and a club within a club. By the newly arrived and by some of the others the privileges are only carefully and sparingly used. To the senior members—and sometimes they are senior only in terms of power and high acceptability—privilege is inexhaustible and can be pressed to almost any limit. I have seen one member, say a Lehman of

---

* Chapter VII, "The Senate and the Club," from *Citadel: The Story of the U.S. Senate,* by William S. White. Copyright © 1956 by William S. White. Reprinted by permission of the publishers, Harper & Brothers.

New York, confined by niggling and almost brutal Senate action to the most literal inhibitions of the least important of all the rules. And again I have seen a vital Senate roll call held off by all sorts of openly dawdling time-killing for hours, in spite of the fact that supposedly it is not possible to interrupt a roll call once it is in motion, for the simple purpose of seeing that a delayed aircraft has opportunity to land at Washington Airport so that a motorcycle escort can bring, say a Humphrey of Minnesota in to be recorded.

Lehman was, of course, a member of the Outer Club, which is composed of all the Senate. But Humphrey is, in part by the mysterious operation of acceptability-by-association, in or very close to the Inner Club. The inequality indicated here has nothing to do with political belief or activity; both Lehman and Humphrey are liberal Democrats and both have records of distinction. Humphrey simply got along better.

The inner life of the Senate—and the vast importance to it of its internal affairs may be seen in the fact that it has on occasion taken longer to decide upon the proper salaries for a handful of Senate employees than to provide billions of dollars for the defense of the United States—is controlled by the Inner Club. This is an organism without name or charter, without officers, without a list of membership, without a wholly conscious being at all.

There is no list of qualifications for membership, either posted or orally mentioned. At the core of the Inner Club stand the Southerners, who with rare exceptions automatically assume membership almost with the taking of the oath of office. They get in, so to speak, by inheritance, but at their elbows within the core are others, Easterners, Midwesterners, Westerners, Republicans or Democrats.

The outer life of the Senate, in which all the members are theoretically more or less equal at the time of decision that comes when a roll-call vote is added up, is defined by its measurable actions on bills and on public policies. But this outer life, even in its most objective aspects, is not free of the subtle influence of the inner life of the Institution.

The inner life is in the command of a distinct minority within this place of the minority. This minority-within-a-minority is the Inner Club. This Inner Club, though in spirit largely dominated by the Southerners, is by no means geographic.

Those who belong to it express, consciously or unconsciously, the deepest instincts and prejudices of "the Senate type." The Senate type is, speaking broadly, a man for whom the institution is a career in itself, a life in itself and an end in itself. This Senate type is not always free of Presidential ambition, a striking case in point having been the late Senator

Taft. But the important fact is that when the Senate type thinks of the Presidency he thinks of it as only *another* and not as really a *higher* ambition, as did Taft and as did Senator Russell of Georgia when, in 1952, he sought the Democratic Presidential nomination.

The Senate type makes the Institution his home in an almost literal sense, and certainly in a deeply emotional sense. His head swims with its history, its lore and the accounts of past personnel and deeds and purposes. To him, precedent has an almost mystical meaning and where the common run of members will reflect twice at least before creating a precedent, the Senate type will reflect so long and so often that nine times out of ten he will have nothing to do with such a project at all.

His concern for the preservation of Senate tradition is so great that he distrusts anything out of the ordinary, however small, as for example a night session. Not necessarily an abstemious man (a sometimes fairly bibulous one as a convivial character *within* the Institution) he will complain that such sessions, especially along toward the closing days of Congress, will be unduly tiring on the elders of the body. Often he really means here that prolonged meetings, tending as they do to send the most decorous of men out to the lounges for a nip, may wind up with one or more distinguished members taking aboard what never in the world would be called a few too many.

This Senate type knows, with the surest touch in the world, precisely how to treat his colleagues, Outer Club as well as Inner Club. He is nearly always a truly compassionate man, very slow to condemn his brothers. And not even the imminent approach of a great war can disturb him more than the approach of what he may regard as adequate evidence that the Senate may in one crisis or another be losing not the affection of the country (for which he has no great care) but the respect of the country.

He measures the degree of respect being shown by the country at any given time not wholly by what he reads and hears through the mass media, and not at all by the indicated attitude of any President, but by what is borne in upon his consciousness by his contact with what he considers to be the more *suitable* conveyors of *proper* public thought. He, the true Senate type, has this partiality toward the few as distinguished from the many all through his career even though he will hide it skillfully in his recurring tests at home when, up for re-election, he *must* depend upon the mass.

As the Southern members of the Inner Club make the ultimate decisions as to what is proper in point of manner—these decisions then infallibly pervading the Outer Club—so the whole generality of the Inner

Club makes the decisions as to what *in general* is proper in the Institution and what *in general* its conclusions should be on high issues. These decisions are in no way overtly or formally reached; it is simply that one day the perceptive onlooker will discover a kind of aura from the Inner Club that informs him of what the Senate is later going to do about such and such.

For an illustration of the point, there was this small but significant incident in 1956: Some of the junior members had set out to put some Congressional check on the Central Intelligence Agency by creating an overseeing Joint Congressional Committee. A majority of the whole body became formally committed to the bill, and all seemed clear ahead. Suddenly, however, some of the patriarchs—among them the venerable Alban Barkley of Kentucky, who was soon to die in his seventy-ninth year while smiting the Republicans from a speaking platform at Washington and Lee University—found themselves disenchanted. They decided, for no very perceptible reason except that they felt they had been inadequately consulted, that a joint committee would not do at all. Under their bleak and languid frowns the whole project simply died; a wind had blown upon it from the Inner Club and its erstwhile sponsors simply left it.

The senate type therefore—and his distillate as found in the Inner Club—is in many senses more an institutional man than a public man in the ordinary definition of such a personage. Some of the Senate's most powerful public men have not been truly Senate types. The late Senator Arthur Vandenberg of Michigan, for all his influence upon foreign relations after he had abandoned isolationism for internationalism, was never in his career a true Senate type, no matter how formidable he was as a public man. Incomparably the truest current Senate type, and incomparably the most influential man on the inner life of the Senate, Senator Russell of Georgia, has never had one-tenth Vandenberg's impact upon public and press in objective, or out-Senate, affairs.

Russell's less palpable and less measurable influence, however, was infinitely greater in the *Senate,* on all matters involving its inner being, than was Vandenberg's, as indeed was Taft's. For Russell could actually command the votes of others upon many matters, even some entirely objective matters. Vandenberg spoke to the country and occasionally to the world. Russell (and other Senate types as well) speaks primarily to the Senate. Going back a good deal farther, Huey Long of Louisiana spoke also beyond the Senate, specifically to the discontented and the dispossessed outside, while one of his greatest critics of the time, Carter Glass of Virginia, spoke to the Senate, as Byrd of Virginia does to this day.

The non-Senate types, it thus may be seen, are in the end influential only to the degree that they may so instruct or so inflame a part of the public sufficiently large to insist upon this or that course of political conduct. The Senate type in the last analysis has the better of it. For not only does his forum generally resist change and all public pressure save the massive and enduring; it also will tend quickly to adopt his proposals unless they are quite clearly untenable.

The Senate Democratic leader in the Eighty-fourth Congress, Lyndon Johnson of Texas, once was able to pass more than a hundred bills, not all of them lacking in controversy, in a matter of a little more than an hour. There were a variety of reasons for this wholly untypical burst of speed in a body devoted to the leisurely approach. But the most important of these reasons was simply "Lyndon wants it." It is hardly necessary to add that "Lyndon" is pre-eminently a Senate type, so much so that, highly realistic politician though he is, he is quite unable to believe that the public is not in utter fascination of the parliamentary procedures of his Institution. . . .

A man . . . may be a Senate type in good standing in the Inner Club if he is wholly out of step on fateful matters with his own Administration (as with Knowland on Asia in regard to Eisenhower). He may be the same if he is wholly out of step with his own party, as for illustration Byrd in regard to the regular Democrats who control the party nationally. He may be the same if, like McClellan of Arkansas, he comes fortuitously and reluctantly to national attention only because he becomes involved in something widely televised, like the Army-McCarthy hearings.

Equally a man may be a powerful Senate type with never a great legislative triumph to his credit, by a mysterious chemical process that seems to be transforming now so relative a newcomer as Payne of Maine. Why such progress for Payne? It is a little awkward to explain; perhaps the explanation is that Payne, who was a rather hard-handed politician as Governor of Maine, simply generates a warmth about him because he so wholeheartedly performs, without fuss or trouble, such Senate chores as are handed over to him.

The converse is similarly so. William Fulbright of Arkansas, a Rhodes Scholar, an ex-university president, a young and literate man with many useful years ahead of him, was credited as a member of the House with promoting this country's turn to internationalism before the Second World War. He has been credited since in the Senate with many achievements, not the least of which is the cumulative achievement of an experience and a seniority that are very likely one day to make him chairman of the Foreign Relations Committee. [He is now chairman.]

He is not, for all of this, quite a Senate type. Nor, for another example, is Paul Douglas of Illinois, with his academic background, his ability in the field of economics, and his not inconsiderable feat in winning re-election in 1954 over assistance given to his opponent by President Eisenhower. Is scholastic achievement or "intellectualism" then—considering the cases of Fulbright and of Douglas—some bar to the Inner Club? Not at all. For, standing well inside the doors of the Inner Club, at least, is Humphrey of Minnesota, who used to teach political science. And at the very heart of the Inner Club in the Eighty-fourth Congress sat the man with what many would consider the most truly intellectual character in the Senate, Eugene Millikin of Colorado.

Does being liberal put a barrier on the way to the Inner Club? No, for few in the Institution can be more liberal than the old indestructible, Senator Theodore Green of Rhode Island, a member of the very hierarchy of the Club.

Does being "unpopular" and remote keep out a man? No. The ordinary conversation of Carl Hayden of Arizona, whose manners are as leathery as his face, consists largely of sour grunts. And Hayden could very nearly be the president of the Club, if only it had officers.

Does wealth or social status count? Not really. One of those men in the Senate who are wholly without commercial instinct and must get along strictly on their salaries is Mike Mansfield of Montana. He spent his young years in the mines of Butte; he largely educated himself—and he, like Humphrey, is well across the threshold of the Inner Club. . . .

Indeed, it may be that . . . one of the keys to the qualities of the Senate type [is] tolerance toward his fellows, intolerance toward any who would in any real way change the Senate, its customs or its way of life. And, right or wrong, it is the moral force of these men that gives to them an ascendancy in the Institution which they never assert and which most of them do nothing consciously to promote.

It is, then, against all this background of the human facts in the cases that answer must be made to the question whether and how the Senate is "the most exclusive club in the world" and whether, indeed it is exclusive in the ordinary understanding at all. . . .

There *is*, however, for all of this, a quality of exclusiveness, too. Though some arrive more or less by accident in the Senate, most have worked a passage that has required more than luck, than money, than family or political position. In a sense at first there is the exclusiveness of success and then, as test succeeds test, the exclusiveness of both success and understanding. All these may be, and are, attained without reaching the final quality of exclusiveness that is involved in acceptance in the Inner Club.

To be in the Inner Club a man must be many things—some important and some mere accidents of life—but the greatest of these things is to have the character that will pass the severest scrutiny (if carried out blandly and seemingly casually) of which nearly five score highly understanding and humanly perceptive men are capable.

It is not character in the sense intended in the forms prepared by personnel offices. It has not got much to do with questions like "Does applicant drink?" or "Does he pay his bills?" It is character in the sense that only the true traditionalists will understand.

It is character in the sense that the special integrity of the person must be in harmony with, and not lesser in its way than, the special integrity of the Institution—the integrity of its oneness. 🖋

The "Inner Club" described by William S. White in the preceding selection may seem rather mystical. There is little doubt, however, that something approximating it has existed for many years. In 1963 Senators Clark and Douglas expressed this concept more concretely when they violated every rule of the "Inner Club" by charging openly in the Senate that it is run by a small minority, dominated by Southern conservative Democrats and conservative Republicans from other parts of the country. This small Senate elite they called the "Establishment." The influence of the "Senate Establishment" is gradually breaking down. The passage of the Civil Rights Bill of 1964 illustrates a declining influence of the South in both the House and Senate. Although there may be an eventual demise of this inner group in the Senate, it will continue to exercise significant power for many years to come. For this reason the following selection is highly pertinent to the contemporary political scene.

THE SENATE ESTABLISHMENT
Senator Joseph S. Clark and others*

M<small>R.</small> <small>CLARK.</small> Mr. President, I desire to address the Senate on the subject of the Senate establishment and how it operates. Perhaps the first thing to do is to state what I mean by "the Senate establishment." Senators may recall that last May, Richard Rovere, the very able reporter who writes for magazines such as the New Yorker and Esquire . . . wrote an article on the establishment of the United States; and in the article he compared those who he thought ran America—although I suspect that to some extent he had his tongue in his cheek—with the British establishment, which is headed by the royal family, and includes the peers, whether hereditary or only for life, and most of the aristocracy, if not the plutocracy, of Great Britain and northern Ireland. . . .

I believe that the concept of an establishment in America is something which all of us who try to understand the sometimes almost inexplicable ways in which we in this country act would do well to contemplate. Just as Great Britain has its establishment and the United States of America perhaps has its establishment, so, as I pointed out last year, the U.S. Senate has its establishment. I wish to discuss today what that establishment is, how it operates, and why in my opinion the present establishment is not operating in the interests of the future of the United States, or the future of the U.S. Senate, and certainly is not operating to the benefit of the future of the Democratic Party.

The Senate establishment, as I see it, after a relatively brief sojourn here—I am now in my seventh year—is almost the antithesis of democracy. It is not selected by any democratic process. It appears to be quite unresponsive to the caucuses of the two parties, be they Republican or Democratic. It is what might be called a self-perpetuating oligarchy with mild, but only mild, overtones of plutocracy. The way it operates is something like this:

There are a number of States, most of them Democratic, but one or two of them Republican, which inevitably and always return to the U.S. Senate members of one party, and under a custom which has grown up over the years of following the rule of seniority in making committee assignments, and in connection with the distribution of other perquisites

* This selection is taken from the Congressional Record, February 19, 20, 21, and 25, 1963.

of Senate tenure, the result has been that those who have been here longest
have become chairmen of committees, and as such chairmen, have exercised
virtual control over the distribution of favors, including committee assignments and other perquisites of office in the Senate, and largely—although
not always, and not entirely, because there are exceptions—determine who
shall be selected to posts of leadership in this body. . . .

As I see it, the Senate establishment pretty well controls the assignment of Members to committees. How is that done? I think it is interesting to note that it is not only the present Senate establishment which does
that. From time to time, going back at least to the early days of the
present century, the same system prevailed. There have always been those
who fought against the establishment, who thought that the Democratic
caucus and the Republican caucus should determine who would select
the members of committees and the other perquisites of office. . . .

It was true then, as it is now, that the establishment was bipartisan.
The senior ranking members of the minority party are a part of the establishment; and they, in conference—usually informal, always friendly—
with their colleagues on the other side of the aisle pretty well decide who
is going to do what to whom.

That is what is happening in the Senate today. That is what has
happened in the Senate many times before. But it does not always happen
in the Senate, and it need not happen in the Senate much longer. Whenever it does happen in the Senate, in a constantly shrinking world, in
which change in inevitable, I suggest that the existence of that kind of
oligarchical rule is a detriment to the national interest.

There was a very famous occasion when the rank and file of the
Senate membership overturned the establishment and in a couple of years
passed legislation—which had long been bottled up in previous Senates—
and important to the welfare of the country as almost any other program
in the long sweep of history.

I shall relate what happened in 1913, after Woodrow Wilson was
elected President aof the United States on a party platform which pledged
to bring into legislative form the New Freedom—the program on which
he defeated both William Howard Taft, seeking reelection to the Presidency, and Theodore Roosevelt, running on the Bull Moose ticket.

In 1913 the Democrats captured control of the Senate for the first
time in 16 years. A majority of the Democratic Senators were progressive
and espoused the progressive principles of the Baltimore platform, but
the committee chairmanships and the important committee posts were
to go to the conservative Democrats under the old seniority system in
the Senate.

Note the striking analogy. A large majority of the Democratic Senators in the 88th Congress are also progressive. A majority of them support the Democratic platform adopted in Los Angeles in 1960. On that platform President Kennedy was swept into office by a very narrow majority.

We now stand at the beginning of the third session of what might be called a Kennedy Congress, but actually it is not a Kennedy Congress, and it seems to me that it is not going to be a Kennedy Congress. The principal reason why it is not going to be a Kennedy Congress, so far as the Senate is concerned, is, in my opinion, that we are operating under archaic, obsolete rules, customs, manners, procedures, and traditions—and because the operation under those obsolete and archaic setups is controlled by this oligarchical Senate establishment, a majority of the Members of which, by and large, are opposed to the program of the President.

I do not wish to overstate the case. There are able and effective Members of the establishment who will support the program of the President in many areas. There are a few Members of the establishment who will support the program of the President in some areas. But, by and large, the two-thirds majority of the Democratic Senators who are Kennedy men, and therefore liberals, and therefore want to get the country moving again, and therefore believe in the inevitability of change, are represented sparsely, if at all, in the Senate establishment.

I return now to a consideration of the situation of 1913. At that time, I point out again, the committee chairmanships and the important committee positions would have gone to conservative Democrats under the old seniority system in the Senate. The progressive Democrats, however united to insure the passage of their progressive legislation and modified the Senate rules to aid in the translation of the Baltimore platform into legislation.

At that time there were 51 Democratic Senators, 44 Republicans, and 1 Progressive. Forty of the Democrats, 10 of the Republicans, and 1 Progressive—a total of 51—could be safely labeled as in sympathy with the important planks of the Baltimore platform and of the policy of President Woodrow Wilson. I refer to the currency, tariff, civil service reform, pure food, and health planks.

In all, the progressives of the three parties had a very slim majority in the Senate of 1913, but that majority was sufficient, and it enabled the Democratic Senators, with the aid of their Progressive colleague and of their friends in the Republican Party, to set aside the seniority system in the Senate, to displace senior committee chairmen, to replace the senior committee chairmen with young men, some of whom had not served in the Senate for more than 2 years; and, as a result of quiet meetings during different evenings in Washington they took over the Senate, reconstituted the membership of all committees, got rid of all the senior chairmen, and put their own men in. . . .

The end results of the revolution of 1913 in the Senate of the United States were: First, emasculation of the old Senate seniority system; second, committee domination by the progressives, which meant the Wilson men; third, the Senate being democratized in terms of its rules and procedures; and fourth, the planks of the Baltimore platform being enacted into legislation.

I plead with my colleagues to do the same thing now—if not now, then next year—if not next year, then the year after—but let us get it done, while President Kennedy is still at the White House, if we want to preserve the Democratic Party for progressive principles, if we want to get the help of a number of our progressive friends on the Republican side—if we want to move this country forward and not be blocked by the hand of the past.

Mr. Douglas. Mr. President, will the Senator yield?

Mr. Clark. I yield to the Senator from Illinois.

Mr. Douglas. Is it not likely that, if it had not been for this successful revolution, in all probability the Federal Reserve System would not have been brought into being?

Mr. Clark. The Senator is quite correct. The establishment in those days had been opposed to the Federal Reserve System.

Mr. Douglas. Is it not likely that the Underwood tariff, which greatly reduced previous tariffs, would not have been put into effect?

Mr. Clark. I think that is quite correct.

Mr. Douglas. Is it not also likely that the Federal Trade Act would not have been passed?

Mr. Clark. The Senator is entirely correct.

Mr. Douglas. Is it not also true that, in all probability the other companion measure, dealing with unfair competitive practices, would not have been passed?

Mr. Clark. I believe that was the Clayton Act, which amended the Sherman Antitrust Act and put teeth into it.

Mr. Douglas. That is correct.

Mr. Clark. The Senator is correct.

Mr. Douglas. Is it not true that, in all probability, the Agricultural Credit Act would not have been passed?

Mr. Clark. I am confident the Senator is correct.

MR. DOUGLAS. In other words, the great domestic achievements of the Wilson administration from 1913 to 1915, before the war diverted the attention of the country from domestic reforms, would not have been possible had it not been for the procedural changes in the designation of committees by the rank and file of the Senators of the Democratic Party?

MR. CLARK. They were dependent upon modernization of the Senate procedures for committee makeup. I thank the Senator for the interjection. . . .

To return to my subject, in 1961, and again this year, the Democratic conference approved a statement of the majority leader to the effect that the composition of the Democratic steering committee should reflect both the geographical distribution and the ideological views of Democratic Members of the Senate. . . .

MR. DOUGLAS. Mr. President, will the Senator yield?

MR. CLARK. I am glad to yield to my friend from Illinois.

MR. DOUGLAS. Is it not true that prior to the establishment of the present steering committee, and prior to the death of Senator Chavez, of the 15 members on the steering committee only 1 was from any of the 12 States which lie between the Alleghenies and the Rockies and can be described as the East and West Central States?

MR. CLARK. The Senator is correct. . . . [T]here are now on the committee 7 out of 15 members from the South, including both Senators from Florida.

Therefore, 47 percent of the total membership of the steering committee comes from those 13 States [including Oklahoma].

If we were to be guided solely on the basis of geography, this section of the country would be entitled to five seats. I point out that without exception these able, charming, friendly Senators from the South, all of whom are good friends of mine, belong to the conservative wing of the Senate Democratic Party. There are three Senators from the Northeast, all members of the liberal wing of the Democratic Party. There are three Senators from the Pacific and Mountain States out of 17 western Senators representing 12 of the 13 Western States. Two of these three Senators, I believe they would agree, are proud members of the conservative wing of the Democratic Party. The other member, the distinguished and able majority leader, is a follower of the President of the United States and of the liberal wing of our party.

As a result of the succession of the Senator from Illinois [Mr. Douglas] to the committee, there are now two Senators from the Midwest, both of them liberals, Senators who support our President, almost always

—Senators Humphrey and Douglas—out of 15 Senators representing 9 of the 12 Middle Western States.

MR. DOUGLAS. Mr. President, will the Senator yield further?

MR. CLARK. I am happy to yield to my friend from Illinois.

MR. DOUGLAS. When I first came to the Senate, in 1949, there was only 1 Democrat from those 12 States, Senator Lucas, of Illinois. We have gained 14 seats since then, so there are now, I believe, 15 Democratic Senators from these States. Indeed, the great gains which the Democratic Party has made since the election of 1946 have been largely and almost exclusively from what is roughly known as the Mississippi Valley, from the territory drained by the Mississippi River and its tributaries. And yet up until a few days ago we had but one representative on the steering committee.

MR. CLARK. If the Senator will permit me to make an interjection at this point, the Senator from Illinois is correct. There are 15 from the Middle West.

MR. DOUGLAS. I appreciate that comment. Prior to the last selection, which I must admit came as a great surprise to me, there was only one representative on the steering committee from the Middle West, which on a geographical basis within our party was the most underrepresented area in the Nation. It is still underrepresented.

MR. CLARK. The Senator is correct.

Turning from geography to ideology, and to recapitulate, of the 15 members on the committee, there are 9 whom, I am confident, any objective observer would classify as conservative: Senators Smathers, Bible, Ellender, Hayden, Holland, Johnston, McClellan, Robertson, and Russell. . . .

According to my count—and some may differ one way or the other— there are at most 27 conservative Democrats out of 67 Democrats in the entire Senate; so 9 out of 15 Senators who are members of the vital committee which selects committee members are from the conservative ranks of our party, and only 6 from the liberal wing . . . the modern wing, which numbers, at a minimum, 40—and I should say more nearly 45—of the 67 Democratic Members of the Senate. Those six are Senators Mansfield, Humphrey, Dodd, Douglas, Williams of New Jersey, and Clark. . . .

I suggest in all candor that . . . the present membership of the steering committee accordingly does not fairly represent either the geography or the ideology of the Democratic Members of the Senate. . . .

Whom does the steering committee of the Democratic Party represent? It represents the Democratic side of the establishment. It represents those who hold the positions of committee chairmen. Senator Mansfield has recently resigned as chairman of the Committee on Rules and Administration. His resignation was effective a few days ago.

Senator Bible is chairman of the Committee on the District of Columbia. Senator Ellender is chairman of the Committee on Agriculture and Forestry. Senator Hayden is chairman of the Committee on Appropriations. Senator Johnston is chairman of the Committee on Post Office and Civil Service. Senator McClellan is chairman of the Committee on Government Operations. Senator Robertson is chairman of the Committee on Banking and Currency. Senator Russell is chairman of the Committee on Armed Services. . . .

. . . [T]his control of the establishment over the Senate requires the support of a dwindling group of Republican conservatives headed by the able and distinguished minority leader, and that as a result of what has happened since the election of 1958, when 18 forward-looking, modern Senators joined this body, and the election of 1960, when the Senator from Rhode Island and several other Senators joined this body, and now because of the election of 1962, when a substantial group of splendid forward-looking liberal Senators joined the Senate, the attrition on the establishment has been very substantial indeed.

Let me point out that since 1958 the establishment has lost control of the Banking and Currency Committee, the Commerce Committee, the Committee on Government Operations, the Interior Committee, and, as of Monday believe it or not, the Judicial Committee. They never had control of the Committee on Labor and Public Welfare. They have lost control of the Public Works Committee.

Therefore time is on our side. Unless catastrophe overtakes the liberals of both parties in the election of 1964, I predict that we are within striking distance of obtaining control of the committee system of the Senate for the liberal and forward-looking elements on both sides of the aisle.

. . . [T]he majority leader . . . asked me to comment on whether the actions of the steering committee had revealed a constant pattern or bias in favor of junior senators who had voted against cloture [and thus supporting the position of the Southern Senate Establishment] and to overlook the claim of Senators, frequently of greater seniority, who had voted for cloture. . . .

. . . I have had prepared a table which shows the names of Senators on the Democratic side who sought [new] committee assignments, what their first, second, and third choices were, and the position they took either for or against a change in rule XXII, and therefore, almost automatically, the position they took on cloture. . . .

Name	New Committee assignments received	Choice	Position on rule XXII	
			For change	Against change
Bartlett	Appropriations	1st		X
Burdick	None		X	
Byrd (West Virginia)	Rules	No. 1		X
Cannon	Commerce (applied for Commerce and Finance)			X
Clark	Rules	No. 2	X	
Engle	None		X	
Hart	Commerce	No. 3	X	
Hayden	Interior	No. 1		X
Jordan	Public Works	No. 1		X
Lausche	None		X	
Long (Missouri)	None		X	
McGee	Post Office and Civil Service	No. 1		X
Moss	None		X	
Mansfield	Appropriations	No. 1	X	
Muskie	None		X	
Neuberger	None		X	
Pell	Government Operations	No. 2	X	
Proxmire	None		X	
Smathers	Foreign Relations	No. 1		X
Thurmond	None			X
Yarborough	None		X	
Young (Ohio)	Armed Services	No. 2	X	

CONCLUSIONS

1. Eight nonfreshmen Senators (Bartlett, Byrd, Cannon, Hayden, Jordan, McGee, Smathers, Thurmond) who opposed rules change submitted eligible bids for new committee assignments. Seven of them (88 percent) got new assignments. Six (75 percent) got the assignments which represented their first choice (only Thurmond was disappointed.)

2. Fourteen nonfreshmen Senators who favored rules change applied for new committee assignments. Five (36 percent) got new assignments (Mansfield, Hart, Pell, Young, and Clark); only one Senator (7 percent) of the group—Senator Mansfield—got the committee which was his first choice.

MR. PROXMIRE. Mr. President . . . this is a startling analysis. . . . The Senator says that eight nonfreshmen Senators who opposed a rules change and supported the South submitted eligible bids for new committee assignments, and that seven of those eight got new assignments, and that six out of the eight, or three-fourths, got their first choice. . . . Then the Senator says that 14 nonfreshmen Senators who favored a rules change applied for new committee assignments, and that in sharp contrast whereas among those who voted with the South on rules change 88 percent, or 7 out of 8 had gotten an assignment they sought. Of those who voted against the South only 5, or nearly 36 percent, or 1 out of 3, got any new assignment. . . . Only one of those Senators, or 1 out of 14, got the committee which was his first choice, and that was the majority leader. . . .

In other words, of all the Senators applying for a committee assignment in the entire Senate who opposed the South, only the majority leader out of the 14 got his first choice. In other words, all the others were turned down, whereas of the Senators who had voted with the South, six out of eight got their first choice. . . . Then there was another elimination, which reinforces the objectivity of this analysis, and that is that the freshman Senators were eliminated from consideration in this particular analysis.

MR. CLARK. I should like now to continue my theme that the South is overrepresented in the committee structure of the Senate in terms of geography and also in terms of the ideological convictions of Members on the Democratic side of the Senate. The overrepresentation has resulted from the strict carrying out of that rule of seniority which the steering committee so frequently violated—on nine committees to be exact—in the course of making committee assignments for the present session of Congress.

I ask unanimous consent that a brief statement showing the overrepresentation may be printed in the Record at this point as a part of my remarks.

There being no objection, the statement was ordered to be printed in the Record, as follows:

Southern Control of Key Senate Committees

There are 23 Democratic Senators from the South, including the 11 States of the Confederacy and Oklahoma and Arkansas. The southern Senators make up 34 percent of the 67-man Democratic block in the Senate at present. The 23 Senators from the South have far more than 34 percent of the seats on the 4 most important standing committees of the Senate, however, and more than their share of the seats of the Democratic leadership committees.

Committee	Southern seats	Entitled	Overrepresentation
Appropriations	9 (50 percent) out of 18	6	3
Armed Services	5 (42 percent) out of 12	4	1
Finance	6 (55 percent) out of 11	4	2
Foreign Relations	5 (42 percent) out of 12	4	1
Policy	3 (33 percent) out of 9	3	0
Steering	7 (47 percent) out of 15	5	2

MR. CLARK. It will be noted that 50 percent of the members of the Democratic representation on the Appropriations Committee are southern Senators; 42 percent are on the Committee on Armed Services; 55 percent are on the Committee on Finance; 42 percent are on the Committee on Foreign Relations; 47 percent are on the steering committee.

I make the comment, not in criticism of any southern Senator, for surely they are entitled to press their own claims for membership on important committees. I make the comment only to show the extent to which the Senate establishment, led by Senators from the South, but very ably abetted by northern Senators of the Republican Party, led by the intrepid minority leader, has a stranglehold on the four most important legislative committees—Appropriations, Armed Services, Finance, and Foreign Relations—and on the very important Democratic steering committee. It is my contention that if we are to advance the program of the President and do justice to the fair claims of Senators from other sections of the country or of a different ideology, the stranglehold of the bipartisan Senate establishment must eventually be broken; and I believe it will eventually be.

MR. DOUGLAS. Mr. President, while I have been listening to the Senator from Pennsylvania [Mr. Clark] for the past 3 days, and have been studying his remarks in the Congressional Record each morning closely, I have been debating with myself whether I should seek recognition from the Presiding Officer to discuss the points which he has brought out.

I am well aware that to speak on this subject is not popular; that it does not advance one in the assignment of positions; and that it tends to be resented by many who occupy influential positions in the Senate and in the country.

Nevertheless, I felt that it was my duty to indicate that the Senator from Pennsylvania did not stand alone in what he said, and that some indication should be given, through the Congressional Record, that there are some—and I believe many—of us who believe in the basic positions which he has been advancing.

Let me say at the very beginning that I have no personal complaints to make so far as my own treatment is concerned. I am a member of two important committees, the Banking and Currency Committee, of which I have been a member ever since I first came to the Senate more than 14 years ago, and the Finance Committee, which I tried to get on for a number of years and had some difficulty in making, but to which I was finally assigned. I am also a member of the Joint Economic Committee.

So I want to make it clear that I have absolutely no complaint about the way I have been assigned to committees, nor have I any complaint whatsoever about the way I have been treated by those who hold different opinions from mine on public policy. Furthermore, I have no animus toward those who are in control of the party senatorial policy. I do not question their motives. I think they are conscientious, according to their lights, and that they have in many ways estimable qualities which deserve recognition.

Nevertheless, the Senator from Pennsylvania has put his finger on one of the weaknesses of our party and one of the weaknesses of the Senate.

The Democratic Party wins its presidential elections by the votes of the great industrial States. It wins those elections on platforms which are believed in by the voters and which pledge to carry out legislative programs which will be in the interest of the great masses of the American people; namely, the wage earners, the small farmers, the white-collar workers, the small businessmen, the housewives, and the consumers. That is how we win our presidential elections. Then the Congress convenes, and we are not able to pass any considerable portion of the program upon which we have gone to the country, and we find that the machinery of the Senate, and I think largely of the House, is in the hands of those who fundamentally do not believe in the program by which the presidential election was won and for which the great mass of voters in the country cast their ballots.

We all know this to be a fact. No one can be around this body for 2 or 3 years—indeed, less than that—without knowing it to be the case. No one can be around here for any space of time without knowing that the combination against such a program operates from both sides of the aisle; that what we have is really a bipartisan alliance, a coalition which is basically opposed to the platform of the Democratic Party.

Many of us have been reading the book "The Deadlock of Democracy" by James Burns, in which I think he correctly states that there are four parties. Even though I think his classification is not precisely accurate, there are four parties. There are the liberal and progressive Democrats, the conservative Democrats, the conservative Republicans, and the liberal Republicans—a small but gallant band. The two center groups, conservative Democrats and conservative Republicans, work in very close alliance with each other, dominate the major committees, control the procedures of the Senate, and in the main stymie the legislation for which the presidential candidate of the Democratic Party has gone to the country.

There is no use, to my mind, in denying these facts, but apparently it is regarded as bad form to call attention to them. I am reminded of the story in Hans Christian Andersen's "Fairy Tales," about the emperor who had a suit of clothes supposedly woven for him which was in reality nonexistent. He paraded in this suit of clothes. Others were expected to admire the suit of clothes. Finally, a very naive boy said, "The emperor has no clothes." Then the illusion was punctured and the people saw the king in his full nakedness. The reluctance of some to discuss the facts of the organization of the Senate is similar to the reluctance to admit that the emperor had no clothes.

Consider the committee chairmanships. Of 14 major chairmen, 10 come from the Southern States, 2 from the Southwestern States, and 2 from States in other parts of the country.

I refer to the bipartisan coalition—I suppose the Senator from Pennsylvania would call it the senatorial establishment—and its followers. I suppose the author of "The Citadel" would call it the club. They mean the same thing and largely refer to the same persons. They control the Senate.

I personally believe the result of permitting the coalition's dominance to continue has been that we have not moved forward in the field of legislation as rapidly as we should have done. I also feel, as a Democrat, that it is of increasing disadvantage to the party in making an appeal to the country, because people are properly saying, "You campaign on these platforms, but you do not or cannot put them into effect when we elect you."

Therefore, the bipartisan alliance, which really carries out the Republican platform, operates against Democratic senatorial and congressional candidates from the North and the West, operates against our presidential candidate, and is indeed an albatross around the neck of the Democratic Party.

Yet we are not supposed to talk about it because we might offend someone or might indicate that matters are decided in a different way from the way they are discussed in public. In short, we should not call attention to the nakedness of the emperor.

However, I happen to be one who believes that the truth in these matters is extremely important and that to recognize the facts is the first step toward cure. We all know it is so in the field of medicine. Diagnosis comes first; cure comes second. As long as one denies he is ill, as long as he believes everything is fine, he will not take steps to cure the situation. Not until evidence piles up, crippling symptoms appear, and real sickness develops are corrective measures adopted. . . .

Mr. President, I think the party and the Senate need a few people who will say, "The emperor has no clothes on," and who will state the truth.

It is not popular to do that. The Senator from Pennsylvania [Mr. Clark] took great risks by making the speech he made. He can always be accused of "sour grapes," and can be told, "The legislation you favor will not go through. The dam your constituents want will not be built. The river improvements your constituents want will not be made." But the Senator from Pennsylvania felt that he must speak out, and I think he has performed a very valuable service.

He did not speak to a crowded Senate; and I am not speaking to a crowded Senate, either, exactly. Very few of the lords of the press are now in the Press Gallery. But our words will appear in the Congressional Record, which some people read; and voices in this country are not entirely muffled.

Mr. President, I wish to say, in all kindness, that the Democratic Party is not served by putting the Congressional structure of the party in opposition to its platform. The Democratic Party is not served by attempting to deny the existence of palpable truths. The Democratic Party is not served when Senators such as the Senator from Utah [Mr. Moss], the Senator from North Dakota [Mr. Burdick], the Senator from Wisconsin [Mr. Proxmire], the Senator from Michigan [Mr. Hart], the Senator from Ohio [Mr. Young], and the Senator from California [Mr. Engle] are discriminated against; nor is the Democratic Party served when Senators who go along with the bipartisan coalition are rewarded. . . .

Unless we put more vitality into the congressional work of our party, it will be very hard to go before the voters in 1964 and urge them to vote for the party. The tragedy is that in 1964, of the 24 now sitting Democratic Senators who then will be running for reelection, 21 come from the North and from the West, and, in the main, represent the progressive wing or the liberal wing of the party; they may pay with their political lives for the sins of others.

Sometimes, Mr. President, in my sardonic moments, I wonder whether this is also a part of the plan—to discredit the party, to defeat the Senators from the North and the Senators from the West who otherwise might threaten the supremacy of the bipartisan alliance, and then to emerge with an even tighter control over the Senate than before, with the bipartisan coalition swollen in numbers and the liberal opposition diminished. . . .

MR. MANSFIELD. What I believe those who complain of an "establishment" are, in the final analysis, complaining against is the ever-present fact of frustration, the frustration of working in this body, the frustration of half a loaf, the frustration of compromise that of necessity is always with us. Who among us does not feel this heavy cloak of dissatisfaction? Less than absolute power to achieve one's will is the essence of frustration. Yet less than absolute power to achieve one's will is also an essential of democracy. The practice of democracy is therefore frustrating, and let us be sure that when it ceases to be so for any group or faction, at that same time there will also have ceased to be a democracy. That same principle pervades all we do here, and we should thank God it does.

Now let us begin the substantive debates of the 88th Congress. I urge the Senate to get off the business of the Senate and get on with the business of the Nation.

CHAPTER EIGHT

The Judiciary

The establishment and maintenance of an independent judicial system is an important part of constitutional government. The United States Supreme Court was created on this basis, with its members given life tenure and guaranteed compensation; however, Congress was given power to structure the entire subordinate judicial system, including control over the appellate jurisdiction of the Supreme Court. Regardless of any initial lack of power, and notwithstanding various attempts made by and through Congress to curb its power, the Supreme Court today occupies a predominant position in the governmental system. This chapter will analyze the evolution of the Court, and indicate the nature and implications of its present powers.

31. Constitutional Background

The Supreme Court and the judicial system play an important part in the intricate separation of powers scheme. Through judicial review both legislative and executive decisions may be overruled by the courts for a number of reasons. To some extent, then, the judiciary acts as a check upon arbitrary action by governmental departments and agents. What was the intent of the framers of the Constitution regarding the role of the judiciary, and more particularly the Supreme Court, in our governmental system? This may be seen in the following selection from *The Federalist*.

FEDERALIST 78

Alexander Hamilton

W E proceed now to an examination of the judiciary department of the proposed government.

In unfolding the defects of the existing confederation, the utility and necessity of a federal judicature have been clearly pointed out. It is the less necessary to recapitulate the considerations there urged; as the propriety of the institution in the abstract is not disputed; the only questions which have been raised being relative to the manner of constituting it, and to its extent. To these points, therefore, our observations shall be confined.

The manner of constituting it seems to embrace these several objects: 1st. The mode of appointing the judges; 2nd. the tenure by which they are to hold their places; 3rd. The partition of the judiciary authority between different courts, and their relations to each other.

First. As to the mode of appointing the judges: This is the same with that of appointing the officers of the union in general, and has been so fully discussed . . . that nothing can be said here which would not be useless repetition.

Second. As to the tenure by which the judges are to hold their places: This chiefly concerns their duration in office; the provisions for their support; the precautions for their responsibility.

According to the plan of the convention, all the judges who may be appointed by the United States are to hold their offices *during good behavior*; which is conformable to the most approved of the state constitutions. . . . The standard of good behavior for the continuance in office of the judicial magistracy is certainly one of the most valuable of the modern improvements in the practice of government. In a monarchy, it is an excellent barrier to the despotism of the prince; in a republic, it is a no less excellent barrier to the encroachments and oppressions of the representative body. And it is the best expedient which can be devised in any government, to secure a steady, upright, and impartial administration of the laws.

Whoever attentively considers the different departments of power must perceive, that, in a government in which they are separated from each other, the judiciary, from the nature of its functions, will always be the least dangerous to the political rights of the constitution; because it will be least in a capacity to annoy or injure them. The executive not only dispenses the honors, but holds the sword of the community. The legislature not only commands the purse, but prescribes the rules by which the duties and rights of every citizen are to be regulated. The judiciary, on the contrary, has no influence over either the sword or the purse; no direction either of the strength or of the wealth of the society; and can take no active resolution whatever. It may truly be said to have neither FORCE NOR WILL, but merely judgment; and must ultimately depend upon the aid of the executive arm for the efficacious exercise even of this faculty.

This simple view of the matter suggests several important consequences: It proves incontestably, that the judiciary is beyond comparison, the weakest of the three departments of power, that it can never attack with success either of the other two; and that all possible care is requisite to enable it to defend itself against their attacks. It equally proves, that, though individual oppression may now and then proceed from the courts of justice, the general liberty of the people can never be endangered from that quarter; I mean so long as the judiciary remains truly distinct from both the legislature and executive. For I agree, that "there is no liberty, if the power of judging be not separated from the legislative and executive powers." It proves, in the last place, that as liberty can have nothing to fear from the judiciary alone, but would have everything to fear from its union with either of the other departments; that, as all the effects of such an union must ensue from a dependence of the former on the latter, notwithstanding a nominal and apparent separation; that as, from the natural feebleness of the judiciary, it is in continual jeopardy of being overpowered, awed or influenced by its co-ordinate branches; that, as nothing can contribute so much to its firmness and independence as PERMANENCY IN OFFICE, this quality may therefore be justly regarded as an indispensable ingredient in its constitution; and, in a great measure, as the CITADEL of the public justice and the public security.

The complete independence of the courts of justice is peculiarly essential in a limited constitution. By a limited constitution, I understand one which contains certain specified exceptions to the legislative authority; such, for instance, as that it shall pass no bills of attainder, no *ex post facto* laws, and the like. Limitations of this kind can be preserved in practice no other way than through the medium of the courts of justice, whose duty it must be to declare all acts contrary to the manifest tenor of the constitution void. Without this, all the reservations of particular rights or privileges would amount to nothing.

Some perplexity respecting the right of the courts to pronounce legislative acts void, because contrary to the constitution, has arisen from an imagination that the doctrine would imply a superiority of the judiciary to the legislative power. It is urged that the authority which can declare the acts of another void, must necessarily be superior to the one whose acts may be declared void. As this doctrine is of great importance in all the American constitutions, a brief discussion of the grounds on which it rests cannot be unacceptable.

There is no position which depends on clearer principles than that every act of a delegated authority, contrary to the tenor of the commission under which it is exercised, is void. No legislative act, therefore, contrary to the constitution, can be valid. To deny this would be to affirm, that the deputy is greater than his principal; that the servant is above his master; that the representatives of the people are superior to the people themselves; that men, acting by virtue of powers, may do not only what their powers do not authorize, but what they forbid.

If it be said that the legislative body are themselves the constitutional judges of their own powers, and that the construction they put upon them is conclusive upon the other departments, it may be answered, that this cannot be the natural presumption, where it is not to be collected from any particular provisions in the constitution. It is not otherwise to be supposed that the constitution could intend to enable the representatives of the people to substitute their *will* to that of their constituents. It is far more rational to suppose that the courts were designed to be an intermediate body between the people and the legislature, in order, among other things, to keep the latter within the limits assigned to their authority. The interpretation of the laws is the proper and peculiar province of the courts. A constitution is, in fact, and must be, regarded by the judges as a fundamental law. It must therefore belong to them to ascertain its meaning, as well as the meaning of any particular act proceeding from the legislative body. If there should happen to be an irreconcilable variance between the two, that which has the superior obligation and validity ought, of course, to be preferred; in other words, the constitution ought to be preferred to the statute, the intention of the people to the intention of their agents.

Nor does his conclusion by any means suppose a superiority of the judicial to the legislative power. It only supposes that the power of the people is superior to both; and that where the will of the legislature declared in its statutes, stands in opposition to that of the people declared in the constitution, the judges ought to be governed by the latter, rather than the former. They ought to regulate their decisions by the fundamental laws, rather than by those which are not fundamental. . . .

It can be of no weight to say, that the courts, on the pretense of a repugnancy, may substitute their own pleasure to the constitutional intentions of the legislature. This might as well happen in the case of two contradictory statutes; or it might as well happen in every adjudication upon any single statute. The courts must declare the sense of the law; and if they should be disposed to exercise WILL instead of JUDGMENT, the consequence would equally be the substitution of their pleasure to that of the legislative body. The observation, if it proved anything, would prove that there ought to be no judges distinct from the body.

If then the courts of justice are to be considered as the bulwarks of a limited constitution, against legislative encroachments, this consideration will afford a strong argument for the permanent tenure of judicial officers, since nothing will contribute so much as this to that independence spirit in the judges, which must be essential to the faithful performance of so arduous a duty.

This independence of the judges is equally requisite to guard the constitution and the rights of individuals, from the effects of those ill-humors which the arts of designing men, or the influence of particular conjunctures, sometimes disseminate among the people themselves, and which, though they speedily give place to better information, and more deliberate reflection, have a tendency, in the meantime, to occasion dangerous innovations in the government, and serious oppressions of the minor party in the community. . . . Until the people have, by some solemn and authoritative act, annulled or changed the established form, it is binding upon themselves collectively, as well as individually; and no presumption, or even knowledge of their sentiments, can warrant their representatives in a departure from it, prior to such an act. But it is easy to see, that it would require an uncommon portion of fortitude in the judges to do their duty as faithful guardians of the constitution, where legislative invasions of it had been instigated by the major voice of the community.

But it is not with a view to infractions of the constitution only, that the independence of the judges may be an essential safeguard against the effects of occasional ill-humors in the society. These sometimes extend no farther than to the injury of the private rights of particular classes of citizens, by unjust and partial laws. Here also the firmness of the judicial magistracy is of vast importance in mitigating the severity, and confining the operation of such laws. It not only serves to moderate the immediate mischiefs of those which may have been passed, but it operates as a check upon the legislative body in passing them; who, perceiving that obstacles to the success of an iniquitous intention are to be expected from the scruples of the courts, are in a manner compelled by the very motives of the injustice they meditate, to qualify their attempts. . . .

That inflexible and uniform adherence to the rights of the constitution, and of individuals, which we perceive to be indispensable in the courts of justice, can certainly not be expected from judges who hold their offices by a temporary commission. Periodical appointments, however regulated, or by whomsoever made, would, in some way or other, be fatal to their necessary independence. If the power of making them was committed either to the executive or legislature, there would be danger of an improper compliance to the branch which possessed it; if to both, there would be an unwillingness to hazard the displeasure of either; if to the people, or to persons chosen by them for the special purpose, there would be too great a disposition to consult popularity, to justify a reliance that nothing would be consulted but the constitution and the laws.

There is yet a further and a weighty reason for the permanency of judicial offices, which is deducible from the nature of the qualifications they require. It has been frequently remarked, with great propriety, that a voluminous code of laws is one of the inconveniences necessarily connected with the advantages of a free government. To avoid an arbitrary discretion in the courts, it is indispensable that they should be bound down by strict rules and precedents, which serve to define and point out their duty in every particular case that comes before them; and it will readily be conceived, from the variety of controversies which grow out of the folly and wickedness of mankind, that the records of those precedents must unavoidably swell to a very considerable bulk, and must demand long and laborious study to acquire a competent knowledge of them. Hence it is, that there can be but few men in the society, who will have sufficient skill in the laws to qualify them for the stations of judges. And making the proper deductions for the ordinary depravity of human nature, the number must be still smaller, of those who unite the requisite integrity with the requisite knowledge. . . .

From *Federalist 78* students can observe that the intent of the framers of the Constitution, at least as expressed and represented by Hamilton, was to give to the courts the power of judicial review, *i.e.,* the power to declare legislative or executive acts unconstitutional. Students should note that this concept was not explicitly written into the Constitution. Although the reason for this omission is not known it is reasonable to assume that the framers felt that the nature of judicial power implied judicial review; further, it is possible that the framers did not expressly spell out the powers of the judiciary in the realm of judicial review because of the need for adoption of the Constitution by the states; judicial power would extend to them as well as to the co-ordinate departments of the national government.

The power of the Supreme Court to invalidate an act of Congress was stated by John Marshall in *Marbury* v. *Madison*, 1 Cranch 137 (1803). At issue was a provision in the Judiciary Act of 1789 which extended the *original jurisdiction* of the Supreme Court by authorizing it to issue writs of mandamus in cases involving public officers of the United States and private persons, a power not conferred upon the Court in the Constitution. Marbury had been appointed a justice of the peace by President Adams under the Judiciary Act of 1801, which was passed by the Federalists after Jefferson and the Republican party won the elections in the fall of 1800, in order to enable President Adams to fill various newly created judicial posts with Federalists before he had to leave office in March, 1801. Marbury was scheduled to receive one of these commissions, but when Jefferson took office on March 4, with Madison as his Secretary of State, it had not been delivered. Marbury filed a suit with the Supreme Court requesting it to exercise its original jurisdiction and issue a writ of mandamus (a writ to compel an administrative officer to perform his duty) to compel Madison to deliver his commission, something which both Jefferson and Madison were opposed to doing. In his decision Marshall, a prominent Federalist, stated that although Marbury had a legal right to his commission, and although mandamus was the proper remedy, the Supreme Court could not extend its original jurisdiction beyond the limits specified in the Constitution; therefore, that section of the Judiciary Act of 1789 permitting the court to issue such writs to public officers was unconstitutional. Incidentally, the Republicans were so outraged at the last-minute appointments of Adams there were threats that Marshall would be impeached if he issued a writ of mandamus directing Madison to deliver the commission. This is not to suggest, of course, that Marshall let such considerations influence him; however, from a political point of view his decision was a masterpiece at reconciling his position as a Federalist with the political tenor of the times.

MARBURY v. MADISON
1 Cranch 137 (1803)

MR. Chief Justice Marshall delivered the opinion of the Court, saying in part:

. . . The authority, therefore, given to the Supreme Court, by the [Judiciary Act of 1789] . . . establishing the judicial courts of the United States, to issue writs of mandamus to public officers, appears not to be warranted by the Constitution [because it adds to the original jurisdiction of the Court delineated by the framers of the Constitution in Article III; had they wished this power to be conferred upon the Court it would be so stated, in the same manner that the other parts of the Court's original jurisdiction are stated]; . . . it becomes necessary to inquire whether a jurisdiction so conferred can be exercised.

The question whether an act repugnant to the Constitution can become the law of the land, is a question deeply interesting to the United States; but, happily, not of an intricacy proportioned to its interest. It seems only necessary to recognize certain principles supposed to have been long and well established, to decide it.

That the people have an original right to establish, for their future government, such principles as, in their opinion, shall most conduce to their own happiness, is the basis on which the whole American fabric has been erected. The exercise of this original right is a very great exertion; nor can it nor ought it to be frequently repeated. The principles, therefore, so established, are deemed fundamental. And as the authority from which they proceed is supreme, and can seldom act, they are designed to be permanent.

This original and supreme will organizes the government, and assigns to different departments their respective powers. It may either stop here, or establish certain limits not to be transcended by those departments.

The government of the United States is of the latter description. The powers of the legislature are defined and limited; and that those limits may not be mistaken, or forgotten, the Constitution is written. To what purpose are powers limited, and to what purpose is that limitation committed to writing, if these limits may, at any time, be passed by those intended to be restrained? The distinction between a government with limited and unlimited powers is abolished, if those limits do not confine the persons on whom they are imposed, and if acts prohibited and acts allowed, are of equal obligation. It is a proposition too plain to be contested, that the Constitution controls any legislative act repugnant to it; or, that the legislature may alter the Constitution by an ordinary act.

Between these alternatives there is no middle ground. The Constitution is either a superior paramount law, unchangeable by ordinary means, or it is on a level with ordinary legislative acts, and, like other acts, is alterable when the legislature shall please to alter it.

If the former part of the alternative be true, then a legislative act contrary to the Constitution, is not law; if the latter part be true, then written constitutions are absurd attempts, on the part of the people, to limit a power in its own nature illimitable.

Certainly all those who have framed written constitutions contemplate them as forming the fundamental and paramount law of the nation, and, consequently, the theory of every such government must be, that an act of the legislature, repugnant to the constitution, is void.

This theory is essentially attached to a written constitution, and is consequently to be considered, by this court, as one of the fundamental principles of our society. It is not, therefore, to be lost sight of in the further consideration of this subject.

If an act of the legislature, repugnant to the Constitution, is void, does it, notwithstanding its invalidity, bind the courts, and oblige them to give it effect? Or, in other words, though it be not law, does it constitute a rule as operative as if it was a law? This would be to overthrow in fact what was established in theory; and would seem, at first view, an absurdity too gross to be insisted on. It shall, however, receive a more attentive consideration.

It is emphatically the province and duty of the judicial department to say what the law is. Those who apply the rule to particular cases, must of necessity expound and interpret that rule. If two laws conflict with each other, the courts must decide on the operation of each.

So if the law be in opposition to the Constitution; if both the law and the Constitution apply to a particular case, so that the court must either decide that case conformably to the law, disregarding the Constitution, or conformably to the Constitution, disregarding the law, the court must determine which of these conflicting rules governs the case. This is of the very essence of judicial duty.

If, then, the courts are to regard the Constitution, and the Constitution is superior to any ordinary act of the legislature, the Constitution, and not such ordinary act, must govern the case to which they both apply.

Those, then, who controvert the principle that the Constitution is to be considered, in court, as a paramount law, are reduced to the necessity of maintaining that courts must close their eyes on the Constitution, and see only the law.

This doctrine would subvert the very foundation of all written constitutions. It would declare that an act which, according to the principles and theory of our government, is entirely void, is yet, in practice, completely obligatory. It would declare that if the legislature shall do what is expressly forbidden, such act, notwithstanding the express prohibition, is in reality effectual. It would be giving to the legislature a practical and real omnipotence, with the same breath which professes to restrict their powers within narrow limits. It is prescribing limits, and declaring that those limits may be passed at pleasure.

That it thus reduces to nothing what we have deemed the greatest improvement on political institutions, a written constitution, would of itself be sufficient, in America, where written constitutions have been viewed with so much reverence, for rejecting the construction. But the peculiar expressions of the Constitution of the United States furnish additional arguments in favor of its rejection.

The judicial power of the United States is extended to all cases arising under the Constitution.

Could it be the intention of those who gave this power, to say that in using it the Constitution should not be looked into? That a case arising under the Constitution should be decided without examining the instrument under which it arises?

This is too extravagant to be maintained.

In some cases, then, the Constitution must be looked into by the judges. And if they can open it at all, what part of it are they forbidden to read or to obey?

There are many other parts of the Constitution which serve to illustrate this subject.

It is declared that "no tax or duty shall be laid on articles exported from any State." Suppose a duty on the export of cotton, of tobacco, or of flour; and a suit instituted to recover it. Ought judgment to be rendered in such a case? Ought the judges to close their eyes on the Constitution, and only see the law?

The Constitution declares "that no bill of attainder or *ex post facto* law shall be passed."

If, however, such a bill should be passed, and a person should be prosecuted under it, must the court condemn to death those victims whom the Constitution endeavors to preserve?

"No person," says the Constitution, "shall be convicted of treason unless on the testimony of two witnesses to the same overt act, or on confession in open court."

Here the language of the Constitution is addressed especially to the courts. It prescribes, directly for them, a rule of evidence not to be departed from. If the legislature should change that rule, and declare one witness, or a confession out of court, sufficient for conviction, must the constitutional principle yield to the legislative act?

From these, and many other selections which might be made, it is apparent that the framers of the Constitution contemplated that instrument as a rule for the government of courts, as well as of the legislature.

Why otherwise does it direct the judges to take an oath to support it? This oath certainly applies in an especial manner to their conduct in their official character. How immoral to impose it on them, if they were to be used as the instruments, and the knowing instruments, for violating what they swear to support!

The oath of office, too, imposed by the legislature, is completely demonstrative of the legislative opinion on this subject. It is in these words: "I do solemnly swear that I will administer justice without respect to persons, and do equal right to the poor and to the rich; and that I will faithfully and impartially discharge all the duties incumbent on me as ———, according to the best of my abilities and understanding, agreeably to the Constitution and laws of the United States."

Why does a judge swear to discharge his duties agreeably to the Constitution of the United States, if that Constitution forms no rule for his government—if it is closed upon him, and cannot be inspected by him?

If such be the real state of things, this is worse than solemn mockery. To prescribe, or to take this oath, becomes equally a crime.

It is also not entirely unworthy of observation, that in declaring what shall be the supreme law of the land, the Constitution itself is first mentioned; and not the laws of the United States generally, but those only which shall be made in pursuance of the Constitution, have that rank.

Thus, the particular phraseology of the Constitution of the United States confirms and strengthens the principle, supposed to be essential to all written constitutions, that a law repugnant to the Constitution is void; and that courts, as well as other departments, are bound by that instrument.

The rule must be discharged. 🦅

32. Powers and Limitations of the Supreme Court

Paul A. Freund, in his book entitled *On Understanding the Supreme Court* (1949), notes that the Supreme Court has a definite political role. He asks: "Is the law of the Supreme Court a reflection of the notions of 'policy' held by its members? The question recalls the controversy over whether judges 'make' or 'find' the law. A generation or two ago it was thought rather daring to insist that judges make law. Old Jeremiah Smith, who began the teaching of law at Harvard after a career on the New Hampshire Supreme Court, properly deflated the issue. 'Do judges make law?' he repeated. ''Course they do. Made some myself.' Of course Supreme Court Justices decide cases on the basis of their ideas of policy." To emphasize this point today is to repeat the familiar. The Court makes policy. It would be difficult to conceive how a Court having the power to interpret the Constitution could fail to make policy, *i.e.,* could fail to make rulings that have *general* impact upon the community as a whole. The essential distinction between policy-making and adjudication is that the former has general effect while the latter affects only a specifically designated person or group.

If the Supreme Court has this power of constitutional interpretation, how is it controlled in its relationships with the other governmental departments and with the community? Is it, as some have claimed, completely arbitrary in rendering many of its decisions? Is it, potentially, a dictatorial body? The late Justice Robert H. Jackson answered some of these questions in the following selection.

THE SUPREME COURT AS A UNIT OF GOVERNMENT
*Robert H. Jackson**

We ought first to inquire what kind of institution the Supreme Court really is, the degree of its independence, the nature of its power, and the limitations on its capacity and effectiveness. . . .

The Supreme Court of the United States was created in a different manner from most high courts. In Europe, most judiciaries evolved as sub-

* From *The Supreme Court in the American System of Government,* by Robert H. Jackson. Copyright © 1955, by William Eldred Jackson and G. Bowdoin Craighill, Jr., Executors. Reprinted by permission of the Executors and the publishers, Harvard University Press.

ordinates to the King, who delegated to them some of his functions. For example, while the English judges have developed a remarkably independent status, they still retain the formal status of Crown servants. But here, the Supreme Court and the other branches of the Federal Government came into existence at the same time and by the same act of creation. "We the People of the United States" deemed an independent Court equally as essential as a Congress or an Executive, especially, I suppose, to "establish Justice, insure domestic Tranquility," and to "secure the Blessings of Liberty to ourselves and to our Posterity." The status of the Court as a unit of the Government, not as an institution subordinate to it, no doubt has given it prestige, for the people do not regard the Justices as employees of the Government of the day or as civil servants, as in continental Europe. Also, federal judges enjoy two bulwarks of independence —life tenure (except for impeachable misbehavior) and irreducible salaries (except by taxation and inflation).

Nonetheless, the Constitution-makers left the Court in vital respects a dependent body. The political branches nominate and confirm the Justices, a control of the Court's composition which results in a somewhat lagging political influence over its trend of decision, and any party that prevails in the Federal Government through several presidential terms will gradually tend to impress its political philosophy on the Court. The political branches also from time to time may alter the number of Justices, and that power was used to influence the course of decision several times before it was again proposed by President Roosevelt.

The Court also is dependent on the political branches for its powers in other vital respects. Its only irrevocable jurisdiction is original, and that reaches only cases affecting Ambassadors, public Ministers, or Consuls, or cases in which a state is a party. In all other cases it has appellate jurisdiction, but "with such exceptions and under such regulations as Congress shall make." One Congress, fearing a decision unfavorable to its post-Civil War enactments, ousted the court of jurisdiction in a case that had already been argued, and the Court submitted. The Court also is dependent upon the political branches for the execution of its mandates, for it has no physical force at its command. The story is traditional that President Jackson once withheld enforcement, saying, "John Marshall has made his decision:—*now let him enforce it!*" Also, the Court, of course, depends upon Congress for the appropriation of funds with which to operate. These all add up to a fairly formidable political power over the Supreme Court, if there were a disposition to exert it.

But perhaps the most significant and least comprehended limitation upon the judicial power is that this power extends only to cases and controversies. We know that this restriction was deliberate, for it was proposed in the Convention that the Supreme Court be made part of a Council of Revision with a kind of veto power, and this was rejected.

The result of the limitation is that the Court's only power is to decide lawsuits between adversary litigants with real interests at stake, and its only method of proceeding is by the conventional judicial, as distinguished from legislative or administrative, process. This precludes the rendering of advisory opinions even at the request of the nation's President and every form of pronouncement on abstract, contingent, or hypothetical issues. It prevents acceptance for judicial settlement of issues in which the interests and questions involved are political in character. It also precludes imposition on federal constitutional courts of nonjudicial duties. Recent trends to empower judges to grant or deny wiretapping rights to a prosecutor or to approve a waiver or prosecution in order to force a witness to give self-incriminating testimony raise interesting and dubious questions. A federal court can perform but one function—that of deciding litigations—and can proceed in no manner except by the judicial process. . . .

While the President or the Congress can take up any subject at any time, a court in our Anglo-American system is a substantially passive instrument, to be moved only by the initiative of litigants. The Supreme Court cannot take most cases until at least one and generally two courts below have heard and decided them, which, with the present congestion of calendars, may be very long indeed. Also, as an appellate court, it properly can act only on the state of facts revealed by the record made in the court below, supplemented sometimes by general information of which it may take judicial notice. Hence a claim of right may be prejudiced by the incompetence, carelessness, or collusion of attorneys, as where they fail to make an adequate record to support the question sought to be raised. The decision of a case also may depend on its peculiarities of fact, for it is still true that hard cases make bad law. And when it is all over, the judicial decree, however broadly worded, actually binds, in most instances, only the parties to the case. As to others, it is merely a weather vane showing which way the judicial wind is blowing—a precedent that the Court in a similar case is likely to follow. Its real weight in subsequent cases, however, will depend on many factors, such as the quality of the prevailing opinion, the strength of any dissent, the acceptance or criticism by the profession, and the experience in application of the rule. Thus, the process of the courts is adapted to the intensive examination of particular legal grievances.

No conclusion as to what can be expected of the Court is valid which overlooks the measure of its incapacity to entertain and decide cases under its traditional working methods. With few exceptions, Congress has found it necessary to make review in the Supreme Court not the right of a litigant but a discretionary matter with the Court itself, in order to keep the volume of its business within its capacity. Last term, review was sought by appeal and certiorari in 1,452 cases, only 119 of which were allowed. It is not necessary to detail the considerations which move the Court to grant review beyond saying that the grant is not intended merely to give a litigant another chance, nor does it depend on the dollars involved or the private interests affected, but upon the importance of the case to a uniform and just system of federal law. . . .

From what I have said it might almost be assumed that the Supreme Court could be ignored in the power equation of the American Government. But in living history this institution has profoundly influenced, for better or for worse, the course of the nation. Not only has it been the center of bitter debate itself, but its decisions have played some part in nearly every great political issue that has vexed our people.

What authority does the Court possess which generates this influence? The answer is its power to hold unconstitutional and judicially unenforceable an act of the President, of Congress, or a constituent state of the Federation. That power is not expressly granted or hinted at in the Article defining judicial power, but rests on logical implication. It is an incident of jurisdiction to determine what really is the law governing a particular case or controversy. In the hierarchy of legal values, if the higher law of the Constitution prohibits what the lower law of the legislature attempts, the latter is a nullity; otherwise, the Constitution would exist only at the option of Congress. Thus it comes about that in a private litigation the Court may decide a question of power that will be of great moment to the nation or to a state.

The assertion of this power over the enactments of the states met with strong resistance, and its application to laws of Congress provoked bitter and persistent opposition. It is needless to trace the evolution of the power as now exercised. The Rooseveltian struggle with the Court did not impair the power, which is as positively asserted today as in pre-Roosevelt days. But neither did that struggle end the controversy over the proper use of the power, a controversy which lies just beneath the surface and is likely to break forth from time to time as long as the Republic shall last.

Public opinion, however, seems always to sustain the power of the Court, even against attack by popular executives and even though the public more than once has repudiated particular decisions. It is inescapable in our form of government that authority exist somewhere to interpret an instrument which sets up our whole structure and defines the powers of the Federal Government in about 4,000 words, to which a century and a half have added only about half as many amendatory words. The people have seemed to feel that the Supreme Court, whatever its defects, is still the most detached, dispassionate, and trustworthy custodian that our system affords for the translation of abstract into concrete constitutional commands.

The Constitution has gone through several cycles of interpretation, each of which is related to the political and economic condition of the period. Federal powers were consolidated and invigorated under Marshall. A reaction marked by conflict over the very nature and binding force of the compact embittered the time of Taney. There followed a period when attention turned to nationalism and to railroad building and industrial growth stimulated by a long period of almost uninterrupted peace. That came to an end in 1914, and we entered the period of international violence which now burdens and vexes us and puts our internal liberties under new strains.

That the Supreme Court, in some instances, can interpose judicial authority between political forces and those whose liberty they would override is a great distinction from those governments abroad which have been subverted by dictatorship. But I have tried to point out that while our judiciary is an effective instrument for applying to the case of an individual the just laws enacted by representatives of a freedom-respecting society, it has grave jurisdictional, procedural, and political shortcomings. These counsel against leaving the protection of liberty wholly to the judiciary, while heedlessly allowing the elected branches of the Government to be constituted without regard to their members' attitudes toward liberty.

Let us take the factor of delay. Since the Court may pronounce a judgment of unconstitutionality only in deciding a case or controversy, obviously it cannot take the initiative in checking what the Justices may know to be constitutional violations. It has no self-starting capacity and must await the action of some litigant so aggrieved as to have a justiciable case. Also, its pronouncement must await the decision in the lower courts. Often it is years after a statute is put on the books and begins to take effect before a decision on a constitutional question can be heard by the Supreme Court. The Smith Act of 1940 was held constitutional for the first time in 1951, and the Alien Registration Act, also of 1940, was passed on in 1952. The run of constitutional litigation, like that of all litigations, is slow and costly.

Such delays often mean that the damage is done before the remedy for invasion of civil liberties is available. For example: In 1951 the Court cast serious doubt upon the legality of the Attorney General's list of subversive organizations promulgated in 1947. But the list had long been widely circulated and accepted, and despite the Court's views it has never ceased to be used in the press, in the executive department, by and before congressional committees, and even in courts to prejudice individuals in their liberty, position, and good name.

Then, too, many of the most vital acts of government cannot be challenged at all by the case and controversy route, because the questions are political or involve the spending power, foreign affairs, or the war power. The Supreme Court is a tribunal of limited jurisdiction, narrow processes, and small capacity for handling mass litigation; it has no force to coerce obedience, and is subject to being stripped of jurisdiction or smothered with additional Justices any time such a disposition exists and is supported strongly enough by public opinion. I think the Court can never quite escape consciousness of its own infirmities, a psychology which may explain its apparent yielding to expediency, especially during war time.

If I may borrow a summation from my former self, I will repeat to you the conclusion of a lecture to the lawyers of the Ministry of Justice of France, delivered at their invitation in April 1946, when they were in the throes of writing a new constitution for France. After discussing the judicial vis-a-vis the political power in our system, I said:

"Opinion, of course, will differ as to the advantages and disadvantages of this constitutional and judicial system. The United States on the whole has been a prosperous country, with varied resources, making a favorable background for any experiment in government. Its inhabitants have not faced the strains that beset some less-favored nations. Even so, our history has not been free of sanguinary internal conflicts. It would not be realistic to contend that judicial power always has been used wisely. The Court has been sharply attacked by Presidents Jefferson, Jackson, Lincoln, and both Roosevelts. Yet no substantial sentiment exists for any curtailment of the Court's powers. Even President Roosevelt in the bitterest conflict with judicial power in our history suggested only change in the Court's composition, none in its constitutional prerogatives. The real strength of the position of the Court is probably in its indispensability to government under a written Constitution. It is difficult to see how the provision of a 150-year-old written document can have much vitality if there is not some permanent institution to translate them into current commands and to see to their contemporary application. Courts will differ from time to time in the emphasis they will place on one or another of the Constitution's provisions, in part no doubt responsive to the atmosphere of the changes in public opinion. Interpretations will change from one generation to another, precedents will sometimes be overruled, innovations will be made that will not always be predictable. This always has been the history of the Supreme Court.

"The legal profession in all countries knows that there are only two real choices of government open to a people. It may be governed by law or it may be governed by the will of one or of a group of men. Law, as the expression of the ultimate will and wisdom of a people, has so far proven the safest guardian of liberty yet devised. I think our constitutional and judicial system has made a valuable and enduring contribution to the science of government under law. We commend it to your notice, not because we think it is perfect, but because it is an earnest effort to fulfill those aspirations for freedom and the general welfare which are a common heritage of your people and of mine." ▶

The Supreme Court, and lower courts as well, are not only controlled through external factors. They may, for various reasons, exercise judicial self-restraint in certain cases to avoid difficult and controversial issues, and, in the final analysis, to avoid outside pressure to limit the powers of the judiciary. The following selection by John P. Roche deals with the background, the nature, and the implications of judicial doctrines of self-restraint.

JUDICIAL SELF-RESTRAINT

John P. Roche*

Every society, sociological research suggests, has its set of myths which incorporate and symbolize its political, economic, and social aspirations. Thus, as medieval society had the Quest for the Holy Grail and the cult of

* Quoted with permission from *The American Political Science Review*, Vol. 49 (September 1955).

numerology, we, in our enlightened epoch, have as significant manifestations of our collective hopes the dream of impartial decision-making and
the cult of "behavioral science." While in my view these latter two are
but different facets of the same fundamental drive, namely, the age-old
effort to exorcise human variables from human action, our concern here is
with the first of them, the pervasive tendency in the American political
and constitutional tradition directed toward taking the politics out of
politics, and substituting some set of Platonic guardians for fallible politicians.

While this dream of objectivizing political Truth is in no sense a
unique American phenomenon, it is surely true to say that in no other
democratic nation has the effort been carried so far and with such persistence. Everywhere one turns in the United States, he finds institutionalized
attempts to narrow the political sector and to substitute allegedly "independent" and "impartial" bodies for elected decision-makers. The so-called
"independent regulatory commissions" are a classic example of this tendency in the area of administration, but unquestionably the greatest hopes
for injecting pure Truth-serum into the body politic have been traditionally reserved for the federal judiciary, and particularly for the Supreme
Court. The rationale for this viewpoint is simple: "The people must be
protected from themselves, and no institution is better fitted for the role of
chaperone than the federal judiciary, dedicated as it is to the supremacy
of the rule of law."

Patently central to this function of social chaperonage is the right of
the judiciary to review legislative and executive actions and nullify those
measures which derogate from eternal principles of truth and justice as
incarnated in the Constitution. Some authorities, enraged at what the
Supreme Court has found the Constitution to mean, have essayed to
demonstrate that the Framers did not intend the Court to exercise this
function, to have, as they put it, "the last word." I find no merit in this
contention; indeed, it seems to me undeniable not only that the authors
of the Constitution intended to create a federal government, but also that
they assumed *sub silentio* that the Supreme Court would have the power
to review both national and state legislation.

However, since the intention of the Framers is essentially irrelevant
except to antiquarians and polemicists, it is unnecessary to examine fur-
ther the matter of origins. The fact is that the United States Supreme
Court, and the inferior federal courts under the oversight of the high
Court, have enormous policy-making functions. Unlike their British and
French counterparts, federal judges are not merely technicians who live in

the shadow of a supreme legislature, but are fully equipped to intervene in the process of political decision-making. In theory, they are limited by the Constitution and the jurisdiction it confers, but, in practice, it would be a clumsy judge indeed who could not, by a little skillful exegesis, adapt the Constitution to a necessary end. This statement is in no sense intended as a condemnation; on the contrary, it has been this perpetual reinvigoration by reinterpretation, in which the legislature and the executive as well as the courts play a part, that has given the Constitution its survival power. Applying a Constitution which contains at key points inspired ambiguity, the courts have been able to pour the new wine in the old bottle. Note that the point at issue is not the legitimacy or wisdom of judicial legislation; it is simply the enormous scope that this prerogative gives to judges to substitute their views for those of past generations, or, more controversially, for those of a contemporary Congress and President.

Thus it is naive to assert that the Supreme Court is limited by the Constitution, and we must turn elsewhere for the sources of judicial restraint. The great power exercised by the Court has carried with it great risks, so it is not surprising that American political history has been sprinkled with demands that the judiciary be emasculated. The really startling thing is that, with the notable exception of the McCardle incident in 1869, the Supreme Court has emerged intact from each of these encounters. Despite the plenary power that Congress, under Article III of the Constitution, can exercise over the appellate jurisdiction of the high Court, the national legislature has never taken sustained and effective action against its House of Lords. It is beyond the purview of this analysis to examine the reasons for congressional inaction; suffice it here to say that the most significant form of judicial limitation has remained self-limitation. This is not to suggest that such a development as statutory codification has not cut down the area of interpretive discretion, for it obviously has. It is rather to maintain that when the justices have held back from assaults on legislative or executive actions, they have done so on the basis of self-established rationalizations. . . .

The remainder of this paper is therefore concerned with two aspects of this auto-limitation: first, the techniques by which it is put into practice; and, second, the conditions under which it is exercised. . . .

TECHNIQUES OF JUDICIAL SELF-RESTRAINT

The major techniques of judicial self-restraint appear to fall under the two familiar rubrics: procedural and substantive. Under the former fall the various techniques by which the Court can avoid coming to grips with substantive issues, while under the latter would fall those methods by which the Court, in a substantive holding, finds that the matter at issue in the litigation is not properly one for judicial settlement. Let us examine these two categories in some detail.

Procedural Self-Restraint. Since the passage of the Judiciary Act of 1925, the Supreme Court has had almost complete control over its business. United States Supreme Court *Rule 38,* which governs the certiorari policy, states, (§5) that discretionary review will be granted only "where there are special and important reasons therefor." Professor Fowler Harper has suggested in a series of detailed and persuasive articles on the application of this discretion [*University of Penna. Law Review,* vols. 99-101; 103] that the Court has used it in such a fashion as to duck certain significant but controversial problems. While one must be extremely careful about generalizing in this area, since the reasons for denying certiorari are many and complex, Harper's evidence does suggest that the Court in the period since 1949 has refused to review cases involving important civil liberties problems which on their merits appeared to warrant adjudication. As he states at one point: "It is disconcerting when the Court will review a controversy over a patent on a pin ball machine while one man is deprived of his citizenship and another of his liberty without Supreme Court review of a plausible challenge to the validity of government action." ...

Furthermore, the Supreme Court can issue certiorari on its own terms. Thus in *Dennis* v. *United States,* appealing the Smith Act convictions of the American Communist leadership, the Court accepted the evidential findings of the Second Circuit as final and limited its review to two narrow constitutional issues. This, in effect, burked the basic problem: whether the evidence was sufficient to demonstrate that the Communist party, U.S.A., was *in fact* a clear and present danger to the security of the nation, or whether the Communists were merely shouting "Fire!" in an empty theater.

Other related procedural techniques are applicable in some situations. Simple delay can be employed, perhaps in the spirit of the Croatian proverb that "delay is the handmaiden of justice." ... However, the technique of procedural self-restraint is founded on the essentially simple gadget of refusing jurisdiction, or of procrastinating the acceptance of jurisdiction, and need not concern us further here.

Substantive Self-Restraint. Once a case has come before the Court on its merits, the justices are forced to give some explanation for whatever action they may take. Here self-restraint can take many forms, notably, the doctrine of political questions, the operation of judicial parsimony, and—particularly with respect to the actions of administrative officers or agencies—the theory of judicial inexpertise.

The doctrine of political questions is too familiar to require much elaboration here. Suffice it to say that if the Court feels that a question before it, *e.g.*, the legitimacy of a state government, the validity of a legislative apportionment, or the correctness of executive action in the field of foreign relations, is one that is not properly amenable to judicial settlement, it will refer the plaintiff to the "political" organs of government for any possible relief. The extent to which this doctrine is applied seems to be a direct coefficient of judicial egotism, for the definition of a political question can be expanded or contracted in accordian-like fashion to meet the exigencies of the times. A juridical definition of the term is impossible, for at root the logic that supports it is circular: political questions are matters not soluble by the judicial process; matters not soluble by the judicial process are political questions. As an early dictionary explained, violins are small cellos, and cellos are large violins.

Nor do examples help much in definition. While it is certainly true that the Court cannot mandamus a legislature to apportion a state in equitable fashion, it seems equally true that the Court is without the authority to force state legislators to implement unsegregated public education. Yet in the former instance the Court genuflected to the "political" organs and took no action, while in the latter it struck down segregation as violative of the Constitution.

Judicial parsimony is another major technique of substantive self-restraint. In what is essentially a legal application of Occam's razor, the Court has held that it will not apply any more principles to the settlement of a case than are absolutely necessary, *e.g.*, it will not discuss the constitutionality of a law if it can settle the instant case by statutory construction. Furthermore, if an action is found to rest on erroneous statutory construction, the review terminates at that point: the Court will not go on to discuss whether the statute, properly construed, would be constitutional. A variant form of this doctrine, and a most important one, employs the "case or controversy" approach, to wit, the Court, admitting the importance of the issue, inquires as to whether the litigant actually has standing to bring the matter up. . . .

A classic use of parsimony to escape from a dangerous situation occurred in connection with the evacuation of the Nisei from the West Coast in 1942. Gordon Hirabayashi, in an attempt to test the validity of the regulations clamped on the American-Japanese by the military, violated the curfew and refused to report to an evacuation center. He was convicted on both counts by the district court and sentenced to three months for each offense, the sentences to run *concurrently*. When the case came before the Supreme Court, the justices sustained his conviction for violating the *curfew*, but refused to examine the validity of the evacuation order on the ground that it would not make any difference to Harabayashi anyway; he was in for ninety days no matter what the Court did with evacuation.

A third method of utilizing substantive self-restraint is particularly useful in connection with the activities of executive departments or regulatory agencies, both state and federal. I have entitled it the doctrine of judicial *inexpertise*, for it is founded on the unwillingness of the Court to revise the findings of experts. The earmarks of this form of restraint are great deference to the holdings of the expert agency usually coupled with such a statement as "It is not for the federal courts to supplant the [Texas Railroad] Commission's judgment even in the face of convincing proof that a different result would have been better." In this tradition, the Court has refused to question *some* exercises of discretion by the National Labor Relations Board, the Federal Trade Commission, and other federal and state agencies. But the emphasis on *some* gives the point away: in other cases, apparently on all fours with those in which it pleads its technical *inexpertise*, the Court feels free to assess evidence *de novo* and reach independent judgment on the technical issues involved. . . .

In short, with respect to expert agencies, the Court is equipped with both offensive and defensive gambits. If it chooses to intervene, one set of precedents is brought out, while if it decides to hold back, another set of equal validity is invoked. Perhaps the best summary of this point was made by Justice Harlan in 1910, when he stated bluntly that "the Courts have rarely, if ever, felt themselves so restrained by technical rules that they could not find some remedy, consistent with the law, for acts . . . that violated natural justice or were hostile to the fundamental principles devised for the protection of the essential rights of property."

This does not pretend to be an exhaustive analysis of the techniques of judicial self-restraint; on the contrary, others will probably find many which are not given adequate discussion here. The remainder of this paper, however, is devoted to the second area of concern: the conditions under which the Court refrains from acting.

THE CONDITIONS OF JUDICIAL SELF-RESTRAINT

The conditions which lead the Supreme Court to exercise auto-limitation are many and varied. In the great bulk of cases, this restraint is an outgrowth of sound and quasi-automatic legal maxims which defy teleological interpretation. It would take a master of the conspiracy theory of history to assign meaning, for example, to the great majority of certiorari denials; the simple fact is that these cases do not merit review. However, in a small proportion of cases, purpose does appear to enter the picture, sometimes with a vengeance. It is perhaps unjust to the Court to center our attention on this small proportion, but it should be said in extenuation that these cases often involve extremely significant political and social issues. In the broad picture, the refusal to grant certiorari in 1943 to the Minneapolis Trotskyites convicted under the Smith Act is far more meaningful than the similar refusal to grant five hundred petitions to prison "lawyers" who have suddenly discovered the writ of habeas corpus. Likewise, the holding that the legality of congressional apportionment is a "political question" vitally affects the operation of the whole democratic process.

What we must therefore seek are the conditions under which the Court holds back *in this designated category of cases*. Furthermore, it is important to realize that there are positive consequences of negative action: as Charles Warren has implied, the post-Civil War Court's emphasis on self-restraint was a judicial concomitant of the resurgence of states' rights. Thus self-restraint may, as in wartime, be an outgrowth of judicial caution, or it may be part of a purposeful pattern of abdicating national power to the states.

Ever since the first political scientist discovered Mr. Dooley, the changes have been rung on the aphorism that the Supreme Court "follows the election returns," and I see no particular point in ringing my variation on this theme through again. Therefore, referring those who would like a more detailed explanation to earlier analyses, the discussion here will be confined to the bare bones of my hypothesis.

The power of the Supreme Court to invade the decision-making arena, I submit, is a consequence of that fragmentation of political power which is normal in the United States. No cohesive majority, such as normally exists in Britain, would permit a politically irresponsible judiciary to usurp decision-making functions, but, for complex social and institutional reasons, there are few issues in the United States on which cohesive majorities exist. The guerrilla warfare which usually rages between Congress and the President, as well as the internal civil wars which are endemic in both the legislature and the administration, give the judiciary considerable room for maneuver. If, for example, the Court strikes down a controversial decision of the Federal Power Commission, it will be supported by a substantial bloc of congressmen; if it supports the

FPC's decision, it will also receive considerable congressional support. But the important point is that *either* way it decides the case, there is no possibility that Congress will exact any vengeance on the Court for its action. A disciplined majority would be necessary to clip the judicial wings, and such a majority does not exist on this issue.

On the other hand, when monolithic majorities do exist on issues, the Court is likely to resort to judicial self-restraint. A good case here is the current tidal wave of anti-Communist legislation and administrative action, the latter particularly with regard to aliens, which the Court has treated most gingerly. About the only issues on which there can be found cohesive majorities are those relating to national defense, and the Court has, as Clinton Rossiter demonstrated in an incisive analysis [*The Supreme Court and the Commander-in-Chief*, Ithaca, 1951], traditionally avoided problems arising in this area irrespective of their constitutional merits. Like the slave who accompanied a Roman consul on his triumph whispering "You too are mortal," the shade of Thad Stevens haunts the Supreme Court chamber to remind the justices what an angry Congress can do.

To state the proposition in this brief compass is to oversimplify it considerably. I have, for instance, ignored the crucial question of how the Court knows when a majority *does* exist, and I recognize that certain aspects of judicial behavior cannot be jammed into my hypothesis without creating essentially spurious epicycles. However, I am not trying to establish a monistic theory of judicial action; group action, like that of individuals, is motivated by many factors, some often contradictory, and my objective is to elucidate what seems to be one tradition of judicial motivation. In short, judicial self-restraint and judicial power seem to be opposite sides of the same coin: it has been by judicious application of the former that the latter has been maintained. A tradition beginning with Marshall's *coup* in *Marbury* v. *Madison* and running through *Mississippi* v. *Johnson* and *Ex Parte Vallandigham* to *Dennis* v. *United States* suggests that the Court's power has been maintained by a wise refusal to employ it in unequal combat. 〽

33. The Process of Judicial Decision Making

The preceding selection should dissuade students from accepting the common assumption that judicial decision making is quasi-scientific, based upon legal principles and precedent, with the judges set apart from the normal political process. The interpretation of law, whether constitutional or statutory, always involves a large amount of discretion. The majority of the Court can always read its opinion into law if it so chooses.

The following selection presents the views of Justice William J. Brennan, a current member of the Supreme Court, on the general role of the Court and the procedures it follows in decision making.

HOW THE SUPREME COURT COMES TO ARRIVE AT DECISIONS
*William J. Brennan Jr.**

THROUGHOUT its history the Supreme Court has been called upon to face many of the dominant social, political, economic and even philosophical issues that confront the nation. But Solicitor General Cox only recently reminded us that this does not mean that the Court is charged with making social, political, economic or philosophical decisions.

Quite the contrary. The Court is not a council of Platonic guardians for deciding our most difficult and emotional questions according to the Justices' own notions of what is just or wise or politic. To the extent that this is a government function at all, it is the function of the people's elected representatives.

The Justices are charged with deciding according to law. Because the issues arise in the framework of concrete litigation they must be decided on facts embalmed in a record made by some lower court or administrative agency. And while the Justices may and do consult history and the other disciplines as aids to constitutional decision, the text of the Constitution and relevant precedents dealing with that text are their primary tools.

It is indeed true, as Judge Learned Hand once said, that the judge's authority "depends upon the assumption that he speaks with the mouth of others: the momentum of his utterances must be greater than any which his personal reputation and character can command; if it is to do the work assigned to it—if it is to stand against the passionate resentments arising out of the interests he must frustrate—he must preserve his authority by cloaking himself in the majesty of an overshadowing past, but he must discover some composition with the dominant trends of his times."

* From *The New York Times,* October 12, 1963. © 1963 by The New York Times Company. Reprinted by permission of the author and *The New York Times.*

Answers Unclear

However, we must keep in mind that, while the words of the Constitution are binding, their application to specific problems is not often easy. The Founding Fathers knew better than to pin down their descendants too closely.

Enduring principles rather than petty details were what they sought.

Thus the Constitution does not take the form of a litany of specifics. There are, therefore, very few cases where the constitutional answers are clear, all one way or all the other, and this is also true of the current cases raising conflicts between the individual and governmental power—an area increasingly requiring the Court's attention.

Ultimately, of course, the Court must resolve the conflicts of competing interests in these cases, but all Americans should keep in mind how intense and troubling these conflicts can be.

Where one man claims a right to speak and the other man claims the right to be protected from abusive or dangerously provocative remarks the conflict is inescapable.

Where the police have ample external evidence of a man's guilt, but to be sure of their case put into evidence a confession obtained through coercion, the conflict arises between his right to a fair prosecution and society's right to protection against his depravity.

Where the orthodox Jew wishes to open his shop and do business on the day which non-Jews have chosen, and the Legislature has sanctioned, as a day of rest, the Court cannot escape a difficult problem of reconciling opposed interests.

Finally, the claims of the Negro citizen, to borrow Solicitor General Cox's words, present a "conflict between the ideal of liberty and equality expressed in the Declaration of Independence, on the one hand, and, on the other hand, a way of life rooted in the customs of many of our people."

Society Is Disturbed

If all segments of our society can be made to appreciate that there are such conflicts, and that cases which involve constitutional rights often require difficult choices, if this alone is accomplished, we will have immeasurably enriched our common understanding of the meaning and significance of our freedoms. And we will have a better appreciation of the Court's function and its difficulties.

How conflicts such as these ought to be resolved constantly troubles our whole society. There should be no surprise, then, that how properly to resolve them often produces sharp division within the Court itself. When problems are so fundamental, the claims of the competing interests are often nicely balanced, and close divisions are almost inevitable.

Supreme Court cases are usually one of three kinds: the "original" action brought directly in the Court by one state against another state or states, or between a state or states and the Federal Government. Only a handful of such cases arise each year, but they are an important handful.

A recent example was the contest between Arizona and California over the waters of the lower basin of the Colorado River. Another was the contest between the Federal Government and the newest state of Hawaii over the ownership of lands in Hawaii.

The second kind of case seeks review of the decisions of a Federal Court of Appeals—there are 11 such courts—or of a decision of a Federal District Court—there is a Federal District Court in each of the 50 states.

The third kind of case comes from a state court—the Court may review a state court judgment by the highest court of any of the 50 states, if the judgment rests on the decision of a Federal question.

When I came to the Court seven years ago the aggregate of the cases in the three classes was 1,600. In the term just completed there were 2,800, an increase of 75 per cent in seven years. Obviously, the volume will have doubled before I complete 10 years of service.

How is it possible to manage such a huge volume of cases? The answer is that we have the authority to screen them and select for argument and decision only those which, in our judgment, guided by pertinent criteria, raise the most important and far-reaching questions. By that device we select annually around 6 per cent—between 150 and 170 cases—for decision.

Petition and Response

That screening process works like this: When nine Justices sit, it takes five to decide a case on the merits. But it takes only the votes of four of the nine to put a case on the argument calendar for argument and decision. Those four votes are hard to come by—only an exceptional case raising a significant Federal question commands them.

Each application for review is usually in the form of a short petition, attached to which are any opinions of the lower courts in the case. The adversary may file a response—also, in practice usually short. Both the petition and response identify the Federal questions allegedly involved, argue their substantiality, and whether they were properly raised in the lower courts.

Each Justice receives copies of the petition and response and such parts of the record as the parties may submit. Each Justice then, without any consultation at this stage with the others, reaches his own tentative conclusion whether the application should be granted or denied.

The first consultation about the case comes at the Court conference at which the case is listed on the agenda for discussion. We sit in conference almost every Friday during the term. Conferences begin at 10 in the morning and often continue until 6, except for a half-hour recess for lunch.

Only the Justices are present. There are no law clerks, no stenographers, no secretaries, no pages—just the nine of us. The junior Justice acts as guardian of the door, receiving and delivering any messages that come in or go from the conference.

Order of Seating

The conference room is a beautifully oak-paneled chamber with one side lined with books from floor to ceiling. Over the mantel of the exquisite marble fireplace at one end hangs the only adornment in the chamber—a portrait of Chief Justice John Marshall. In the middle of the room stands a rectangular table, not too large but large enough for the nine of us comfortably to gather around it.

The Chief Justice sits at the south end and Mr. Justice Black, the senior Associate Justice, at the north end. Along the side to the left of the Chief Justice sit Justices Stewart, Goldberg, White and Harlan. On the right side sit Justice Clark, myself and Justice Douglas in that order.

We are summoned to conference by a buzzer which rings in our several chambers five minutes before the hour. Upon entering the conference room each of us shakes hands with his colleagues. The handshake tradition originated when Chief Justice Fuller presided many decades ago. It is a symbol that harmony of aims if not of views is the Court's guiding principle.

Each of us has his copy of the agenda of the day's cases before him. The agenda lists the cases applying for review. Each of us before coming to the conference has noted on his copy his tentative view whether or not review should be granted in each case.

The Chief Justice begins the discussion of each case. He then yields to the senior Associate Justice and discussion proceeds down the line in order of seniority until each Justice has spoken.

Voting goes the other way. The junior Justice votes first and voting then proceeds up the line to the Chief Justice, who votes last.

Each of us has a docket containing a sheet for each case with appropriate places for recording the votes. When any case receives four votes for review, that case is transferred to the oral argument list. Applications in which none of us sees merit may be passed over without discussion.

Now how do we process the decisions we agree to review?

There are rare occasions when the question is so clearly controlled by an earlier decision of the Court that a reversal of the lower court judgment is inevitable. In these rare instances we may summarily reverse without oral argument.

Each Side Gets Hour

The case must very clearly justify summary disposition, however, because our ordinary practice is not to reverse a decision without oral argument. Indeed, oral argument of cases taken for review, whether from the state or Federal courts, is the usual practice. We rarely accept submissions of cases on briefs.

Oral argument ordinarily occurs about four months after the application for review is granted. Each party is usually allowed one hour, but in recent years we have limited oral argument to a half-hour in cases thought to involve issues not requiring longer argument.

Counsel submit their briefs and record in sufficient time for the distribution of one set to each Justice two or three weeks before the oral argument. Most of the members of the present Court follow the practice of reading the briefs before the argument. Some of us often have a bench memorandum prepared before the argument. This memorandum digests the facts and the arguments of both sides, highlighting the matters about which we may want to question counsel at the argument.

Often I have independent research done in advance of argument and incorporate the results in the bench memorandum.

We follow a schedule of two weeks of argument from Monday through Thursday, followed by two weeks of recess for opinion writing and the study of petitions for review. The argued cases are listed on the conference agenda on the Friday following argument. Conference discussion follows the same procedure I have described for the discussions of certiorari petitions.

Opinion Assigned

Of course, it is much more extended. Not infrequently discussion of particular cases may be spread over two or more conferences.

Not until the discussion is completed and a vote taken is the opinion assigned. The assignment is not made at the conference but formally in writing some few days after the conference.

The Chief Justice assigns the opinions in those cases in which he has voted with the majority. The senior Associate Justice voting with the majority assigns the opinions in the other cases. The dissenters agree among themselves who shall write the dissenting opinion. Of course, each Justice is free to write his own opinion, concurring or dissenting.

The writing of an opinion always takes weeks and sometimes months. The most painstaking research and care are involved.

Research, of course, concentrates on relevant legal materials—precedents particularly. But Supreme Court cases often require some familiarity with history, economics, the social and other sciences, and authorities in these areas, too, are consulted when necessary.

When the author of an opinion feels he has an unanswerable document he sends it to a print shop, which we maintain in our building. The printed draft may be revised several times before his proposed opinion is circulated among the other Justices. Copies are sent to each member of the Court, those in the dissent as well as those in the majority.

Some Change Minds

Now the author often discovers that his work has only begun. He receives a return, ordinarily in writing, from each Justice who voted with him and sometimes also from the Justices who voted the other way. He learns who will write the dissent if one is to be written. But his particular concern is whether those who voted with him are still of his view and what they have to say about his proposed opinion.

Often some who voted with him at conference will advise that they reserve final judgment pending the circulation of the dissent. It is a common experience that dissents change votes, even enough votes to become the majority.

I have had to convert more than one of my proposed majority opinions into a dissent before the final decision was announced. I have also, however, had the more satisfying experience of rewriting a dissent as a majority opinion for the Court.

Before everyone has finally made up his mind a constant interchange by memoranda, by telephone, at the lunch table continues while we hammer out the final form of the opinion. I had one case during the past term in which I circulated 10 printed drafts before one was approved as the Court opinion.

Uniform Rule

The point of this procedure is that each Justice, unless he disqualifies himself in a particular case, passes on every piece of business coming to the Court. The Court does not function by means of committees or panels. Each Justice passes on each petition, each time, no matter how drawn, in long hand, by typewriter, or on a press. Our Constitution vests the judicial power in only one Supreme Court. This does not permit Supreme Court action by committees, panels, or sections.

The method that the Justices use in meeting an enormous caseload varies. There is one uniform rule: Judging is not delegated. Each Justice studies each case in sufficient detail to resolve the question for himself. In a very real sense, each decision is an individual decision of every Justice.

The process can be a lonely, troubling experience for fallible human beings conscious that their best may not be adequate to the challenge.

"We are not unaware," the late Justice Jackson said, "that we are not final because we are infallible; we know that we are infallible only because we are final."

One does not forget how much may depend on his decision. He knows that usually more than the litigants may be affected, that the course of vital social, economic and political currents may be directed.

This then is the decisional process in the Supreme Court. It is not without its tensions, of course—indeed, quite agonizing tensions at times.

I would particularly emphasize that, unlike the case of a Congressional or White House decision, Americans demand of their Supreme Court judges that they produce a written opinion, the collective expression of the judges subscribing to it, setting forth the reason which led them to the decision.

These opinions are the exposition, not just to lawyers, legal scholars and other judges, but to our whole society, of the bases upon which a particular result rests—why a problem, looked at as disinterestedly and dispassionately as nine human beings trained in a tradition of the disinterested and dispassionate approach can look at it, is answered as it is.

It is inevitable, however, that Supreme Court decisions—and the Justices themselves—should be caught up in public debate and be the subjects of bitter controversy.

Freund's View

An editorial in The Washington Post did not miss the mark by much in saying that this was so because "one of the primary functions of the

Supreme Court is to keep the people of the country from doing what they would like to do—at times when what they would like to do runs counter to the Constitution. . . . The function of the Supreme Court is not to count constituents; it is to interpret a fundamental charter which imposes restraints on constituents. Independence and integrity, not popularity, must be its standards."

Certainly controversy over its work has attended the Court throughout its history. As Professor Paul A. Freund of Harvard remarked, this has been true almost since the Court's first decision:

"When the Court held, in 1793, that the State of Georgia could be sued on a contract in the Federal courts, the outraged Assembly of that state passed a bill declaring that any Federal marshal who should try to collect the judgment would be guilty of a felony and would suffer death, without benefit of clergy, by being hanged. When the Court decided that state criminal convictions could be reviewed in the Supreme Court, Chief Justice Roane of Virginia exploded, calling it a 'most monstrous and unexampled decision. It can only be accounted for by that love of power which history informs us infects and corrupts all who possess it, and from which even the eminent and upright judges are not exempt.' "

But public understanding has not always been lacking in the past. Perhaps it exists today. But surely a more informed knowledge of the decisional process should aid a better understanding.

It is not agreement with the Court's decisions that I urge. Our law is the richer and the wiser because academic and informed lay criticism is part of the stream of development.

Consensus Needed

It is only a greater awareness of the nature and limits of the Supreme Court's function that I seek.

The ultimate resolution of questions fundamental to the whole community must be based on a common consensus of understanding of the unique responsibility assigned to the Supreme Court in our society.

The lack of that understanding led Mr. Justice Holmes to say 50 years ago:

"We are very quiet there, but it is the quiet of a storm center, as we all know. Science has taught the world skepticism and has made it legitimate to put everything to the test of proof. Many beautiful and noble reverences are impaired, but in these days no one can complain if any institution, system, or belief is called on to justify its continuance in life. Of course we are not excepted and have not escaped.

Painful Accusation

"Doubts are expressed that go to our very being. Not only are we told that when Marshall pronounced an Act of Congress unconstitutional he usurped a power that the Constiution did not give, but we are told that we are the representatives of a class—a tool of the money power.

"I get letters, not always anonymous, intimating that we are corrupt. Well, gentlemen, I admit that it makes my heart ache. It is very painful, when one spends all the energies of one's soul in trying to do good work, with no thought but that of solving a problem according to the rules by which one is bound, to know that many see sinister motives and would be glad of evidence that one was consciously bad.

"But we must take such things philosophically and try to see what we can learn from hatred and distrust and whether behind them there may not be a germ of inarticulate truth.

"The attacks upon the Court are merely an expression of the unrest that seems to wonder vaguely whether law and order pay. When the ignorant are taught to doubt they do not know what they safely may believe. And it seems to me that at this time we need education in the obvious more than investigation of the obscure."

Judicial decision making involves the disposition of specific cases and controversies. Groups more than individuals are often involved in this process. Litigation is a time-consuming and expensive process, requiring financial resources and endurance for survival. It is a rare individual who has the capacity and motivation to use the judicial process. For this reason individual interest in court cases is often represented by pressure groups. Other aspects of our political system also lead to extensive group rather than individual participation before courts, which becomes clear in the following selection.

LITIGATION AS A FORM OF PRESSURE GROUP ACTIVITY

Clement E. Vose*

THE conventional judicial process is distinguished from legislative and administrative processes by features which forbid, conceal, or control the participation of organized pressure groups. Justice Robert H. Jackson warned that "perhaps the most significant and least comprehended limitation upon the judicial power is that this power extends only to cases and controversies." This limitation has meant that the Supreme Court of the United States refuses to provide advisory opinions and avoids what judges are fond of calling "political questions." It cannot be overstressed that the Supreme Court's only power is to decide lawsuits between adversaries with real interests at stake. Under the case system that marks American jurisprudence, a court is a "substantially passive instrument, to be moved only by the initiative of litigants." This contrasts with the power of the President and the Congress to deal with any subject as desired.

Despite this limiting prerequisite, the Supreme Court does possess considerable control over the particular cases to be decided. The Judiciary Act of 1925 gave the Court almost complete discretionary control of its appellate business through grant or denial of the writ of certiorari. This statute settled the modern principle that the Supreme Court's function was: "not to see justice done in every case, but to decide the more important policy issues presented within the frame of a 'case' or 'controversy,' concerning the federal balance, the relations of the branches of the federal government, or the fundamental rights of the individual in relation to government." [From James Willard Hurst, *The Growth of American Law*, Boston, 1950.] Elaborating upon the function of deciding important policy issues, Chief Justice Fred M. Vinson, in 1949, told the bar that the Supreme Court is interested only in "those cases which present questions whose resolution will have immediate importance beyond the particular facts and parties involved." Vinson added that "what the Court is interested in is the actual practical effect of the disputed decision—its consequences for other litigants and in other situations." This meant that lawyers whose petitions for certiorari were granted by the Supreme Court were representing not only their clients, "but tremendously important

* From Clement E. Vose, "Litigation as a Form of Pressure Group Activity," *Annals of the American Academy of Political and Social Science*, Vol. 319 (September, 1958). Quoted with permission of the publishers.

principles, upon which are based the plans, hopes and aspirations of a great many people throughout the country."

It is the thesis of this article that organizations—identifiable by letterhead—often link broad interests in society to individual parties of interest in Supreme Court cases. Since the American judicial system is built upon specific cases with specific facts, it is assumed that study of the role of specific organizations is relevant to understanding.

REASONS ORGANIZATIONS GO TO COURT

Organizations support legal action because individuals lack the necessary time, money, and skill. With no delays a case takes an average of four years to pass through two lower courts to the Supreme Court of the United States. A series of cases on related questions affecting the permanent interest of a group may extend over two decades or more. The constant attention that litigation demands, especially when new arguments are being advanced, makes the employment of regular counsel economical. This may be supplemented by a legal staff of some size and by volunteer lawyers of distinction. Parties also pay court costs and meet the expense of printing and briefs. Organizations are better able to provide the continuity demanded in litigation than individuals. Some individuals do maintain responsibility for their own cases even at the Supreme Court level, but this is difficult under modern conditions.

The form of group participation in court cases is set by such factors as the type of proceeding, standing of the parties, legal or constitutional issues in dispute, the characteristics of the organization, and its interest in the outcome. . . . The cases have sometimes placed organizations as parties, but more often the organization supports a member or an officer in litigation. One example must suffice.

The constitutional concept of religious freedom has been broadened in recent years by the Supreme Court decisions in cases involving members of the sect known as Jehovah's Witnesses. Most of the cases began when a Jehovah's Witness violated a local ordinance or state statute. Since 1938, the Witnesses, incorporated as the Watchtower Bible and Tract Society and represented by its counsel, Hayden Cooper Covington, have won forty-four of fifty-five cases in the United States Supreme Court. As a result Jehovah's Witnesses now enjoy: "the rights to solicit from house to house, to preach in the streets without a license, to canvass apartment buildings regardless of the tenants' or owners' wishes, to be recognized as ministers of an accredited religion and thus be exempt from the draft, to decline to serve on juries, and to refuse to salute or pledge allegiance to the flag."

THE NAACP

Since 1909 the National Association for the Advancement of Colored People has improved the legal status of Negroes immeasurably by the victories it has won in more than fifty Supreme Court cases. During its early years, the NAACP relied upon prominent volunteer lawyers like Moorfield Storey, Louis Marshall, and Clarence Darrow to represent Negroes in the courts. Limited success coupled with its failure to win gains from Congress led the NAACP in the 1930's to make court litigation fundamental to its program. A separate organization, the NAACP Legal Defense and Educational Fund, was incorporated for this purpose. The goal of the NAACP was to make Negroes "an integral part of the nation, with the same rights and guarantees that are accorded to other citizens, and on the same terms." This ambition meant that beginning in 1938 Thurgood Marshall as special counsel for the NAACP Legal Defense and Educational Fund held what was "probably the most demanding legal post in the country." . . .

By presenting test cases to the Supreme Court, the NAACP has won successive gains protecting the right of Negroes in voting, housing, transportation, education, and service on juries. Each effort has followed the development of new theories of legal interpretation and required the preparation of specific actions in the courts to challenge existing precedent. The NAACP Legal Defense Fund has accomplished these two tasks through the co-operation of associated and allied groups. First, as many as fifty Negro lawyers practicing in all parts of the country have been counsel in significant civil rights cases in the lower courts. . . . Second, the NAACP has long benefited from its official advisory group, the National Legal Committee composed of leading Negro and white lawyers. . . . Third, other organizations with no direct connection with the Legal Defense Fund have sponsored a few cases. State and local chapters of the NAACP have often aided Negroes who were parties in cases, especially in the lower courts. The St. Louis Association of Real Estate Brokers was the chief sponsor of the important restrictive covenant case of *Shelley* v. *Kraemer*. A Negro national college fraternity, Alpha Phi Alpha, sponsored quite completely the successful attack on discrimination in interstate railway dining cars. . . .

THE AMERICAN LIBERTY LEAGUE

The experience of the American Liberty League, organized in 1934 by conservative businessmen to oppose the New Deal, provides another variation on the theme of organizations in litigation. When the League proved unable to prevent enactment of economic regulation by Congress, a National Lawyers' Committee was formed to question the constitutionality of the legislation. . . .

Members of the National Lawyers' Committee of the American Liberty League, but not the organization itself, participated in litigation. The Committee's first public announcement had stated that "it will also contribute its services in test cases involving fundamental constitutional questions." Although the intention was to offer free legal services to citizens without funds to defend their constitutional rights, members of the National Lawyers' Committee actually represented major corporations which challenged the constitutionality of New Deal legislation in the Supreme Court. . . .

AIDING THE GOVERNMENT DEFENSE

Judicial review in the United States constitutes an invitation for groups whose lobbying fails to defeat legislation to continue opposition by litigation. The NAACP has taken advantage of this in questioning state segregation laws, and, especially before 1937, business groups of various sizes—the American Liberty League, trade associations, and corporations —contested the constitutionality of state and federal regulatory legislation. This exploitation of judicial review has been balanced by the practice of victorious groups in legislation continuing to support administrative agencies in charge of enforcement. When statutes are challenged, organizations often support the Justice Department in Washington or a state Attorney General in defending them. This is to say that when losers in legislation have brought test cases in the courts, the legislative winners have aided the official legal defense.

THE NATIONAL CONSUMERS' LEAGUE

The efforts of the National Consumers' League to defend the validity of protective labor legislation affords an example of this private organizational aid to the public defense of legislation. Organized by society women in 1899 to improve the lot of women and children in industry, the National Consumers' League sought first to boycott goods produced under substandard conditions and then to persuade state legislatures to control factory practices through legislation. When employers in the hotel and laundry business organized to defeat legislation in the courts, the National Consumers' League, in 1908, organized a Committee on Legislation and Legal Defense of Labor Laws to "assist in the defense of the laws by supplying additional legal counsel and other assistance."

The leaders of the National Consumers' League . . . learned to prod state Attorneys General in order to gain adequate defense for statutes under fire in the courts. . . .

ORGANIZATIONS AS "FRIENDS OF THE COURT"

The appearance of organizations as *amici curiae* has been the most noticed form of group representation in Supreme Court cases. This does not concern the technical office of *amicus curiae* for which an attorney is appointed to assist the court in deciding complex and technical problems. Today, the Supreme Court does sometimes, as in formulating its decree in the School Segregation Cases, issue a special invitation to the Solicitor General or to state Attorneys General to act as *amici curiae*. Of interest here is the rule under which individuals, organizations, and government attorneys have been permitted to file briefs and/or to make oral argument in the Supreme Court. During the last decade *amici curiae* have submitted an average of sixty-six briefs and seven oral arguments in an average total of forty cases a term.

The frequent entrance of organizations into Supreme Court cases by means of the *amicus curiae* device has often given litigation the distinct flavor of group combat. This may be illustrated by the group representation in quite different cases. In 1943, when a member of the Jehovah's Witnesses challenged the constitutionality of a compulsory flag salute in the schools, his defense by counsel for the Watchtower Bible and Tract Society was supported by separate *amici curiae*, the American Civil Liberties Union and the Committee on the Bill of Rights of the American Bar Association. The appellate state board of education was supported by an *amicus curiae* brief filed by the American Legion. In 1951, in a case testing state resale price maintenance, the United States was an *amicus* against a Louisiana statute while the Commonwealth of Pennsylvania, the Louisiana State Pharmaceutical Association, American Booksellers, Inc., and the National Association of Retail Druggists entered *amici curiae* briefs in support of the statute.

Many *amici curiae* briefs are workmanlike and provide the Court with helpful legal argument and material. Yet writers who favor their use by organizations and recognize that "the *amicus curiae* has had a long and respected role in our own legal system and before that, in the Roman law," believe that many briefs in recent years display a "timewasting character." Another authority has said that after 1947 there were multiplying signs "that the brief *amicus curiae* has become essentially an instrumentality designed to exert extrajudicial pressure on judicial decisions."

Concern over this by the Members of the Supreme Court was shown in 1946 when Justice Robert H. Jackson, in a dissenting opinion, criticized an *amicus curiae* brief by the American Newspaper Publishers Association: ". . . Of course, it does not cite a single authority not available to counsel for the publisher involved, and does not tell us a single new fact except this one: 'This membership embraces more than 700 newspaper publishers whose publications represent in excess of eighty per cent of the total daily and Sunday circulation of newspapers published in this country. The Association is vitally interested in the issue presented in this case, namely, the right of newspapers to publish news stories and editorials pending in the courts.' " Justice Jackson told his colleagues, "this might be a good occasion to demonstrate the fortitude of the judiciary." [*Craig* v. *Harney*, 331 U.S. 367, 397 (1946)].

REGULATION OF ORGANIZATIONS IN THE COURTS

Judges, lawyers, legislators, and citizens have reacted to appearances that organizational activity in court cases touches the integrity of the judicial process. A number of limitations have resulted. But in protecting the legal system against these dangers, regulations may be too harsh on organizations and interfere unduly with the freedom of association their functioning represents. . . .

Picketing of federal courthouses. During the trial of the leaders of the Communist party under the Smith Act in the Federal District Court for the Eastern District of New York located at Foley Square in New York City, picketing and parading outside the court was a daily occurrence. When the Senate Judiciary Committee was considering bills to limit this practice, it received many statements like the following: "Assuming under our form of representative government pressure groups must be tolerated in our legislative and executive branches, I feel there is no good reason why our courts should be subjected to such pressures." In accord with this view, Congress, in 1959, enacted legislation prohibiting any person from parading, picketing, or demonstrating in or near a federal courthouse with the intent of "interfering with, obstructing, or impeding" the administration of justice or of "influencing any judge, juror, witness, or court officer" in the discharge of his duty.

Mass petitions to the Supreme Court. In 1953, the National Committee to Secure Justice in the Rosenberg Case addressed a petition claimed to have the support of 50,000 persons to the Supreme Court. Among many condemnations of this was one urging that "the Court must consult its own collective conscience on such matters without reference to the number of persons who are willing to sign a petition. No rule prevents groups from such indecorous action but Justice Hugo Black has expressed the intense disapproval of the Supreme Court. In 1951, when granting a stay of execution to Willie McGhee, a Negro under the death penalty in Mississippi, Justice Black lamented the "growing practice of sending telegrams to judges in order to have cases decided by pressure." Declaring that he would not read them, he said that "the courts of the United States are not the kind of instruments of justice that can be influenced by such pressures." Justice Black gave an implied warning to the bar by noting that "counsel in this case have assured me they were not responsible for these telegrams." . . .

CONCLUSION

There is a logical relationship of organizational interest in litigation and the importance of courts in forming public policy. Although courts act only in cases between parties with concrete interests at stake, organizations concerned with the impact of the outcome may become quite active participants. Organizations may do this by sponsoring a "test case" brought in the name of a private party, they may aid the government attorney in a case, or they may file a brief as an *amicus curiae*. Considering the importance of the issues resolved by American courts, the entrance of organizations in these ways seems in order. Indeed the essential right of organizations to pursue litigation would appear to follow from the generous attitude of American society toward the freedom of individuals to form associations for the purpose of achieving common goals. Of course, traditional judicial procedures should be followed and the attorneys for organizations, as well as for individuals, must address their arguments to reason. If these standards of conduct are followed there is no incompatibility between the activity of organizations in litigation and the integrity or independence of the judiciary.

CHAPTER NINE

Government and Policy

The theory and practice of the American political system have been analyzed in preceding selections. The purpose of this concluding chapter is to discuss the dimensions of several important problems in economic and foreign policy. The political system places constraints upon policy makers, substantially affecting the kind of policy that is made. Administrators and elected officials must be responsive to the forces in their constituencies. Students should attempt to relate this aspect of our government to the problems discussed in the following selections.

34. Economic Policy: Government Control or Laissez Faire?

The growth of economic interdependence has resulted throughout our history in demands being made upon the government to act as an umpire for conflicting interests. Regulation has not been established by unilateral government decree, but by governmental response to pressure of various kinds from the community. The following selections debate the question of the extent to which there should be economic planning by the central government. The resolution of this problem will ultimately stem from the balance of political forces favoring or opposing various forms of planning.

ECONOMIC CONTROL AND TOTALITARIANISM
*Friedrich A. Hayek**

Most planners who have seriously considered the practical aspects of their task have little doubt that a directed economy must be run on more or less dictatorial lines. That the complex system of interrelated activities, if it is to be consciously directed at all, must be directed by a single staff of experts, and that ultimate responsibility and power must rest in the hands of a commander-in-chief whose actions must not be fettered by democratic procedure, is too obvious a consequence of underlying ideas of central planning not to command fairly general assent. The consolation our planners offer us is that this authoritarian direction will apply "only" to economic matters. One of the most prominent economic planners, Stuart Chase, assures us, for instance, that in a planned society "political democracy can remain if it confines itself to all but economic matter." Such assurances are usually accompanied by the suggestion that, by giving up freedom in what are, or ought to be, the less important aspects of our lives, we shall obtain greater freedom in the pursuit of higher values. On this ground people who abhor the idea of a political dictatorship often clamor for a dictator in the economic field.

The arguments used appeal to our best instincts and often attract the finest minds. If planning really did free us from the less important cares and so made it easier to render our existence one of plain living and high thinking, who would wish to belittle such an ideal? If our economic activities really concerned only the inferior or even more sordid sides of life, of course we ought to endeavor by all means to find a way to relieve ourselves from the excessive care for material ends and, leaving them to be cared for by some piece of utilitarian machinery, set our minds free for the higher things of life.

Unfortunately, the assurance people derive from this belief that the power which is exercised over economic life is a power over matters of secondary importance only, and which makes them take lightly the threat to the freedom of our economic pursuits, is altogether unwarranted. It is largely a consequence of the erroneous belief that there are purely economic ends separate from the other ends of life. Yet, apart from the pathological care of the miser, there is no such thing. . . .

... Economic values are less important to us than many things precisely because in economic matters we are free to decide what to us is more, and what less, important. Or, as we might say, because in the present society it is *we* who have to solve the economic problems of our lives. To be controlled in our economic pursuits means to be always controlled unless we declare our specific purpose. Or, since when we declare our specific purpose we shall also have to get it approved, we should really be controlled in everything.

The question raised by economic planning is, therefore, not merely whether we shall be able to satisfy what we regard as our more or less important needs in the way we prefer. It is whether it shall be we who decide what is more, and what is less, important for us, or whether this is to be decided by the planner. Economic planning would not affect merely those of our marginal needs that we have in mind when we speak contemptuously about the merely economic. It would, in effect, mean that we as individuals should no longer be allowed to decide what we regard as marginal.

The authority directing all economic activity would control not merely the part of our lives which is concerned with inferior things; it would control the allocation of the limited means for all our ends. And whoever controls all economic activity controls the means for all our ends and must therefore decide which are to be satisfied and which not. This is really the crux of the matter. Economic control is not merely control of a sector of human life which can be separated from the rest; it is the control of the means for all our ends. And whoever has sole control of the means must also determine which ends are to be served, which values are to be rated higher and which lower—in short, what men should believe and strive for. Central planning means that the economic problem is to be solved by the community instead of by the individual; but this involves that it must also be the community, or rather its representatives, who must decide the relative importance of the different needs.

The so-called economic freedom which the planners promise us means precisely that we are to be relieved of the necessity of solving our own economic problems and that the bitter choices which this often involves are to be made for us. Since under modern conditions we are for almost everything dependent on means which our fellow-men provide, economic planning would involve direction of almost the whole of our life. There is hardly an aspect of it, from our primary needs to our relations with our family and friends, from the nature of our work to the use of our leisure, over which the planner would not exercise his "conscious control."

The power of the planner over our private lives would be no less complete if he chose not to exercise it by direct control of our consumption. Although a planned society would probably to some extent employ rationing and similar devices, the power of the planner over our private lives does not depend on this and would be hardly less effective if the consumer were nominally free to spend his income as he pleased. The source of this power over all consumption which in a planned society the authority would possess would be its control over production.

Our freedom of choice in a competitive society rests on the fact that, if one person refuses to satisfy our wishes, we can turn to another. But if we face a monopolist we are at his mercy. And an authority directing the whole economic system would be the most powerful monopolist conceivable. While we need probably not be afraid that such an authority would exploit this power in the manner in which a private monopolist would do so, while its purpose would presumably not be the extortion of maximum financial gain, it would have complete power to decide what we are to be given and on what terms. It would not only decide what commodities and services were to be available and in what quantities; it would be able to direct their distribution between districts and groups and could, if it wishes, discriminate between persons to any degree it liked. If we remember why planning is advocated by most people, can there be much doubt that this power would be used for the ends of which the authority approves and to prevent the pursuits of ends which it disapproves? . . .

Not only in our capacity as consumers, however, and not even mainly in that capacity, would the will of the authority shape and "guide" our daily lives. It would do so even more in our position as producers. These two aspects of our lives cannot be separated; and as for most of us the time we spend at our work is a large part of our whole lives, and as our job usually also determines the place where and the people among whom we live, some freedom in choosing our work is, probably, even more important for our happiness than freedom to spend our income during the hours of leisure.

No doubt it is true that even in the best of worlds this freedom will be very limited. Few people ever have an abundance of choice of occupation. But what matters is that we have some choice, that we are not absolutely tied to a particular job which has been chosen for us, or which we may have chosen in the past, and that if one position becomes quite intolerable, or if we set our heart on another, there is almost always a way for the able, some sacrifice at the price of which he may achieve his goal. . . .

That in a competitive society most things can be had at a price—though it is often a cruelly high price we have to pay—is a fact the importance of which can hardly be overrated. The alternative is not, however, complete freedom of choice, but orders and prohibitions which must be obeyed and, in the last resort, the favor of the mighty.

It is significant of the confusion prevailing on all these subjects that it should have become a cause for reproach that in a competitive society almost everything can be had at a price. If the people who protest against having the higher values of life brought into the "cash nexus" really mean that we should not be allowed to sacrifice our lesser needs in order to preserve the higher values, and that the choice should be made for us, this demand must be regarded as rather peculiar and scarcely testifies to great respect for the dignity of the individual. That life and health, beauty and virtue, honor and peace of mind, can often be preserved only at considerable material cost, and that somebody must make the choice, is as undeniable as that we all are sometimes not prepared to make the material sacrifice necessary to protect those higher values against all injury.

To take only one example: We could, of course, reduce casualties by automobile accidents to zero if we are willing to bear the cost—if in no other way—by abolishing automobiles. And the same is true of thousands of other instances in which we are constantly risking life and health and all the fine values of the spirit, of ourselves and of our fellow-men, to further what we at the same time contemptuously describe as our material comfort. Nor can it be otherwise, since all our ends compete for the same means; and we could not strive for anything but these absolute values if they were on no account to be endangered.

That people should wish to be relieved of the bitter choice which hard facts often impose upon them is not surprising. But few want to be relieved through having the choice made for them by others. People just wish that the choice should not be necessary at all. . . .

We should be seriously deceiving ourselves if for these apprehensions we sought comfort in the consideration that the adoption of central planning would merely mean a return, after a brief spell of a free economy, to the ties and regulations which have governed economic activity through most ages, and that therefore the infringements of personal liberty need not be greater than they were before the age of laissez faire. This is a dangerous illusion. Even during the periods of European history when the regimentation of economic life went furthest, it amounted to little more than the creation of a general and semipermanent framework of rules within which the individual preserved a wide free sphere. The apparatus of control then available would not have been adequate to impose more than very general directions. And even where the control was most complete it extended only to those activities of a person through which he took part in the social division of labor. In the much wider sphere in which he then still lived on his own products, he was free to act as he chose.

The situation is now entirely different. During the liberal era the progressive division of labor has created a situation where almost every one of our activities is part of a social process. This is a development which we cannot reverse, since it is only because of it that we can maintain the vastly increased population at anything like present standards. But, in consequence, the substitution of central planning for competition would require central direction of a much greater part of our lives than was ever attempted before. It could not stop at what we regard as our economic activities, because we are now for almost every part of our lives dependent on somebody else's economic activities. The passion for the "collective satisfaction of our needs," with which our socialists have so well prepared the way for totalitarianism, and which wants us to take our pleasures as well as our necessities at the appointed time and in the prescribed form, is, of course, partly intended as a means of political education. But it is also the result of the exigencies of planning, which consists essentially in depriving us of choice, in order to give us whatever fits best into the plan and that at a time determined by the plan.

It is often said that political freedom is meaningless without economic freedom. This is true enough, but in a sense almost opposite from that in which the phrase is used by our planners. The economic freedom which is the prerequisite of any other freedom cannot be the freedom from economic care which the socialists promise us and which can be obtained only by relieving the individual at the same time of the necessity and of the power of choice; it must be the freedom of our economic activity which, with the right of choice, inevitably also carries the risk and the responsibility of that right. ▉

Although the political implications of total planning are dictatorial, there are definite arguments to be made for partial government intervention in economic life. In the latter instance the centers of economic power are still largely dispersed, with many private groups counteracting governmental power. The following selection discusses the justifications for and implications of government regulation of the economy.

DEMOCRACY AND THE PLANNED ECONOMY
*Robert M. MacIver**

THE arguments on which this plea [for total economic planning and socialism] rests are mainly of three kinds. One is that capitalism puts an increasing concentration of wealth into the hands of a small elite: those who head the great industrial corporations, the international cartels, the banking syndicates, and an entity known as "Wall Street." The gross disparity of power they wield makes our democracy only a façade for a plutocracy that at any moment may resort to fascism if its power is threatened.

A second argument is that the capitalistic system is proving increasingly incapable of meeting the conditions and needs of modern civilization. The recurrent crises of the "business cycle" are evidences of its incapacity. Modern technology creates an elaborate mechanism of interdependence. A failure or inadequacy anywhere can throw the whole system out of gear. Breakdowns are inevitable without over-all planning. Otherwise there is a drift to chaos.

The third argument claims that the prospective breakdown is not only economic but also moral and social. Indeed, we are already, according to its proponents, in a state of social disintegration. The capitalism system with its competitive detachment of every unit from every other, with its heartlessness, has undermined the moral foundations of society. It has destroyed man's essential loyalties, his sense of community. It breeds what the French call *anomie*, a total loosening of the social bond....

The advocates of total over-all planning talk much of the power of big business and the power of high finance. They warn us of the dangers of concentrated private economic power; they would abolish it on that score. Certainly there is need for control to avoid such dangers, and an alert democracy will invoke various governmental controls for that purpose. But those who are alarmed by the perils of private power seem to have no fear of public power, no matter how vast and concentrated it may become. Thomas Hobbes said of Leviathan, the great state: "There is no power on earth that may be compared with it." The power of government

* Reprinted from *Democracy and the Economic Challenge,* by Robert M. MacIver, by permission of Alfred A. Knopf, Inc. Copyright 1951 by Alfred A. Knopf. Inc.

is comprehensive and final, different in kind from any other power, more terrible in its abuse than any other power. It is armed with new techniques of control that make it potentially more formidable than it ever was in the past. Over many centuries men have learned to put a bit in the mouth of Leviathan. Will the bit hold it if political functions are vastly increased? Or will Leviathan enslave them again, as it does today in those countries which have abolished private economic power? When economic power and political power are totally combined, then there is no social *power* left in the community itself. Power has become monolithic. Can democracy restrain monolithic power? . . .

The reply may be made that after all the executive itself, or at least its policy-making leaders, would still depend, given the democratic structure, on election by the people. But mere elections are no safeguard of democracy unless the conditions are present for the maintenance and development of an alert and critical public opinion. The danger is that the concentration of power in the executive would curb the emergence of any effective opposition, in which case elections would become as nugatory as those of Soviet Russia or of certain Latin-American republics.

The organizational impetus of this concentrated power would mean that the ambitious leader—every leader and every new aspirant to leadership—is now under strong persuasions to keep in step with the establishment. The roads to power and position and wealth all lead through government service. The multitude of boards and commissions and managerial positions insure that leaders can climb the ladder only inside the establishment. Under these conditions Michels's iron law of oligarchy would come fully into its own.

Besides the leaders there are the rank and file; consider the new pressures that they in turn, bereft as they would be of independent leadership, must endure. You need new leaders to revolt from old leadership—would they have a chance to emerge? The usual democratic guarantees of civil rights would not suffice to protect workers who showed signs of independence. The constitution might proclaim that no one would suffer or be disadvantaged for his opinions; but it would now be very risky to rely on such a guarantee. There are so many grounds that could be allowed to justify demotion or punitive action. To whom could one appeal with much hope of success?

In short, when the government is the sole employer the word of the employer is law. There may be a façade of democratic liberties but there is inevitably a heavy disability attached to dissent, and conformity is the condition of every award. Moreover, there are more subtle influences that strongly abet the spirit of acceptance. Every means of communication is geared to the interests of government. Dissent becomes lonely and furtive and sinful. . . .

Under democracy part of the economy is always socialized and all the economy is subject to control. It controls whatever it has the will to control. If here and there it falls short, is that still not a lesser evil than to embark on a course which, once followed, is exceedingly difficult to reverse and which will assuredly imperil its very existence? . . .

It is not the way of democracy to change by one stroke the whole order of things. Democracy does not work by blueprints. It pursues a course of continuous adaptation as conditions change and as its perception of needs changes. No hard and fast lines can be laid down to determine what government should take over, what it should curb, what it should regulate. But there are principles that can guide us, and in the first place there are broad distinctions to be made.

We should in the first place learn to distinguish more clearly between the welfare state and the socialist state. It is one thing that government should protect and insure and actively foster the health and security and general well-being of the people. It is an entirely different thing that government should take over and run the steel industry and the oil industry and the building industry and all the rest. When government can achieve its ends by proper regulation it may well be a confession of failure to nationalize instead.

There are of course special cases where it is desirable or necessary that government should take the responsibility for some area of economic activity. Such cases fall mainly into two types:

1. Where an industry is a natural monopoly of such a kind as to preclude effective competition while at the same time it is not amenable to effective price regulation if privately operated. This is a rather rare situation. It is more likely to occur in industrially undeveloped countries, when a new source of mineral wealth, say, is discovered. A present instance in the United States would be the manufacture and sale of the isotopes and other commercially utilizable products of the atomic pile. Indeed, the present stage in the production of atomic energy in any form has characteristics that make it inevitably a state monopoly.

2. Where the economic returns from an industry, professional activity, or other service mature slowly over a long period, or where the full cost of such a service cannot properly be assessed against those who receive it, or where the service itself has such wide implications for the national well-being that the latter would be impaired if the immediate beneficiaries

were required to pay their proportion of the full cost. We have here a series of closely related conditions that everywhere have led governments to take responsibility for the supply of certain economic services instead of leaving them to private initiative. An obvious case is education, which is only modestly qualified by the fact that many governments permit private groups to provide it, in accordance with acceptable standards, alongside of the universal provision they make themselves. Other obvious cases are the post office and the highways, while various governments extend the area of public ownership to the railroads and other means of communication.

In this cursory sketch we cannot develop this theme. It is enough for our purpose to point out that if we apply the principles stated above with reasonable discretion, they leave intact a very considerable area of private economic power where the general regulatory function of government is sufficient to prevent any serious evils from private exploitation.

In short, the defects and weaknesses of our democracy on which the total planners enlarge do not call for the total planning they extol. Our democracy is not in such desperate condition that it needs to resort to this drastic surgery, which offers no assurance of the future health of the patient while it certainly threatens to kill him in the process of "recovery."

There is a kind of idealism that is three parts impatience and one part good intentions. It wants quick results and embraces whatever means may promise them. It falls in love with the means—they are so simple and clean-cut, so free from ambiguities and perplexities of the social reality to which they are to be applied. Presently they confuse the goal with the means.

The goal is not socialism nor capitalism nor any neat blueprint of economic organization. The goal is the freer and fuller life of man in his society, equipped with all the means that liberate his capacities. Anything that advances this goal is to be welcomed. It is foolish to shout "socialism," "communism," when any particular measure is proposed which might further the end—when, for example, it is a question of some form of social insurance or protection against discrimination which would relieve men of anxiety or helplessness of any kind. It is equally foolish to approve any scheme because it means more planning or more socialism. Some people have a passion for planning. It is a passion for tidiness, a kind of social puritanism.

If instead we sincerely face each need as it arises, the ever emergent society will not be capitalism, will not be socialism, but a flexible system far more suited for the promotion of human values and far more expressive of the particular genius of each people than any imposed and pre-determined pattern. Democracy is the long emergent way, proceeding stage by stage, moving this way and that, sometimes hesitant and sometimes confused, but feeling the pulse of the ever changing present, always seeking, never fully attaining, never forgetting its own fallibility and never unwilling to correct its mistakes, always aspiring and never fulfilled. For such is the gift of life and such is the spirit that animates man. ✍

35. Foreign Policy: Problems and Prospects

The goals of American foreign policy cannot be set forth in any objective fashion. They will depend upon the President and his top advisers. They will also depend upon the world situation. The following selection is taken from President Kennedy's famous American University speech, given in June of 1963. In it the President announced the beginning of discussions that eventually led to the Nuclear Test Ban Treaty, which was signed at Moscow on August 5, 1963, and later ratified by the Senate.

TOWARD A STRATEGY OF PEACE

John F. Kennedy*

THERE are few earthly things more beautiful than a university," wrote John Masefield, in his tribute to the English universities—and his words are equally true here. He did not refer to spires and towers, to campus greens and ivied walls. He admired the splendid beauty of the university, he said, because it was "a place where those who hate ignorance may strive to know, where those who perceive truth may strive to make others see."

I have, therefore, chosen this time and this place to discuss a topic on which ignorance too often abounds and the truth is too rarely perceived—yet it is the most important topic on earth: World peace.

What kind of peace do I mean? What kind of peace do we seek? Not a Pax Americana enforced on the world by American weapons of war. Not the peace of the grave or the security of the slave. I am talking about genuine peace, the kind of peace that makes life on earth worth living, the kind that enables men and nations to grow and to hope and to build

* This is the text of an address made by President Kennedy at American University, Washington, D.C., June 10, 1963.

a better life for their children—not merely peace for Americans but peace for all men and women, not merely peace in our time but peace for all time.

I speak of peace because of the new face of war. Total war makes no sense in an age when great powers can maintain large and relatively invulnerable nuclear forces and refuse to surrender without resort to those forces. It makes no sense in an age when a single nuclear weapon contains almost 10 times the explosive force delivered by all of the Allied air forces in the Second World War. It makes no sense in an age when the deadly poisons produced by a nuclear exchange would be carried by the wind and water and soil and seed to the far corners of the globe and to generations yet unborn.

Today the expenditure of billions of dollars every year on weapons acquired for the purpose of making sure we never need to use them is essential to keeping the peace. But surely the acquisition of such idle stockpiles—which can only destroy and never create—is not the only, much less the most efficient, means of assuring peace.

I speak of peace, therefore, as the necessary rational end of rational men. I realize that the pursuit of peace is not as dramatic as the pursuit of war, and frequently the words of the pursuer fall on deaf ears. But we have no more urgent task.

Some say that it is useless to speak of world peace or world law or world disarmament—and that it will be useless until the leaders of the Soviet Union adopt a more enlightened attitude. I hope they do. I believe we can help them do it. But I also believe that we must reexamine our own attitude, as individuals and as a nation, for our attitude is as essential as theirs. And every graduate of this school, every thoughtful citizen who despairs of war and wishes to bring peace, should begin by looking inward—by examining his own attitude toward the possibilities of peace, toward the Soviet Union, toward the course of the cold war, and toward freedom and peace here at home.

The Possibilities of Peace

First: Let us examine our attitude toward peace itself. Too many of us think it is impossible. Too many think it unreal. But that is a dangerous, defeatist belief. It leads to the conclusion that war is inevitable, that mankind is doomed, that we are gripped by forces we cannot control.

We need not accept that view. Our problems are manmade; therefore they can be solved by man. And man can be as big as he wants. No problem of human destiny is beyond human beings. Man's reason and spirit have often solved the seemingly unsolvable, and we believe they can do it again.

I am not referring to the absolute, infinite concept of universal peace and good will of which some fantasies and fanatics dream. I do not deny the values of hopes and dreams, but we merely invite discouragement and incredulity by making that our only and immediate goal.

Let us focus instead on a more practical, more attainable peace, based not on a sudden revolution in human nature but on a gradual evolution in human institutions—on a series of concrete actions and effective agreements which are in the interest of all concerned. There is no single, simple key to this peace, no grand or magic formula to be adopted by one or two powers. Genuine peace must be the product of many nations, the sum of many acts. It must be dynamic, not static, changing to meet the challenge of each new generation. For peace is a process, a way of solving problems.

With such a peace there will still be quarrels and conflicting interests, as there are within families and nations. World peace, like community peace, does not require that each man love his neighbor; it requires only that they live together in mutual tolerance, submitting their disputes to a just and peaceful settlement. And history teaches us that enmities between nations, as between individuals, do not last forever. However fixed our likes and dislikes may seem, the tide of time and events will often bring surprising changes in the relations between nations and neighbors.

So let us persevere. Peace need not be impracticable, and war need not be inevitable. By defining our goal more clearly, by making it seem more manageable and less remote, we can help all peoples to see it, to draw hope from it, and to move irresistibly toward it.

Common Interests of the United States and the Soviet Union

Second: Let us reexamine our attitude toward the Soviet Union. It is discouraging to think that their leaders may actually believe what their propagandists write. It is discouraging to read a recent authoritative Soviet text on military strategy and find, on page after page, wholly baseless and incredible claims—such as the allegation that "American imperialist circles are preparing to unleash different types of wars . . . that there is a very real threat of a preventive war being unleashed by American imperialists against the Soviet Union . . . [and that] the political aims of the American imperialists are to enslave economically and politically the European and other capitalist countries . . . [and] to achieve world domination . . . by means of aggressive wars."

Truly as it was written long ago: "The wicked flee when no man pursueth." Yet it is sad to read these Soviet statements—to realize the extent of the gulf between us. But it is also a warning—a warning to the American people not to fall into the same trap as the Soviets, not to see only a distorted and desperate view of the other side, not to see conflict as inevitable, accommodation as impossible, and communication as nothing more than an exchange of threats.

No government or social system is so evil that its people must be considered as lacking in virtue. As Americans we find communism profoundly repugnant as a negation of personal freedom and dignity. But we can still hail the Russian people for their many achievements—in science and space, in economic and industrial growth, in culture and in acts of courage.

Among the many traits the peoples of our two countries have in common, none is stronger than our mutual abhorrence of war. Almost unique among the major world powers, we have never been at war with each other. And no nation in the history of battle ever suffered more than the Soviet Union suffered in the course of the Second World War. At least 20 million lost their lives. Countless millions of homes and farms were burned or sacked. A third of the nation's territory, including nearly two-thirds of its industrial base, was turned into a wasteland—a loss equivalent to the devastation of this country east of Chicago.

Today, should total war ever break out again—no matter how—our two countries would become the primary targets. It is an ironical but accurate fact that the two strongest powers are the two in the most danger of devastation. All we have built, all we have worked for, would be destroyed in the first 24 hours. And even in the cold war, which brings burdens and dangers to so many countries—including this Nation's closest allies—our two countries bear the heaviest burdens. For we are both devoting massive sums of money to weapons that could be better devoted to combating ignorance, poverty, and disease. We are both caught up in a vicious and dangerous cycle in which suspicion on one side breeds suspicion on the other and new weapons beget counterweapons.

In short, both the United States and its allies, and the Soviet Union and its allies, have a mutually deep interest in a just and genuine peace and in halting the arms race. Agreements to this end are in the interests of the Soviet Union as well as ours, and even the most hostile nations can be relied upon to accept and keep those treaty obligations, and only those treaty obligations, which are in their own interest.

So let us not be blind to our differences, but let us also direct attention to our common interests and to the means by which those differences can be resolved. And if we cannot end now our differences, at least we can help make the world safe for diversity. For in the final analysis our most basic common link is that we all inhabit this planet. We all breathe the same air. We all cherish our children's future. And we are all mortal.

The Pursuit of Peace

Third: Let us reexamine our attitude toward the cold war, remembering that we are not engaged in a debate, seeking to pile up debating points. We are not here distributing blame or pointing the finger of judgment. We must deal with the world as it is and not as it might have been had the history of the last 18 years been different.

We must, therefore, persevere in the search for peace in the hope that constructive changes within the Communist bloc might bring within reach solutions which now seem beyond us. We must conduct our affairs in such a way that it becomes in the Communists' interest to agree on a genuine peace. Above all, while defending our own vital interests, nuclear powers must avert those confrontations which bring an adversary to a choice of either a humiliating retreat or a nuclear war. To adopt that kind of course in the nuclear age would be evidence only of the bankruptcy of our policy—or of a collective death wish for the world.

To secure these ends, America's weapons are nonprovocative, carefully controlled, designed to deter, and capable of selective use. Our military forces are committed to peace and disciplined in self-restraint. Our diplomats are instructed to avoid unnecessary irritants and purely rhetorical hostility.

For we can seek a relaxation of tensions without relaxing our guard. And, for our part, we do not need to use threats to prove that we are resolute. We do not need to jam foreign broadcasts out of fear our faith will be eroded. We are unwilling to impose our system on any unwilling people, but we are willing and able to engage in peaceful competition with any people on earth.

Meanwhile we seek to strengthen the United Nations, to help solve its financial problems, to make it a more effective instrument of peace, to develop it into a genuine world security system—a system capable of resolving disputes on the basis of law, of insuring the security of the large and the small, and of creating conditions under which arms can finally be abolished.

At the same time we seek to keep peace inside the non-Communist world, where many nations, all of them our friends, are divided over issues which weaken Western unity, which invite Communist interven-tion, or which threaten to erupt into war. Our efforts in West New Guinea, in the Congo, in the Middle East, and in the Indian subcontinent have been persistent and patient despite criticism from both sides. We have also tried to set an example for others—by seeking to adjust small but significant differences with our own closest neighbors in Mexico and in Canada.

Speaking of other nations, I wish to make one point clear. We are bound to many nations by alliances. Those alliances exist because our concern and theirs substantially overlap. Our commitment to defend Western Europe and West Berlin, for example, stands undiminished because of the identity of our vital interests. The United States will make no deal with the Soviet Union at the expense of other nations and other peoples, not merely because they are our partners but also because their interests and ours converge.

Our interests converge, not only in defending the frontiers of freedom but in pursuing the paths of peace. It is our hope—and the purpose of allied policies—to convince the Soviet Union that she, too, should let each nation choose its own future, so long as that choice does not interfere with the choices of others. The Communist drive to impose their political and economic system on others is the primary cause of world tension today. For there can be no doubt that, if all nations could refrain from interfering in the self-determination of others, the peace would be much more assured.

This will require a new effort to achieve world law, a new context for world discussions. It will require increased understanding between the Soviets and ourselves. And increased understanding will require increased contact and communication. One step in this direction is the proposed arrangement for a direct line between Moscow and Washington, to avoid on each side the dangerous delays, misunderstandings, and misreadings of the other's actions which might occur at a time of crisis.

We have also been talking in Geneva about other first-step measures of arms control, designed to limit the intensity of the arms race and to reduce the risks of accidental war. Our primary long range interest in Geneva, however, is general and complete disarmament, designed to take place by stages, permitting parallel political developments to build the new institutions of peace which would take the place of arms. The pursuit of disarmament has been an effort of this Government since the 1920's. It has been urgently sought by the past three administrations. And however dim the prospects may be today, we intend to continue this effort—to continue it in order that all countries, including our own, can better grasp what the problems and possibilities of disarmament are.

The one major area of these negotiations where the end is in sight, yet where a fresh start is badly needed, is in a treaty to outlaw nuclear tests. The conclusion of such a treaty—so near and yet so far—would check the spiraling arms race in one of its most dangerous areas. It would place the nuclear powers in a position to deal more effectively with one of the greatest hazards which man faces in 1963, the further spread of nuclear arms. It would increase our security: it would decrease the prospects of war. Surely this goal is sufficiently important to require our steady pursuit, yielding neither to the temptation to give up the whole effort nor the temptation to give up our insistence on vital and responsible safeguards.

I am taking this opportunity, therefore, to announce two important decisions in this regard.

First: Chairman Khrushchev, Prime Minister Macmillan, and I have agreed that high-level discussions will shortly begin in Moscow looking toward early agreement on a comprehensive test ban treaty. Our hopes must be tempered with the caution of history, but with our hopes go the hopes of all mankind.

Second: To make clear our good faith and solemn convictions on the matter, I now declare that the United States does not propose to conduct nuclear tests in the atmosphere so long as other states do not do so. We will not be the first to resume. Such a declaration is no substitute for a formal binding treaty, but I hope it will help us achieve one. Nor would such a treaty be a substitute for disarmament, but I hope it will help us achieve it.

Peace and Human Rights

Finally, my fellow Americans, let us examine our attitude toward peace and freedom here at home. The quality and spirit of our own society must justify and support our efforts abroad. We must show it in the dedication of our own lives as many of you who are graduating today will have a unique opportunity to do, by serving without pay in the Peace Corps abroad or in the proposed National Service Corps here at home.

But wherever we are, we must all, in our daily lives, live up to the age-old faith that peace and freedom walk together. In too many of our cities today the peace is not secure because freedom is incomplete.

It is the responsibility of the executive branch at all levels of government—local, State, and National—to provide and protect that freedom for all of our citizens by all means within their authority. It is the responsibility of the legislative branch at all levels, wherever that authority is not now adequate, to make it adequate. And it is the responsibility of all citizens in all sections of this country to respect the rights of all others and to respect the law of the land.

All this is not unrelated to world peace. "When a man's ways please the Lord," the Scriptures tell us, "he maketh even his enemies to be at peace with him." And is not peace, in the last analysis, basically a matter of human rights—the right to live out our lives without fear of devastation, the right to breathe air as nature provided it, the right of future generations to a healthy existence?

While we proceed to safeguard our national interests, let us also safeguard human interests. And the elimination of war and arms is clearly in the interest of both. No treaty, however much it may be to the advantage of all, however tightly it may be worded, can provide absolute security against the risks of deception and evasion. But it can, if it is sufficiently effective in its enforcement and if it is sufficiently in the interests of its signers, offer far more security and far fewer risks than an unabated, uncontrolled, unpredictable arms race.

The United States, as the world knows, will never start a war. We do not want a war. We do not now expect a war. This generation of Americans has already had enough—more than enough—of war and hate and oppression. We shall be prepared if others wish it. We shall be alert to try to stop it. But we shall also do our part to build a world of peace where the weak are safe and the strong just. We are not helpless before that task or hopeless of its success. Confident and unafraid, we labor on —not toward a strategy of annihiliation but toward a strategy of peace. 🖋

Foreign policy making must take place within the framework of a very broad popular consensus. The government cannot adopt positions that smack of appeasement, nor can it be too belligerent. The following selection is taken from a highly controversial speech given by the Chairman of the Senate Foreign Relations Committee, Senator J. W. Fulbright, in March of 1964. In it he suggested that Americans reevaluate some of their long-held attitudes concerning foreign policy.

FOREIGN POLICY—OLD MYTHS AND NEW REALITIES

*J. W. Fulbright**

THERE is an inevitable divergence, attributable to the imperfections of the human mind, between the world as it is and the world as men perceive it. As long as our perceptions are reasonably close to objective reality, it is possible for us to act upon our problems in a rational and appropriate manner. But when our perceptions fail to keep pace with events, when we refuse to believe something because it displeases or frightens us, or because it is simply startlingly unfamiliar, then the gap between fact and perception becomes a chasm, and action becomes irrelevant and irrational.

There has always—and inevitably—been some divergence between the realities of foreign policy and our ideas about it. This divergence has in certain respects been growing, rather than narrowing; and we are handicapped, accordingly, by policies based on old myths, rather than current realities. This divergence is, in my opinion, dangerous and unnecessary—dangerous, because it can reduce foreign policy to a fraudulent game of imagery and appearances; unnecessary, because it can be overcome by the determination of men in high office to dispel prevailing misconceptions by the candid dissemination of unpleasant, but inescapable, facts.

Before commenting on some of the specific areas where I believe our policies are at least partially based on cherished myths, rather than objective facts, I should like to suggest two possible reasons for the growing divergence between the realities and our perceptions of current world politics. The first is the radical change in relations between and within the Communist and the free world; and the second is the tendency of too many of us to confuse means with ends and, accordingly, to adhere to prevailing practices with a fervor befitting immutable principles.

Although it is too soon to render a definitive judgment, there is mounting evidence that events of recent years have wrought profound changes in the character of East-West relations. In the Cuban missile crisis of October 1962, the United States proved to the Soviet Union that a policy of aggression and adventure involved unacceptable risks. In the signing of the test ban treaty, each side in effect assured the other that it was

* From the *Congressional Record*, March 25, 1964.

prepared to forego, at least for the present, any bid for a decisive military or political breakthrough. These occurrences, it should be added, took place against the background of the clearly understood strategic superiority—but not supremacy—of the United States.

It seems reasonable, therefore, to suggest that the character of the cold war has, for the present, at least, been profoundly altered: by the drawing back of the Soviet Union from extremely aggressive policies; by the implicit repudiation by both sides of a policy of "total victory"; and by the establishment of an American strategic superiority which the Soviet Union appears to have tacitly accepted because it has been accompanied by assurances that it will be exercised by the United States with responsibility and restraint. These enormously important changes may come to be regarded by historians as the foremost achievements of the Kennedy administration in the field of foreign policy. Their effect has been to commit us to a foreign policy which can accurately—though perhaps not prudently—be defined as one of "peaceful coexistence."

Another of the results of the lowering of tensions between East and West is that each is now free to enjoy the luxury of accelerated strife and squabbling within its own domain. The ideological thunderbolts between Washington and Moscow which until a few years ago seemed a permanent part of our daily lives have become a pale shadow of their former selves. Now instead the United States waits in fascinated apprehension for the Olympian pronouncements that issue from Paris at 6-month intervals while the Russians respond to the crude epithets of Peiping with almost plaintive rejoinders about "those who want to start a war against everybody."

These astonishing changes in the configuration of the postwar world have had an unsettling effect on both public and official opinion in the United States. One reason for this, I believe, lies in the fact that we are a people used to looking at the world, and indeed at ourselves, in moralistic rather than empirical terms. We are predisposed to regard any conflict as a clash between good and evil rather than as simply a clash between conflicting interests. We are inclined to confuse freedom and democracy, which we regard as moral principles, with the way in which they are practiced in America—with capitalism, federalism, and the two-party system, which are not moral principles but simply the preferred and accepted practices of the American people. There is much cant in American moralism and not a little inconsistency. It resembles in some ways the religious faith of the many respectable people who, in Samuel Butler's words, "would be equally horrified to hear the Christian religion doubted or to see it practiced."

Our national vocabulary is full of "self-evident truths" not only about "life, liberty, and happiness," but about a vast number of personal and public issues, including the cold war. It has become one of the "self-evident truths" of the postwar era that just as the President resides in Washington and the Pope in Rome, the Devil resides immutably in Moscow. We have come to regard the Kremlin as the permanent seat of his power and we have grown almost comfortable with a menace which, though unspeakably evil, has had the redeeming virtues of constancy, predictability, and familiarity. Now the Devil has betrayed us by traveling abroad and, worse still, by dispersing himself, turning up now here, now there, and in many places at once, with a devilish disregard for the laboriously constructed frontiers of ideology.

We are confronted with a complex and fluid world situation and we are not adapting ourselves to it. We are clinging to old myths in the face of new realities and we are seeking to escape the contradictions by narrowing the permissible bounds of public discussion, by relegating an increasing number of ideas and viewpoints to a growing category of "unthinkable thoughts." I believe that this tendency can and should be reversed, that it is within our ability, and unquestionably in our interests, to cut loose from established myths and to start thinking some "unthinkable thoughts"—about the cold war and East-West relations, about the under-developed countries and particularly those in Latin America, about the changing nature of the Chinese Communist threat in Asia and about the festering war in Vietnam.

The master myth of the cold war is that the Communist bloc is a monolith composed of governments which are not really governments at all but organized conspiracies, divided among themselves perhaps in certain matters of tactics, but all equally resolute and implacable in their determination to destroy the free world.

I believe that the Communist world is indeed hostile to the free world in its general and long-term intentions but that the existence of this animosity in principle is far less important for our foreign policy than the great variations in its intensity and character both in time and among the individual members of the Communist bloc. Only if we recognize these variations, ranging from China, which poses immediate threats to the free world, to Poland and Yugoslavia, which pose none, can we hope to act effectively upon the bloc and to turn its internal differences to our own advantage and to the advantage of those bloc countries which wish to maximize their independence. It is the responsibility of our national leaders both in the executive branch and in Congress, to acknowledge and act upon these realities, even at the cost of saying things which will not win immediate widespread enthusiasm.

For a start, we can acknowledge the fact that the Soviet Union, though still a most formidable adversary, has ceased to be totally and implacably hostile to the West. It has shown a new willingness to enter mutually advantageous arrangements with the West and, thus far at least, to honor them. It has therefore become possible to divert some of our energies from the prosecution of the cold war to the relaxation of the cold war and to deal with the Soviet Union, for certain purposes, as a normal state with normal and traditional interests.

If we are to do these things effectively, we must distinguish between communism as an ideology and the power and policy of the Soviet state. It is not communism as a doctrine, or communism as it is practiced within the Soviet Union or within any other country, that threatens us. How the Soviet Union organizes its internal life, the gods and doctrines that it worships, are matters for the Soviet Union to determine. It is not Communist dogma as espoused within Russia but Communist imperialism that threatens us and other peoples of the non-Communist world. Insofar as a great nation mobilizes its power and resources for aggressive purposes, that nation, regardless of ideology, makes itself our enemy. Insofar as a nation is content to practice its doctrines within its own frontiers, that nation, however repugnant its ideology, is one with which we have no proper quarrel. We must deal with the Soviet Union as a great power, quite apart from differences of ideology. To the extent that the Soviet leaders abandon the global ambitions of Marxist ideology, in fact if not in words, it becomes possible for us to engage in normal relations with them, relations which probably cannot be close or trusting for many years to come but which can be gradually freed of the terror and the tensions of the cold war.

In our relations with the Russians, and indeed in our relations with all nations, we would do well to remember, and to act upon, the words of Pope John in the great Encyclical, Pacem in Terris:

"It must be borne in mind," said Pope John, "that to proceed gradually is the law of life in all its expressions, therefore, in human institutions, too, it is not possible to renovate for the better except by working from within them, gradually. Violence has always achieved only destruction, not construction, the kindling of passions, not their pacification, the accumulation of hate and ruin, not the reconciliation of the contending parties. And it has reduced men and parties to the difficult task of rebuilding, after sad experience, on the ruins of discord."

Important opportunities have been created for Western policy by the development of "polycentrism" in the Communist bloc. The Communist nations, as George Kennan has pointed out, are, like the Western nations, currently caught up in a crisis of indecision about their relations with countries outside their own ideological bloc. The choices open to the satellite states are limited but by no means insignificant. They can adhere slavishly to Soviet preferences or they can strike out on their own, within limits, to enter into mutually advantageous relations with the West.

Whether they do so, and to what extent, is to some extent at least within the power of the West to determine. If we persist in the view that all Communist regimes are equally hostile and equally threatening to the West, and that we can have no policy toward the captive nations except the eventual overthrow of their Communist regimes, then the West may enforce upon the Communist bloc a degree of unity which the Soviet Union has shown itself to be quite incapable of imposing—just as Stalin in the early postwar years frightened the West into a degree of unity that it almost certainly could not have attained by its own unaided efforts. If, on the other hand, we are willing to reexamine the view that all Communist regimes are alike in the threat which they pose for the West—a view which had a certain validity in Stalin's time—then we may be able to exert an important influence on the course of events within a divided Communist world.

We are to a great extent the victims, and the Soviets the beneficiaries, of our own ideological convictions, and of the curious contradictions which they involve. We consider it a form of subversion of the free world, for example, when the Russians enter trade relations or conclude a consular convention or establish airline connections with a free country in Asia, Africa, or Latin America—and to a certain extent we are right. On the other hand, when it is proposed that we adopt the same strategy in reverse—by extending commercial credits to Poland or Yugoslavia, or by exchanging Ambassadors with a Hungarian regime which has changed considerably in character since the revolution of 1956—then the same patriots who are so alarmed by Soviet activities in the free world charge our policymakers with "giving aid and comfort to the enemy" and with innumerable other categories of idiocy and immorality.

It is time that we resolved this contradiction and separated myth from reality. The myth is that every Communist state is an unmitigated evil and a relentless enemy of the free world; the reality is that some Communist regimes pose a threat to the free world while others pose little or none, and that if we will recognize these distinctions, we ourselves will be able to influence events in the Communist bloc in a way favorable to the security of the free world.

It could well be argued . . . —

Writes George Kennan—

That if the major Western Powers had full freedom of movement in devising their own policies, it would be within their power to determine whether the Chinese view, or the Soviet view, or perhaps a view more liberal than either would ultimately prevail within the Communist camp —George Kennan, "Polycentrism and Western Policy," Foreign Affairs, January 1964, page 178.

There are numerous areas in which we can seek to reduce the tensions of the cold war and to bring a degree of normalcy into our relations with the Soviet Union and other Communist countries—once we have resolved that it is safe and wise to do so. We have already taken important steps in this direction: the Antarctic and Austrian treaties and the nuclear test ban treaty, the broadening of East-West cultural and educational relations, and the expansion of trade.

On the basis of recent experience and present economic needs, there seems little likelihood of a spectacular increase in trade between Communist and Western countries, even if existing restrictions were to be relaxed. Free world trade with Communist countries has been increasing at a steady but unspectacular rate, and it seems unlikely to be greatly accelerated because of the limited ability of the Communist countries to pay for increased imports. A modest increase in East-West trade may nonetheless serve as a modest instrument of East-West detente—provided that we are able to overcome the myth that trade with Communist countries is a compact with the Devil and to recognize that, on the contrary, trade can serve as an effective and honorable means of advancing both peace and human welfare.

Whether we are able to make these philosophic adjustments or not, we cannot escape the fact that our efforts to devise a common Western trade policy are a palpable failure and that our allies are going to trade with the Communist bloc whether we like it or not. The world's major exporting nations are slowly but steadily increasing their trade with the Communist bloc and the bloc countries are showing themselves to be reliable customers. Since 1958 Western Europe has been increasing its exports to the East at the rate of about 7 percent a year, which is nearly the same rate at which its overall world sales have been increasing.

West Germany—one of our close friends—is by far the leading Western nation in trade with the Sino-Soviet bloc. West German exports to bloc countries in 1962 were valued at $749.9 million. Britain was in second place—although not a close second—with exports to Communist countries amounting to $393 million in 1962. France followed with exports worth $313.4 million, and the figure for the United States—consisting largely of surplus food sales to Poland under Public Law 480—stood far below at $125.1 million.

Our allies have made it plain that they propose to expand this trade, in non-strategic goods, wherever possible. West Germany, in the last 16 months, has exchanged or agreed to exchange trade missions with every country in Eastern Europe except Albania. Britain has indicated that she will soon extend long-term credits to Communist countries, breaching the 5-year limit which the Western allies have hitherto observed. In the light of these facts, it is difficult to see what effect the tight American trade restrictions have other than to deny the United States a substantial share of a profitable market.

The inability of the United States to prevent its partners from trading extensively with the Communist bloc is one good reason for relaxing our own restrictions, but there is a better reason: the potential value of trade— a moderate volume of trade in nonstrategic items—as an instrument for reducing world tensions and strengthening the foundations of peace. I do not think that trade or the nuclear test ban, or any other prospective East-West accommodation, will lead to a grand reconciliation that will end the cold war and usher in the brotherhood of man. At the most, the cumulative effect of all the agreements that are likely to be attainable in the foreseeable future will be the alleviation of the extreme tensions and animosities that threaten the world with nuclear devastation and the gradual conversion of the struggle between communism and the free world into a safer and more tolerable international rivalry, one which may be with us for years and decades to come but which need not be so terrifying and so costly as to distract the nations of the world from the creative pursuits of civilized societies.

There is little in history to justify the expectation that we can either win the cold war or end it immediately and completely. These are favored myths, respectively, of the American right and of the American left. They are, I believe, equal in their unreality and in their disregard for the feasibilities of history. We must disabuse ourselves of them and come to terms, at last, with the realities of a world in which neither good nor evil is absolute and in which those who move events and make history are those who have understood not how much but how little it is within our power to change. . . .

Latin America is one of the areas of the world in which American policy is weakened by a growing divergency between old myths and new realities.

The crisis over the Panama Canal has been unnecessarily protracted for reasons of domestic politics and national pride and sensitivity on both sides—for reasons, that is, of only marginal relevance to the merits of the dispute. I think the Panamanians have unquestionably been more emotional about the dispute than has the United States. I also think that there is less reason for emotionalism on the part of the United States than on the part of Panama. It is important for us to remember that the issue over the canal is only one of a great many in which the United States is involved, and by no means the most important. For Panama, on the other hand, a small nation with a weak economy and an unstable government, the canal is the preeminent factor in the nation's economy and in its foreign relations. Surely in a confrontation so unequal, it is not unreasonable to expect the United States to go a little farther than halfway in the search for a fair settlement.

We Americans would do well, for a start, to divest ourselves of the silly notion that the issue with Panama is a test of our courage and resolve. I believe that the Cuban missile crisis of 1962, involving a confrontation with nuclear weapons and intercontinental missiles, was indeed a test of our courage, and we acquitted ourselves extremely well in that instance. I am unable to understand how a controversy with a small and poor country, with virtually no military capacity, can possibly be regarded as a test of our bravery and will to defend our interests. It takes stubbornness but not courage to reject the entreaties of the weak. The real test in Panama is not of our valor but of our wisdom and judgment and commonsense.

We would also do well to disabuse ourselves of the myth that there is something morally sacred about the treaty of 1903. The fact of the matter is that the treaty was concluded under circumstances that reflect little credit on the United States. It was made possible by Panama's separation from Colombia, which probably could not have occurred at that time without the dispatch of U.S. warships to prevent the landing of Colombian troops on the isthmus to put down the Panamanian rebellion. The United States not only intervened in Colombia's internal affairs but did so in violation of a treaty concluded in 1846 under which the United States had guaranteed Colombian sovereignty over the isthmus. President Theodore Roosevelt, as he boasted, "took Panama," and proceeded to negotiate the canal treaty with a compliant Panamanian regime. Panamanians contend that they were "shotgunned" into the treaty of 1903 as the price of U.S. protection against a possible effort by Colombia to recover the isthmus. The contention is not without substance.

It is not my purpose here to relate the events of 60 years ago but only to suggest that there is little basis for a posture of injured innocence and self-righteousness by either side and that we would do much better to resolve the issue on the basis of present realities rather than old myths.

The central reality is that the treaty of 1903 is in certain respects obsolete. The treaty has been revised only twice, in 1936 when the annual rental was raised from $250,000 to $430,000 and other modifications were made, and in 1955 when further changes were made, including an increase in the annual rental to $1.9 million, where it now stands. The canal, of course, contributes far more to the Panamanian economy in the form of wages paid to Panamanian workers and purchases made in Panama. The fact remains, nonetheless, that the annual rental of $1.9 million is a modest sum and should probably be increased. There are other issues, relating to hiring policies for Panamanian workers in the zone, the flying of flags, and other symbols of national pride and sovereignty. The basic problem about the treaty, however, is the exercise of American control over a part of the territory of Panama in this age of intense nationalist and anti-colonialist feeling. Justly or not, the Panamanians feel that they are being treated as a colony, or a quasi-colony, of the United States, and this feeling is accentuated by the contrast between the standard of living of the Panamanians, with a per capita income of about $429 a year, and that of the Americans living in the Canal Zone—immediately adjacent to Panama, of course, and within it—with a per capita income of $4,228 a year. That is approximately 10 times greater. It is the profound social and economic alienation between Panama and the Canal Zone, and its impact on the national feeling of the Panamanians, that underlies the current crisis.

Under these circumstances, it seems to me entirely proper and neces-sary for the United States to take the initiative in proposing new arrange-ments that would redress some of Panama's grievances against the treaty as it now stands. I see no reason—certainly no reason of "weakness" or "dishonor"—why the United States cannot put an end to the semantic debate over whether treaty revisions are to be "negotiated" or "discussed" by stating positively and clearly that it is prepared to negotiate revisions in the canal treaty and to submit such changes as are made to the Senate for its advice and consent.

I think it is necessary for the United States to do this even though a commitment to revise the treaty may be widely criticized at home. It is the responsibility of the President and his advisers, in situations of this sort, to exercise their own best judgment as to where the national interest lies even though this may necessitate unpopular decisions.

An agreement to "negotiate" revisions is not an agreement to nego-tiate any particular revision. It would leave us completely free to deter-mine what revisions, and how many revisions, we would be willing to accept. If there is any doubt about this, one can find ample reassurance in the proceedings at Geneva, where several years of "negotiations" for "general and complete disarmament" still leaves us with the greatest arse-nal of weapons in the history of the world.

The problem of Cuba is more difficult than that of Panama, and far more heavily burdened with the deadweight of old myths and prohibitions against "unthinkable thoughts." I think the time is overdue for a candid reevaluation of our Cuban policy even though it may also lead to dis-tasteful conclusions.

There are and have been three options open to the United States with respect to Cuba: first, the removal of the Castro regime by invading and occupying the island; second, an effort to weaken and ultimately bring down the regime by a policy of political and economic boycott; and finally, acceptance of the Communist regime as a disagreeable reality and annoyance but one which is not likely to be removed in the near future because of the unavailability of acceptable means of removing it.

The first option, invasion, has been tried in a halfhearted way and found wanting. It is generally acknowledged that the invasion and occu-pation of Cuba, besides violating our obligations as a member of the United Nations and of the Organization of American States, would have explosive consequences in Latin America and elsewhere and might pre-cipitate a global nuclear war. I know of no responsible statesman who advocates this approach. It has been rejected by our Government and by public opinion and I think that, barring some grave provocation, it can be ruled out as a feasible policy for the United States.

The approach which we have adopted has been the second of those mentioned, an effort to weaken and eventually bring down the Castro regime by a policy of political and economic boycott. This policy has taken the form of extensive restrictions against trade with Cuba by United States citizens, of the exclusion of Cuba from the inter-American system and efforts to secure Latin American support in isolating Cuba politically and economically, and of diplomatic efforts, backed by certain trade and aid sanctions, to persuade other free world countries to maintain economic boycotts against Cuba.

This policy, it now seems clear, has been a failure, and there is no reason to believe that it will succeed in the future. Our efforts to persuade our allies to terminate their trade with Cuba have been generally rebuffed. The prevailing attitude was perhaps best expressed by a British manufacturer who, in response to American criticisms of the sale of British buses to Cuba, said: "If America has a surplus of wheat, we have a surplus of buses."

In cutting off military assistance to Great Britain, France, and Yugoslavia under the provisions of Section 620 of the Foreign Assistance Act of 1963, the United States has wielded a stuffed club. The amounts of aid involved are infinitesimal; the chances of gaining compliance with our boycott policy are nil; and the annoyance of the countries concerned may be considerable. What we terminated with respect to Britain and France, in fact, can hardly be called aid; it was more of a sales promotion program under which British and French military leaders were brought to the United States to see—and to buy—advanced American weapons. Terminating this program was in itself of little importance; Britain and France do not need our assistance. But terminating the program as a sanction against their trade with Cuba can have no real effect other than to create an illusory image of "toughness" for the benefit of our own people.

Free world exports to Cuba have, on the whole, been declining over recent years, but overall imports have been rising since 1961. . . .

The figures provide little basis for expecting the early termination of free world trade with Cuba. The export table shows U.S. exports to Cuba in both 1962 and 1963 exceeding those of any other free world country. These American exports consisted almost entirely of ransom payments for the Bay of Pigs prisoners and should not be confused with normal trade.

There is an interesting feature to this table, which may not be well known. It is that the exports from Cuba to various allies of ours, particularly Japan, the United Kingdom, Morocco, and others, have been going up, and have been very substantial. This reflects, I believe, the importation from Cuba of sugar to a great extent, and also accounts for the accumulation by Cuba of substantial foreign aid as a result of the dramatic increase in the price of sugar during the past couple of years.

The exports from the free world to Cuba have been going up in similar instances, in the case of Japan, but generally speaking they have not been increasing. Of course, since 1958, when we accounted for more than half of Cuba's exports, they have gone down rather dramatically. In any case, the tables will speak for themselves.

I should like to make it very clear that I am not arguing against the desirability of an economic boycott against the Castro regime but against its feasibility. The effort has been made and all the fulminations we can utter about sanctions and retaliation against free world countries that trade with Cuba cannot long conceal the fact that the boycott policy is a failure.

The boycott policy has not failed because of any "weakness" or "timidity" on the part of our Government. This charge, so frequently heard, is one of the most pernicious myths to have been inflicted on the American people. The boycott policy has failed because the United States is not omnipotent and cannot be. The basic reality to be faced is that it is simply not within our power to compel our allies to cut off their trade with Cuba, unless we are prepared to take drastic sanctions against them, such as closing our own markets to any foreign company that does business in Cuba, as proposed by Mr. Nixon. We can do this, of course, but if we do, we ought first to be very sure as apparently Mr. Nixon is, that the Cuban boycott is more important than good relations with our closest allies. In fact, even the most drastic sanctions are as likely to be rewarded with defiance as with compliance. For practical purposes, all we can do is to ask other countries to take the measures with respect to Cuba which we recommend. We have done so and in some areas have been successful. In other areas, notably that of the economic boycott, we have asked for the full cooperation of other free world countries and it has been largely denied. It remains for us to decide whether we will respond with a sustained outburst of hollow and ill-tempered threats, all the while comforting ourselves with the myth that we can get anything we want if we only try hard enough—or, in this case, shout loud enough—or we can acknowledge the failure of our efforts and proceed, coolly and rationally, to reexamine the policies which we now pursue in relation to the interests they are intended to serve.

The prospects of bringing down the Castro regime by political and economic boycott have never been very good. Even if a general free world boycott were successfully applied against Cuba, it is unlikely that the Russians would refuse to carry the extra financial burden and thereby permit the only Communist regime in the Western Hemisphere to collapse. We are thus compelled to recognize that there is probably no way of bringing down the Castro regime by means of economic pressures unless we are prepared to impose a blockade against nonmilitary shipments from the Soviet Union. Exactly such a policy has been recommended by some of our more reckless politicians, but the preponderance of informed opinion is that a blockade against Soviet shipments of nonmilitary supplies to Cuba would be extravagantly dangerous, carrying the strong possibility of a confrontation that could explode into nuclear war.

Having ruled out military invasion and blockade, and recognizing the failure of the boycott policy, we are compelled to consider the third of the three options open to us with respect to Cuba: the acceptance of the continued existence of the Castro regime as a distasteful nuisance but not an intolerable danger so long as the nations of the hemisphere are prepared to meet their obligations of collective defense under the Rio Treaty.

In recent years we have become transfixed with Cuba, making it far more important in both our foreign relations and in our domestic life than its size and influence warrant. We have flattered a noisy but minor demagog by treating him as if he were a Napoleonic menace. Communist Cuba has been a disruptive and subversive influence in Venezuela and other countries of the hemisphere, and there is no doubt that both we and our Latin American partners would be better off if the Castro regime did not exist. But it is important to bear in mind that, despite their best efforts, the Cuban Communists have not succeeded in subverting the hemisphere and that in Venezuela, for example, where communism has made a major effort to gain power through terrorism, it has been repudiated by a people who in a free election have committed themselves to the course of liberal democracy. It is necessary to weigh the desirability of an objective against the feasibility of its attainment, and when we do this with respect to Cuba, I think we are bound to conclude that Castro is a nuisance but not a grave threat to the United States and that he cannot be gotten rid of except by means that are wholly disproportionate to the objective. Cuban communism does pose a grave threat to other Latin

American countries, but this threat can be dealt with by prompt and vigorous use of the established procedures of the inter-American system against any act of aggression.

I think that we must abandon the myth that Cuban communism is a transitory menace that is going to collapse or disappear in the immediate future and face up to two basic realities about Cuba: first, that the Castro regime is not on the verge of collapse and is not likely to be overthrown by any policies which we are now pursuing or can reasonably undertake; and second, that the continued existence of the Castro regime, though inimical to our interests and policies, is not an insuperable obstacle to the attainment of our objectives, unless we make it so by permitting it to poison our politics at home and to divert us from more important tasks in the hemisphere.

The policy of the United States with respect to Latin America as a whole is predicated on the assumption that social revolution can be accomplished without violent upheaval. This is the guiding principle of the Alliance for Progress and it may in time be vindicated. We are entitled to hope so and it is wise and necessary for us to do all that we can to advance the prospects of peaceful and orderly reform.

At the same time, we must be under no illusions as to the extreme difficulty of uprooting long-established ruling oligarchies without disruptions involving lesser or greater degrees of violence. The historical odds are probably against the prospects of peaceful social revolution. There are places, of course, where it has occurred and others where it seems likely to occur. In Latin America, the chances for such basic change by peaceful means seem bright in Colombia and Venezuela and certain other countries; in Mexico, many basic changes have been made by peaceful means, but these came in the wake of a violent revolution. In other Latin American countries, the power of ruling oligarchies is so solidly established and their ignorance so great that there seems little prospect of accomplishing economic growth or social reform by means short of the forcible overthrow of established authorities.

I am not predicting violent revolutions in Latin America or elsewhere. Still less am I advocating them. I wish only to suggest that violent social revolutions are a possibility in countries where feudal oligarchies resist all meaningful change by peaceful means. We must not, in our preference for the democratic procedures envisioned by the Charter of Punta del Este, close our minds to the possibility that democratic procedures may fail in certain countries and that where democracy does fail violent social convulsions may occur.

We would do well, while continuing our efforts to promote peaceful change through the Alliance for Progress, to consider what our reactions might be in the event of the outbreak of genuine social revolution in one or more Latin American countries. Such a revolution did occur in Bolivia, and we accepted it calmly and sensibly. But what if a violent social revolution were to break out in one of the larger Latin American countries? Would we feel certain that it was Cuban or Soviet inspired? Would we wish to intervene on the side of established authority? Or would we be willing to tolerate or even support a revolution if it was seen to be not Communist but similar in nature to the Mexican revolution or the Nasser revolution in Egypt?

These are hypothetical questions and there is no readily available set of answers to them. But they are questions which we should be thinking about because they have to do with problems that could become real and urgent with great suddenness. We should be considering, for example, what groups in particular countries might conceivably lead revolutionary movements, and if we can identify them, we should be considering how we might communicate with them and influence them in such a way that their movements, if successful, will not pursue courses detrimental to our security and our interests.

The Far East is another area of the world in which American policy is handicapped by the divergence of old myths and new realities. Particularly with respect to China, an elaborate vocabulary of make believe has become compulsory in both official and public discussion. We are committed, with respect to China and other areas in Asia, to inflexible policies of long standing from which we hesitate to depart because of the attribution to these policies of an aura of mystical sanctity. It may be that a thorough reevaluation of our Far Eastern policies would lead us to the conclusion that they are sound and wise, or at least that they represent the best available options. It may be, on the other hand, that a reevaluation would point up the need for greater or lesser changes in our policies. The point is that, whatever the outcome of a rethinking of policy might be, we have been unwilling to undertake it because of the fear of many Government officials, undoubtedly well founded, that even the suggestion of new policies toward China or Vietnam would provoke a vehement public outcry.

I do not think the United States can, or should, recognize Communist China, or acquiesce in its admission to the United Nations under present circumstances. It would be unwise to do so, because there is nothing to be gained by it so long as the Peiping regime maintains its attitude of implacable hostility toward the United States. I do not believe, however, that this state of affairs is necessarily permanent. As we have seen in our relations with Germany and Japan, hostility can give way in an astonishingly short time to close friendship; and, as we have seen in our relations with China, the reverse can occur with equal speed. It is not impossible that in time our relations with China will change again—if not to friendship, then perhaps to "competitive coexistence." It would therefore be extremely useful if we could introduce an element of flexibility, or, more precisely, of the capacity to be flexible, into our relations with Communist China.

We would do well, as former Assistant Secretary Hilsman has recommended, to maintain an "open door" to the possibility of improved relations with Communist China in the future. For a start, we must jar open our minds to certain realities about China, of which the foremost is that there really are not "two Chinas," but only one—mainland China; and that it is ruled by Communists, and is likely to remain so for the indefinite future. Once we accept this fact, it becomes possible to reflect on the conditions under which it might be possible for us to enter into relatively normal relations with mainland China. One condition, of course, must be the abandonment by the Chinese Communists, tacitly, if not explicitly, of their intention to conquer and incorporate Taiwan. This seems unlikely now; but far more surprising changes have occurred in politics, and it is quite possible that a new generation of leaders in Peiping and Taipei may put a quiet end to the Chinese civil war, thus opening the possibility of entirely new patterns of international relations in the Far East.

Should such changes occur, they will open important opportunities for American policy; and it is to be hoped that we shall be able and willing to take advantage of them. It seems possible, for instance, that an atmosphere of reduced tensions in the Far East might make it possible to strengthen world peace by drawing mainland China into existing East-West agreements in such fields as disarmament, trade, and educational exchange.

These are long-range prospects, which may or may not materialize. In the immediate future, we are confronted with possible changes in the Far East resulting from recent French diplomacy.

French recognition of Communist China, although untimely and carried out in a way that can hardly be considered friendly to the United States, may nonetheless serve a constructive long-term purpose, by unfreezing a situation in which many countries, none more than the United States, are committed to inflexible policies by long-established commitments and the pressures of domestic public opinion. One way or another, the French initiative may help generate a new situation in which the United States, as well as other countries, will find it possible to reevaluate its basic policies in the Far East.

The situation in Vietnam poses a far more pressing need for a reevaluation of American policy. Other than withdrawal, which I do not think can be realistically considered under present circumstances, three options are open to us in Vietnam: First, continuation of the antiguerrilla war within South Vietnam, along with renewed American efforts to increase the military effectiveness of the South Vietnamese Army and the political effectiveness of the South Vietnamese Government; second, an attempt to end the war, through negotiations for the neutralization of South Vietnam, or of both North and South Vietnam; and, finally, the expansion of the scale of the war, either by the direct commitment of large numbers of American troops or by equipping the South Vietnamese Army to attack North Vietnamese territory, possibly by means of commando-type operations from the sea or the air.

It is difficult to see how a negotiation, under present military circumstances, could lead to termination of the war under conditions that would preserve the freedom of South Vietnam. It is extremely difficult for a party to a negotiation to achieve by diplomacy objectives which it has conspicuously failed to win by warfare. The hard fact of the matter is that our bargaining position is at present a weak one; and until the equation of advantages between the two sides has been substantially altered in our favor, there can be little prospect of a negotiated settlement which would secure the independence of a non-Communist South Vietnam.

Recent initiatives by France, calling for the neutralization of Vietnam, have tended to confuse the situation, without altering it in any fundamental way. France could, perhaps, play a constructive mediating role if she were willing to consult and cooperate with the United States. For somewhat obscure reasons, however, France has chosen to take an independent initiative. This is puzzling to Americans, who recall that the United States contributed $1.2 billion to France's war in Indochina of a decade ago—which was 70 percent of the total cost of the conflict. Whatever its motivation, the problem posed by French intervention in southeast Asia is that while France may set off an unforeseeable chain of events, she is neither a major military force nor a major economic force in the Far East, and is therefore unlikely to be able to control or greatly influence the events which her initiative may precipitate.

It seems clear that only two realistic options are open to us in Vietnam in the immediate future: the expansion of the conflict in one way or another, or a renewed effort to bolster the capacity of the South Vietnamese to prosecute the war successfully on its present scale. The matter calls for thorough examination by responsible officials in the executive branch; and until they have had an opportunity to evaluate the contingencies and feasibilities of the options open to us, it seems to me that we have no choice but to support the South Vietnamese Government and Army by the most effective means available. Whatever specific policy decisions are made, it should be clear to all concerned that the United States will continue to meet its obligations and fulfill its commitments with respect to Vietnam.

These, I believe, are some, although by no means all, of the issues of foreign policy in which it is essential to reevaluate longstanding ideas and commitments in the light of new and changing realities. In all the issues which I have discussed, American policy has to one degree or another been less effective than it might have been because of our national tendency to equate means with ends and therefore to attach a mythological sanctity to policies and practices which in themselves have no moral content or value except insofar as they contribute to the achievement of some valid national objective. I believe that we must try to overcome this excessive moralism, which binds us to old myths and blinds us to new realities and, worse still, leads us to regard new and unfamiliar ideas with fear and mistrust.

We must dare to think about "unthinkable" things. We must learn to explore all of the options and possibilities that confront us in a complex and rapidly changing world. We must learn to welcome rather than fear the voices of dissent and not to recoil in horror whenever some heretic suggests that Castro may survive or that Khrushchev is not as bad a fellow as Stalin was. We must overcome our susceptibility to "shock"—a word which I wish could be banned from our newspapers and magazines and especially from the CONGRESSIONAL RECORD.

If Congress and public opinion are unduly susceptible to "shock," the executive branch, and particularly the Department of State, is subject to the malady of chronic and excessive caution. An effective foreign policy is one which concerns itself more with innovation abroad than with concilliation at home. A creative foreign policy—as President Truman, for one, knew—is not necessarily one which wins immediate general approval. It is sometimes necessary for leaders to do unpleasant and unpopular things, because, as Burke pointed out, the duty of the democratic politician to his constituents is not to comply with their every wish and preference but to give them the benefit of, and to be held responsible for, the exercise of his own best judgment.

We must dare to think about "unthinkable things," because when things become "unthinkable," thinking stops and action becomes mindless. If we are to disabuse ourselves of old myths and to act wisely and creatively upon the new realities of our time, we must think and talk about our problems with perfect freedom, remembering, as Woodrow Wilson said, that "The greatest freedom of speech is the greatest safety because, if a man is a fool, the best thing to do is to encourage him to advertise the fact by speaking." ▰

AMERICAN FOREIGN AID DOCTRINES

Edward C. Banfield*

THIS essay examines critically the premises of American foreign aid doctrines. By foreign aid (or simply "aid") is meant technical assistance and loans and grants to underdeveloped countries for nonmilitary purposes. Aid programs may, of course, bear little resemblance to the doctrines by which they are justified; but it is *doctrines*, not *programs*, that are under discussion here.

The essay is in three parts. The first discusses the doctrines which place the ultimate justification of aid in its contribution to national defense. The second discusses those which place it on other grounds (altruism, the moral law, and improvement of American life). The last part appraises the general character of the discussion about aid and endeavors to show that the nature of American democracy makes a rational approach to the subject impossible.

I. AID JUSTIFIED BY NATIONAL SECURITY

Those who find the ultimate justification for aid in its contribution to national security rely upon one or another of two incompatible doctrines. One doctrine asserts that the security purpose can be served by using aid to transform the fundamental character of the culture and

* Reprinted from *Why Foreign Aid?* ed. Robert A. Goldwin (Chicago: Rand McNally, 1963). Copyright © 1962 by the Public Affairs Conference Center, The University of Chicago. All rights reserved.

institutions of the recipient country. The other takes the fundamental character of the recipient society as given and without seeking to change the culture or institutions of the country endeavors to achieve the purpose by influencing either its government or its public opinion. In this part of the essay, these two doctrines will be discussed in turn and then the logical alternative to both (that is, no aid at all) will be considered.

The Doctrine of Indirect Influence

One widely held view, which I will call the doctrine of indirect influence, asserts that aid can bring about in the outlook and institutions of the underdeveloped countries changes which will encourage the spread of freedom and democracy, thereby promoting peace and ultimately serving the vital security interest of the United States. Max F. Millikan and W. W. Rostow, who advance this argument in their influential book, *A Proposal*, say that it is a serious misconception to believe that the mere creation of wealth will satisfy people's expectations; "some" increase of wealth is essential, they say, but the real importance of aid is that it will set off social, political, and psychological changes that will energize the society, point it in the direction of democracy, and incline it toward peace.

To estimate the likelihood of achieving the end ultimately sought (the greater security of the United States) in the manner prescribed by this doctrine, one must make judgments of four separate probabilities: (1) that aid will raise incomes by at least the minimum that is necessary for the other, energizing changes to occur; (2) that these changes (social, political, and psychological) will lead to freedom and democracy; (3) that freedom and democracy will lead to peace; and (4) that peace will serve the vital defense interests or the security interests of the United States. Let us consider these assumptions one by one.

1. The increase in wealth that is necessary must occur not simply in aggregate national incomes but in the actual incomes of ordinary men. Three factors are therefore involved: the productivity of the economy, the size of the population, and the evenness with which income is distributed. In most parts of the underdeveloped world all three of these factors will have to change.

Aggregate income has been increasing in most underdeveloped countries, but the gains have been offset, or nearly so, by increases of population. Although their aggregate incomes are rising, the underdeveloped countries have not increased their per capita food supplies very significantly. P. N. Rosenstein-Rodan has estimated that if the underdeveloped countries get all the aid they can absorb, if they use it reasonably well, and if their populations increase by one-fourth, their gross national product may rise from an average of $140 per capita in 1961 to $192 in 1976*. Whether, even assuming no further rise in the "aspiration level" of the underdeveloped countries, this would be enough to change their outlook and institutions profoundly may well be doubted.

If one believes that modernization of the economies of the underdeveloped areas (not merely "some" improvement in their levels of living) will be required to produce the social and psychological effects that are sought, the case is even more discouraging. Some societies may never enter fully into modern ways. The American Indian, for example, has had extensive aid for decades, but he is still in most cases very far from belonging to the modern world.

It is at least plausible to suppose that certain cultural prerequisites must be met in order for self-sustaining economic development to occur. One such prerequisite is probably the presence in the society of at least a few people who have the talents and incentives to organize, innovate, and take risks. Other prerequisites (which, incidentally, probably must be met in order for such a class to arise or to function effectively) are: widespread desire for material improvement, widespread belief that economic activity is worthy of respect, willingness to cooperate to some extent for the common welfare, and ability to maintain a certain degree of political stability. All of these prerequisites are critically lacking in the underdeveloped countries.

Where cultural conditions do not allow of it, economic development will not take place, no matter how much aid is given. On the other hand, where cultural conditions are right for it, development will occur rapidly in the absence of any aid. Japan and Russia both developed rapidly without aid. No country is too poor to accumulate capital if its people are disposed to save and to invest, and the technical knowledge of the Western world is easily available to the underdeveloped countries—indeed, could not be withheld from them—if they are willing to avail themselves of it. Where populations have a "will" not to propagate excessively, the population problem will solve itself; where they do not have such a will, nothing much can be done about the population problem. The existence of a cheap and effective oral contraceptive does not put it within the power of a government—certainly not of our government—to reduce births among people who do not want to reduce them.

* See Max F. Millikan and Donald L. M. Blackmer, eds., *The Emerging Nations* (Boston: Little, Brown, 1961), p. 154.

Aid doctrine tends greatly to overvalue the importance of both technical assistance and foreign capital in the development process. Only in the most backward countries can either make a crucial difference, and it is in these countries, of course, that the prospects of bringing about development are poorest. In countries like Mexico, where the likelihood of ultimate success is good, outside aid is not necessary in order for development to occur at what the leaders of the countries consider to be a satisfactory rate. Mexico, for example, has not accepted any aid. It is true that there is an important middle group of countries—India is a conspicuous example—which can absorb large amounts of aid and which also show fair promise of eventual development. Nevertheless, there is in general an element of perversity in the situation: the more aid can be absorbed, the poorer the prospects for its eventual success.

There is also some possibility . . . that aid may be so misapplied as to stifle initiative and entrepreneurship, thereby reducing the rate of growth to less than it would be if there were no aid at all.

Even if it does begin, economic development may not last very long or get very far. Continued growth . . . involves discovery and use of new ideas. The developing society must produce a social outlook, institutions, and economic organization which, generation after generation, will bring to the fore men who will produce new ideas. That such men come to the fore in one generation . . . is no guarantee that they will in the next. The long-run economic prospect, therefore, is very uncertain in any society, including of course a highly developed one like our own.

2. Even if economic growth does occur it will not necessarily lead to the spread of freedom and democracy. If what is meant by these is "respect for the individual" and its expression in some form of "government by discussion," there is no basis for optimism. Respect for the individual is unique to the Judaeo-Christian tradition, and in the underdeveloped parts of the world, where the worthlessness of the individual human life is an obvious fact of everyday experience, the concept of the dignity of man is not likely to be generally intelligible for generations to come.

If by "democracy" is meant something much less—that institutions are representative in the sense that they take some account of the wants and interests of the major elements of the population—then the outlook is better. But democracy, even in this very attenuated sense, will probably be of slow growth. Political institutions cannot be copied in the way technical practices can. It took the West several hundred years to arrive at its imperfect democracy; the underdeveloped areas may perhaps learn something from this experience, but, even so, they are not likely to do in decades what took us centuries.

The outlook for democracy is best in the cultures which share our fundamental moral premises. But even in Latin America, which has participated in Western civilization for 400 years, its prospects, short run or long run, are not encouraging.

There is, indeed, much reason to expect that economic development, to the extent that it occurs, will prove incompatible with freedom and democracy. The spread of literacy, an indispensable accompaniment of economic growth, hastens the decay of tradition and other forms of authority. As Millikan and Rostow observe,

> The education which accompanies economic change contributes to unrest. People who can't read can't be subverted by literature. Once they can read, the process of widening knowledge and changing ideas of what the world is like and what is possible in it proceeds with great rapidity.*

In India, Asia, Africa, and Latin America . . . the relatively developed regions have shown themselves most prone to violence.

The realistic question is not whether democracy can be brought into being in the foreseeable future in the underdeveloped countries—the answer almost everywhere is clearly, "No"—but whether there can be brought into being political systems that are capable of modernizing the countries at all. "No new state," Edward A. Shils has written, "can modernize itself and remain or become liberal and democratic without an elite of force of character, intelligence, and high moral qualities." Very few of the underdeveloped countries, he adds, have such elites; those that do have them may under favorable circumstances enjoy democracy that is to some extent tutelary, and in time, if the elite has a very powerful will to be democratic, the enormous gap between it and the masses of the population may be overcome. The less democratic and much more probable alternatives will not, he thinks, provide stable government at all:

> The alternatives are disorderly oligarchies, each promising and aspiring to maintain order and to modernize, but doing so only by sweeping the disorder temporarily into a box from which it recurrently springs out into full strength. The totalitarian oligarchy by the ruthlessness of its elite and by the vigor of its party machine as well as by the organizational and material aid which it would get from the Soviet Union, would appear to

* *A Proposal,* p. 22.

have the best chance to maintain itself, once it gets into power. But it too would have to compromise markedly with the human materials which traditional society gives it. It could build monuments and suppress open dissatisfaction but it could not realize its ideal.*

Some of the measures which may be necessary (or, more likely, which may be *thought* necessary) to induce rapid economic development are likely to discourage the growth of democracy. If a government thinks that the amount of voluntary saving is not enough to produce the rate of development that is sought, it is likely to use fraud or force to increase the amount of savings. Ruthless dictatorship will be defended as the only way, or the fastest and hence, in the long run, the least painful way to bring about self-sustained economic growth and modernization.

Other tendencies toward totalitarianism will be encouraged by the new technology of communications. For the first time in history it is now possible to rule a vast area by propaganda. People too poor to be ruled by force (force requires a police organization, something expensive to maintain) may now be ruled by radio and television, provided, of course, that those in control are skilled in playing upon the emotions of the masses. Whether "constructive" appeals (for example, for national crusades against poverty, disease, and ignorance) will prove as useful as campaigns of hate directed against the white, the capitalist, the foreigner, and the American, may well be doubted. As compared to the Communists, the West is at a great and probably hopeless disadvantage in the propaganda war. The Marxist ideology . . . is a *natural* one for backward societies because it provides what is, from the standpoint of people undergoing transition from pre-industrial to industrial society, an intelligible account of their experience. Democracy and freedom are too foreign to the experience of backward peoples to make sense to them.

In some of the underdeveloped countries the religion of nationalism is a dominant force. The leaders of these countries, and perhaps the people as well, are moved less by a desire for better living standards than by an urge to create a mystic bond, to assert the glory of the nation, and to demonstrate the superiority of the chosen people to all others. Where there is fervent nationalism, hate for the white man, the Westerner, indeed for all foreigners, is indispensable to the making of the new nation. Our enmity may (as Castro seems to think) be more valuable than our friend-

* "Political Developments in the New States," *Comparative Studies in Society and History*, Vol. II (1960), pp. 407 and 410.

ship in unleashing the energies by which a regime can maintain itself in power and, perhaps, make a nation.

3. Even if aid leads to economic development and even if economic development leads to freedom and democracy, peace may not be promoted. Disparities in the wealth of nations do not cause wars: poor, pre-industrial nations do not attack rich, industrial ones. Nor does a high level of economic and political development give any assurance at all that a nation will not be aggressive if it can be so with impunity. Millikan and Rostow have no basis for believing either that democratic societies "can be relied upon not to generate conflict because their own national interests parallel ours and because they are politically healthy and mature," or that as nations "gain confidence" they become easier to deal with.* The Soviet Union is a confident nation, and all the more dangerous for that. What counts is not the "maturity" or "confidence" of nations but their relative power and the purposes for which they would use that power.

There is even reason to think that our aid may already have been a cause of one war and that it may be leading to others. It is arguable that Israel could not have attacked Egypt if we had not given her aid. Similarly, the arms race between India and Pakistan seems to have been touched off by our aid to India; in any case, it is being financed on both sides by us. (We give nonmilitary aid to India, but this frees Indian funds for the purchase of arms. For several years India's military spending has offset, or somewhat more than offset, the amount of our aid.)

4. Even if the ultimate effect of aid were to make the countries in question entirely peaceful, our security might not be enhanced thereby and it might even be jeopardized. It would not be enhanced if the threat of nuclear retaliation is enough to protect us: warlike nations are no more dangerous than peaceable ones when the price of aggression is obliteration. Our security would actually be reduced by the peaceableness of these countries if the alternative (an unlikely one, to be sure) were that they would risk war in support of us. "Aggressive" countries, in other words, might in some circumstances be preferable to peaceable ones from the standpoint of American security interests, provided, of course, that they were agressive *on our side*.

The confidence one has in the doctrine of indirect influence will depend, then, upon the assessments one makes of each of these probabilities. If (to assign numbers for illustrative purposes only) there is one

* *A Proposal,* pp. 4 and 32.

chance in ten that aid will produce economic growth, one chance in ten that economic growth will produce freedom and democracy, one chance in ten that democracy will produce peace, and one chance in ten that peace will add to our security, then the chance that aid will serve our national interest (in the manner prescribed) is one in ten thousand.

Whatever outcome one comes to, it is necessary to consider the element of time. It is wildly optimistic to think that the results intended can be secured in less than a generation or two. What, then, is the value of these results on the most optimistic estimate of them for dealing with the crisis of today and tomorrow? Even if it were absolutely certain that aid would produce all the results sought, it would be wise not to extend it if the results could not accrue in time to help us in the present crisis and if the giving of aid in the manner prescribed by the doctrine of indirect influence would prevent us from taking measures that might be effective in the short run.

The Doctrine of Direct Influence

The doctrine of direct influence, that is, that aid should make its effect directly by influencing governments or public opinions and not indirectly by transforming cultures and institutions, takes several distinct forms:

1. *Quid Pro Quo.* The aid is part of a bargain between two governments in which there are clearly specified advantages to both sides. For example, we might agree to build a system of highways in return for assurances that the Soviet Union would not be allowed to penetrate the country. Bribery is a special case. Here the bargain is with politicians in the underdeveloped country who act from personal interest rather than duty.

2. *Business Friendship.* The aid is given to create or maintain with a government a relationship that is expected to have mutual advantages over a period of time. The aid is, so to speak, a payment on an open account, it being tacitly understood that political advantages will be given in return.

3. *Maintenance of Friendly Governments.* The aid is intended to strengthen and to keep in power a government which is friendly, or at least not unfriendly. This may be done by undertaking, including of course economic development, that will increase the prestige of the recipient government or increase the confidence of its public in it.

4. *Prestige.* The aid is intended to exhibit dramatically the power of the giver and thereby to increase it. As Hobbes said, "Reputation of power

is power, because it draweth with it the adherence of those that need protection."

5. *Good Will.* The aid is intended to make the recipient feel well disposed toward the giver and to put him under an implied obligation to return kindness for kindness. Governments are seldom thought to be moved by sentiments such as gratitude, but it is sometimes thought that public opinion may be so moved and that this may have some effect on the policy of governments.

6. *Moral Force.* The aid is expected to affect public opinion by exerting moral force. The giver expects that the nobility of his action will inspire the recipient to act upon equally high moral principles.

Those who write about aid tend to rank these methods on an ascending scale of moral worth. David Lilienthal, for example, deplores the spectacle of "the representatives of a noble nation up to their elbows in the cynical international bazaar, there to bargain and haggle and make deals by which we trade our money or credit or technical aid for 'friendship'"; aid, he says, "should provide a demonstration of the kind of people our system of political and economic freedom is capable of producing."* It is hard to understand these judgments. If a government is willing to trade favors in foreign policy for material assistance, why should it or the country with which it trades be criticized? The expression "friendly governments" means, Aristotle remarked, not governments that love each other but ones that exchange favors. A trade, moreover, is the outcome of free action by the governments involved; one government does not manipulate the other in the sense of using the other without the other's knowledge or consent. Efforts to exercise influence by "good will" or "moral force," on the other hand, *do* involve manipulation. One who is placed under a diffuse obligation by the receipt of a favor is obviously less free than one who has made a definite exchange in a bargaining process.

From the standpoint both of morality and American national interest we ought to prefer to give aid on a *quid pro quo* basis. The possibilities of doing this, however, are extremely limited. Most of the underdeveloped countries are pathologically sensitive about "honor" and accordingly will not tolerate any suggestion that we should get something for our money. The few governments which will sell favors are reactionary ones which cannot long survive. Doing business with these may be necessary, but will

* "Needed: A New Credo for Foreign Aid," *New York Times Magazine,* June 26, 1960.

probably make it harder for us to get on a satisfactory basis with those that will replace them. The *quid pro quo* principle is therefore not one which can be relied upon very far or very long.

To use aid to increase American prestige is foolish. Our power, military and economic, is not doubted anywhere. The trouble is that those who appreciate our power are nevertheless in a position to ignore it because they know that we cannot or will not use it. Cuba is a case in point. Reminders of our power will not change the situation.

"Good will" and "moral force" can make an effect only by working upon public opinion in the recipient countries and not by influencing governments directly. But "public opinion" may accept American aid—conceivably even accept it gratefully—without viewing our foreign policy in a more favorable light. Moreover, in the countries in question, a favorable public opinion would not mean any change of government policy. In the underdeveloped countries, public opinion does not include the opinion of the masses of people, most of whom are peasants. The only opinion that counts is that of the small ruling elites. These elites will not be grateful to us and will not respect us for saving peasants from starvation. Although they are largely Western-educated, they do not entirely share our moral standards. What we think is noble, they may think merely foolish. The very idea of public-spiritedness is unintelligible to educated people in most parts of the world, including some that share the Judaeo-Christian tradition.

The effect of aid upon opinion in the underdeveloped countries is at least as likely to be unfavorable as to be favorable. Having to feel grateful is not a pleasant position to be in; it implies inferiority. The underdeveloped countries, precisely because their inferiority is already so obvious, will be made more hostile by every reminder of it.

The Alternative of No Aid

However dim the prospects of improving our security by the methods of indirect or of direct aid, these methods—either or both—would nevertheless have to be relied upon if it could be shown that the alternative is likely to be national disaster. Criticism of aid must therefore consider, if only very briefly, the alternative of no aid at all.

If the United States were to follow such a policy, the worst that could happen is that the underdeveloped countries would all fall to the Communists and be organized by them into an aggressive military and economic alliance to bring about our destruction. There are tremendous military advantages to us in having military missile bases, tracking stations, and other installations in some parts of the underdeveloped world (not, however, in Africa south of the Sahara, India, or Latin America) and, to a lesser extent, in not having Soviet installations close to us. Valuable as they are, however, our survival as a nation probably does not depend upon these installations. It depends upon our nuclear deterrent, and this would be about the same (although more costly) if instead of having bases abroad we had more and larger missiles within our borders and on our submarines.

The economic disadvantages of withdrawal from the underdeveloped countries would be far less serious than the military ones. Economists say that if all of our trade with the underdeveloped areas ceased, our national income would not stop rising, although it might rise somewhat more slowly than otherwise. It is even arguable that "no aid and no trade" would leave us better off than "aid and trade."

The cultural losses that we would suffer by withdrawal can also easily be overestimated. The contribution of the underdeveloped countries to the enrichment of our culture has been small, and will certainly remain so for a long time to come.

It is often said that the United States could not long stand isolated in a totalitarian world: our confidence in our institutions and traditions and our respect for freedom would, it is said, sooner or later give way under the strenuous propaganda that would stream from all directions. This supposition is plausible, but so also is the contrary supposition. Our response to Hitler and, thus far, to the Soviets has been to extend and reaffirm our faith in democracy, and there is no reason to expect a change. Withdrawal from the underdeveloped areas might indeed give aid and comfort to paranoid and native-Fascist elements in the United States. But if the withdrawal were justified on reasonable and humanitarian grounds, as the least among evils, and if it were supported by the majority of decent and well-intentioned people, its political significance could afford the native Fascists no satisfaction at all.

The real danger to our morale and institutions would come not from a calculated withdrawal but from being pushed from one country after another after having lavished good will and wealth in futile efforts to remain. A long series of humiliating failures might cause us to lose confidence and self-respect and might lead to recriminations and to loss of trust in each other. If the dynamic of the processes of transition from pre-industrial to industrial society proves such as to make it virtually certain that we will fail politically even if we succeed economically, then it would certainly be better to withdraw with dignity than to be forced out in failure.

The case for withdrawal depends, it should be noted, upon the assumption that conditions will arise to make the alternative of not withdrawing relatively undesirable. In other words, withdrawal is not good in itself. It would be far better for us to maintain a close association with the underdeveloped areas if we could do so at a cost (not alone in money, of course) not unreasonably high in relation to the advantages to be derived from the association.

This is the worst that can happen if we give no aid. It is not likely to happen, however. Neither the Soviets nor any other country could, even if we withdrew from the underdeveloped parts of the world, organize all or even most of it into a cohesive bloc. (This is not to say, of course, that the Soviets, the Chinese, or others might not take possession of some countries and exercise much direct or indirect influence in others.) The Soviets are no more able than we to command the tides of nationalism; even among the presently Communist countries there are differences of interest and ideology that prevent concerted action. What is more, the Soviets cannot bring about the economic development of the underdeveloped countries for the same reasons, among others, that we cannot bring it about; and in the unlikely event that they should try, they will probably make themselves hated, just as we will probably make ourselves hated if we persist in trying. If it were possible for us to bestow the underdeveloped areas upon them it might well be to our advantage to do so in order that they might suffer the expense and incur the hatred that will otherwise be ours.

II. OTHER ULTIMATE JUSTIFICATIONS

We turn now to a consideration of the doctrines justifying aid on grounds other than its contribution to national security.

Altruism as a Basis for Aid

Some say that we ought to extend aid for humanitarian reasons even if there is no possibility of any advantage to us from doing so. Two major objections may be made to this doctrine. One is that "doing good" may be impossible because we do not know even in general terms what it consists of for another culture; because, even if we do know what it consists of concretely in the particular circumstances of time and place; or because, even if we know what it consists of concretely, we cannot bring about the effects we intend, or can bring them about only at the risk of bringing about other, unintended effects which will make the situation worse on the whole than before. Doing good cannot be equated to obvious physical improvements like better diet. It must be relative to some conception of the good life and the good society or, rather, of the best life and the best society possible under the circumstances. Are we in a position to judge for other cultures what is best absolutely or best under the circumstances? Assuming for purposes of argument that the answer to both questions is "Yes," do we know how to proceed? Will we be doing good, if, for example, we prevent starvation without at the same time reducing the rate of population increase, and thus lower average incomes and perhaps thereby prevent the occurrence of radical adjustments without which there is no possibility of sustained economic growth? Will we be doing good if we set in motion a process which leads to totalitarian repression in the manner of the Chinese?

If we try to improve matters and fail, perhaps thereby making people worse off, that our intentions were good will not in the least lessen the suffering we will have caused. From our point of view, the goodness of our intention is very important. But from the point of view of the peoples being acted upon, it is not what we want to achieve but what we are likely to achieve that is important.

The other major objection that may be made to the doctrine of altruism is that our political philosophy does not give our government any right to do good for foreigners. Since the seventeenth century, Western political thought has maintained that government may use force or the threat of force to take the property of some and give it to others only if doing so somehow serves the common good, meaning, of course, the good of those from whom the property is taken as well as the good of those to whom it is given. Those who do not belong to a given political community—that is, those who are not its citizens—cannot, under this theory, be given, *for purely altruistic reasons*, the property of those who do belong to it; such giving could not, by definition, serve the common good of the community. In short, government may take from citizens and give to foreigners when doing so serves the common good of the citizens, but it may not do so if (as the doctrine of altrism assumes) all advantage will accrue to foreigners and none to citizens.

That aid cannot be justified under the federal Constitution unless some national interest will be served by it goes without saying. But even our state governments, which we are prone to think can do anything not given to the federal government to do, cannot act except to serve the common good of their peoples.

These considerations may seem legalistic or antiquarian. If Americans wish to do good abroad through the instrumentality of their government they will certainly not be prevented by theoretical considerations. But the theoretical problem must sooner or later be faced, for presumably no American believes that there is no limit whatever to the right of the state to coerce its citizens.

Aid "Because It Is Right"

This doctrine asserts that the United States should give aid because the moral law requires doing so. A nation as rich as ours, this doctrine says, sins if it does not sacrifice for the sake of the poor.

Whether the origin of this obligation to be charitable is believed to arise from the will of God or from nature, it is placed upon *persons* and not upon organizational entities like corporations and governments. Aid has moral significance only as it expresses the intention of *persons* as distinguished from *office-holders*. One can imagine a government giving aid without the knowledge or consent of its citizens and perhaps even over their strong opposition. Aid so given would be morally meaningless. One who taxes Peter to give to Paul does not thereby gain moral credit either for himself or for Peter.

Those who advocate aid "because it is right" should favor making it a matter for voluntary contributions. To the extent that a government takes more from some (and less from others) than they would wish to give, it deprives the aid of moral significance.

Aid for National Self-Improvement

Another ultimate justification for aid is that the giving of it will improve the quality of American life. Millikan and Rostow regard this justification as second only to the promotion of national security in importance. "American society," they say, "is at its best when wrestling with the positive problems of building a better world"; we need "the challenge of world development to keep us from the stagnation of smug prosperity."*

Those who take this view seem to have one or another of two kinds of improvement in mind. Some think that drawing the individual into a great, idealistic national endeavor will turn him from the frivolous and demoralizing distractions characteristic of a commercial culture and by so doing will strengthen and deepen his attachment to what may be called collective values. Whether the dangers of commercialism and of individualistic alienation from society are really as great as this assumes and whether, even if they are, foreign aid is a suitable way of dealing with

* *A Proposal,* pp. 7 and 8.

them, will appear extremely doubtful to people whose conception of the
good society does not stress the values associated with collective life.

Improvement in our national life, other proponents of aid say, would
occur through the strengthening of the impulse to reform and of the
institutions through which reformers work, which would be an accompaniment of extensive aid. Just as the atom bomb strengthened the position of scientists and of science in our society, so, it is argued, aid on a
vast scale would strengthen those who want to make the society over.
This argument, too, cuts both ways: those who do not want to see
reformers and reform institutions strengthened will oppose aid if they take
the argument seriously.

III. DEMOCRACY AND AID DOCTRINE

Nothing that has been said constitutes a decisive argument against
aid. Reasonable men having the same information and the same general
values may well come to opposite policy conclusions. That many thoughtful people favor giving aid does not, then, require any explanation. But
that few thoughtful and public-spirited people oppose giving it, or have
serious misgivings about it, and that after more than ten years of aid there
has been practically no serious discussion of aid doctrines—this *does*
require explanation.

The most influential writings about aid doctrine are full of clichés
and sweeping statements that turn out on close examination to be meaningless or else entirely unsupported by evidence. Economists who write
on aid generally take it for granted that the whole problem is one of
raising incomes. Whether this will contribute to the welfare of the recipient peoples, to the peace of the world, or to the security of the United
States they rarely seem to consider.

In most of the discussion, the hard choices that must be made are
obscured by a fog of moralizing. Moralizing is advocacy, as a basis for
action, of principles that do not take into account features of the concrete
situation that render them inapplicable or inappropriate. The moralizer
averts his gaze from the features of the real situation that constitute the
crux of the practical problem, and then, unhampered, tells us how we
ought to act in a world that is not the one in which we must act. He warns
severely against extending aid to corrupt tyrannies or reactionary ruling
oligarchies. This would be good advice if the real choice were between a
corrupt tyranny and an honest democracy. Alas, it seldom is, and when it
is, his advice is not needed. A genuine problem exists only when the
choice must be made between, say, a corrupt tyranny and a Communist

one—and in such cases the advice of the moralizer is confusing or pernicious. He, however, refuses to acknowledge the existence of the genuine
problem. If it is pointed out to him that supporting a corrupt tyranny may
in some circumstances be necessary to avert something worse, he replies
blandly that "the proper and the practical courses coincide." If it is pointed
out to him that there may be an incompatibility between the security
interests of the United States and the development needs of some underdeveloped countries, he assures us that "as long as our policies are designed
to help these societies develop in directions which meet the real interests
of their own people, our political and our moral interests coincide."

Aid doctrine does not face up to the tragic facts which constitute the
problem: that vast areas of the world will probably not achieve a very
significant and widespread improvement in levels of living for at least
several generations; that they will probably not learn to govern themselves even tolerably well; that such development as occurs is as likely
to be inspired by hate as by good will or moral respect; that it may therefore prove to be a disaster for the United States and for all mankind; and
that the measures which promise the most present advantage to the West
in its struggle for survival are in general the ones that are least likely to
lead to self-sustained economic growth in the underdeveloped countries.
Instead of looking squarely at these tragic facts and dealing with them
politically—instead, that is, of framing courses of action that may not be
admirable by absolute standards (and may indeed be downright evil by
the standards of the moralizers) but are nevertheless workable and the
best that the situation allows of—the writers on aid tell us that if only we
are more generous, more enterprising, and more aware of the needs and
interests of other cultures, all will be well both for them and for us.

The reason for the unsatisfactory character of discussion—for its
optimistic, moralizing, and apolitical tone—is to be found in the nature of
the American political system. Our political system works best when
"interests" (the concrete and usually material advantages that individuals
seek for themselves) rather than "principles" (general ideas about what
would be good for the society) are at stake. When interests clash, the
interested parties are highly motivated to make the strongest possible case
for what they want and to find weaknesses and loopholes in the arguments
of their opponents. This competition usually results in a thorough scrutiny
of every aspect of the issue. By the same token, when the interested parties
are all on the same side of the question or when the matter is decided on
the basis of principle rather than interest, the system is likely to work in a
slipshod way, few pros and cons being pressed because no one has as much

incentive to press them. This has been the situation with regard to aid. The parties most keenly interested in it (farmers and manufacturers wanting subsidized markets) have been in favor of it; opposition has been mainly on grounds of principle.

For another thing, it is in the nature of our political system to bring to the fore issues which the President can use to generate a public opinion that will support him. Presidents have always had to find ways of overcoming by informal means the extreme decentralization of formal authority—the checks and balances and divided powers—so skillfully contrived by the Founding Fathers. Party loyalty, patronage, and logrolling are among the ways this has been done. Today voters and politicians are more than ever concerned with political principle and therefore the old devices for overcoming the decentralization of authority no longer suffice and must be supplemented by others. As Sir Henry Sumner Maine observed three-quarters of a century ago, to Party and Corruption, the influences which have hitherto shown themselves capable of bringing a large number of men into civil discipline, democracy has added a third: "generalization, the trick of rapidly framing, and confidently uttering, general propositions on political subjects."* Foreign aid is a subject (space exploration seems to be another) that is extremely serviceable in creating the "levity of assent" required nowadays to strengthen the power of the Executive.

There are doubtless several reasons why it is so serviceable. The most important, perhaps, is that it appeals to a millennial tendency in the American mind. Americans, as Kenneth W. Thompson has pointed out, have always abhorred force, distrusted diplomacy, and put their faith in comprehensive formulas for solving the world's problems. Confident that they can regenerate the world without resort to force, they have advanced one millennial idea after another; foreign aid is for the present decade what the United Nations was for the last one and what arbitration and the World Court were for the 1920's.

Our political system has brought this millennial tendency constantly to the fore. It has done so in part by preventing the formation of an elite of statesmen who might have a considerable leeway to decide matters on the basis of a professional view. Our statesmen have instead been mostly amateurs who shared the popular ideals and myths. The system has also given importance to the millennial tendency by admitting the general public to an extraordinarily close participation in the making of foreign policy and in its day-to-day conduct.

* *Popular Government* (New York: Henry Holt, 1886), pp. 107 and 108.

Americans are apt to feel that they should participate in the making of foreign policy just as they should in the making of, say, farm policy. There is great danger in this. It arises because *goodness*, morality in ordinary personal relations (e.g., kindness, sympathy, liberality, and the desire to see justice done), is sometimes incompatible with *virtue*, morality in matters of state. Private persons ought to act on the principles of goodness, but rulers—those who have accepted responsibility for protecting a society from its enemies—do not have the right to enjoy the luxury of goodness when goodness might endanger the society. They must do what the welfare of their society demands (that is, they must act virtuously) even though this may require of them actions which, by the standards of ordinary personal relations, are unjust or without kindness. As Churchill has written, "The Sermon on the Mount is the last word in Christian ethics. Everyone respects the Quakers. Still, it is not on these terms that Ministers assume their responsibilities of guiding states."*

It *is* on these terms, however, that public opinion guides states. So far as it acts morally, a public acts from goodness, not virtue. It may, of course, act amorally or immorally, as, for example, when it is self-deceived or in a fit of passion. But it cannot calmly and reflectively decide to violate its own fundamental principles and to profane what it holds sacred. It is hard even for the experienced statesman to acknowledge to himself the occasional necessity of subordinating goodness to virtue (that is, of doing what by the standards of ordinary personal relations is evil in order to secure the public welfare); for a whole people to see and accept this necessity is beyond the bounds of possibility. And even if it were possible, it would lead to the eventual disintegration of the society, for once the principles of goodness had been publicly challenged and found unacceptable as criteria by which to decide a great public question, their authority in the ordinary relations of private life would be weakened or destroyed. When, therefore, consideration must be given to transgressing the moral principles of a society, the considering must be done by an elite set apart for the purpose —one which, like a bomb decontamination squad, having special skills that fit it for its task, is willing to endanger itself for the sake of the society. Professional statesmen—those of them who know their job and do it—belong to such an elite.

The goodness of democracy, or, more precisely, the subordination of virtue to goodness that occurs when public opinion enters into the making and the execution of policy, is particularly dangerous in foreign relations.

* Winston S. Churchill, *The Gathering Storm* (Boston: Houghton Mifflin, 1948), p. 320.

The inveterate goodness of American public opinion accounts to a large extent not only for the deficiencies in our national discussion about aid doctrines but also for the general atmosphere of all such discussions, an atmosphere marked by millennial fervor; unreasoning confidence that right, reason, and democracy will eventually prevail; abhorrence of force even in the best of causes; profound distrust of diplomacy, of bargaining, and of self-interest; and naive confidence in the efficacy of good examples, noble sentiments, and benevolence as means of exerting influence.

These distortions in our national view of things are likely to cause us to do great injury to ourselves and to others. But if the analysis here is correct, there is nothing that can be done to change the situation fundamentally. Warning the public that its goodness will lead to disaster can have no effect. For the public's very goodness will prevent it from seeing the necessity sometimes of putting trust not in goodness but in men capable of doing what the welfare of mankind requires.

APPENDIX

The Constitution
of the United States

WE THE PEOPLE of the United States, in Order to form a more perfect Union, establish Justice, insure domestic Tranquility, provide for the common defence, promote the general Welfare, and secure the Blessings of Liberty to ourselves and our Posterity, do ordain and establish this CONSTITUTION for the United States of America.

Article I

SECTION 1. All legislative Powers herein granted shall be vested in a Congress of the United States, which shall consist of a Senate and House of Representatives.

SECTION 2. (1) The House of Representatives shall be composed of Members chosen every second Year by the People of the several States, and the Electors in each State shall have the Qualifications requisite for Electors of the most numerous Branch of the State Legislature.

(2) No Person shall be a Representative who shall not have attained to the Age of twenty-five Years, and been seven Years a Citizen of the United States, and who shall not, when elected, be an Inhabitant of that State in which he shall be chosen.

(3) [Representatives and direct Taxes[1] shall be apportioned among the several States which may be included within this Union, according to their respective Numbers, which shall be determined by adding to the whole Number of free Persons, including those bound to Service for a Term of Years, and excluding Indians not taxed, three fifths of all other Persons.][2] The actual Enumeration shall be made within three Years after the first Meeting of the Congress of the United States, and within every subsequent Term of ten Years, in such Manner as they shall by Law direct. The Number of Representatives shall not exceed one for every thirty Thousand, but each State shall have at Least one Representative; and until such enumeration shall be made, the State of New Hampshire shall be entitled to choose three,

[1] The Sixteenth Amendment replaced this with respect to income taxes.
[2] Repealed by the Fourteenth Amendment.

Massachusetts eight, Rhode-Island and Providence Plantations one, Connecticut five, New-York six, New Jersey four, Pennsylvania eight, Delaware one, Maryland six, Virginia ten, North Carolina five, South Carolina five, and Georgia three.

(4) When vacancies happen in the Representation from any State, the Executive Authority thereof shall issue Writs of Election to fill such Vacancies.

(5) The House of Representatives shall choose their Speaker and other Officers; and shall have the sole Power of Impeachment.

SECTION 3. (1) The Senate of the United States shall be composed of two Senators from each State, [chosen by the Legislature]³ thereof, for six Years; and each Senator shall have one Vote.

(2) Immediately after they shall be assembled in Consequence of the first Election, they shall be divided as equally as may be into three Classes. The Seats of the Senators of the first Class shall be vacated at the Expiration of the second Year, of the second Class at the Expiration of the fourth Year, and of the third Class at the Expiration of the sixth Year, so that one-third may be chosen every second Year; [and if Vacancies happen by Resignation, or otherwise, during the Recess of the Legislature of any State, the Executive thereof may make temporary Appointments until the next Meeting of the Legislature, which shall then fill such Vacancies]⁴

(3) No person shall be a Senator who shall not have attained to the Age of thirty Years, and been nine Years a Citizen of the United States, and who shall not, when elected, be an Inhabitant of that State for which he shall be chosen.

(4) The Vice President of the United States shall be President of the Senate, but shall have no Vote, unless they be equally divided.

(5) The Senate shall choose their other Officers, and also a President pro tempore, in the absence of the Vice President, or when he shall exercise the Office of President of the United States.

(6) The Senate shall have the sole Power to try all Impeachments. When sitting for that Purpose, they shall be on Oath or Affirmation. When the President of the United States is tried, the Chief Justice shall preside: And no Person shall be convicted without the Concurrence of two thirds of the Members present.

(7) Judgment in Cases of Impeachment shall not extend further than to removal from Office, and disqualification to hold and enjoy any Office of honor, Trust or Profit under the United States: but the Party convicted shall nevertheless be liable and subject to Indictment, Trial, Judgment and Punishment according to Law.

SECTION 4. (1) The Times, Places and Manner of holding Elections for Senators and Representatives, shall be prescribed in each State by the Legislature thereof; but the Congress may at any time by Law make or alter such Regulations, except as to the Places of Choosing Senators.

(2) The Congress shall assemble at least once in every Year, and such Meeting shall [be on the first Monday in December,]⁵ unless they shall by Law appoint a different Day.

SECTION 5. (1) Each House shall be the Judge of the Elections, Returns and

---

³ Repealed by the Seventeenth Amendment, Section 1.

⁴ Changed by the Seventeenth Amendment.

⁵ Changed by the Twentieth Amendment, Section 2.

Qualifications of its own Members, and a Majority of each shall constitute a Quorum to do Business; but a smaller number may adjourn from day to day, and may be authorized to compel the Attendance of absent Members, in such Manner, and under such Penalties as each House may provide.

(2) Each House may determine the Rules of its Proceedings, punish its Members for disorderly Behavior, and, with the Concurrence of two thirds, expel a Member.

(3) Each House shall keep a Journal of its Proceedings, and from time to time publish the same, excepting such Parts as may in their Judgment require Secrecy; and the Yeas and Nays of the Members of either House on any question shall, at the Desire of one fifth of those Present, be entered on the Journal.

(4) Neither House, during the Session of Congress, shall, without the Consent of the other, adjourn for more than three days, nor to any other Place than that in which the two Houses shall be sitting.

Section 6. (1) The Senators and Representatives shall receive a Compensation for their Services, to be ascertained by Law, and paid out of the Treasury of the United States. They shall in all Cases, except Treason, Felony and Breach of the Peace, be privileged from Arrest during their Attendance at the Session of their respective Houses, and in going to and returning from the same; and for any Speech or Debate in either House, they shall not be questioned in any other Place.

(2) No Senator or Representative shall, during the Time for which he was elected, be appointed to any civil Office under the Authority of the United States, which shall have been created, or the Emoluments whereof shall have been increased during such time; and no Person holding any Office under the United States, shall be a Member of either House during his Continuance in Office.

Section 7. (1) All Bills for raising Revenue shall originate in the House of Representatives; but the Senate may propose or concur with Amendments as on other Bills.

(2) Every Bill which shall have passed the House of Representatives and the Senate, shall, before it become a Law, be presented to the President of the United States; If he approve he shall sign it, but if not he shall return it, with his Objections to that House in which it shall have originated, who shall enter the Objections at large on their Journal, and proceed to reconsider it. If after such Reconsideration two thirds of that House shall agree to pass the Bill, it shall be sent, together with the Objections, to the other House, by which it shall likewise be reconsidered, and if approved by two thirds of that House, it shall become a Law. But in all such Cases the Votes of both Houses shall be determined by Yeas and Nays, and the Names of the Persons voting for and against the Bill shall be entered on the Journal of each House respectively. If any Bill shall not be returned by the President within ten Days (Sundays excepted) after it shall have been presented to him, the Same shall be a Law, in like Manner as if he had signed it, unless the Congress by their Adjournment prevent its Return, in which Case it shall not be a Law.

(3) Every Order, Resolution, or Vote to which the Concurrence of the Senate and House of Representatives may be necessary (except on a question of Adjournment) shall be presented to the President of the United States; and before the Same shall take Effect, shall be approved by him, or being disapproved by him, shall be repassed by two thirds of the Senate and House of Representatives, according to the Rules and Limitations prescribed in the Case of a Bill.

SECTION 8. (1) The Congress shall have Power To lay and collect Taxes, Duties, Imposts and Excises, to pay the Debts and provide for the common Defence and general Welfare of the United States; but all Duties, Imposts and Excises shall be uniform throughout the United States;

(2) To borrow money on the credit of the United States;

(3) To regulate Commerce with foreign Nations, and among the several States, and with the Indian Tribes;

(4) To establish an uniform Rule of Naturalization, and uniform Laws on the subject of Bankruptcies throughout the United States;

(5) To coin Money, regulate the Value thereof, and of foreign Coin, and fix the Standard of Weights and Measures;

(6) To provide for the Punishment of counterfeiting the Securities and current Coin of the United States;

(7) To establish Post Office and post Roads;

(8) To promote the Progress of Science and useful Arts, by securing for limited Times to Authors and Inventors the exclusive Right to their respective Writings and Discoveries;

(9) To constitute Tribunals inferior to the supreme Court;

(10) To define and punish Piracies and Felonies committed on the high Seas, and Offenses against the Law of Nations;

(11) To declare War, grant Letters of Marque and Reprisal, and make Rules concerning Captures on Land and Water;

(12) To raise and support Armies, but no Appropriation of Money to that Use shall be for a longer Term than two Years;

(13) To provide and maintain a Navy;

(14) To make Rules for the Government and Regulation of the land and naval Forces;

(15) To provide for calling forth the Militia to execute the Laws of the Union, suppress Insurrections and repel Invasions;

(16) To provide for organizing, arming, and disciplining the Militia, and for governing such Part of them as may be employed in the Service of the United States, reserving to the States respectively, the Appointment of the Officers, and the Authority of training the Militia according to the discipline prescribed by Congress;

(17) To exercise exclusive Legislation in all Cases whatsoever, over such District (not exceeding ten Miles square) as may, by Cession of particular States, and the acceptance of Congress, become the Seat of the Government of the United States, and to exercise like Authority over all Places purchased by the Consent of the Legislature of the State in which the Same shall be, for the Erection of Forts, Magazines, Arsenals, dock-Yards, and other needful Buildings;—And

(18) To make all Laws which shall be necessary and proper for carrying into Execution the foregoing Powers, and all other Powers vested by this Constitution in the Government of the United States, or in any Department or Officer thereof.

SECTION 9. (1) The Migration or Importation of such Persons as any of the States now existing shall think proper to admit, shall not be prohibited by the Congress prior to the Year one thousand eight hundred and eight, but a tax or duty may be imposed on such Importation, not exceeding ten dollars for each Person.

(2) The privilege of the Writ of Habeas Corpus shall not be suspended, unless when in Cases of Rebellion or Invasion the public Safety may require it.

(3) No Bill of Attainder or ex post facto Law shall be passed.

(4) No capitation, or other direct, Tax shall be laid, unless in Proportion to the Census or Enumeration herein before directed to be taken.[6]

(5) No Tax or Duty shall be laid on Articles exported from any State.

(6) No Preference shall be given by any Regulation of Commerce or Revenue to the Ports of one State over those of another: nor shall Vessels bound to, or from, one State, be obliged to enter, clear, or pay Duties in another.

(7) No Money shall be drawn from the Treasury, but in Consequence of Appropriations made by Law; and a regular Statement and Account of the Receipts and Expenditures of all public Money shall be published from time to time.

(8) No Title of Nobility shall be granted by the United States: And no Person holding any Office of Profit or Trust under them, shall, without the Consent of the Congress, accept of any present, Emolument, Office, or Title, of any kind whatever, from any King, Prince, or foreign State.

SECTION 10. (1) No State shall enter into any Treaty, Alliance, or Confederation; grant Letters of Marque and Reprisal; coin Money; emit Bills of Credit; make any Thing but gold and silver Coin a Tender in Payment of Debts; pass any Bill of Attainder, ex post facto Law, or Law impairing the Obligation of Contracts, or grant any Title of Nobility.

(2) No State shall, without the Consent of the Congress, lay any Imposts or Duties on Imports or Exports, except what may be absolutely necessary for executing its inspection Laws: and the net Produce of all Duties and Imposts, laid by any State on Imports or Exports, shall be for the Use of the Treasury of the United States; and all such Laws shall be subject to the Revision and Control of the Congress.

(3) No State shall, without the Consent of Congress, lay any duty of Tonnage, keep Troops, or Ships of War in time of Peace, enter into any Agreement or Compact with another State, or with a foreign Power, or engage in War, unless actually invaded, or in such imminent Danger as will not admit of delay.

Article II

SECTION 1. (1) The executive Power shall be vested in a President of the United States of America. He shall hold his Office during the Term of four Years, and, together with the Vice-President, chosen for the same Term, be elected, as follows

(2) Each State shall appoint, in such Manner as the Legislature thereof may direct, a Number of Electors, equal to the whole Number of Senators and Representatives to which the State may be entitled in the Congress: but no Senator or Representative, or Person holding an Office of Trust or Profit under the United States, shall be appointed an Elector.

[The Electors shall meet in their respective States, and vote by Ballot for two persons, of whom one at least shall not be an Inhabitant of the same State with themselves. And they shall make a List of all the Persons voted for, and of the Number of Votes for each; which List they shall sign and certify, and transmit sealed to the Seat of the Government of the United States, directed to the President of the Senate. The President of the Senate shall, in the Presence of the Senate and

[6] Changed by the Sixteenth Amendment.

House of Representatives, open all the Certificates, and the Votes shall then be counted. The Person having the greatest Number of Votes shall be the President, if such Number be a Majority of the whole Number of Electors appointed; and if there be more than one who have such Majority, and have an equal Number of Votes, then the House of Representatives shall immediately choose by Ballot one of them for President; and if no Person have a Majority, then from the five highest on the List the said House shall in like Manner choose the President. But in choosing the President, the Votes shall be taken by States, the Representation from each State having one Vote; A quorum for this Purpose shall consist of a Member or Members from two-thirds of the States, and a Majority of all the States shall be necessary to a Choice. In every Case, after the Choice of the President, the Person having the greatest Number of Votes of the Electors shall be the Vice President. But if there should remain two or more who have equal Votes, the Senate shall choose from them by Ballot the Vice-President.][7]

(3) The Congress may determine the Time of choosing the Electors, and the Day on which they shall give their Votes; which Day shall be the same throughout the United States.

(4) No person except a natural born Citizen, or a Citizen of the United States, at the time of the Adoption of this Constitution, shall be eligible to the Office of President; neither shall any Person be eligible to that Office who shall not have attained to the Age of thirty-five Years, and been fourteen Years a Resident within the United States.

(5) In case of the Removal of the President from Office, or of his Death, Resignation, or Inability to discharge the Powers and Duties of the said Office, the same shall devolve on the Vice President, and the Congress may by Law provide for the Case of Removal, Death, Resignation or Inability, both of the President and Vice President, declaring what Officer shall then act as President, and such Officer shall act accordingly, until the Disability be removed, or a President shall be elected.

(6) The President shall, at stated Times, receive for his Services, a Compensation, which shall neither be increased nor diminished during the Period for which he shall have been elected, and he shall not receive within that Period any other Emolument from the United States, or any of them.

(7) Before he enter on the Execution of his Office, he shall take the following Oath or Affirmation:—"I do solemnly swear (or affirm) that I will faithfully execute the Office of President of the United States, and will to the best of my Ability, preserve, protect and defend the Constitution of the United States."

SECTION 2. (1) The President shall be Commander in Chief of the Army and Navy of the United States, and of the Militia of the several States, when called into the actual Service of the United States; he may require the Opinion in writing, of the principal Officer in each of the executive Departments, upon any subject relating to the Duties of their respective Offices, and he shall have Power to Grant Reprieves and Pardons for Offenses against the United States, except in Cases of Impeachment.

(2) He shall have Power, by and with the Advice and Consent of the Senate, to make Treaties, provided two-thirds of the Senators present concur; and he shall nominate, and by and with the Advice and Consent of the Senate, shall appoint Ambassadors, other public Ministers and Consuls, Judges of the supreme Court, and

[7] This paragraph was superseded in 1804 by the Twelfth Amendment.

all other Officers of the United States, whose Appointments are not herein otherwise provided for, and which shall be established by Law: but the Congress may by Law vest the Appointment of such inferior Officers, as they think proper, in the President alone, in the Courts of Law, or in the Heads of Departments.

(3) The President shall have Power to fill up all Vacancies that may happen during the Recess of the Senate, by granting Commissions which shall expire at the End of their next Session.

SECTION 3. He shall from time to time give to the Congress Information of the State of the Union, and recommend to their Consideration such Measures as he shall judge necessary and expedient; he may, on extraordinary Occasions, convene both Houses, or either of them, and in Case of Disagreement between them, with Respect to the Time of Adjournment, he may adjourn them to such Time as he shall think proper; he shall receive Ambassadors and other public Ministers; he shall take Care that the Laws be faithfully executed, and shall Commission all the Officers of the United States.

SECTION 4. The President, Vice President and all civil Officers of the United States, shall be removed from Office on Impeachment for, and Conviction of, Treason, Bribery, or other high Crimes and Misdemeanors.

Article III

SECTION 1. The judicial Power of the United States, shall be vested in one supreme Court, and in such inferior Courts as the Congress may from time to time ordain and establish. The Judges, both of the supreme and inferior Courts, shall hold their Offices during good Behavior, and shall, at stated Times, receive for their Services a Compensation which shall not be diminished during their Continuance in Office.

SECTION 2. (1) The judicial Power shall extend to all Cases, in Law and Equity, arising under this Constitution, the Laws of the United States, and Treaties made, or which shall be made, under their Authority;—to all Cases affecting Ambassadors, other public Ministers and Consuls;—to all Cases of admiralty and maritime Jurisdiction;—to Controversies to which the United States shall be a Party;—to Controversies between two or more States;—[between a State and Citizens of another State];[8]—between Citizens of different States;— between Citizens of the same State claiming Lands under Grants of different States, and [between a State, or the Citizens thereof, and foreign States, Citizens or Subjects.][9]

(2) In all Cases affecting Ambassadors, other public Ministers and Consuls, and those in which a State shall be Party, the supreme Court shall have original Jurisdiction. In all the other Cases before mentioned, the supreme Court shall have appellate Jurisdiction, both as to Law and Fact, with such Exceptions, and under such Regulations as the Congress shall make.

(3) The trial of all Crimes, except in Cases of Impeachment, shall be by Jury; and such Trial shall be held in the State where the said Crimes shall have been committed; but when not committed within any State, the Trial shall be at such Place or Places as the Congress may by Law have directed.

[8] Restricted by the Eleventh Amendment.
[9] Restricted by the Eleventh Amendment.

SECTION 3. (1) Treason against the United States, shall consist only in levying War against them, or in adhering to their Enemies, giving them Aid and Comfort. No Person shall be convicted of Treason unless on the Testimony of two Witnesses to the same overt Act, or on Confession in open Court.

(2) The Congress shall have power to declare the Punishment of Treason, but no Attainder of Treason shall work Corruption of Blood, or Forfeiture except during the Life of the Person attainted.

Article IV

SECTION 1. Full Faith and Credit shall be given in each State to the public Acts, Records, and judicial Proceedings of every other State. And the Congress may by general Laws prescribe the Manner in which such Acts, Records and Proceedings shall be proved, and the Effect thereof.

SECTION 2. (1) The Citizens of each State shall be entitled to all Privileges and Immunities of Citizens in the several States.

(2) A Person charged in any State with Treason, Felony, or other Crime, who shall flee from Justice, and be found in another State, shall on demand of the executive Authority of the State from which he fled, be delivered up, to be removed to the State having Jurisdiction of the Crime.

(3) [No Person held to Service or Labor in one State, under the Laws thereof, escaping into another, shall, in Consequence of any Law or Regulation therein, be discharged from such Service or Labor, but shall be delivered up on Claim of the Party to whom such Service or Labor may be due.]10

SECTION 3. (1) New States may be admitted by the Congress into this Union; but no new State shall be formed or erected within the Jurisdiction of any other State; nor any State be formed by the Junction of two or more States, or parts of States, without the Consent of the Legislatures of the States concerned as well as of the Congress.

(2) The Congress shall have Power to dispose of and make all needful Rules and Regulations respecting the Territory or other Property belonging to the United States; and nothing in this Constitution shall be so construed as to Prejudice any Claims of the United States, or of any particular State.

SECTION 4. The United States shall guarantee to every State in this Union a Republican Form of Government, and shall protect each of them against Invasion; and on Application of the Legislature, or of the Executive (when the Legislature cannot be convened) against domestic Violence.

Article V

The Congress, whenever two-thirds of both Houses shall deem it necessary, shall propose Amendments to this Constitution, or, on the Application of the Legislatures of two-thirds of the several States, shall call a Convention for proposing Amendments, which, in either Case, shall be valid to all Intents and Purposes, as part of this Constitution, when ratified by the Legislatures of three-fourths of the several States, or by Conventions in three-fourths thereof, as the one or the other Mode of Ratification may be proposed by the Congress; Provided that no Amendment which may be made prior to the Year One thousand eight

10 This paragraph has been superseded by the Thirteenth Amendment.

hundred and eight shall in any Manner affect the first and fourth Clauses in the Ninth Section of the first Article; and that no State, without its Consent, shall be deprived of its equal Suffrage in the Senate.

Article VI

(1) All Debts contracted and Engagements entered into, before the Adoption of this Constitution, shall be as valid against the United States under this Constitution, as under the Confederation.

(2) This Constitution, and the Laws of the United States which shall be made in Pursuance thereof; and all Treaties made, or which shall be made, under the Authority of the United States, shall be the supreme Law of the Land; and the Judges in every State shall be bound thereby, any Thing in the Constitution or Laws of any State to the Contrary notwithstanding.

(3) The Senators and Representatives before mentioned, and the Members of the several State Legislatures, and all executive and judicial Officers, both of the United States and of the several States, shall be bound by Oath or Affirmation, to support this Constitution; but no religious Test shall ever be required as a Qualification to any Office or public Trust under the United States.

Article VII

The Ratification of the Conventions of nine States, shall be sufficient for the Establishment of this Constitution between the States so ratifying the Same.

DONE in Convention by the Unanimous Consent of the States present the Seventeenth Day of September in the Year of our Lord one thousand seven hundred and Eighty seven and of the Independence of the United States of America the Twelfth. In Witness whereof We have hereunto subscribed our Names.

Go WASHINGTON
Presidt and deputy from Virginia

ARTICLES IN ADDITION TO, AND AMENDMENT OF, THE CONSTITUTION OF THE UNITED STATES OF AMERICA, PROPOSED BY CONGRESS, AND RATIFIED BY THE LEGISLATURES OF THE SEVERAL STATES, PURSUANT TO THE FIFTH ARTICLE OF THE ORIGINAL CONSTITUTION.

Article I[11]

Congress shall make no law respecting an establishment of religion, or prohibiting the free exercise thereof; or abridging the freedom of speech, or of the press; or the right of the people peaceably to assemble, and to petition the Government for a redress of grievances.

Article II

A well regulated Militia, being necessary to the security of a free State, the right of the people to keep and bear Arms, shall not be infringed.

[11] The first ten amendments were adopted in 1791.

Article III

No Soldier shall, in time of peace be quartered in any house, without the consent of the Owner, nor in time of war, but in a manner to be prescribed by law.

Article IV

The right of the people to be secure in their persons, houses, papers, and effects, against unreasonable searches and seizures, shall not be violated, and no Warrants shall issue, but upon probable cause, supported by Oath or affirmation, and particularly describing the place to be searched, and the persons or things to be seized.

Article V

No person shall be held to answer for a capital, or otherwise infamous crime, unless on a presentment or indictment of a Grand Jury, except in cases arising in the land or naval forces, or in the Militia, when in actual service in time of War or public danger; nor shall any person be subject for the same offence to be twice put in jeopardy of life or limb; nor shall be compelled in any criminal case to be a witness against himself, nor be deprived of life, liberty, or property, without due process of law; nor shall private property be taken for public use, without just compensation.

Article VI

In all criminal prosecutions, the accused shall enjoy the right to a speedy and public trial, by an impartial jury of the State and district wherein the crime shall have been committed, which district shall have been previously ascertained by law, and to be informed of the nature and cause of the accusation; to be confronted with the witnesses against him; to have compulsory process for obtaining witnesses in his favor, and to have the Assistance of Counsel for his defence.

Article VII

In suits at common law, where the value in controversy shall exceed twenty dollars, the right of trial by jury shall be preserved, and no fact tried by a jury, shall be otherwise reexamined in any Court of the United States, than according to the rules of the common law.

Article VIII

Excessive bail shall not be required, nor excessive fines imposed, nor cruel and unusual punishments inflicted.

Article IX

The enumeration in the Constitution, of certain rights, shall not be construed to deny or disparage others retained by the people.

Article X

The powers not delegated to the United States by the Constitution, nor prohibited by it to the States, are reserved to the States respectively, or to the people.

Article XI[12]

The Judicial power of the United States shall not be construed to extend to any suit in law or equity, commenced or prosecuted against one of the United States by Citizens of another State, or by Citizens or Subjects of any Foreign State.

Article XII[13]

The Electors shall meet in their respective states and vote by ballot for President and Vice-President, one of whom, at least, shall not be an inhabitant of the same state with themselves; they shall name in their ballots the person voted for as President, and in distinct ballots the person voted for as Vice-President, and they shall make distinct lists of all persons voted for as President, and of all persons voted for as Vice-President, and of the number of votes for each, which lists they shall sign and certify, and transmit sealed to the seat of the government of the United States, directed to the President of the Senate;— The President of the Senate shall, in presence of the Senate and House of Representatives, open all the certificates and the votes shall then be counted;—The person having the greatest number of votes for President, shall be the President, if such number be a majority of the whole number of Electors appointed; and if no person have such majority, then from the persons having the highest numbers not exceeding three on the list of those voted for as President, the House of Representatives shall choose immediately, by ballot, the President. But in choosing the President, the votes shall be taken by states, the representation from each state having one vote; a quorum for this purpose shall consist of a member or members from two-thirds of the states, and a majority of all the states shall be necessary to a choice. [And if the House of Representatives shall not choose a President whenever the right of choice shall devolve upon them, before the fourth day of March next following, then the Vice-President shall act as President, as in the case of the death or other constitutional disability of the President.][14]— The person having the greatest number of votes as Vice-President, shall be the Vice-President, if such number be a majority of the whole number of Electors appointed, and if no person have a majority, then from the two highest numbers on the list, the Senate shall choose the Vice-President; a quorum for the purpose shall consist of two-thirds of the whole number of Senators, and a majority of the whole number shall be necessary to a choice. But no person constitutionally ineligible to the office of President shall be eligible to that of Vice-President of the United States.

Article XIII[15]

SECTION I. Neither slavery nor involuntary servitude, except as a punishment for crime whereof the party shall have been duly convicted, shall exist within the United States, or any place subject to their jurisdiction.

[12] Adopted in 1798.
[13] Adopted in 1804.
[14] Superseded by the Twentieth Amendment, Section 3.
[15] Adopted in 1865.

SECTION 2. Congress shall have power to enforce this article by appropriate legislation.

Article XIV[16]

SECTION 1. All persons born or naturalized in the United States, and subject to the jurisdiction thereof, are citizens of the United States and of the State wherein they reside. No state shall make or enforce any law which shall abridge the privileges or immunities of citizens of the United States; nor shall any State deprive any person of life, liberty, or property, without due process of law; nor deny to any person within its jurisdiction the equal protection of the laws.

SECTION 2. Representatives shall be apportioned among the several States according to their respective numbers, counting the whole number of persons in each State, excluding Indians not taxed. But when the right to vote at any election for the choice of electors for President and Vice-President of the United States, Representatives in Congress, the Executive and Judicial officers of a State, or the members of the Legislature thereof, is denied to any of the male inhabitants of such State, being twenty-one years of age, and citizens of the United States, or in any way abridged, except for participation in rebellion, or other crime, the basis of representation therein shall be reduced in the proportion which the number of such male citizens shall bear to the whole number of male citizens twenty-one years of age in such State.

SECTION 3. No person shall be a Senator or Representative in Congress, or elector of President and Vice-President, or hold any office, civil or military, under the United States, or under any State, who, having previously taken an oath, as a member of Congress, or as an officer of the United States, or as a member of any State legislature, or as an executive or judicial officer of any State, to support the Constitution of the United States, shall have engaged in insurrection or rebellion against the same, or given aid or comfort to the enemies thereof. But Congress may by a vote of two-thirds of each House, remove such disability.

SECTION 4. The validity of the public debt of the United States, authorized by law, including debts incurred for payment of pensions and bounties for services in suppressing insurrection or rebellion, shall not be questioned. But neither the United States nor any State shall assume or pay any debt or obligation incurred in aid of insurrection or rebellion against the United States, or any claim for the loss or emancipation of any slave; but all such debts, obligations and claims shall be held illegal and void.

SECTION 5. The Congress shall have power to enforce, by appropriate legislation, the provisions of this article.

Article XV[17]

SECTION 1. The right of citizens of the United States to vote shall not be denied or abridged by the United States or by any State on account of race, color, or previous condition of servitude—

SECTION 2. The Congress shall have power to enforce this article by appropriate legislation.

[16] Adopted in 1868.
[17] Adopted in 1870.

Article XVI[18]

The Congress shall have power to lay and collect taxes on incomes, from whatever source derived, without apportionment among the several States, and without regard to any census or enumeration.

Article XVII[19]

The Senate of the United States shall be composed of two Senators from each State, elected by the people thereof, for six years; and each Senator shall have one vote. The electors in each State shall have the qualifications requisite for electors of the most numerous branch of the State legislatures.

When vacancies happen in the representation of any State in the Senate, the executive authority of such State shall issue writs of election to fill such vacancies: *Provided,* That the legislature of any State may empower the executive thereof to make temporary appointments until the people fill the vacancies by election as the legislature may direct.

This amendment shall not be so construed as to affect the election or term of any Senator chosen before it becomes valid as part of the Constitution.

Article XVIII[20]

SECTION 1. After one year from the ratification of this article the manufacture, sale, or transportation of intoxicating liquors within, the importation thereof into, or the exportation thereof from the United States and all territory subject to the jurisdiction thereof for beverage purposes is hereby prohibited.

SECTION 2. The Congress and the several States shall have concurrent power to enforce this article by appropriate legislation.

SECTION 3. This article shall be inoperative unless it shall have been ratified as an amendment to the Constitution by the legislatures of the several States, as provided in the Constitution, within seven years from the date of the submission hereof to the States by the Congress.

Article XIX[21]

The right of citizens of the United States to vote shall not be denied or abridged by the United States or by any State on account of sex.

Congress shall have power to enforce this article by appropriate legislation.

Article XX[22]

SECTION 1. The terms of the President and Vice President shall end at noon on the 20th day of January, and the terms of Senators and Representatives at noon on the 3d day of January, of the years in which such terms would have ended if this article had not been ratified; and the terms of their successors shall then begin.

[18] Adopted in 1913.
[19] Adopted in 1913.
[20] Adopted in 1919. Repealed by Section 1 of the Twenty-first Amendment.
[21] Adopted in 1920.
[22] Adopted in 1933.

Section 2. The Congress shall assemble at least once in every year, and such meeting shall begin at noon on the 3d day of January, unless they shall by law appoint a different day.

Section 3. If, at the time fixed for the beginning of the term of the President, the President elect shall have died, the Vice President elect shall become President. If a President shall not have been chosen before the time fixed for the beginning of his term, or if the President elect shall have failed to qualify, then the Vice President elect shall act as President until a President shall have qualified; and the Congress may by law provide for the case wherein neither a President elect nor a Vice President elect shall have qualified, declaring who shall then act as President, or the manner in which one who is to act shall be selected, and such person shall act accordingly until a President or Vice President shall have qualified.

Section 4. The Congress may by law provide for the case of the death of any of the persons from whom the House of Representatives may choose a President whenever the right of choice shall have devolved upon them, and for the case of the death of any of the persons from whom the Senate may choose a Vice President whenever the right of choice shall have devolved upon them.

Section 5. Sections 1 and 2 shall take effect on the 15th day of October following the ratification of this article.

Section 6. This article shall be inoperative unless it shall have been ratified as an amendment to the Constitution by the legislatures of three-fourths of the several States within seven years from the date of its submission.

Article XXI[23]

Section 1. The eighteenth article of amendment to the Constitution of the United States is hereby repealed.

Section 2. The transportation or importation into any State, Territory, or possession of the United States for delivery or use therein of intoxicating liquors, in violation of the laws thereof, is hereby prohibited.

Section 3. This article shall be inoperative unless it shall have been ratified as an amendment to the Constitution by conventions in the several States, as provided in the Constitution, within seven years from the date of the submission hereof to the States by the Congress.

Article XXII[24]

Section 1. No person shall be elected to the office of the President more than twice, and no person who has held the office of President, or acted as President, for more than two years of a term to which some other person was elected President shall be elected to the office of the President more than once. But this Article shall not apply to any person holding the office of President when this Article was proposed by the Congress, and shall not prevent any person who may be holding the office of President, or acting as President, during the term within which this Article becomes operative from holding the office of President or acting as President during the remainder of such term.

[23] Adopted in 1933.
[24] Adopted in 1951.

SECTION 2. This article shall be inoperative unless it shall have been ratified as an amendment to the Constitution by the legislatures of three-fourths of the several States within seven years from the date of its submission to the States by the Congress.

Article XXIII[25]

SECTION 1. The District constituting the seat of Government of the United States shall appoint in such manner as the Congress may direct:

A number of electors of President and Vice President equal to the whole number of Senators and Representatives in Congress to which the District would be entitled if it were a State, but in no event more than the least populous State; they shall be in addition to those appointed by the States, but they shall be considered, for the purposes of the election of President and Vice President, to be electors appointed by a State; and they shall meet in the District and perform such duties as provided by the twelfth article of amendment.

SECTION 2. The Congress shall have power to enforce this article by appropriate legislation.

Article XXIV[26]

SECTION 1. The right of citizens of the United States to vote in any primary or other election for President or Vice President, for electors for President or Vice President, or for Senator or Representative in Congress, shall not be denied or abridged by the United States or any state by reasons of failure to pay any poll tax or other tax.

SECTION 2. The Congress shall have power to enforce this article by appropriate legislation.

[25] Adopted in 1961.
[26] Adopted in 1964.

Table of Cases